Proceedings

32nd Applied Imagery Pattern Recognition Workshop

"Image Data Fusion"

AIPR 2003

www.aipr-workshop.org

Back cover image from

"Sensor and Classifier Fusion for Outdoor Obstacle Detection:
An Application of Data Fusion to Autonomous Off-Road Navigation"

by Cristian S. Dima, Nicolas Vandapel, and Martial Hebert

Figure 1. A typical scene from the road detection dataset: the color image (top-left), the IR image (top-right), the 3D point cloud in which points are colorized based on the color image (bottom).

Proceedings

32nd Applied Imagery Pattern Recognition Workshop

**October 15-17, 2003
Washington, DC**

**Sponsored by
IEEE Computer Society Technical Committee on
Pattern Analysis and Machine Intelligence**

**Presented by
AIPR — Applied Imagery Pattern Recognition**

http://computer.org

Los Alamitos, California

Washington • Brussels • Tokyo

Copyright © 2004 by The Institute of Electrical and
Electronics Engineers, Inc.
All rights reserved

Copyright and Reprint Permissions: Abstracting is permitted with credit to the source. Libraries may photocopy beyond the limits of US copyright law, for private use of patrons, those articles in this volume that carry a code at the bottom of the first page, provided that the per-copy fee indicated in the code is paid through the Copyright Clearance Center, 222 Rosewood Drive, Danvers, MA 01923.

Other copying, reprint, or republication requests should be addressed to: IEEE Copyrights Manager, IEEE Service Center, 445 Hoes Lane, P.O. Box 133, Piscataway, NJ 08855-1331.

The papers in this book comprise the proceedings of the meeting mentioned on the cover and title page. They reflect the authors' opinions and, in the interests of timely dissemination, are published as presented and without change. Their inclusion in this publication does not necessarily constitute endorsement by the editors, the IEEE Computer Society, or the Institute of Electrical and Electronics Engineers, Inc.

IEEE Computer Society Order Number P2029
ISBN 0-7695-2029-4
Library of Congress Number 2004100407

Additional copies may be ordered from:

IEEE Computer Society	IEEE Service Center	IEEE Computer Society
Customer Service Center	445 Hoes Lane	Asia/Pacific Office
10662 Los Vaqueros Circle	P.O. Box 1331	Watanabe Bldg., 1-4-2
P.O. Box 3014	Piscataway, NJ 08855-1331	Minami-Aoyama
Los Alamitos, CA 90720-1314	Tel: + 1-732-981-0060	Minato-ku, Tokyo 107-0062
Tel: + 1-714-821-8380	Fax: + 1-732-981-9667	JAPAN
Fax: + 1-714-821-4641	http://shop.ieee.org/store/	Tel: + 81-3-3408-3118
E-mail: cs.books@computer.org	customer-service@ieee.org	Fax: + 81-3-3408-3553
		tokyo.ofc@computer.org

Individual paper REPRINTS may be ordered at: reprints@computer.org

Editorial production by Bob Werner
Cover art production by Joe Daigle/Studio Productions
Printed in the United States of America by Applied Digital Imaging

Table of Contents

32nd Applied Imagery Pattern Recognition Workshop — AIPR 2003

Preface ix

AIPR Executive Committee x

Astronomy
Session Chair: John Evans, Department of Physics and Astronomy, George Mason University

Space Weather Research: A Major Application of Imagery and Data Fusion 3
    A. Poland, G. Withbroe, and J. Evans

Military Applications
Session Chairs: Neelam Gupta Army Research Lab and John Irvine SAIC

Next Generation IR Focal Plane Arrays and Applications 7
    J. Caulfield

Multisensor and Spectral Image Fusion and Mining: From Neural Systems to Applications 11
    D. Fay, R. Ivey, N. Bomberger, and A. Waxman

Fused Spectropolarimetric Visible Near-IR Imaging 21
    N. Gupta

Fusion Techniques for Automatic Target Recognition 27
    S. Rizvi and N. Nasrabadi

Eigenviews for Object Recognition in Multispectral Imaging Systems 33
    R. Ramanath, W. Snyder, and H. Qi

Quantum Image Processing (QuIP) 39
    G. Beach, C. Lomont, and C. Cohen

Registration of Range Data from Unmanned Aerial and Ground Vehicles 45
    A. Downs, R. Madhavan, and T. Hong

Projectile Identification System 51
    G. Beach, C. Cohen, G. Moody, and M. Henry

Vehicle Detection Approaches Using the NVESD Sensor Fusion Testbed 56
    P. Perconti, J. Hilger, and M. Loew

3-Dimensional Object Reconstruction from Frequency Diverse RF Systems 62
    R. Bonneau

Imaging of Moving Targets Using a Doppler Compensated Multiresolution Method 66
    R. Bonneau

Posters
Session Chair: Carlos Maraviglia, Naval Research Lab

Dual Band (MWIR/LWIR) Hyperspectral Imager 73
   M. Hinnrichs, N. Gupta, and A. Goldberg

Remote Sensing
Session Chairs: Harvey Rhody, RIT and John Schott, RIT

Superresolution from Image Sequence 81
   N. Bose

Data Association for Fusion in Spatial and Spectral Imaging 87
   A. Schaum

Band Selection Using Independent Component Analysis for Hyperspectral Image Processing 93
   H. Du, H. Qi, X. Wang, R. Ramanath, and W. Snyder

Quantitative Fusion of Performance Results from Actual and Simulated Image Data 99
   P. Blake and T. Brown

Automated Multisensor Image Registration 103
   K. Walli

Historical Research
Session Chair: David Schaefer

Multispectral Imaging of the Archimedes Palimpsest 111
   R. Easton, K. Knox, and W. Christens-Barry

Medical Applications
Session Chairs: Larry Clarke, National Cancer Institute and Murray Loew, George Washington University

Heterogeneity of MR Signal Intensity Mapped onto Brain Surface Models 119
   A. Rebmann and J. Butman

The Research of Semantic Content Applied to Image Fusion 125
   Y. Miao and Y. Miao

Photo-Realistic Representation of Anatomical Structures for Medical
Education by Fusion of Volumetric and Surface Image Data 131
   A. Wetzel, G. Nieder, G. Durka-Pelok, T. Gest, S. Pomerantz,
   D. Nave, S. Czanner, L. Wagner, E. Shirey, and D. Deerfield

Data Fusion Using Neural Networks
Session Chair: Donald Gerson, Gerson Imaging Solutions

Neural Network Based Skin Color Model for Face Detection 141
   M. Seow, D. Valaparla, and V. Asari

Real Time Face Detection from Color Video Stream Based on PCA Method 146
   R. Gottumukkal and V. Asari

Associative Memory Based on Ratio Learning for Real Time Skin Color Detection 151
   M. Seow and V. Asari

Performance Evaluation of Color Based Road Detection Using Neural Nets and Support Vector Machines — 157
P. Conrad and M. Foedisch

Posters
Session Chair: Carlos Maraviglia, Naval Research Lab

Defect Detection on Patterned Jacquard Fabric — 163
H. Ngan, G. Pang, S. Yung, and M. Ng

A Hybrid Approach to Character Segmentation of Gurmukhi Script Characters — 169
N. Davessar, S. Madan, and H. Singh

Modified Luminance Based MSR for Fast and Efficient Image Enhancement — 174
L. Tao and V. Asari

Fusion for Registration of Medical Images- A Study — 180
R. Kapoor, A. Dutta, D. Bagai, and T. Kamal

Visual Learning in Humans and Machines
Session Chair: Jim Aanstoos, Cary Academy

Visual Literacy: An Overview — 189
J. Aanstoos

Children's Understanding of Imagery in Picture Books — 194
L. Levin

Spectral Histogram Representations for Visual Modeling — 199
X. Liu and Q. Zhang

A Survey of Recent Developments in Theoretical Neuroscience and Machine Vision — 205
J. Colombe

Homeland Security
Session Chair: Joan Lurie, GAC Inc.

Perspectives on the Fusion of Image and Non-Image Data — 217
D. Hall

Quick Response Airborne Deployment of Viper Muzzle Flash Detection and Location System During DC Sniper Attacks — 221
M. Pauli, M. Ertem, and E. Heidhausen

Fusing Face and ECG for Personal Identification — 226
S. Israel, W. Scruggs, W. Worek, and J. Irvine

Image Formation through Walls Using a Distributed Radar Sensor Array — 232
A. Hunt

Access Control System with High Level Security Using Fingerprints — 238
Y. Gil, D. Ahn, S. Pan, and Y. Chung

Geo-spatial Active Visual Surveillance on Wireless Networks — 244
T. Boult

A Real-time Wide field of View Passive Millimeter-wave Imaging Camera 250
   S. Clark, C. Martin, V. Kolinko, J. Lovberg, and P. Costianes

Sensor and Classifier Fusion for Outdoor Obstacle Detection:
An Application of Data Fusion to Autonomous Off-Road Navigation 255
   C. Dima, N. Vandapel, and M. Hebert

Stereo Mosaics with Slanting Parallel Projections from Many Cameras or a Moving Camera 263
   Z. Zhu

License Plate Surveillance System Using Weighted Template Matching 269
   Y. Kim and M. Ko

Tracking and Handoff between Multiple Perspective Camera Views 275
   S. Guler, J. Griffith, and I. Pushee

Personal Authentication Using Feature Points on Finger and Palmar Creases 282
   J. Doi and M. Yamanaka

Author Index 289

Preface

The theme for the 2003 AIPR Workshop was Imagery and Data Fusion. The ability to organize information that has been collected from more than one source is a prime achievement of modern computers. The 2003 AIPR workshop explored the fusing of inputs where at least one of the inputs is an image. Examples include the fusion of images from many spectral bands, various sensors, preprocessing techniques such as polarization, image processing techniques such as Quantum and time varying processing, the fusing of images and external parameters such as GPS, historical data collected about the image, expert knowledge of the image, etc., and the fusing of X-rays and MRI generated images. Data Mining and other techniques used to compare previously captured images and data to the current image. The workshop featured more than fifty papers from seven different application areas on Image data fusion.

The Applied Imagery Pattern Recognition Workshop is held annually in Washington DC and is dedicated to facilitating the interchange between government, industry, and academia. The 2003 workshop combined image data fusion presentations from such diverse applications areas such as Homeland Security, Medical Applications, Military Applications, Remote Sensing, Historical Research, Astronomy, and Visual Learning In Humans And Machines. Dr Robert Hummel led off the workshop presenting the first Mike Hord Memorial Keynote Address. Mike Hord was one of the founding fathers of AIPR more than 30 years ago. Dr Hummel gave a good overview of the current status of Image Data Fusion. He started his discussion by stating that Image Data Fusion is not the next hot topic in image understanding.

John Evans, Art Poland, and George Withbroe of George Mason presented a three part discussion on the use of multispectral images from both ground based and space based sensors and other various data types that are combined to predict solar weather. Neelam Gupta, Army Research Lab was the session chair for military applications using image data fusion. John Caulfield and Neelam Gupta described the use of dual band focal plane arrays with on chip processing and the use of spectropolarimetric image fusion in the infrared and visible near-IR bands. David Fay described methods for fusion of multispectral imagery based on concepts derived from neural models.

The second day of the workshop started with a talk and demonstration by Thad Starner from Georgia Tech on a mobile one-way translator for American Sign Language. N.K Bose of Penn State University led off the Remote Sensing Session chaired by Harvey Rhody of RIT with a good presentation on Superresolution from Image Sequences. Roger Easton presented a paper on the use of multispectral imaging in an historical research application — revealing the writings of Archimedes from a 1000-year-old parchment that had been re-used. The afternoon workshop started with an invited talk by Andrea Rebmann from NIH on image data fusion of MR images of the brain surface to lead off the medical applications session. The daytime program concluded with a session on neural network methods, including papers on face recognition and road detection applications. The day ended with a wonderful banquet and talk by Dr. Steve Rogers on the topic of intelligence amplification applied to early detection of breast cancer.

The third and final day of the workshop started with the Visual Learning in Humans and Machines session chaired by Jim Aanstoos of Cary Academy. Jim introduced the session with an overview of research in Visual Literacy. Lori Levin from Kansas State University presented a visual learning in humans paper titled Children's understanding of imagery in picture books. Jeffrey Colombe from Mitre Corporation ended the session with a survey of recent developments in theoretical neuroscience and machine vision. Joan Lurie chaired the last session of the workshop, Homeland Security, and David Hall from Penn State University presented a good discussion on the perspectives of fusing image and non-image data.

Two excellent poster sessions accompanied the evening receptions, which were well-attended and proved to be good opportunities for enthusiastic interaction.

On behalf of the AIPR Executive Committee; we hope you enjoy and gain insights on the subject of image data fusion by reading the proceedings of the 32nd AIPR Workshop.

Elmer Williams
Program Chair, 32nd AIPR Workshop

AIPR Executive Committee

Chairman: James Aanstoos, Cary Academy

Deputy Chair: Neelam Gupta, Army Research Labs

Program Chair: Elmer Williams, Naval Research Lab

Secretary: Carlos Maraviglia, Naval Research Lab

Treasurer: Paul Anuta, TITAN Systems

Local Arrangements: Donald J. Gerson, Gerson Imaging Solutions

Publicity: William Oliver, Armed Forces Institute of Pathology

Web Master: Charles J. Cohen, Cybernet

Members

Bill Alschuler, California Institute of the Arts
Eamon Barrett, Lockheed Martin
Bob Bonneau, AFRL
Larry Clarke, NCI
Peter Costianes, AFRL, Rome Research Site
Larry Davis, Univ. of Maryland
Robert Evans, NRL
Cliff Greve, SAIC
Robert Haralick, U. of Washington
John Huth, Veridian
John Irvine, SAIC
Heidi Jacobus, Cybernet
Michael D. Kelly, IKCS
Yeongji Kim, ATP
Murray H. Loew, GWU
Joan Lurie, Remote Sensing Consultant
Don Malkoff, Boeing
Robert Mericsko, NIMA
Robert Meyer, BAE Systems
Keith Monson, FBI
James Pearson, Remote Sensing Consultant
Harvey Rhody, RIT
David Schaefer, GMU
J. Michael Selander, Mitre
Faina Shtern, DHHS
Harold Stone, NEC

Astronomy

⌘ ⌘ ⌘ ⌘ ⌘ ⌘ ⌘ ⌘

Space Weather Research: A Major Application of Imagery and Data Fusion

Arthur I. Poland, George Withbroe, and John C. Evans
George Mason University, Fairfax, Virginia, USA
apoland@gmu.edu, gwithbro@gmu.edu, jevans@gmu.edu

Abstract

Space weather research involves the study of the Sun and Earth from a systems viewpoint to improve the understanding and prediction of solar-terrestrial variability. There are a wide variety of solar-terrestrial imagery, spectroscopic measurements, and in situ space environmental data that can be exploited to improve our knowledge and understanding of the phenomena and processes involved in space weather.

1. Space Weather Research

The Sun is a magnetic variable star whose varying output of electromagnetic radiation, solar wind, and energetic particles generates variability in the geospace environment and upper terrestrial atmosphere. This variability, space weather, can affect a variety of human activities and technology such as spacecraft, GPS signals, electric power grid, high frequency radio signals, radiation exposures of astronauts in orbit and crews in high altitude aircraft, and is believed to be a major source of the natural variability in terrestrial climate.

There is an international fleet of spacecraft observing the Sun and making measurements in the heliospheric environment between Sun and Earth and in the Earth's space environment. Their observations of transient phenomena in the solar atmosphere along with the complementary observations and measurements of geospace variability are improving knowledge and understanding of the behavior of the connected Sun-Earth system. Relevant solar transient phenomena include solar flares, which can produce solar energetic particles and generate enhanced x-ray radiation affecting conditions in the terrestrial ionosphere, and coronal mass ejections (CME's), which can cause geomagnetic storms when the ejected solar material reaches Earth. CME's can also be a source of solar energetic particles.

We are now able to probe not only the solar atmosphere, but also the solar interior. The latter is accomplished by using spectroscopic imaging data to measure the properties of waves at the solar surface to provide information on conditions in the solar interior via helioseismology techniques. This provides valuable information for developing models for the solar dynamo believed to be responsible for solar variability.

The geospace environment is studied by *in situ* and remote sensing instruments on spacecraft orbiting Earth at a variety of altitudes and inclinations to observe the behavior of the terrestrial upper atmosphere and plasma and energetic particles in the Earth's magnetosphere and its interface with solar wind flowing outward from the Sun. Interactions between the variable solar wind, solar energetic particles, and Earth's atmosphere and magnetic field generate space weather phenomena such as aurorae and the radiation belts.

The challenge is to develop techniques for optimally exploiting the diverse solar terrestrial data base to improve understanding of the characteristics and underlying physical processes of the phenomena involved in space weather. Much progress has been achieved as a result of simultaneous measurements of the variability of the Sun, heliosphere, and geospace provided by currently flying space missions. As a result of the fusion of these various types of data we now have much better insights as to what to measure with the next generation of solar terrestrial space missions and what new tools are needed for data fusion and analysis and the complementary theoretical modeling. For more information see reference [1] and the NASA Sun Earth Connection website (http://sec.gsfc.nasa.gov/).

2. References

[1] P. Song, H. J. Singer, G. L. Siscoe (eds), *Space Weather*, American Geophysical Union, Washington DC, 2001.

Military Applications

⌘⌘⌘⌘⌘⌘⌘⌘

Next Generation IR Focal Plane Arrays and Applications

John T. Caulfield
Raytheon Vision Systems
jtcaulfield@raytheon.com

Abstract

Raytheon Vision Systems (RVS) has invented and demonstrated a new class of advanced focal plane arrays. These Advanced FPAs are sometimes called 3rd Generation or "Next Generation" FPAs because they have integrated onto the FPA the ability to sense multiple IR spectrums, and conduct image processing on the FPA ROIC. These Next Generation of IRFPAs are allowing more functionality and the detection of a more diverse set of data than previously possible with 2nd Gen FPAs. Examples and history of 3rd Gen FPAs are shown including RVS' Multispectral, Uncooled, and Adaptive Sensors.

1.0 Next Generation IRPFA Introduction and Requirements

There are several definitions of what determines if a FPA is 3rd Generation. There is general agreement that 3rd Generation means an FPA with advanced image detection and processing such as multispectral, Temporal or Spatial processing built onto the FPA could be considered 3rd Gen FPAs. The user community needs and capabilities follow a common theme.

A new generation of requirements for IR focal plane arrays (IRFPAs) has emerged that affects the development of both the detectors and readout integrated circuits (ROICs). Because these applications have varying requirements, a set of FPAs cannot be made to satisfy all needs, and custom designs are needed.

The industry is receiving more demands in the areas of larger formats, increased sensitivity, smaller pixels, and higher functionality. Many users desire more functionality on the FPA/Sensor System to improve on many FPA attributes. These attributes are sensitivity, spectral agility, correctability, as well as decreasing the power, size, and weight of next generation FPAs. These must be met in addition to achieving production quantities at a low cost.

The FPA community has embraced 2nd Gen FPA and created the push towards the next generation of sensors. Figure 1 provides a simple history of IR Sensor technology.

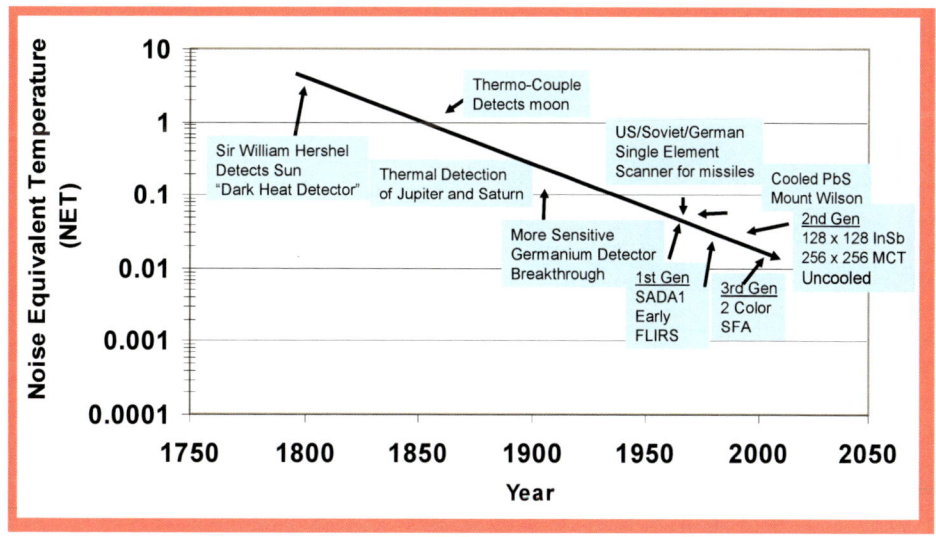

Figure 1. Simple history of IR detectors – NEDT vs. Era.

There is a impetus for developing advanced or 3rd Gen FPAs. The system rational and expected benefits for developing next generation IRFPAs include (but are not limited to):
- More functionality on FPAs for higher performance sensors
- Superiority in IR target detection
- More functionality on FPAs to support migration of the systems function onto the FPA
- Will allow upgrading smaller platforms with ultra high performance IRFPAs (UAVs, Unattended Sensors)
- Will open up IR sensor capability to other new applications due to size, weight reduction, and increased user friendliness
- Will drive down costs and improve reliability

2.0 Biological Inspired Vision Systems

RVS has turned to the biological retina for answers as to how to improve man made sensors. There are several retina attributes worth considering. These attributes are: Curved Retina- insures minimal optical aberrations, Temporal and Spatial Processing, Color Processing (back in optic nerve), WFOV with Foveated Pixel regions for variable acuity, motion/Moving target sensing, Rod/Cone Dark and Light adaptation, and stereoscopic sensors for range estimation.

A schematic of the eye is shown in Figure 2 illustrating the on retina processing. It is these types of processing paradigms that RVS wishes to exploit in order to improve our Advanced Sensors. While we don't yet fully understand all the biological functions, research into this area is ongoing. We call these sensors that attempt to exploit eye functions biologically inspired sensors. In fact, RVS has several programs that mimic several attributes of the human eye [1][2][3].

3.0 Multispectral Sensors

RVS has designed and fabricated Dual Band Multispectral IRFPAs. These FPAs can be used to detect different flux levels in disparate bands, and use spectral information for advanced discrimination. Figure 3 shows a snapshot of imagery taken at an airport with a Dual Band IRFPA.

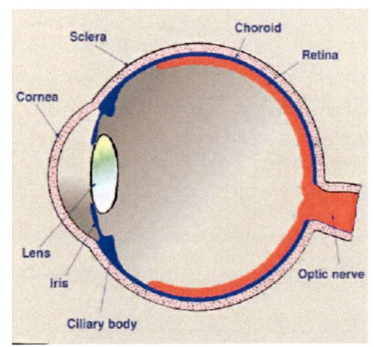
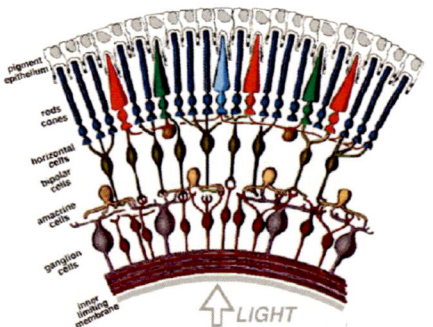

Figure 2. Biological Vision performs multiple color, temporal, spatial, opponent, and other processing in the Retinal Cells.

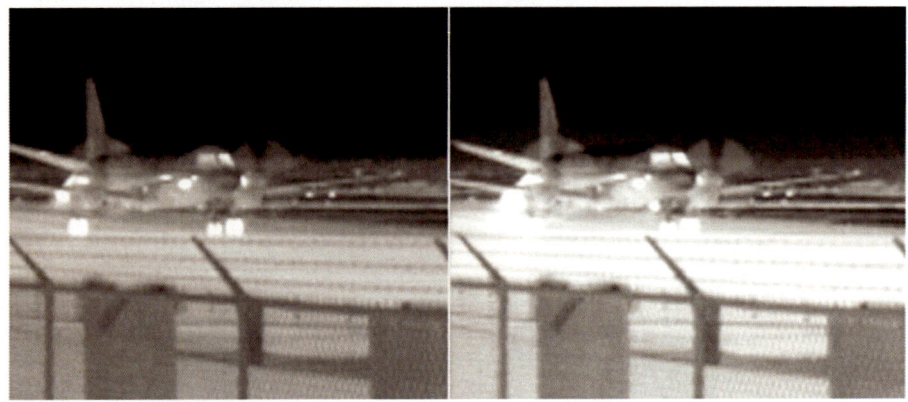

Figure 3. Imagery from RVS' Dual Band Sensor Technology.

4.0 Uncooled Sensors

Raytheon Vision Systems has developed a family of uncooled microbolometer FPAs. These FPAs have been designed to address commercial and high-performance military applications. These devices have been used as single color uncooled image cameras and also in multispectral applications [4]. These FPAs has been fabricated with several microbolometer pixel designs that allow optimization of either sensitivity or response time. These FPAs have been integrated into a variety of prototype sensors. Figure 4 illustrates the high quality imagery obtained from one of Raytheon's Microbolometer camera systems.

5.0 Smart Sensors with On-FPA processing

RVS has developed Smart Sensors with Adaptive pixel-based processing. One program recently completed is the Adaptive IR Sensor (AIRS). The AIRS (on the FPA processing) pixel-based processing has resulted in a Multifunctional FPA with selectable modes of operation. The modes of operation are illustrated in Figure 5.

Figure 4. Large Format microbolometer FPA Exhibits excellent uniformity and sensitivity.

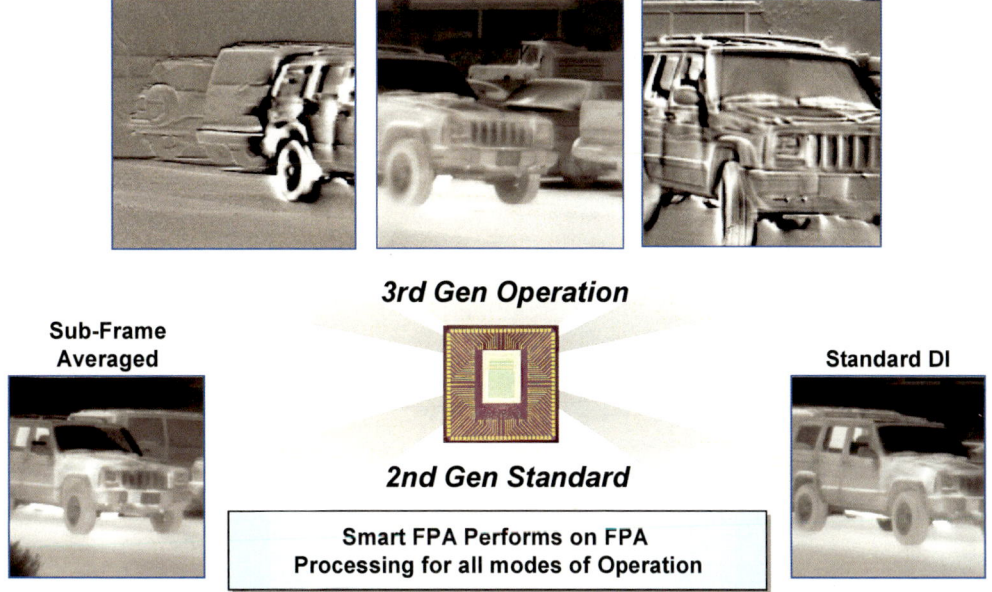

Figure 5. Smart FPA provides the user with multiple imaging functions including improving the sensor FPA sensitivity using subframe averaging.

Performance breakthroughs of the AIRS Smart FPA have been demonstrated in the following four modes of operation.

- **Direct Injection (DI).** The AIRS operates as a standard 2nd Generation imaging FPA.
- **Adaptive THP Scene-Based Non-Uniformity Correction.** This mode allows adaptive reduction of the Low frequency noise and drift component from the scene. The fixed pattern noise (FPN) is significantly reduced in the temporal high pass filter mode (THPF). The THPF lowers the temporal noise making marginal pixels (i.e., low responsivity or high noise) perform sufficiently for use.
- **Subframe Averaging.** This mode offers a tremendous advantage over existing designs. By averaging subframes, high photon shot noise is reduced and sensitivity is improved. Using low noise electronics vastly improved sensitivity of 3 x in NEDT in the subframe accumulation mode is possible.
- **Motion Detection/Edge Enhancement:** This mode offers the ability to remove all stationary scene clutter and only detect moving targets and edges. This mode is the THP mode running at a very high update rate.

6.0 Applications for Next Generation Sensors

Using the next generation FPA technology can provide benefits in numerous 21st century missions. The maturation of Multispectral, Uncooled, and Smart FPAs with On FPA pixel-based processing is enabling more refined sensing and processing which can be utilized to extract unique Spectral, Spatial, and Temporal features in imagery. Table 1 illustrates the various systems that could be improved or enabled with 3rd Gen Sensors:

Table 1. Next generation sensor requirements and constraints

Application	Constant Driver
•Homeland Defense	Cost
–Perimeter Security	Performance
•Unattended Ground Sensor	Power
–First responders	
•Firefighters	Cost, size
•Police	Cost
•Search and rescue	Size
•Military	Performance
–Driving and navigation	Performance, cost
–Weapons sights	Performance weight
–Long range acquisition sights	Performance
–Targeting	Performance, weight
–Track and seek	Performance, size

7.0 Summary

Raytheon has demonstrated an ability to do processing on the FPA that has previously been done in the FPA warm electronics. DOD funding has resulted in dramatic improvement in both MWIR and LWIR detectors. However, the IR detector industry is asymptotically approaching the upper limit of performance and operability. What is needed now are advanced ROICs that actually improve the performance of detectors and increase useful operability of FPAs. Also, with the DOD's desire for smaller, smarter, and lower power sensors, more image processing needs to be moved onto the FPA.

Raytheon's advanced sensor development efforts have demonstrated significant breakthroughs using advanced spectral, spatial, and temporal processing on the FPA:

- Multispectral Starting IRFPAs
- Uncooled Staring IRFPAs
- Multifunctional FPAs with On FPA Signal Processing

The excellent results achieved with Raytheon's Advanced FPA products illustrate that Next Generation FPAs are maturing and offer more capability than existing 2nd generation IRFPAs.

8.0 ACKNOWLEDGEMENTS

We would like to recognize the efforts of the Raytheon Advanced Technology teams developing Multispectral, Uncooled, and On FPA Signal Processing for making the new technology work. Raytheon also thanks the various sponsors for their continued support.

9.0 REFERENCES

1. J. Dowling, *The Retina: An Approachable Part of the Brain*, Belknap Press of Harvard University Press, Cambridge, MA, 1987.

2. Biological vision system information at http://www.webvision.med.utah.edu.

3. J. T. Caulfield, J. Fisher, J. A. Zadnik, E. S. Mak, D. A. Scribner, "Digital Characterization of a Neuromorphic IRFPA", Proceedings of the 1995 SPIE Aerosense Meeting, Orlando, FL. April, 1995.

4. D. Murphy, W. Radford, J. Finch, A. Kennedy, J. Wyles, M. Ray, R. Wyles, G. Polchin, N. Hua, and C. Peterson, "Multi-spectral Uncooled Microbolometer Sensor for the Mars 2001 Orbiter THEMIS Instrument", Proceedings of the 2000 SPIE Aerosense Meeting, Orlando, FL. April, 2000.

Multisensor & Spectral Image Fusion & Mining: From Neural Systems to Applications

David A. Fay, Richard T. Ivey, Neil Bomberger, and Allen M. Waxman
Cognitive Fusion Technology Directorate
ALPHATECH, Inc.
Burlington, MA, U.S.A.
{fay, rivey, neilb, waxman}@alphatech.com

Abstract

We have continued development of a system for multisensor image fusion and interactive mining based on neural models of color vision processing, learning and pattern recognition. We pioneered this work while at MIT Lincoln Laboratory, initially for color fused night vision (low-light visible and uncooled thermal imagery) and later extended it to multispectral IR and 3D ladar. We also developed a proof-of-concept system for EO, IR, SAR fusion and mining. Over the last year we have generalized this approach and developed a user-friendly system integrated into a COTS exploitation environment known as ERDAS Imagine. In this paper, we will summarize the approach and the neural networks used, and demonstrate fusion and interactive mining (i.e., target learning and search) of low-light visible/SWIR/MWIR/LWIR night imagery, and IKONOS multispectral and high-resolution panchromatic imagery. In addition, we will demonstrate how target learning and search can be enabled over extended operating conditions by allowing training over multiple scenes. This will be illustrated for the detection of small boats in coastal waters using fused visible/MWIR/LWIR imagery.

1. Introduction

We report here our progress on integrating our methods [1]-[6] for multisensor and multispectral image fusion and interactive image mining into a commercial GIS software environment, ERDAS *Imagine*. This allows us to leverage all of *Imagine*'s existing geospatial tools and quickly reach an entire user community already familiar with *Imagine*. We include add-on modules for *Image Conditioning*, *Image Fusion*, extraction of *Context Features*, and interactive *Image Mining*. Together, these modules create a work flow enabling a user to create vector products of foundation features (e.g., roads, rivers, and forests) and highlighted target detections from raw multisensor or multispectral imagery. In Section 3, examples of processed multispectral imagery will help illustrate this new fusion and mining environment.

As we have demonstrated in the past, multisensor image fusion and mining is also relevant to night vision applications [5][6]. We have presented work on fusion of two, three, and four sensors, including: low-light visible, short-wave infrared (SWIR), mid-wave infrared (MWIR), and long-wave infrared (LWIR) [5]. New results on fusion of these sensors, in two, three, and four sensor combinations, using a double-opponent color fusion architecture within the *Image Fusion* module will be presented in Section 4. We will also show image mining results, searching for men and a truck in a night scene, and describe the limitations in training on data selected from a single scene. A method for overcoming this limitation will be demonstrated in Section 5, along with results on image mining under extended operating conditions using a data set containing visible, MWIR and LWIR imagery of kayaks in coastal waters.

2. Neural Architectures

Our image fusion methods are motivated by biological examples of Visible/IR fusion in snakes [7], and color processing in the primate visual system [8][9]. We have, in the past, used these methods for both realtime fusion of multiple night vision sensors [5][6], and off-line exploitation of surveillance imagery including EO, IR, MSI, HSI, and SAR modalities [1]-[4].

Image fusion is based on the visual processes of spatial- and spectral-opponent networks, as realized in the retina and primary visual cortex. This serves to contrast enhance and adaptively normalize the wide-dynamic range imagery and also decorrelate the cross-modality interactions that occur in two stages, as shown in **Figure 1**. These opponent-color interactions can also be thought of as spectral contrast enhancement, as well as estimation of reflectance slope and curvature (i.e., they approximate local spatial derivatives with normalization). The opponent interactions are modeled using center-surround shunting neural networks [10][11] in a local feed-forward architecture to form a nonlinear image processing operator. This same operator is used repeatedly in the fusion architecture shown in **Figure 1**.

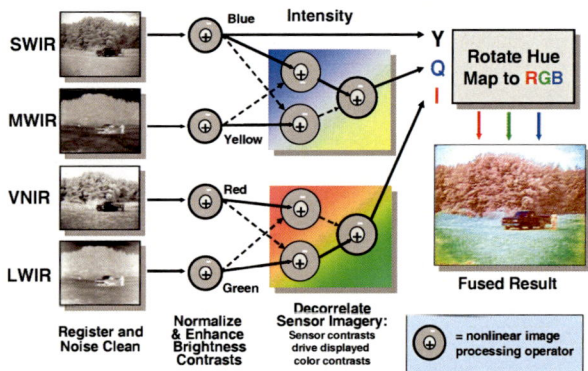

Figure 1. Double-opponent color architecture for image fusion constructed from center-surround shunting neural networks. This architecture can be modified to fuse imagery from two to five different sensors or spectral bands.

The outputs of all the opponent operators shown in **Figure 1** form registered image layers that contribute to the growing registered data stack shown in **Figure 2**. In addition, we extract spatial context features from the enhanced imagery, opponent-color imagery, and (if available) 3D information, in the form of extended contours, periodic textures, grayscale variance, and surface steepness and curvatures. Visual processing models of oriented contrast and contours on multiple scales are implemented as neural networks [12]-[14] to extract these context features. These context features augment the layered set of feature imagery that resembles a stack of spectral imagery (which can also be incorporated into the stack), and can be visualized as shown in **Figure 2**. A vertical cut through the stack corresponds to a feature vector at each pixel, which will serve as input to the neural pattern classifier described below.

Through the use of a simple point-and-click graphical user interface or GUI (to be illustrated in the next section), feature vectors can be selected to correspond to examples and counter-examples of targets of interest in the fused imagery. This training data is then fed to a pattern learning and recognition network in order to train a target detector (i.e., *search agent*) that can then be used to search extended areas for more of those targets. We utilize a combination of *Fuzzy ARTMAP* neural networks [15][16] and an algorithm which exploits the signatures of both target and context [4], to discover a much reduced feature subspace that is sufficient to learn the training data selected. This serves to accelerate the search for targets, highlights salient features of the target in context, and has implications for sensor tasking. The process of training data selection, pattern learning and subspace projection occurs very quickly, and is suitable for an interactive environment in which a human teaches the computer to find targets of interest.

A simplified version of the *Fuzzy ARTMAP* neural network is shown in **Figure 3**. It consists of a lower *ART* module, which performs unsupervised clustering of feature vectors into categories, and an upper layer in which the learned categories form associations with one or the other class for a target of interest. This approach enables the network to learn a compressed representation of the target class in the context of non-targets in the scene. That is, it learns to discriminate the target from the context, using the multisensor data and spatio-spectral features. A target of interest is typically represented by a few learned categories, as are the non-targets. Also shown are the match-tracking attentional pathways that modulate the matching criterion (vigilance) when predictive errors occur during training [16], leading to further category search or creation of new categories. *Simplified Fuzzy ARTMAP* [17] combines unsupervised category learning with supervised class association in hierarchy.

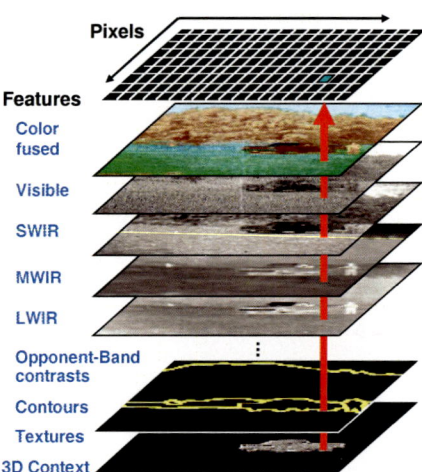

Figure 2. Layered stack of registered, processed, multisensor imagery and spatial context features, augmented by 3D features when available. A vertical cut through the stack corresponds to a feature vector at each pixel.

3. ERDAS Imagine Implementation

In order to enable widespread dissemination and use of our neural methods for multisensor/spectral image fusion and mining, we have refined and enhanced our prototype system [2], and reimplemented it within an extensible commercial image exploitation environment, ERDAS *Imagine*. This allows us to take advantage of the significant software infrastructure and capabilities of the *Imagine* suite, while supporting technology transfer to users already familiar with this exploitation environment.

The process workflow for image fusion and mining is shown in **Figure 4**, where the red and green boxes correspond to our own modules, and the blue boxes are modules developed from existing *Imagine* functionality. These modules are reflected in the software toolbar and pop-up menu, shown in **Figure 5**.

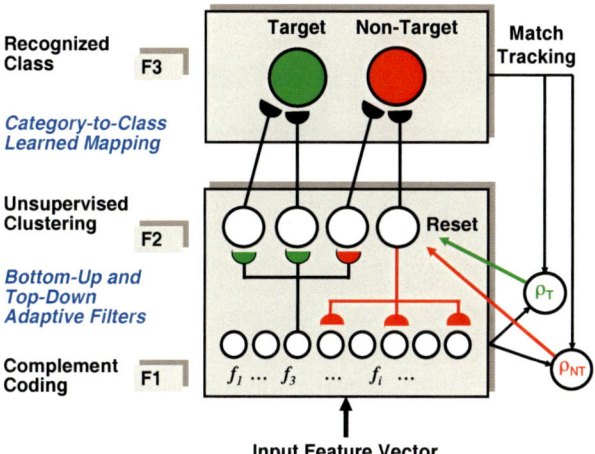

Figure 3. *Simplified Fuzzy ARTMAP* neural network used for interactive training of search agents that discriminate targets from non-targets in context.

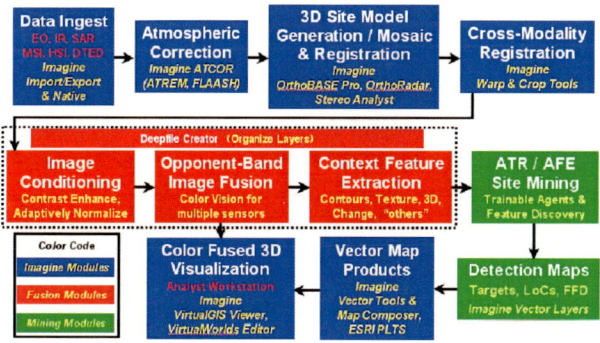

Figure 4. Workflow for multisensor and multispectral image fusion (red boxes) and mining (green boxes), integrated into the ERDAS *Imagine* environment (blue boxes).

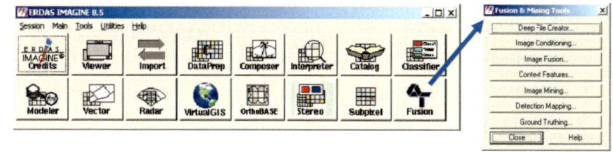

Figure 5. Toolbar for ERDAS *Imagine*, augmented with a Fusion button that launches our menu of *Fusion & Mining Tools*. Each menu button launches one of the corresponding modules.

Here we illustrate a few of the GUIs for these image fusion and mining tools. **Figure 6** illustrates the *Image Fusion* module user interface, with an area in Monterey, CA, imaged in four spectral bands (red, green, blue, near-IR) and a panchromatic band, being fused into a color presentation. This module, based on opponent-color processing, supports mixed-resolution imagery as collected by the IKONOS satellite.

Figure 6. User interface for image fusion of up to 5 sensors or spectral bands. Opponent-sensor pairs are mapped to human opponent-colors *red vs. green* and *blue vs. yellow*. An additional channel supports a high-resolution intensity band. The viewers show a site overview (upper-right), main window (left), and detail area (lower-right window) of Monterey, CA.

After image fusion and context features are generated using the various modules, and layered onto the geodatabase we call a deepfile, the user begins the process of interactive *Image Mining* by launching the GUI shown in **Figure 7**. A *search agent* (5 ARTMAP networks) is easily trained to find targets pointed out by example and counter-example. Also, a subset of sufficient feature layers is discovered that is able to support 99-100% correct categorization of the selected training examples and counter-examples, and the user is then informed of these important feature layers, as shown in **Figure 8**. As the user points out mistakes or missed targets in subsequent search areas, the mining system learns to improve its performance and refines the trained search agent. This training process is very rapid. The trained agent can then be used to search for targets over the entire scene.

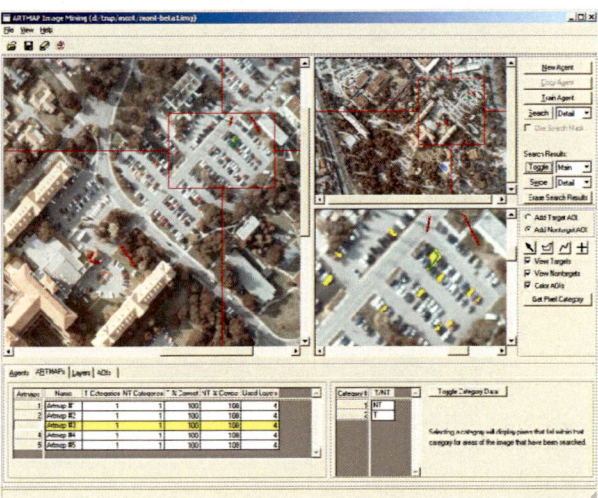

Figure 7. GUI for interactive *Image Mining* using *ARTMAP* pattern learning & recognition. The user selects training pixels, examples (in green) and counter-examples (in red). Each pixel has an associated feature vector. In this case the agent has learned to find red cars (detections shown in yellow in the lower-right detail window) in Monterey, CA.

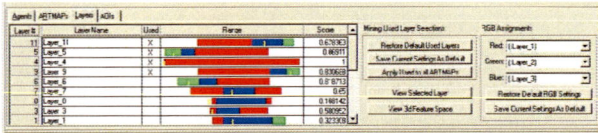

Figure 8. The *Layers* tab in the *Image Mining* GUI shows the system discovered that only 4 of the original 20 layers were needed to find the red car targets in context. The GUI supports the user in understanding the feature space, the categories generated, and their relation to the training data. Interactive 3D viewing of data clusters and learned categories is supported as well (and will be illustrated in Figure 13 for a different example).

Following the search process, detections can be filtered using morphological processing and then converted to vectors for editing, attributing, and map-making. Multiple search agents are trained and used in order to construct maps of multiple classes. To add new target classes to a map, one need only train a new search agent for the new class, and multiple agents could be constructed simultaneously by multiple operators exploiting the same data set. **Figure 9** illustrates the GUI used to convert raster detections into vectors for map-making. This example utilizes IKONOS imagery (4-band MSI at 4-meter resolution in conjunction with a panchromatic image at 1-meter resolution) of a steel plant outside Charleston, South Carolina. In this example, a first-time user trained an agent to find piles of iron ore (outlined with yellow vectors), and discovered trains carrying ore to the plant (as indicated in the lower-right detail window).

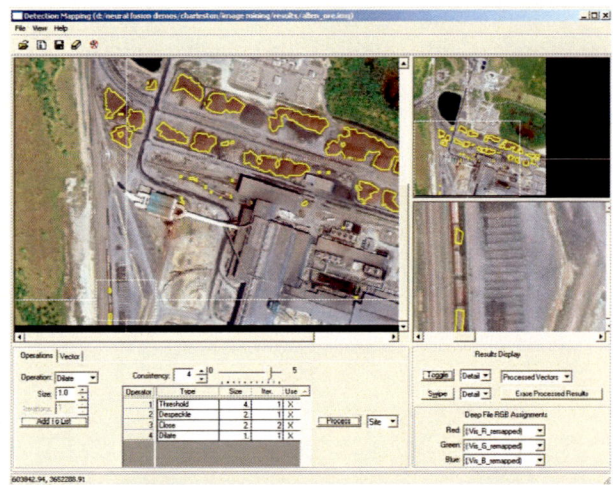

Figure 9. IKONOS imagery has been fused and combined with spatial context features for mining. A first-time user rapidly trained the system to search for iron ore. This *Detection Mapping* module supports morphological filtering of the detections and conversion to vectors for map-making. Iron ore detections have been outlined by vectors in yellow, and train cars are found carrying ore to the plant (as revealed in the lower-right detail window).

4. Application to Night Vision

The *Image Fusion* and *Mining* software described above is also able to support ground based sensors that do not have georeferencing capabilities, as long as the imagery can be registered. We previously reported results on two, three, and four sensor fusion for night vision applications [5]. For that work, multiple variations of the fusion architecture were used depending on the number and types of sensors employed. Using our current implementation inside the ERDAS *Imagine* environment, we can now support fusion of two, three, four, or five sensors with the same fusion architecture shown in **Figure 1**. **Figure 10** shows the fused result of imagery from SWIR and LWIR sensors taken at night under 2/3-moon (27 mLux) lighting conditions. The *Image Fusion* GUI includes pull-down menus for selecting images to feed the five input channels of the fusion architecture. In the dual-band example shown in **Figure 10**, the SWIR image is used as input to the *Red*, *Blue*, and *Intensity* channels (see the architecture diagram in **Figure 1**). Opponency is created between the SWIR and LWIR images by feeding the *Green* and *Yellow* channels with the LWIR image and its reverse (black-hot). The color fused result retains and enhances the complementary information contained in the original SWIR and LWIR images (see **Figure 1**) and produces a strong visual separation between the truck, men, and background.

Figure 10. *Image Fusion* GUI illustrating fusion of two sensors: SWIR and LWIR. Mappings between the input images and the opponent channels (see fusion architecture diagram in Figure 1) are determined by selections in the lower-left of the GUI. For example, the SWIR conditioned image is used as input to the *Red*, *Blue*, and *Intensity* channels.

The left side of **Figure 11** shows fused results for a tri-sensor (Low-light Visible-NIR, SWIR, and LWIR) system created using the same fusion architecture with different input pairings. Results from quad-sensor (Low-light Visible-NIR, SWIR, MWIR, and LWIR) fusion are shown on the right of **Figure 11**.

The image fusion results are combined with image conditioning results and extracted context features to form a multi-layered data structure (as in **Figure 2**) which serves as input to the *Image Mining* module. **Figure 12** shows detection results for the dual-sensor system (SWIR & LWIR) after training a search agent to recognize men in the scene. The search agent was trained with examples from the man standing next to the truck and counter-examples from the truck, tress, ground, and sky. After training, the search of the entire scene detects both the man standing and the man in the truck, and only a few false detections in the trees.

Figure 11. *Left*: Tri-sensor (Low-light Visible-NIR, SWIR, and LWIR) fusion results. *Right*: Quad-sensor (Low-light Visible-NIR, SWIR, MWIR, and LWIR) fusion results. All results are created with the fusion architecture of Figure 1.

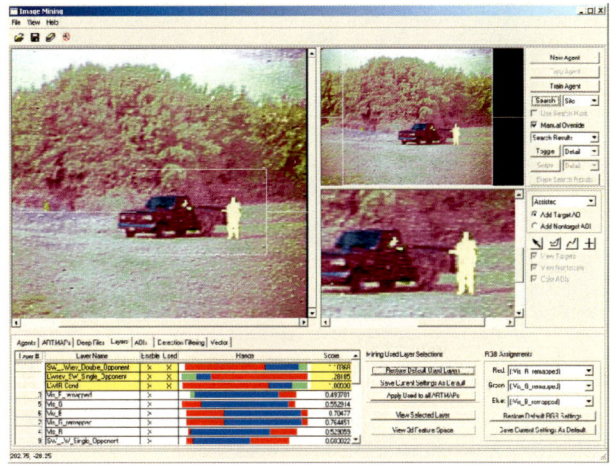

Figure 12. *Image Mining* GUI showing detection results for a search agent trained to find man targets in the dual-sensor (SWIR & LWIR) data. The *Layers* tab indicates which layers were discovered to be important by our feature selection algorithm for one of the *ARTMAP* networks. The 3D feature space created by the three highlighted features is shown in Figure 13 along with the target and non-target category boxes.

In the lower-left of the *Image Mining* GUI shown in **Figure 12**, the Layers tab shows the 3 layers, discovered by our feature selection algorithm, that are sufficient for one of the *ARTMAP* networks to discriminate between targets and non-targets in the training data. They include single and double opponent results and the thermal LWIR conditioned results. In order to visualize the relationship between the target and non-target categories in feature space, using just these three features, the *Image Mining* module contains an interactive 3D category viewer, as shown in **Figure 13**. For the selected *ARTMAP* network, there is only one target category (green box) and four non-target categories (overlapping red boxes) learned. **Figure 14** shows very similar performance results for detecting men in the scene using the tri-sensor and quad-sensor systems described above. This improvement and consistency in performance, as compared to our earlier results [5], can be attributed to the use of a unified fusion architecture and to improvements in the methods for extracting spatial context features.

5. Fusion and Mining under Extended Operating Conditions

The night vision image mining examples presented above demonstrate training under a single set of operating conditions and searching under those same conditions. In this section we will present results on extending the range of operating conditions under which a trained *search agent* can be successfully employed. This will be accomplished by allowing training examples to be selected from more than one image, thus increasing opportunities for encountering a variety of collection conditions.

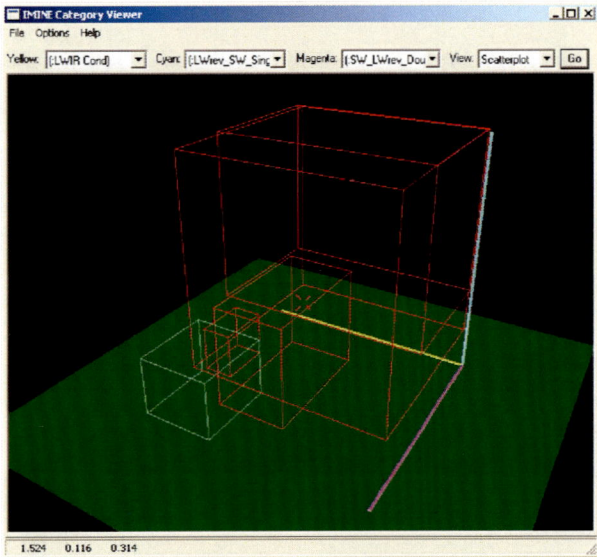

Figure 13. Interactive *Category Viewer* showing target (green boxes) and non-target (red boxes) category boxes in 3D feature space.

Figure 14. *Left*: *Image Mining* results for man target search using three sensors. *Right*: *Image Mining* results for quad-sensor. The search for the man targets is successful in all three sensor configurations (dual-, tri-, and quad-sensor), and also finds a deer hiding in the trees at night.

Figure 15. Conditioned images (whole scene on left, detail on right) from one of the Den Helder scenes (scene 4130a) showing three kayaks in the water near a buoy (triangular object on the right). *Top*: Visible imagery. *Middle*: MWIR imagery. *Bottom*: LWIR imagery. The MWIR imagery is the sharpest and has the highest contrast between the kayaks and the water.

The data set used for these experiments includes imagery from three sensors: Visible, MWIR, and LWIR, collected under overcast skies in the late afternoon and early evening. The images were collected by Alexander Toet in Den Helder, The Netherlands, for his study on detecting point targets on the water using multisensor fusion [17]. **Figure 15** shows an example image from each sensor after they have been processed with our *Image Conditioning* module. The left column shows the entire coastal scene with three men in kayaks paddling near a buoy (triangular shape). The right column shows a zoomed in view of the rectangular area indicated in the full images on the left. The visible image has the most literal appearance, but has the weakest contrast between the kayaks and the surrounding water. The kayaks appear sharpest and have the highest contrast in the MWIR image, making the kayaks easier to detect and identify. Hundreds of images were collected over a period of approximately three hours in which the illumination and environmental conditions changed dramatically. In addition, camera settings were adjusted during the collection, creating a wide variety of operating conditions.

We selected four representative triplets of images from this large data set and processed them with our *Image Conditioning*, *Image Fusion*, and *Context Feature* modules to create co-registered data structures (*deepfiles*) for multiple scenes. The assignment of the three sensors to the double-opponent color fusion architecture is as follows: Visible to *Red* channel, LWIR to *Green* channel, MWIR to *Blue* channel, and reverse-LWIR to *Yellow* channel. Color fused results for each triplet are shown in **Figure 16**. The variety in collection conditions yields fused images with slightly different appearances, yet all still have strong color contrasts between the kayaks and the background.

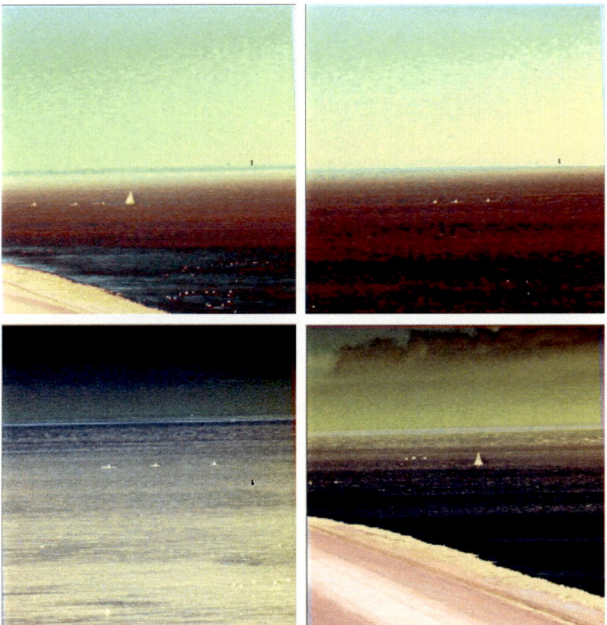

Figure 16. Color fused results for the four Den Helder scenes (4130a, 3624a, 8548a, and a424a) collected under different environmental and lighting conditions. While the appearances of each scene are different, they all have strong color contrast between the three dim point targets (kayaks) and the surrounding water.

A search agent is created in the *Image Mining* module for detecting the kayaks using examples and counter-examples selected from only a single scene, 4130a, shown in Figures 15 and 16. Examples are chosen from each of the three kayaks in the scene and counter-examples are taken from the sky, the water, the beach, and the buoy. After training is completed satisfactorily, all four scenes are searched. The first column in **Figure 17** shows a close up of the three kayaks from the color fused results for each of the four scenes. The second column shows the masked search results for each of the scenes, using the search agent created from scene 4130a, with targets being highlighted in colors ranging from red to yellow. The lighter colors indicate higher *confidence* detections. The top image in the second column shows that all three kayaks are detected with high confidence. The next result image down the second column contains search results for scene 3624a using the kayak search agent from scene 4130a. In this case, only two of the three kayaks are detected with low confidence and there are numerous false detections throughout the full scene. Search results from scenes 8548a and a424a, shown in the lower two images of the second column, do not contain target detections on any of the kayaks, yet there are many false detections. The poor performance on the other three scenes searched, using the kayak search agent created with examples from only scene 4130a, can be attributed to using a sparse set of training data. In this example, the training data from scene 4130a did not provide enough coverage in the regions of feature space occupied by the feature vectors from the other three scenes. To alleviate this problem we increase the variety of training data by allowing selection of training samples from multiple fused scenes.

Target and non-target training data is selected from all four scenes collected under different environmental conditions. After training a search agent for kayak targets, all four scenes were again searched, as shown in column three at the right of **Figure 17**. All three kayaks were detected with high confidence in each of the four scenes, with no false alarms. *This example shows that successful target learning and search can be achieved over extended operating conditions by increasing the variety of training data.*

In order to gain further insight into why performance improved when training data was selected over different environmental conditions, we can look at the how the Fuzzy ARTMAP categories change as more training data is added. The top image in **Figure 18** shows the target and non-target category boxes in 3D feature space using the three salient features discovered for one of the Fuzzy ARTMAP networks trained using data from only scene 4130a. There are two target category boxes (dark green) and nine non-target category boxes (dark red). The green and red points inside the category boxes indicate the locations of the target and non-target training data within this 3D feature space. Although two target categories were created, there is essentially only one cluster of target training data. However, the non-target training data is distributed throughout most of the 3D feature space, forming multiple clusters.

The previous target cluster has expanded due to the increased variety in training data. In addition, a new target cluster has formed (upper-left) indicating a more drastic change to the target signatures under one of the collection conditions. This increased coverage of the target categories leads to the improved detections of the kayaks across the extended operating conditions. The number of non-target categories has increased to 21, further refining the representation of the non-target signatures, which ultimately leads to fewer false alarm detections.

For the experiments described here, increased variety in the training data was accomplished by selecting examples from subsequent images collected at later times under different environmental and illumination conditions. In future work, we will explore the use of a single scene while simulating changes in operating conditions for situations when collecting data over variable environmental conditions is not possible.

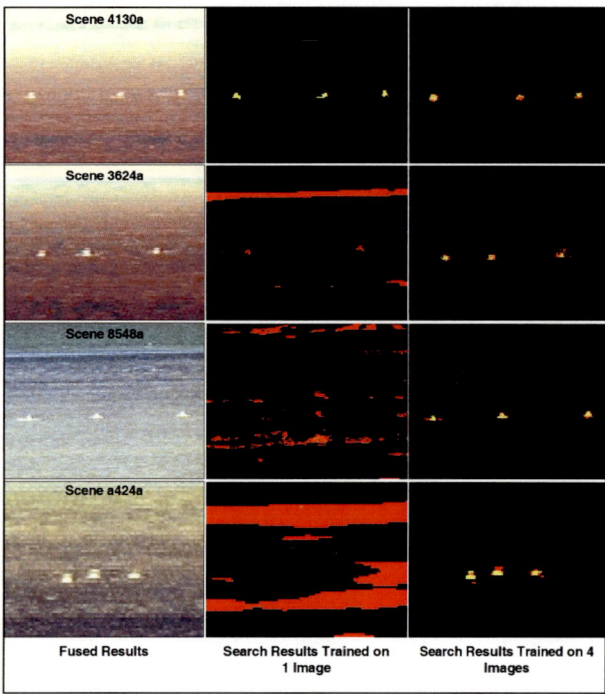

Figure 17. Target search under extended operating conditions. *Left column*: Color fused results of cropped area around the three kayaks for all four scenes. *Middle column*: Search results for kayaks using an agent created with examples from only scene 4130a showing many missed and false detections. *Right column*: Improved search results for kayaks using an agent created with examples from all four scenes. All three kayaks are detected and there no false alarms. By selecting training examples from multiple scenes, the ARTMAP networks are able to learn a more robust representation of the targets across extended operating conditions.

The bottom image in **Figure 18** shows the category boxes for the same Fuzzy ARTMAP network after further training with data from the other three scenes. There are now 19 target categories covering the target training data.

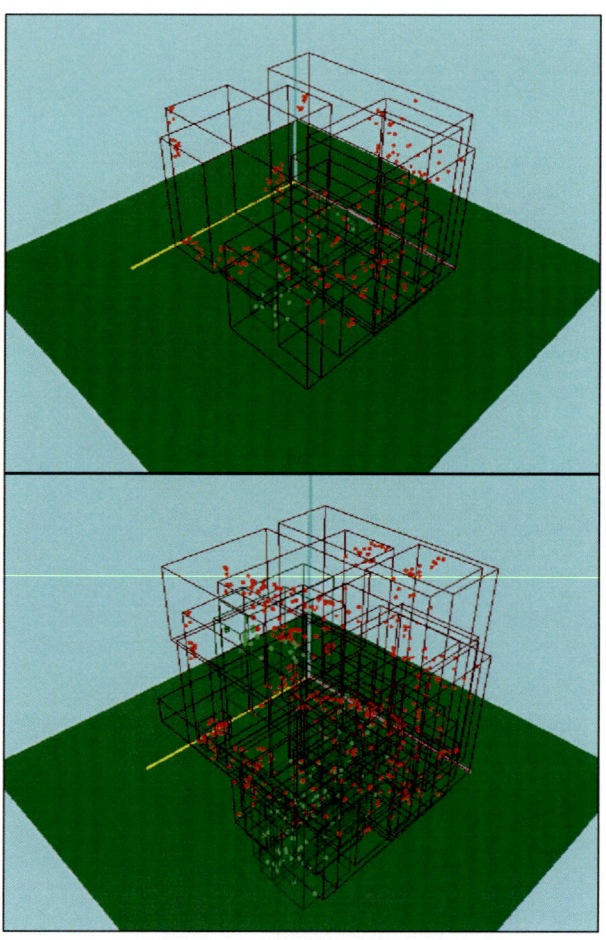

Figure 18. A more robust representation of the target is learned after training across multiple scenes. *Top*: Target (green) and non-target (red)

categories created by a Fuzzy ARTMAP network trained with data from a single scene shown in 3D feature space. *Bottom*: **Categories for the same network after further training with data from three other scenes collected under extended operating conditions.**

6. Conclusions

We have summarized an architecture and approach for multisensor image fusion and mining that is based on biological vision processing and pattern learning & recognition paradigms, and modeled using adaptive neural networks. These methods have now been integrated into the commercial exploitation environment of ERDAS *Imagine*, and applied to surveillance imagery collected by airborne and space-based platforms. We presented results on image fusion and mining for night vision applications, using the same double-opponent color fusion architecture for two, three, and four sensor combinations. Finally, we demonstrated how multisensor image mining can be successful across extended operating conditions by selecting training data from multiple scenes. Future work will explore image mining based on multispectral imagery modified by simulated environmental conditions.

7. Acknowledgements

The authors would like to thank Alexander Toet from the TNO for providing the data set presented in Section 5.

8. References

[1] A.M. Waxman, D.A. Fay, B.J. Rhodes, T.S. McKenna, R.T. Ivey, N.A. Bomberger, V.K. Bykoski, and G.A. Carpenter, *Information fusion for image analysis: Geospatial foundations for higher-level fusion,* in 5th International Conference on Information Fusion, Annapolis, 2002.

[2] A.M. Waxman, J.G. Verly, D.A. Fay, F. Liu, M.I. Braun, B. Pugliese, W. Ross, and W. Streilein, *A prototype system for 3D color fusion and mining of multisensor/spectral imagery,* in 4th International Conference on Information Fusion, Montreal, 2001.

[3] W. Ross, A. Waxman, W. Streilein, J. Verly, F. Liu, M. Braun, P. Harmon, and S. Rak, *Multisensor image fusion for 3D site visualization and search,* in 3rd International Conference on Information Fusion, Paris, 2000.

[4] W. Streilein, A. Waxman, W. Ross, F. Liu, M. Braun, J. Verly, and C.H. Read, *Fused multisensor image mining for feature foundation data,* in 3rd International Conference on Information Fusion, Paris, 2000.

[5] D.A. Fay, A.M. Waxman, M. Aguilar, D.B. Ireland, J.P. Racamato, W.D. Ross, W.W. Streilein, and M.I. Braun, *Fusion of 2-/3-/4-Sensor Imagery for Visualization, Target Learning and Search,* in Proceeds of the SPIE Conference on Enhanced and Synthetic Vision 2000, **SPIE-4023**, pp.106-115, 2000.

[6] D.A. Fay, A.M. Waxman, J.G. Verly, M.I. Braun, J.P. Racamato, and C. Frost, *Fusion of visible, infrared and 3D LADAR imagery,* in 4th International Conference on Information Fusion, Montreal, 2001. Also see (same authors) *Fusion of Multisensor Passive and Active 3D Imagery,* in Proceeds of the SPIE Conference on Enhanced and Synthetic Vision 2001, **SPIE-4363**, pp. 219-230, 2001.

[7] E.A. Newman and P.H. Hartline, *The infrared vision of snakes,* Scientific American, **246** (March), 116-127, 1982.

[8] P. Schiller, and N.K. Logothetis, *The color-opponent and broad-band channels of the primate visual system,* Trends in Neuroscience, **TINS-13**, 392-398, 1990.

[9] P. Gouras, *Color vision,* Chapter 31 in **Principles of Neural Science** (E.R. Kandel, J.H. Schwartz and T.M. Jessell, editors), pp. 467-480, New York: Elsevier Science Publishers, 1991.

[10] S. Grossberg, *Nonlinear neural networks: Principles, mechanisms and architectures,* Neural Networks, **1**, 17-61, 1988.

[11] D.S. Levine, **Introduction to Neural and Cognitive Modeling**, 2nd edition, Mahwah, NJ: Lawrence Erlbaum Associates, 2000.

[12] J.G. Daugman, *Uncertainty relation for resolution in space, spatial frequency, and orientation optimized by two-dimensional visual cortical filters,* J. Optical Society of America A, **2**, pp. 1160-1169, 1985.

[13] S. Grossberg and E. Mingolla, *Neural dynamics of perceptual grouping: Textures, boundaries and emergent segmentations,* Perception & Psychophysics, **38**, 141-171, 1985.

[14] A.M. Waxman, M.C. Seibert, A. Gove, D.A. Fay, A.M. Bernardon, C. Lazott, W.R. Steele, and R.K. Cunningham, *Neural processing of targets in visible, multispectral IR and SAR imagery,* Neural Networks, **8**, 1029-1051, 1995.

[15] G.A. Carpenter, S. Grossberg, and D.B. Rosen, *Fuzzy ART: Fast stable learning and categorization of analog patterns by an adaptive resonance system,* Neural Networks, **4**, 759-771, 1991.

[16] G.A. Carpenter, S. Grossberg, N. Markuzon, J.H. Reynolds, and D.B. Rosen, *Fuzzy ARTMAP: A neural network architecture for incremental supervised learning of analog multidimensional maps,* IEEE Transactions on Neural Networks, **3**, pp. 698-713, 1992.

[17] T. Kasuba, *Simplified Fuzzy ARTMAP*, AI Expert, pp. 18-25, Nov 1993.

[18] A. Toet, *Detection of dim point targets in cluttered maritime backgrounds through multisensor image fusion*, in Proceeds of SPIE Conference on Targets and Backgrounds 2002, **SPIE-4718**, pp. 118-129, 2002.

Fused Spectropolarimetric Visible Near-IR Imaging

Neelam Gupta
Sensors and Electron Devices Directorate
U.S. Army Research Laboratory,
2800 Powder Mill Road, Adelphi, MD 20783
ngupta@arl.army.mil

Abstract

We report on the development and characterization of a compact, lightweight, robust, and field-portable spectropolarimetric imaging system at the U.S. Army Research Laboratory (ARL). It operates in the 400 to 900 nm region with a passband of 10 nm at 600 nm. This automated imager is designed using a tellurium dioxide (TeO_2) acousto-optic tunable filter (AOTF) as an agile spectral selection element and a commercial nematic liquid-crystal variable retardation (LCVR) plate as a tunable polarization selection device with an off-the-shelf uncooled charge coupled device (CCD) camera and optics. Image acquisition with both spectral and polarization features facilitates significant improvement in target detection. Here we will describe the design concept and our program, with a detailed description of the VNIR imager, and present images obtained from it and the analysis of the results.

1. Introduction

In order to perform better target detection imaging sensors need to be designed that can capture not only spatial and spectral but also polarization information from the objects in the scene. Fusion of the spectral and polarization information in the images results in better target identification and recognition and can save lives. Spectral features arise due to the material properties of objects based on the chemical composition as a result of the emission, reflection, and absorption of light, while the polarization features arise from the physical nature of the object surfaces (whether they are smooth or rough) and edges that influence the polarization properties of the reflected, scattered, or emitted light. In general, man-made objects have more defined polarization signatures due to their well defined regular contours than natural objects such as soil and vegetation that generally have irregular shapes. These natural objects often make up background scenarios of interest in many applications. Besides their shapes, objects and backgrounds have unique spectral signature information that can be used for discrimination and identification. Using hyperspectral imaging one can acquire images with narrow spectral bands and take advantage of the characteristic spectral signatures of different materials making up objects and backgrounds. By combining both polarization and hyperspectral detection capabilities in one single imager, we can perform much better object detection and identification than by using either polarization or hyperspectral capability alone. Traditional hyperspectral imaging systems use gratings and prisms and acquire images in hundreds of bands, requiring a huge amount of data processing. In general, object detection requires spectral images at a few bands that change based on the object and background scenarios. This clearly establishes a need to design adaptive imaging systems.

An imager designed using an acousto-optic tunable filter (AOTF) is ideally suited to provide both agile spectral and polarization signatures. At the U.S. Army Research Laboratory (ARL), we are developing small, vibration-insensitive, robust, remotely controlled, and programmable hyperspectral imagers covering the ultraviolet (UV) to the long wave infrared (LWIR) spectral regions for Army specific applications. These imagers require minimum amount of data processing because they can collect data at only select wavelengths of interest and the selected wavelengths can be changed based on the scenes of interest. The time needed to change wavelengths is very short (in tens of μs). This agility in data collection is quite critical for hyperspectral applications because it greatly reduces the data processing requirements associated with the vast quantity of data collection and utilization associated with traditional hyperspectral imaging systems. An AOTF is also a polarization sensitive device because the diffracted beams from it are orthogonally polarized. By combining it with another polarizing device, a polarizer/analyzer system can be developed to obtain polarization information from the scene of interest. Such imagers have applications in various other fields as well, such as astronomy, atmospheric sciences, geology, museums, medicine, remote sensing, chemical analysis, etc.

At ARL, a number of different noncollinear AOTFs fabricated in different birefringent crystals with different cameras are used to cover the wavelengths from UV to LWIR. We use a potassium dihydrophosphate (KDP) AOTF with an extended range response Si charge coupled device (CCD) camera to cover the UV to visible region from 220 to 480 nm, a tellurium dioxide (TeO$_2$) AOTF with an off-the-shelf Si CCD camera to cover the visible to near-infrared (VNIR) region from 400 to 900 nm, a TeO$_2$ AOTF to cover the short wave IR (SWIR) region from 900 to 1700 nm with a room temperature InGaAs camera, another TeO$_2$ AOTF with a liquid nitrogen-cooled indium antimonide (InSb) camera to cover the mid wave IR (MWIR) region from 2 to 4.5 µm, and a thalium arsenic selenide (TAS) AOTF with a liquid nitrogen-cooled mercury cadmium telluride (HgCdTe) camera to cover the LWIR region from 7.8 to 9.7 µm. Each imager has a suitable optical train. We have used a nematic liquid crystal variable retarder (LCVR) as the first polarization element to cover wavelength regions from 400 nm to 1700 nm and developed a prototype LCVR for the 2–4.5 µm spectral region. The operation of each imager and its image acquisition is computer controlled.

The VNIR imager is the most developed imaging system. It has a 10-nm spectral resolution at 600 nm, and uses a TeO$_2$ AOTF for spectral selection and an electronically tunable nematic crystal commercial LCVR to change the incident polarization. Each spectral image is acquired with two retardation values, corresponding to the horizontal and vertical incident polarizations. The wavelength is controlled by changing the radio frequency (rf) signal applied to the AOTF, which can be done either locally or remotely. RF electronics and control and image processing software have been developed for automated image capture, acquisition, and storage. The operation of the imager and image acquisition is completely computer controlled. Here we will describe our concept in designing a spectropolarimetric imager, give a detailed description of the VNIR imager, and present raw images obtained with it and the analysis of these images.

2. Spectropolarimetric Imager Concept

To understand the wavelength tuning operation of such imagers, it is important to know how a noncollinear AOTF works. In an AOTF, a radio frequency (rf) signal is applied to a piezoelectric transducer that is attached to a birefringent crystal to produce an ultrasonic wave that travels through the crystal. This sets up a moving diffraction grating in the crystal. An acoustic absorber absorbs the sound wave after it traverses the crystal. When unpolarized white light is incident on such a crystal, it is diffracted by the traveling acoustic wave, and it produces two diffracted beams with orthogonal polarizations—one with a Doppler upshifted and the other with a Doppler downshifted optical frequency for a given applied rf—based on the phase-matching condition. (The Doppler shift is negligible for the optical frequencies.) The diffracted optical wavelength can be tuned by changing the applied rf [1,2]. There is also an undiffracted light beam that contains all the incident wavelengths minus the one that is diffracted. In our imager design, we use one of the diffracted beams to image the spectral scene in a time domain using a CCD camera and block the second diffracted as well as the undiffracted beam as shown in figure 1. To obtain the polarimetric information we use another polarizing element—an electronically controlled spectrally dependent retarder—in the optical train before the AOTF [3]. Another approaches is to image both the diffracted beams on separate cameras to obtain the polarimetric information [4,5].

The spectrally tunable nematic LCVR in front of the AOTF is a commercial off-the-shelf component that is used to obtain two retardance values corresponding to the horizontal and vertical polarizations for each diffracted wavelength. The tuning of such a retarder is done by changing the applied voltage. The LCVR passes most of the incident light with very little absorption. The diffracted beam from the AOTF is imaged on a commercial CCD camera. Since the wavelength filtered by the AOTF can be tuned to any value within the tuning range, we can acquire a spectropolarimetric image cube by tuning over the wavelength range. Since both the retarder and the AOTF are tuned electronically, no moving parts are involved. This makes our imager adaptive and robust as compared to other traditional hyperspectral imagers. We have also set up another spectropolarimetric imaging experiment using three separate cameras to image the two diffracted beams and the undiffracted zero order beam. The camera used for the undiffracted beam can be a higher resolution camera to provide a high resolution regular image of the scene under observation. This camera can be either a CCD camera or an IR camera depending on the particular application and the AOTF. In our table top imaging setup, we use one AOTF with broad spectral coverage (we have two AOTFs that operate over more than two octave in wavelength and cover visible to MWIR range). The images from the zero order imaging camera can be used to improve the spatial resolution of both the spectral images that in general are obtained with lower resolution cameras.

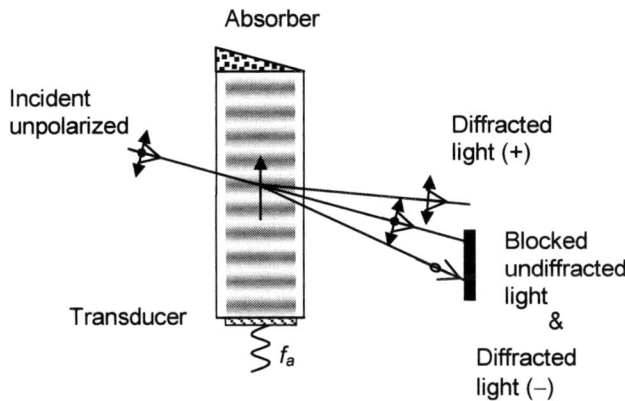

Figure 1. Filtering operation of a noncollinear AOTF.

3. Imager Development

At ARL, we are developing AOTF-based spectropolarimetric/hyperspectral imagers covering wavelength regions from UV to LWIR using different birefringent acousto-optic (AO) materials, as listed in table 1 [6–9]. Spectral range, spectral resolution, AOTF crystal material, retarder, and camera focal plane array (FPA) with its temperature of operation for each of these imagers are listed in this table.

Table 1: ARL spectropolarimetric imagers

Imager	Spect. Range (μm)	Spect. Resolu-tion (nm)	AOTF Xtal	Retard-er	FPA
UV	0.22–0.48	1.4 at 0.3 μm	KDP		Si CCD Rm. Temp
VNIR	0.4–0.9	10 at 0.6 μm	TeO$_2$	Nemat-ic LC	Si CCD Rm. Temp.
SWIR	0.9–1.7	10.4 at 1.3 μm	TeO$_2$	Nemat-ic LC	InGaAs Rm. Temp.
MWIR	2.0–4.5	77 at 3 μm	TeO$_2$	Nemat-ic LC	InSb 77 K
LWIR	8.0–10.0	80 at 10 μm	TAS		MCT 77 K

With our collaborators (Moscow State University, Northrop Grumman Corporation, etc.) we are developing new AOTF cells and materials for fabricating such cells.

So far both KDP and MgF$_2$ cells operating from vacuum UV to visible wavelengths [10–12], TeO$_2$ AOTF cells with multiple transducers operating with greater than one octave range in wavelength from visible to MWIR, and TAS cells for LWIR have been developed [13]. Now Hg$_2$Br$_2$ crystals are being grown to fabricate AOTFs operating in the range from 0.4 to 30 μm [14,15]. We have characterized an LCVR operating in the MWIR region and investigated LWIR retarder options under an SBIR program.

4. VNIR Spectropolarimetric Imager

As mentioned earlier, the VNIR imager is the most developed among all the imagers listed in table 1. Now, we will focus on this imager. The most important requirement for designing an imaging AOTF cell is a large light throughput. Since we bin the entire spectral region into narrow bands, the intensity in each of these narrow bands in quite low. In order to obtain a reasonably high signal-to-noise ratio, we need to design the cell with a relatively broad bandpass and large linear and angular apertures. These requirements need to be translated into the cell design by choosing an appropriate birefringent material and computer modelling to obtain the optimum cell design.

The AOTF used in this imager was fabricated in TeO$_2$ for a wide-angle AO diffraction geometry with a Bragg polar incidence angle of 14°. The LiNbO$_3$ transducer makes a tilt angle of 6° with respect to the optical axis in the (1 $\overline{1}$0) interaction plane of the crystal. The input aperture of the AOTF is 1.5×1.5 cm^2. Both the electrical and acoustic impedance matching were done carefully to couple most of the applied rf power into the crystal as acoustic power. The electrical impedance matching was done to match the impedance of the transducer to 50 Ω over the full operational rf range. The angular separation between the diffracted and the incident beams in the air is 4.2°. A wedge is formed on the output facet by rotating it 4.3° with respect to the input facet. This wedge minimizes the spectral scene shift of the output diffracted beam. The filter was designed to operate with the ordinary (vertically) polarized incident beam and the extraordinary (horizontally) polarized diffracted beam. Figure 2 shows the layout and figure 3 shows a photograph of an AOTF filter.

The filter operates in the rf range from 44 to 126.5 MHz, corresponding to the wavelength range from 420 to 880 nm. The experimentally measured tuning curve for this filter is shown in figure 2. The spectral bandpass of the filter is 10 nm at 600 nm. The diffraction efficiency of the filter is close to 95% with 0.9 W of rf power. The acoustic velocity in this crystal is 650 m/s, and for a 1.5

cm aperture we can change the frequency every 23 μs. In other words, we can obtain 4.33×10^4 spectral image frames per second.

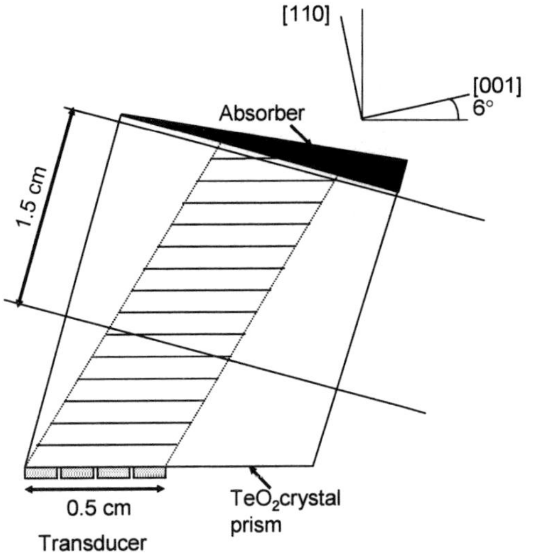

Figure 2. Layout of TeO$_2$ AOTF.

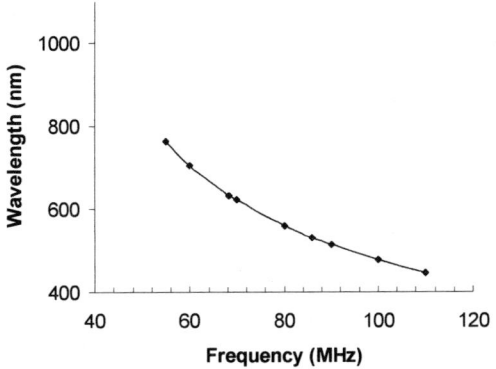

Figure 3. TeO$_2$ AOTF.

The optical layout of the imager is shown in Figure 5 and a photograph of the optical package is shown in figure 6. We use two irises to define the field of view for the incident beam and to block the unwanted beams after the AOTF (as shown in figure 1) in this imager. Also, two single lenses are used in a confocal configuration, such that the light from a distant object is first imaged at the center of the AOTF crystal and then re-imaged on a commercial 640×480-pixel Si-CCD camera with an objective lens. The entire optical system is packaged in a 15×20×10 cm^3 box and weighs around 2 kg. Less than 1 W of rf power is used to drive the AOTF. The imaging system is completely automated. Both the rf synthesizer and the LCVR are controlled using a personal computer. RF is changed between 50 and 120 MHz to correspond to the desired optical wavelength range. The CCD output is captured using a frame grabber and stored on a hard drive.

We developed a graphical user interface for the seamless operation of the imager. A photograph of the imager mounted on a camera tripod is shown in figure 7.

Figure 4. Experimentally measured tuning curve.

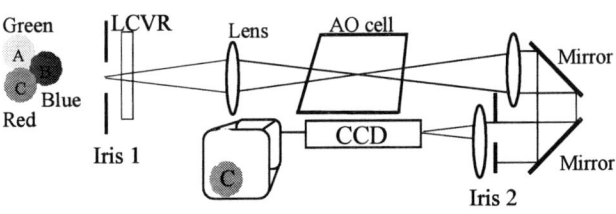

Figure 5. Optical layout of the VNIR imager.

Figure 6 Optical breadboard of the VNIR imager.

5. Data collection and analysis

We have carried out a number of data collection exercises using the VNIR AOTF imager. Analyses of

24

these data have clearly shown that manmade objects have strong polarimetric signatures [7,9] and these signatures are affected by the viewing conditions [9]. Also, it is found that the natural backgrounds like foliage do not have polarization signatures [8]. Here we present one example of the outdoor data collected by the VNIR imager and the results of a detailed analysis of these data.

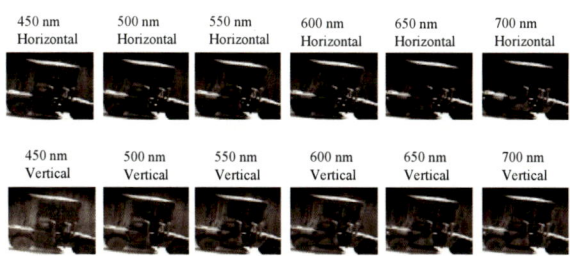

Figure 8. Spectropolarimetric images of a HMMWV and a white trailer.

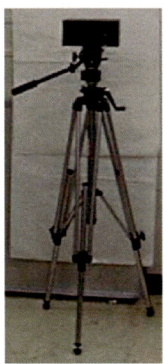

Figure 7. The VNIR imager mounted on a tripod.

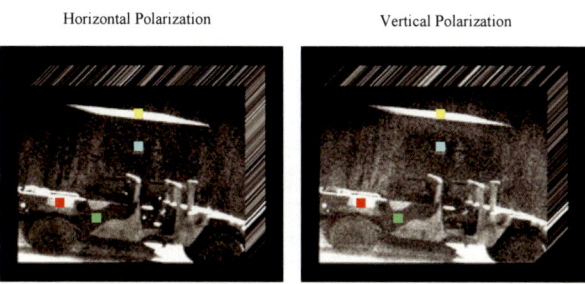

Figure 9. Image cubes for the two polarizations.

This example is from a data collection carried out on a clear sunny day on September 13, 2001 around 3 PM. Images were collected from 400 to 800 nm with a 10 nm step. We collected each image with both the horizontal and the vertical polarizations. The scene consisted of an open top HMMWV with a white trailer in the back sitting on a white asphalt top parking lot. Some sample raw images at two polarizations are shown in figure 8. The two image cubes shown in figure 9 were formed using the raw images corresponding to the horizontal and the vertical incident polarizations. Each cube contains images at 41 different spectral bands from 400 to 800 nm with a 10 nm interval. The size of each image cube is 12.6 MBytes. There are four colored squares marked on each of the two image cubes corresponding to the four points for which spectral profiles have been plotted in figure 10.

We computed the spectral profiles for both these image cubes. These profiles are uncalibrated and included here to show the effect of changes in both the spectral and polarimetric signatures of various pixels in the image. Each profile is an average of 5×5 pixels for the center point of each of the colored squares. These results clearly illustrate that both the HMMWV and the trailer exhibit spectropolarimatric signatures. The difference in spectropolarimetric signatures is largest for the highly reflecting top of the trailer and relatively small for the side of the trailer and the two painted portions on the side of the HMMWV.

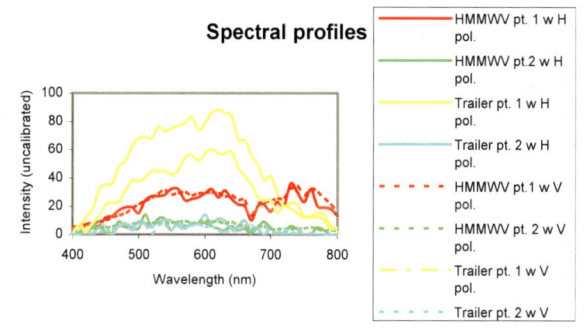

Figure 10. Spectral profiles for both horizontal and vertical polarization for points shown in figure 9.

6. Conclusions

We developed a compact, portable, agile VNIR spectropolarimetric imager using an AOTF for light dispersion and a liquid crystal variable retarder for polarization selection. Outdoor images were acquired in the spectral range from 400 to 800 nm with polarization settings of 0° and 90° at each wavelength. These images clearly show both the spectral and polarization signatures for various features in a scene. Most natural backgrounds show no polarization signatures because of random distribution of shapes and features [8], whereas man-made objects such as cars with regular shapes and edges, show polarization signatures [7,9]. Our compact spectropolarimetric imager is useful for collecting spectral as well as polarization signatures in the laboratory and outdoors. We have also developed similar imagers operating in the UV [10–12] as well as in three IR regions. We are carrying out research in growing better birefringent materials and in development of new AOTF cells [14,15].

References

[1] N. Gupta, "Acousto-Optic Tunable Filters," Opt. Photon. News, 8, 23–27, 1997.

[2] M. S. Gottlieb, Design and Fabrication of Acousto-Optic Devices, Marcel Dekker, New York, 1994.

[3] L. J. Denes, M. Gottlieb, B. Kaminsky, and P. Metes, "AOTF Polarization Difference," Proceedings of SPIE 3584, 106–115, 1999.

[4] D. A. Glenar, J. J. Hillman, B. Saif, and J. Bergstralh, "Acousto-Optic Imaging Spectropolarimetry for Remote Sensing," Appl. Opt. 33, 7412–7424, 1994.

[5] M.A. Sturgeon, L. J. Cheng, P. A. Durkee, M. K. Hamilton, J. F. Huth, C. Mahoney, R. C. Olsen, G. Reyes, "Spectral and polarimetric analysis of hyperspectral data collected by an acousto-optic tunable filter system," Proceedings of SPIE 2231, 167–176, 1994.

[6] N. Gupta and R. Dahmani , "Tunable Infrared Hyperspectral Imagers," in Proceedings of International Symposium on Spectral Sensing Research 2001, Quebec City, Canada, June 11–15, 2001, pp.233-236.

[7] N. Gupta, R. Dahmani, and S. Choy, "Acousto-optic tunable filter based visible-to near-infrared spectropolarimetric imager," Opt. Eng. 41, pp. 1033-1038, 2002.

[8] N. Gupta, "Remote sensing using hyperspectral and polarization images," Proceedings of SPIE 4574, pp.184-192, 2001.

[9] N. Gupta, L. Denes, M. Gottlieb, D. Suhre, B. Kaminsky, and P. Metes, "Object detection using a field-portable spectropolarimetric imager," App. Opt.40, pp.6626-6632, 2001

[10].N, Gupta and V. Voloshinov, "Tunable ultraviolet hyperspectral imagers," Digest Of 2003 Conference on Electro-optics and Lasers (CLEO), Baltimore, MD, June 2003.

[11] V. Voloshinov and N. Gupta, "Ultraviolet/Visible Imaging Acousto-Optic Tunable Filters in KDP," paper submitted to Appl. Optics, June 2003.

[12] N. Gupta and V. Voloshinov, "Hyperspectral Imager from Ultraviolet to Visible Using KDP AOTF," paper submitted to Appl. Optics, August 2003.

[13] N. B. Singh, D. Suhre, Neelam Gupta, W. Rosch, and M. Gottlieb, "Performance of TAS crystal for AOTF imaging," J. Crysal Growth, **225,** 124-128 (2002).

[14] N. Gupta, H. Zhang, N. B. Singh, A. Berghmans, D. Kahler, T. Waite, and J. H. Meacham, "Growth of mercurous bromide crystals for acousto-optic applications, Proc. Of CTA Symposium Advaned Sensors, p.59, April 2003.

[15] N. Gupta, N.B.Singh, H. Zhang, A. Berghmans and D. Kahler, "Development of High Efficiency Crystals for AOTF Applications," Proc.of MSS meeting in Tuscon , AZ, Mar 2003.

Fusion Techniques for Automatic Target Recognition

Syed A. Rizvi
Department of Engineering Science and Physics
College of Staten Island of City University of New York
2800 Victory Blvd., Staten Island, NY 10314
Email: rizvi@postbox.csi.cuny.edu

Nasser M. Nasrabadi
U.S. Army Research Laboratory, ATTN: AMSRL-SE-SE
2800 Powder Mill Road, Adelphi, MD 20783
Email: nnasraba@arl.army.mil

Abstract

In this paper, we investigate several fusion techniques for designing a composite classifier to improve the performance (probability of correct classification) of FLIR ATR. In this research, we propose to use four ATR algorithms for fusion. The individual performance of the four contributing algorithms ranges from 73.5% to about 77% of probability of correct classification on the testing set. We propose to use Bayes classifier, committee of experts, stacked-generalization, winner-takes-all, and ranking-based fusion techniques for designing the composite classifiers. The experimental results show an improvement of more than 6.5% over the best individual performance.

1. Introduction

Automatic target recognition (ATR) systems generally consist of three stages as shown in Fig. 1 [1]: (1) a preprocessing stage (target detection stage) that operates on the entire image and extracts regions containing potential targets, (2) a clutter[1] rejection stage that uses a sophisticated classification technique to identify true targets by discarding the clutter images (false alarms) from the potential target images provided by the detection stage, and (3) a classification stage that determines the type of the target.

Automatic target recognition (ATR) using forward-looking infrared (FLIR) imagery is an integral part of the ongoing research at U.S. Army Research Laboratory (ARL) for digitization of the battlefield. The real-life FLIR imagery (for example the database available at the ARL, see Figs. 2 and 3) demonstrates a significantly high level of variability of target thermal signatures. The high variability of target thermal signatures is due to several reasons, including meteorological conditions, times of the day, locations, ranges, etc. This highly unpredictable nature of thermal signatures makes FLIR ATR a very challenging problem. In recent years a number of FLIR ATR algorithms have been developed by the scientists at ARL as well as by the researchers in academia and industry working under ARL-sponsored research. These research activities have used a common development set of FLIR data (17,318 target images). The performance of these independently developed algorithms is measured in terms of the probability of correct classification using a common testing FLIR data collected under relatively unfavorable conditions. The testing FLIR data is not used during the algorithm development. The performance of these algorithms seems to be topped off around 77% of probability of correct classification.

In this paper, we investigate several fusion techniques for designing a composite classifier to improve the performance (probability of correct classification) of FLIR ATR. The motivation behind the fusion of ATR algorithms is that if each contributing technique in a fusion algorithm (composite classifier) emphasizes on learning at least some features of the targets that are not learned by other contributing techniques for making a classification decision, a fusion of ATR algorithms may improve overall probability of correct classification of the composite classifier. In this research, we propose to use four ATR algorithms for fusion with individual performance of the four contributing algorithms ranging from 73.5% to about 77% of probability of correct classification on the testing set.

The first algorithm uses a multi-layer convolution neural network (MLCNN) [2] for designing the ATR system [3]. The next classification algorithm is based on learning vector quantization (LVQ) algorithm [4]. The third classification algorithm used in the fusion is based on *modular neural network* (MNN) approach in which the classification of targets is realized hierarchically [5]. The fourth technique uses expansion matching (EXM) filtering and Karhunen-Loeve transform (KLT) for feature extraction [6].

This paper is organized as follows: Section II presents several fusion techniques proposed in this paper. Section III presents the experimental results and section IV concludes the paper discussing the future research directions.

---

[1] A clutter is anything that mimics a target but is not a real target.

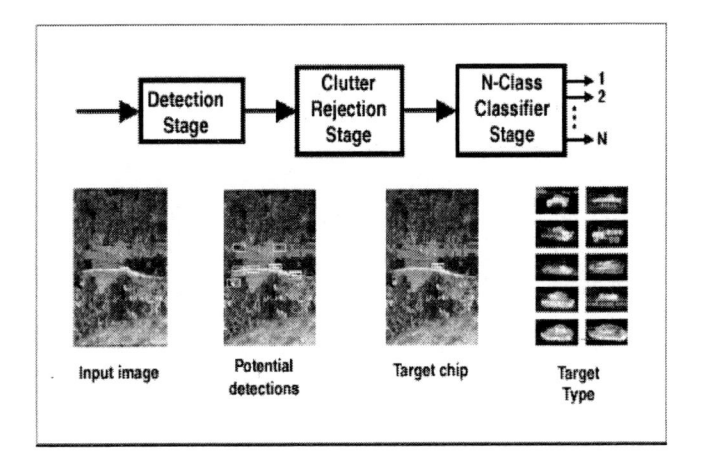

Figure 1: An ATR System.

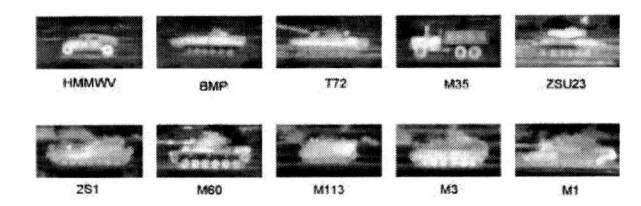

Figure 2: Example of 10 target types taken under favorable conditions.

Figure 3: Examples of 5 target types taken under relatively less favorable conditions.

2. Composite Classifiers

Several approaches have been used in the previous research for improving generalization performance of a classification system. For example, the boosting and committee-of-experts techniques have been used successfully in character recognition applications for improving generalization performance [7]. These approaches generally require that a number of experts be trained on subsets of the training data, where these subsets could be disjoint as well as overlapping. These approaches may be grouped into two basic approaches: *classifier fusion* and *classifier selection* [8], [9]. In a classifier fusion algorithm, all classifiers are executed and a mixing algorithm combines all the outputs from all the classifiers. Since all the classifiers contribute their outputs to a mixing algorithm, the computational complexity is no less than the sum of the computational complexities of all the classifiers. In a classifier selection algorithm, a separate selection component chooses the appropriate classifier to classify each particular target image. The computational complexity of this approach is much lower than that of the classifier fusion algorithms, since not all the classifiers participate in classifying a target image. The performance of the classification selection algorithm depends on the accuracy of the selection component. However, the design of selection component with a sufficiently high level of accuracy is not trivial. Therefore, when compared to the classification selection algorithms with non-optimal selection component, the classifier fusion algorithms tend to have better performance. In this research we focus on classifier fusion techniques.

Let us define the notation that is used in this section. Suppose that we have a set of K classifiers, C_k, each of which classifies targets into one of Q distinct classes, where $k = 1, 2, ..., K$. The output vector of classifier C_k, given a target $\mathbf{X}$, is represented by a column vector

$$\mathbf{y}_k = \{y_{k,q}; q = 1, 2, ..., Q\}, \quad (1)$$

where qth component of the output vector, $y_{k,q}$, represents the estimated posteriori probability that target $\mathbf{X}$ belongs to the class q, estimated by classifier C_k. We can then express the estimated posteriori probability as the desired posteriori probability $p(q|\mathbf{X})$ plus an error $\varepsilon_{k,q}(\mathbf{X})$:

$$y_{k,q} = p(q|\mathbf{X}) + \varepsilon_{k,q}(\mathbf{X}). \quad (2)$$

For notational convenience, we do not explicitly express the dependence of outputs $y_{k,q}$ upon variable $\mathbf{X}$, where $\mathbf{X}$ is the input of each individual classifier C_k. The ground truth class of a target $\mathbf{X}$ is θ_T. The output vector of a composite classifier, C_k, given a target $\mathbf{X}$, is represented by a column vector

$$\mathbf{y}(\mathbf{X}) = \{y_q(\mathbf{X}); q = 1, 2, ..., Q\}, \quad (3)$$

where $y_q(\mathbf{X})$, the qth component of the output vector, is the estimated posteriori probability that target $\mathbf{X}$ belongs to the class q. The classification decision of classifier C_k is

$$\theta_k = \arg\max_{1 \leq q \leq Q} y_{k,q}. \quad (4)$$

The final decision of a composite classifier C is

$$\theta = \arg\max_{1 \leq q \leq Q} y_q. \quad (5)$$

The first step in the design of the composite classifier is to express the outputs of the different classifiers in terms of the probability of correct classification. In one classifier, the classification may be based on the highest score. In the other classifier, however, it may be based on the minimum mean squared error (MSE) etc. Scores can be expressed as probabilities if an appropriate transformation (linear or nonlinear) is applied. Therefore, the MSEs given by any classifier are first converted to scores, and these scores are then expressed as the probabilities of correct classification by applying an appropriate transformation. Let $S_{k,q}$ be the qth unconstrained output (score) of the classifier k. In order to express the output of the classifier k as the estimated posteriori probability, $y_{k,q}$, we apply a transformation $\Psi(.)$ given by

$$y_{k,q} = \Psi(S_{k,q}), \quad (6)$$

where the transformation $\Psi(.)$ can be linear or nonlinear, and $y_{k,q}$ must satisfy the following two requirements: (1) $0 \leq y_{k,q} \leq 1$ and (2) $\Sigma_q y_{k,q} = 1$. The following transformations $\Psi_k(.)$ can used:

$$\Psi_1(S_{k,q}) = \frac{S_{k,q}}{\sum_j S_{k,j}} \quad (7)$$

$$\Psi_2(S_{k,q}) = \frac{\exp(S_{k,q})}{\sum_j \exp(S_{k,j})} \quad (8)$$

$$\Psi_3(S_{k,q}) = \frac{(S_{k,q})^n}{\sum_j (S_{k,j})^n}. \quad (9)$$

In above mentioned transformations, $\Psi_1(.)$ is a linear transformation; however, $\Psi_2(.)$ and $\Psi_3(.)$ are nonlinear transformations. When compared to linear transformation, nonlinear transformation provides more *amplification* of the classification decisions with higher scores (higher confidence) and dampens the classification decisions with lower scores (less confident decisions). In this way, the outputs of the classifiers are made *biased* towards classification decisions with higher scores (high confidence). In these experiments, the nonlinear transformation given by $\Psi_3(.)$ was used. Figure 4 shows the effect of applying the linear and nonlinear transformations to a set of typical unconstrained outputs of the neural network. The outputs of the contributing classifiers are finally mixed together through a fusion technique. Figure 5 shows the complete functional diagram of the composite ATR system.

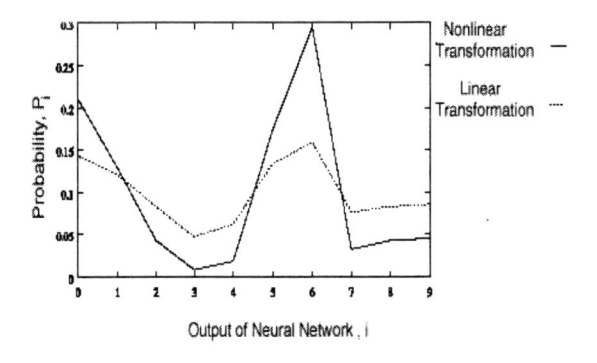

Figure 4: Effect of the linear and nonlinear transformations that are applied to typical unconstrained outputs of the neural network. $\Psi(i)$ represents the probability that the target class is "i," where i = 0,1,2,...9.

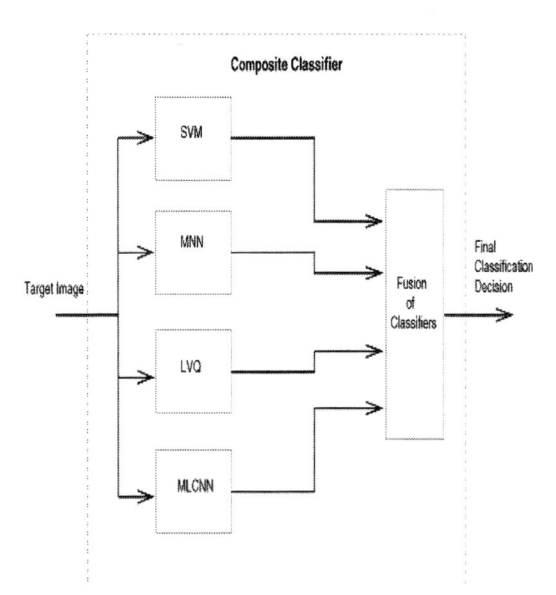

Figure 5: Functional block diagram of the composite classifier using four classifiers.

A. Winner-takes-all strategy

This strategy assumes that the score assigned to a given class by a particular network is a reasonable measure of the probability of correct classification. This technique works as follows: First, the class θ_k is determined for the classifier k using Eq. 4. The θ_kth output of the kth classifier is denoted by y_k^θ. The final classification decision is then made using y_k^θ's for all k as

$$\theta = \arg\max_{1 \leq k \leq K} y_k^\theta. \quad (10)$$

B. Averaged Bayes classifier

This simple mixing algorithm takes the average outputs of a set of classifiers as a new estimated posteriori probability of a composite classifier.

$$\mathbf{y} = \frac{1}{K}\sum_{k=1}^{K}\mathbf{y}_k, \quad (11)$$

or equivalently,

$$y_q = \frac{1}{K}\sum_{k=1}^{K}y_{k,q}, \quad (12)$$

That is, each individual classifier is weighted equally. The final decision C made by this composite classifier is given by Eq. 13,

$$\theta = \arg\max_{1 \leq q \leq Q} y_q. \quad (13)$$

This mixing algorithm is called an averaged Bayes classifier by Xu et al [10], where they assumed that all individual classifiers are Bayes classifiers. Perrone in Ref.

[11] has shown theoretically that the averaging over the outputs of a set of neural networks can improve the performance of a neural network, in terms of any convex cost function. This algorithm not only provides better performance but also better generalization than a single classifier.

C. Ranking based

In this technique, for the classifier "k" a new vector, z_k is generated in which each component is assigned a score that is based on the rank of that component in the output vector $\mathbf{y}_k = \{y_{k,q}; q = 1,2,....,Q\}$. That is, $\mathbf{z}_k = R(\mathbf{y}_k)$, where R is a ranking operator that takes in a vector $\mathbf{y}_k = \{y_{k,q}; q = 1,2,....,Q\}$ and replaces it with a new vector $\mathbf{z}_k = \{z_{k,q}; q = 1,2,....,Q\}$, where the vector components $z_{k,q}$ are computed as follows:

- Define a ranking vector $\mathbf{r} = \{r_q; q = 1,2,....,Q\}$
- Set $r_q = 0$ for all q.
- for i := 1 step 1 until Q

begin

$$r_i := \arg \max_{1 \le q \le Q \text{ and } q \ne r_i} y_{k,q} \text{ for all i}$$

$z_{k,ri} := Q - (i-1)$

end

This process is repeated for all the contributing networks. A tie between two classes is broken by randomly selecting one of the two classes. A final decision is then made by employing an averaged Bayes classifier that uses the vectors z_k's instead of $\mathbf{y}_k$'s.

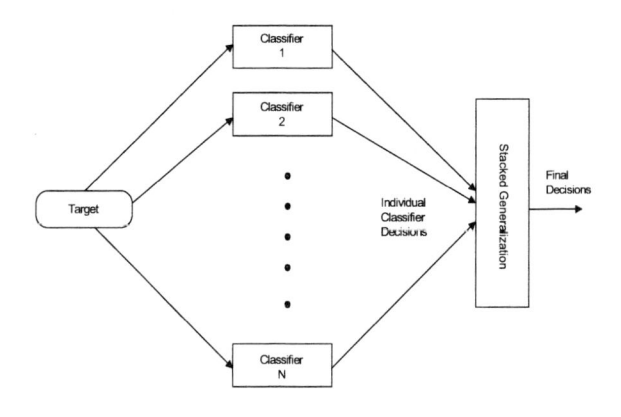

D. Stacked generalization method

The averaged Bayes classifier algorithm treats each individual classifier equally. However, it is possible that some classifiers can make better decisions than others for some targets. Thus, we can reduce the probability of misclassification if we assign larger weightings to some classifiers than to other classifiers for some targets. Two approaches that provide linear weighting to individual classifiers are explored in Ref. 11 and 12. The first approach, called *generalized committee* [11], obtains the weighting of each component classifier by solving the error correlation matrix. The second approach, similar to the generalized committee, is supported by consensus theory [12]. The optimal weighting is obtained by solving the Weiner-Hopf equation. Better performance can be expected if nonlinear weighting is applied to individual classifiers, since a linear function is a special case of a nonlinear function. The stacked generalization method [13] is a general approach to combine a set of classifiers to obtain a final decision. A multi-layer perceptron (MLP)

neural network that receives the output of all classifiers can be trained to implement the combination. That is,

$$\mathbf{y} = \Phi(\mathbf{y}_1, \mathbf{y}_2, ..., \mathbf{y}_k), \qquad (14)$$

where $\Phi(.)$ is an MLP that implements the stacked generalization. This MLP provides a nonlinear weighting to the outputs of individual classifiers. The architecture is shown in Fig. 6.

Figure 6: Stacked Generalization.

E. Committee of experts

In this technique, a potential target is presented to all classifiers (experts). Each expert can cast one vote in the classification decision. All votes carry an equal weight. The decision about the class of the potential target is then made on a majority vote of the contributing classifiers. For example, in the case of four experts used in this research, if three or more classifiers agree on a class then that classification decision constitutes the final classification decision. However, there is a possibility that for some potential targets, some or all experts may have a differing opinion and, therefore, there may not be a clear majority vote. In this situation we propose to employ two strategies: (1) use averaged Bayes classifier, (2) use winner-takes-all strategy (see Fig. 7). A more detailed analysis of committee of experts approach can be found in Ref. 14.

3. Experimental results

In all experiments performed, we have used a total of 17,318 target images from U.S. Army Comanche data set as our development set. The development set consists of two database (1) SIG, which is collected under favorable conditions and has 13,862 target images (10 target types), (2) ROI, which is collected under less favorable conditions and has 3,456 target images (5 target types). Specifically, this data set contains 10 military ground vehicles viewed from a ground-based second-generation FLIR. The targets are viewed from arbitrary aspect angles, which are recorded in the ground truth (rounded to the nearest 5°). The images contain cluttered backgrounds and some partially obscured targets. The contributing classifiers were trained using SIG data set. ROI data set was used to evaluate the generalization capability of the classifiers. Figure 2 shows the examples of 10 target types. The performance is reported in terms of probability of correct classification. The probability of correct classification, P_i, of the class i is computed as follows:

$$P_i = \frac{C_i}{T_i} \times 100 \qquad (15)$$

Figure 8 shows the performance of the contributing classifiers on the test data. The Fig. shows that the more than half of the test chips are correctly identified by all classifiers. Another 38 percent or so of the test chips are correctly identified by at least one of the contributing classifiers. This suggests that one can achieve as much as 15 percent improvement in performance over the best individual performance of the contributing classifiers, if one can appropriately *weight* the classification decisions given by these algorithms (if one is able to choose the best classifier for a given target chip). In practice, however, the improvement may be significantly less than that, depending on the data and the approach used to *mix* the outputs of the experts.

Table 1 presents the overall performance of the contributing classifiers that range from the probability of correct classification of 73.5% to 77.3%. Table 2 presents the overall performance of all the fusion techniques investigated in this paper. As can be seen in Table 2 that the ranking- based technique performed the best among all fusion techniques investigated in this paper (probability of correct classification = 82.3 %) with committee of experts with averaged Bayes classifier providing comparable performance (probability of correct classification = 82.1 %). The performance improvement over the best contributing classifier is ((82.3-77.3)/(77.3)) X 100 = 6.5%.

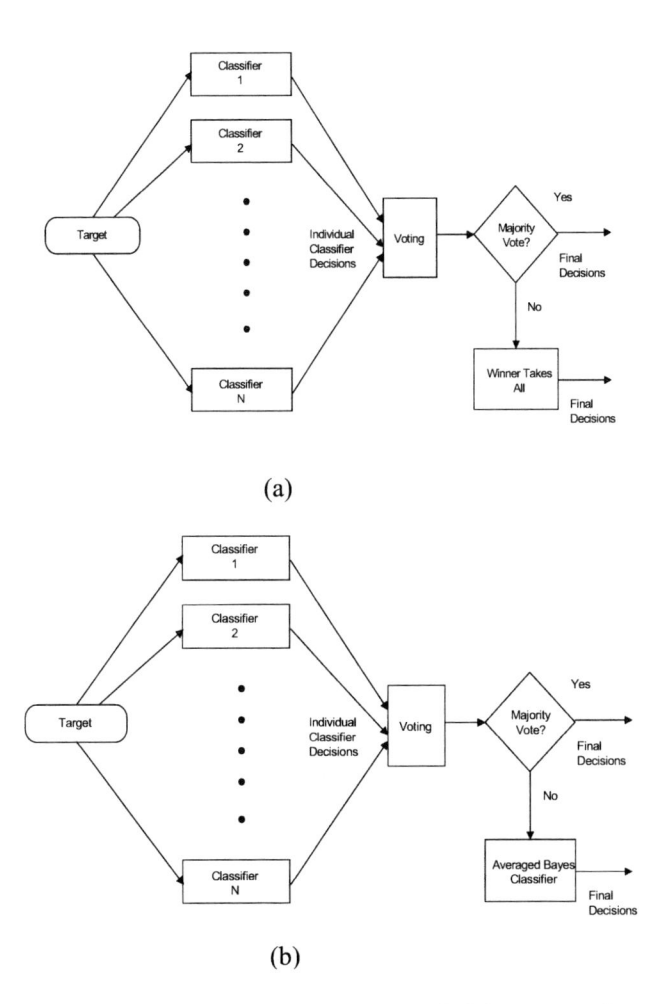

Figure 7: Committee of experts with (a) averaged Bayes classifier and (b) winner-takes-all classifier.

where C_i represents the correctly identified targets of class i and T_i represents the total number of targets of class i tested.

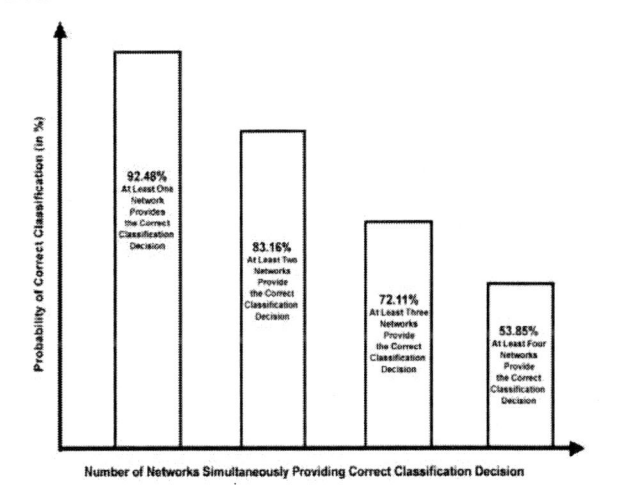

Figure 8: Conditional classification decisions for at least one, two, three, or four networks together providing the correct classification decision.

4. Conclusions

In this paper, we have investigated six different fusion techniques and demonstrated that the performance of an ATR system can be improved by using a fusion algorithm. We obtained about 6.5% improvement over the best performing contributing classifier, which is a significant improvement considering the difficult testing data used in the experiments performed in this paper. An interesting observation was that the stacked generalization technique did not perform better than the averaged Bayes classifier (see Table 2). As mentioned earlier, in the averaged Bayes composite classifier the output vectors from the contributing classifiers are given equal weights. Stacked generalization technique, on the other hand, attempts to provide a better set of weights for the output vectors of the contributing classifiers through a nonlinear (neural network) processing. The behavior of stacked generalization technique can be explained by the fact that the neural networks in the stacked generalization technique were trained using the training data on which all the contributing networks provide almost perfect performance (see Table 1). And, therefore, there may not be much for the neural networks in stacked generalization technique to learn from the training data that can significantly improve the generalization (the performance on the testing data) capability of the stacked generalization composite classifier.

Table 1: Performance of the contributing classifiers.

Contributing Classifier	Probability of Correct Classification (Training Data)	Probability of Correct Classification (Testing Data)
MLCNN	96.40 %	73.5 %
LVQ	99.71 %	75.1 %
MNN	94.25	75.5 %
SVM	98.10 %	77.3 %

Table 2: Performance of the fusion techniques.

Fusion Technique	Probability of Correct Classification
Averaged Bayes	81.5 %
Ranking Based	82.3 %
Winner-Takes-All	79.6 %
Stacked Generalization	81.0 %
Committee of Experts (With Averaged Bayes)	82.1 %
Committee of Experts (Winner-Takes-All)	81.5 %

It should be noted that in all the fusion techniques presented in this paper, the contributing algorithms were not re-trained (as mentioned earlier, the contributing classifiers were independently developed by different research groups). The behavior of stacked generalization technique, however, suggests that a re-training (possibly jointly) of the contributing algorithms during the fusion process may be necessary for further improving the generalization capability of the fusion techniques. This is the focus of our future research.

References

1. B. Bhanu, "Automatic target recognition: state of the art survey," *IEEE Trans. Aerospace and Electronic Systems*, vol. AES-22, no. 4, pp. 364—379, 1986.
2. Y. Le Cun, "Generalization and network design strategies," R. Preifer, Z. Schreter, F. Fogelman, and L. Steels, Editors, *Connectionism in Perspective*, Elsevier, Zurich, Switzerland, 1989.
3. V. Mirelli and S. A. Rizvi, "Automatic target recognition using a multi-layer convolution neural network," in *Proc. SPIE's Symp. Aerospace/Defense Sensing and Controls* (Orlando, Florida), April 8—12, 1996, vol. 2755, pp. 106—125.
4. L. A. Chan, N. M. Nasrabadi and V. Mirelli, "Multi-stage target recognition using modular vector quantizers and multilayer perceptrons," in *Proc. Computer Vision Pattern Recognition*, pp. 114—119, 1996.
5. L.-C. Wang, S. Der, N. M. Nasrabadi, and S. A. Rizvi, "Automatic target recognition using neural networks," in *Proc. SPIE Conference on Algorithms, Devices, and Systems for Optical Information Processing*, (San Diego) July 1998, pp. 278—289.
6. L. Carin "FLIR classification using physics-motivated features and support vector machines," Presentation at U.S. Army Research Laboratory, October 2001.
7. H. Drucker, C. Cortes, L. D. Jackel, Y. LeCun, and V. Vapnik, "Boosting and other ensemble methods," *Neural Comp.*, vol. 6, pp. 1289—1301, 1994.
8. T. K. Ho, J. J. Hull and S. N. Srihari, "Decision combination in multiple classifier systems," *IEEE Trans. Pattern Analysis and Machine Intelligence*, vol. PAMI-16, no. 1, pp. 66—75, 1994.
9. K. Woods, W. P. Kegelmeyer Jr. and K. Bowyer, "Combination of multiple classifiers using local accuracy estimates," *IEEE Trans. Pattern Analysis and Machine Intelligence*, vol. PAMI-19, no. 4, pp. 405—410, 1997.
10. L. Xu, A. Krzyżak and C. Y. Suen, "Methods of combining multiple classifiers and their applications to handwriting recognition," *IEEE Trans. Systems, Man, and Cybernetics*, vol. SMC-22, no. 2, pp. 418—435, 1992.
11. M. P. Perrone, "General averaging results for convex optimization," in *Proc. Connectionist Models Summer School*, 364—371, 1993.
12. J. A. Benediktsson, J. R. Sveinsson, O. K. Ersoy and P. H. Swain, "Parallel consensual neural networks," *IEEE Trans. Neural Networks*}, NN-8 (1), pp. 54—64, 1997.
13. D. H. Wolpert, "Stacked generalization," *Neural Networks* no. 5, pp. 241—259, 1992.
14. J. A. Benediksson and I. Kanellopoulos, "Decision fusion methods in classification of multisource and hyperdimensional data," *IEEE Trans. Geoscience and Remote Sensing*, vol. 37, no. 3, pp. 1367—1377, May 1999.

Eigenviews for Object Recognition in Multispectral Imaging Systems

Rajeev Ramanath   Wesley E. Snyder
Dept. of Electrical and Computer Engineering
NC State University
Box 7911, Raleigh, NC 27695-7911
rajeev.ramanath@ieee.org, wes@ncsu.edu

Hairong Qi *
Dept. of Electrical and Computer Engineering
The University of Tennessee
Knoxville, TN 37996-2100
hqi@utk.edu

Abstract

We address the problem of representing multispectral images of objects using eigenviews for recognition purposes. Eigenviews have long been used for object recognition and pose estimation purposes in the grayscale and color image settings. The purpose of this paper is two-fold: firstly to extend the ideologies of eigenviews to multispectral images and secondly to propose the use of dimensionality reduction techniques other than those popularly used. Principal Component Analysis (PCA) and its various kernel-based flavors are popularly used to extract eigenviews. We propose the use of Independent Component Analysis (ICA) and Non-negative Matrix Factorization (NMF) as possible candidates for eigenview extraction. Multispectral images of a collection of 3D objects captured under different viewpoint locations are used to obtain representative views (eigenviews) that encode the information in these images. The idea is illustrated with a collection of eight synthetic objects imaged in both reflection and emission bands. A Nearest Neighbor classifier is used to perform the classification of an arbitrary view of an object. Classifier performance under additive white Gaussian noise is also tested. The results demonstrate that this system holds promise for use in object recognition under the multispectral imaging setting and also for novel dimensionality reduction techniques. The number of eigenviews needed by various techniques to obtain a given classifier accuracy is also calculated as a measure of the performance of the dimensionality reduction technique.

1. Introduction

With the increasing availability of data and decreasing costs of sensors to perform such data capture, multispectral imaging is gaining rapid popularity for surveillance, maintenance, inspection and military uses. Fig. 1 shows a sample multispectral image of an object generated using a simulator that has been developed by the authors as part of this project. The authors are not aware of a "standard" database that has both reflection and emission band images with the images captured from multiple views. Different poses of ob-

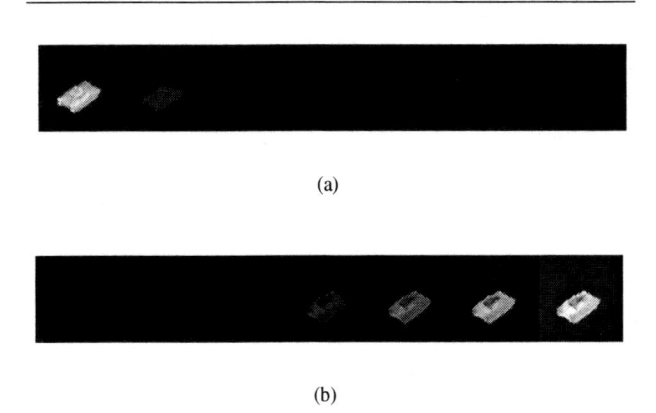

Figure 1. Sample 7-band synthetic image of a tank (left to right: bands uniformly spaced between 0.4μm to 12μm). The image has been min-max scaled over all bands. (a) Reflection images (b) Emission Images

jects provide information about different physical features, which may be used in an object recognition task. In the work reported here, the object is centered at the origin, with the camera looking at the centroid of the object along the radial lines of an imaginary viewing hemisphere of radius r and at an elevation of ϕ and an azimuth of θ [20]. The variables that are allowed to change are θ and ϕ. In this work, it is assumed that the object can be segmented from the scene accurately and that this segmentation has been performed.

---

* This work was supported by grant DASG60-02-1-0005 from the US Army Space and Missile Defense Command.

While little is known about how the human visual system extracts a representation of an object and requires little or no effort to distinguish one object from the other; it is relatively clear that the appearance of the object plays a crucial role in its "memorization". In this paper, we extend popular work on appearance-based matching to multispectral imaging systems and also investigate more recently published dimension-reduction techniques than those popularly used literature [18, 23, 24].

In Section 2, a brief description of the various techniques used to generate eigenviews is presented. Section 3 describes the dataset used in this work. Section 4 describes the various experiments performed along with the effects of noise and the number of eigenviews used. We conclude the paper in Section 5 with suggestions for future work.

2. Eigenviews

All possible views of an object $\mathcal{O}_i$ may be denoted by a set of multispectral images

$$\mathcal{Z}_{\mathcal{O}_i} = \left\{ I_{\mathcal{O}_i}(\theta, \phi) \right\}_{\theta=0, \phi=0}^{\theta=\pi, \phi=2\pi}. \quad (1)$$

Consider a countable subset $\mathcal{Y} : \mathcal{Y} \subset \bigcup_{i=1}^{O} \mathcal{Z}_{\mathcal{O}_i}$ (we have M views of O objects). Denote the cardinality of this set (of images corresponding to different views of various objects) as MO and the size of each image I, as $R \times C \times K$.

As traditionally used, the term eigenfaces refers to the use of a smaller, more representative set of images extracted from linear combinations of face images. Eigenfaces were proposed by Sirovich and Kirby [23] and extended by Turk and Pentland over a decade ago to represent a set of images of faces [24]. In the work presented here, we shall use the term "eigen" without the restriction of the traditionally used reference to the Karhunen-Loeve transform or to Principal Component Analysis [23]. Instead, in this work, the term eigenimages is used to denote "representative" images (either faces or objects) that encode information in its broadest sense.

The work by Turk and Pentland was later extended to generate eigenviews of images of objects [17]. Turk and Pentland proposed using Principal Component Analysis (PCA) to generate eigenfaces, which essentially accounted for the variance in the data. The system they developed projected a given set of face images onto a feature space that spans the variations in the images. The projection operation characterizes a face by a weighted sum of eigenface features and does not recognize the details (individual components of a face). This has been known to perform with good accuracy on face images [19, 24]. Murase and Nayar's eigenviews are generated by linear combinations of elements of $\mathcal{Y}$. Here, we extend this work to perform recognition of objects viewed from arbitrary locations on the viewing hemisphere using their multispectral images.

We generate a lexical representation (column vectors of length RCK) for each image $I \in \mathcal{Y}$. These vectors are now stacked into a matrix $\mathbf{I}$ of size $RCK \times MO$. Approximate factorizations for this input data matrix are now found such that

$$\mathbf{I} \approx \mathbf{VW} \quad (2)$$

where $\mathbf{V}$ is a matrix of size $RCK \times M'$ and $\mathbf{W}$ is a matrix of size $M' \times MO$. The columns of $\mathbf{V}$ are the lexical representations of the $M' < MO$ eigenviews and $\mathbf{W}$ may be regarded as a weight matrix that stores the weight that is used in a linear combination with each eigenview to generate the original images (in $\mathbf{I}$). Let us denote by $\mathcal{I}'$, the space spanned by these eigenviews.

Different mappings from $\mathcal{Y} \rightarrow \mathcal{I}'$ generate different eigenviews. The manner in which $\mathbf{V}$ and $\mathbf{W}$ (the mapping) are generated is investigated in this work. PCA, Independent Component Analysis (ICA) [13, 5] and Nonnegative Matrix Factorization (NMF) [14] have been considered as techniques for factorizing $\mathbf{I}$ and therefore generating different eigenviews.

2.1. Principal Component Analysis

As $\mathbf{I}$ is not a full-rank matrix, Singular Value Decomposition is used to extract the eigenvalues and eigenvectors. In traditional notation of SVD, we may factorize[1] the $RCK \times MO$ zero-mean matrix $\mathbf{I}_0$ as

$$\mathbf{I}_0 = \mathbf{U}_1 \mathbf{\Lambda} \mathbf{U}_2^T \quad (3)$$

where $\mathbf{\Lambda}$ is an $RCK \times MO$ diagonal matrix with diagonal elements λ_i such that $\lambda_1 \geq \lambda_2 \geq \ldots \geq \lambda_{\min(RCK, MO)} \geq 0$ and $\mathbf{U}_1$ and $\mathbf{U}_2$ are orthogonal matrices of size $RCK \times RCK$ and $MO \times MO$, respectively. The λ_i are called *singular values* and the first $\min(RCK, MO)$ columns of $\mathbf{U}_1$ and $\mathbf{U}_2$ are called the *left* and *right singular vectors*. Putting this in the framework of Eqn. 2, we have $\mathbf{V} = \mathbf{U}_1 \mathbf{\Lambda}$ and $\mathbf{W} = \mathbf{U}_2^T$. This however is an exact decomposition. What we are after is a condensed representation of $\mathbf{I}$. We hence pick the largest $M' < MO$ singular values and vectors and now have

$$\mathbf{I}_0 \approx \mathbf{U}_1' \mathbf{\Lambda}' \mathbf{U}_2'^T \quad (4)$$

where $\mathbf{U}_1'$ is of size $RCK \times RCK$, $\mathbf{\Lambda}$ is of size $RCK \times M'$ and $\mathbf{U}_2'$ is of size $M' \times M'$. The columns of $\mathbf{V} = \mathbf{U}_1' \mathbf{\Lambda}'$ are now the eigenviews and those of $\mathbf{U}_2'$ are the encodings. Eigenviews generated in such a manner account for directions that have the largest variance. The eigenviews generated using PCA have the property that they involve linear

---

1 Without loss of generality, we consider only real-valued images, this eliminates the need for the Hermitian transpose

combinations that involve complex cancellations and do not correspond to views that have intuitive meaning (although this is not the goal of the problem at hand).

Computing the singular values and vectors for an $RCK \times MO$ matrix comes at a very high computational cost. To reduce the computational cost of such a process, the following setup is often used. Instead of computing the eigenvectors and eigenvalues of $\Sigma = \mathbf{I}_0 \mathbf{I}_0^T$, consider the matrix $\Sigma' = \mathbf{I}_0^T \mathbf{I}_0$. The eigenvalues λ' and eigenvectors ψ' of Σ' satisfy the condition

$$\Sigma' \psi' = \lambda' \psi'. \quad (5)$$

Pre-multiplying both sides by $\mathbf{I}_0$, we get

$$\begin{aligned} \mathbf{I}_0 \Sigma' \psi' &= \mathbf{I}_0 \lambda' \psi' \\ \text{i.e.} \quad \mathbf{I}_0 \left(\mathbf{I}_0^T \mathbf{I}_0 \right) \psi' &= \mathbf{I}_0 \lambda' \psi' \\ \text{i.e.} \quad \left(\mathbf{I}_0 \mathbf{I}_0^T \right) \mathbf{I}_0 \psi' &= \lambda' \mathbf{I}_0^T \psi' \\ \text{i.e.} \quad \Sigma \mathbf{I}_0 \psi' &= \lambda' \mathbf{I}_0 \psi' \end{aligned} \quad (6)$$

which shows us that the eigenvalues for the two matrices are the same while the eigenvectors of Σ may be calculated from those Σ', which is computationally much more feasible. The remainder $RCK - M'$ eigenvalues (or $\min(RCK, MO)$ singular values) are zero.

2.2. Independent Component Analysis

In contrast to decorrelation techniques such as PCA, which ensures that output pairs are uncorrelated, Independedt Component Analysis (ICA) imposes a much stronger criterion that the multivariate probability density function of output variables is independent (it can be factored) [10]. ICA is essentially a linear formation model that describes the data by a linear combination of a collection of independent "sources" through a mixing matrix given by

$$\mathbf{I} = \mathbf{AS} \quad (7)$$

where $\mathbf{A}$ denotes the mixing matrix that is a collection of scalars and $\mathbf{S}$ is a collection of independent sources. The problem of ICA is to estimate not only $\mathbf{A}$ but also $\mathbf{S}$. The enforcement of independence is done so as to remove redundant information (as is also the case with PCA). The fundamental restriction in ICA is that the independent components must be non-Gaussian for ICA to be possible. In [12], Hyvarinen et al. provide a simple explanation as to why Gaussian variables are forbidden.

The measured data, $\mathbf{I}$ is usually correlated while the assumption of ICA is that the sources, the columns of $\mathbf{S}$ are not. Consider that we can come up with a matrix $\mathbf{W}$, that makes the columns of $\mathbf{Z} = \mathbf{WI}$ statistically independent, we can recover the original sources (columns of $\mathbf{S}$) up to a multiplicative constant. The statistical properties of $\mathbf{Z}$ can be described by its moments or, more conveniently, by its cumulants $C(\mathbf{Z})$. Cumulants form tensors of varying ranks based upon the order of the cumulant and the diagonal elements of the tensor characterize the distribution of single components. For example, $C(\mathbf{Z})_i$ is the mean, $C(\mathbf{Z})_{ii}$ is the variance, $C(\mathbf{Z})_{iii}$ is the skewness and $C(\mathbf{Z})_{iiii}$ is the kurtosis of the ith column of $\mathbf{Z}$. The off-diagonal elements characterize the statistical dependencies between components. Clearly, if and only if the off diagonal elements are zero, the columns of $\mathbf{Z}$ are statistically independent (assuming infinite amount of data). Thus, ICA is equivalent to finding an unmixing matrix that diagonalizes the cumulant tensors. The conventional KL transform may be considered as an ICA process operating on the second-order cumulant.

Kurtosis is commonly used as a measure of non-Gaussinity and an often used objective function. For a random variable x, it is given by $E\{x^4\} - 3(E\{x^2\})^2$. For a Gaussian random variable, it is zero and typically positive for densities with heavy tails and a peak at zero and negative for flatter densities with lighter tails. There are researchers who do not support the use of Kurtosis as an objective function due to the sheer nature of the random variables and the fact that we have a finite sample of the random variables and are hence limited in the estimate of the Kurtosis [9]. However, due to the strong global convergence properties of using such an objective function and the mathematical simplicity of such a formulation [6, 11], in this work, the Kurtosis is used as a measure of non-Gaussinity. Other measures include Negentropy and Mutual Information [10].

In this work, the ICA problem is solved using a popular algorithm called Joint Approximate Diagonalization of Eigenmatrices (JADE). The advantage of this approach is that it requires no knowledge of the probability densities of the independent components. This algorithm works by jointly diagonalizing the maximal set of cumulant matrices (fourth order cumulants are used as the Givens rotations can now be computed in closed form). The interested reader is referred to the work reported by Cardoso and Souloumiac [5].

2.3. Non-negative Matrix Factorization

NMF is a recently proposed technique to factorize an all-positive matrix (hence well-suited for images) into all-positive factors [14, 15]. NMF restricts the entries in $\mathbf{V}$ and $\mathbf{W}$ to be non-negative by making the assumption that an image pixel is generated by adding Poisson noise to the factored image. In other words, the pixels I_{ij} are obtained from a Poisson process of mean $(\mathbf{VW})_{ij}$. An objective function related to the likelihood of generating the pixels in $\mathbf{I}$ from

V and **W** given by

$$\log P(I_{ij}|(\mathbf{VW})_{ij}) = \sum_{i=1}^{RCK} \sum_{j=1}^{MO} \left(I_{ij} \log (\mathbf{VW})_{ij} - (\mathbf{VW})_{ij} - \log I_{ij}! \right).$$

Clearly, $I_{ij}!$ does not affect the optimization and can be dropped, giving us a cost function that is iteratively minimized usually using gradient descent techniques or multiplicative update rules [15]. In [15], Lee and Seung prove convergence properties of such a minimization and also illustrate that this cost function is identical to the Kullback-Liebler distance between two distributions if the matrices are normalized to unity. This technique has been shown to be powerful and at the same time extract meaningful representations of data. Various other authors have used this technique to extract additive "parts" of datasets that make intuitive sense for reflectivity functions [4, 22], face image datasets [7, 8] and gene expression analysis [2] to name a few. Note though that **V** is of size $RCK \times M'$ and **W** is of size $M' \times MO$ — the loss of dimensions accounts for the approximation in Eqn. 2.

Subspace techniques have been used in the past with high recognition rates [18, 23, 24]. Recently, Bischof and Leonardis proposed a radial basis function network for representing 3D object views with considerable success [3]. Moghaddam and Pentland have used a parametric normal-distribution setting to formulate this problem in a face-recognition scenario [16]. However, its use in a setting as the one proposed here is not suitable as the difference between different views of objects is much less normal than the difference between various orientations of a face image. Existing techniques however are not established or tested for multi– or hyperspectral images.

2.4. Classification

We call the space spanned by these M' eigenviews (images) as an eigenspace. The eigenspaces represent the image data in the "best" possible manner depending upon the technique used. The images used for generating these M' eigenviews are projected into the eigenspace and serve as a training set which is later used for classification. Given a new (earlier unseen) view of one of these O objects, the image may now be projected into the eigenspace. This projection describes the contribution of each eigenview in representing the new view. A simple means of classifying this new image (its projection), is to assign it to the class that its projection is "closest" to. Due to the non-parametric nature of this space, an obvious choice for a classifier is the 1-Nearest Neighbor (NN) classifier that uses the L_2 norm as a distance measure.

In other words, given a database of images as a matrix **I**, of size $RCK \times MO$; we compute eigenimages **V** that is a matrix of size $RCK \times M'$. The columns of **V** span the eigenspace. Projecting **I** onto this space will form a training set. When presented with a new image I', we project it onto the eigenspace and assign class labels according to the following

$$Label(I') = Label\left(\mathop{\arg\min}_{l = 1 \ldots MO} \|\mathbf{V}^T I' - \mathbf{V}^T I_l\|_2 \right) \quad (8)$$

which is the naive Nearest Neighbor (NN) rule. In the case of PCA however, the mean image needs to be subtracted. As an illustration of this technique, a dataset of eight objects (as described in later chapters) is used for classification purposes. The dataset consists of 128 views of eight objects. It is partitioned into a training and a test set in a 60-40 ratio. Eigenviews are generated using the training data and the test data is classified using the NN rule.

3. Dataset

A simulator has been created that loads the 3D model of objects and displays those objects at any arbitrary value of θ and ϕ, at a fixed value of r, where r, θ and ϕ are the spherical coordinates of the camera on the viewing hemisphere (radius, azimuth and elevation, respectively). The simulator generates reflection and emission images independently and then adds them to obtain the combined image. The thermal profiles for the objects are hand-generated and mapped onto various parts of the objects. Eight objects (shown in Fig. 3) are used, each with a different thermal profile. The

Figure 2. The eight objects used in our experiment. They have been shown as a single-band reflection image for display purposes.

reflectance spectrum assigned to the surfaces of each object is tabulated in Table 1. The spectral reflectance functions were obtained from the ASTER spectral Library [1] and were subsampled depending upon the number of bands that were needed. Fig. 3 shows a plot of these spectra along with that of the D55 illuminant (black body radiator at 5500 K).

The dataset used in this work consisted of capturing 128 (32×32 size) 7-band images (reflection+emission) of each object from randomly generated views (with no repetitions). This gives us 1024 7-band images. The images are normalized for size to fit in a 32×32 image and the intensity in

Class Label	Object	Material Type
11	DC-10	Galvanized Steel
12	747	Oxidized Galvanized Steel Metal
2	F-15	Oxidized Galvanized Steel Metal
3	Biplane	Aluminum Metal
4	Jeep	Aluminum Metal
51	Tank-0	Olive Green Paint
52	Tank-1	Olive Green Paint
53	Tank-2	Olive Green Paint

Table 1. Spectra assignment to the surfaces of the objects used in the database

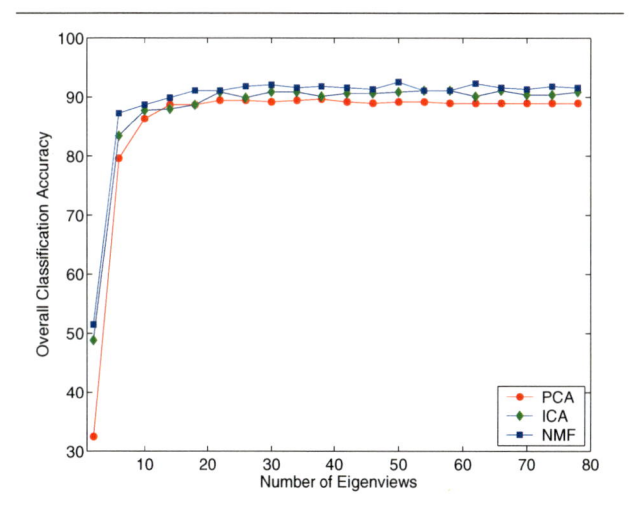

Figure 4. Classification accuracies for various values of M' — the number of eigenviews for PCA, ICA and NMF.

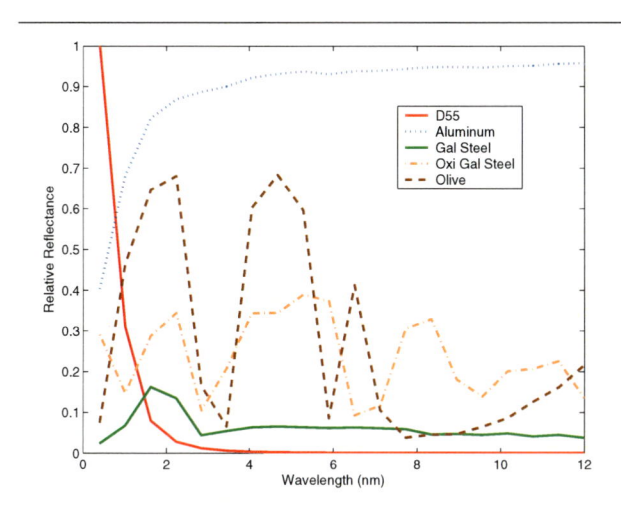

Figure 3. Spectral Power Distributions of the D55 illuminant superimposed upon the relative reflectance functions of the various materials used.

each band is normalized so as to have unit energy, as described in [17]. The dataset is divided into a training set and a test set in a 60-40 ratio with no overlaps.

4. Experiments

Eigenviews (with $M' = 78$) are generated using PCA, ICA and NMF with the training data. The test data is now projected onto the bases that are generated and the images are classified using a simple Nearest Neighbor (NN) classifier. The overall classification accuracy for PCA, ICA and NMF are found to be 90.14%, 90.87% and 91.59%, respectively, averaged over 5 runs.

The second experiment consisted of adding Gaussian noise to the test images and performing classification, while keeping the training set unchanged. White Gaussian noise with SNR of 20dB was added to the test data. Negative values were clipped. In reality, different sensors (and hence different bands of the images) will have different noise characteristics. However at this stage, we have assumed that all bands have the same noise properties. The classification accuracies for PCA, ICA and NMF using $M' = 78$ are 89.42%, 87.02% and 90.31%, respectively. This demonstrates that the eigenview system is relatively robust to noise — this may be explained by the fact that the projections of the noise on the eigenviews is relatively insignificant when compared to the contributions of the images, hence changing the projection on the eigenspace only slightly. In other words, as the eigenviews explain the image data, the projections noise are relatively insignificant.

The third experiment consists of determining the influence of the value of M' on the classification accuracy. In other words, studying how the number of eigenviews stored affects the recognition accuracy. Various values of M' are chosen and the classification accuracy evaluated. The results are plotted in the graph shown in Fig. 4. As is seen, the three algorithms perform with comparable accuracies (within a few percentage points of each other) although NMF appears to out-perform both PCA and ICA for almost all values of M'.

5. Conclusions and Future Work

The fundamental differences in the manner in which PCA, ICA and NMF are used makes a direct comparison difficult. PCA and ICA require that the data to have zero mean while NMF has no such restriction. In fact, NMF requires the data to be non-negative. In PCA, the basis functions are the same independent of the M' chosen, while in both ICA and NMF, depending upon the M' used, different basis functions are generated. However, as pointed out earlier, NMF performs marginally better than PCA and ICA.

The results presented here clearly illustrate the potential for eigenviews in performing object recognition. The application of the proposed technique to perform object recognition especially under restricted conditions of a limited number of views (a sparse sampling of the views over the viewing hemisphere) and a computational and storage restriction on eigenviews, has been demonstrated to be efficient. In the work reported here, a nearest neighbor classifier (a simple classifier) has been implemented – other non-parametric classifiers like the Reduced Coulomb Energy Classifier or the Nearest Feature Line classifier need to be investigated for possibly improved performance. The interested reader is referred to [21] for detailed discussions. Classification accuracies can be easily improved with larger databases.

References

[1] ASTER Spectral Library. Data on website http://speclib.jpl.nasa.gov/, 1998.

[2] S. Bergmann, J. Ihmels, and N. Barkai. Iterative signature algorithm for the analysis of large-scale gene expression data. *Physical Review E*, 67(3), 2003. ARTICLE No. 031902 Part 1.

[3] H. Bischof and A. Leonardis. View-based object representations using rbf networks. *Image and Vision Computing*, 19:619–629, 2001.

[4] G. Buschbaum and O. Bloch. Color categories revealed by non-negative matrix factorization of Munsell color spectra. *Vision Research*, 42(5):559–563, 2002.

[5] J. Cardoso and A. Couloumiac. Blind beamforming for non-gaussian signals. *Proceedings of the IEEE-F*, 140:362–370, 1993.

[6] N. Delfosse and P. Loubaton. Adaptive blind sepataion of independent sources: A deflation approach. *Signal Processing*, 45:59–83, 1995.

[7] A. Graf and F. Wichmann. Gender classification of human faces. *Lecture Notes on Computer Science*, 2525:491–500, 2002.

[8] D. Guillamet and J. Vitria. Non-negative matrix factorization for face recognition. *Lecture Notes on Artificial Intelligence*, 2504:336–344, 2002.

[9] A. Hyvarinen. One unit contrast function for independent component analysis: A statistical analysis. In *Proceedings of the IEEE Workshop on Neural Networks and Signal Processing*, pages 388–397, 1997.

[10] A. Hyvarinen, J. Karhunen, and E. Oja. *Independent Component Analysis*. John Wiley and Sons Inc., 2001.

[11] A. Hyvarinen and E. Oja. Simple neuron models for independent component analysis. *International Journal of Neural Systems*, 7(6):671–687, 1996.

[12] A. Hyvarinen and E. Oja. Independent component analysis: Algorithms and applications. *Neural Networks*, 13:411–430, 2000.

[13] T. Jaaskelainen, J. Paarkkinen, and S. Toyooka. Vector subspace model for color representation. *Journal of the Optical Society of America A*, 7:725–730, 1990.

[14] D. Lee and H. Seung. Learning the parts of objects by non-negative matrix factorization. *Nature*, 401:788–791, 1999.

[15] D. Lee and H. Seung. Algorithms for non-negative matrix factorization. *Advances in Neural Information Processing Systems*, 13:556–562, 2001.

[16] B. Moghaddam and A. Pentland. Probabilistic visual learning for object representation. *IEEE Transactions on Pattern Analysis and Machine Intelligence*, 19(7):696–710, 1997.

[17] H. Murase and S. Nayar. Learning object models from appearance. In *Proceedings of AAAI*, pages 836–843, 1993.

[18] H. Murase and S. Nayar. Visual learning and recognition of 3d objects from appearance. *International Journal of Computer Vision*, 14(1):5–24, 1995.

[19] A. Pentland, B. Moghaddam, and T. Starner. View-based and modular eigenspaces for face recognition. In *Proceedings of the IEEE Conference on Computer Vision and Pattern Recognition*, pages 84–91, 1994.

[20] T. Poggio and S. Edelman. A network that learns to recognize three-dimensional objects. *Nature*, 343(263–266), 1990.

[21] R. Ramanath. *A Framework for object characterization and matching in multi–and hyperspectral imaging systems*. PhD thesis, NC State University, Raleigh, 2003.

[22] R. Ramanath, R. Kuehni, W. Snyder, and D. Hinks. Spectral spaces and color spaces. *to appear Color Research and Application*, 29(1), 2004.

[23] L. Sirovich and M. Kirby. Low dimensional procedure for the characterization of human faces. *Journal of Optical Society of America*, 4(3):519–524, 1987.

[24] M. Turk and A. Pentland. Eigenfaces for recognition. *Journal of Cognitive Neuroscience*, 3(1):71–86, 1991.

Quantum Image Processing (QuIP)

Glenn Beach, Dr. Chris Lomont, Dr. Charles Cohen
Cybernet Systems Corporation
727 Airport Blvd., Ann Arbor, MI 48108
gbeach@cybernet.com, clomont@cybernet.com, ccohen@cybernet.com

Abstract

Moore's law states that computing performance doubles every 18 months. While this has held true for 40 years, it is widely believed that this will soon come to an end. Quantum computation offers a potential solution to the eventual failure of Moore's law. Researchers have shown that efficient quantum algorithms exist and can perform some calculations significantly faster than classical computers. Quantum computers require very different algorithms than classical computers, so the challenge of quantum computation is to develop efficient quantum algorithms. Cybernet is working with the Air Force Research Laboratory (AFRL) to create image processing algorithms for quantum computers. We have shown that existing quantum algorithms (such as Grover's algorithm) are applicable to image processing tasks. We are continuing to identify other areas of image processing which can be improved through the application of Quantum Computing.

1. Introduction

Image processing is a critical technology for the Air Force, as well as other branches of the military and the commercial sector. It is used in many key Air Force areas, such as surveillance, target acquisition, target tracking, and navigation. There are many image processing systems currently in use by the military. However, there are many desired applications that may never be possible on a classical computer. This may include tasks like sophisticated model based target acquisition with a large set of possible models.

Quantum computers theoretically have the ability to perform computations much faster than classical computers. Therefore, quantum computers may be able to realistically solve some of these intractable classical problems.

This paper details our work towards applying quantum computation to image processing tasks. We call this Quantum Image Processing (QuIP). Section 2 reviews the basics of quantum computation and provides specifics on the well-known Grover's algorithm. Section 3 provides details on Cybernet's model-based machine vision system and how Grover's algorithm can be applied to greatly increase the speed of the recognition. Section 4 discusses the concept of creating quantum versions of the classical correlation and convolution algorithms. Section 5 discusses other issues related to Quantum Image Processing.

2. Quantum computation

Quantum computing is a new approach to computation that has the possibility to revolutionize the field of computer science. The late Nobel Prize winning physicist Richard Feynman, who was interested in using a computer to simulate quantum systems, first investigated using quantum systems to do computation in 1982 [2]. He realized that the classical storage requirements for quantum systems grow exponentially in the number of particles. So while simulating twenty quantum particles only requires storing a million values, doubling this to a forty particle simulation would require a trillion values. Interesting simulations, say using a hundred or thousand particles, would not be possible, even using every computer on the planet. Thus he suggested making computers that utilized quantum particles as a computational resource that could simulate general quantum systems in order to do large simulations, and the idea of using quantum mechanical effects to do computation was born. The exponential storage capacity, coupled with some spooky effects like quantum entanglement, has led researchers to probe deeper into the computing power of quantum systems. Quantum computing has blossomed over the past 20 years, demonstrating the ability to solve some problems exponentially faster than any current computer could ever do. The most famous algorithm, the integer-factoring algorithm of Peter Shor, would allow the most popular encryption methods in use today to be cracked easily, if large enough quantum computers can be constructed. Thus the race is on to develop the theory and hardware that would enable quantum computing to become as widespread as PCs are today.

Classical computers, which include all current mainstream computers, work on discrete pieces of information, and manipulate them according to rules laid out by John Von Neumann in the 1940's. In honor of his groundbreaking work, current computers are said to run on a "Von Neumann architecture", which is modeled on an abstraction of discrete pieces of information. However, in recent years, scientists have changed from this abstraction of computing, to realizing that since a computer must ultimately be a physical device, the rules governing computation should be derived from physical law. Quantum mechanics is one of the most fundamental physical theories, and thus was a good choice to study what computational tasks could be physically achieved. This study led to the profound discovery that quantum mechanics allows much more powerful machines than the Von Neumann abstraction.

Another amazing quantum algorithm, besides the factoring algorithm of Shor, is Lov Grover's search algorithm, which greatly reduces the work needed to search for a specific item. For example, to search through one million unsorted names for a specific name averages about 500,000 compares with a classical computer, and there is no better way to do it under the Von Neumann model of computing. However, the same name can be found with only 1,000 compares using Grover's algorithm under the quantum model, which exploits the parallel nature of quantum mechanics. For bigger lists Grover's algorithm beats the classical one by an even greater amount.

Quantum computing today is a vast and varied field. There researchers working on areas ranging from making physical devices, using numerous technologies such as trapped ions and quantum dots, to people working on the theory side, solving thorny algorithm questions and trying to determine the exact power of quantum computation. It has been proven that quantum computers are strictly more powerful than classical ones, but how far that power reaches is still an open question. And how to build a big quantum computer is a hard technological problem.

So quantum computation is just in its infancy, much like classical computing with the vacuum tube computers like ENIAC and the Harvard MARK I computers of the 1940's. If the technological hurdles are overcome, in the same manner that many decades of work refined the classical computer from the slow lumbering vacuum-tube behemoths of the 1940's to the sleek, speedy transistorized computers that are currently widespread, then perhaps quantum computation will one day replace all current computation methods with a superior form of computation. All this from quantum mechanics, with weird rules and methods rooted in the weirdness of Nature Herself. Only time can tell what computers will be derived from deeper physical theories like quantum field theory or superstring theory.

2.1. Grover's algorithm

Grover's algorithm is known as the quantum search algorithm (Note that this section is derived largely from [1]). Classically, searching an unstructured database with N entries for a particular entry takes on the order of N checks. On a quantum computer this same search can be performed in the order of $\sqrt{N}$ checks. The remaining parts of this section provide details on Grover's algorithm. With Grover's algorithm, the search is performed over an index to the database elements rather than the elements themselves.

The oracle in Grover's algorithm is typically thought of as a black box with the capability of recognizing the solutions to a search problem. That is, the black box cannot calculate solutions, but it can verify that a proposed solution is correct. For any given index, the oracle, f(x) returns 1 if x is a solution to the search and 0 if x is not a solution. In the searches in our pose determination system, this oracle typically consists of checking to see if the error stored at the index x is less than a certain threshold. If so, then our oracle returns a 1 indicating a solution. Otherwise, it returns a 0 signifying that the index does not point to a solution.

The recognition is typically signaled through the use of an oracle qubit. A qubit is the quantum analog to the classical bit; however, a qubit can store both 0 and 1 with some probability, typically written as $a|0\rangle + b|1\rangle$. Therefore, a qubit can store much more information than a classical bit. The oracle is a unitary operator, O, defined by its action on the computational basis:

$$|x\rangle|q\rangle \xrightarrow{O} |x\rangle|q \oplus f(x)\rangle$$

where $|x\rangle$ is the index register, $\oplus$ denotes addition modulo 2, and the oracle qubit $|q\rangle$ is a single qubit that is flipped if f(x) = 1, and is unchanged otherwise.

Therefore, we can check to see if x is a solution to the problem by preparing $|x\rangle|0\rangle$, applying the oracle, and checking to see if the oracle qubit has been flipped to $|1\rangle$. We say that the oracle marks the solutions to the search problems by shifting the phase of the solution.

The goal of the algorithm is to find a solution to the search problem using the minimum number of applications of the oracle. The algorithm begins with the computer in the state $|0\rangle^{\otimes n}$. The Hadamard transform is used to put the computer in the equal superposition state of:

$$|\psi\rangle = \frac{1}{N^{1/2}} \sum_{x=0}^{N-1} |x\rangle$$

Finally, the repeated iterations of the Grover iteration or operator are applied to the system. This occurs in basically 4 steps:
   1. Application of the oracle.

2. Application of the Hadamard transform $H^{\otimes n}$.
3. Perform a conditional phase shift on the computer with every computation basis state except $|0\rangle$ receiving a phase shift of -1.
4. Application of the Hadamard transform $H^{\otimes n}$.

3. Cybernet's model-based vision system

This section describes Cybernet's vision-based pose determination and reality registration system for identifying objects in an unstructured visual environment. This vision system can be used in a wide variety of applications for military and civilian use including: vehicle identification, aircraft identification, manufacturing (identification of good and bad parts/objects), traffic safety, and video searches...or anywhere where there is a need for visual identification of objects.

The reality registration and pose determination system utilizes one or more cameras as its inputs. A wire-frame template of the object to be identified is compared to the input images. If it is found, an output of the object's position and orientation is computed. The placement of the template can be performed by a human in-the-loop, or through a real-time front end system.

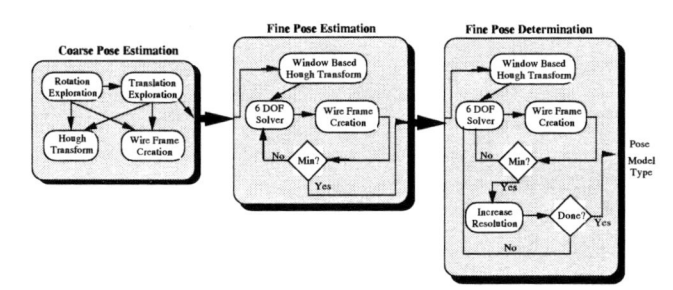

Figure 1. Three module classification and recognition.

The vision system uses three modules to classify and determine the pose of an object (see Figure 1). The first module in the sequence uses input images and models to generate a coarse pose estimate for the object. Since there is no constraint in the first module on the object's pose, and the module only estimates the rough pose of the object, the module is referred to as the Coarse Pose Estimation module. The second module uses the estimates from the coarse pose estimation module, input images, and the model to further refine the pose to a small degree of error. It is therefore called the Fine Pose Estimation module. The last module in the sequence uses the fine pose estimation, the images, and the model to determine an exact match between the model and the image, thereby determining an answer. This is called the Fine Pose Determination module.

The coarse pose estimation module calculates a rough pose using two steps: a rotational exploration of the problem space followed by a translational exploration of the problem space. The output is a ranked set of potential poses of the object.

The rotational exploration of the problem space attempts to identify the correct pitch, roll and yaw of the object that may yield a correct overall position/orientation. The Hough transform of the image(s) and a wireframe projection are used to calculate the orientation information. The Hough transform converts an image from xy pixel space into a representation which contains information about the lines found within the image. Using the lines from the image, and lines from a simple wireframe projection, the rotational parameters are solved by using an exhaustive search.

To efficiently solve for the translational parameters (x,y,z), the translational exploration is constrained using the results of the rotational exploration. As with the rotational exploration, the translation exploration uses the lines from the image(s) and the lines from the wireframe to perform a search and calculate the translational parameters. By constraining the exploration, we avoid unrealistic exhaustive combinatoric approaches.

The fine pose estimation module is the second in the sequence of three modules in the machine vision system. It uses input images, models, and pose hypotheses to match the wireframe of the model to the image(s). The fine pose estimation system is designed to calculate the pose of the object very quickly and accurately, though not as precisely as possible. The first step in the fine pose estimation is to overlay a grid onto the image(s) to divide them into small regions called windows. A Hough transform is calculated in each window to identify the strongest line within that window. The line information from all windows is passed to a 6 degree-of-freedom solver that attempts to search the problem space for the correct x, y, z, pitch, roll, and yaw. To match the wireframe of the model to the lines from the image(s) windows, the 6 DOF solver uses a modified Newton-Raphson solver. The wireframe creation module is used to project wireframes into the image windows. As the x, y, z, roll, pitch, yaw solution space is searched, the solver attempts to minimize a distance function. After each iteration in the solver, a check is made to determine if a minimum has been found (the algorithm has found a solution). When a minimum is located, the x, y, z, roll, pitch, and yaw are passed to the fine pose determination module. If a minimum is not reached, the solver identifies the next pose to be tested.

The fine pose determination module is the third in the sequence of the three machine vision modules. It uses the input image(s), model(s) and pose information from the fine pose estimation module to exactly match the model's wireframe to the image(s). The fine pose determination module is designed to search a very small section of the x, y, z, pitch, roll, yaw search space at higher and higher resolutions to calculate the most accurate possible solution. The majority of the fine pose determination calculations are very similar to the fine pose estimation calculations. More specifically, the window-based Hough transform, 6 DOF solver, wireframe construction, and minimization are all the same. What is different is the logic used to increase the resolution of the search in order to find a more exact solution. After a minimum is located at a given resolution, the resolution is increased, and the search for a finer minimum continues. The increase in resolution continues until increasing the resolution no longer increases the accuracy of the solution. The output from this module is the exact pose of the object or fuse and a match confidence for classification purposes.

3.1. Application of Grover's algorithm

This section provides details about how we applied Grover's quantum search algorithm to perform searches within our pose determination system. In the broadest sense, the pose determination algorithm can be thought of as a brute force comparison between every possible pose (at some level of discreteness) of the object and the appearance of the object in the image. A good solution is represented by a low error in the comparison of the projection of the model at a specified pose and the edges visible in the image.

For simplicity, we'll assume that the 3D position (x,y,z) is known and we are only attempting to identify the orientation (roll, pitch, yaw). This assumption actually reduces the benefits of the quantum implementation because it reduces the size of the search space. However, it makes the analysis simpler by removing a level of algorithmic complexity. In the current classical implementation, the system performs the following general steps (there are many function calls built into these steps):

1. Select an orientation to test.
2. Calculate the 3D location of the vertices in the model (their location will be dependent on orientation).
3. Calculate the 3D edges that connect the vertices.
4. Compare the model edges to the image edges and generate an error.
5. Compare the error to an error threshold. If the error is below the threshold, then we can exit the algorithm with the current pose as a solution. If not, then repeat the calculations with the next orientation.

In the quantum implementation, the algorithm gets reformatted as follows:
1. Simultaneously calculate the 3D location of the vertices of the model for all of the possible orientations.
2. Simultaneously calculate the 3D edges that connect the vertices for all of the possible orientations.
3. Simultaneously calculate the error for all orientations.
4. Search for an orientation with an error level below the specified threshold.

If we assume that there are M solutions within the set of possible orientations with a low enough error, then the classical approach will take on the order of N/M iterations. The quantum approach will take on the order of $\sqrt{N/M}$ iterations.

The quantum implementation leverages a few techniques from quantum computing. These techniques include quantum memory, quantum parallelism, and Grover's algorithm. The quantum approach requires the system to store all of the 3D positions for every vertex in the model for all orientations. As an example, let's assume the following:

1. We have a relatively simple object, such as a 3D hexagon with 12 vertices.
2. Each vertex is stored as a structure containing 3 floats representing roll, pitch, and yaw. Therefore, each vertex requires 12 bytes of information for storage.
3. We will use a relatively coarse resolution in the increments for the rotation. We will perform 1 degree increments in roll, pitch, and yaw across a 360x360x180 degree space. Therefore, there are 23,328,000 orientations to check.

In the classical sense, we would need 12*12*23,328,000 = 3,359,232,000 bytes of information. In order to store this for efficient use within the program, we would need approximately 3.1 GBytes of conventional RAM for just storing the vertices. However, in the quantum paradigm this information can be stored in only 35 qubits ($2^{35} = 34,359,738,368$ bits or about 4 GBytes). The amount of classical memory required will increase dramatically if we decrease the increment size (say to ½ degree) or consider the 3D position to be unknown. For example, if the increment were ½ degree then we would need approximately 25 GBytes of classical RAM to hold the vertex information for all orientations, but we would only need 38 qubits to hold the information.

Once the information is contained in quantum memory, then we can use quantum parallelism to calculate the scores for each orientation. Quantum parallelism allows us to apply a function to all states of a system simultaneously. This function could be responsible for calculating the error rate between the image edges and edges for each of the potential solutions. Once we have calculated all of the errors, then we can use Grover's algorithm to search the space for a correct answer.

Again, we assume a known 3D position, orientation increments of 1 degree, and only one orientation meets our criteria (this could be relaxed without significantly changing the example). Again, we have 360*360*180 = 23,328,000 orientations to check. Applying Grover's algorithm produces the same determination in 4829 checks (or about 2% of the classical approach). Again, if we include the effects of searching through x,y,z, then the improvements become more important.

4. Quantum convolution and correlation

Classical convolution and correlation leverage the classical Fast Fourier Transform to perform many image processing tasks, such as noise reduction, simple edge detection, sobel filters, laplacian filters, gradient detection, despeckle, edge blurring, smoothing, edge sharpening, contrast enhancement, spatial averaging, and template matching. As part of our work in quantum image processing, we have shown that it is not possible to perform convolution and correlation on a physically realizable quantum computer. Due to space limitations, this paper only includes a discussion of the proof.

The Fast Fourier Transform (FFT) is arguably the most important algorithm in computer science. Many applications, from image processing, signal processing, pattern matching, polynomial multiplication, and many others are accomplished efficiently by utilizing FFT to compute a Discrete Fourier Transform (DFT) of some set of data. Naively, the DFT of $N = 2^n$ complex values has complexity $O(N^2)$, but the famous paper by Cooley and Tukey introduced the Fast Fourier Transform, reducing the complexity to $\Theta(N \log N) = \Theta(n 2^n)$, making Fourier transforms extremely useful in computer algorithms. This efficiency is the basis of fast convolution and correlation with complexity $O(N \log N)$.

In the last decade, quantum computing has become well known due to the integer factoring algorithm of Shor and the database search of Grover, both of which have complexities much better than their classical counterparts. There are other problems for which quantum computers perform exponentially better than any classical (Turing) computer. A quantum Fourier Transform (QFT) can be done on a quantum state consisting of $N = 2^n$ complex values with complexity $O(\log^2 N) = O(n^2)$, making it exponentially faster than the classical counterpart, but unfortunately the peculiarities of quantum mechanics disallows using this algorithm as a direct replacement for all FFT algorithms. In fact, after the breakthrough algorithms of Shor and Grover, no algorithms of similar importance have been found, although there has been intense work in that direction.

Since the QFT and inverse QFT are more efficient than their classical counterparts, and the FFT and inverse FFT are the cornerstones for convolution and correlation algorithms, it is reasonable to attempt to construct quantum analogues of convolution and correlation algorithms that outperform their classical counterparts. The key point of our work is that there is no physically realizable method to compute the normalized convolution or correlation of the coefficients of two quantum states. Thus replacing classical algorithms that rely on convolution or correlation cannot be done in a simple, direct algorithm replacement manner, but must be approached by more sophisticated techniques.

Please note, that this relates to convolution and correlation directly, not the image processing tasks that they are typically used to perform. For example, pattern recognition is frequently performed through correlation. The section states that correlation is not possible on a quantum computer, but makes no claims about pattern recognition. Suppose you have an NxN-pixel image, and are searching for a n x n-pixel pattern. The brute force method of looking over all pixels and comparing each time requires $O(N^{2n^2})$ steps. The convolution method requires something like $O(Nn \log(Nn))$ steps.

Instead we could use Grover search, and take as an oracle the function that takes an (i,j) pixel location, and returns 1 if and only if this is the upper left corner of a match for the pattern. This oracle can be the usual brute force search using O(n^2) time. But since Grover requires O(N) calls versus the usual O(N^2), this should result in a final algorithm of O(N n^2), which is a lot better for small matches in large images.

This is not the exponential speedup we had hoped for using some Fourier transform idea, but it is still a speedup. Also, there may be a way to speed up the oracle using Grover recursively, perhaps to get an O(Nn) algorithm.

6. Current status and additional work

As part of the ongoing effort, we have developed a number of other tools and investigated other quantum algorithms. These include the following:

1. A quantum programming language, called Q++, which includes programming tools for creating code related to quantum algorithms.
2. A quantum simulator written in Q++ that allows us to test quantum algorithms as if they were being executed on an actual quantum computer. Of course, simulating a quantum computer on a classical computer results in slow execution.
3. A bright spot finding algorithm written in Q++ and simulated on our simulator.
4. A method for using Grover's algorithm to perform image template matching.

As the project progresses we will be studying many other image and signal processing algorithms to determine which ones are good candidates for quantum computing. Additionally, we will be examining the applicability of quantum computation to areas such as automatic route planning, collision detection, and object interactions.

7. References

[1] I.L. Chuang and M.A. Nielson, *Quantum computation and quantum information*, Cambridge University Press, Cambridge, 2000.

[2] R. Feynman, Simulating physics with computers. *International Journal of Theoretical Physics 21,* 6&7, pp. 467-488.

Registration of Range Data from Unmanned Aerial and Ground Vehicles*

A. Downs, R. Madhavan and T. Hong
Intelligent Systems Division
National Institute of Standards and Technology
Gaithersburg, MD 20899-8230.
Email: {raj.madhavan, tsai.hong, mike.shneier}@nist.gov

Abstract

In the research reported in this paper, we propose to overcome the unavailability of Global Positioning System (GPS) using combined information obtained from a scanning LADAR rangefinder on an Unmanned Ground Vehicle (UGV) and a LADAR mounted on an Unmanned Aerial Vehicle (UAV) that flies over the terrain being traversed. The approach to estimate and update the position of the UGV involves registering range data from the two LADARs using a combination of a feature-based registration method and a modified version of the well-known Iterative Closest Point (ICP) algorithm. Registration of range data thus guarantees an estimate of the vehicle's position even when only one of the vehicles has GPS information. Additionally, such registration over time (i.e., from sample to sample), enables position information to be maintained even when both vehicles can no longer maintain GPS contact. The approach has been validated by conducting systematic experiments on complex real-world data.

1. Introduction

With funding from the Army Research Laboratory (ARL) and the Defense Advanced Research Projects Agency (DARPA), the National Institute of Standards and Technology (NIST) is developing architectures and algorithms for unmanned vehicles. The research makes use of the NIST Highly Mobile Multi-Wheeled Vehicle (HMMWV) and an eXperimental Unmanned Vehicle (XUV) developed under the Army's Demo III program [8]. The position estimation for these Unmanned Ground Vehicles (UGVs) relies on fusing Global Positioning System (GPS) reported estimates with other on-board navigation sensors. The required accuracy of the GPS estimates cannot be guaranteed for the entirety of a particular mission as the direct line of sight to the satellites cannot be maintained at all times. GPS can be lost due to multipathing effects and terrain conditions, especially for on-road driving tasks. In order to account for such unavailability and unreliability of GPS, another form of position estimation becomes imperative.

To overcome this problem, the UGV can use aerial survey maps constructed using a downward-looking LADAR (LAser Detection And Ranging) sensor mounted on an Unmanned Aerial Vehicle (UAV). If the LADAR range images from the UGV can be registered to those from the UAV, then these results can serve as secondary position estimates in the event of absence or degradation of GPS. This paper describes a position estimation algorithm that works by registering a scanning LADAR rangefinder on an UGV and a LADAR mounted on an UAV that flies over the terrain being traversed. We propose a hybrid approach which is a combination of both feature-based and point cloud-based Iterative Closest Point (ICP) algorithm for registering two sets of LADAR range images.

The value of aerial imagery obtained via active range sensing for aiding ground vehicle navigation is being recognized within the UGV community. For example, in [11], aerial and ground views from unmanned vehicles are registered by extracting a geometrically consistent set of correspondences using surface signatures from which a registration transformation is estimated. It is not clear, given the computational burden associated with the extraction of surface signatures, whether

---

* Commercial equipment and materials are identified in this paper in order to adequately specify certain procedures. Such identification does not imply recommendation or endorsement by the National Institute of Standards and Technology, nor does it imply that the materials or equipment identified are necessarily the best available for the purpose.

this approach can be implemented in real-time. In [10], an aerial vehicle, a Flying Eye (FE), flies ahead of an UGV acting as a "scout" to detect difficult obstacles from an overhead perspective thus benefitting ground vehicle navigation. The above paper briefly mentions the need for registering the data from the FE to the ground vehicle but the details of the registration process are not presented. The hybrid approach proposed in this paper exploits the simplicity and speed of the iterative closest point algorithm thus lending itself to real-time implementation.

The paper is organized as follows: Section 2 describes registration of 3D LADAR range images using a modified ICP algorithm. Section 3 describes a feature extraction and alignment methodology for accurate registration. Section 4 describes the experimental results. Finally, Section 5 concludes the paper by summarizing the contributions and suggesting further research efforts.

2. Iterative Registration

The iterative algorithm for registering two sets of 3D LADAR data denoted by **M** (model) and **D** (data) can be summarized by the following steps [2] :

1. For each point in **D**, compute its closest point in **M**. This is usually accomplished via 3D nearest point search from the set comprising $N_\mathbf{D}$ data and $N_\mathbf{M}$ model points.
2. Compute the incremental transformation (**R**,**T**) using Singular Value Decomposition (SVD) using correspondences obtained in step **1**.
3. Apply the incremental transformation from step **2.** to **D**.
4. If relative changes in **R** and **T** are less than a threshold, terminate. Else go to step **1**.

To deal with spurious points/false matches and to account for occlusions and outliers, the least-squares objective function that is to be minimized is weighted such that [12]:

$$min_{(\mathbf{R},\mathbf{T})} \sum_i w_i \, ||\mathbf{M}_i - (\mathbf{R}\mathbf{D}_i + \mathbf{T})||^2 \qquad (1)$$

where **R** is a 3 × 3 rotation matrix, **T** is a 3 × 1 translation vector and the subscript i refers to the corresponding points of the sets **M** and **D**.

If the Euclidean distance between a point x_i in one set and its closest point y_i in the other, denoted by $d_i \triangleq d(x_i, y_i)$, is bigger than the maximum tolerable distance threshold $\mathcal{D}_{max}$, then w_i is set to zero in Equation (1). This means that an x_i cannot be paired with a y_i since the distance between reasonable pairs cannot be very big. The value of $\mathcal{D}_{max}$ is set adaptively in a robust manner by analyzing distance statistics.

Let $\{x_i, y_i, d_i\}$ be the set of original points, the set of closest points and their distances, respectively. The mean and standard deviation of the distances are computed as:

$$\mu = \frac{1}{N}\sum_{i=1}^{N} d_i; \quad \sigma = \sqrt{\frac{1}{N}\sum_{i=1}^{N}(d_i - \mu)^2}$$

where N is the total number of pairs. The pseudo-code for the adaptive thresholding of the distance $\mathcal{D}_{max}$ is given below:

```
        if  μ  <   D
 D^itn_max   =   μ  + 3σ;
    elseif μ  <  3D
 D^itn_max   =   μ  + 2σ;
    elseif μ  <  6D
 D^itn_max   =   μ  + σ;
    else D^itn_max  =   ε;
```

where *itn* denotes the iteration number, $\mathcal{D}$ is defined as the average distance between the scan points to be registered and is a function of the resolution of the range data. During implementation, $\mathcal{D}$ was selected based on the following two observations: (i) If $\mathcal{D}$ is too small, then several iterations are required for the algorithm to converge and several good matches will be discarded, and (ii) if $\mathcal{D}$ is too big, then the algorithm may not converge at all since many spurious matches will be included. For more details on the effect and selection of $\mathcal{D}$ and ϵ on the convergence of the algorithm, see [12]. At the end of this step, two corresponding point sets, $\mathbf{P_M}$:$\{\mathbf{p}_i\}$ and $\mathbf{P_D}$:$\{\mathbf{q}_i\}$ are available.

The incremental 3D transformation (rotation and translation) of step **2.** is obtained as follows [1]:
• Calculate $\mathbf{H} = \sum_{i=1}^{N_D}(\mathbf{p}_i - \mathbf{p}_c)(\mathbf{q}_i - \mathbf{q}_c)^T$; $(\mathbf{p}_c, \mathbf{q}_c)$ are the centroids of the point sets $(\mathbf{P_M}, \mathbf{P_D})$.
• Find the SVD of $\mathbf{H}$ such that $\mathbf{H} = \mathbf{U}\mathbf{\Omega}\mathbf{V}^T$.
• The rotation matrix relating the two point sets is given by $\mathbf{R} = \mathbf{V}\mathbf{U}^T$.
• The translation between the two point sets is given by $\mathbf{T} = \mathbf{q}_c - \mathbf{R}\mathbf{p}_c$.

This process is iterated as stated in step **4.** until the mean Euclidean distance between the corresponding point sets $\mathbf{P_M}$ and $\mathbf{P_D}$ is less than or equal to a predetermined distance or until a given number of iterations is exceeded. For further details, see [5].

3. Air to Ground Feature-based Registration

The underlying assumption in the iterative registration algorithm is that the rotation angle between the range images that need to be registered is not too large

(a)

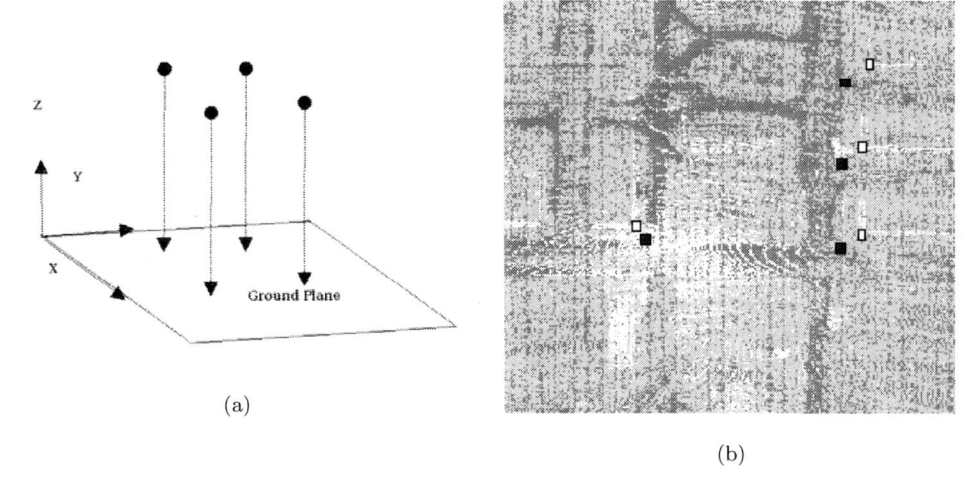

(b)

Figure 1. Projection of LADAR data to base ground planes is shown in (a). The extracted features (corners) from the UGV and UAV LADARs are shown as white and black squares, respectively, in (b).

and also that these images are not too far apart. For the current case of UAV and UGV LADAR data, this assumption is overly restrictive and an aiding mechanism for the registration of the range images becomes necessary.

The correspondence determination step is the most difficult and computationally expensive step of the iterative algorithm. Despite the apparent simplicity of this problem, establishing reliable correspondences is extremely difficult as the UGV is subjected to heavy pitching and rolling motion characteristic of travel over undulating terrain. This is further exacerbated by the uncertainty of the location of the sensor platform relative to the global frame of reference. In addition to these factors, noise inherently present in LADAR range images complicates the process of determining reliable correspondences. One solution to overcome the above deficiencies is to extract naturally occurring view-invariant features, for example, corners, from the LADAR scans. Such *control points* can then be used for establishing reliable registration.

Towards guaranteeing robust and accurate registration, we first obtain the z translation value by estimating the ground z values on the UGV and UAV LADAR data in the vicinity of the UGV's current location. For the UGV, the ground values are obtained from the LADAR points that are within a given radius immediately in front of the vehicle and those for the UAV are obtained by finding the minimum of the LADAR values. Then we project the UAV and UGV LADAR data into the base ground planes as depicted in Figure 1(a) and construct the feature planes by using the Canny edge detector [3]. The corner features are detected based on the intersections of lines formed by edges. The corner features are independently extracted from both LADAR data sets by considering those points that are above a given height from the ground as shown in Figure 1(b).

The two sets of the projected corner points (UAV LADAR set: $\mathbf{A}$ and UGV LADAR set: $\mathbf{G}$) are used to estimate a 2D translation. Given two sets of 2D corner points:

$$\mathbf{A} \triangleq \mathbf{a}_j = \begin{bmatrix} a_{1j} \\ a_{2j} \\ \vdots \\ a_{nj} \end{bmatrix} ; \ j = 1, 2, \cdots n;$$

$$\mathbf{G} \triangleq \mathbf{g}_k = \begin{bmatrix} g_{1k} \\ g_{2k} \\ \vdots \\ g_{nk} \end{bmatrix} ; \ k = 1, 2, \cdots n;$$

To find a translation along the x and y directions, we first calculate the means of sets $\mathbf{A}$ and $\mathbf{G}$:

$$\bar{\mathbf{a}} = \frac{1}{n}\sum_{j=1}^{n} \mathbf{a}_j; \quad \bar{\mathbf{g}} = \frac{1}{n}\sum_{k=1}^{n} \mathbf{g}_k;$$

The difference between the means of x, y and that between the aerial and ground z values provide a rough estimate of the required 3D translation between the two sets of LADAR data. The 3D translational offset when applied to the UGV range image enables the ICP algorithm to provide reliable registration results.

4. Experimental Setup and Results

The UAV LADAR produces a 3D point cloud (range image) at up to 6000 pts/sec with a 100 meter scanning range. The UGV is equipped with a long-range 3D Riegl image sensor (LMS-Z420i) which provides 10000 pts/sec with range up to 800 meters. For additional details on the UAV and UGV LADARs, see [6] and [7], respectively. The UAV LADAR provides an aerial survey map with significant information about existing topology and structures.

Figure 2 shows a top view of unregistered LADAR range images obtained from the UGV (in white) and UAV (in black) LADARs, respectively. Figures 3(a)-(d)

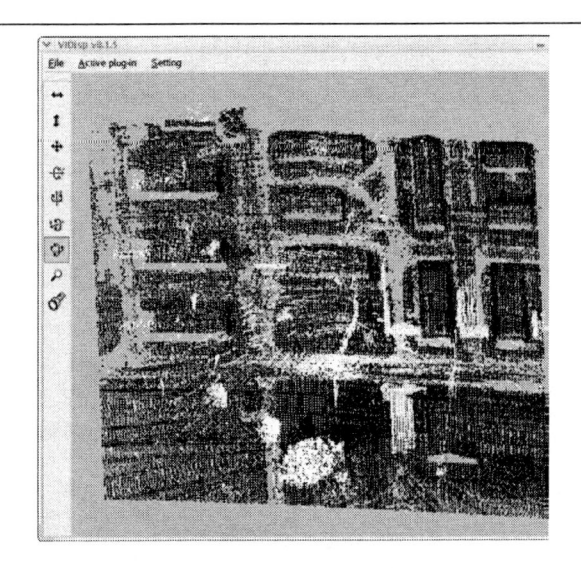

Figure 2. Top view of unregistered range images of UGV and UAV LADARs

depict the results of the feature-based registration algorithm. Figure 3(a) shows a top view of the LADAR range images after applying the translation obtained using the corner features. Figure 3(c) shows the results of the iterative registration algorithm applied to the LADAR range images in (a). Figures 3(b) and (d) show a magnified view of stages depicted in Figures 3(a) and (c), respectively. From Figures 2 and 3, it is evident that the LADAR range images are registered.

A similar sequence of results presented in Figure 4 again shows the efficacy of the proposed feature-based iterative algorithm in registering aerial and ground LADAR range images.

5. Conclusions and Further Research

A hybrid iterative algorithm for registering 3D LADAR range images obtained from unmanned aerial and ground vehicles was proposed in this paper. Combined with a feature-based approach, the algorithm was shown to produce accurate registration for the two sets of LADAR data. Registration of the UGV LADAR to the aerial survey map minimizes the dependency on GPS for position estimation especially when the GPS estimates are unreliable or unavailable. The results presented in the paper demonstrated the potential of this approach lending itself to real-time implementation.

For practical purposes, the LADAR data utilized in this paper can be assumed to be of the same resolution even though typically the aerial data tend to be of lower resolution than that of the UGV LADAR. To address this issue, we are currently developing schemes for use within the ICP algorithm that will inherently account for varying resolution in data sets that need to be registered. Towards this, we are also developing corner detection schemes using the Harris [4] and SUSAN [9] corner detectors.

References

[1] K. Arun, T. Huang, and S. Bolstein. Least-Squares Fitting of Two 3-D Point Sets. *IEEE Trans. on Pattern Analysis and Machine Intelligence*, 9(5):698–700, 1987.

[2] P. Besl and N. McKay. A Method for Registration of 3-D Shapes. *IEEE Trans. on Pattern Analysis and Machine Intelligence*, 14(2):239–256, 1992.

[3] J. Canny. A Computational Approach to Edge Detection. *IEEE Trans. on Pattern Analysis and Machine Intelligence*, 8(6):679–698, Nov. 1986.

[4] C. Harris and M. Stephens. A Combined Corner and Edge Detector. In *Proc. of the Fourth Alvey Vision Conf.*, pages 147–151, Sept. 1988.

[5] R. Madhavan and E. Messina. Iterative Registration of 3D LADAR Data for Autonomous Navigation. In *Proc. of the IEEE Intelligent Vehicles Symp.*, pages 186–191, June 2003.

[6] R. Miller and O. Amidi. 3D Site Mapping with the CMU Autonomous Helicopter. In *Proc. of the 5th Intl. Conf. on Intelligent Autonomous Systems*, June 1998.

[7] M. Shneier, T. Chang, T. Hong, G. Cheok, H. Scott, S. Legowik, and A. Lytle. A Repository of Sensor Data for Autonomous Driving Research. In *Proc. of the SPIE Unmanned Ground Vehicle Technology V*, Apr. 2003.

[8] C. Shoemaker and J. Bornstein. The Demo III UGV Program: A Testbed for Autonomous Navigation Research. In *Proc. of the IEEE ISIC/CIRA/ISAS Joint Conf.*, pages 644–651, Sept. 1998.

[9] S. Smith and J. Brady. SUSAN - A New Approach to Low Level Image Processing. *Intl. Jrnl. of Comp. Vision*, pages 45–78, May 1997.

[10] A. Stentz et al. Real-Time, Multi-Perspective Perception for Unmanned Ground Vehicles. In *Proc. of the AUVSI Unmanned Systems Conf.*, July 2003.

(a)

(b)

(c)

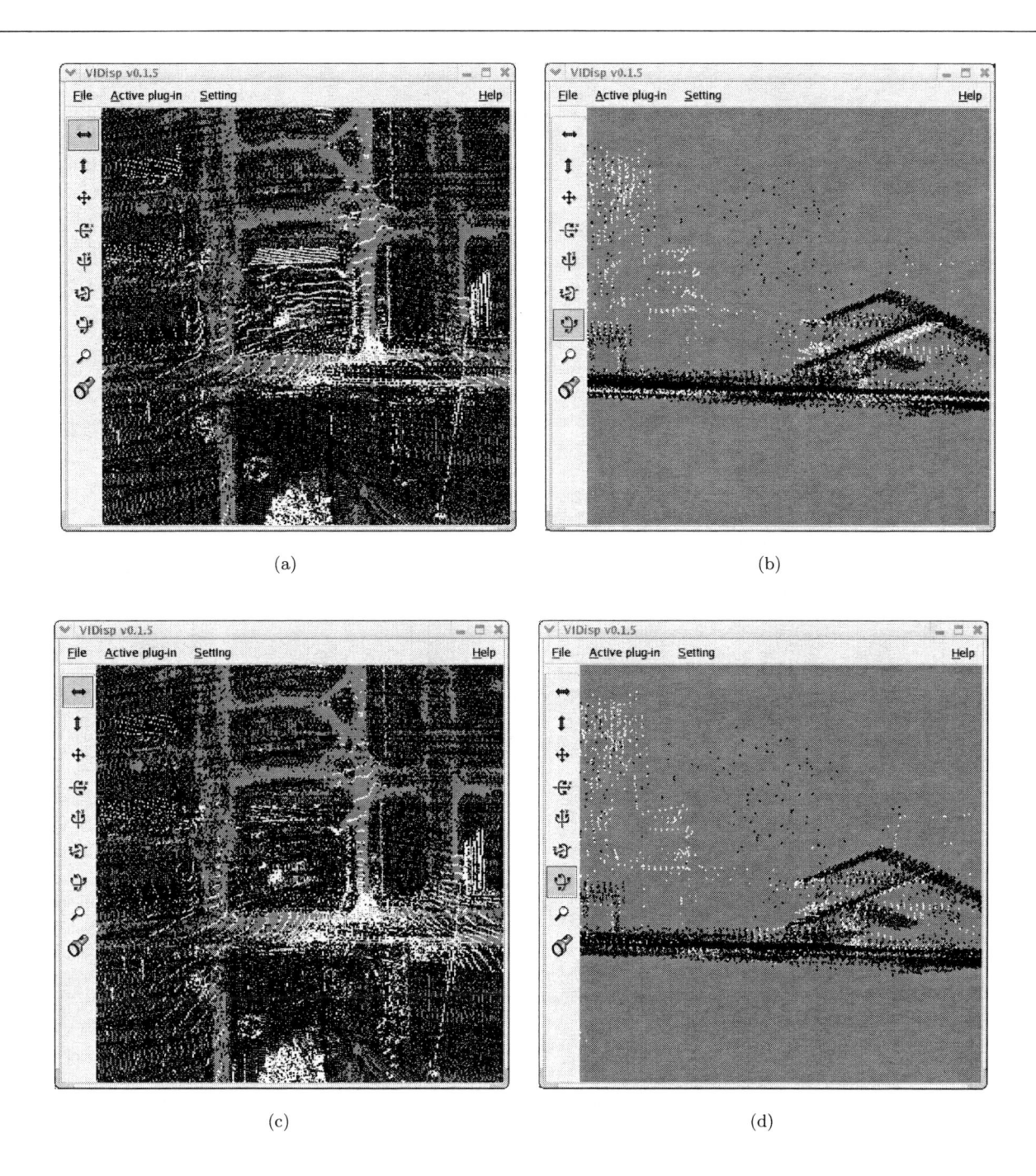

(d)

Figure 3. A top view of the feature-based translation obtained using the extracted corners is shown in (a) and a magnified side view of the same is shown in (b). (c) shows a top view of the registered UAV and UGV LADAR range images obtained by utilizing the feature-based translation results and (d) is a magnified view of (c). See text for further details.

[11] N. Vandapel, R. Donamukkala, and M. Hebert. Experimental Results in Using Aerial LADAR Data for Mobile Robot Navigation. In *Proc. of the Intl. Conf. on Field and Service Robotics*, July 2003.

[12] Z. Zhang. Iterative Point Matching for Registration of Free-Form Curves and Surfaces. *Intl. Jrnl. of Comp. Vision*, 13(2):119–152, 1994.

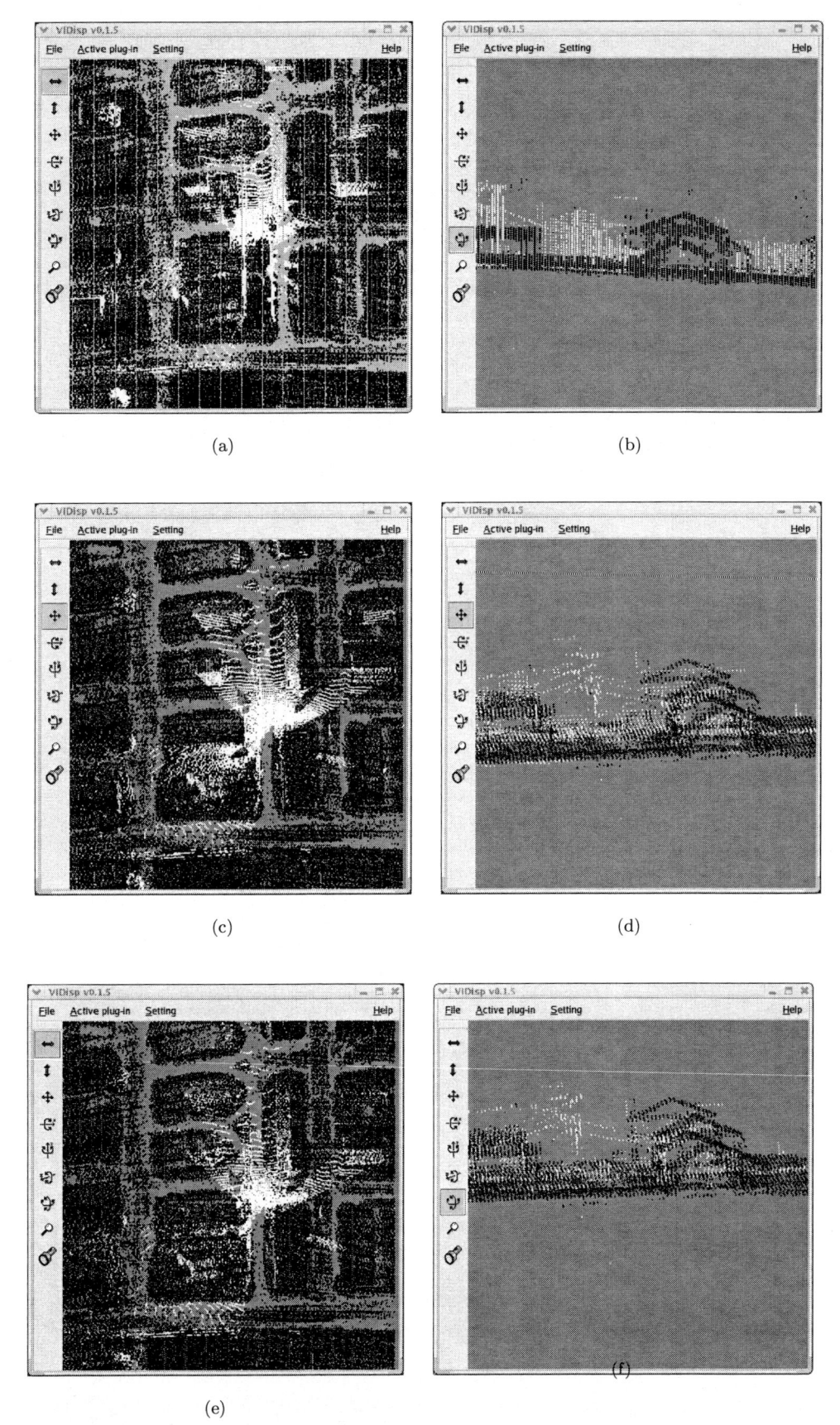

Figure 4. A top view of unregistered range images of UGV and UAV LADARs, the feature-based translation obtained using the extracted corners, and the registered UAV and UGV LADAR range images obtained by utilizing the feature-based translation results are shown in (a), (c) and (e), respectively. (b), (d) and (f), respectively, show magnified side views of their counterparts in the left column.

Projectile Identification System

Glenn Beach, Dr. Charles J. Cohen, Gary Moody, Martha Henry
Cybernet Systems Corporation
727 Airport Blvd., Ann Arbor, MI 48108
gbeach@cybernet.com, ccohen@cybernet.com, gmoody@cybernet.com, mhenry@cybernet.com

Abstract

The U.S. Army plans for the needs of future warfare to retain its technological superiority. Future Combat Systems (FCS) is a major effort designed to meet this need. FCS includes multiple automated fire weapons. On current systems, a human typically enters information about each projectile loaded. This is a slow process, placing the soldier and the weapon in danger. Cybernet (through funding by TACOM-ARDEC) has created a vision system that leverages multiple simple and mature image processing techniques to recognize the projectile type as it is loaded into the system's magazine. The system uses a combination of shape detection, color detection, and character identification, along with knowledge of the projectile (such as CAD model, text location, coloring, etc.) to identify the projectile. The system processes the data in real-time, allowing the soldier to load the projectiles as quickly as possible. The system has been designed with a modular recognition framework.

1. Introduction

The U.S. Army is developing or considering developing a number of weapons platforms with the capability of automated fire control. These include programs such as Dragon Fire, Responsive Accurate Mission Module (RAMM), Non-Line-of-Sight (NLOS) Cannon, and Multi-Role Armament and Ammunition System (MRAAS). These systems are capable of automatically loading a projectile from an internal magazine into the barrel to be fired. However, they require a human in the loop to load the projectiles into the magazine.

Most of these systems support more than one type of projectile. For example, the RAMM fires 120 mm mortar shells that come in many variations, such as high explosive, illumination, and smoke. Therefore, the fire control system must be able to request a particular type of projectile from the magazine. If the mission is to illuminate an area over friendly troops, shooting a high explosive round by mistake would be disastrous.

Currently, the human loader is required to manually input information about the projectile to inform the magazine what type of munition is in each location. There are two main drawbacks to this solution. First, the text entry for each projectile can take on the order of one minute. This produces a lengthy downtime during reloading, since many of these systems can hold more than 40 projectiles in their magazine. Additionally, these systems are designed to launch projectiles rapidly. For example, the Dragon Fire can launch up to 10 rounds per minute. Therefore, the ratio of time when the system is ready to engage the enemy versus the reloading time is too low.

Second, it can be anticipated that the human loaders will be operating under conditions of high stress (either due to enemy fire or rapid pace). This high level of stress increases the chance that a human may enter erroneous information. This could produce extremely undesirable results if this causes the wrong type of projectile to be launched.

In this paper, we discuss an optical projectile identification system (PIDS) that solves the problems discussed above. Section 2 provides an overview of this vision system. Section 3 provides details about the architecture of the system. Section 4 provides details about the specific recognition modules. Finally, section 5 provides details about future work and other areas where the technology is applicable.

2. PIDS

The Projectile IDentification System (PIDS) provides projectile identification capability and interfaces for the communication of identification data. The PIDS consists of a combination of sensor hardware and innovative software algorithms. The architecture for this system is modular and allows us to easily add new recognition modules. This increases the usefulness of the system to other areas.

The hardware for the current system includes 3 high resolution, high frame rate, color Atmel AviivA C2 CL 4010 line scan cameras, 3 Matrox Meteor II CameraLink frame grabbers, a standard PC, a set of illuminators, and a user interface display. Figure 1 provides a conceptual picture of the production version of the PIDS. In this system, the PC is replaced with a DSP to enable direct integration with the weapon system.

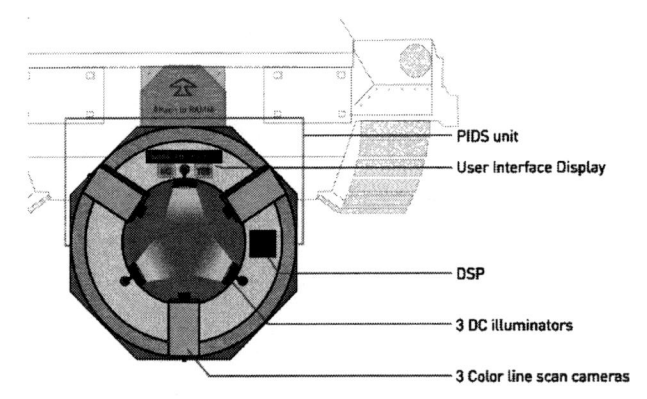

Figure 1. PIDS hardware concept

The PIDS hardware is designed to mount over the projectile loading port of the weapon system. The physical loading process remains the same for the user. That is, the user slides the projectile into a circular opening. However, the user is no longer responsible for manually entering the necessary projectile information.

The PIDS software applies various image processing algorithms to determine various properties of the projectile (this includes projectile type, fuze type, lot number, etc.). The system leverages differences in the visible characteristics of the projectiles to determine the information. In the current version, the system leverages shape recognition, color matching, and text recognition to perform the identification task. The system is capable of properly identifying the necessary information even in cases where all modules cannot make a positive identification. The modular nature of the system allows support for new recognition modules (such as a barcode reader).

3. Software system architecture

The PIDS software foundation is called the Projectile Identification Framework (PIF). The PIF coordinates and controls all of the PIDS software modules (see Figure 2). This includes the hardware driver modules, the recognition modules, and the user interface modules. The PIF also manages the communication between the PIDS and the weapon systems mission control system (MCS).

The PIF monitors the data captured by the PIDS hardware to determine when an object passes by the line scan cameras. This detection occurs through a simple background separation algorithm. Once the presence of an object is detected, the system builds three images of the object (one from each camera) from the line scan data. The PIF then sends these images to the recognition modules to score the new object against a set of metrics (in our current case, shape, color, and text match against a known model). The results from the recognition modules are sent to the decision module that is responsible for determining the identity of the detected object through fusion of the results from the multiple recognition modules.

The PIF sends the result of the decision module to the user interface. If the user accepts the determination, then the identity of the projectile is sent to the mission control system. The manual confirmation step is required to insure safety.

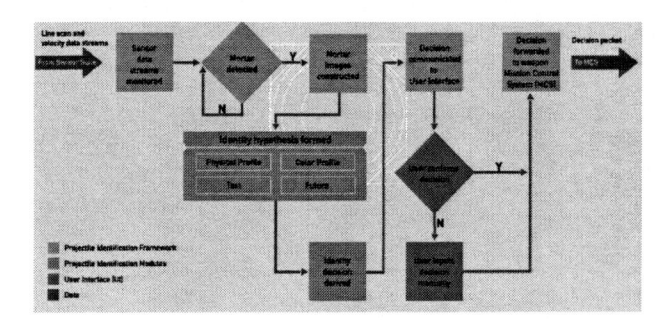

Figure 2. PIDS process flow chart

4. Recognition modules

The PIF system is designed in a modular fashion so that recognition modules can be added to or removed from the system. The main purpose for this is to allow for easy expansion of the projectile recognition system. Additionally, this capability allows the system to be easily modified to support other applications.

For our current application, the system uses three recognition modules. The first compares the shape of the projectile to each shape profile stored in the projectile profile database. The second compares the color pattern of the projectile to each color profile stored in the projectile profile database. The third identifies the text written on the projectile. We chose this set of recognition modules because they were capable of identifying the features physically visible on the munitions. That is, the projectile type can be determined through color and/or shape and the unique identity of the projectile (its lot number) can be detected through text recognition.

A barcode reading module is another module that at first appears like a logical choice to be included in the system. However, the U.S. Army has millions of existing projectiles without barcodes in its arsenal. It is not logistically reasonable to put bar codes on all of these existing modules. Therefore, other means of recognition are required. However, it is likely that newly designed projectiles will include barcodes. Therefore, we have included the ability to support barcode readers in the future.

4.1. Shape recognition module

The shape recognition module processes the image to create a 2D outline of the projectile. The projectile outline is compared against each profile in the projectile profile database to determine a match score for each possible projectile type. Since the projectiles are all axially symmetric (neglecting fins), a single 2D perspective provides all of the necessary information for recognition. The system automatically creates the profiles in the database when a known projectile passes through the system during training mode. The technician manually enters the pertinent projectile information and the system stores a profile that includes the identification information and the physical characteristics needed for recognition. This training process is only required once for each type of projectile. The recognition process occurs as follows:

1. The camera detects an object passing underneath it and generates an image of the object.
2. The system binarizes each image to create images where object pixels are white and background is black. Due to the controlled lighting within the PIDS, we are able to use a single intensity threshold value.
3. The system blurs the resulting binary image to remove noise (such as isolated pixels).
4. The system processes the image in a left to right, top to bottom manner to detect the location of the first object pixel in each image row.
5. The system normalizes the length of the object to 1 to compensate for velocity differences between runs. Figure 3 provides an example of a binary image and the extracted normalized profile.
6. The system regenerates the physical profile information at 0.001 increments. This step requires the system to interpolate and extrapolate the actual collected physical profile points.
7. The system compares this "corrected physical profile" to the templates for each object. The system determines a match based on the absolute difference of the physical profile values between the current physical profile and the template for each increment and then divides the sum of these differences by the number of increments (1000).
8. The template with the lowest error is considered to be the match. This assumes that the error is below a certain threshold. If it is not, then the system assumes that a new object type has been inserted and no match is declared.

We are currently adding a subsystem to the PIDS that can determine the velocity of the projectile as it is inserted. Once this is complete, the system will not need to normalize for velocity. Then the actual speed can be used to create a true physical profile.

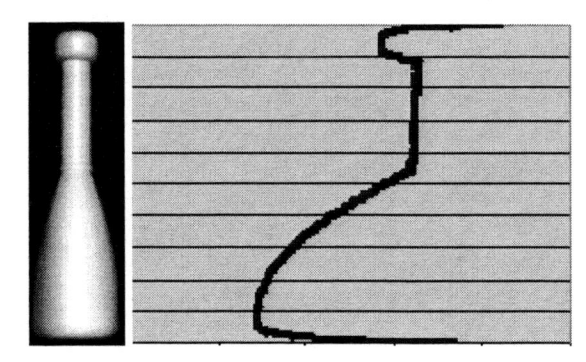

Figure 3. Binary image and extracted profile

4.2. Color recognition module

The color recognition module processes the image to create a color profile of the projectile. The projectiles of interest in our project are color-coded depending on type. For example, a M934 HE mortar shell is olive green and the XM930 illumination mortar shell is white. Some of the projectiles have color bands that represent some property of the projectile.

The projectile's color profile is compared against each color profile in the color profile database to determine a match score for each possible projectile type. The system automatically creates the color profiles in the database when a known projectile passes through the system during training mode (this occurs simultaneously with the creation of the shape profile). The technician manually enters the pertinent projectile information and the system stores a color profile that includes the identification information and the physical characteristics needed for recognition. This training process is only required once for each type of projectile.

The recognition process starts by segmenting out a vertical slice of the object. The colors on each row are averaged to create a single value for each row in the image. A color profile is derived from this averaged slice by determining segment boundaries within the target and then deriving RGB averages across all pixels that are contained within boundary pairs. The first pixel in the slice is always considered a segment boundary pixel. We then compare subsequent pixels to the segment boundary pixel until we encounter a pixel that does not match the segment boundary pixel. If this condition does not occur we will consider the last pixel to be the rightmost boundary. This pixel will be considered a segment boundary pixel because it signifies the end of the current segment and in some cases the beginning of a new segment. The identified segment that lies between the last two discovered segment boundaries must meet a predefined length constraint or it will be ignored. If the length constraint is met, we then derive an RGB average representation for all pixels that lie between the last two segment boundary pixels that were discovered. The RGB average becomes the next entity within the color profile, and if we have not processed the last pixel of the slice, we proceed to identify the next segment, that may have its RGB average representation added to the profile, using the method that we just described.

The system then creates a match score by comparing the projectile's color slice to the color profiles stored in the database. The system compares the color segment averages of color profile pairs such that the detection of ordered color segment sequences increases their match score. This process requires the allowance for missed segments (which can occur due to light source variation) or dropped segments (which can occur when a segment fails to meet the minimal segment length constraint which can be caused by high scan velocities) that may occur in one profile but not the other. Thus, color segment sequences do not require contiguous profile color segments. However, matching color segments must occur as ordered in their respective profiles. Colors are matched by comparing their vectors within the three dimensional RGB space. Vectors of similar colors will have a small or no angular difference. Color intensity changes due to illumination changes will appear as a movement along the colors RGB vector. A threshold of 0.995 is used to specify the maximum allowable angular difference for a color match.

4.3. Text recognition module

The text recognition module is responsible for classifying the type of projectile and capturing projectile data that can only be obtained directly from the text (such as lot number). There are two main pieces of the text recognition module. The first uses information about text placement to help identify the type of projectile. That is, all of the projectiles are stamped at certain locations with text that identifies the nature of the projectile. These locations are identified in the manufacturing specifications for the projectiles. Therefore, determining placement of the text on the detected projectile can be used to support the projectile identity determined by the shape and color recognition modules.

The second portion of the text recognition module uses a commercially available text recognition engine to identify the individual characters stamped on the projectile. This information is not required to identify the type of projectile, but does provide support information, such as lot number.

4.4. Decision module

The decision module is responsible for analyzing the results returned from the individual recognition modules to produce a final determination of the projectile type. The current decision module was designed to leverage the properties of the projectiles that are of interest to our project. However, due to the modular nature of our design, new decision modules can easily be added to support new applications.

In the current system, the decision module leverages the following:
1. The shape profile recognition module is the most reliable system. Specifically, the recognition rate between projectiles of different shape is 100%.
2. Not all projectiles are different in shape, so shape alone is not sufficient to determine type.
3. The color recognition module is also highly reliable, but less so than the shape profile recognition module.
4. The character recognition module is the least reliable for many reasons. First, even under ideal conditions character recognition is not 100% accurate. Second, the system will be used in extreme conditions where characters may become occluded (such as by mud).

Therefore, the current decision module behaves as follows:
1. The module analyzes the results of the shape profile recognition module to identify the set of possible projectile types.
2. The module analyzes the results of the color recognition module against this set of potential projectile types to identify the most likely candidate.
3. The module analyzes multiple parts of the result from the character recognition module.
   a. The location of the characters on the shell is used to verify the suspected identity. This information is only used as a secondary check because it is not a unique identifier.
   b. The actual text is used to determine the shell type stamped on the projectile and other properties (such as lot number).
   c. If the text result contradicts the result from step 2, then the decision module decides that no valid identification can be made. For example, if step 2 implies that the projectile is an M934, but the text recognition clearly recognizes M929 then there is sufficient reason to doubt the results from step 2.

d. If the text result confirms the result from step 2, then the decision module reports the projectile identity from step 2.
e. If the text recognition module is not capable of determining the written text, then the decision module reports the projectile identity from step 2. This is acceptable due to the high recognition rate of the color and shape recognition modules.

Typically, the result after step 2 remains correct and the text recognition module is only used to collect additional information about the projectile, such as the lot number.

5. Follow-on work

To date, we have proven the feasibility of the concept by building a demonstration unit that utilizes off-the-shelf hardware and standard PCs. We will be evolving this system to utilize embedded electronics that can be used to create the production version of the PIDS. The production version will be a self-contained hardware/processing unit that can be mounted to a weapon platform during loading. The final system will be designed to be easily installed and removed from a platform so that it can be carried on resupply vehicles and installed on a weapon platform when needed.

6. Conclusion

The current version of the projectile identification system has been shown to be capable of determining the type of a projectile passed through the system. The technology that enables this is basically a fusion of multiple simple recognition modules that leverage knowledge of the physical properties of the projectiles. We are currently working on making this system into a production ready prototype.

Vehicle Detection Approaches Using the NVESD Sensor Fusion Testbed

Philip Perconti, James Hilger
RDECOM/CERDEC NVESD
{pperconti, hilger}@nvl.army.mil
Murray Loew
George Washington University
loew@seas.gwu.edu

Abstract

The US Army RDECOM CERDEC Night Vision & Electronic Sensors Directorate (NVESD) has a dynamic applied research program in sensor fusion for a wide variety of defense & defense related applications. This paper highlights efforts under the NVESD Sensor Fusion Testbed (SFTB) in the area of detection of moving vehicles with a network of image and acoustic sensors. A sensor data collection was designed and conducted using a variety of vehicles. Data from this collection included signature data of the vehicles as well as moving scenarios. Sensor fusion for detection and classification is performed at both the sensor level and the feature level, providing a basis for making tradeoffs between performance desired and resources required. Several classifier types are examined (parametric, nonparametric, learning). The combination of their decisions is used to make the final decision.

1. Introduction

There are multiple areas of applied sensor fusion research at the US Army RDECOM CERDEC Night Vision & Electronic Sensors Directorate (NVESD). These areas include internal efforts, collaborative efforts with universities, as well as contract efforts with private industry. Many of the early efforts at NVESD during the 1980's and 1990's showed that multiple collocated sensors could be utilized to improve system performance in detecting targets. These early efforts fused image data with non-image data in order to improve the performance of algorithms processing the image data. Current efforts use multiple, more robust types of sensor data and fusion techniques in order to improve overall system performance as measured by Probability of Detection (P(d)) and False Alarm Rate (FAR). All of these efforts highlight the trend within the Department of Defense (DoD) of using multiple sensors, either collocated or dispersed, to detect objects of interest. This trend has fueled efforts such as those focused on mine and minefield detection (countermine) [1,2,3,4], mounted and dismounted soldiers, and unattended ground systems.

Unattended Ground Systems (UGS) are attractive in the sense that they can be deployed in an area for surveillance purposes over long periods of time. These sensors consist of sensor nodes with imaging (IR, visible) and non-imaging (seismic, acoustic, magnetic) sensors and communication capability to establish sensor networks with each other as well as command and control facilities. When UGS are deployed, they self configure into a network to perform surveillance to improve situational awareness. Collaboration between UGS allows for multi-sensor, multi-look data to be passively collected and fused such that target characterization can occur at the node. A research area at NVESD utilizing a sensor fusion testbed is focused on demonstrating vehicle detection and identification algorithms as well as studying long-term deployment impacts for these sensor systems.

2. Sensor Fusion Testbed

The Sensor Fusion Testbed (SFTB) is an environment consisting of three outdoor nodes and an indoor base-station and associated software to support the development and testing of imaging and non-imaging sensors and algorithms. Its purpose is to provide a consistent and well-defined testing facility for advanced sensors and associated detection and fusion algorithms. The SFTB will evolve in the sense that it will be augmented with additional nodes of varying capability and algorithms over time. Through the SFTB, analysis of the impact to advanced sensors and associated algorithms deployed over long periods of time on station in urban and rural environments can be accomplished.

2.1 SFTB nodes and base-station

The SFTB nodes have imaging and non-imaging sensors and associated computer hardware. Two of the nodes have advanced uncooled Infrared (IR) cameras. The IR cameras have 40 degrees horizontal by 30 degrees vertical field of view and output 160 by 120 pixel images where each pixel is 12 bits in length. The other node has a color camera with 52.06 degrees horizontal and 30.45 degrees vertical field of view. The full resolution 640 by 480 pixel digital output can be down sampled to produce a 160 by 120 pixel image where each pixel is 24 bits (8 bits red, 8bits green, 8bits blue). The IR and color cameras are attached to 2-axis, pan and tilt, gimbals controlled by software. Each node has an acoustical array consisting of 7 microphones arranged such that 6 microphones are equally spaced along the periphery of a 4-foot diameter circle and one microphone is in the center of the array. Figure 1 shows a picture of one of the nodes. The camera and gimbal sit atop a tripod with the acoustical array mounted at the base of it as shown in the figure. Each node has a Global Positioning System (GPS) and a personal computer, ruggedized for outdoor use, to hold the necessary interface electronics as well as provide a processor for those applications that want to do processing of the sensor data at the node. The personal computer also has data storage to record both sensor input data as well as any algorithm processing results. Cabling shown in Figure 1 are sensor interface cables to the personal computer in order to allow it to be up to 50 feet away from the sensor nodes.

The SFTB nodes are connected to a base-station through a wireless Ethernet link. The base-station is a personal computer inside a building that provides the SFTB with a number of capabilities and services. A user interface has been written to allow each SFTB node to be controlled from the base-station. Sensor outputs can be transmitted to the base-station to provide another level of sensor fusion capability for those applications that require it. With sensor data processing capability at each node as well as at the base-station, multiple kinds of sensor fusion applications can be setup for analysis and demonstration. Weather data is obtained from a weather station whose output weather measurements are input to the base-station.

Figure 1. Sensor fusion testbed node.

2.2 SFTB deployment

The SFTB is deployed initially in a triangular location illustrated in Figure 2. The nodes are labeled 1 through 3 with the imaging sensor type in parenthesis. Again, all nodes have a 7 element acoustical array. The order of the nodes can be switched around for testing purposes depending on the particular application. The triangular location represents a complex area with various backgrounds, road directions, building structures and noise sources. The surrounding area has numerous continuous and periodic man made noise sources, various buildings at different distances, aspect angles, shapes and construction materials, various traffic patterns and road surfaces, various vegetation, and wildlife. Due to the road structure around the triangular location, various distances and directions to objects of interest can be setup for testing purposes. The nearby parking lots provide additional opportunities for testing.

While the triangular location was chosen in part due to the complexity offered from a myriad of noise sources, types of clutter, and movement of objects of interest, the SFTB is also portable. Portability allows the nodes and base-station to be taken to other locations for more focused data collections, detection and fusion algorithm focused data collections, detection and fusion algorithm tests and/or analysis. This enables other types of environmental conditions from more rural to more urban compared to the triangular location to be included in any analysis.

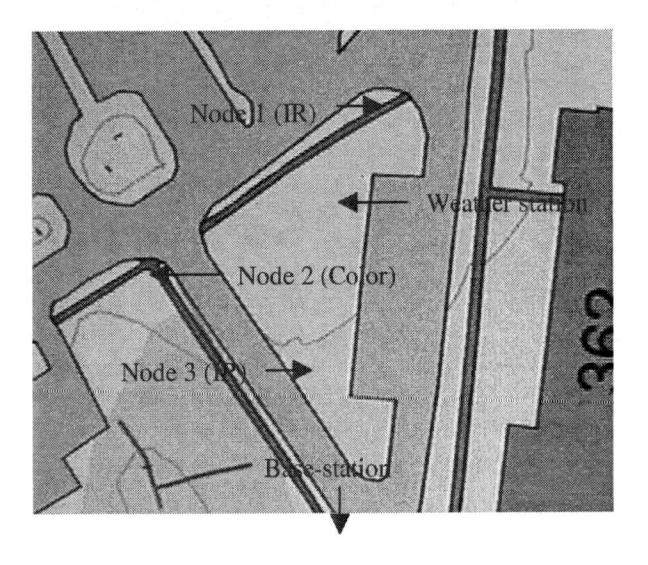

Figure 2. Sensor fusion testbed deployment.

2.3 SFTB vehicle detection demonstration

A vehicle detection demonstration has been implemented into the SFTB during its development and integration. This simple demonstration was implemented to ensure components within the SFTB were functioning properly, demonstrate the utility of the SFTB in such a system application, serve as a baseline application to guide algorithm enhancements and experiments, as well as guide the integration of the SFTB into the NVESD algorithm evaluation facility. The vehicle detection demonstration exercises all nodes within the SFTB as well as the base-station. This demonstration serves as the baseline for which to compare other sensor fusion algorithm and node concepts.

The vehicle detection demonstration uses outputs from the processing of the acoustical data to cue the imaging sensors to point in a particular direction and snap a picture. Figure 3 illustrates the concept. The power spectrum of the acoustical signal from one acoustical array is shown in the top of the figure. The snapshots are those of a light truck passing the node. The truck approaches the node cueing the imaging sensor to point in the direction of arrival. The imaging sensor follows the noise truck as it passes, continuously snapping pictures based on the processing of acoustical data. It should be noted that Figure 3 shows the outputs of only a single node to illustrate the concept. Outputs from the others nodes are available also and are used in the vehicle demonstration.

To accomplish this concept, each of the three sensor nodes within the SFTB has been programmed with a version of the MUSIC algorithm that has been adapted by the U. S. Army Research Laboratory to determine the angle of arrival for vehicles of interest [5,6]. Acoustical data at each node is processed using this MUSIC algorithm. The resultant angle of arrival from each node is transmitted via wireless Ethernet to the base-station. The base-station then charts the angles of arrival to determine if any intersect. If two or more angles intersect, then a detection is declared. The angles of arrival are displayed in a graphical user's interface for the operator.

2.4 SFTB data analysis

The SFTB was designed to support development and testing of imaging and non-imaging detection and fusion algorithms. This also includes collection of data to do offline algorithm development and evaluation as well as data analysis. Algorithms and demonstrations developed and implemented on the SFTB support the focus of studying the phenomenology of an area's environmental impact to sensors and associated detection and fusion algorithms. This addresses the shortfall of knowledge, and supporting data, of how well detection and fusion algorithms perform when deployed over long periods of time. Since the driver for sensor fusion is increased system performance in terms of false alarm rates and detection probabilities, through the SFTB these metrics can be analyzed in terms of variables such as road types, environmental conditions, random natural and man made noise sources, sensor data characteristics over seasonal changes, as well as the resulting physical system level attributes such as average power consumed.

The analysis will focus on a "top 10" list of variables. Objects of interest are vehicles from 4 classes: car, pickup, SUV, and light truck as well as human. Each object is in a state as determined by tire type, tire air pressure, and general overall condition. Surface types of interest include asphalt, concrete, gravel, dirt, and grass. The objects of interest could be operating near noise sources that are man made or naturally occurring.

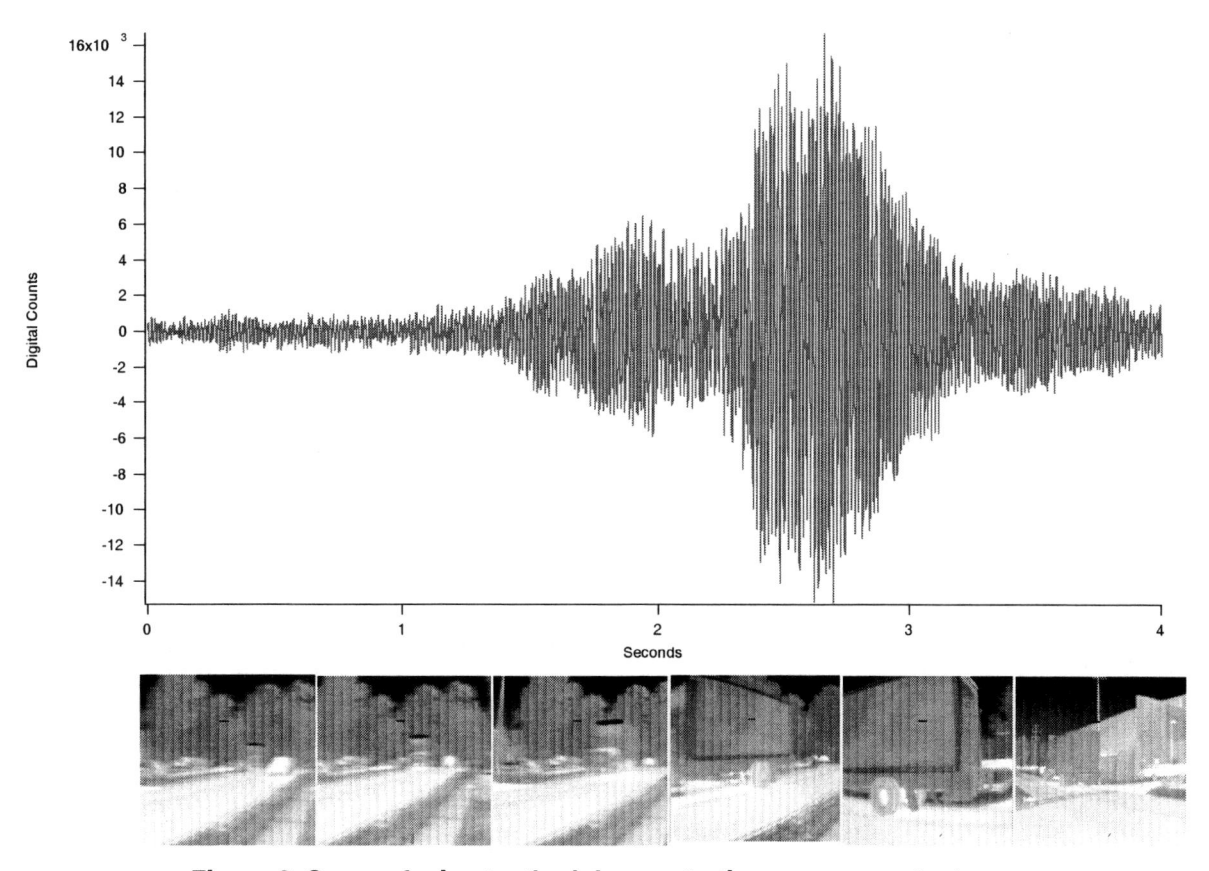

Figure 3. Sensor fusion testbed demonstration program outputs.

during the four seasons. All of this would be monitored using sensor nodes in any number of possible arrangements. Each sensor node could be composed of sensors of differing capabilities such as seismic, acoustic, imaging IR, proximity IR, and visible both black and white and color. Each node could be collaborating with its neighbor, groups of neighbors, or command station. This leads to what data to fuse, how to fuse it such that a minimal number of sensor nodes are required to effectively cover an area under surveillance. Also of interest is the possibility of learning the background noise, both periodic and non-periodic, over extended periods of time in order to eliminate information not of interest.

Whenever sensor nodes are deployed in the field, the variables listed above are those that impact overall system performance. Understanding the impacts over long periods of time will help improve overall sensor nodes and their capability. Collecting data to aid experiments addressing these variables will be accomplished through data collections using the SFTB and the NVESD algorithm evaluation facility.

3. Sensor Fusion Data Collection

The purpose of the sensor fusion data collection is the generation of problem sets having simultaneously collected image and non-image sensor data for work in multi sensor fusion for vehicle detection. This provides data for initial research and developments addressing the "top 10" list of variables from the previous section. Problem set data is typically divided into development and training data and sequestered data for algorithm evaluation. The initial data collection is referred to as the SFTB Local Site (SFTBLS) data collection and will be repeated over the year such that seasonal conditions are captured.

3.1 SFTB local site data collection

The SFTBLS data collection allowed for the generation of a problem set containing what is referred to as signature data as well as testing data. These data were collected in a controlled fashion with known vehicles moving at known predetermined speeds operating on a predetermined course. The SFTB sensor nodes were setup at known locations and surveyed in such that pointing angles and distances between nodes are known. The imaging sensors were pointed in a fixed direction such that vehicles entered and moved out of the sensor node's field of view. Data was collected in 2-minute segments to allow time for vehicles to traverse the predetermined course at the slowest rate and keep the data in manageable segments for fusion algorithm development purposes. Each vehicle traversed the predetermined course at 5, 10, 15, 20 and 25 miles per hour. The course had parallel asphalt and gravel road surfaces. Data was also collected with multiple vehicles traversing the course at one time. All vehicle positions and movements were recorded through the use of Global Positioning System (GPS) units. Acoustical data was collected simultaneously with the image data. The acoustical data recorded was from the outputs of the 7 microphones after digitalization.

The signature sensor data also included data on each of the vehicles as they are rotated about their center axis at 45-degree intervals at a fixed distance from a sensor node with a visible camera and a sensor node with an IR camera. Acoustical data was also collected from each vehicle as it was rotated with the engine being revved from idle to 2000 RPM. Turntable like data is important in that it highlights a vehicle itself rather than the vehicle in its surroundings so that pristine vehicle signatures can be obtained.

3.2 SFTB future data collections

The SFTB will be utilized for future data collections to generate other problem sets whose data further addresses the "top 10" list of variables. Future collections will occur at the same location as the SFTBLS and else where. Along with location additional sensors, sensor nodes, and vehicles from the 4 classes will be utilized. These controlled, multi sensor problem sets will be such that everything about the data will be known and recorded.

The SFTBLS data collection generated an initial set of data that can be provided to others for use in sensor fusion efforts. At the completion of every data collection, the data are checked and ground truthed. A portion is sequestered for evaluation purposes. The rest is made available to interested parties working in the sensor fusion community. As additional data collections are accomplished, those data will also be made available.

4. Sensor Fusion Data Analysis

As indicated above, acoustic data will cue and then guide the IR and visible sensors, which will acquire imagery, extract features, and decide whether this is a detection or false alarm. Multiple acquisitions over time for a given stimulus can be made and multiple classifiers used to fuse features from each of the sensors and make a decision. The training data is analyzed to identify the useful features to support and guide the design of the fusion algorithms. All techniques will be evaluated using jackknife procedures in combination with the sequestered data set.

4.1 Fusion errors

Image features are intended to describe points, lines, areas, and their temporal behavior. The ability to extract some of those features (e.g., texture) is dependent on resolution (and hence range). Postulation of various minimum target dimensions will enable bounds to be established for the extraction of resolution-dependent features. The maximum range for IR and visible measurements will depend on the specifications of the system. Sensor separation (baseline) will be determined in part by sensor resolution to ensure that the precision provided by each is comparable.

It is possible to compute the maximum location error when the fields of view of the sensors in an array are known. For example, for the typical SFTB geometry shown in Figure 4 (an isosceles triangle with two 100-unit legs) and for an assumed sensor field-of-view of 1.2 mrad, the contours of iso-error shown in Figure 5 result. The three axes of the plot use the same units.

4.2 Fusion approaches

As stated earlier, all data collected with the SFTB have associated ground truth in order to determine the image truth for vehicle location. Features are being extracted from the time-synchronized source data pertaining to vehicles and backgrounds. In both the IR and CCD images, segmentation of the vehicle(s) from the background is essential, since any vehicle-classification method will use information extracted from the segmented region(s). The effectiveness of segmentation

direct function of the proportion of the visible vehicle(s) actually identified as vehicle(s), and as an inverse function of the proportion of non-vehicle (background) identified as vehicle. This requires that

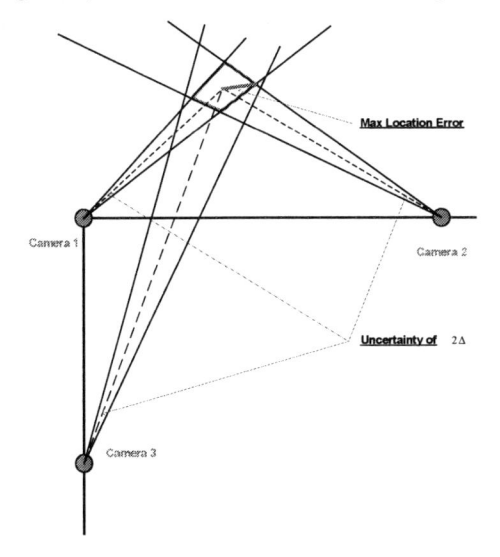

Figure 4. SFTB geometry showing errors.

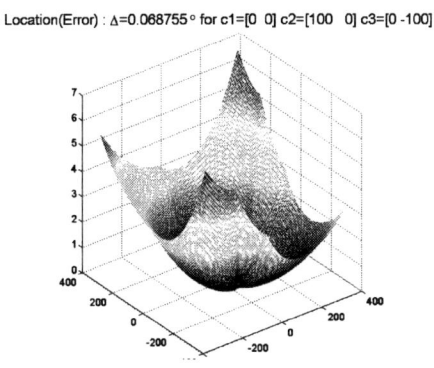

Figure 5. Contours of iso-errors for SFTB.

the true extent of each vehicle is known, at least in some sample images. A set of IR and CCD images comprising a variety of vehicle types, orientations, and environments (clutter) are hand-segmented and used as a reference set. That set is being used to evaluate each candidate segmentation algorithm, yielding a ranking of the algorithms. Although the evaluation does not guarantee that the hierarchy of performance will hold for each image in the overall data set, if the reference set is representative the ranking will provide a generally useful measure.

Each image is time-stamped at the moment of acquisition. Errors may be introduced into the time-stamp data for a variety of reasons (e.g., processing delays, data misalignment). Traveling at modest velocities, vehicles imaged with time-stamp errors incur time-related position errors that are small enough to define usable spatial regions of uncertainty. Those regions are combined with the iso-error regions to yield overall position uncertainties. This contributes to estimates of uncertainty of vehicle identification, since templates or features extracted from each image then have an overall measure of concordance (i.e., agreement as to vehicle) assigned.

5. Conclusions

This paper presented sensor fusion research using the SFTB at the US Army RDECOM CERDEC Night Vision & Electronic Sensors Directorate. The SFTB is being utilized to develop and evaluate vehicle detection algorithms as well as understand the long-term impact of fusion algorithms in deployed UGS.

6. References

[1] Maksymonko, G. B. et. al., "Robust detection and fusion of mine images", Proc SPIE Vol 4742, p 142-149, Detection and Remediation Technologies for Mines and Minelike Targets VII, Aug 2002.

[2] Witten, T. R. et. al., "Fusion of ground penetrating radar and acoustics data", Proc SPIE Vol 4742, p 903-910, Detection and Remediation Technologies for Mines and Minelike Targets VII, Aug 2002.

[3] Bradley, M. R. et. al., "Fusion of acoustic/seismic and ground-penetrating radar sensors for antitank mine detection", Proc SPIE Vol 4394, p 979-990, Detection and Remediation Technologies for Mines and Minelike Targets VI, Oct 2001.

[4] Williams, A. C. et. al., "Development of a robust algorithm for detection of mine targets in image data from electro-optic and acoustic sensors", Proc SPIE Vol 4394, p 943-951, Detection and Remediation Technologies for Mines and Minelike Targets VI, Oct 2001.

[5] T. Pham and B. Sadler, "Aeroacoustic wideband array processing for detection and tracking of ground vehicles", Journal of the Acoustical Society of America, Vol. 98, No. 5, pt. 2, p 2969, 1995.

[6] T. Pham and M Fong, " Real-time implementation of MUSIC for wideband acoustic detection and tracking" SPIE AeroSense 97: Automatic Target Recognition VII, April 1997.

3-Dimensional Object Reconstruction From Frequency Diverse RF Systems

Robert J. Bonneau

Air Force Research Lab
Radar Signal Processing Branch
Rome, NY 13441
bonneaur@rl.af.mil

Abstract

Conventional phased arrays operate on narrow bandwidth principles to achieve resolution in imaging of buildings and other objects of interest. Unfortunately, such narrow bandwidth methods to not allow sufficient resolution to reconstruct objects of interest in 3 dimensions at low frequencies and with small apertures. We propose a method that is computationally efficient and allows dynamic use of spectrum to achieve high resolution 3 dimensional reconstruction of objects from small or distributed apertures. This method also allows available spectrum bands to be used on a non-interference basis.

1. Introduction

We will first develop the methodology for a composite chirp signal and show how this method produces a narrow high resolution pulse for multiple narrow bandwidth signals. We will then show how this composite pulse can be inserted into an array geometry either uniform or non-uniform to increase resolution on a target in 3 dimensions. Finally we will show different array configurations and how spatial array distribution can be traded for bandwidth.

2. Chirp Signal

The basis optimization algorithm begins by defining a linear FM or 'chirp' signal with sufficient bandwidth to provide the desired resolution on the target being observed. The chirp waveform with carrier frequency ω_0 can be described as

$$f_n(t) = \tilde{u}(t/T) e^{jbt^2} e^{jt\omega_0} \tag{1}$$

where $\tilde{u}(t)$ denotes a rectangular pulse of unit height and width, T, centered at the origin b is the chirp slope describing the rate over the frequency interval between $\omega_i \leq \omega \leq \omega_{i+n}$. Because the chirp is over the time interval $-T/2 \leq t \leq T/2$, the instantaneous frequency varies over a bandwidth given by

$$B_c = bT \tag{2}$$

To achieve wider bandwidth response we have multiple chirp increments of n = 1,.....,N where all chirp increments are combined in post processing. If we have an impulse response $I(t)$ then our received signal for each chirp increment, is equal to

$$h_n(t) = f_n(t) \otimes I(t) \tag{3}$$

where $\otimes$ denotes the convolution operation. We also define the vector of outputs from the correlation over a finite window of time. If we now Fourier transform $h_n(t)$ you have $H_n(\omega)$. Combining each chirp increment we have

$$\tilde{H}(\omega) = \sum_{n=1}^{N} H_n(\omega) \tag{4}$$

We inverse Fourier transform (4) to obtain $\tilde{r}(t)$ the impulse response of the combined chirp function. In the case of a target response we have

$$s_n(t) = f_n(t) \otimes T(t) \tag{5}$$

If we now Fourier transform $s_n(t)$ you have $S_n(\omega)$. The combined target response function from our object is then

$$\tilde{S}(\omega) = \sum_{n=1}^{N} S_n(\omega) \tag{6}$$

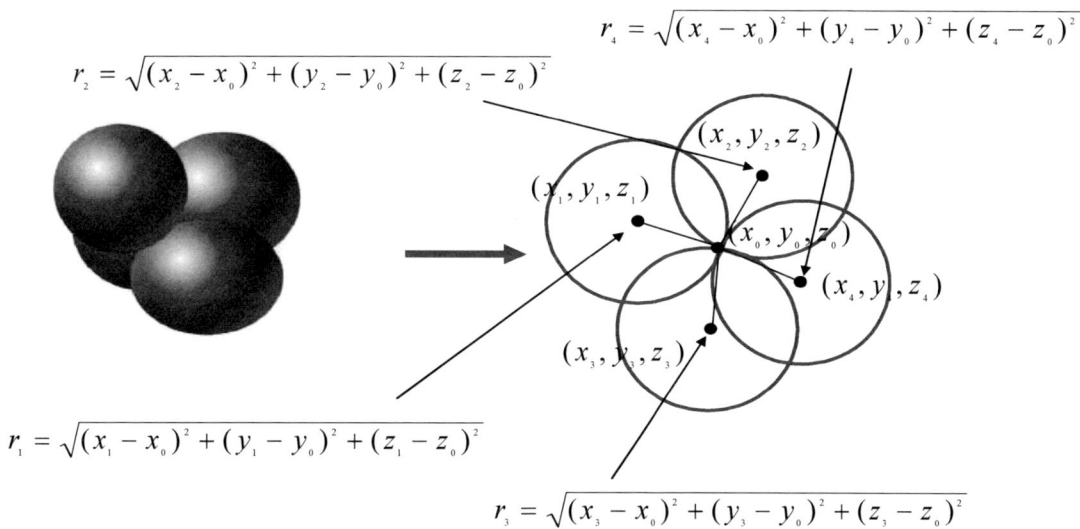

Figure 1 3 Dimensional distance estimation to any point in space requires 4 points.

The matched filter response of the target function in the Fourier domain is then

$$\tilde{K}(\omega) = F(\tilde{s}(t))F(\tilde{h}(-t)) \quad (7)$$

Inverse Fourier transforming $k(t)$ is the combined target response. It is important to note that even though we have a high resolution pulse, this technique does not require high sampling rates due to the ability to sample the chirp pulses over slow time intervals thus reducing the real time computational burden on the algorithm.

3. Time Delay Array Structure

We now develop a measurement process for signal returns from an object radiated by a composite chirp signal. As is shown in Figure 1, to locate a signal return in three dimensions we need to measure the time delay between the signal at 4 points in space which is the unique intersection point between 4 spheres. The distance between the point and any one of the spheres is shown in equation 8.

$$r_n = \sqrt{(x_n - x_0)^2 + (y_n - y_0)^2 + (z_n - z_0)^2} \quad (8)$$

The corresponding time delay to each point is given by.

$$t_n = \frac{r_n}{c} \quad (9)$$

The angle to the target in 4 dimensions is given by the following two equations

$$\tilde{\theta}_x(n) = \sin^{-1}\frac{x_n}{r_n} \quad (10)$$

$$\tilde{\theta}_y(n) = \cos^{-1}\frac{y_n}{r_n} \quad (11)$$

If we now assume our signal is a single frequency measured from the radiation center of two dimensional rectangular isotropic phased array with spacing d at wavelength λ with radiation pattern as

$$G(\theta_x, \theta_y) = \frac{\sin[N\pi(d/\lambda)\sin\theta_y]^2}{N^2\sin[\pi(d/\lambda)\sin\theta_y]^2}\frac{\sin[M\pi(d/\lambda)\sin\theta_x]^2}{M^2\sin[\pi(d/\lambda)\sin\theta_x]^2} \quad (12)$$

where N = the number of vertical columns of the array that give rise to the vertical angle θ_y and M = the number of horizontal rows that generate the angle θ_x. The above relationship assumes that the spacing between elements in the two directions is the same. Unfortunately such a pattern for element spacings that are not equal to $\frac{\lambda}{4}$ results in repeated grating lobes as is shown in Figure 2.

If we now introduce the composite chirp signal from the previous section as is shown in the following equation the combination of phased array signals as the intersect at the phased center of any element in 3 dimensions in space. The impulse response of this signal

Linear Array 1 Axis

Dyadic Lobe Structure, 2 Elements With Lambda Factors of 2

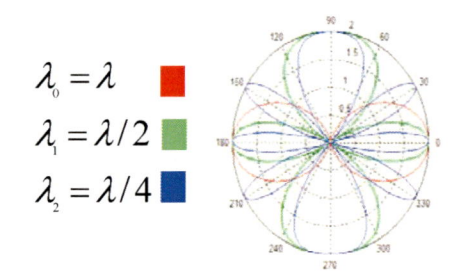

$\lambda_0 = \lambda$
$\lambda_1 = \lambda/2$
$\lambda_2 = \lambda/4$

Figure 2 Grating lobe structure for uniform linear array

delayed by the amount that causes all of the return pulses to intersect at the time according to their distances from the reflector is.

$$h(\tau) = h(\tau-t_1) + h(\tau-t_2) + \ldots h(\tau-t_N) \quad (13)$$

The corresponding correlated target response from a point reflector in space is:

$$k(\tau) = k(t_1-\tau) + k(t_2-\tau) + \ldots k(t_N-\tau) \quad (14)$$

The advantage of using the composite chirp pulse is that it allows multiple narrowband signals to be brought together to form a wideband pulse. Figure 3 shows the composite chirp implementation in terms of a phased array. We see this process in Figure 3 where each part of the composite chirp signal adds resolution to the measurement such that the entire signal provides a high resolution image. This allows the individual signals to be treated like narrowband signals as in the single frequency case.

4. Results

We first showed how the composite chirp method works with a linear array and reasonably little bandwidth. As we can see from Figure 4a, this method gives reasonable results with the composite representation of the test target having good fidelity. We next made the array non-uniform with relatively low instantaneous bandwidth as is shown in Figure 4b. We can see that this approach does not allow for high resolution on the test target since grating lobe effects start to occur. Finally we simulate a non-uniform array with relatively high bandwidth and we are able to replace the irregularities in the array with the increased resolution provided by the collective bandwidth of the composite chirp to obtain the total response of the target. as is shown in Figure 4c.

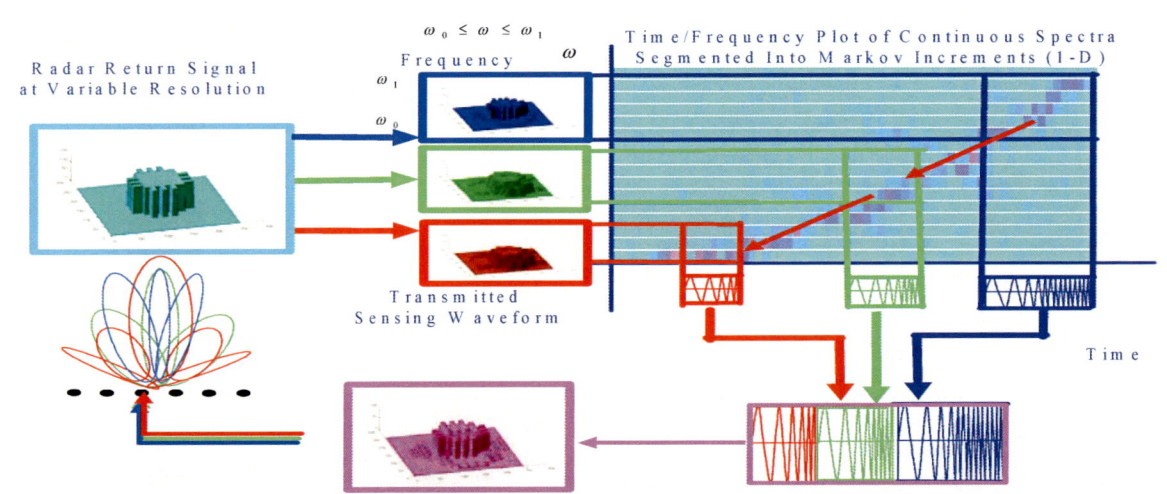

Figure 3 Integrated chirp pulse radiating test target from uniform array.

5. Conclusion

We have shown how a high resolution pulse can be created through multiple narrowband chirp signals to improve spatial resolution in antenna arrays. This approach allows high resolution 3 Dimensional imaging response from targets in situations that were not previously possible due to antenna characteristics, frequency allocations, or computational burdens.

6. References

1. Brown, R.D., Lynch E.D., Mokry, D.W., VanDamme J.M., Schneible R.A., Wicks M.C., "Near field focusing algorithm for ground penetration imaging radar", Radar Conference 1999.

2. Skolnik, M., *Introduction to Radar Systems 3rd Ed.*, McGraw Hill, Boston, 2001.

3. Soumekh, M., *Synthetic Aperture Radar Signal Processing with Matlab Algorithms*, Wiley, New York, 1999.

4. Steinburg, B., *Microwave Imaging With Large Antenna Arrays Radio Camera Principles and Techniques*, Wiley, New York, 1984.

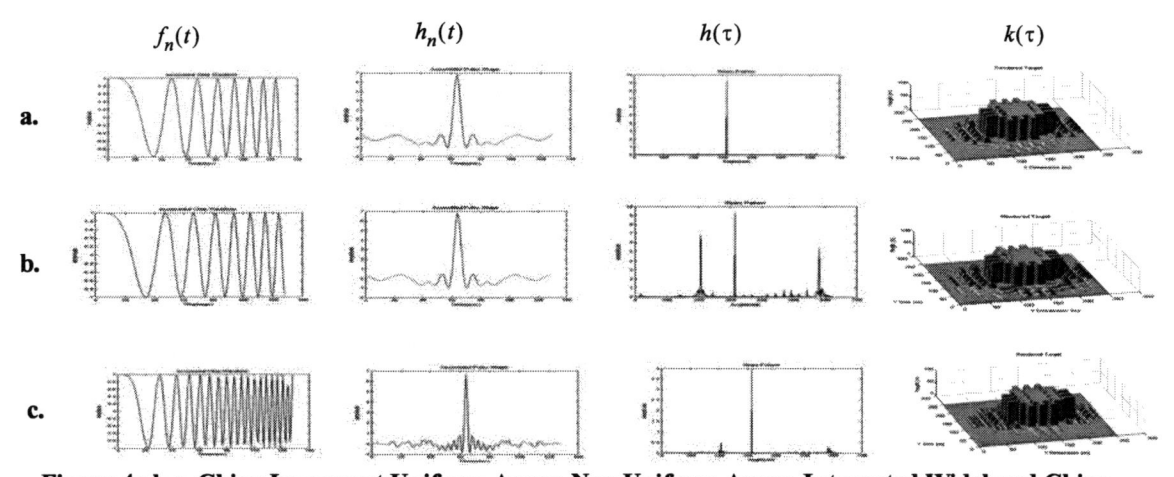

Figure 4a,b,c Chirp Increment Uniform Array, Non Uniform Array, Integrated Wideband Chirp

Imaging of Moving Targets Using a Doppler Compensated Multiresolution Method

Robert J. Bonneau

Air Force Research Lab
Radar Signal Processing Branch
Rome, NY 13441
bonneaur@rl.af.mil

Abstract

Traditional radar imaging has difficulties in imaging moving targets due to doppler shifts induced in the imagery and limited spatial resolution of the target. We propose a method that uses a multiresolution processing technique that sharpens the ambiguity function of moving objects to remove doppler induced imaging errors and improves instantaneous resolution. This method allows for instantaneous imaging of both static an moving objects in a computationally efficient manner thereby allowing more real time radar imagery generation.

1. Introduction

We will first develop the methodology for a composite chirp signal and show how this method produces a narrow high resolution pulse for multiple narrow bandwidth signals. We will then include a doppler compensation technique within this approach and then show how this composite pulse can be inserted into an array geometry either uniform or non-uniform to increase resolution on a target in 3 dimensions. Finally we will show different array configurations and derive an expression for exploiting integrated spatial measurements.

2. Chirp Signal

The basis optimization algorithm begins by defining a linear FM or 'chirp' signal with sufficient bandwidth to provide the desired resolution on the target being observed. The chirp waveform with carrier frequency ω_0 can be described as

$$f_n(t) = \tilde{u}(t/T)e^{jbt^2}e^{jt\omega_0} \qquad (1)$$

where $\tilde{u}(t)$ denotes a rectangular pulse of unit height and width, T, centered at the origin b is the chirp slope describing the rate over the frequency interval between $\omega_i \leq \omega \leq \omega_{i+n}$. Because the chirp is over the time interval $-T/2 \leq t \leq T/2$, the instantaneous frequency varies over a bandwidth given by

$$B_c = bT \qquad (2a)$$

Now including the effect of doppler shift we have

$$\omega_d = \frac{2\upsilon_r \omega}{c} \qquad (2b)$$

where υ_r is the radial velocity of the target with respect to the radar, and c is the speed of light. To achieve wider bandwidth response we have multiple chirp increments of n = 1,.....,N where all chirp increments are combined in post processing. If we have an impulse response $I(t)$ then our received signal for each chirp increment, is equal to

$$h_n(t) = f_n(t) \otimes I(t) \qquad (3)$$

where $\otimes$ denotes the convolution operation. We also define the vector of outputs from the correlation over a finite window of time. If we now Fourier transform $h_n(t)$ you have $H_n(\omega)$. Combining each chirp increment we have

$$\tilde{H}(\omega) = \sum_{n=1}^{N} H_n(\omega) \qquad (4)$$

We inverse Fourier transform (4) to obtain $\tilde{h}(t)$ the impulse response of the combined chirp function. In the case of a target response we have

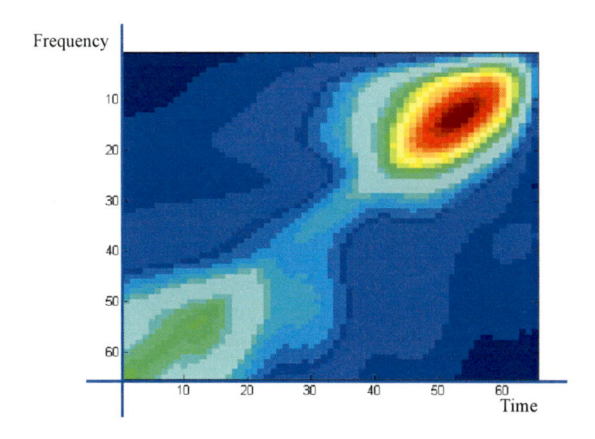

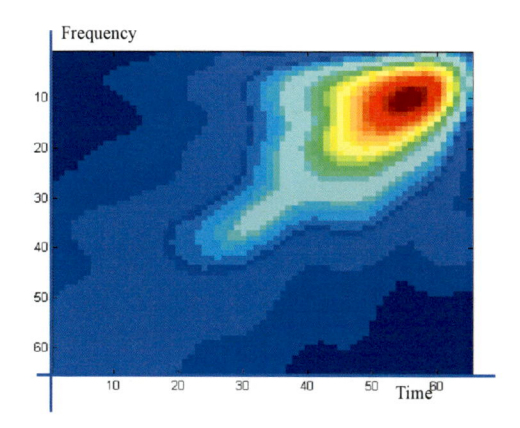

Figure 1a/b Ambiguity Function of Narrowband Increment/Ambiguity Function of Integrated Wideband Response

$$s_n(t) = f_n(t) \otimes T(t) \quad (5)$$

If we now Fourier transform $s_n(t)$ you have $S_n(\omega)$. The combined target response function from our object is then

$$\tilde{S}(\omega) = \sum_{n=1}^{N} S_n(\omega) \quad (6)$$

The matched filter response of the target function in the Fourier domain is then

$$\tilde{K}(\omega) = F(\tilde{s}(t))F(\tilde{h}(-t)) \quad (7)$$

Inverse Fourier transforming $k(t)$ is the combined target response. Using a doppler velocity filter approach, we can filter out the relative doppler velocities of targets by varying $H(\omega)$ with frequencies over a range $-\omega_d < \omega < \omega_d$ thus the doppler velocity filter of interest would result in maximizing the target response. Thus for a target with $S(\omega_d)$ we maximize the response k(t) with $H(\omega_d)$.

It is important to note that even though we have a high resolution pulse, this technique does not require high sampling rates due to the ability to sample the chirp pulses over slow time intervals thus reducing the real time computational burden on the algorithm. We now analyze the effect of the waveform design method on the ambiguity function of our signal.

We now define equation 3 with

$$\hat{f}_n(t) = f_n(t-\tau)e^{i2\pi f_d t} \quad (8)$$

Where τ is the range delay and f_D is the doppler frequency shift. The correlation between the transmitted and received signal is then

$$\Phi(\tau, f_d) = \int_{-\infty}^{\infty} f^*(t-\tau)f(t)e^{2\pi f_d t}dt \quad (9)$$

and an ambiguity function of

$$\chi(\tau, f_d) = |\Phi(\tau, f_d)|^2 \quad (10)$$

We can see that in Figure 1, the, greater the number of frequencies in the chirp signal, the higher and the narrower the peak of the ambiguity function. Thus as bandwidth increases resolution improves as expected. Compensating over possible doppler frequency shifts, the peak is sharper when the doppler frequency of the vehicle is accurately compensated. When the vehicle is not adequately compensated the resolution of the target decreases. Doppler mismatches often result in blurry patches in SAR imagery or blur "streaks" where moving targets do not correspond to the doppler of the rest of the imagery.

3. Time Delay Array Structure

We now develop a measurement process for signal returns from an object radiated by a composite

$$r_2 = \sqrt{(x_2-x_0)^2+(y_2-y_0)^2+(z_2-z_0)^2}$$

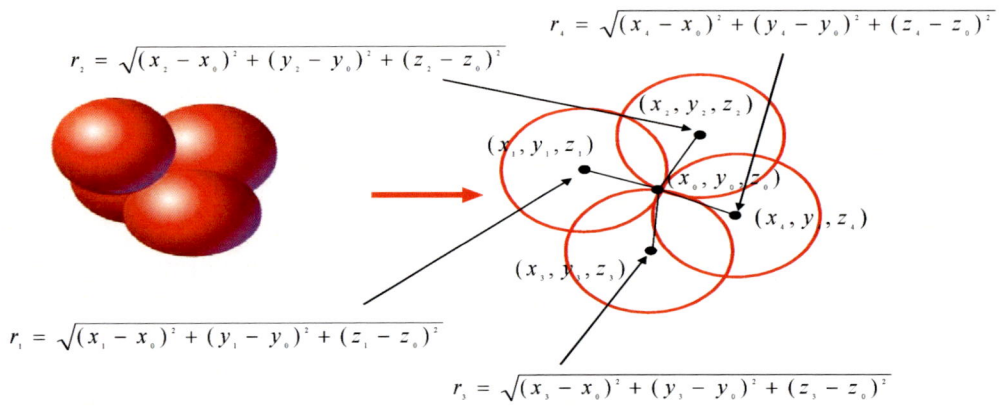

$$r_4 = \sqrt{(x_4-x_0)^2+(y_4-y_0)^2+(z_4-z_0)^2}$$

$$r_1 = \sqrt{(x_1-x_0)^2+(y_1-y_0)^2+(z_1-z_0)^2}$$

$$r_3 = \sqrt{(x_3-x_0)^2+(y_3-y_0)^2+(z_3-z_0)^2}$$

Figure 2 Multi-frequency observation of target form various positions.

chirp signal. As is shown in Figure 2, to locate a signal return in three dimensions we need to measure the time delay between the signal at 4 points in space which is the unique intersection point between 4 spheres. The distance between the point and any one of the spheres is shown in Equation 11.

$$r_n = \sqrt{(x_n-x_0)^2+(y_n-y_0)^2+(z_n-z_0)^2} \qquad (11)$$

The corresponding time delay to each point is given by.

$$t_n = \frac{r_n}{c} \qquad (12)$$

The angle to the target in 4 dimensions is given by the following polar coordinates

$$\tilde{\theta}_x(n) = \sin^{-1}\frac{z_n}{r_n} \qquad (13)$$

$$\tilde{\theta}_z(n) = \tan^{-1}\frac{y_n}{x_n} \qquad (14)$$

If we now introduce the composite chirp signal from the previous section as is shown in the following equation the combination of phased array signals as the intersect at the phased center of any element in 3 dimensions in space.

$$\hat{f}(t_n) = \sum_{i=1}^{M} f_i(t_n) \qquad (15)$$

The composite sync signal is then convolved with the target function in polar coordinates for antenna element at a given position $T_k(r_{nm}, \theta_{xnm}, \theta_{ynm})$ as is shown in Figure 4 and a sync function at time t_n and observed at position m thereby giving Equation 16 as

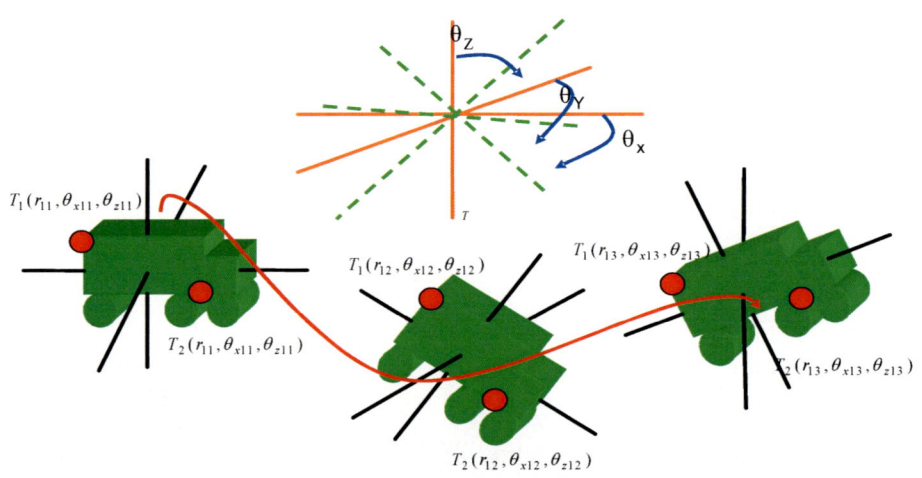

Figure 3 Spatial Diversity Generated by Different Perspectives on Vehicle

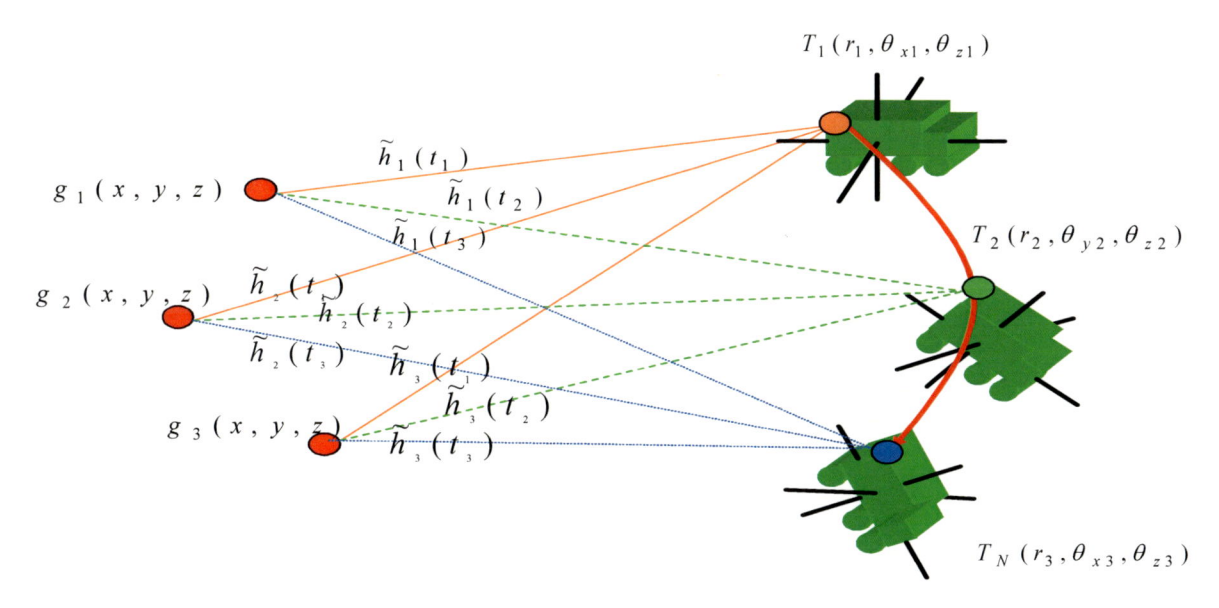

Figure 4 Frequency/Spatial Diversity Scenario

$$\hat{s}_m(t_n) = \hat{f}(t_n) \otimes T_k(r_{nm}, \theta_{xnm}, \theta_{ynm}) \quad (16)$$

We can image the target spatially through Fourier integration at each diffraction limited point T_k with

$$\hat{K}_m(\omega) = \sum_{n=1}^{N} F(\hat{s}_m(t_n - \tau_m))\tilde{H}(-\omega) \quad (17)$$

We can observe the target through bandwidth increments from multiple spatial time delays with

$$\widehat{K}_n(\omega) = \sum_{m=1}^{M} F(\hat{s}_m(t_n - \tau_m))\tilde{H}(-\omega) \quad (18)$$

Combining both equations 17 and 18 we have

$$K(\omega) = \sum_{m=1}^{M} \sum_{n=1}^{N} F(\hat{s}_m(t_n - \tau_m))\tilde{H}(-\omega) \quad (19)$$

Thus target characteristics not observable through spatial diversity can be observed through frequency diversity and visa versa. The entire geometry is shown in Figure 4 with dynamic doppler velocity filtering for target and or observation platform motion compensation.

4. Results

Figure 5 shows the algorithm sequence. We first see the original target in 5a, and then the target with a moderate doppler shift introduced in Figure 5b followed by the target over a number of observation angles in 5c and then with the integrated pulse in Figure 5c. We see a dramatic improvement in image quality with each of the compensating techniques applied in succession.

5. Conclusion

We have shown how a high resolution pulse can be created through multiple narrowband chirp signals to improve spatial resolution in antenna arrays. This approach allows high resolution 3 Dimensional imaging response from targets in situations that were not previously possible due to antenna characteristics, frequency allocations, or computational burdens.

6. References

1. Brown, R.D., Lynch E.D., Mokry, D.W., VanDamme J.M., Schneible R.A., Wicks M.C., "Near field focusing algorithm for ground penetration imaging radar", Radar Conference 1999.

2. Skolnik, M., *Introduction to Radar Systems 3rd Ed.*, McGraw Hill, Boston, 2001.

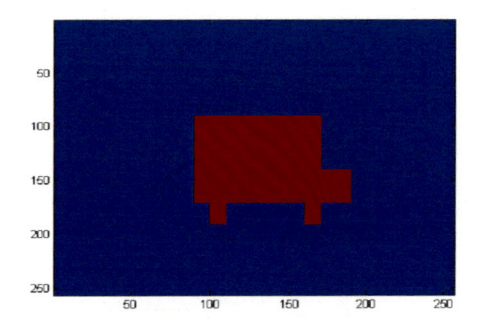

5a Original Object

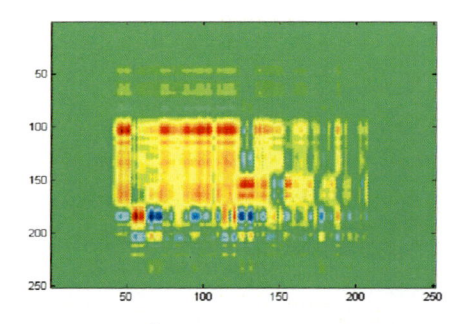

5b $\hat{K}_m(\omega)$ **No Doppler Compensation**

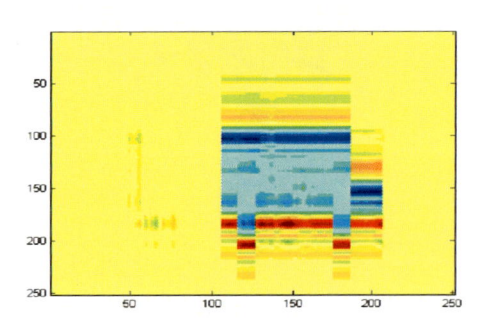

5c $\hat{K}_m(\omega)$ **With Doppler Compensation**

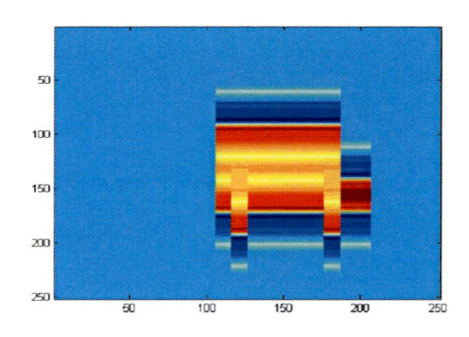

5d $K(\omega)$ **With Doppler Compensation**

3. Soumekh, M., *Synthetic Aperture Radar Signal Processing with Matlab Algorithms,* Wiley, New York, 1999.

4. Steinburg, B., *Microwave Imaging With Large Antenna Arrays Radio Camera Principles and Techniques,* Wiley, New York, 1984.

Posters

⌘ ⌘ ⌘ ⌘ ⌘ ⌘ ⌘ ⌘

Dual Band (MWIR/LWIR) Hyperspectral Imager

Michele Hinnrichs
Pacific Advanced Technology
micheleh@patinc.com
Neelam Gupta
Army Research Laboratory
ngupta@arl.army.mil
Arnold Goldberg
Army Research Laboratory
arniecy@arl.army.mil

Abstract

The demonstration of a dual band, MWIR/LWIR hyperspectral imaging system with a single lens and single focal plane array was performed at the Army Research Laboratory in the spring of 2003. To our knowledge this is the first time that a single two color focal plane array has been used for hyperspectral imaging. The ability of the IMSS diffractive optic to image both bands (MWIR/LWIR) simultaneously has allowed this new and innovative technique to work. The diffractive lens images the first order in the longwave infrared and the second order in the midwave infrared. Since the light is dispersed along the optical axis, as opposed to perpendicular to the optical axis, both color bands are imaged in parallel.

This paper reports on this work showing a demonstration of a dual band hyperspectral image.

1. Summary

For one week in May of 2003 Pacific Advanced Technology, in collaboration with the Army Research Laboratory, conducted experiments to prove the concept that an IMSS (**I**mage **M**ulti-**s**pectral **S**ensing) lens can be used to collect hyperspectral images in both the MWIR (mid wave infra red) and LWIR (long wave infra red) spectral region simultaneously using a single lens and single dual-band (MWIR/LWIR) focal plane array (FPA). The significance of this work has shown that a smaller, lighter more compact hyperspectral imaging systems that covers the two primary bands of the thermal infrared (3 to 5 and 8 to 12 microns) can be built with an IMSS diffractive optical element coupled to a dual band FPA.

The IMSS lens diffracts the first order in the LWIR and the second order in the MWIR and both spectral regions can be collected simultaneously allowing for complete spatial registration between the two spectral regions.

Figure 1. The ARL Dual Band (MWIR/LWIR) camera control electronics and the IMSSS lens with data acquisition system.

Shown in the picture in figure 1 is the ARL Dual Band infrared camera, dual band FPA supplied by DRS, FPA control and processing electronics supplied by SE-IR. The IMSS lens system replaced the conventional dual band infrared lens on the camera and the HyPAT data acquisition system [1] was used to grab frames synchronous with the lens motion. The HyPAT data acquisition computer is shown in the foreground with the camera and control and processing electronics are shown in the background.

The spectral calibration of the system was performed using the ARL dual band monochromater. After calibration, spectral data was collected on miscellaneous objects and sources that were available in the laboratory. A sample of the data is presented here.

The concept that a single lens can be used in conjunction with a dual band focal plane array to collect hyperspectral images in multiple spectral regions was experimentally demonstrated. Unfortunately, the windows and lens used in the IMSS system were coated only for the LWIR spectral region and the MWIR spectral region was attenuated. In spite of this drawback, we were able to prove the concept which was the primary objective of the test.

2. Concept Theory

It is the unique capability of Pacific Advanced Technology's (PAT's) Image Mult-spectral Sensing IMSS lens technology that a dual band MWIR/LWIR hyperspectral imaging system with minimum components can be developed, that results in a greater throughput and a simpler more robust design than any other deployed technolgy. The IMSS technology is described in brief here.

Shown in figure 2 is a diffractive optic element that has both imaging power and dispersion in a single lens. Such an element focuses different colors at different focal lengths. By translating the lens with respect to the focal plane, different spectral bins can be imaged. A diffractive optical element is made up of a blazed circular grating etched on a transparent substrate. The blazed grating can be made using either diamond turning, laser writing or photo lithographic techniques.

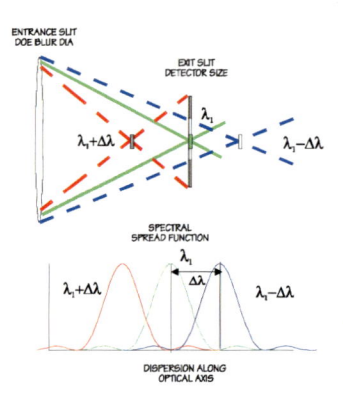

Figure 2. Diffractive optic chromatic aberration exploited for agile spectral tuning.

Figure 3 shows how a diffractive optical element can be used as a dual band hyperspectral imaging lens. The lens is designed with a first order blaze at the longer wavelength and the second order transmission should fall at half that wavelength as shown. For this case the lens was designed with a first order blaze at 7.5 microns so that both the LWIR and MWIR spectral bands can be covered with high diffraction efficiency of over 80% for LWIR and greater than 40% for the spectral region below 3.5 microns, (in this case diffraction efficiency is equal to the spectral transmission of the lens).

When the lens is tuned to a focal length for 8 microns in the LWIR band it will also be tuned for 4 microns in the MWIR band. When used in conjunction with a dual band MWIR and LWIR FPA both 8 and 4 micron light will be imaged at the same time. As the lens is translated along the optical axis, light from first order in the LWIR and second order in the MWIR is detected by each of the layers on the focal plane array. In this manner tuned

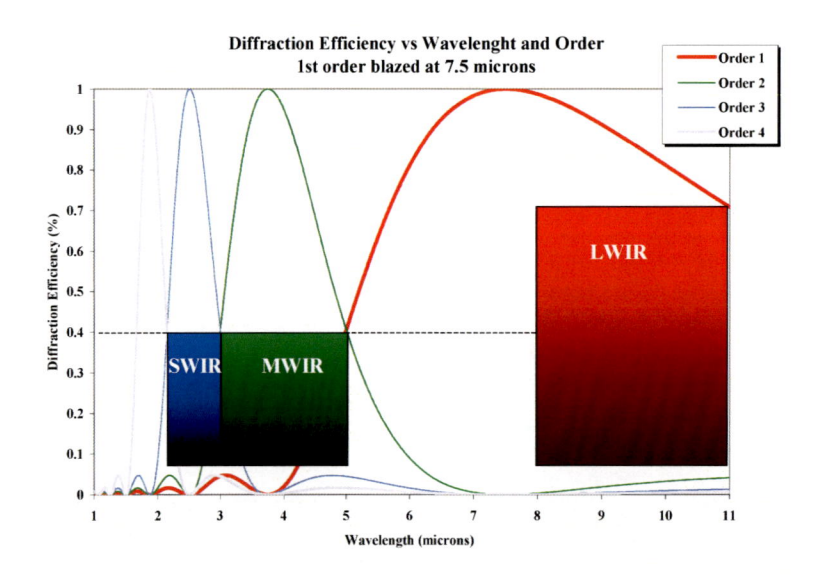

Figure 3. Multiple orders of a diffractive optics and be used to cover both the MWIR and LWIR bands.

hyperspectral images in both the MWIR and LWIR spectral regions can be collected simultaneously. By adaptively changing the focal length of the lens, different spectral bins in both the MWIR and LWIR bands can be selected.

Pacific Advanced Technology has developed a dual band MWIR/LWIR diffractive optical element for a tactical missile seeker applications under a Phase II SBIR for Eglin AFB. This lens was designed using a

3. Calibration

The IMSS system was calibrated using a monochromater. After the calibration, coefficients were determined for the LWIR bands. Then the monochromater was used to measure the spectral response for both the LWIR and MWIR spectral regions. These spectral response curves are shown in figures 4 and figure 5. It is important to note that the spectral band-pass measured is that of the monochromater and not of

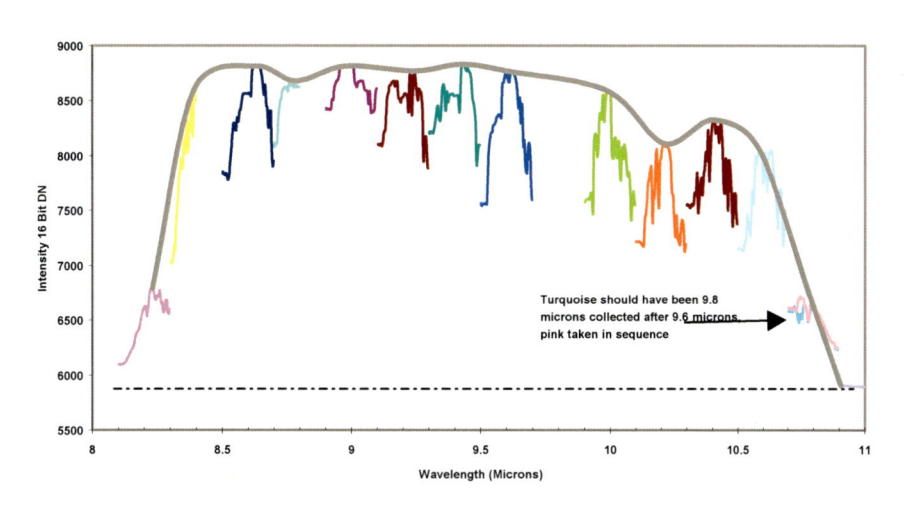

Figure 4. Spectral response for the LWIR band.

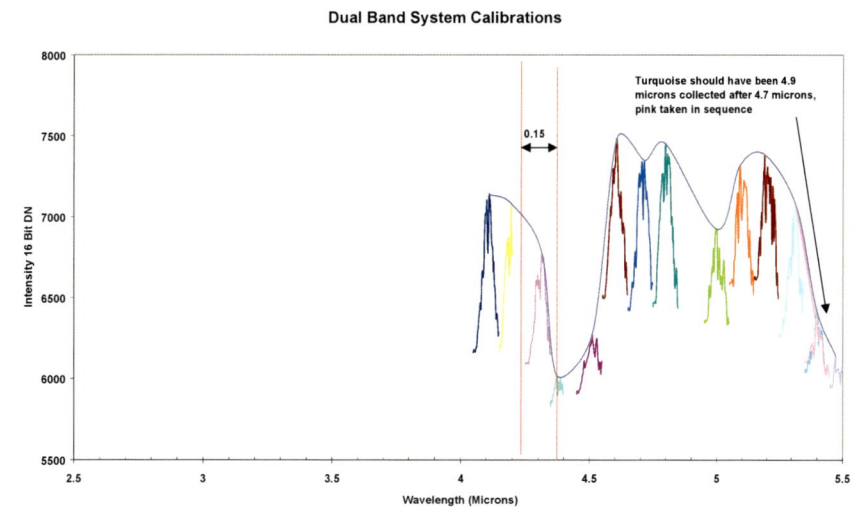

Figure 5. Spectral response for the MWIR band.

Germanium substrate and the blaze was diamond turned. The focal length of the lens was 100 mm. It was this lens that was used in the demonstration proof of concept.

the spectral resolution of the IMSS because the monochromater band-pass was left wide open to insure a good strong signal.

It also should be noted that the MWIR spectral response is not exactly, as theory would predict, a value of half the LWIR wavelength. By looking at the CO_2 absorption it was noticed that the MWIR spectral response curve is short by about 0.15 microns. This would indicate that the MWIR diffracted second order wavelength is really equal to half the sum of the LWIR wavelength plus 0.30 microns, i.e.:

$$MWIR = \frac{LWIR + 0.3}{2}$$

4. Examples of Dual Band Hyperspectral Images

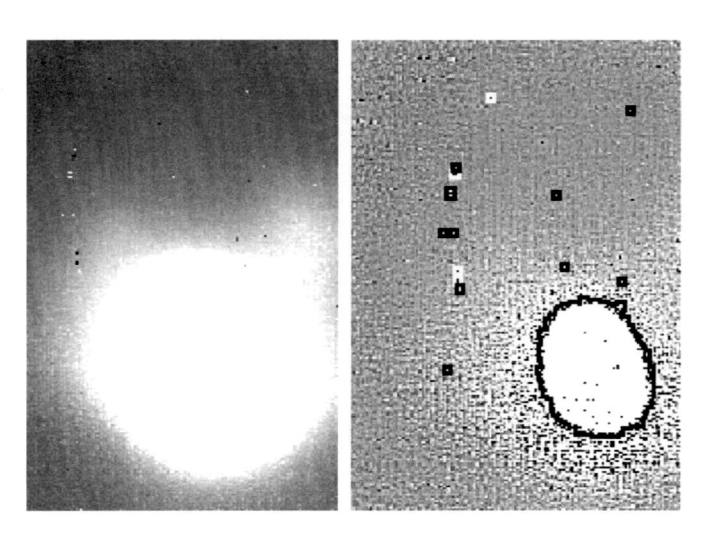

MWIR (4.43 microns)
raw image on left processed image on right.

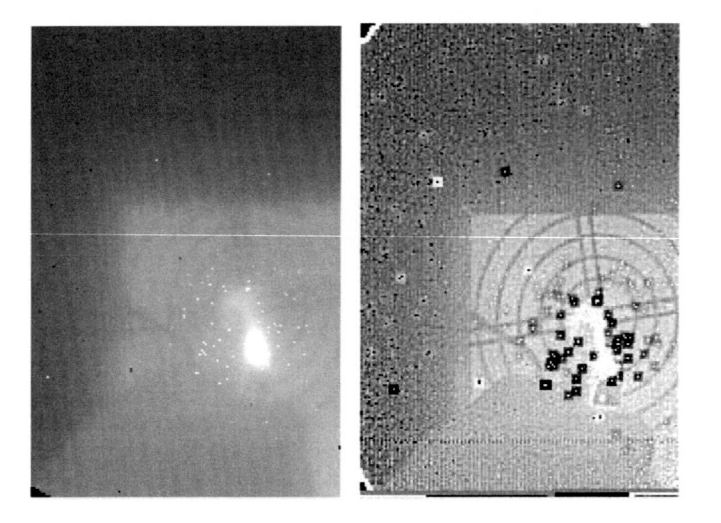

LWIR (8.862 microns)
raw image on left processed image on right.

Figure 6. Representative spectral images of a butane lighter in front of a circular wire screen in both the MWIR and LWIR with narrow spectral images centered at 4.43 microns and 8.862 microns.

Using a butane lighter as a strong midwave infrared signal, hyperspectral data was collected to show the difference between a butane flame in both the MWIR and LWIR spectral regions. Shown in figure 6 are a sequence of images at 4.43 microns for the MWIR band and taken at the same time at 8.824 microns in the LWIR band, raw image on the left and processed image on the right. The flame saturates the image in the MWIR at 4.43 microns, where CO_2 emission is strong. Even after processing the core of the flame is still saturated. Had we gotten further away or reduced the integration time we would have been able to measure the constituent species of the flame.

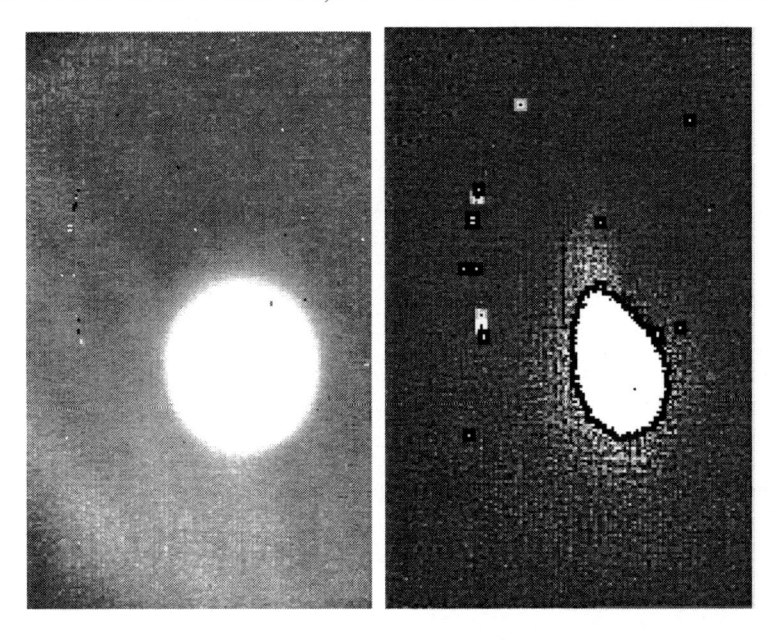

MWIR (5.38 microns)
raw image on left processed image on right.

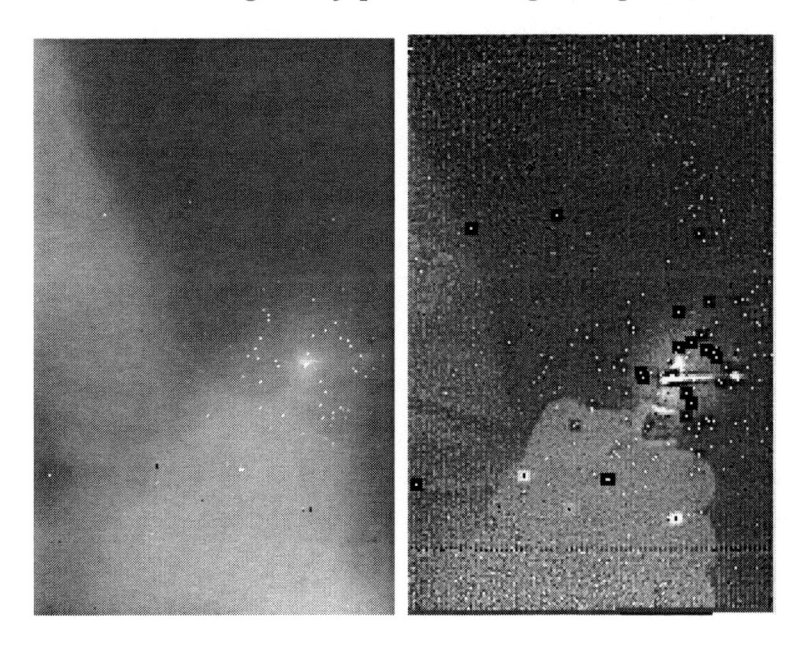

LWIR 10.76 microns)
raw image on left processed image on right.

Figure 7. Dual-band Hyperspectral images of a wire embedded in a butane flame shown in narrow spectral bands in both the MWIR and LWIR centered at 5.38 and 10.76 microns.

(Most of the butane is burned as CO_2, however, there usually are unburned by products that show up as soot or unburned butane in this case). For the LWIR spectral region the hand and the wire screen in the background can be seen in figure 7. It is important to point out that both of these images were taken simultaneously, showing that hyperspectral data on a butane flame in both the MWIR and LWIR can be collected using a dual-band FPA and the IMSS lens technology.

It should be noted that the bad pixels were not corrected for and thus give an artifact in the image. Unfortunately, there were many bad pixels in the center of the image where the region of interest is.

Another scan was taken with a wire embedded in the flame to show that spectral tuning can pull the wire out of the flame and make it clearly visible in the LWIR spectral region, even when the signal is saturated in MWIR region. The image taken at 5.38 microns, even though it is well beyond the CO_2 band, still gives a saturated signal, where the 10.76 micron band shows the wire clearly.

5. Acknowledgements

The authors would like to acknowledge the support given this work by the Missile Defense Agency Small Business Innovative Research Phase I program. It was funding from this program along with internal funding from the Army Research Laboratory that allowed us to demonstrate this concept.

6. References:

[1] http://www.patinc.com

[2] Michele Hinnrichs, "Handheld Imaging Spectrometer", AIPR 2002.

[3] Michele Hinnrichs, "Imaging Spectrometer for Fugitive Gas Leak Detection", Industrial and Environmental and Industrial Sensing, SPIE, Boston September 19-20, 1999.

[4] Michele Hinnrichs "Remote Sensing for Gas Plume Monitoring Using State-of-the-art Infrared Hyperspectral Imaging", SPIE, Industrial and Environmental Monitors and Biosensors Nov 2-5, 1998.

[5] Michele Hinnrichs, Mark Massie "New Approach to Imaging Spectroscopy Using Diffractive Optics", SPIE San Diego, July 1997.

[6] Hinnrichs, Michele, Mark Massie and Jeff Frank (Amber), "Hyperspectral Imaging Radiometer Using Staring 128 x 128 InSb Focal Plane Array and Dispersive Techniques", SPIE AeroSense 1995, Imaging Spectroscopy Session, Orlando, 1995.

Remote Sensing

⌘ ⌘ ⌘ ⌘ ⌘ ⌘ ⌘ ⌘

SUPERRESOLUTION FROM IMAGE SEQUENCE

N. K. Bose

The Pennsylvania State University
Department of Electrical Engineering
University Park, PA 16802
nkb1@psu.edu

Abstract

Due to cost of hardware, size, and fabrication complexity limitations, imaging systems like CCD detector arrays or digital cameras often provide only multiple low-resolution (LR) degraded images. However, a high-resolution (HR) image is indispensable in many applications including health diagnosis and monitoring, military surveillance, and terrain mapping by remote sensing. Other intriguing possibilities include substituting expensive high-resolution instruments like scanning electron microscopes by their cruder, cheaper counterparts and then applying technical methods for increasing the resolution to that derivable with much more costly equipment. This paper will present in a comparison between the various popular approaches to the attaining of superresolution following image acquisition.

1. Introduction

Image superresolution refers to methods that increase spatial resolution by fusing information from a sequence of images, acquired in one or more of several possible ways. The low-resolution images are either captured as a temporal sequence or simultaneously with different sensors. The high resolution filtered image is constructed from the aliased (undersampled) noisy and blurred frames with subpixel shifts. The process for obtaining a HR image from a sequence of LR frames is referred to as *superresolution imaging*. The term, superresolution, used here is different from the usage in optics of the same term that implies recovery of information beyond the diffraction limit. The HR image realizes an increase in *spatial resolution* (distinct from *temporal resolution* that sets the frame rate or number of frames captured per second), measured in pixels per unit distance. In current imaging technologies, it is difficult for a single CCD (Charged Coupled Device) sensor to capture a SHD (Super High Definition) image because of the physical restrictions on the size of current CCD sensing elements. Therefore, high resolution image reconstruction from a set of frames acquired by currently available image sensors has been an interesting topic of research.

The spatial resolution of an image is often determined by imaging sensors. In a CCD camera, the image resolution is determined by the size of its photo-detector. Although CCD cameras for HD (High Definition) images has already been developed, it is necessary to increase the resolution further for SHD images. One way to increase resolution is by reducing the size of pixels (photo-detectors). However, with decreasing pixel size, the amount of light available for each pixel is less and the picture quality is degraded due to shot-noise. Therefore, new schemes are needed to synthesize a high resolution image beyond the physical device performance bound by incorporating signal processing techniques.

The geometry of sensors, where each sensor has a subarray of sensing elements of suitable size has recently been popular in the task of attaining spatial resolution enhancement from the acquired low-resolution degraded images that comprise the set of observations. The multisensor array technology is particularly suited for use in a broad spectrum of applications ranging from satellite imaging to microelectromechanical systems (MEMS) where accuracy, reliability, and low transducer failure rates are essential. This also extends to chronic implantable sensors, monitoring of semiconductor processes, mass-flow sensors, optical cross-connect switches, pressure and temperature sensors. The benefits include application of the methods for development to any sensor array or cluster, reduced calibration and periodic maintenance costs (desirable especially for space-based prefabricated multisensor arrays), higher confidence in sensor measurements based on statistical average on multiple sensors, extended life of the array compared to a single-sensor system, improved fault tolerance, lower failure rates, and low measurement drift. Further research is required on the incorporation of robustness and efficiency, features that are crucial in multispectral sensing and subsequent multiframe processing. The sparseness and structure of the matrix in the image deblurring and superresolution problem needs to be exploited. Rapid progress in computer and semiconductor technology is making it possible to implement image sequence processing tasks reasonably quickly, but the need for processing in real time requires attention to design of efficient and robust algorithms for implementation on current and future generations of computational architectures.

2. Problem Setup

Given a set of LR frames $\{f_k \in \mathbb{R}^{M \times N} \mid k = 1, 2, \ldots, P\}$ where P is the number of available frames. The sought resolution enhancement factor is r (usually r is set to 2, 3, or 4). Interpolate a HR image x of size $rM \times rN$. Assume that the *geometric transformations* T_k (due to camera motion) between the LR frames to the chosen LR reference frame are known.

The processing memory requirement is the extra memory over and above that required to store a set of LR images, (current) HR image and geometric transformations. Singularity problem is based on the assumption that the LR samples on the HR grid are all distinct.

3. Kim, Bose and Valenzuela [1]

The continuous-space original image x^c, is assumed to be bandlimited. That is, its continuous Fourier transform (CFT), $X^c(u, v)$, satisfies

$$|X^c(u,v)| = 0, \quad |u| > r\omega_x/2, |v| > r\omega_y/2, \quad (3.1)$$

where $\omega_x = 2\pi/\Delta_x$ and $\omega_y = 2\pi/\Delta_y$, r is an even integer and Δ_x and Δ_y are the sampling intervals along the x and y axes.

3.1. Algorithm

The kth LR frame is $f_k[i,j] = x^c(i\Delta_x + \delta_{xk}, j\Delta_y + \delta_{yk})$, where δ_{xk} and δ_{yk} are the horizontal and vertical subpixel displacements of the kth frame with respect to a reference frame. The CFT of f_k is

$$F_k^c(u,v) = e^{j2\pi(\delta_{xk}u + \delta_{yk}v)} X^c(u,v). \quad (3.2)$$

From the aliasing relationship, the CFT and DFT are related by

$$F_k[m,n] = \frac{1}{\Delta_x \Delta_y} \sum_{i=-\infty}^{\infty} \sum_{l=-\infty}^{\infty} F_k^c\left(\frac{2\pi m}{M\Delta_x} + i\omega_x, \frac{2\pi n}{N\Delta_y} + l\omega_y\right), \quad (3.3)$$

for $m = 0, 1, \ldots, M-1$, $n = 0, 1, \ldots, N-1$. The infinite summations in Eq. (3.3) can be reduced to finite summations, i.e. $-r/2 \leq i, l \leq r/2 - 1$, by assuming the bandlimitedness of HR image x^c. By substituting Eq. (3.2) into Eq. (3.3) and assuming the bandlimitedness of x^c, the matrix form of Eq. (3.3) is

$$F_P = \frac{1}{\Delta_x \Delta_y} \Phi X^c \quad (3.4)$$

where $F_P \in \mathbb{C}^P$, $\Phi \in \mathbb{C}^{P \times r^2}$, and $X^c \in \mathbb{C}^{r^2}$. First, the initial HR image is reconstructed by choosing any r^2 LR frames such that matrix Φ is nonsigular (set $P = r^2$ in Eq. (3.4)). The rest of the LR frames (other than first r^2 frames) are sequentially fed into the algorithm by applying the recursive update procedure (no matrix inversion involved) developed in [1] using sequential estimation theory in the wavenumber domain.

3.2. Features

1. The method is recursive. The subpixel displacements of frames with respect to a reference frame are assumed known. The camera motion model is translational. Noise filtering is possible, if the number of available LR frames $P > r^2$. Noise filtering is done by implementing minimum least squares procedure.

2. Singularity problem (Robustness): In 1-D there is no singularity problem because matrix Φ has a Vandermonde structure. In 2-D certain structures of shift patterns can cause singularity of matrix Φ (see [2] for more detail). However, an initial HR image can be first reconstructed using r^2 LR frames with a nonsingular shift pattern. Then the recursive update scheme is applied on a suitable subset of the unused LR frames and, in this phase, the singularity problem will not occur because there is no matrix inversion involved.

3. Speed: The initial HR image (in wavenumber domain) X^c is obtained by solving Eq. (3.4) MN times independently (pixel by pixel). Therefore, the algorithm is endowed with a massively parallel computational capability. This scheme is of low complexity since there is no matrix inversion involved. Finally, the HR image in spatial domain can be obtained in FFT speed.

4. Since the algorithm is implemented pixel by pixel (in wavenumber domain), the method is local. and also it does not have the capability for extrapolation.

5. Memory required in processing: The algorithm needs memory to store the LR frames and the current HR image in wavenumber domain whose sizes are the same as that of the corresponding spatial domain images. During processing, the matrix Φ of size $r^2 \times r^2$ requires very low memory for storage.

4. Irani and Peleg [3][4]

This procedure uses iterative back-projection (IBP), previously used in tomographic image reconstruction.

4.1. Algorithm

To make this superresolution algorithm fall into an interpolation framework, the blur PSF (point spread function) and back-projection PSF are assumed to be identity. The HR image $x^{(n+1)}$ at the $(n+1)$th iteration is given by

$$x^{(n+1)} = x^{(n)} + \frac{1}{P}\sum_{k=1}^{P} T_k^{-1}[(\uparrow r)(f_k - f_k^{(n)})] \quad (4.1)$$

where the kth simulated LR frame at the nth iteration $f_k^{(n)}$ is

$$f_k^{(n)} = (\downarrow r)T_k(x^{(n)}). \quad (4.2)$$

Here $(\uparrow r)$ denotes the interpolation or upsampling operator that produces the image at a sampling rate that is higher by a factor r while $(\downarrow r)$ is the downsampling operator that decimates by a factor r. The initial HR image $x^{(0)} = (\uparrow r)(f_m)$ where f_m is the reference frame in the sequence of LR images. Choose the HR image so that the simulated LR frames are as close as desired to the actual LR frames. Strictly speaking,

$$x = \arg\min_{x} \sum_{k=1}^{P} \|(\downarrow r)T_k(x^{(n)}) - f_k\|_2^2. \quad (4.3)$$

Convergence is guaranteed if the camera motion model is affine.

4.2. Features

1. The method is iterative. Noise filtering is done via image averaging. An affine camera motion model guarantees convergence.

2. The algorithm does not suffer from any singularity problem and is robust.

3. Speed: mostly depends on the geometric transformation operation and its inverse. The algorithm converges at an exponential rate.

4. Does not possess capability for extrapolation. It is a global method. It does not have parallel computational capability.

5. Memory required in processing: needs to store a set of simulated LR frames $\{f_k^{(n)} \mid k = 1, 2, \ldots, P\}$ and the current HR image $x^{(n)}$, before update. The memory required during processing is very low.

5. Nguyen, Milanfar, and Golub [5]

By allowing $\sigma = 2^m\pi$ to vary for integer values of m, the Paley-Wiener space of bandlimited functions $\mathcal{B}_2^\sigma$ can be transferred to the setting of wavelet subspaces for multiresolution analysis, which consists of a family of embedded closed subspaces, $V_m \triangleq \mathcal{B}_2^{2^m\pi}$, satisfying the ascending chain condition,

$$\{0\} \subset \cdots V_{-1} \subset V_0 \subset V_1 \cdots \subset L_2(\mathbb{R}),$$

so that their intersection is the empty set and the closure of their union covers $L_2(\mathbb{R})$, i.e.,

$$\text{clos}(\bigcup_{k\in\mathcal{Z}} V_k) = L_2(\mathbb{R}) \quad \text{and} \quad \bigcap_{k\in\mathcal{Z}} V_k = \{0\}.$$

The orthogonal complement of subspace V_{j-1} in subspace V_j will be denoted by W_{j-1}, so that

$$V_j = V_{j-1} \oplus W_{j-1},$$

which is equivalent to, $V_j = V_{j-1} + W_{j-1}$ and $W_{j-1} \perp V_{j-1}$.

The signal $x \in V_{J+1}$ for some interger J.

Any 1-D signal $x(t) \in L_2(\mathbb{R})$ can be expanded as

$$x(t) = \sum_{k\in\mathcal{Z}} a_{J,k}\phi_{J,k}(t) + \sum_{j\geq J}\sum_{k\in\mathcal{Z}} b_{j,k}\psi_{j,k}(t), \quad (5.1)$$

where $\{a_{J,k}\}$ and $\{b_{j,k}\}$ are the *scaling coefficients* and the *wavelet coefficients*.

It is noted that the first term in the left-hand side of Eq. (5.1) is the projection of $x(t)$ onto the subspace V_J which represents a *coarse* approximation of $x(t)$ and the second term is the projection of $x(t)$ onto the subspaces $W_j, j \geq J$ which provides the *added detail* of $x(t)$. When the number of coefficients is infinite, the problem becomes very difficult to handle. A remedy is to choose finitely supported $\phi(t)$ and $\psi(t)$ and this constrains the number of coefficients to be finite. Let $t_{min} = \min\{t_i\}$ and $t_{max} = \max\{t_i\}$, where $0 \leq t_{min} < t_{max}$ and the cardinality of set $S_j = \{k \in \mathbb{Z} \mid \exists t \in [t_{min}, t_{max}], \phi_{j,k}(t) \neq 0\}$ is denoted by $|S_j|$.

The multiresolution concept can be extended to the 2-D case. For any 2-D signal belonging to $L_2(\mathbb{R}^2)$, the subspace V_{j+1} can be decomposed into four subspaces. That is

$$V_{j+1} = V_j \oplus W_j^h \oplus W_j^v \oplus W_j^d \quad (5.2)$$

where the superscripts h, v, and d denote *horizontal, vertical*, and *diagonal*, respectively.

5.1. Algorithm

After transforming all samples of LR frames into the HR grid, according to the multiresolution structure, the HR image $x \in V_{J+1}$ can be expressed as

$$x = \sum_{k \in S_{J,k}} \sum_{l \in S_{J,l}} a_{J,k,l} \phi_{J,k,l} + \sum_{k \in S_{J,k}} \sum_{l \in S_{J,l}} b^h_{J,k,l} \psi^h_{J,k,l} + \sum_{k \in S_{J,k}} \sum_{l \in S_{J,l}} b^v_{J,k,l} \psi^v_{J,k,l} + \sum_{k \in S_{J,k}} \sum_{l \in S_{J,l}} b^d_{J,k,l} \psi^d_{J,k,l}, \quad (5.3)$$

where integer J is chosen such that the cardinality $|S_{J,k}||S_{J,l}| \leq PMN$ (the numbers of LR samples in HR grid). The set $S_{J,k}$ is

$$S_{J,k} = \{k \in \mathbb{Z} \mid -L + \lceil 2^J t_{min} \rceil \leq k \leq \lfloor 2^J t_{max} \rfloor\}, \quad (5.4)$$

where the support of both ϕ and ψ is the closed interval $[0, L]$. The set $S_{J,l}$ is defined in a similar fashion. The matrix form of Eq. (5.3) is

$$\mathbf{x} = G_J \mathbf{a}_J + H^h_J \mathbf{b}^h_J + H^v_J \mathbf{b}^v_J + H^d_J \mathbf{b}^d_J, \quad (5.5)$$

where

$$\mathbf{x} \in \mathbb{R}^{PMN}$$
$$G_J, H^h_J, H^d_J, H^v_J \in \mathbb{R}^{PMN \times |S_{J,k}||S_{J,l}|}. \quad (5.6)$$

First, solve scaling coefficient vector approximant $\hat{\mathbf{a}}_J$ by ignoring last three terms in the right hand side of above equation, then calculate the residual $\mathbf{x} - G_J \hat{\mathbf{a}}_J$ for solving $\mathbf{b}^h_J$ by ignoring the last two terms in the right hand side of above equation. The procedure is repeated in similar fashion until the last coefficient vector $\mathbf{b}^d_J$ is solved.

5.2. Features

1. This is an one step method. Noise filtering is performed implicitly because the resulting HR image is projected onto subspace V_{J+1}. Therefore, the noise wavenumber falling outside the passband of V_{J+1} will be suppressed. Even though the camera motion model can be the projective model, the fast algorithm applies only to the translational model for camera motion parameter estimation.

2. Singularity problem (robustness): Matrix G_J is very likely to be either singular or rank-deficient. Tikhonov regularization must be applied to the problem in general. Note that even in the 1-D case, matrix G_J is rank-deficiency-prone if there is a big gap in the irregular sampling structure.

3. Speed: Because of the huge size of matrix $G_J \in \mathbb{R}^{PMN \times |S_{J,k}||S_{J,l}|}$, solving $\mathbf{x} = G_J \hat{\mathbf{a}}_J$ is not easy. That is, to calculate the minimum least squares solution $\hat{\mathbf{a}}_J = (G_J^T G_J + \lambda I)^{-1} G_J^T \mathbf{x}$ requires a lot of memory. Moreover, if the scaling and wavelet functions ϕ and ψ are not explicitly described by formulae, constructing matrices G_J, H^h_J, H^v_J, H^d_J can be very computation-intensive. For example, if one chooses the Daubechies scaling and wavelet class, the $\phi(t)$ and $\psi(t)$ are the solution of two-scale equations which do not have an explicit solution. The solution can be obtained by using iterative filter banks. Since each entry in matrix G_J is calculated from ϕ directly, therefore, the speed of constructing matrix G_J depend on how fast the function ϕ can be calculated. Similar arguments apply to the other matrices (H^h_J, H^v_J, H^d_J).

4. The method can extrapolate. It is also a global method. It does not have parallel computational capability.

5. Memory required in processing: Large memory required to store G_J and others matrices. Huge memory required to do matrix inversion of $(G_J^T G_J + \lambda I)$ and some other operations.

6. Sandwell [6]

The original signal $x \in$ minimum curvature space. It is equivalent to bicubic spline 2-D interpolation which guarantees $\mathcal{C}^2$ smoothness, where $\mathcal{C}^2$ is the space of continuous and twice differentiable functions.

6.1. Algorithm

After transforming all samples of LR frames into a HR grid, one can treat them as the set of scattered samples $\{(x_i, y_i)\}$ for $i = 1, 2, \ldots, PMN$. To avoid notational confusion, the HR image x at location (x_i, y_i) will be denoted by z_i. The HR image at arbitrary location $\mathbf{x}^T = [xy]$ is given by

$$z(\mathbf{x}) = \sum_{j=1}^{PMN} a_j \phi(\|\mathbf{x} - \mathbf{x}_j\|_2). \quad (6.1)$$

The function $\phi : \mathbb{R}^+ \to \mathbb{R}$ is considered to be a *radial basis* of a minimum curvature space. It is given by

$$\phi(d) = d^2(\ln(d) - 1) \quad (6.2)$$

which is derived from the *biharmonic equation*. It is noted that, according to Eq. (6.2), $\phi \in \mathcal{C}^\infty$. After substituting $z_i = z(\mathbf{x}_i)$ for $i = 1, 2, \ldots, PMN$ into Eq. (6.1) and writing in matrix form, one gets

$$\mathbf{z} = \Phi \mathbf{a}, \quad (6.3)$$

where $\mathbf{z} \in \mathbb{R}^{PMN}$ and $\Phi \in \mathbb{R}^{PMN \times PMN}$.

6.2. Features

1. It cannot filter noise. The camera motion model is projective. This is an one step method.

2. Singularity problem (robustness): No singularity problem. It is a very robust algorithm.

3. Speed: Like in Nguyen *et al.* [5] case, the size of matrix Φ is very large. However, it is nonsingular and much better conditioned than in the case of Nguyen *et al.*

4. It has extrapolation capability. The method is global without parallel computational capability.

5. Memory required in processing: Due to the size of matrix $\Phi \in \mathbb{R}^{PMN \times PMN}$, the coefficient vector $\mathbf{a} = \Phi^{-1}\mathbf{z}$ requires a lot of memory in its calculation.

7. Delaunay Triangulation [7][10]

The image $x \in \mathcal{C}^n$ for some integer $n \geq 1$.

7.1. Algorithm

After transforming all samples of LR frames into a HR grid, one can treat them as the set of scattered samples (vertices) $\{(x_i, y_i)\}$ for $i = 1, 2, \ldots, PMN$. To avoid notational confusion, the HR image x at location (x_i, y_i) will be denoted by z_i. The algorithm is briefly described next.

1. Generate the Delaunay triangulation on the set of scattered vertices.

2. Estimate the gradients at each vertex of the triangulation.

3. Approximate each triangle patch in the triangulation by a $\mathcal{C}^n$-smoothness surface, subject to the smoothness constraints (gradients information).

4. Interpolate the value at each HR grid point.

7.2. Features

1. It cannot filter noise. The camera motion model is projective. This is a recursive method.

2. Singularity problem (robustness): There is no problem with sigularity and it is a very robust algorithm.

3. Speed: The algorithm can be implemented very fast because it is done on each triangle patch independently.

4. Extrapolation capability: The algorithm cannot extrapolate the values outside the convex hull of the set of vertices.

5. Local method. The algorithm is performed on each triangle patch, independently. It has parallel computational capability.

6. Memory required in processing: The algorithm needs to store the following variables during processing.
    - Each vertex needs to store the gradients up to nth order along both directions.
    - Each edge needs to store the gradient normal to the direction of the edge up to nth order.
    - Each triangle needs to store coefficient vector $\mathbf{c}$ whose length is more or less $\frac{1}{2}(n+1)(n+2)$ depending on the bivariate polynomial used to model smooth surface.

In Delaunay triangulation,
- the number of vertices is $\aleph := PMN$,
- the number of triangle patches is $2\aleph - \aleph_b - 2$,
- the number of edges is $3\aleph - \aleph_b - 3$,

where $\aleph_b$ is the number of vertices on the boundary of the convex hull.

8. Conclusions

This paper provides a comparison of the performance, features, and constraints of several superresolution algorithms that have been popularized during the last decade or so. The reader should not get the impression that other superresolution algorithms do not exist. In fact, the prolific research activity in this area [9] cannot be adequately described within the framework of a paper like this one that has imposed constraints on the number of allowed pages. It should be emphasized that the dynamism in this area of research is substantiated by not only the voluminous past activity within a reasonably short time span but also the realized need to meet many other remaining challenges.

Nonuniform spacing of the data samples in frames is at the heart of superresolution, and this may be coupled with presence of data dropouts or missing data. The wavelet basis offers considerable promise in the fast interpolation of unevenly spaced data. Papers so far used only first generation wavelets and have not adequately subscribed to the need for selecting the mother wavelet to optimize performance. The wavelet superresolution algorithm proposed by Nguyen *et al* [5] ignored the effects of using different choices of mother wavelets and scaling functions. In their work, only the Daubechies wavelet and scaling function were applied and tested. From the implementational standpoint of superresolution algorithms, *small and finite support*, and *explicit and simple expression* properties of scaling function and wavelet are preferred. In addition, other common desirable properties of mother scaling function and wavelet are: *symmetry (or linear phase), orthogonality, high regularity (smoothness), low approximation error,* and *high time-frequency localization*. A detailed comparison of the desirable properties in superresolution has recenly been made [10] for several finitely supported scaling function and wavelet families (Haar, Daubechies, Symlets, Coiflets, and B-splines). Among the scaling functions of the same order $L > 1$, the support size of the B-spline scaling function is the smallest in comparison to others.

It has been concluded from this and several other considerations that the most suitable choice of scaling function and wavelet for superresolution algorithm is the B-spline family because of the following properties. First, its scaling function has the shortest possible finite support size. Moreover, its corresponding wavelet's support size can be selected as low as L while the supports of Daubechies, Symlets, and Coiflets wavelets are fixed at $2L-1$, $2L-1$, and $3L-1$, respectively. Second, the B-spline scaling function and wavelet have explicit expressions which are very useful from the computational standpoint. Third, the B-spline family has the highest regularity (or smoothness) for order $L \geq 3$ and lowest approximation constant C_ϕ when compared with other families for a chosen order L. Finally, the B-spline scaling function is considered to be the optimal time-frequency localization in comparison to others having the common order L. Specifically, as the approximation order $L \to \infty$, the B-spline scaling function of order L, constructed from the L-time convolutions of Box functions, converges to the Gaussian function which achieves the optimal time-frequency localization. It is reported in [11] that the time-frequency localization of cubic-spline scaling function ($L = 4$) is already within 2% range of the lower bound.

Wavelet Transform (WT) is also used for blind image restoration under the condition that the blur function has zero-phase. With its sensitivity to the perceptual importance of edges to human eyes, WT can be applied to estimation of subpixel displacement errors and reconstructing "edge-preserving" high resolution images from multisensor arrays; this needs to be vigorously pursued in the future. The advantage s of second generation waveletss (like adaptation to nonsmooth domains, irregularly sampled data, and weighted measures, as opposed to only translation-invariant Haar-Lebesgue measures)) in superresolution has only been realized very recently and they are expected to provide the framework for attaining robust superresolution to data acquired with different types of sensors and fused Infrared (IR) sensors are indispensable under nocturnal and limited visibility conditions while electro-optic (EO) sensing systems using both absorption lidar and infrared spectroscopy have been widely used in both active and passive sensing of industrial and atmospheric pollutants, detection of concealed explosives for airport security applications, detection of land mines, and weather monitoring through the sensing and tracking of vapor clouds.

9. Acknowledgement

This research was supported by US Army Research Office Grant No. DAAD19-03-1-0261. The author thanks Surapong Lertrattanapanich for his contributions to this research effort and Mahesh B. Chappalli for proofreading this paper.

References

[1] S. P. Kim, N. K. Bose, and H. M. Valenzuela. Recursive reconstruction of high resolution image from noisy undersampled multiframes. *IEEE Transactions on Acoustics, Speech, and Signal Processing*, 38:1013–1027, 1990.

[2] S. P. Kim and N. K. Bose. Reconstruction of 2-D bandlimited discrete signals from nonuniform samples. *IEE Proceedings*, 137(3):197–204, June 1990.

[3] Michal Irani and Shmuel Peleg. Improving resolution by image registration. *CVGIP: Graphical Models and Image Processing*, 53(3):231–239, May 1991.

[4] Michal Irani and Shmuel Peleg. Motion analysis for image enhancement: Resolution, occlusion, and transparency. *Journal of Visual Communication and Image Representation*, 4:324–335, December 1993.

[5] Nhat Nguyen and Peyman Milanfar. A wavelet-based interpolation-restoration method for superresolution (wavelet superresolution). *Circuits Systems Signal Process*, 19(4):321–338, 2000.

[6] David T. Sandwell. Biharmonic spline interpolation of Geo-3 and Seasat altimeter data. *Geophysical Research Letters*, 14(2):139–142, February 1987.

[7] S. Lertrattanapanich and N. K. Bose. High resolution image formation from low resolution frames using Delaunay Triangulation. *IEEE Transactions on Image Processing*, 17(2):1427–1441, December 2002.

[8] M. K. Ng and N. K. Bose. Mathematical analysis of super-resolution methodology. *IEEE Signal Processing Magazine*, 62-74, May 2003.

[9] N. K. Bose. Multidimensional Systems Theory and Applications. *Kluwer Academic Publishers*, November 2003.

[10] S. Lertrattanapanich. Superresolution from Degraded Image Sequence Using Spatial Tessellations and Wavelets *Ph. D. Dissertation, Department of Electrical Engineering, Pennsylvania State University, University Park, PA, USA*, May 2003.

[11] M. Unser . Ten good reasons for using spline wavelets *Proc. SPIE Conf. Math. Imaging: Wavelet Applications in Signal and Image Processing V, San Diego, CA*, 422-431, 1997.

Data Association for Fusion in Spatial and Spectral Imaging

A. Schaum, *Member, IEEE*

Abstract—Conventional spatial imaging of the same object at different times or with different sensing modalities often requires the identification of corresponding points within a solid object. A mathematically similar problem occurs in the remote hyperspectral imaging of one scene at two widely separated time intervals. In both cases the information can be interpreted using linear vector spaces, and the differences in sensed signals can be modeled with linear transformations of these spaces. Here we explore first, how much can be deduced about the transformations based solely on the multivariate statistics of the two data sets. Then we solve application-specific models for each of conventional and hyperspectral applications.

Index Terms—Covariance equalization, Data Association, Registration, Hyperspectral Imaging, Point set matching

I. INTRODUCTION

THE generic problem addressed in this paper is how to find a linear transformation that approximately connects two multivariate data sets. Making the connection is a crucial step in many data fusion problems. Associations between specific pairs of points from the two sets that are related by the transformation are assumed to be unavailable. In imaging applications, for example, this may be caused by an unknown rotation and change of scale. Finding the rotation and magnification may be considered equivalent to solving the association problem.

A general mathematical treatment of the problem, based on a comparison of first- and second-order statistics, is useful up to a point. Further progress requires problem-specific models of the transformation. We discuss two such examples: conventional (spatial) volumetric imaging, with especially medical and computer graphics applications in mind, and hyperspectral imaging, with change detection and target tracking as the principal applications.

For spatial imaging, each point of either data set corresponds to a physical location, typically within a solid object, and is represented as a 3-dimensional vector. In hyperspectral imaging, each point is N-dimensional, where N is the number of spectral channels collected by an imaging spectrometer. The coordinates in this space represent the intensities in each wavelength. The value of N can be in the hundreds, although in most applications the spectral space is mathematically blurred or undersampled to correspond to, at most, a few dozen manageable dimensions.

The prototype association problem in spatial imaging requires the correlation of points within an object whose locations have been recorded in two images, the difference being a shift, a rotation, and a magnification, the combined effect of which can be represented by a linear transformation of mean-centered coordinates. For example, physiological structures can be studied with different medical sensing modalities [1] or with the same modality at different times.

In hyperspectral imaging (HSI) applications, two images collected at widely separated times can generate different spectral (vector) signals at every pixel. The evolution of the signals can often be modeled with a linear transformation describing changes both in illumination and in atmospheric effects. Finding the transformation can facilitate anomalous change detection [2], [3], [4] over long time intervals, and it can be used to evolve target signatures for tracking.

II. MATHEMATICAL DEVELOPMENT

A. General Framework

We assume that two associated data sets

$$\{x(i)\}, \{y(j)\} \qquad (1)$$

are available for analysis. The generic problem is: Which $x(i)$ corresponds to which $y(j)$?

We treat x and y as stochastic variables whose realizations in (1) are elements of an N-dimensional vector space. They are assumed to be related by an unknown linear transformation T, according to

$$y = Tx + O, \qquad (2)$$

with O an unknown offset. Subtracting from Equation (2) its mean value shows that it can be written as $y - \mu_Y = T(x - \mu_X)$. Therefore, by always choosing mean-centered coordinates, we can consider the linear equation

$$y = Tx \qquad (3)$$

Manuscript received October 15, 2003. A. Schaum is with the Naval Research Laboratory, Washington D.C., 20375, USA (Phone: 202-767-9366; e-mail: schaum@nrl.navy.mil).

without loss of generality.

We will consider multivariate Gaussian models of the x and y distributions. The general form is

$$P(z) \propto (\|(M)\|)^{-\frac{1}{2}} \exp\left[-(z-\mu)^t \frac{M^{-1}}{2}(z-\mu)\right], \quad (4)$$

where μ and M are the mean vector and covariance matrix for the random variable z, $\|\ \|$ means determinant, and ^{t} indicates matrix transposition.

Solving the association problem could amount to specifying parameters in a model-based estimate of T. However, the approach could also be purely statistical. For example, if we treat T as an estimator of y from x, we can approximate it with the well-known matrix Wiener filter

$$T_W = R_{yx} R_{xx}^{-1}, \quad (5)$$

which minimizes the mean squared prediction error. Here the covariance matrices are defined as

$$R_{xx} \equiv \langle xx^t \rangle, \quad R_{yx} \equiv \langle yx^t \rangle, \quad (6)$$

where the symbol $\langle\ \rangle$ denotes expected value.

However, the answer in Equation (5) is of no use in the problem of associating each x-value with a y-value, because calculating R_{yx} (see Equation (6)) requires this information a priori. In this paper we study methods of estimating T that depend only on the individual statistics of the two data sets in (1), not the cross-correlations between them.

Because we further specialize our study to Gaussian distributions for these data sets, we can restrict the statistics considered to those of the first- and second-order, which completely define Gaussians. By always using mean-centered coordinates, we reduce the problem to a study of estimates of T based on the covariance matrices R_{xx} and R_{yy}, which encode all the second-order statistics of the random variables x and y.

The first question then is: Of the N^2 degrees of freedom associated with a general N×N matrix T that maps the set $\{x(i)\}$ onto $\{y(j)\}$, how many are fixed by the values of R_{xx} and R_{yy}?

Multiplying Equation (3) by its transpose and averaging produces the relation

$$T R_{xx} T^t = R_{yy}. \quad (7)$$

Define singular value decompositions (SVD) of the symmetric nonnegative covariance matrices:

$$\begin{aligned} R_{xx} &= U_x D_x U_x^t \\ R_{yy} &= U_y D_y U_y^t, \end{aligned} \quad (8)$$

in which the U matrices are orthonormal ($UU^t = I$), and the D matrices are nonnegative diagonal. The columns of U are also known as principal components. They are the eigenvectors of the corresponding covariance matrix. It should be noted that the representations in Equation (8) are not unique. (For example, the columns of U, along with the diagonals of D can be permuted.) Nevertheless, they can be used to define unambiguous square-root matrices, for example $R_{xx}^{\pm\frac{1}{2}} \equiv U_x D_x^{\pm\frac{1}{2}} U_x^t$, which are unique, i.e., independent of the particular SVD representation. Then Equation (7) is equivalent to [3]

$$\left(R_{yy}^{-\frac{1}{2}} T R_{xx}^{\frac{1}{2}}\right)\left(R_{yy}^{-\frac{1}{2}} T R_{xx}^{\frac{1}{2}}\right)^t = I. \quad (9)$$

This is the definition of orthonormality for each matrix factor, meaning that

$$T = \left(R_{yy}^{\frac{1}{2}} \Lambda R_{xx}^{-\frac{1}{2}}\right), \quad (10)$$

with Λ some orthonormal matrix. Notice that Equation (9) needs to be true only if R_{yy} is invertible. However, even if it is not, an orthonormal Λ can always be found to make Equation (10) true. (We always assume that R_{xx} is invertible. If it is not, we make it so by working in a lower-dimensional space obtained by projecting out the degenerate dimensions, which are those in which $\{x(i)\}$ exhibits no variability.)

Furthermore, the form for T in Equation (10) satisfies Equation (7) for *any* orthonormal Λ. It follows that Equations (7) and (10) are equivalent statements, so that, given R_{xx} and R_{yy}, all uncertainty in T has been concentrated in the $\frac{N}{2}(N-1)$ degrees of freedom associated with the orthonormal matrix Λ in Equation (10), which is called the "data-dependent decomposition" [3] of the matrix T. For any data set with covariance matrix R_{xx}, the effect any linear transformation T has on it can be decomposed into a whitening/rotation/coloring sequence, corresponding to the three factors in Equation (10).

In the case of volumetric imaging, the data correspond to points within or on a physical object. If this object can rotate, then a natural choice for Λ is that rotation $U_x U_y^t$ which maps the eigenvectors of R_{xx} onto those of R_{yy}. These are just the principal moments of inertia. This choice makes (10) mathematically equivalent to the transformation proposed by Moshfeghi and Rusinek [1, page 81]. Our preferred method is derived in Section *B*.

We remark that, for hyperspectral imaging, the choice $\Lambda = I$ (the identity matrix) has worked well [3], [5]. This choice is also convenient, because the resultant $T = R_{yy}^{\frac{1}{2}} R_{xx}^{-\frac{1}{2}}$ is unambiguous, independent of the SVDs used to calculate the square root matrices. In §*B.1* below, we show that this is not the case for volumetric imaging.

B. Model-based Methods

When x_i and y_i are linearly related, as in Equation (3), the transform must satisfy Equation (7), and so the general solution must be of the form (10), which contains $\frac{N}{2}(N-1)$ unknown parameters. To deduce more detailed properties of T, we must invoke a model based on the particular phenomenology under consideration.

In the following, we derive specific estimates of T by invoking a constrained version of the principle of maximum likelihood estimation. The standard version estimates an unknown set of parameters by choosing those values that maximize the log likelihood function

$$L \equiv \ln\left[\prod_i P(x_i, y_i)\right] = \ln\left[\prod_i P(y_i \mid x_i) P(x_i)\right], \quad (11)$$

in which the probabilities are modeled as Gaussians. The solution to this problem is Expression (5), but that depends on the covariance R_{yx}, the calculation of which (see Equation (6)) begs the association question.

In the following two model-based examples, we avoid a dependence on R_{yx} by maximizing $\prod_i P(y_i)$, instead of $\prod_i P(x_i, y_i)$, while using Equation (7) to define the covariance of the y-data in terms of the x-data. The general solution to (7) (Equation (10)) allows $\frac{N}{2}(N-1)$ degrees of freedom. That is, it exhausts $N^2 - \frac{N}{2}(N-1) = \frac{N}{2}(N+1)$ of the original parameters. The following models can contain fewer than this number of parameters. In such cases, the covariance structures of real data usually do not support (except in anomalous cases) Equation (7). Nevertheless, the solution to the maximum likelihood problem is well-defined, as the following examples illustrate.

1) Spatial Imaging: The mR Model

In many conventional imaging applications, the principal difference between two images can be attributed to changes in aspect and range. Thus, the general transform in Equation (3) can be replaced by a more specific model,

$$T = mR, \quad (12)$$

with m an unknown positive number representing magnification, and R an unknown rotation (and hence orthonormal) matrix. (The effect of any overall shift s is accounted for by use of mean-centered coordinates.) The general transformation, which has $N^2 = 9$ parameters, is thus replaced by one with a total of only $\frac{N}{2}(N-1) + 1 = 4$ free parameters in this magnification/rotation (mR) model.

To find the maximum likelihood estimates of m and R, we make the usual Gaussian assumption for the y distribution and maximize the likelihood function $L \equiv \ln\left[\prod_i P(y_i)\right]$ for the aggregate of N_S sample values of y, substituting the expression (7) for the covariance matrix. Then, from Equation (4),

$$L \approx -\frac{N_S}{2} \ln\left\| m^2 R R_{xx} R^t \right\| - \frac{1}{2} \sum_i y_i^t \left(m^2 R R_{xx} R^t \right)^{-1} y_i. \quad (13)$$

Using various properties of determinants, traces, and the orthonormality of rotation matrices, we can simplify the log likelihood function to

$$L \approx -\frac{N_S}{2}\left[\ln(m^{2N}) + \ln\|R_{xx}\|\right] - \frac{N_S}{2m^2} tr\left(R_{yy} R R_{xx}^{-1} R^t\right). \quad (14)$$

(No distinction has been made between the covariance matrix R_{yy} and its maximum likelihood estimate $\frac{1}{N_s}\sum_{i=1}^{N_s} y_i y_i^t$.)

Equation (14) is easily maximized over m^2 by differentiation, with the result

$$m^2 = \frac{1}{N} tr\left(R_{yy} R R_{xx}^{-1} R^t\right). \quad (15)$$

Substituting this into (14) reduces the problem of maximizing L to one of minimizing the expression

$$tr\left(R_{yy} R R_{xx}^{-1} R^t\right) \quad (16)$$

over all orthonormal matrices R. This can be simplified with the help of Equation (8) to

$$g(Q) = tr\left(D_y Q D_x^{-1} Q^t\right) \quad (17)$$

with

$$Q \equiv U_y^t R U_x \quad (18)$$

which, being the product of orthonormal matrices, is itself orthonormal. The orthonormality constraint on R, therefore, translates into one for Q

$$Q Q^t = I, \quad (19)$$

and to incorporate it into the minimization process we introduce one LaGrange multiplier λ_{ij} for each component of the matrix equation (19).

Therefore, we want to minimize

$$g_\lambda(Q) = tr(D_y Q D_x^{-1} Q^t) - \sum_{ij} \lambda_{ij}(QQ^t - I)_{ji}$$
$$= tr[(D_y Q D_x^{-1} Q^t) - \lambda(QQ^t - I)] \quad (20)$$

Note that the anti-symmetric part of the matrix λ does not contribute to this equation, because it is annihilated on contraction with a symmetric matrix. Therefore, we can assume without loss of generality that it is symmetric:

$$\lambda = \lambda^t. \quad (21)$$

Then, setting to zero the derivative of Equation (20) with respect to the matrix elements Q_{ij} produces the matrix equation

$$D_y Q D_x^{-1} = \lambda Q \quad (22)$$

for any orthonormal Q that extremizes (20). Because of Equations (21) and (19), this means that $D_y Q D_x^{-1} Q^t$ is symmetric. That is,

$$D_y Q D_x^{-1} Q^t = Q D_x^{-1} Q^t D_y. \quad (23)$$

This also means that the matrices D_y and $QD_x^{-1}Q^t$ commute. A standard theorem of linear algebra states that commuting symmetric matrices A and B can always be simultaneously diagonalized by an orthonormal matrix U. That is, there is such a U that makes both UAU^t and UBU^t diagonal.

Now note that D_y is already diagonal. Assume for the moment that all its diagonal entries are distinct. It is known [6] that then the only orthonormal matrices U that keep $UD_y U^t$ diagonal have columns that are permutations and/or inversions of the columns of the identity matrix. We will call such a matrix a PI matrix. Therefore, for some PI matrix U, $UD_y U^t$ and $U(QD_x^{-1}Q^t)U^t$ are both diagonal. The latter, $= (UQ)(D_x^{-1})(UQ)^t$, is also in SVD form and, assuming further that the diagonals of D_x^{-1} are distinct, now it is UQ that must be a PI matrix. Because products and inverses of PI matrices are also PI matrices, this means that Q must be a PI matrix.

Therefore $QD_x^{-1}Q^t$ is a diagonal matrix

$$QD_x^{-1}Q^t = \tilde{D}_x^{-1}, \quad (24)$$

whose diagonal elements $\{(\tilde{D}_x^{-1})_{ii}\}$ are some permutation of $\{(D_x^{-1})_{ii}\}$. Consequently, it follows from Equation (17) that all extremal values of the trace must be of the form $\sum_i (D_y)_{ii} (\tilde{D}_x^{-1})_{ii}$. It is easy to show that the choice of PI matrix that minimizes the sum occurs when the largest values of $\{(\tilde{D}_x^{-1})_{ii}\}$ are matched with the smallest of $\{(D_y)_{ii}\}$. This choice therefore globally minimizes (16) and, combined with (15), defines the maximum likelihood solution to the mR model.

From Equation (18), and the fact that Q is a PI matrix, the optimal R is seen to be

$$R = U_y Q U_x^t = U_y \tilde{U}_x^t \quad (25)$$

with $\tilde{U}_x^t$ a row-permuted version of U_x^t. R rotates the eigenvectors of R_{xx}^{-1} (with eigenvalues $(\tilde{D}_x^{-1})_{ii}$) into corresponding eigenvectors of R_{yy}, associating each pair according to the reverse order of the eigenvalue magnitudes. This is the same as rotating the eigenvectors of R_{xx} (which are the same as those of R_{xx}^{-1}) into the eigenvectors of R_{yy} by associating each pair according to the *same* order of the eigenvalues.

Using Equations (8), (24) and (25), the magnification estimate in Equation (15) can now be computed:

$$m^2 = \frac{1}{3} tr[D_y \tilde{D}_x^{-1}] \quad (26)$$

The answer can be simplified if we remove some of the arbitrariness from the SVD definitions for R_{xx} and R_{yy} in Equation (8). We choose a form that orders the eigenvalues along the diagonals of D_x and D_y (by permuting the columns of the U matrices, if necessary) in the same way—either increasing or decreasing. With this choice, the solution to the mR problem:

$$y \approx mRx \quad (27)$$

can be written

$$R = U_y U_x^t \quad (28)$$

and

$$m = \left\{ \frac{1}{3} \sum_{i=1}^{3} (D_y)_{ii} (D_x^{-1})_{ii} \right\}^{\frac{1}{2}} = \frac{1}{3} tr(D_y D_x^{-1}). \quad (29)$$

To summarize, we have shown that a rotation defined by the intuitively natural association of eigenvectors, based on ordering the corresponding eigenvalues by size, follows from a maximum likelihood principle applied to the magnification/rotation/shift model of Equation (12).

A pure rotation of the data from $\{x(i)\}$ to $\{y(i)\}$ constitutes a rigid-body transformation, which preserves shape information. In particular, the principal component eigenvectors undergo the same rotation, and their eigenvalues are not changed. If, as we have assumed, these are all distinct, then associating eigenvectors according to eigenvalue is equivalent to associating them by order of their size. Finally, any magnification m preserves this order, and so it is reasonable to define R as that rotation which maps eigenvectors of R_{xx} into those of R_{yy}, with the association of pairs based on rank-order of respective eigenvalue magnitudes.

The final ambiguity lies in choosing the signs of the columns of U_x and U_y. Generally this detail requires more information than we have assumed. For example, rotations of either 90° and -90° about the third principal axis each interchange the other two (non-directional) axes, and so the eigenvectors alone—whose signs are arbitrary (except that $\|R\|$ should equal +1)—cannot be used to distinguish the two rotations. The extra information required to define the rotation unambiguously could rely on higher-order moments of the distributions, or on prior knowledge, e.g., that the rotations are small.

We note further that this ambiguity problem is much more severe if two of the eigenvalues are close in value. Measurement noise can reorder them, and ambiguity in $U_y U_x^t$ grows to include any rotation in the plane of the corresponding eigenvectors. Also, if real noise with mean square value comparable to the smaller values of $(D_x)_{ii}$ corrupts the estimate of R_{xx}, then the estimate in (29) can be sensitive to the measurement process. Equation (29) should be thought of as a high SNR (signal-to-noise ratio) solution.

If the SNR is low compared to measured data variances, we suggest replacing Equation (29) with

$$m = \left\{\frac{tr(R_{yy})}{tr(R_{xx})}\right\}^{\frac{1}{2}} = \left\{\frac{\sum_i (D_y)_{ii}}{\sum_i (D_x)_{ii}}\right\}^{\frac{1}{2}}. \quad (30)$$

This mitigates the error in the magnification estimate in the case that noise substantially corrupts all the eigenvalues of the covariance matrices.

Finally, if one can at least rely on the largest eigenvalue being much larger than the noise, both Equations (29) and (30) suggest truncating the sum and using

$$m = \left\{\frac{\underset{i}{Max}(D_y)_{ii}}{\underset{i}{Max}(D_x)_{ii}}\right\}^{\frac{1}{2}}. \quad (31)$$

To summarize: Our formulation of the maximum likelihood problem generates a solution to the mR model (Equation (27)) that is defined by the prescription:
1. Use mean centered coordinates x and y to account for any possible shift in the data.
2. Solve the eigenvalue problems for the covariance matrices

$$R_{xx} \equiv \langle xx^t \rangle = U_x D_x U_x^t$$
$$R_{yy} \equiv \langle yy^t \rangle = U_y D_y U_y^t, \quad (32)$$

ordering the eigenvectors (the columns of U_x and U_y) so that the corresponding eigenvalues appear in the same order in both diagonal D matrices. Resolve the residual sign ambiguity as suggested above.
3. Choose for the rotation

$$R = U_y U_x^t. \quad (33)$$

4. Estimate the magnification m according to SNR:

	High	Intermediate	Low
Equation	(29)	(31)	(30).

2) Hyperspectral Imaging: The Diagonal Chromodynamics Model

As a second example of the model-based approach, we let $\{x(i)\}$ represent spectral radiance vectors at different pixels in a natural scene. The same scene is measured at a second time, with the result $\{y(j)\}$.

The principal differences in the radiance profiles of two such images collected at different times arise from changes in: (a) path radiance (haze), which is independent of the background terrain spectral characteristics, (b) illumination level, and (c) atmospheric attenuation of ground-leaving energy. Each of these effects can depend on wavelength.

If the intrinsic reflectivity at any pixel is unchanged, (a) changes the mean value of the distribution, an effect already accounted for in the present development by use of mean-centered coordinates. Both (b) and (c) can be represented at any wavelength by scale factors. In the context of Equation (3), the matrix T can therefore be modeled with a diagonal matrix D. Thus the analog of Equation (27) for our model of spectral dynamics is

$$y \approx Dx \quad (D \text{ diagonal}), \quad (34)$$

We again maximize $\prod_i P(y_i)$, as in §IIB.1. Now the variance constraint in Equation (7) becomes

$$R_{yy} \approx D R_{xx} D, \quad (35)$$

and Equation (13) is replaced by

$$L \approx -\frac{N_s}{2} \ln\|D R_{xx} D\| - \frac{1}{2}\sum_{i=1}^{N_s} y_i^t (D R_{xx} D)^{-1} y_i. \quad (36)$$

Ignoring an additive term independent of D reduces this to:

$$L \approx -\frac{N_S}{2}\sum_{i=1}^{N}\ln(D_{ii})^2 - \frac{N_S}{2}tr\left((DR_{xx}D)^{-1}R_{yy}\right). \quad (37)$$

(Recall the development following Equation (14).) To extremize this equation, we differentiate with respect to the variables D_{ii} to arrive at the equation

$$D = diag\left(R_{xx}^{-1}D^{-1}R_{yy}\right), \quad (38)$$

in which the diagonalizing matrix operation *diag* is defined by:

$$\left(diag(M)\right)_{ij} \equiv M_{ij}\delta_{ij}, \quad (39)$$

with δ the Kronecker delta.

No closed form solution to Equation (38) is currently known, except for the cases $N=1,2$. However, these solutions are instructive.

For $N=2$, Equation (38) defines a pair of coupled equations in the two unknowns D_{11} and D_{22}. Simple substitution produces quadratic equations that can be solved easily. The result is:

$$D_{ii} = \frac{\sigma_{y_i}}{\sigma_{x_i}}\left\{\frac{1-\rho_x\rho_y}{1-\rho_x^2}\right\}^{\frac{1}{2}} \quad (i=1,2), \quad (40)$$

where

$$\sigma_{x_i} = R_{x_ix_i}^{\frac{1}{2}}, \quad \sigma_{y_i} = R_{y_iy_i}^{\frac{1}{2}}, \quad (41)$$

and the correlation coefficients are defined by

$$\rho_x = \frac{R_{x_1x_2}}{\sqrt{R_{x_1x_1}R_{x_2x_2}}}, \rho_y = \frac{R_{y_1y_2}}{\sqrt{R_{y_1y_1}R_{y_2y_2}}}. \quad (42)$$

The first ratio in Equation (40) is, for $i=1$, the one-dimensional ($N=1$) solution. That is, the maximum likelihood estimate of the scale factor D_{11} is just the ratio of the standard deviations of the *y*-data and the *x*-data, an intuitively appealing result that agrees with Equation (10) for $N=1$.

Returning to the $N=2$ case, Equation (40) tells us that the one-dimensional solutions also apply to each component of the two-dimensional case if and only if either: (a) the *x*-data are uncorrelated ($\rho_x = 0$), or (b) the diagonal matrix D transforms each *x* data point to an associated *y* data point exactly, thereby preserving the correlation ($\rho_x = \rho_y$). It can be shown that both these properties generalize to higher dimensions.

Equation (40) reveals the interesting fact that, despite a diagonal model of spectral dynamics, the maximum likelihood estimate of the parameter associated with one color generally depends on the other colors.

For higher-dimensional problems, Equation (38) suggests an iterative approach. Replace the left-hand D with the next iteration of the right-hand D. That is, on iteration $i+1$ let

$$D^{(i+1)} = diag\left(R_{xx}^{-1}\left(D^{(i)}\right)^{-1}R_{yy}\right). \quad (43)$$

This is known to fail in an important case. Whenever the argument of *diag* happens to be a diagonal matrix (for example, whenever R_{xx} and R_{yy} are), Equation (43) reduces to N parallel problems, to wit, finding the square roots of $\frac{R_{y_iy_i}}{R_{x_ix_i}}$. And in this case, the iterates in Equation (43) simply alternate between two values and do not converge to the answer.

However, motivated by this example, we propose a different iterative technique:

$$D^{(i+1)} = \frac{1}{2}\left[diag\left(R_{xx}^{-1}\left(D^{(i)}\right)^{-1}R_{yy}\right) + D^{(i)}\right],$$

with $D^{(0)} = I$. For $N=1$ (and for the diagonal argument case described above) this certainly converges, because it reduces to Newton's method of finding square roots. However, as of this writing, the conditions under which this method converges in higher dimensions are not generally known.

III. Summary and Future

We have defined a new methodology for estimating linear transformations that connect two point data sets. It is based on a constrained maximum likelihood principle. The general form of the solution was derived for the case of an unconstrained transform, and two different particular models were explored. A volumetric imaging problem was solved completely. In a second model, of spectral dynamics, some general properties of the solutions were obtained, and the exact solutions were found in one and two dimensions. Iterative approaches to the general problem were suggested. Future research will seek solutions to the general N-dimensional chromodynamics model, and will incorporate noise models into the general problem statement.

Reference

[1] M. Moshfeghi, H. Rusinek, *Philips J. Res. 47* (1992), pp. 81-97.
[2] A. Schaum, Alan Stocker, Long-Interval Chronochrome Target Detection, *Proc. 1997 International Symposium on Spectral Sensing Research*, 1998.
[3] A. Schaum, Alan Stocker, Linear Chromodynamics Models for Hyperspectral Target Detection, IEEE Aerospace Conference, IEEE Catalog Number: 03TH8652C; ISBN: 0-7803-7652-8, 19 FEBRUARY, 2003.
[4] A. Schaum, Alan Stocker, Hyperspectral Multi-Pass Mapping for Target Detection, *Algorithms and Technologies for Multispectral, Hyperspectral, and Ultraspectral*, SPIE AeroSense Annual Meeting, April, 2003.
[5] A. Schaum, Alan Stocker, Estimating Hyperspectral Target Signature Evolution with a Background Chromodynamics Model, *Proc. International Symposium on Spectral Sensing Symposium*, June 1, 2003.
[6] A. Schaum, private notes.

Band Selection Using Independent Component Analysis for Hyperspectral Image Processing

Hongtao Du, Hairong Qi, Xiaoling Wang
Dept. of Elec. and Comp. Engineering
University of Tennessee
Knoxville, TN 37996-2100
{hdu1, hqi, xwang1}@utk.edu

Rajeev Ramanath, Wesley E. Snyder[*]
Dept. of Elec. and Comp. Engineering
North Carolina State University
Raleigh, NC 27695-7914
rajeev.ramanath@ieee.org, wes@eos.ncsu.edu

Abstract

Although hyperspectral images provide abundant information about objects, their high dimensionality also substantially increases computational burden. Dimensionality reduction offers one approach to Hyperspectral Image (HSI) analysis. Currently, there are two methods to reduce the dimension, band selection and feature extraction. In this paper, we present a band selection method based on Independent Component Analysis (ICA). This method, instead of transforming the original hyperspectral images, evaluates the weight matrix to observe how each band contributes to the ICA unmixing procedure. It compares the average absolute weight coefficients of individual spectral bands and selects bands that contain more information. As a significant benefit, the ICA-based band selection retains most physical features of the spectral profiles given only the observations of hyperspectral images. We compare this method with ICA transformation and Principal Component Analysis (PCA) transformation on classification accuracy. The experimental results show that ICA-based band selection is more effective in dimensionality reduction for HSI analysis.

1. Introduction

In the past few years, hyperspectral sensor systems have advanced many remote sensing applications by providing images with a large number of spectral bands. Therefore, we can detect targets and classify materials with potentially higher accuracy. However, high dimensionality of hyperspectral images also substantially increases computational burden. In many cases, it is unnecessary to process all the spectral bands of a hyperspectral image, since most materials have specific characteristics only at certain bands, which makes the remaining spectral bands somewhat redundant. As an important pre-processing step in HSI analysis, dimensionality reduction intends to eliminate these redundant bands and diminish computational burden [12]. Methods of dimensionality reduction can be divided into two categories, *feature extraction* and *band selection*. Feature extraction methods extract features from the original spectral band to construct a lower-dimension feature space, thereby transforming the original data onto the destination feature space through projections like Projection Pursuit (PP) [14], Principal Component Analysis (PCA) [8], wavelet transform[2] and Independent Component Analysis (ICA) [13]. These projections preserve most desired information but change the physical meaning of each spectral band. Compared to feature extraction, band selection methods identify absorption bands which is a subset of the original spectral bands that contains most of the characteristics. This paper will focus on the discussion of band selection methods for dimensionality reduction.

We summarize approaches to band selection as distance measure methods and spectral band ranking methods. The distance measure methods compute either the separability between spectral bands or the signal-to-noise ratio (SNR) losses. Swain and King [18] propose the Jeffreys-Matusita Distance (JM-Distance) separability measure based on divergence and derive two criteria for band selection, the average separability criterion and the saturating transform of divergence. In the spectral space, Keshava [11] quantifies the distance between the spectra of two materials at corresponding spectral bands, and then analyzes the separability of these two spectra using the Spectral Angle Mapper (SAM) metric. The spectral bands are selected in order to maximize the SAM metric, that is, the angle between the two spectra. Stein et al. [17] apply Spectral Matched Filter (SMF) which is the likelihood ratio detection statistics for a known additive signal in a Gaussian background. They then evaluate the SNR losses, and select spectral bands in order to optimize an objective function which is defined in terms

---

[*] This work was supported by a US Army Space and Missile Defense Command grant DASG60-02-1-0005.

of probability of detection.

As the other category of band selection, the spectral band ranking methods always construct and evaluate an objective matrix based on corresponding criteria, where the spectral band-related vectors are ranked and selected. In [4], Chang et al. use eigenanalysis to decompose the hyperspectral data matrix into an eigenform matrix according to two PCA-based criteria [Maximum-Variance PCA (MVPCA) and Maximum-SNR PCA (MSNRPCA)] or classification-based criteria [Minimum-Misclassification Canonical Analysis (MMCA) and Orthogonal-Subspace Projection (OSP)], thereby constructing a loading-factor matrix which prioritizes individual spectral band. All bands are then ranked by their associated priorities. By computing the correlation matrix of different spectral bands, an Adaptive Subspace Decomposition (ASD) method is also presented in [21].

Among band selection methods, ICA is one of the most popular techniques. It is a technique that extracts independent source signals by searching for a linear or nonlinear transformation which minimizes the statistical dependence between components [6]. ICA is first proposed by Pierre Comon in 1994, and has been used in a variety of applications such as BSS [9], recognition [1], etc. In [5] and [13], Chiang et al. and Lennon et al. use ICA as a feature extraction method, in which hyperspectral images are represented in a lower dimensional feature space. The spectral profile of all pixels in the hyperspectral image is treated as the observed signal and used to estimate the unmixing matrix. The hyperspectral image is then transformed onto a lower dimensional space which is constructed by the desired materials (source signals). Since for some hyperspectral images taken over a large area the number of materials existed may be unknown, it is hard to determine the dimensionality of the feature space in this case, thereby raising another challenging problem of intrinsic dimensionality determination [3].

In this paper, we present an ICA-based method for band selection. This method avoids transforming the original hyperspectral images to the feature space that is related to the unknown number of materials. Instead, it compares the average absolute weight coefficients of individual spectral bands and selects the independent bands which contain the maximum information, thereby reducing the dimensionality but retaining most spectral features of hyperspectral images.

The rest of this paper is organized as follows. Section 2 briefly introduces the ICA and FastICA algorithms. Section 3 presents the ICA-based band selection method. Section 4 conducts various experiments to evaluate the performance of ICA-based band selection compared to ICA transformation and PCA transformation. The evaluation is conducted through through classification accuracy comparisons. Section 5 concludes this paper.

2. Independent Component Analysis and the FastICA Algorithm

Suppose m is the number of source signals, n is the number of observed signals, and the observed signals are linear mixtures of the source signals. Then, the observed signal $\mathbf{X} = (\mathbf{x}_1, \cdots, \mathbf{x}_n)^T$ and the source signal $\mathbf{S} = (\mathbf{s}_1, \cdots, \mathbf{s}_m)^T$ are represented in the following ICA unmixing model,

$$\mathbf{S}_{m \times p} = \mathbf{W}_{m \times n} \mathbf{X}_{n \times p} \qquad (1)$$

where $\mathbf{W} = [\mathbf{w}_1, \cdots, \mathbf{w}_m]^T$ is the unmixing matrix, or weight matrix, and $\mathbf{w}_i = [w_{i1}, \cdots, w_{in}], i = 1, \cdots, m$.

In the ICA transformation model, the components $\mathbf{s}_i$ are assumed to be statistically independent and no more than one component is Gaussian distributed. If information on a component $\mathbf{s}_i$ in $\mathbf{S}$ does not give any information on the other components, then $\mathbf{s}_i$ is considered independent of these components. According to the assumption of nongaussianity, the desired independent components $\mathbf{s}_i$ contains the least Gaussian components.

The main work of ICA is to estimate the weight matrix $\mathbf{W}$ and a measure of nongaussianity is the key. The classical measure of nongaussianity is kurtosis, which is the fourth order statistics and has zero value for Gaussian distribution. However, kurtosis is sensitive to outliers. Since a Gaussian variable has the largest entropy among all random variables of equal variance [7], negentropy can be used as a measure of nongaussianity. The negentropy is defined as Eq. 2,

$$J(\mathbf{X}) = H(p_{\mathbf{X}_{gauss}}) - H(p_{\mathbf{X}}) \qquad (2)$$

where $H(p_{\mathbf{X}_{gauss}})$ is the entropy of a Gaussian random variable with the same covariance matrix as $\mathbf{X}$, and $H(p_{\mathbf{X}})$ is the differential entropy. Since the negentropy is difficult to compute, an approximation is used instead [10].

$$J(\mathbf{X}) \approx \{E[G(\mathbf{X})] - E[G(\mathbf{X}_{gauss})]\}^2 \qquad (3)$$

where $G(\mathbf{X})$ is a non-quadratic function.

In order to maximize the objective function shown in Eq. 3, Hyvärunen [9] developed the so-called FastICA algorithm, which is claimed to be the fastest practical ICA method so far. FastICA consists of two processes, the one unit process and the decorrelation process.

The one unit process estimates and normalizes the weight vector $\mathbf{w}_i$ with Eqs. 4 and 5.

$$\mathbf{w}_i^+ = E\{\mathbf{X}g(\mathbf{w}_i^T\mathbf{X})\} - E\{g'(\mathbf{w}_i^T\mathbf{X})\}\mathbf{w}_i, \quad g(.) = \tanh(.) \qquad (4)$$

$$\mathbf{w}_i = \mathbf{w}_i^+ / \|\mathbf{w}_i^+\| \qquad (5)$$

While the one unit process estimates individual weight vectors, the decorrelation process keeps different weight vectors from converging to the same maximal. Given p

decorrelated weight vectors and the $(p+1)^{th}$ weight vector estimated by the one unit process, the $(p+1)^{th}$ weight vector is decorrelated from p weight vectors by Eqs. 6 and 7.

$$\mathbf{w}_{p+1}^{+} = \mathbf{w}_{p+1} - \sum_{i=1}^{p} \mathbf{w}_{p+1}^{T} \mathbf{w}_i \mathbf{w}_i \qquad (6)$$

$$\mathbf{w}_{p+1} = \mathbf{w}_{p+1}^{+} / \|\mathbf{w}_{p+1}^{+}\| \qquad (7)$$

3. ICA-based Band Selection

When ICA is used to reduce dimensionality of hyperspectral images, the number of observed signals n is the original dimensionality. The observed signal $\mathbf{X}$ is the spectral profile of all pixels in the hyperspectral images. The source signal $\mathbf{S}$ resides in a lower dimensional space corresponding to the present materials in the hyperspectral image, and each independent component $\mathbf{s}_i$ is distinctive for one material. Since the number of present materials may be unknown, we avoid transforming the original hyperspectral images to the source signal $\mathbf{S}$ which is related to the number of materials m. Instead, we randomly assume m but evaluate the weight matrix $\mathbf{W}$ to observe how each original band contributes to the ICA transformation described above.

Suppose the number of materials in an n-band hyperspectral image is m, we obtain the corresponding weight matrix $\mathbf{W}_{m \times n}$ using FastICA. In the ICA unmixing procedure, we estimate the source $\mathbf{S}$ (pure materials) from the observation $\mathbf{X}$ (pixels in the hyperspectral image) with the weight matrix $\mathbf{W}$,

$$\begin{bmatrix} s_{11} & . & . & . & s_{1p} \\ . & . & . & . & . \\ . & . & s_{ik} & . & . \\ . & . & . & . & . \\ s_{m1} & . & . & . & s_{mp} \end{bmatrix} = \begin{bmatrix} w_{11} & . & . & . & w_{1n} \\ . & . & . & . & . \\ w_{i1} & . & w_{ij} & . & w_{in} \\ . & . & . & . & . \\ w_{m1} & . & . & . & w_{mn} \end{bmatrix} \begin{bmatrix} x_{11} & . & x_{1k} & . & x_{1p} \\ . & . & . & . & . \\ . & . & x_{jk} & . & . \\ . & . & . & . & . \\ x_{n1} & . & x_{nk} & . & x_{np} \end{bmatrix}$$

where p is the number of pixels in the hyperspectral image.

The kth element s_{ik} of the independent component $\mathbf{s}_i$ is obtained by

$$s_{ik} = \sum_{j=1}^{n} w_{ij} x_{jk}, \quad i = 1 \cdots m \qquad (8)$$

where w_{ij} denotes the weight of the jth band regarding to component $\mathbf{s}_i$. In other words, w_{ij} shows how much information the jth band contains about the ith material. Therefore, we can estimate the importance of each spectral band for all materials by calculating the average absolute weight coefficient $\bar{w}_j$, which is shown in Eq. 9,

$$\bar{w}_j = \frac{1}{m} \sum_{i=1}^{m} |w_{ij}| \qquad (9)$$

where $j = 1 \cdots n$.

By sorting the average absolute weight coefficients for all spectral bands, we obtain a band weight sequence

$$[\bar{w}_1, \cdots, \bar{w}_j, \cdots, \bar{w}_n] \qquad (10)$$

where $\bar{w}_1 \geq \cdots \geq \bar{w}_j \geq \cdots \geq \bar{w}_n$. In this sequence, the bands with higher average absolute weight coefficients contribute more to the ICA transformation than other bands do. That means these bands contain more spectral information than other bands. Therefore, we pick the spectral bands with the highest average absolute weight coefficients for the purpose of band selection. Because typical hyperspectral analysis methods treat each spectral band as an independent variable, we call these selected bands independent bands. The set of selected independent bands is a subset of the original set of spectral bands and characterizes most features of the original spectral profile without changing its physical property. From the selected bands, we generate a new spectral image with lower dimension, therefore achieve the purpose of dimensionality reduction.

4. Experiments

The proposed ICA-based band selection is applied to reduce the dimension of a multispectral image set collected at North Carolina State University [15]. The multispectral sensor system consists of a custom-made Pulnix digital color camera and an infrared camera sensitive in the 3~5μm range combined with filters obtained from ThermoOriel, as shown in Fig. 1. This system provides us multispectral im-

Figure 1. IR camera with filters [15].

ages of 6 bands: red, green, blue, and three infrared bands of 3~3.2μm, 3.2~4.2μm and 4.2~5μm [15].

The image acquisition system tries to emulate a "smart" missile equipped with a multispectral camera closing in on a target. We obtained a multispectral image set consisting of 41 images in a close-in sequence, which is collected by taking a sequence of multispectral images as the camera is moving closer to the targets [16]. Three scenes imaged in a close-in sequence are shown in Fig. 2. These scenes are

(a) Far distance image.

(b) Middle distance image.

(c) Close distance image.

Figure 2. The scenes of some multispectral images in the close-in sequence.

composed of 10 materials, listed in Table 1.

We conducted two experiments. The first experiment tries to show the effectiveness of the data set. In this experiment, we divide images in the close-in sequence into three subsets, far distance, middle distance and close distance images. We choose object 2 as the "target", and further classify different parts of the target into 4 subcategories, cabin, payload, frame and tire. We then apply the k-Nearest-Neighbor (kNN) algorithm on each subset using the leave-one-out method. In this experiment we use all the 6 original spectral bands. Three example label images from each subset derived from kNN are shown in Fig. 3, where the white color denotes non-target pixels and the gray scales denote different components of the target.

The second experiment tries to evaluate the efficiency of the proposed ICA-based band selection. During the band selection procedure, how many bands is enough to represent the original spectral profile depends on different data sets and raises another discussion. In this paper, we assume 4 independent bands, instead of the original 6 bands, are enough to represent the information. We first apply the proposed ICA-based band selection on the original 6-band multispectral image set. Figure 4(a) shows the importance of

Category	Material	Note
1	box	
2	grass	
3	brick	
4	tree	
5	sky	
6	window	
7	metal	
8	object 1	warm water in steel vessel, left on grass
9	object 2	toy truck, middle on grass
10	object 3	cold water in steel vessel, right on grass

Table 1. Categories in NCSU multispectral images.

the 6 original spectral bands in descending order based on the band weight sequence (Eq. 10). We pick the four most important bands which are red, IR3 ($4.2 \sim 5\mu$m), blue, IR2 ($3.2 \sim 4.2\mu$m), from left to right. Figure 4(b) demonstrates the reflectance spectra of the selected independent bands on four different materials, brick, grass, sky and window. We can see that the selected bands contain most of the more dramatic maxima and minima in the reflectance spectra, thus retaining spectral information such as the absorption bands and spectra shapes.

To evaluate the band reduced data set obtained by ICA-based band selection, we apply both kNN classifier using the leave-one-out method and discriminant function to both the original multispectral data set with 6 spectral bands and the ICA-based band selection data set with 4 independent bands. In addition, we estimate 4 independent components by the ICA unmixing model, then generate the ICA transformed data set. We also extract 4 principal components from the eigenvectors corresponding to the maximum eigenvalues in the covariance matrix of the original 6-band data set, thus setting up the PCA transformed data set. The two classifiers mentioned above are then applied to the ICA transformed data set with 4 independent components and the PCA transformed data set with 4 principal components as well.

In this experiment, we try to classify the materials into the 10 categories listed in Table 1. Figure 5 compares the overall classification accuracy between kNN and discriminant function classifications using these four data sets. The detailed classification accuracy comparisons of each category are illustrated in Fig. 6. Observing both figures, we find that the difference between the classification results using the original 6-band data set and the 4-independent band data set is much less than those of the original 6-band data set and the ICA transformed data set, or the PCA trans-

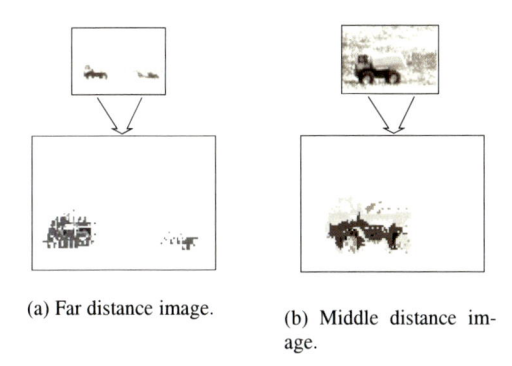

(a) Far distance image.

(b) Middle distance image.

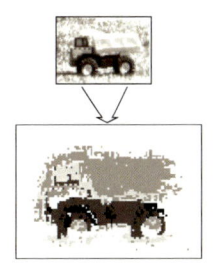

(c) Close distance image.

Figure 3. The label images from kNN classification.

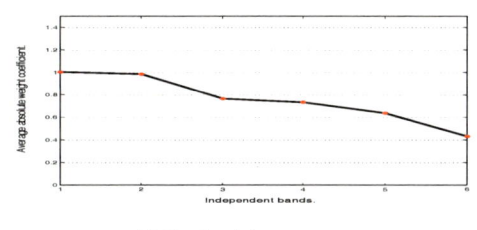

(a) Band weight sequence.

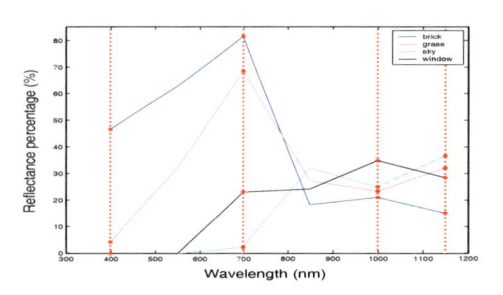

(b) Four independent bands in reflectance spectrum.

Figure 4. ICA-based band selection for the multispectral image.

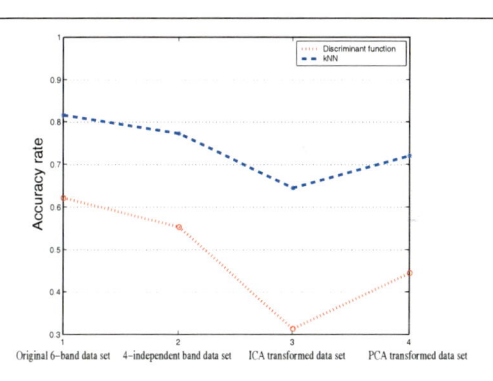

formed data set. In other words, the 4-independent band data set reserves more information than the ICA or PCA transformed data sets.

5. Conclusion

This paper presents an ICA-based band selection method for hyperspectral image analysis which is different from the commonly used ICA methods in dimensionality reduction. First, this method evaluates the weight matrix **W** to observe the importance of each original band. Second, it avoids transforming the original hyperspectral image to the source signal **S** which is related to the unknown number of materials m. Third, the selected independent bands contain the maximum information of the original hyperspectral images. The experimental results show that the ICA-based band selection is more effective than the ICA and the PCA transformations in dimensionality reduction for HSI analysis.

References

[1] M. S. Bartlett and T. J. Sejnowski. *Viewpoint invariant face recognition using independent component analysis and attractor networks*, chapter Neural Information Processing

Figure 5. Overall classification accuracy comparison.

Systems-Natural and Synthetic 9, pages 817–823. MIT Press, Cambridge, MA, 1997.

[2] L. Bruce, C. Koger, and J. Li. Dimensionality reduction of hyperspectral data using discrete wavelet transform feature extraction. *IEEE Transactions on Geoscience and Remote Sensing*, 40(10):2331–2338, October 2002.

[3] C.-I. Chang and Q. Du. A noise subspace projection approach to determination of intrinsic dimensionality for hyperspectral imagery. In *EOS/SPIE Symosium on Remote Sensing, Conference on Image and Signal Processing for Remote Sensing V.*, volume 3871, pages 34–44, Florence, Italy,

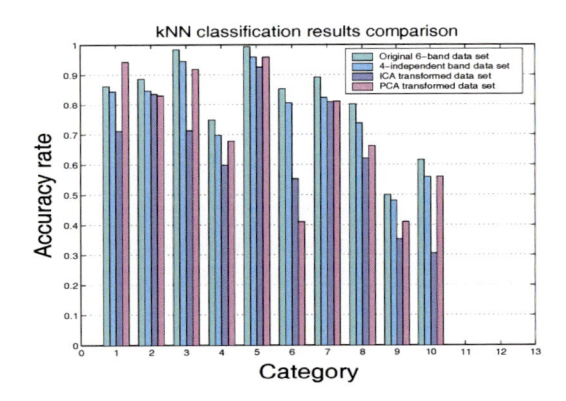

(a) kNN classification results comparison.

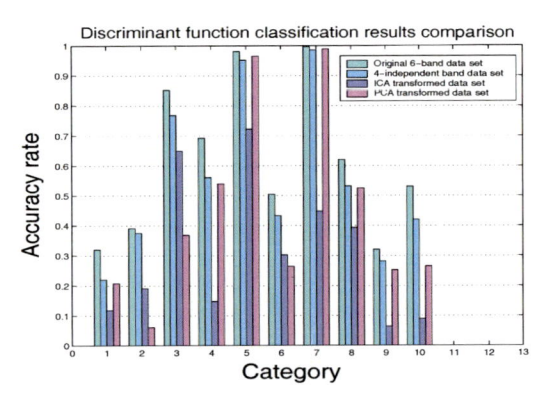

(b) Discriminant function classification results comparison.

Figure 6. Classification results comparison for four data sets: original 6-band data set, 4-independent band data set, ICA transformed data set and PCA transformed data set.

Sep 20-24 1999.

[4] C.-I. Chang, Q. Du, T.-L. Sun, and M. Althouse. A joint band prioritization and band-decorrelation approach to band selection for hyperspectral image classification. *IEEE Transactions on Geoscience and Remote Sensing*, 37(6):2631–2641, November 1999.

[5] S. Chiang, C. Chang, and I. W. Ginsberg. Unsupervised hyperspectral image analysis using independent component analysis. In *Geoscience and Remote Sensing Symposium, Proc. IGARSS 2000*, volume 4, pages 3136 – 3138, Honolulu, HI, USA, 24-28 July 2000. IEEE.

[6] P. Common. Independent component analysis, a new concept? *Signal Processing*, 36(3):287–314, April 1994. Special Issue on High-order Statistics.

[7] T. M. Cover and J. A. Thmoas. *Element of Information Theory*. John Wiley & Sons, 1991.

[8] T. El-ghazawi, S. Kaewpijit, and J. Le Moigne. Parallel and adaptive reduction of hyperspectral data to intrinsic dimensionality. In *Proceeding, 3rd IEEE International Conference on Cluster Computing CLUSTER'01*, pages 102–109, Newport Beach, CA, Oct 8-11 2001.

[9] A. Hyvärinen and E. Oja. A fast fixed-point algorithm for independent component analysis. *Neural Computation*, 9:1483–1492, 1997.

[10] A. Hyvärunen and E. Oja. Independent component analysis: Algorithms and applications. *Neural Networks*, 13(4-5):411–430, 2000.

[11] N. Keshava. Best bands selection for detection in hyperspectral processing. In *Proc. IEEE Int. Conf. on Acoustics, Speech, and Signal Processing*, volume 5, pages 3149–3152, 2001.

[12] D. Landgrebe. Hyperspectral image data analysis as a high dimensional signal processing problem. *Special Issue of the IEEE Signal Processing Magazine*, 19(1):17–28, January 2002.

[13] M. Lennon, G. Mercier, M. C. Mouchot, and L. Hubert-Moy. Independent component analysis as a tool for the dimensionality reduction and the representation of hyperspectral images. In *SPIE Remote Sensing*, volume 4541, pages 2893–2895, Toulouse, France, Sept 19-21 2001.

[14] J. Luis and D. Landgrebe. Supervised classification in high dimensional space: Geometrical, statistical, and asymptotical properties of multivariate data. *IEEE Trans. on System, Man, and Cybernetics*, 28, Part C(1):39–54, February 1998.

[15] H. Qi and W. E. Snyder. Quarterly report: Smart automated target recognition using weighted spectral and geometric information. Other research members: Rajeev Ramanath, Cheolha Pedro Lee and Hongtao Du, July 2002.

[16] H. Qi and W. E. Snyder. Quarterly report: Smart automated target recognition using weighted spectral and geometric information. Other research members: Rajeev Ramanath, Cheolha Pedro Lee and Hongtao Du, December 2002.

[17] D. Stein, S. Stewart, G. Gilbert, and J. Schoonmaker. Band selection for viewing underwater objects using hyperspectral sensors. In *SPIE Conference on Airborne and In-Water Underwater Imaging*, volume 3761, pages 50–61, Denver, Colorado, July 1999.

[18] P. Swain and R. King. Two effective feature selection criteria for multispectral remote sensing. In *International Joint Conference On Pattern Recognition*, Washington, DC, November 1973. LARS Technical Note 042673.

[19] Y. Tan and J. Wang. Nonlinear blind source separation using higher order statistics and a genetic algorithm. *IEEE Transactions on Evolutionary Computation*, 5(6):600–612, 2001.

[20] M. Velez-Reyes, L. O. Jimenez, D. M. Linares, and H. T. Velazquez. Comparison of matrix factorization algorithms for band selection in hyperspectral imagery. In *SPIE 14th Annual Int. Symp. on Aerospace/Defense Sensing, Simulation and Controls*, volume 4049(2000), pages 288–297, Orlando, Florida, April 2000.

[21] Y. Zhang, M. Desai, J. Zhang, and M. Jin. Adaptive subspace decomposition for hyperspectral data dimensionality reduction. In *Proceedings, International Conference on Image Processing (ICIP 99)*, volume 2, pages 326–329, Oct 24-28 1999.

Quantitative Fusion of Performance Results from Actual and Simulated Image Data

Dr. Pamela L. Blake
Terry W. Brown
The Boeing Company
pamela.l.blake@boeing.com
terry.w.brown@boeing.com

Abstract Simulated imagery is a useful adjunct to actual imagery collected from a sensor platform. Simulation allows control of multiple parameters and combinations of parameters that might otherwise be difficult to capture in an actual measurement, leading to a fuller understanding of processes and phenomenology under consideration. However, the complexity that exists in actual, measured imagery can be difficult to capture in simulation. Such complexity, coupled with the other natural ambiguities of measured data, makes it difficult to compare results achieved from algorithms applied to simulated imagery with algorithmic results achieved with actual data. We demonstrate the use of Sequential Quantitative Performance Assessment (SQPA) as a means of fusing results from simulated and actual imagery.

1. Introduction

There is an ongoing need for tools to quantitatively assess the results obtained from analysis of spectral imagery. We present in this paper an approach for leveraging spectral and spatial simulations to bound the results obtained for AVIRIS data. The objective of the AVIRIS analysis is to identify pixels in a largely urban scene showing evidence of vegetation stress. The Sequential Quantitative Performance Assessment (SQPA) methodology we describe here is based on the set of tools typically known as "Design of Experiment (DOE)" tools (e.g. see Box et al., 1978 or Wu and Hamada, 2000). The basic SQPA approach is given in Figure 1.

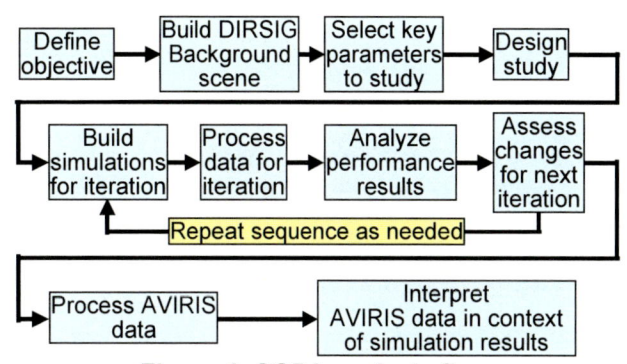

Figure 1. SQPA analysis flow

2. Data

The data for this study consist of an AVIRIS scene acquired for Rochester, NY and a DIRSIG-generated scene simulation for a portion of the same area (for DIRSIG see Schott et al. 1992). The Rochester Institute of Technology (RIT) provided these data to us as an element of Boeing's participation with RIT's laboratory for Advanced Spectral Studies (LASS). Figures 2 and 3 show true-color composites of these data.

Figure 2. True-color composite of portion of AVIRIS scene used for study

Figure 3. True-color composite of DIRSIG-generated scene

3. Study Design

For purposes of this study, we chose to investigate the effects of three key parameters on the ability of the Spectral Angle Mapper (SAM) algorithm, as implemented in ENVI® (ENVI® is a registered trademark of Research Systems, Inc). The three parameters and the factorial design structure are given in Figure 4.

Treatment #	B	V	T	Result
1	—	—	—	y1
2	+	—	—	y2
3	—	+	—	y3
4	+	+	—	y4
5	—	—	+	y5
6	+	—	+	y6
7	—	+	+	y7
8	+	+	+	y8

Figure 4. Variables and design structure for 2^3 factorial design (B = # of bands; V = visibility in km; T = SAM threshold in degrees; result is false alarm rate)

4. Analysis

Figure 5 shows the values for each of the parameters used and the resulting false alarm rates (FAR) for the first iteration of the sequential analysis. Each "treatment" consisted of a DIRSIG-simulated scene prepared with the MODTRAN (Berk et al., 1989) mid-latitude summer model and the visibility as shown in Figure 5. SAM was applied with the thresholds as given in the figure and the resultant pixel alarms were compared to the known locations for stressed vegetation in the scene to arrive at the FAR determination.

Treatment #	B	V	T	Result
1	3	0.5	5	16.3%
2	128	0.5	5	0.0%
3	3	23	5	15.7%
4	128	23	5	6.2%
5	3	0.5	20	94.3%
6	128	0.5	20	71.0%
7	3	23	20	79.7%
8	128	23	20	47.2%

Figure 5. Parameter values and results for Iteration 1

Figure 6 shows the computed interactions amongst the three parameters for Iteration 1. As can be seen from the table, the three variables each have a strong influence on the performance of the SAM algorithm, and the threshold parameter also strongly interacts with the other two parameters in affecting SAM performance. Based on these results and in order to optimize algorithm performance for the AVIRIS scene with unknown conditions, we perform a second iteration with the conditions and results given in Figure 7.

Effects	FAR
Main Effects	
Bands B	-20.4%
Visibility V	-8.1%
Threshold T	63.5%
Two-factor Interactions	
B x V	-0.6%
B x T	-7.5%
V x T	-11.0%
Three-factor Interaction	
B x V x T	-4.0%

Figure 6. Computed effects of experiment parameters on SAM performance, Iteration 1

Treatment #	B	V	T	Result
1	12	10	5	1.5%
2	128	10	5	0.8%
3	12	23	5	6.3%
4	128	23	5	6.2%
5	12	10	10	10.8%
6	128	10	10	7.4%
7	12	23	10	14.5%
8	128	23	10	14.4%

Figure 7. Parameter values and results for Iteration 2

Figure 8 shows the computed interactions amongst the three parameters for Iteration 2. As can be seen by these results, tightening the acceptable range of the SAM threshold, and the atmospheric visibility reduces the effect each of these parameters has on SAM performance and dramatically reduces the interaction effects amongst the parameters. There is also little improvement in performance in using 128 bands instead of 12 bands. Based on the results of these two iterations, we conclude that we can have confidence in the AVIRIS analysis using either 12 or 128 of the total available bands, and using a SAM threshold of 5 degrees.

Effects	FAR
Main Effects	
Bands B	-1.1%
Visibility V	4.0%
Threshold T	8.1%
Two-factor Interactions	
B x V	1.0%
B x T	-0.6%
V x T	0.1%
Three-factor Interaction	
B x V x T	0.7%

Figure 8. Computed effects of experiment parameters on SAM performance, Iteration 2

Applying SAM to the AVIRIS data at a threshold of 5 degrees results in an alarmed image with 205 identified pixels exhibiting vegetation stress. This detection image is shown in Figure 9, with the input image for comparison. A zoomed portion of these images is shown in Figure 10.

Figure 9. (Right) Results of AVIRIS analysis using the bounding constraints derived from the sequential simulation analysis. (Left) 3-color composite for comparison. Areas that appear somewhat yellow in the composite image exhibit the stressed vegetation signature.

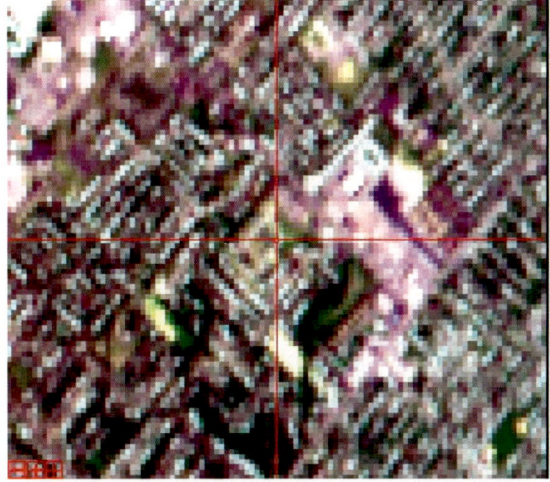

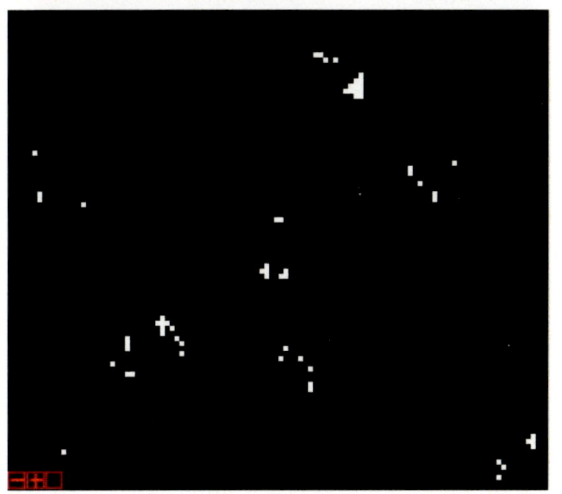

Figure 10. Expanded area from scene showing details of alarmed pixels

5. Summary

The SQPA technique demonstrated here facilitates the partitioning and interpretation of error and variance sources and parameter sensitivities using detailed and controlled image simulations. The results of analysis under the controlled conditions can then be used to optimize the analysis of remotely acquired spectral imagery.

6. Acknowledgements

We thank Dr. John Schott, Dr. Harvey Rhody, and Mr. Michael Richardson of RIT, for their support in providing us the DIRSIG application, the "MegaScene," and the AVIRIS data for use in this analysis. We also thank our

Boeing teammates, Mr. Jack Yin, Ms. Corissa Hines, Ms. Marjorie Green, and Mr. Steven Sedlack for assisting us in processing the data.

7. References

Berk, A., L.S. Bernstein, and D.C. Robertson (1989). "MODTRAN: a Moderate Resolution Model for LOWTRAN 7," GL-TR-89-0122, Spectral Sciences.

Box, George E. P., W. G. Hunter, and J.S. Hunter (1978), **Statistics for Experimenters, An Introduction to Design, Data Analysis, and Model Building**, New York: John Wiley and Sons.

Schott, J.R., R. Raqueno, and C. Salvaggio (1992), "Incorporation of time-dependent thermodynamic model and a radiation propagation model into infrared three-dimensional synthetic image generation," **Optical Engineering**, vol. 31, no. 7, pp. 1505-1516.

Wu, C.F. Jeff and M. Hamada (2000), **Experiments: Planning, Analysis, and Parameter Design Optimization**, Wiley Interscience.

Automated Multisensor Image Registration

Karl C. Walli
USAF
kawalli@netzero.net

Abstract

This paper develops a technique for the registration of multisensor images utilizing the Laplacian of Gaussian (LoG) filter to automatically determine semi-invariant ground control points (GCPs). These points are then related through the development of point matching techniques and statistical analysis. Through the use of matrix transformations, efficient management of multiple affine operations can be obtained and stored in a composite transform. Wavelet theory is used to enable the multi-resolution analysis critical for multisensor image registration and predictive transformations.

Multiple methods will be discussed to test the accuracy of the resulting image registration. Benefits of this technique against parallax and moving objects within the scene will also be highlighted. Finally, an example of 'wavelet sharpening' will be demonstrated that preserves radiometric integrity.

1. Introduction

With the current diversity of both airborne and satellite sensors and the copious amount of images that are being produced, it is becoming more urgent than ever before to develop techniques for automated multisensor image registration.

Because the registration process can be very slow and tedious when done manually, it is the attempt of this research to add additional automation techniques to the registration process through the use of spatial frequency analysis, edge filtering, point matching, and statistical analysis.

The proposed registration technique utilizes comparison of semi-invariant features (edge detail) within a scene to relate images/spectral bands. With the increasing processing speeds of today's computers and the continuing sophistication of edge detection/filtering techniques, point matching, and statistical analysis, it is possible to fully automate this once tedious task.

2. Isolating Semi-Invariant GCPs

The LoG is a combination filter with good edge detection and noise mitigation qualities. By utilizing the LoG digital filter on an image, it is possible to accent and threshold edge features for isolation (figure 1).

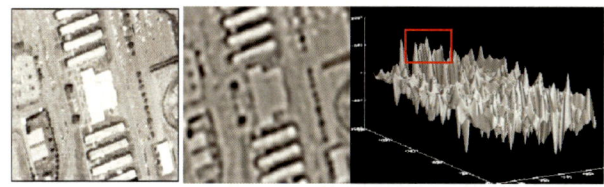

Figure 1. An image that has be filtered with the LoG.

Since the LoG filter approximates a second derivative function, the edges in the image will become zero crossings and the resulting peaks and valleys can be extracted by shaving off the top and bottom portions (5%, 10%, etc). These extracted regions can then be utilized to determine GCPs through 'connected components' analysis and isolation of the pixel in each region that represent a minima or maxima (Figure 2).

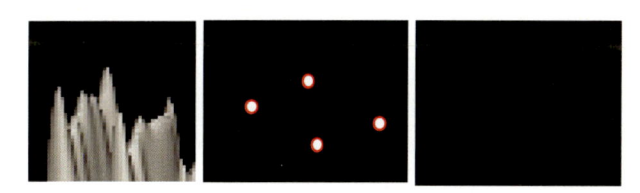

Figure 2. Threshold peaks, isolate regions and GCPs.

It should be noted that the lower the threshold is set for point extraction, more regions and hence more points can be obtained for point matching. By adaptively thresholding two related images independently until the same number of points have been extracted, it is possible to obtain similar point-sets for matching. This assumes that the two images have similar spatial features across a significant portion of the image. Now that the images have been reduced to representative point-sets, the true job of relating the images can begin with point matching techniques.

3. Point Matching

Now that the point-sets, representing the semi-invariant features, have been extracted, the challenge of matching related points begins. The point-sets are fed through a battery of tests in an attempt to related similar points. The first, and most critical test, is a comparison of relative distances between each point and every other point in a set. This is done because the relative distance between semi-invariant features should remain constant if the images are at the same scale. Additional aspects of scale will be covered in Section 6.

A useful technique to accomplish this relative distance comparison was implemented by Chandrasekhar (1999) in his research on the registration of infrared starfield images. This technique involves the creation of two arrays, $n \times n$ and $m \times m$, which represent the distances comparisons of n GCPs, in the reference image, and m GCPs in the warp image (figure 3).

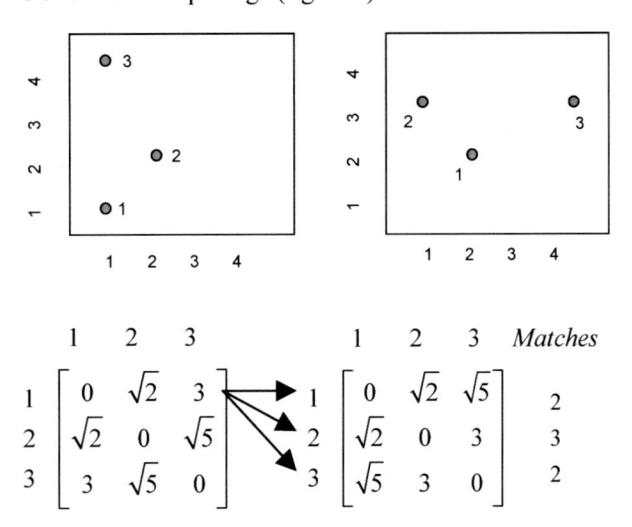

Figure 3. Distance Matrix Comparison to relate GCPs.

For this example case, Image1-GCP1 is related to Image2-GCP2, since these two rows have the most distance matches. In real images, distances between similar features may vary slightly. So, a match between like GCPs should be allowed within some error (~ +/- 2 pix) to increase the robustness of this technique. The resulting matched points provide an initial list of related GCPs. This list is then further refined, utilizing additional tests, to remove bad-matches and gain confidence in the relationship between images.

Utilizing the technique above, scale can also be automatically computed since the ratio of distances between features at different resolutions does not change even though the distance between features does. Also, a similar comparison can be accomplished for comparing relative angles between matching GCPs. The primary difference here is that angle comparison requires a 3-D matrix comparison (vs. the 2-D matrix comparison used above), since three points are required to define an angle.

An additional technique that can be used to identify bad-matches is a comparison of the magnitudes of the LoG filtered images at the location of the matched GCPs. If this comparison deviates by more than a predetermined value (~ +/- 15%) the match can be rejected.

Finally, various statistical analysis tools can be utilized to further prune away the bad matches and to increase the accuracy of the final registration. One such tool, that proves useful for images without rotational variation, involves comparing the mean distance between matched points. If this distance deviates by more than one standard deviation (1STD), it can be deleted

Global statistical analysis involves the computation of the RMS Distance Error (RMSDE) associated with each individual matching pair when compared to the transform model of the entire set of matching points. If the matched pair deviates from the model by more than 1STD it can probably be removed. It is also possible to us RMSDE analysis to increase the accuracy of the registration by removing the matches with greatest error, even if those matches are not anomalous. This can be done by placing a constraint on the maximum allowable error on the transform model (~ 1 pix). In this way the matched GCPs with greatest error are iteratively removed and the RMSDE for the points and model recomputed until the average error is less than the threshold.

By running the matched GCPs through this battery of tests it is reasonable to assume that the anomalous matches have been removed. Now it is possible to use the resulting set of matched points to determine a polynomial transform to relate the images.

4. Using GCPs to Determine a Transform

Once a valid set of matched GCPs have been obtained, it is possible to utilize these points to develop a transform to warp the working image into the spatial domain of the reference image. This polynomial expression is covered in several pieces of literature (Schott 1997, Schowengerdt 1997) and takes the following form.

$$x_{warp} = \sum_{i=0}^{N} \sum_{j=0}^{N-1} a_{ij} x_{ref}^{j} y_{ref}^{i} + \varepsilon_x$$

$$y_{warp} = \sum_{i=0}^{N} \sum_{j=0}^{N-1} b_{ij} x_{ref}^{j} y_{ref}^{i} + \varepsilon_y$$

This paper will utilize a subset of the general polynomial expressions, commonly referred to as affine transforms. The affine coefficients are the linear relationships that allow for shift, scale, rotation and skew between two images of interest.

$$x_{warp} = a_0 + a_1x + a_2y$$
$$y_{warp} = b_0 + b_1y + b_2x$$

The focus on affine transforms for this research is twofold. First, the automated techniques that were developed for point matching are limited to shift, scale and rotation. Secondly, affines have a useful commutative property, which allows them to be combined into composite transforms through matrix multiplication. This property is instrumental to the concept of predictive transforms, which will be addressed in Section 6.

A simple way to solve for affine coefficients is to use a 3 x 3 matrix form of the psuedo-inverse solution to the least squares problem (Wolberg 1990).

$$\begin{bmatrix} x'_1 & y'_1 & 1 \\ x'_2 & y'_2 & 1 \\ x'_3 & y'_3 & 1 \\ \vdots & \vdots & \vdots \\ x'_N & y'_N & 1 \end{bmatrix} = \begin{bmatrix} x_1 & y_1 & 1 \\ x_2 & y_2 & 1 \\ x_3 & y_3 & 1 \\ \vdots & \vdots & \vdots \\ x_N & y_N & 1 \end{bmatrix} \begin{bmatrix} a_2 & b_2 & 0 \\ a_1 & b_1 & 0 \\ a_0 & b_0 & 1 \end{bmatrix}$$

$$U = WA$$

$$A = U^{-1}W$$

$$A = (U^TU)^{-1}U^TW$$

Once the affine coefficients have been solved, it is simply a matter of utilizing the sampling method of choice (i.e. Nearest Neighbor, Bilinear, Bicubic), to transform the working image into the reference image space.

5. Judging Registration Accuracy

Although both qualitative and quantitative methods for judging registration accuracy can be utilized; automation routines must rely heavily on analytical methods. Two methods have been implemented here, the first analyzes global GCP statistics and the second compares pixel intensity values.

The first method assumes that the matched GCPs represent similar features within the two images and that the points can be used to determine a transform model from one image to the other. Once a mathematical model has been developed to describe that relationship, each individual matched point-set can be compared to the model to determine how much error exists between what the model predicts and what was obtained through the point extraction and matching process. This is accomplished for each GCP, in order to determine the RMSDE for itself and the average RMSDE for all of the matched GCPs. Note that this metric only measures how well the overall model agrees with each matched GCP and depends heavily on having over-constrained least-squares problems. But, if the semi-invariant features that have been extracted relate to each other mathematically with high precision, it is normally indicative of an accurate registration. In this way it is possible to register two images to sub-pixel accuracy if the image-wide average RMSDE is less than one pixel (reference RMSDE Plot and GCP Error Image - figure 6).

The second quantitative metric assumes that if two images are well registered, their overlapping area should have similar intensity, or grayscale, values. This would especially hold true if they have been 'histogram matched' for comparison. The absolute mean variance (AMV) between the grayscale of the two overlapping areas should minimize when the images are well registered.

Although qualitative methods are limited in there utility for automation, it is noteworthy to mention that both the AMV 'difference image' and a flicker test can highlight very small discrepancies to the human eye! The flicker test is accomplished by overlaying the reference image with the warped image repeatedly at a fairly high refresh rate (~ 5hz).

6. Multiresolution Registration

Once the scale variation between the two images has been determined through automated techniques or apriori knowledge, it is possible to resample a high-resolution (Hi-Res) image to the same scale as a low-resolution (Lo-Res) image for automatic LoG registration. By retaining the original scale modifier, it is then possible to predict the transform necessary to warp the original Hi-Res image. Once this is accomplished, the low-resolution image can be resampled to a comparable scale for fusion and analysis (figure 4).

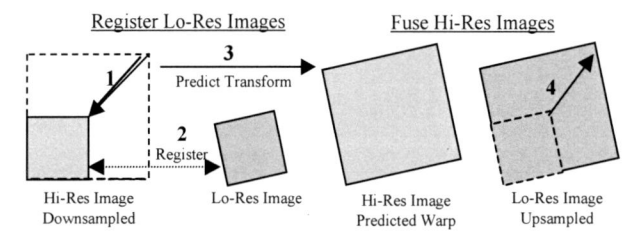

Figure 4. Register at same scale to predict transform.

The predictive transform is computed using matrix multiplication using the commutative property of the affines. Because of this, the registration at Lo-Res must be accomplished with an affine transform. The computation for both composite (M_{comp}) and predictive affine transforms is shown below, for a scale modifier of 2x (which represents a Hi-Res image at twice the scale of the Lo-Res image):

$$M_{comp} = \begin{bmatrix} a_2 & b_2 & 0 \\ a_1 & b_1 & 0 \\ a_0 & b_0 & 1 \end{bmatrix} \begin{bmatrix} 1 & 0 & 0 \\ 0 & 1 & 0 \\ 0 & 0 & 2 \end{bmatrix}$$

For data sets like LANDSAT, having panchromatic Multispectral (MS), and thermal image bands with integer scale relationships, this technique can be utilized to great advantage. It is simply a matter of registering the band of most similarity to a reference image. The resulting affine transform can then be used to relate all the bands of data to the reference image, with only a slight modification for scale. As can be imagined, this technique is very useful for fusion applications, since only one transform is required to relate all the data.

7. Wavelet Sharpening

Utilizing wavelet theory for multiresolution processing and analysis offers several advantages for multisensor image registration. Foremost, its spatial frequency structure allows for image scale analysis at several levels. So, even if the image resolutions are inherently different, they can still be related. Choosing the Fast Wavelet Transform (FWT), to execute wavelet decimation of an image, enables quick and efficient image processing. But, it requires that spatial frequency subbands be stripped off of the image dyadically. The following image is portrayed as a multiresolution pyramid (Mallat 1990), it separates the detail planes into the horizontal, vertical, and diagonal components after each FWT decimation.

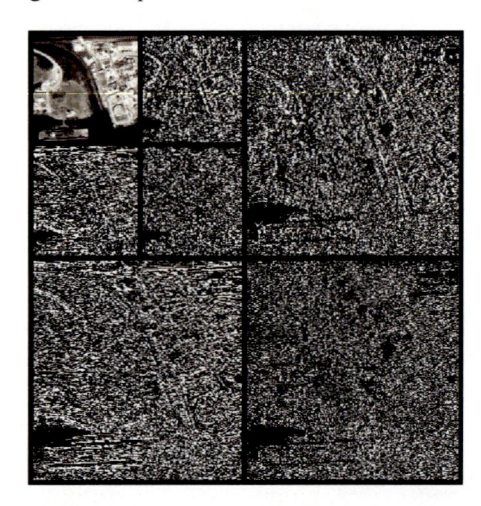

Figure 5. Image Decomposition using the FWT.

Now that the Hi-Res image has been decimated twice, the reduced scale subband (LL2) can be automatically registered with the Lo-Res image, which is now at the same scale. Also, since wavelet decimation retains the high spatial frequency subbands, it is possible to transfer this information to the Lo-Res image.

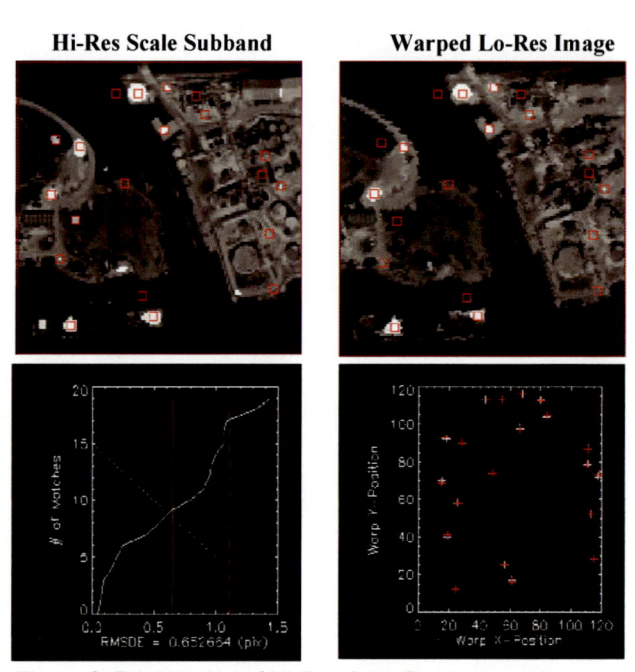

Figure 6. Registration of Hi-Res & Lo-Res Image w/metrics

Once the Lo-Res image has been warped into the same image space as the LL2 subband, the Lo-Res image can be swapped for the LL2 subband in the FWT multiresolution pyramid. Now the FWT^{-1} can be applied to fuse the high spatial frequency subband information into the Lo-Res image at dyadic levels (figure 8).

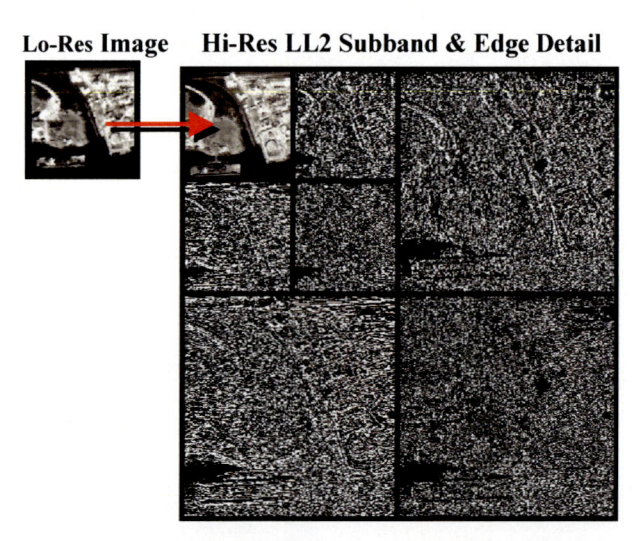

Figure 7. Swapping of Hi-Res Subband w/Lo-Res Image.

If the data are taken nearly at the same time, some cross-sensor resolution enhancement techniques are able to produce a merged image as close as possible to what would be a high spatial resolution hyperspectral image...Multiresolution Wavelet Decomposition is the most interesting tool to perform this process (Peytavin 1996). This technique has been shown, on average, to produce radiometrically accurate "sharpening" of Lo-Res spectral data (Walli 2003).

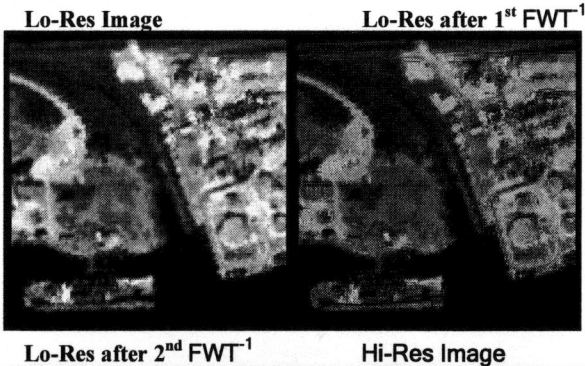

Figure 8. Sharpening of the Lo-Res Image w/FWT^{-1}.

8. Conclusion

By utilizing the LoG filter to extract semi-invariant GCPs, combined with robust point matching techniques, it is possible to automatically register multisensor images. Once the images have been spatially related through registration, it is also possible to 'sharpen' the resolution of the Lo-Res image.

This is accomplished by processing a Hi-Res image, of the same area, using wavelet decimation and transferring the edge detail to the Lo-Res image. This technique can be utilized for radiometrically accurate fusion and sharpening of Lo-Res spectral datasets with Hi-Res panchromatic images.

Benefits to using this automated registration process include robust performance in the presence of noise (due to the LoG filter), parallax, and moving objects. The reliance on relative distance comparison, as the initial point matching criteria, guarantees that any moving objects from one image to the next will automatically be rejected from consideration as an invariant feature. The same rationale is utilized for rejection of features with parallax. Parallax can also be mitigated through use of global statistics as long as the terrain relief is localized within the image.

Finally, as with any automated technique, the processing speed is critical. The initial computer code was generated in IDL with ease of use (GUI interfaces) and flexibility as critical goals. However, code optimized for specific processes and minimal interaction, have resulted in 512x512 images (or image chips) being processed in as little as 20 seconds. This processing was accomplished on a high-end desktop with 50 initial GCPs in each image.

References

Chandrasekhar, A. (1999). "Point Extraction and Matching for Registration of Infrared Astronomical Images," Masters Thesis, Rochester Institute of Technology.

Mallat, S. E. (1989). "A Theory for Multiresolution Signal Decompositon: The Wavelet Representation." IEEE Transactions on Pattern Analysis and Machine Intelligence **11**(7): 674-693.

Peytavin, L. (1996). "Cross-Sensor Resolution Enhancement of Hyperspectral Images using Wavelet Decomposition." SPIE Algorithms for MS & HS Imagery II(2758): 193-203.

Schott, J. R. (1997). Remote sensing : the image chain approach. New York, Oxford University Press.

Schowengerdt, R. A. (1997). Remote sensing, models, and methods for image processing. San Diego, Academic Press.

Walli, K. C. (2003), "Multisensor Image Registration Utilizing the LoG Filter and FWT," Masters Thesis, Rochester Institute of Technology.

Wolberg, G. (1990). Digital Image Warping. California, IEEE Computer Society Press.

Historical Research

⌘⌘⌘⌘⌘⌘⌘⌘

Multispectral Imaging of the Archimedes Palimpsest

Roger L. Easton, Jr.
Chester F. Carlson Center for Imaging Science
Rochester Institute of Technology, Rochester, NY
rlepci@rit.edu

Keith T. Knox
Boeing LTS, Kihei, HI
keithknox@compuserve.com

William A. Christens-Barry
Equipoise Imaging, LLC and Johns Hopkins University
Baltimore, MD
equipoise@rcn.com

Abstract:

Multispectral imaging techniques are being applied to improve the readability of the text in a tenth-century manuscript that includes seven treatises of Archimedes. The manuscript was erased and overwritten about 200 years later with the text of a Christian prayer book. This talk reports on the results of the multispectral imaging techniques used on the Archimedes palimpsest.

1. Introduction

The Archimedes Palimpsest is a thousand-year-old manuscript written on parchment that includes the oldest known copies of parts of seven treatises of Archimedes. Two of these are extraordinarily important in the history of mathematics [1]: the oldest copy of *On Floating Bodies* in the original Greek and the only known text of the *Method of Mechanical Theorems*, where Archimedes describes the mechanical analogues he used to perform his calculations [2]. A scribe in Constantinople copied it from an unknown source in the tenth century. Approximately two hundred years after the original transcription, during the time of the Crusades, the book was sacrificed to use the parchment for copies of Christian texts. The manuscript was disbound and erased by washing off the original ink. Each page was cut in half along the original binding, rotated 90°, and overwritten with the text of a Christian prayer book, the *Euchologion*. The prayer book was used in Christian services for hundreds of years at the Greek Orthodox monastery at Mar Saba in the Judean desert. It was later returned to Constantinople, probably early in the 1800s, and the text of Archimedes was first recognized by a Western scholar when the Danish philologist Johan Ludvig Heiberg visited the library in 1906. Heiberg published his readings of the manuscript, obtained probably with no more assistance than a magnifying glass. He also photographed some of the pages.

The manuscript was damaged significantly over the years, but most particularly (and sadly) during the 20th century. Since Heiberg's examination, many pages of the manuscript have been consumed by mold. In addition, forged paintings of the four Gospels now obscure four pages of text. These were painted during or after the 1920s in an apparent misguided attempt to increase the value of the book.

The manuscript had disappeared from scholarly view during World War I and did not resurface until the 1990s, when it was auctioned by Christie's in New York. This provided the first exposure of the manuscript to two of the authors (RLE and KTK), as we provided some of the images used in the auction catalogue. The manuscript was sold to an anonymous collector for $2M in October 1998.

The new owner pledged to make the manuscript available for scholarly study and contracted with the Walters Art Museum (WAM) in Baltimore MD in 1999 to conserve the manuscript and to recover as much of the original Archimedes' text as possible by noninvasive methods. WAM is also charged with interpreting and publishing new findings of the works of Archimedes. The authors of this paper form the imaging team that captures and enhances the erased writings of Archimedes in this manuscript, primarily by multispectral imaging methods.

2. Multispectral Imaging Applied to the Palimpsest

The imaging methods used to recover the original text have evolved over the three years of this project. The original plans called for a variety of imaging modalities, including multispectral processing of narrowband images taken in the visible spectrum, confocal microscopy, and magnetic mapping.

The original goal of all modalities was to extract the original text from the page so that the overwriting "disappeared" into the background. The potential utility of multispectral of the palimpsest can be seen from the images in Figure 1, which were taken with a SenSys™. scientific digital camera from the Photometrics division of Roper Scientific. The images are of the same section of a page of text as seen in four wavelengths from the ultraviolet through the visible to the infrared regions of the spectrum. The Archimedes text (running horizontally) is more visible at short wavelengths and most visible when viewed under longwave ultraviolet light (LWUV, $\lambda = 365$nm). This last observation is due to the fluorescence of the parchment when illuminated with this wavelength. The presence of ink or ink traces attenuates both the incident LWUV light and the visible fluorescence, thus amplifying the visibility of the text. Note that the "overwriting" (running vertically) is quite visible in the images at all wavelengths. The increase in reflectance (and consequent decrease in visibility) of the original text with increasing wavelength confirms the observation that the original ink is "redder" than the overwriting. The goal of the multispectral imaging is to use this small difference in spectral response of the two inks to extract the desired writings.

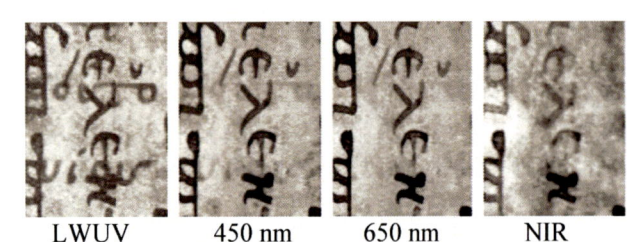

LWUV   450 nm   650 nm   NIR

Figure 1. Spectral signature of the inks: the horizontal Archimedes text is more visible at short wavelengths, particularly in the ultraviolet image due to the fluorescence of the parchment.

2.1 Pseudocolor Imaging

The scholars reviewed the results of the original experiments, and their comments led to establishment of a new goal for the "standard" imaging protocol. As it happens, the scholars benefit from seeing the overwriting and the Archimedes text simultaneously. This helps them distinguish if "gaps" in the ink lines are due to obscurations by the overwritten text. The scholars want to have additional cues that help them differentiate between the texts. Based on their comments, a simpler imaging method was adopted that has proven to be sufficient for reading most of the text. The new method combines channels extracted from two broadband color digital images: one each obtained under visible and ultraviolet illumination. The resulting pseudocolor images highlight the erased text in color and are thus easier for the scholars to read.

Images are collected with a color digital camera commonly used for photojournalism (Eastman Kodak DCS 760) after removing the antialiasing filter that also blocks infrared radiation. Color (RGB) images are collected of the parchment under both LWUV and tungsten illumination. The color images are split into their constituent RGB channels. The red channel of the tungsten image shows very little Archimedes text because of the relative "redness" of the ink. In other words, the pixels containing Archimedes text show mainly the lighter parchment. Only the blue channel of the LWUV image contains information due to the dominance of blue in the fluorescence, and pixels with both overwriting and Archimedes text are dark. After balancing their means and variances, these two channels (shown in Figure 2) are combined to create a pseudocolor image: the red channel of the tungsten image is placed in the red channel of the output, while the blue channel of the LWUV image is placed in both the green and blue channels. Pixels of the overwriting appear dark in all three bands of the pseudocolor image and appear neutral gray. Pixels of Archimedes text are light in the red channel and dark in green and blue, and thus show a reddish or magenta tint. The resulting image is shown in Figure 3. Scholars use this color "cue" to distinguish the two texts.

This method works well for perhaps 80% of the text, but fails in regions that have been damaged by mold or other means. In addition, the method cannot "see" Archimedes text beneath the obscuring overwriting.

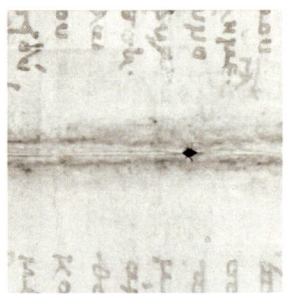

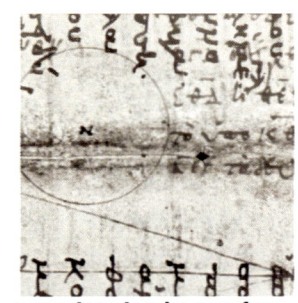

Figure 2. Channels used in pseudocolor image for 093verso-092recto. Red tungsten channel (left) is placed in red channel of pseudocolor image; blue LWUV channel (right) (showing Archimedes text) is in green and blue channels of pseudocolor image.

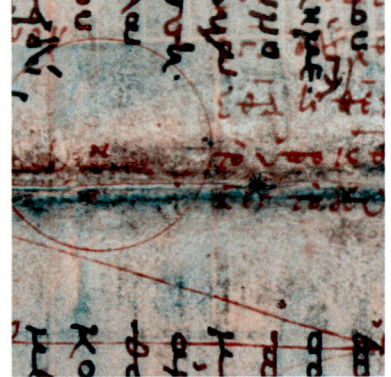

Figure 3. Pseudocolor image created from the channels shown in Figure 2.

2.2 Narrowband Multispectral Imaging

Multispectral techniques using narrowband images taken in visible light are currently being investigated for reading the difficult areas of the manuscript. The images are processed with linear spectral unmixing algorithms. The immediate goal of the study is to determine if multispectral techniques can be adapted to the specific case of inks on parchment and if these methods can be modified to enable the output images to better reveal the erased text. The results of this study showed that a constrained least squares algorithm, that constrains the output images to lie between zero and unity, does enable the output images to be combined in ways that do enhance the visibility of the erased text.

We have constructed an experimental testbed that illuminates a small region of the parchment with narrowband illumination ($\Delta\lambda$=50nm). By filtering the illumination rather than inserting filters at the camera, the spectral separations are guaranteed to be registered. This system is modeled on the "VASARI" illumination system ("Visual Arts Systems for Archiving & Retrieval of Images") that was developed at the National Gallery of London [3] for capturing digital images of artwork.

3. Unconstrained Least Squares Algorithms

The linear mixing model [4] is an assumption that each pixel, which contains several spectral components, can be expressed as a linear combination of the spectral signatures of the component materials, i.e. the two inks, the parchment, etc. For this model, the measured spectral reflectance r_i of the object at each pixel is:

$$r_i = \sum_j S_{ij} \alpha_j$$

where S_{ij} is the matrix of spectral signatures and α_j is the percentage abundance of the material in class j at a given pixel. Each column in the matrix S_{ij} is the signature of a particular material, e.g., ink, parchment, etc. A signature is determined by supervised classification: the class memberships of some set of pixels in the image are identified.

A simple modification is required to adapt this model to the case of ink on parchment because the interaction of ink and parchment is actually multiplicative. This is converted to a sum by evaluating the logarithm of the pixel values and the spectral signatures: the logarithm of r_i becomes a linear combination of the logarithms of the spectral signatures. The linear mixing model may then be appropriately applied.

In the overdetermined case, there are more spectral bands than classes to be identified. The matrix S_{ij} has more rows than columns, and the least squares solution for α is given by the Moore-Penrose pseudoinverse:

$$\alpha = \left[S^T S \right]^{-1} S^T r \equiv S^\dagger r$$

The solution for class membership α is the unconstrained least squares solution. The abundance of a given class at a given pixel is given by multiplying the pseudoinverse $S^\dagger$ by the pixel spectral values. This requires one matrix multiplication at each pixel to calculate the abundances for all classes and this one matrix is applied to the entire image.

The calculated abundances minimize the mean square difference between the actual pixel values and the predicted values from the model, but there are no other constraints on their values. Ideally, the values of α would be restricted to the range $0 \leq \alpha \leq 1$, but the calculated values can lie in the interval $-\infty \leq \alpha \leq +\infty$.

The unconstrained least squares algorithm works well in many cases. The calculated abundances are used to create images of the different classes of object (Archimedes text, parchment, mold, etc.) for the scholars to view. The abundances for a given class, such as Archimedes text, are used as an exponent, scaled and displayed as a raster image. This image can then be viewed to read the text. A pixel-wise image of the abundances, such as this, is also called a fraction map.

There are some significant disadvantages to the unconstrained least squares algorithm. The first is that because the calculated abundances are not constrained to $0 \leq \alpha \leq 1$. To minimize the squared differences for the model at a given pixel location, the abundance of a particular class may be very negative or much greater than unity. This may not matter for a single fraction map, which is displayed after normalizing the maximum and minimum values, but it prevents different fraction maps from being combined. Significantly out-of-range values in one map will overwhelm the values of any other map in a combination. In those cases where this is not an issue, we have found that combinations of fraction maps together allows the Archimedes text to be highlighted and makes it more visible to the scholars.

The second disadvantage of the unconstrained algorithm is that it is not always possible to select pixels that are representative of single classes for the entire leaf, i.e., the spectrum of the parchment or a given ink may vary across the page. In such a case, the writing can be very clear in one section of the fraction map and fade away in another. The solution to this problem is to include many more representative examples and step between the different choices to look for the best fit.

4. Constrained Least Squares Algorithms

Two algorithms were combined to process the multispectral data: Stepwise Linear Unmixing [5] and Constrained Least Squares [6]. The stepwise algorithm is used to attack the problem of spectral signatures that vary across the page, while the constrained least squares algorithm keeps the output abundance values within the range of zero to unity.

A library of spectral signatures is created in the stepwise algorithm if there are several choices for each class. A pseudoinverse solution is constructed for a representative signature from each class and the matrix is applied to the pixel vector. The error that remains unexplained by this solution is the sum of the squared differences between the model predictions and the actual pixel values. The output is saved if the error is less than the current solution. The case with the least error is used for a given pixel. The final abundances for each pixel are normalized to sum to unity.

Within each case, the pseudoinverse solution is calculated and the abundance values are tested to see if any are negative. All negative abundances are set to zero and the corresponding signatures removed. For example, if the abundance of Euchologion text is found to be negative, then it is set to zero and a new pseudoinverse matrix is computed that does not include the Euchologion signature in matrix S.

These loops are computed for each pixel, independently. The results for one pixel are computed for one pixel before moving to the subsequent pixels. Of course, it is not necessary to actually compute the pseudoinverse matrix within the loops. All possible pseudoinverses can be pre-computed and retrieved by lookup table.

The number of combinations of the spectral signatures is given by the product of the number of spectral signatures within each class. For example, if there are 5 signatures in each of 4 classes then there will be $5^4 = 625$ cases to be computed. For each of these cases, there may be as many as 3 (i.e., one less than the number of classes) additional cases to be tested, depending on the occurrence of negative values. As a result, as the number of spectral signatures within a class is increased, the number of cases to be tested and the time to execute could grow exponentially.

It takes a long time to compute, but this algorithm provides high-quality fraction maps of the abundances that can be combined together without being swamped by optimization errors.

5. Combining Fraction Maps

The figures show the fraction maps derived for a leaf of the palimpsest. An image of the leaf in visible light is shown in Figure 4. The red patches on the parchment are regions that contain mold. In this orientation, the Euchologion text is vertical and the Archimedes text is horizontal.

Figure 5 shows the parchment fraction map. Brighter areas are regions of high abundance, i.e. where the image is bright has been classified as parchment. The black regions within this image occur where other classes have been determined, such as text and mold.

Figure 6 and Figure 7 show the class maps of Euchologion and Archimedes text, respectively. The image of the former is quite well defined; the algorithm had little or no difficulty identifying this text. The Archimedes text was hard for the algorithm to identify. Some text is visible, but there are large regions of the image that are noisy and unclear.

The mold fraction map is shown in Figure 8. The white regions nicely correspond to the patches in Figure 4. If this technique could "see through" the mold, then characters would be visible in this figure. Euchologion characters visible, but no Archimedes characters are seen.

The residual errors are shown in Figure 9. Ideally, the gray values of all pixels in this image would be zero, indicating no residual error. In fact, this map can be used to identify regions of parchment or text that have not been explained by the model and new signatures can be added to the library to improve the fit.

Once these fraction maps are calculated, it is possible to combine them together to enhance the Archimedes writing. Since all of the abundance values are between zero and unity and the sum of all the abundance values at each pixel sum to unity, any combination of fraction maps can be added together.

One method of combining the faction maps is to create a pseudocolor image. If fraction maps for parchment (Figure 5) and mold (Figure 8) are added, the resulting image is all white except where there is text. This sum is then written equally into the three RGB color separations of a color image. Since all three separations are the same, these non-text regions are seen as a neutral gray.

The Archimedes fraction map (Figure 7) is added to the red separation. Since the Archimedes text is white, it cancels the Archimedes text in that separation, making it light. Being light only in the red separation, however, make the Archimedes text red in the pseudocolor image. The Euchologion text is left alone and it remains neutral gray and dark.

The resultant pseudocolor image is shown in Figure 10. The Archimedes text is quite visible as red, highlighted text. In fact, it is much easier to read the Archimedes text in the pseudocolor image than it is in the Archimedes fraction map (Figure 7).

A comparison of the Archimedes fraction map and the pseudocolor image is shown in Figure 11. Note the Archimedes characters on the third horizontal line of characters in the middle of the image on each side of the figure. In the fraction map, this line of text is illegible. The characters are faint and confused with other faint characters of Euchologion that were not removed. In the pseudocolor image, on the right, these characters are still faint, but they are now quite legible due to the highlighting in red.

6. Conclusions

A constrained least squares algorithm for spectral unmixing produces normalized and non-negative fraction maps of text and parchment that make it possible to combine different fraction maps together. The combination of these fraction maps can be used to highlight different classes, in this case, the Archimedes text.

The use of pseudocolor greatly enhanced the legibility of the text. With a proper combination, the undesirable non-text elements can be rendered as a neutral gray, while the Archimedes text is highlighted in color, making it more visible. This visibility is greater than simply rendering the Archimedes text in gray. With other combinations of the fraction maps, it may be possible to increase visibility of the text in other ways, as well.

The only drawback of this technique is computation time. For the images shown in this paper, the unconstrained algorithm executed on a 466 MHz Macintosh G4 in less than a minute. The constrained least squares algorithm on the same computer with thousands of combinations to try at each pixel, took around 10 hours. Since each pixel is calculated independently, this is a clear candidate for parallel computing.

7. Acknowledgments

We wish to acknowledge the many contributions from other people to this work. The Archimedes Palimpsest team includes William Noel and Abigail Quandt of the Walters Art Museum, Reviel Netz of Stanford University, Nigel Wilson of Oxford University, Natalie Tchernetska of Cambridge University, Michael Toth of R.B. Toth Associates, and the owner of the Archimedes Palimpsest.

8. References

[1] Netz, R, "The Origins of Mathematical Physics: New Light on an Old Question", **Physics Today 53** (6), 32-37, 2000.

[2] Netz, R., Saito, K. and Tchernetska, N., "A New Reading of Method Proposition 14: Preliminary Evidence from the Archimedes Palimpsest", **SCIAMVS 2**, 9-29, 2001.

[3] Martinez, K., Cupitt, J. Saunders, D. and Pillay, R., "Ten Years of Art Imaging Research", **Proc. IEEE 90** (1), 28-41, 2002.

Robert Schowengerdt, **Remote Sensing**, Academic Press, San Diego, CA, 1997, p. 447.

[4] Gross, H.N., "An Image Fusion Algorithm for Spatially Enhancing Spectral Mixture Maps," Doctoral Dissertation, Rochester Institute of Technology, 1996.

[5] Shimabukuro, Y. E. and Smith, J. A., "The Least-Squares Mixing Models to Generate Fraction Images Derived From Remote Sensing Multispectral Data", **IEEE Trans. Geosci. Rem. Sens. 29** (1) 16-20, 1991.

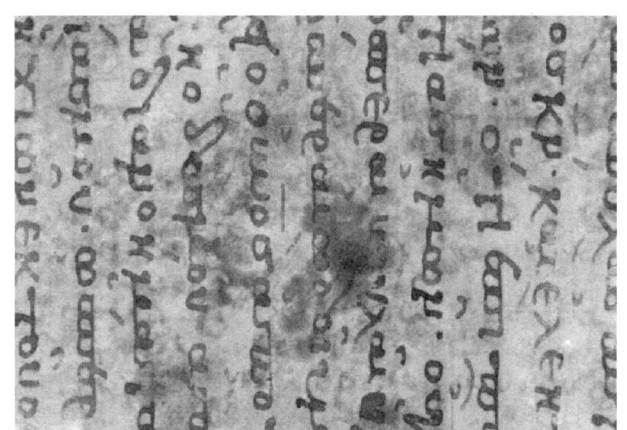

Figure 4. Section of page 028verso in visible light

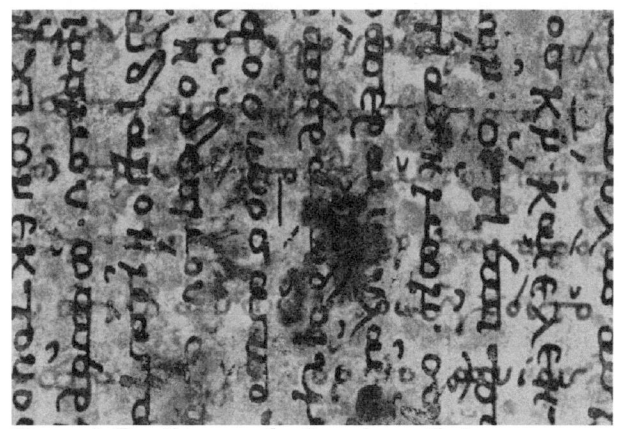

Figure 5. Fraction map for "parchment" class

Figure 6. Fraction map, "Euchologion text"

Figure 7. Fraction map, "Archimedes text"

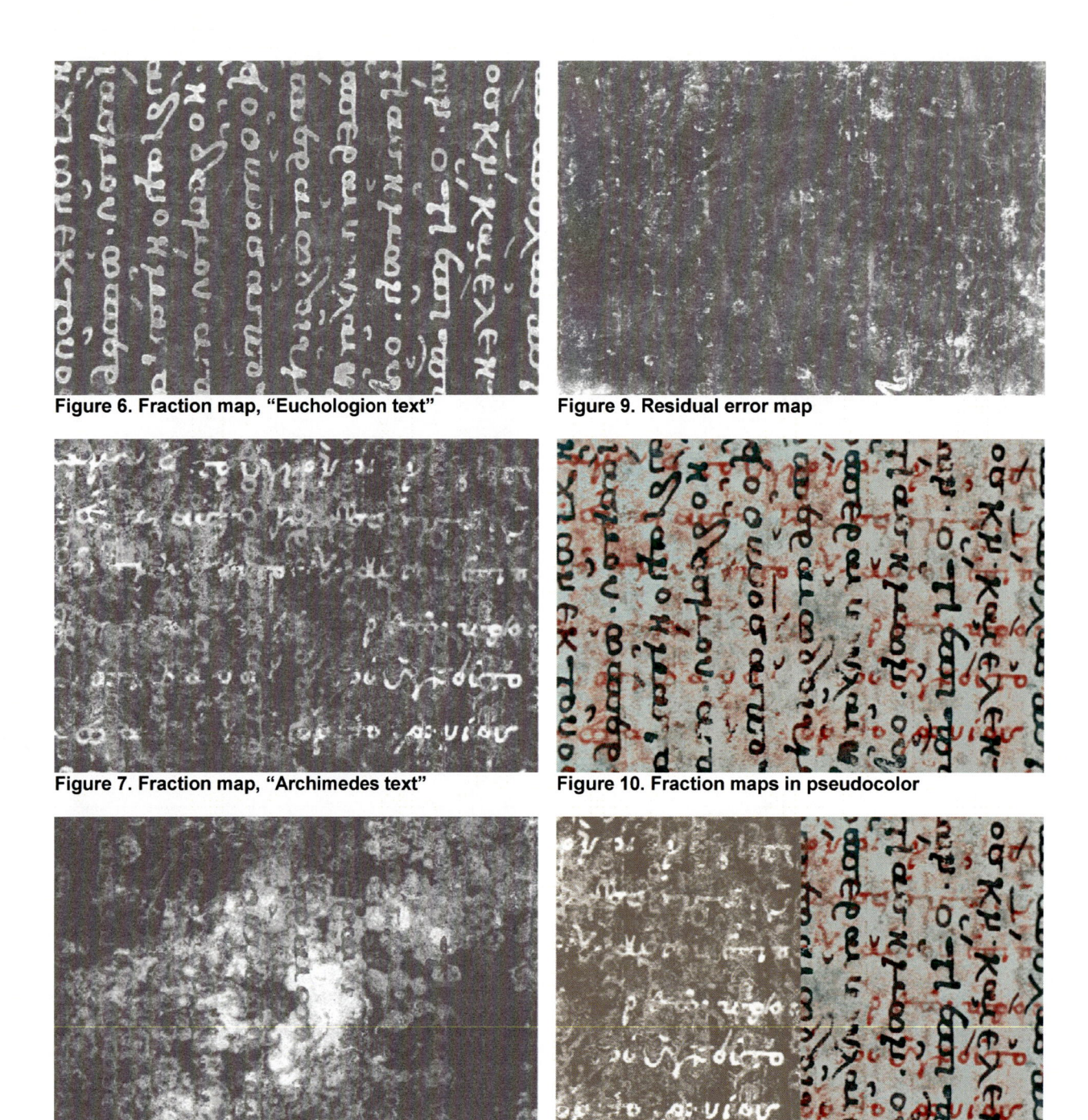

Figure 8. Fraction map, "mold"

Figure 9. Residual error map

Figure 10. Fraction maps in pseudocolor

Figure 11. Comparison of one region of monochrome fraction map of Archimedes text (Figure 7) and pseudocolor mapping (Figure 10)

Medical Applications

Heterogeneity of MR Signal Intensity Mapped onto Brain Surface Models

Rebmann AJ, Butman JA
Diagnostic Radiology Department
The National Institutes of Health
Bethesda, MD
arebmann@cc.nih.gov

Abstract

Heterogeneity of gray matter signal intensity can be demonstrated on some MR sequences, particularly FLAIR. Quantifying this heterogeneity is of interest as it may distinguish among different cortical areas. Gray matter segmentation fails on FLAIR data due to overlap of gray and white matter signal intensity. This overlap also compromises region of interest based approaches. Although volume rendering can visualize some of these differences, it is non quantitative and averaging gray and white matter cannot be avoided.

To overcome these obstacles we obtained T1 weighted data in addition to FLAIR data. T1 weighted data provides strong gray/white contrast, allowing a cortical surface to be extracted. Volume based registration of the FLAIR data set to the T1 data allows FLAIR signal intensity data to be mapped onto the surface generated from the T1 dataset. This allows regional FLAIR signal intensity differences to be visualized and to be compared across subjects.

1. Introduction

Although the brain is a complex 3D structure, the cerebral cortex (gray matter) is topologically equivalent to a sphere, with a thickness on the order of 5 mm. Therefore, 2D surfaces generated from 3D volumetric MR data are currently used in the neuroimaging community to represent the cortex. Conceptually, any coregistered 3D volume data of the cortex can be mapped onto a 2D surface representation of the cortex. For instance, regions of brain activation obtained with functional MRI can be mapped onto such surfaces. Because MR generates volume based data, different forms of MR data can theoretically be mapped onto coregistered surfaces.

Magnetic resonance imaging (MRI) non-invasively images the brain by generating signal dependent on intrinsic tissue properties such as T1 and T2 relaxation rates, and proton density. Because different tissues vary in these and other magnetic resonance properties, tissue contrast is generated allowing anatomic visualization.

The MRI technique is based on the interaction of protons (often referred to as spins because of their magnetic moment) with an external magnetic field (B_0) and a series of radiofrequency (RF) pulses. Protons introduced into a B_0 field, align themselves with the main magnetic field, resonating at a characteristic frequency determined by their gyromagnetic ratio and the field strength. RF pulses tuned to this frequency perturb these spins, and signal is generated as the spins relax or realign with the B_0 field. This relaxation rate is referred to as the T1 or spin-lattice relaxation rate. To generate an image, external gradients are applied to spatially map the location of the spins. Because a given voxel of tissue has many spins, signal can only be measured as long as these spins stay in phase. The rate at which phase coherence is lost is termed T2, or spin-spin, relaxation. Contrast in an image is generated by exciting the tissue with RF pulses in different patterns to modulate the effects of T1 and T2 relaxation on signal. In a T1 weighted image, atoms in a tightly bound matrix relax back most quickly, and typically give the strongest signal, appearing bright in the image (e.g. white matter), and those in a fluid matrix, relax back more slowly, and give a weaker signal thus appearing darker in the image (e.g. cerebrospinal fluid) [1].

T1 weighted images, in particular, have high signal to noise per unit time, and clearly distinguish gray and white matter in the brain. Recently there has been data indicating that MRI signal differences can be distinguished, not just between gray and white matter, but also among different gray matter regions [2-4]. In particular, FLAIR sequences generate tissue signal which is a complex mix of intrinsic T1, T2 and magnetization transfer properties. Some gray matter regions, e.g. motor cortex, are hypo-intense on FLAIR while other areas, e.g. insular cortex, are relatively hyper-intense. It is well known that the cortex can be divided into approximately 40 to 50 different areas based on cytoarchitectonic features identified microscopically on tissue specimens. Our goal is to use surface representations to investigate whether

MRI signal variations in gray matter correspond to these different areas. Here we demonstrate successful mapping of FLAIR image data onto surfaces derived from T1 weighted MR data.

2. Methods

2.1 Subjects

Six healthy volunteers (3 female, 3 male; age range = 31.0 ± 6.8 years, weight = 68.03 ± 16.4 kg, height = 171.5 ± 8.9 cm) participated in this study. Informed consent was obtained under an IRB approved protocol.

2.2 MRI Technique

Subjects were placed supine in a 1.5 T MR imager (Signa 9.0; GE Medical Systems, Milwaukee, WI, USA) using a quadrature head coil. T1 weighted images were acquired using 3D Inversion Recovery Prepped Fast Gradient Recalled Echo (IR-GRE) sequence (Figure 1): TR = 12.2 ms, TE = 5.2 ms, TI = 250 ms, flip Angle = 20, FOV = 22x22 mm, matrix = 256x192, slice thickness = 1.2 mm, number of slices = 248, 1 NEX, ZIPx2, time = 6:34 per volume, 2 volumes, native resolution = [0.86 1.45 1.2] mm, interpolated resolution = [0.86 0.86 0.6] mm.

Because this is a gradient echo technique, B_0 field inhomogeneity is not compensated for, resulting in a slight variation in signal intensity across the image. To correct for this, a nonlinear uniformity correction was applied to the data to correct this (N3 correction, MINC) [5].

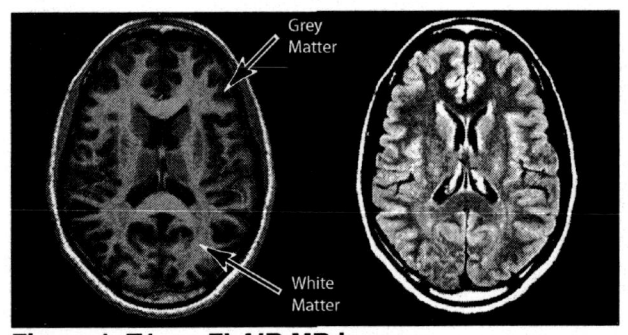

Figure 1. T1 vs. FLAIR MR images.
On T1 weighted imaging (*left*) gray matter is homogeneously intermediate in signal intensity. CSF is hypo-intense. On FLAIR imaging and, gray matter is relatively hyperintense to gray matter, but there is significant heterogeneity so that there is no contrast between gray and white matter in the occipital lobes (*arrows*).

FLAIR images were acquired using 2D fast spin echo Fluid Attenuated Inversion Recovery (FLAIR) sequence (Figure 1): TR = 9000 ms, TE = 140 ms, TI =2200 ms, FOV = 22x22 mm, matrix = 256x256, slice thickness = 2.5 mm, number of slices = 56, number of acquisitions = 5, 2 NEX, echo train length = 22, time = 13:12 per volume, 5 volumes, native resolution = [.86 .86 2.5] mm. Following registration, data was resampled to match the T1 data set.

Because FLAIR is a multislice 2D technique, the first slice in each acquisition has slightly different signal intensity than the remainder of the slices in that acquisition. As five acquisitions were used, care was taken to insure that the bottom five slices of the imaging volume were placed below the cerebral cortex so that signal intensity in the cortex was not affected by this artifact.

2.3 Registration

Automatic registration was performed both inter-modality (e.g. T1 to T1) and cross modality (e.g. FLAIR to T1), using a 3D rigid body volume based registration algorithm (3dvolreg, AFNI) [6]. The transformation was obtained by an iterated linearized weighted least squares algorithm to correct for small motions between two volumes. This procedure is based on a 6 parameter rigid body transformation determined by shifts along the x, y, and z axes, and by rotations about the x, y, and z axes.

Manual registration was performed cross modality also utilizing a 6 parameter rigid body transformation. Between 6 to 12 corresponding points were identified in both volumes, using identifiable anatomical landmarks (e.g. anterior commissure, posterior commissure, Virchow-Robin spaces, sulci). The selected points were distributed throughout the volume. The transformation was computed by a least squares minimization of distances between corresponding points [7].

2.4 Surface Extraction

Two corresponding surfaces defining the cerebral cortex were generated from the T1 data. One surface corresponded to the inner margin of the cerebral cortex, at the boundary of gray and white matter. The second surface corresponds to the outer margin of the cortex (anatomically referred to as the pia) corresponding to the boundary between gray matter and the surrounding cerebrospinal fluid. These surfaces were obtained separately for the right and left cortical hemispheres and were obtained from the T1 weighted images using a semi-automated tool set (FreeSurfer) [8, 9]. We briefly outline this process. First, the T1 volume was deskulled such that all non brain matter is removed, and then white matter segmentation is performed. A surface is tessellated such that faces, e.g. triangles, separate voxels classified as white matter from those classified as gray matter. An inflated view of this surface was created for each hemisphere separately representing sulci and gyri as a smooth surface. This surface was inspected for defects stemming from segmentation errors (i.e., non-white matter voxels incorrectly classified as white matter) and non-cortical anatomic structures (e.g., basal ganglia, ventricles). In addition, small bumps can be seen on the inflated surface when gray matter voxels are classified as white matter. It was necessary to manually edit the white matter image by filling in the holes or removing the pixels representing the bumps and handles. The editing process resulted in a topologically correct surface without holes or handles (i.e., topology equivalent to a sphere, and not a higher order structure such as a torus). To obtain a corresponding outer cortical (pial) surface, each node in the white matter tessellation was inflated to a point at which it now separated grey matter from cerebrospinal fluid, creating a corresponding node on the outer edge of the gray matter surface.

2.4 Volume Rendering

Volume rendering was performed by a method which paints signal intensity of a given depth onto a rendered volume (MRIcro) [10]. Initially FLAIR data were volume rendered following deskulling the brains with the Brain Extraction Tool [11]. Following surface definition, the surfaces were used to create a binary mask using the pial and white matter surfaces as the outer and inner boundaries, and applied to FLAIR images by multiplying the FLAIR dataset by its corresponding gray matter binary mask. A volume rendered image was created as in the first case.

2.6 Intensity Mapping

As the T1 and FLAIR volumetric data have been coregistered, the inner and outer cortical surfaces defined from the T1 data correspond to the inner and outer cortical surface in the FLAIR dataset. To demonstrate the FLAIR signal intensity within the gray matter (not at the boundaries) we chose to assign FLAIR signal intensity from within the cortical gray matter to each node on the surface. To obtain this intensity, a line segment was defined from corresponding nodes on the inner and outer cortical surfaces.

In an ideal surface representation, all points along this segment represent gray matter. To avoid signal variation near the cortical boundaries as well as to correct for slight errors in the surfaces, only the central 60% of this line was used for calculations. This line segment was divided into 10 equally spaced points and these locations were referenced to the coregistered FLAIR volume to obtain FLAIR signal intensity at each point (possibly indexing into the same voxel more than once). These ten values were averaged and assigned to the corresponding surface node.

Surface mapping software (SUMA) [12] was utilized for viewing the calculated FLAIR gray matter intensity on the 3D surface model. These values were mapped onto the surface on the intensity scale from half maximum to maximum frequency for each subject.

3. Results

Figure 2 shows corresponding 2D sections of the T1 and FLAIR datasets following registration, averaging, resampling, smoothing, and non-linear non-uniform intensity normalization correction. On the T1, acquired in 12 minutes, gray matter is distinguished from white matter. Signal is relatively uniform throughout the gray matter. On the FLAIR, acquired over 65 minutes, signal intensity varies across gray matter. For instance, pre and post central gyri are hypo-intense. The occipital lobe (V1) is hypo-intense. The insula and cingulate are hyper-intense. Note that on T1, these regions are relatively uniform in signal intensity.

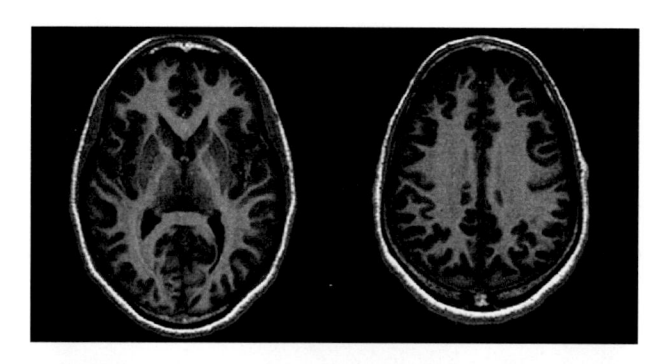

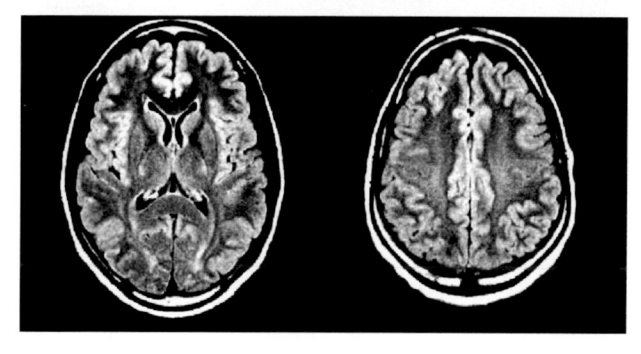

Figure 2. T1 vs. FLAIR MR images.
On T1 weighted imaging (*top*) gray matter is homogeneously intermediate (gray) in signal intensity. White matter is relatively hyperintense (white) and CSF is hypo-intense.
On FLAIR imaging (*bottom*) gray matter is relatively hyper-intense to gray matter in many locations, but there is significant heterogeneity so that there is no contrast between gray and white matter in the occipital lobes (*arrows*) and sensorimotor cortex for example.

White matter signal intensity is relatively homogeneous on T1 but varies on FLAIR. For instance, cingulate white matter is hypo-intense, increasing gray/white contrast while in the precentral gyrus (M1) white matter and gray matter are iso-intense and there is virtually no demarcation between gray and white matter. Gray matter/CSF contrast is clear on FLAIR. On the T1, gray matter is relatively dark and gray matter/CSF contrast, although present, was not optimal.

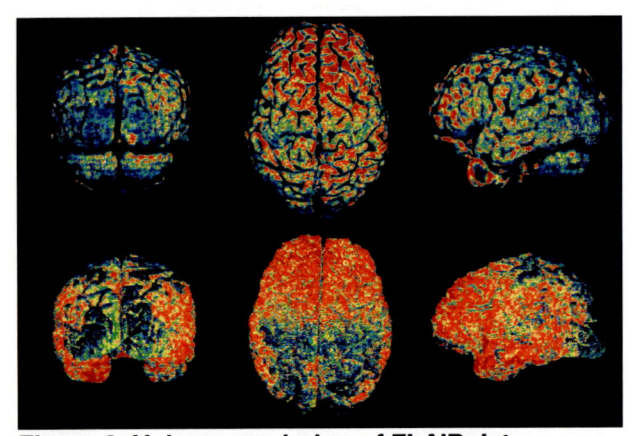

Figure 3. Volume rendering of FLAIR data
Volume rendering of deskulled data obtained directly from the FLAIR data (*top*) shows some similarities to, but is noisier than, volume rendering of FLAIR data following segmentation of gray matter from FLAIR data based on T1 data (*bottom*)

Volume rendering of FLAIR data was performed following skull removal using BET (Figure 3). Although we could not find parameters to remove all non brain tissue without at least partial removal of brain tissue, these volumes were adequate for volume rendering purposes to demonstrate signal variation over the superficial gray matter. As can be seen, the hypo-intensity in the pre and post central gyri and the occipital lobe are identifiable, as would be expected from the axial source images.

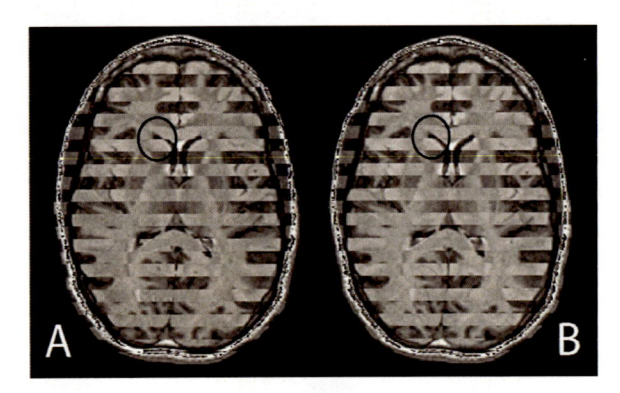

Figure 4. Coregistration demonstrated by alternating stripes of T1 and FLAIR.
Following automated coregistration (A), image misregistration is still present (*circles*). Most of this is eliminated following the manual landmark based registration (B).

Figure 4A shows checkerboard fusion of coregistration, where the T1 and FLAIR datasets are presented as alternating stripes. Following automatic registration, offsets on the order of 2-3 mm are seen, for instance the right frontal horn and left occipital horn of the lateral ventricles. Figure 4B shows improvement following manual registration. Note, the misalignment has been corrected for. However, there is persistent slight misregistration of scalp fat.

Figure 5 shows surface rendering of the brain derived from the T1 dataset with the color scale defined by the FLAIR signal intensity. As with the volume rendering, we see expected areas of hyper- and hypo-intensity. Within regions of hyper-intensity and hypo-intensity, there is relatively uniform signal intensity. Boundaries between regions of different signal intensity appear to be present, and in some locations clearly correspond to well known boundaries between different cortical areas.

Hypo-intensity (blue) is seen in the primary motor (M1) and primary sensory (S1) cortical areas as well as most of the visual cortex (V1) and the medial superior areas of the parietal lobe. Hyper-intensity (red) is seen in the cingulate gyrus, medial and inferior frontal lobes in addition to the inferior temporal lobes. Intermediate signal (green/yellow) is seen in association areas. Figure 5 shows that this pattern is relatively consistent across subjects.

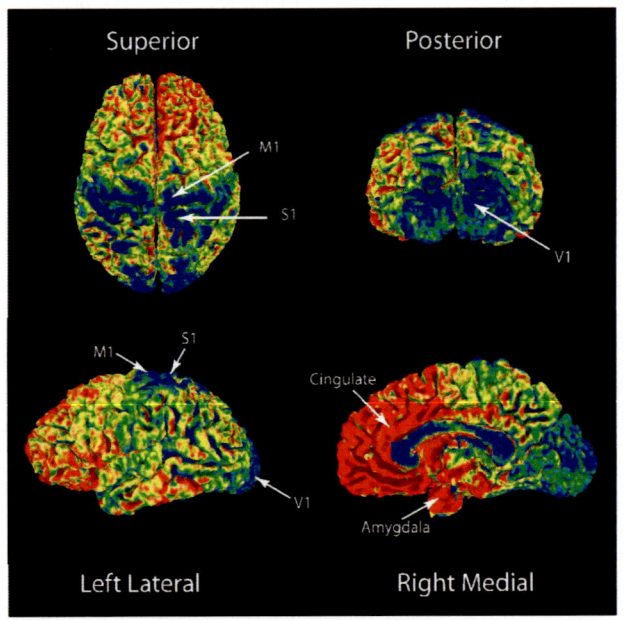

Figure 5. FLAIR intensity mapped onto cortical surface
Different cortical regions have different signal intensities corresponding to known anatomic landmarks.

4. Discussion

Our goal was to generate a mapping of FLAIR signal intensity from volumetric datasets onto a 2D representation of the cortical surface. We were able to successfully map FLAIR signal intensity onto surface representations of the cerebral cortex. In doing so, heterogeneity of this cortical signal can easily be assessed and can be compared. Placing FLAIR signal intensity onto a 2D representation potentially provides more flexibility in analysis, allowing for coregistration across subjects, warping to atlases, and "flat-mapping" of the cortex as well as quantitative and geometric analyses.

In developing this map of cortical FLAIR signal intensity, we desired to obtain as high a resolution a map as possible. Since FLAIR is an intrinsically noisy technique, the use of 2.5 mm slices results in a relatively noisy dataset. Therefore we obtained 5 such volumes requiring over 60 minutes of scanning. Because patient motion is unavoidable on such time scales, image registration was used to average the 5 volumes resulting in a very high SNR dataset.

FLAIR signal heterogeneity was clearly identifiable on these images. Volume rendering suggested that these regional differences in gray matter signal were distinguishable. As the signal intensity in the cortex on FLAIR images have heterogeneous intensity throughout the entirety of the brain as the signal intensities of gray and white matter overlap it is impossible to segment the brain into gray and white matter based on signal intensity. Therefore it is impossible to generate a surface from the FLAIR data alone. Cortical surfaces have been successfully generated from T1 datasets, and there are a number of approaches to do this in a semi automated way [8, 9, 13].

T1 weighted images optimize contrast differences between gray and white matter and preserve the homogeneity of gray and white matter. This is an ideal dataset which enables gray matter, white matter, and cerebrospinal fluid to be segmented. Therefore, we obtained high resolution T1 volumes to generate surfaces onto which FLAIR data could be mapped. 3D T1 gradient echo sequences can provide strong gray white contrast to allow for segmentation and surface extraction. Our T1 datasets were optimized for contrast between gray and white matter. However, this sequence was not optimized for contrast between gray matter and the pial surface. This made brain extraction more difficult in addition to causing some problems with creating the surfaces because some areas of skull were mislabeled as gray matter and additional manual editing was required. In addition, the number of bumps and handles was increased due to suboptimal contrast. A number of methods could be used to improve gray matter/CSF contrast including altering the inversion time, using a post acquisition delay, or increasing the number of signal averages. These methods all come at the expense of increased imaging time or with relatively poorer gray-white contrast at the same imaging time. Despite these difficulties we were able to extract acceptable surfaces from our T1 datasets.

In order to map the FLAIR data onto the surfaces, coregistration of the FLAIR and T1 data sets must exist. Because the cortical ribbon is so thin and convoluted, even submillimeter misregistration of the two data sets is problematic. Since T1 and FLAIR contrast is grossly similar (bright fat, dark CSF, intermediate brain signal intensity), automated registration was expected to succeed. However, small misregistrations were present following automated registration of T1 and FLAIR data. Because scalp fat appeared slightly misregistered even when the brain was registered (manually), we believe there was an unanticipated chemical shift difference between the T1 and FLAIR images. Fat and water components of the MR images are always slightly misregistered along the frequency encode direction of an MRI scan. Even though we tailored the T1 and FLAIR MRI sequences to generate equal magnitudes of chemical shift displacement, slight changes in slice angulations would generate slight differences in the direction of this shift. Suppressing signal from fat is possible with MR (at the expense, as always, of other changes in imaging parameters such as acquisition time). Elimination of fat either by segmentation techniques or by MRI acquisition techniques should be able to eliminate this source of error in the automated registration process.

The mapping procedure uses positions in space defined by the T1 surface, and retrieves FLAIR signal intensity from the coregistered FLAIR volume data. We would like to ensure that the mapped value truly corresponds to gray matter FLAIR signal intensities not white matter or CSF. Ideally, the surface generated would run through the middle of the cortical gray matter ribbon. In effect, we achieved this by using line segments extending from the inner cortical surface (gray / white junction) and the outer cortical surface (gray matter / CSF junction), and sampling data from FLAIR data at points along the central portion of this line.

Successful mapping of the FLAIR dataset onto the T1 surface achieves two goals. First it allows for visualization. While heterogeneity is observable on the axial source images, it is difficult to identify the extent of these signal variations with respect to surface neuroanatomy which is the common frame of reference. Volume rendering can be used to visualize the surface distribution of gray matter signal intensity as in Figure 3. In fact there is a fair degree of similarity between the volume rendered map of FLAIR signal intensity (Figure 3 lower) and the final surface map (Figure 5). While the volume rendering is technically less demanding, it is a non-quantitative method of analysis, and there is no method to extract signal intensities corresponding to locations in space on a volume rendered image. Furthermore, the quality of volume rendering depended to a significant degree on the amount of preprocessing and segmentation. To the extent which this is required, the advantages of volume rendering diminish.

Second, it allows the potential for regional based quantification of these signal intensity variations across the cortex. FLAIR signal heterogeneity varies not only across gray matter, but across white matter as well. Signal intensities of gray and white matter overlap. Therefore it is impossible to segment these images into gray matter, white matter, and cerebrospinal fluid. Region of interest (ROI) analysis has been used to determine gray matter signal intensity [2-4], but in order to avoid the inclusion of white matter signal intensity, expert placement of the ROI is required. While this can be done, it is an arduous task to define ROIs distributed across the entire cortex. In fact, because of poor contrast between gray and white matter, it may be impossible to prospectively place an ROI in gray matter based on the FLAIR image alone, necessitating at the minimum coregistered T1 data upon which the ROI can be defined.

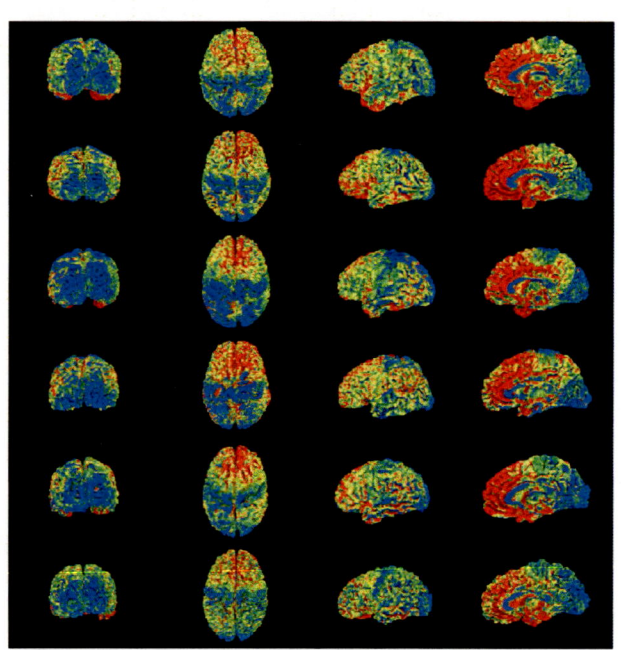

Figure 6. Consistency of heterogeneity in FLAIR signal intensity across 6 subjects

This method of calculating and mapping FLAIR signal intensity is acceptable for the visualization and quantification of structural differences within the brain. Although there were some obstacles to overcome, this new method is reliable for distinguishing and quantifying the heterogeneity inherent in FLAIR images.

5. Acknowledgements

David Thomasson for technical MRI discussions. AFNI guys for their AFNIness. Sandy Jones for volunteer recruitment.

6. References

[1] D. G. Mitchell, MRI principles, Saunders, Philadelphia 1999.

[2] M. Bendersky, C. Rugilo, S. Kochen, G. Schuster and R. E. Sica, *Magnetic resonance imaging identifies cytoarchitectonic subtypes of the normal human cerebral cortex*. J Neurol Sci *211*, 75-80 (2003).

[3] T. Hirai, Y. Korogi, K. Yoshizumi, Y. Shigematsu, T. Sugahara and M. Takahashi, *Limbic lobe of the human brain: evaluation with turbo fluid-attenuated inversion-recovery MR imaging*. Radiology *215*, 470-475 (2000).

[4] E. Karaarslan and A. Arslan, *Perirolandic cortex of the normal brain: low signal intensity on turbo FLAIR MR images*. Radiology *227*, 538-541 (2003).

[5] J. G. Sled, A. P. Zijdenbos and A. C. Evans, *A nonparametric method for automatic correction of intensity nonuniformity in MRI data*. IEEE Trans Med Imaging *17*, 87-97 (1998).

[6] R. W. Cox, *AFNI: software for analysis and visualization of functional magnetic resonance neuroimages*. Comput Biomed Res *29*, 162-173 (1996).

[7] M.J. McAuliffe, F.M. Lalonde, D. McGarry, W. Gandler, K. Csaky, B.L. Trus, *Medical Image Processing, Analysis & Visualization in Clinical Research*. IEEE Computer-Based Medical Systems (CBMS) 381-386 (2001).

[8] A. M. Dale, B. Fischl and M. I. Sereno, *Cortical surface-based analysis. I. Segmentation and surface reconstruction*. Neuroimage *9*, 179-194 (1999).

[9] B. Fischl, M. I. Sereno and A. M. Dale, *Cortical surface-based analysis. II: Inflation, flattening, and a surface-based coordinate system*. Neuroimage *9*, 195-207 (1999).

[10] C. Rorden and M. Brett, *Stereotaxic display of brain lesions*. Behav Neurol *12*, 191-200 (2000).

[11] S. M. Smith, *Fast robust automated brain extraction*. Hum Brain Mapp *17*, 143-155 (2002).

[12] Z. Saad. SUMA (Surface Mapper) Software. http://afni.nimh.nih.gov/ssc/ziad/SUMA . 2003.

[13] D. C. Van Essen, H. A. Drury, J. Dickson, J. Harwell, D. Hanlon and C. H. Anderson, *An integrated software suite for surface-based analyses of cerebral cortex*. J Am Med Inform Assoc *8*, 443-459 (2001).

THE RESEARCH OF SEMANTIC CONTENT APPLIED TO IMAGE FUSION

Yumei Miao

College of Remote Sensing Information, Wuhan University
yumei_miao@hotmail.com

Yusong Miao

Wuhan Communication College

Abstract

The diagnostic value of CT (Computed Tomography) checking for encephalic illness is affirmative. For clinical doctors, they are in urgent need of a good approach for this monomodality medical image fusion at an acceptable accuracy, in order to obtain some visual comparison about a patient in normal and pathologic conditions, tracing the development of focus, determining the regimen and so on. Thus is also the purpose of this paper. The usual method is merging images at pixel-level or feature-level. In this paper, we develop a semantic - level fusion technique that is matched with semantic descriptions associated to images. Content-based semantic information can be used on image segmentation and similarity matching image retrieval through prior-knowledge support. Then we apply a weighted complex similarity retrieval algorithm (WK-NN) to implement. Finally, the integrated images with semantic information are presented.

Keywords: *medical image fusion, brain CT image, semantic-level, prior-knowledge support, similarity matching image retrieval, WK-NN*

1. Introduction

It is necessary that to research the monomodality medical image fusion. For example, brain CT images fusion. Since the diagnostic value of CT (computed tomography) checking for encephalic illness (such as cerebral hemorrhage, infarction) is affirmative. CT images have density resolution highly, and can tell hemorrhage region from natural brain tissue. But traditional brain CT image observation □ handling processing is dependent on radiology doctor □ it is subjected to the inherent inaccuracy and uncertainty of human vision system [1]. In the past few years, PACS (picture archiving and communication system) has speedily been developed. Albeit it resolves the issue of medical image storage and communication, but for image fusion, PACS is fully dependent on artificial registration. Artificial registration on every image in the huge size of image databases is impossible. For clinical doctors, they are in urgent need of a good approach for this monomodality medical image fusion at an acceptable accuracy, in order to obtain some visual comparison about a patient in normal and pathologic conditions, tracing the development of focus, determining the regimen and so on. Thus is also the purpose of this paper.

Image fusion is a time consuming processing. The usual

method is merging images at pixel-level or feature-level. Some person applied the mutual information [2], some one used chamfer matching [3], and many other methods [4, 5, 6]. In this paper, we develop a semantic-level fusion technique that is matched with semantic descriptions associated to images. (See figure 1).

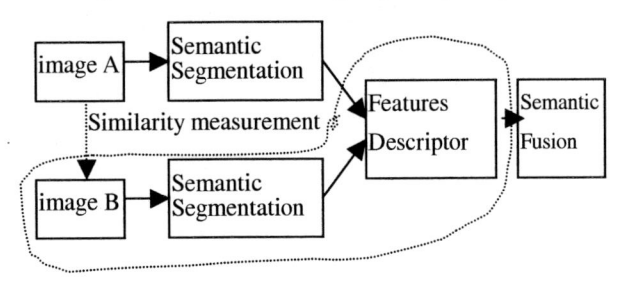

Figure 1. Semantic-level CT images fusion

And our semantic-level fusion has three steps:
(1) Segment the reference image using semantic, thus these segmentation regions correspond to interesting objects in the image, and extract feature vectors;
(2) According to these (visual or semantic) feature vectors, search for matching images in brain CT image database. This is a similarity retrieval processing;
(3) Fused two or more similarity images using feature match.
In section 2, we discuss the semantic-based image segmentation; this is followed by the similarity matching image retrieval in section3. In section 4, we applied the WK-NN to give fused image.

2. Semantic-based Image Segmentation

According to the image content, brain CT slices have some priori knowledge. That is, hemorrhage region reflects high-density in image; brain has symmetry structure; the maximum and minimum values of CBF (cerebral blood flow) area or diameter can be achieved; hemorrhage region has regular location and shape; and so on. It implies that we can use these descriptors, compute the conditional probabilities of objects in image, and can segment image with interpretations, so these regions correspond to those interesting objects in image respectively (such as hemorrhage, lateral-ventricle, etc.) [7]. Let we suppose, a region R_i has properties X_i, its possible labels are described $\theta_i \in \{\omega_1,...,\omega_R\}$, P($\theta_i = \omega_k$) represents the probability that the interpretation of the region R_i is ω_k. Compare with traditional region-based segmentation, the semantic segmentation algorithm has difference as follow:(merge all adjacent regions with their semantic)

(1) For all adjacent regions R_i and R_j, compute the conditional probability P that their mutual border B_{ij} separates them into two regions of the same interpretation ($\theta_i = \theta_j$). Let P_t denote the probability that the remain boundary, P_f denote the false boundary probability, X(B_{ij}) denote the properties of B_{ij}, so

$$p = P_f / (P_t + P_f) \qquad (2-1)$$

In (2-1),

$$P_f = \sum_{k=1}^{R} P[\theta_i = \theta_j | X(B_{ij})] P(\theta_i = \omega_k | X_i) P(\theta_j = \omega_k | X_j)$$

$$P_t = \sum_{k=1}^{R} \sum_{\substack{l=1 \\ k \neq l}}^{R} P[\theta_i = \omega_k\, and\, \theta_j = \omega_l | X(B_{ij})] \quad (2-2)$$
$$P(\theta_i = \omega_k | X_i) P(\theta_j = \omega_l | X_j)$$

If $P > T_2$ (T_2 is a threshold), then merge regions R_i and R_j; if no two regions can be so merged, continue with step (2).

(2) For each region R_i, compute the initial conditional probabilities, $P(\theta_i = \omega_k | X_i)$ k=1,...,R (2-3)

(3) Repeat until all regions are labeled as final. Find a non-final region R_i, R_i has the highest confidence C_i in its interpretation. (θ_i^1, θ_i^2 Represent the two most probable interpretations of region R_i), then C_i is:

$$C_i = \frac{P(\theta_i^1 | X_i)}{P(\theta_i^2 | X_i)} \quad (2-4)$$

After label the R_i with its interpretation and mark it as final, interpretation probabilities of all its neighbors R_j (with non-final labels) are updated to maximize the objective function:

$$P_{new}(\theta_j) = P_{old}(\theta_j) P(B_{ij} | X(B_{ij})) \quad (2-5)$$

Now, from these semantic regions, we can extract feature vectors and form some descriptors. For example, figure 2 represents edges of brain and hemorrhage regions.

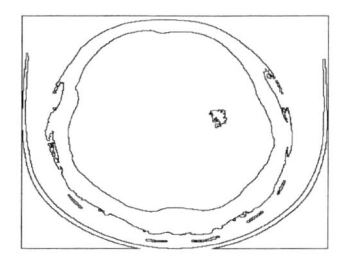

Figure 2. Extract edge feature

3. Semantic retrieval for matching images

For clinical doctors, search for matching images to merge in huge size CT image database is not an easy task. To improve the matching efficiency, doctors want to decrease mismatch images beforehand. Sometimes doctors use the reference image to query the similar image in CT database; sometimes doctors merely use the content descriptor (such as 'large CBF' or 'near lateral_ventricle'.) of reference image to retrieve. (See figure 3)

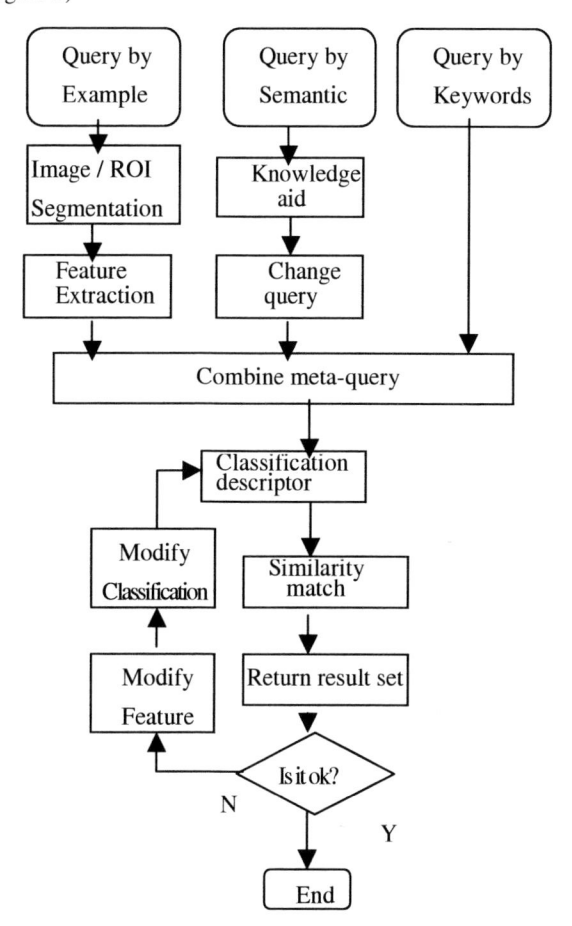

Figure3. Processing of complex similarity query

These content-based semantic descriptions not as same as low-level image visual features, they reflect a high-level of image interpretation and model visual content at a conceptual level [8]. Image feature layer can extract perceptive features. Semantic layer can extract at different levels of meaning through a suitable set of rules. An example rule as follow:

Rule 011: IF density > 0.6 THEN this region is hemorrhage region   With Confidence (0.5)

Construction rules depend on the specific data domain of

knowledge layer. These rules can support retrieval sentences using semantic concept or spatial relationship representations among semantic objects.

3.1 Concept abstraction hierarchy

Some query in CBIR is semantic, we have to change them into clear feature retrieval. The rule of query change is mapping into concept hierarchy tree. We found in different abstraction hierarchy, domain of describing concept feature is different. Domain could be a fuzzy set. For example, in brain CT images, doctors care about the diameter size of CBF, if the diameter of CBF more than 2 cm, it is the index point for surgical operation. Then the concept items of semantic index using large, medium and small, its concept abstraction hierarchy (CAH) is shown in figure 4 (the attribute 'size' indicated the diameter size

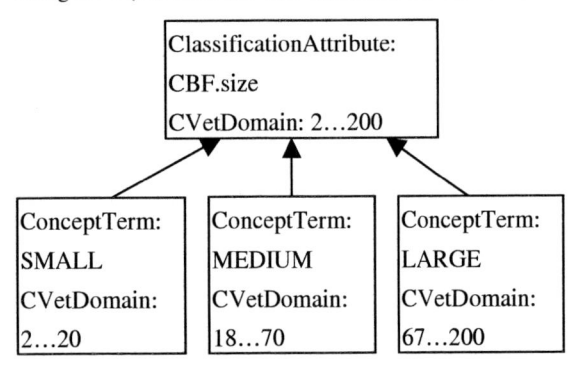

```
ClassificationAttribute:
CBF.size
CVetDomain: 2...200
```

```
ConceptTerm:    ConceptTerm:    ConceptTerm:
SMALL           MEDIUM          LARGE
CVetDomain:     CVetDomain:     CVetDomain:
2...20          18...70         67...200
```

Figure4. Concept abstraction hierarchy for CBF.size

of CBF, unit is mm). And CAH will accelerate the mining processing, though it lost some detail data, but this abstraction data is easily be interpret, and storage space for feature data is decreased.
If a SQL sentence as follow:

```
Select h.patient, h.image
from hemorrhage h
```

where h.size IS 'LARGE';

Then analyses this SQL sentence, search the concept hierarchy tree of CBF.size in knowledge database, and found the node of 'ConceptTerm: LARGE' in the tree, change the SQL sentence as: (unit is mm)

```
Select h.patient, h.image
from hemorrhage h
where h.size>67;
```

3.2 Spatial relationship representations (SRR)

There are various association relations among each semantic object, such as aggregation, generalization, composite, spatial and so on. Doctors care the spatial position of focus. If we know the areal coordinates for semantic object A and B is (x_A, y_A) and (x_B, y_B), then spatial distance for A, B is:

$$SRR(A,B) = tg^{-1}(\frac{y_B - y_A}{x_B - x_A}) \qquad (3-1)$$

Spatial topological relationship::={near, faraway, intersect, overlap, contain,...}, and spatial direction relationship ::={top, down, left, right, front, back, ...}.

Suppose spatial relationship for A and B is SR_k, then we can define metric similarity distance between A and B is [9]:

$$S = \frac{1}{|SRR(A,B) - M_k| + \theta} \qquad (3-2)$$

In (3-2), where M_k is median of SRR (A, B), θ is a small plus. If a SQL sentence as follow:

```
Select h.patient, h.image
from hemorrhage h, lateral_ventrice l
```

where h NEAR l;

Then analyses this SQL sentence, found 'NEAR' is a semantic feature that contains spatial relationship, then use (3-2) and change the SQL sentence as: (unit is mm)

```
Select h.patient, h.image
from hemorrhage h, lateral_ventrice l
```

where s<2;

3.3 WK-NN algorithm

Based on primary visual feature (such as texture, sharp, area of focus, intensities, and so on) or semantic feature (need to change query predicate) of reference image, this is similar query [10, 11, 12]. In our image databases, we use WK-NN algorithm to combine all query type, and the processing of query is used dynamic programming to obtain an optimal query path (global minimum cost) among various meta-query strategies. The major drawback in K-NN (K-nearest neighborhood) algorithm is lack of weight of meta-query; it supposed that weight for all meta-query type is equal. In fact, we know, query by keywords is faster than query by example (QBE). (See figure 5, we indexed the high dimension feature

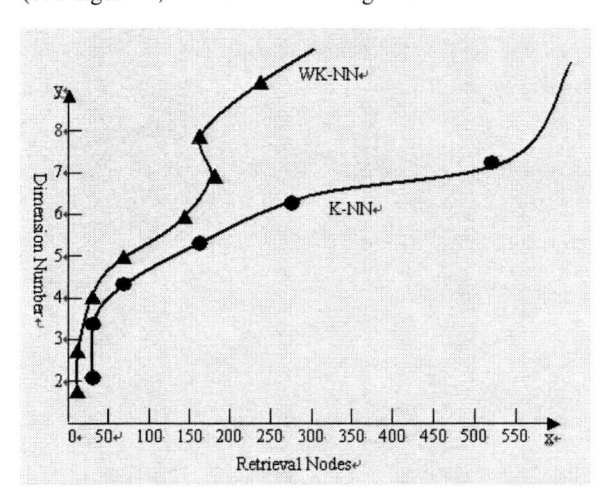

Figure 5. K-NN versus WK-NN for similarity retrieval

vectors using R*-TREE, then used the two algorithms to similarly retrieve, require to return 10 nearest similarity images). It indicates that compares with k-NN, WK-NN algorithm can reduce the radius of searching fast, and upgrade the cost efficiency of query algorithm

WK-NN searching algorithm (m, A, K)
// m is the number of query conjunction word; A is the
//set of A_i; A_i is the meta-query under the query
//predicate i; K is the number of similarity images after
//querying;

(1) Initialization.
  for i=1 to m do {

  index A_i using weight factor W A_i; save as a query queue WA;

  x_i =null}

(2) Search for k matches
  for i=1 to m do{

  Search for the maximum value W A_i in WA;

  G_i = Nearest searching (A_i, K)

  $x_i = x_i \Box G_i$ }

  if (|L| < K) then L= $\bigcap_{i=1}^{m} S_i(x)$

  //L is the intersection of x_i;

(3) Computing the similarity of candidate object

$$Y = \left\{ x \middle| x \in \bigcup_{i=1}^{m} x_i \right\}$$

  j = the object number in Y

  // S_i is similarity fraction for x_i in Y;

  for i =1 to j do {computing S_i, and storing (x_i, S_i) into Y}   // $S_{A_1 \cap A_2 \cap ... A_N}(x) = \Pi S_i(x)$

(4) Search for k nearest similar objects
  if WA ≠ null then repeat (2)
else return {k objects for maximum similarity fraction}.
See figure 6, which is returned result set (10 nearest similarity images) with WK-NN algorithm. The left-top corner image is QBE image.

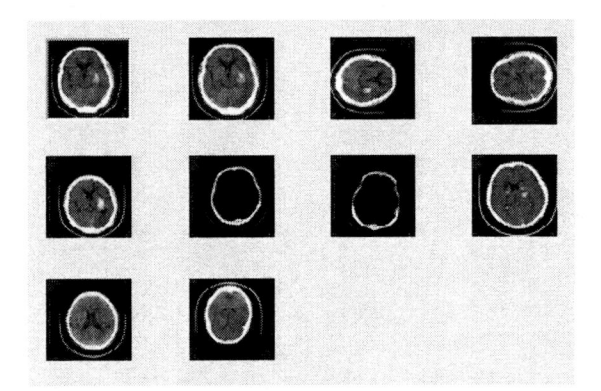

Figure6. Result set with WK-NN query algorithm

4. Conclusion

After find in the most similarity matching image, we can merge these content-correlated images. Result is shown in figure 7c. In figure 7c, hemorrhage region reflected the merging for hemorrhage regions in 7a and

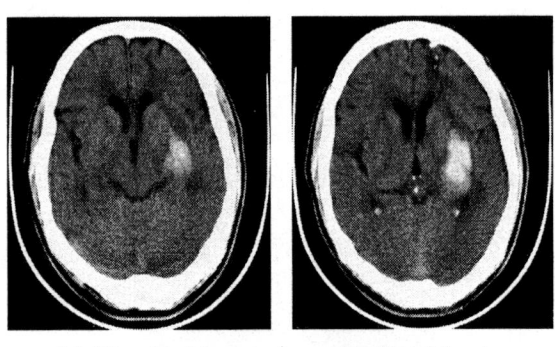

(a) Standard image (b) Matching image

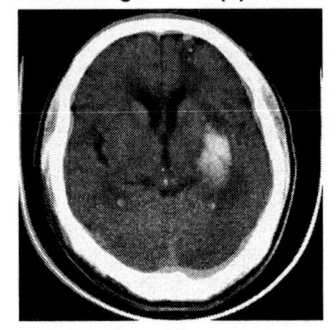

(c) Fused image

Figure7. Semantic content applied to image fusion

7b, like the other semantic regions. Above 7c, we can do some measurements and draw some interesting conclusions for doctor. Of course, we merely research in a small proportion of problem. There is much future work to fulfillment, especially to merge by complex image data and higher accuracy.

5. REFERENCES

[1] Chen Zhenchen, et al., Applications and Development of Artificial Intelligence for medical image expert systems, Biomedical Engineering, 2001,5: 201-206

[2] Wu Feng, et al., Multimodality medical image registration based on mutual information and simulated annealing, Journal of Fourth Military University, 2002

[3] Duan Feng, et al., Application of chamfer matching in the registration of CT and MRI, Journal of Air Force Engineering University, Dec. 2001:74-77

[4] Frederik M, et al., Multimodality image registration by maximization of mutual information, IEEE Transaction of Medical Imaging, 1997,16(2):187-198

[5] Maurer AC, et al., Registration of head CT images to physical space using a weighted combination of points and surfaces, IEEE Transaction of Medical Imaging, 1998,17(5): 753-761

[6] Milan Sonka, et al., Image processing, analysis, and machine vision (Second Edition), Thomson Learning Co., 2001

[7] George F. Luger, Artificial intelligence structures and strategies for complex problem solving (fourth edition), China Machine Press, 2003

[8] J. Han, M. Kamber, Data mining: concepts and techniques, China Machine Press, 2001

[9] Gao Yongying, Zhang Yujin, Progressive image content understanding based on multi-level image description model, Acta Electronica Sinica, October 2001, 1376-1380

[10] Liu Shilin, Image retrieval based on content, Journal of Jiamusi University, 2001,19(3): 257-259

[11] Del Bimbo AD, et al., Visual image retrieval by elastic matching of user sketches, IEEE Transaction on Pattern Analysis and Machine Intelligence, 1997, 19(2): 121-132

[12] Han Shuihua, Chen Chunbo, A retrieval mechanism for complex similarity queries in image databases, Chinese J. Computers, 2001, 24-27

Photo-Realistic Representation of Anatomical Structures for Medical Education by Fusion of Volumetric and Surface Image Data

Arthur W. Wetzel[1], Gary L. Nieder[2], Geri Durka-Pelok[3], Thomas R. Gest[3], Stuart M. Pomerantz[1], Demian Nave[1], Silvester Czanner[1], Lynn Wagner[2], Ethan Shirey[1] and David W. Deerfield[1]

[1]The Pittsburgh Supercomputing Center, [2]Wright State University, [3]The University of Michigan
E-mail: awetzel@psc.edu, gary.nieder@wright.edu, gest@umich.edu

Abstract

We have produced improved photo-realistic views of anatomical structures for medical education combining data from photographic images of anatomical surfaces with optical, CT and MRI volumetric data such as provided by the NLM Visible Human Project. Volumetric data contains the information needed to construct 3D geometrical models of anatomical structures, but cannot provide a realistic appearance for surfaces. Nieder has captured high quality photographic sequences of anatomy specimens over a range of rotational angles. These have been assembled into QuickTime VR Object movies that can be viewed statically or dynamically. We reuse this surface imagery to produce textures and surface reflectance maps for 3D anatomy models to allow viewing from any orientation and lighting condition. Because the volumetric data comes from different individuals than the surface images, we have to warp these data into alignment. Currently we do not use structured lighting or other direct 3D surface information, so surface shape is recovered from rotational sequences using silhouettes and texture correlations. The results of this work will be used to improve the appearance and generality of models used for anatomy instruction with the PSC Volume Browser.

1. Introduction

We are building an anatomical visualization system to improve students' understanding of the relationships and function of anatomical structures. Our approach integrates volumetric data sources with realistic surface textures derived from photographs of anatomical specimens.

In 1991 the National Library of Medicine (NLM) initiated the Visible Human Project to provide a complete full body volumetric data resource for medical education and anatomical research [1]. Under an NLM contract the University of Colorado captured two data sets, the Visible Male and Visible Female, using three image modalities, optical, CT and MRI [2]. Each modality is best suited to particular types of study. For example, skeletal structures are most easily segmented from the CT data due to the high x-ray contrast of bones. However, relatively little information about soft tissue structures can be seen in that data. Soft tissues present much better contrast in MRI but the resolution is low. Optical cryoplanar images, captured by photographing the sectioning surfaces of the frozen Visible Female, provide color imagery of the entire body at 0.33mm isotropic resolution (CCD images).

The educational need to map and model structural relationships from these data volumes in order to understand function was a primary motivation behind the Visible Human project [3]. However, the 2-dimensional nature of raw Visible Human slice data limits the ability to learn and understand the 3-dimensional object structure of the body. Therefore, a large part of work done by users of the Visible Human has been directed to segmenting the volumetric data to build 3D models that can be seen in the context of surrounding tissues and organs.

A number of visualization environments, including the Pittsburgh Supercomputing Center Volume Browser (PSC-VB) [4], and the University of Michigan Edgewarp [5] and iVoxel programs, have been developed to provide full body dynamic navigation through the Visible Human data and display arbitrary cutting plane images, along with 3D anatomical models produced from data segmentation. These models can be seen from any orientation or scale in superposition with their Visible Human context. PSC-VB is currently used at the University of Michigan as a teaching aid in anatomy courses [6][7]. However, the current model surfaces are non-textured and in a single color that does not provide a realistic surface appearance.

Creation of improved colored and textured surfaces derived from the Visible Human datasets has been an ongoing research project for a number of groups, including Project Vesalius™ at Columbia University [8]. The logical approach is to segment each structure from the volume and then color its surface according to the intersecting voxels. For example, determining the appropriate surface color for bone adjacent to surrounding tissue is sketched in Figure 1. In this simplified example we illustrate the concept by supposing that bone directly touches muscle. Choosing voxels that intersect the segmentation surface uses the color and texture from the "A" and "B" voxels. Since "A" voxels are primarily muscle this would produce a surface with splotchy red regions instead of the classical tan color. If, instead, one requires that each voxel be primarily from the structure being colored, bone in this case, then voxels "B" and "C" could be used. Again, since each "B" voxel contains some mixed portion of muscle and bone the surface would still take on some of the reddish muscle color.

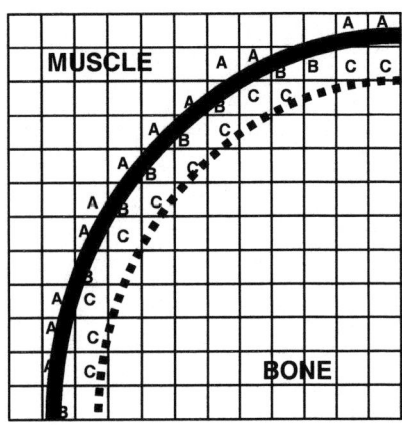

Figure 1. Example (e.g., bone in muscle) of a surface (bold solid line) overlaid on underlying voxel data. The surface coloring will be taken from a selected set of voxels.

A next logical step is to move one voxel layer deeper into the bone. However, this runs the risk of using portions of other substructures (e.g., the marrow in the bones). One difficulty in automatically selecting these voxels is that the subsurfaces, such as marrow, are often close to the surface being colored both spatially and in color space. The actual situation is much more complex because there are interface layers and membranes, often thinner than the voxel size, that cover the entire surface of every structure. Material even one voxel into most structures has different characteristics from the actual surface. There is additional mixing of voxel information in the original transverse planes due to the point-spread function of the camera system and axially due to light penetration. This all adds to the fundamental problem that any voxel close to a surface will contain more than one tissue type. Except for serendipitous surfaces that coincident with cryo-planing, true surface textures are totally lost in the volumetric data. Finally, there is a question of precisely which anatomical surface one wants to present for a particular application. Thus, the coloring of surfaces using only information from the original volumetric data is difficult and ambiguous.

Using the best of these algorithms we have extracted a voxel colored surface from the Visible Female humerus shown in Figure 2a. Although this technique produces a better surface appearance than the abstract solid model approach, many important anatomical details smaller than the voxel resolution are still not visible and the quality is clearly inferior to the surface photograph in Figure 2b. At the full 0.33mm resolution the voxel surface also has transverse striation artifacts due to the slicing of the Visible Female body and some loss of data, such as the black saw kerf from the original sectioning of the body.

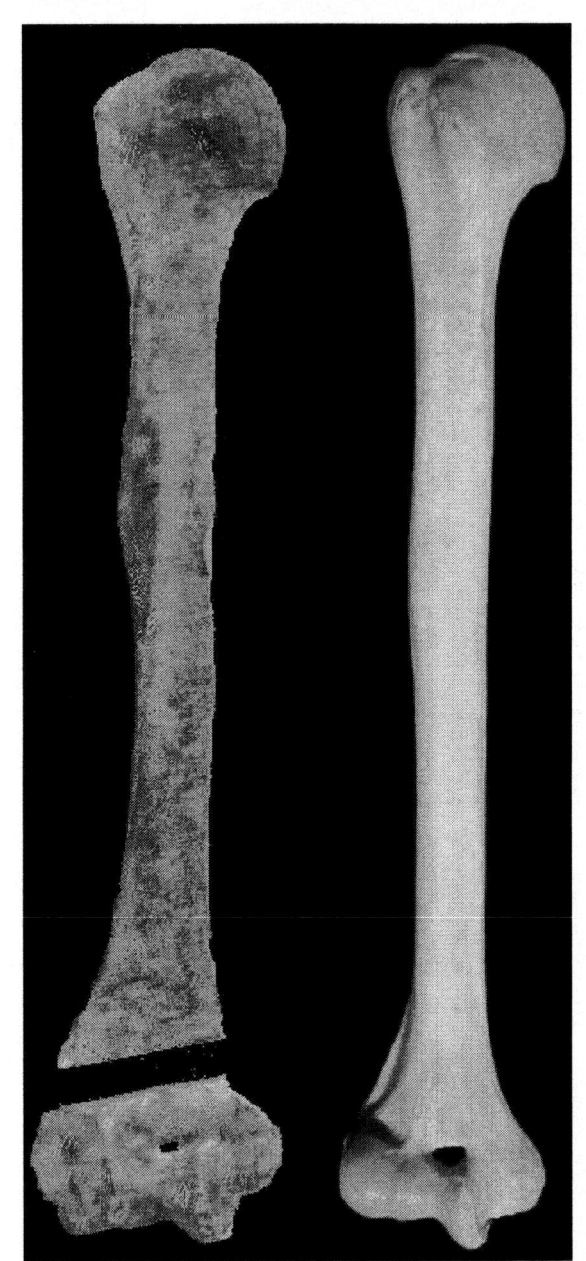

Figure 2a. Visible Female humerus voxel surface (left) Figure 2b. photograph of a dried humerus specimen (right)

Since the humeri of Figure 2a and 2b are from different individuals they demonstrate typical individual differences at a detailed level. The deltoid tuberosity is more pronounced in **Figure 2a**. Color discriminations along the Visible Female's humerus are very obvious and most likely typify the connective tissue plane of fascia that intervenes between muscle and bone. This fascial tissue penetrates into the humerus surface in channels (pits) called Volkman's Canals and represents the periosteum fascial cover of bones like the humerus forming an anchor system. The pits are visible in the gross anatomy sense. Hence, muscle does not physically touch the actual bone surface except at the point of attachment of tendons, or flattened tendons (an aponeurosis) to bone. A component of the voxel data would therefore be the periosteum. The **Figure 2b** photograph of the dried humerous has had the periosteum fascia stripped from its surface providing a smooth bone surface with pits or perforations through the surface of the humerus. Certain pits are dedicated channels for neurovascular structures entering and exiting bone.

Nieder has taken a different approach to producing surface views for computer assisted anatomy instruction by assembling systematically taken photographic series of laboratory specimens into QuickTime Virtual Reality (QTVR) movies [9][10]. Nieder has assembled a substantial collection of QTVR movies of anatomical objects, which is accessible over the web from the Wright State QTVR Anatomical Resource [11]. These QTVR renditions, currently used for anatomy instruction at both Wright State and the University of Michigan, can be manipulated to any viewpoint captured by the original photography. Typically, 36 views at 10-degree increments around a rotational axis are used to give a reasonable degree of rotational control. One reduced image from a humerus series was shown in **Figure 2b** for comparison to the voxel surface **Figure 2a**. The QTVR method enhances the educational experience because of its photographic quality and the interaction of the student during viewing.

A major strength of QTVR objects is the ability to capture them from many specimen sources with relative ease. This is especially important when the application expands from normal anatomy to include anomalies and pathological specimens. Researchers can prepare and non-destructively process interesting specimens from any cadaver into an object movie with simple equipment and minimal time investment. This is a significant advantage compared to the time and specialized equipment needed for capturing voxel data, such as the Visible Human.

Models of this photographic type surpass current "painted" skins covering anatomical models created by animators and computer programmers. There is no additional segmentation, model construction, or surface cleanup processing required. Furthermore, the definition of which surface to represent is resolved. In the case of "wet" specimens surface membranes may be left intact or removed as desired. Any glossy or translucent appearance is also correctly shown. With appropriate specimens and manual effort it is also possible to capture anatomical motions using stop motion photography. In this technique a specimen, such as the articulated knee included on the Wright State QTVR Anatomical Resource web site, is incrementally repositioned between each photograph so it can be displayed to show the actual relative movement of bones, cartilage and ligaments.

There are still some limitations to the QTVR method since students can only see the images from the vantage points used in the original photography. In addition, QTVR sequences 1) cannot be viewed in a surrounding 3D context of Visible Human or other volumetric data, 2) cannot be repositioned in relation to models of related or connecting structures, and 3) cannot be further processed by other computational techniques. Also, the compression levels typically used to build QTVR movies limits the range of effective zoom scales so the full detail of the original photographic resolution is usually not presented.

2. Methods

The PSC, Wright State University, and the University of Michigan are creating a digital hybrid where 3D models, constructed using volumetric datasets from the National Library of Medicine's Visible Human Project or other sources, are combined with texture-mapped surfaces derived from photographs of anatomical specimens. This fusion of photographic imagery, volumetric data and surface models overcomes limitations of current practice to provide accurate and realistic depictions of anatomical structures for improved anatomical instruction. Our approach attempts to encompass the best features from all of the methods currently in use by the collaborators.

A limited linkage between PSC-VB's display of the Visible Female and the Wright State QTVR data has already been demonstrated [12]. Our current work, however, is much more ambitious since it reuses the Wright State image collection outside of the QTVR environment to recover the 3D surface geometry of each object together with its accurate surface texture. These surface models can be used to reconstruct the appearance of that object from any viewpoint but can also be mapped onto object models from other sources. Enhancements to PSC-VB provide an interface by which these models can be accessed anywhere over the Internet and viewed embedded into the Visible Human data volumes.

The Wright State photographs were taken using a rotating specimen stage with a controlled lighting configuration depicted in **Figure 3**. A black velvet backdrop and painted stage ensure that only the specimen of interest appears in the images on a clean black background. A Kodak/Nikon DCS 315 digital camera produces high quality images, with an effective resolution of ~200 pixels per inch at the distance of the stage axis.

Since this camera supports interchangeable lenses, an appropriate lens is selected according to the size of each specific specimen. The lighting setup provides illumination with a good compromise between soft fill and a predominant lighting direction that provides visual shape cues from shading differences.

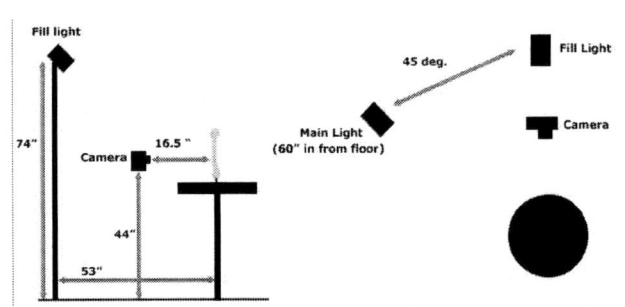

Figure 3. Side (left) and top down view (right) of the rotating stage photographic arrangement

Specimens from the Wright State anatomy lab, or those on loan from the University of Michigan and elsewhere, are mounted on the stage and photographed through a full 360-degree rotation with equal step sizes and a uniform camera elevation. For most objects, a 10-degree step is sufficient. For some specimens additional image series are taken with a higher and lower camera elevation so the top and bottom of the object can be seen more clearly. This is the same standard process and configuration used at Wright State for their regular QTVR production.

We wanted to take advantage of the large existing QTVR image collection. Therefore, we have been recovering object shape using only the information in the photographs and knowledge of the relative geometry of the stage, camera and lighting sources. Because the vast majority of the QTVR archive predates our current work, no effort was made to incorporate structured lighting, 3D digitization or other mechanisms that could simplify the process of object shape recovery and the associated construction of texture to object mappings.

Our initial goal is to produce fully textured models of the skeletal system. The skeletal system is a natural choice from the anatomy perspective since it provides a relatively rigid framework for all of the other body structures. Unlike other organs, dried bone specimens can be re-measured, re-photographed, or re-digitized at a later time to check the accuracy of the process or recover from problems. A number of the other objects in the Wright State QTVR collection are from unpreserved soft tissue specimens that may not be available for further study and, since they are deformable, could not be easily repositioned into a reproducible configuration for further analysis.

A greatly reduced 3-image portion from a 36-image sequence of a humerus specimen is shown in Figure 4 along with a tiny sample of the full resolution imagery.

Clearly, the bone surface is not a uniform bone color but contains many small pores and other features previously discussed in relation to Figure 2a. These details are more effectively represented by surface texturing rather than by building an excessively complex geometry of the surface.

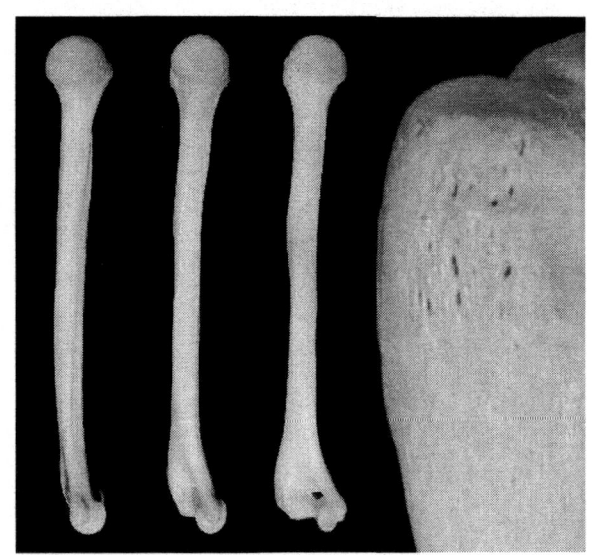

Figure 4. Greatly reduced partial humerus image series (left) and full resolution sample (right)

Even if some small surface details are not anatomically consistent between individuals, they still provide an immediately recognizable visual appearance that is similar to other specimens. Of course, the specific appearance depends on many factors including the age of the specimen and method of preservation. By photographing different specimens that cover the range of anatomical age and other variables, we hope to capture a enough interchangeable surface textures and models to depict the variations that anatomy students will encounter as they continue their career. Students will be able to page through this collection to see them each placed in their correct anatomical context in the Visible Human volumes.

In order to map the photographic textures onto models taken from, or inserted into, a volumetric context we have to recover geometric models of corresponding structures from both the volumetric and image data sources. We chose the humerus due to simplicity and availability of QTVR datasets. We used PSC-VB to produce segmented slice contours of the humerus from the Visible Female. The contours were then processed with the Powercrust program [13][14] to produce a mesh model. Powercrust uses properties of the Voronoi complex to generate a polygonal mesh approximating the surface sampled by the point set. The mesh is guaranteed to converge to the original surface as the point set density approaches infinity. In cases where the mesh is overly complex, we simplify it using Mike Garland's Qslim program [15].

Models of the structures photographed for QTVR production were built using a different process. In simple cases, such as the humerus, most of the surface can be recovered from silhouettes of the bone in the rotational image series. Our process uses rays computationally projected into 3D perspective space from the camera position to carve around the silhouette of each image successively removing volume regions that are outside the bone. An iterative process is used to obtain a consistent camera position and rotational axis since these were not known with adequate precision from prior measurements of the capture rig. The surface of the remaining volume is flood painted to recover the surface point cloud that is further processed using the same Powercrust and Qslim procedure used previously. Of course, this mechanism is sufficient only for regions with convex cross sections.

The ability to model concave surfaces is achieved by correlating pixels between successive rotational images to determine positional displacements so we can recover depth by triangulation. This process requires surface positions to be visible and identifiable in at least two images. Typically the same surface position can be seen in as many as 12 of the 36 images which improves the length of the triangulation baseline. Since we know that all points on the surface follow axis-centered circular trajectories, the search range for this correlation process is tightly constrained. In image space, pixels at the height of the camera simply move in a horizontal sinusoidal path with a slight correction for perspective rather than orthographic image projection. Pixels above and below the camera level travel along portions of increasingly open ellipses.

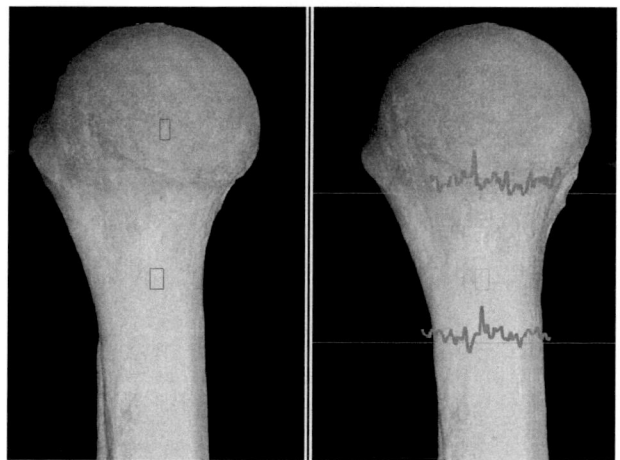

Figure 5. Correlation of surface patches between rotational steps in rough and smooth regions

Use of image correlations to recover shape assumes an adequate level of surface texture so that strong peaks in the correlations can be found. Fortunately, even relatively smooth objects, like the central shafts of the humeri, contain sufficient texture at the resolution of our source image data. Two graphs of typical correlations across a series of target positions are illustrated in Figure 5. The two sample patches in the left image were correlated along each potential rotational trajectory in the right image that is the next 10 degree step from a rotational image series. We have found a similar accuracy of position correlation over the entire bone surface except in regions of specular reflection. The assumption of surface continuity from surrounding regions easily bridges those small gaps.

Once the surface point cloud and model have been produced, we back project into the original images to recover pixel color and intensity values. Corresponding pixel values recovered from multiple views are not all the same due to changes in direction of illumination, specular reflection, and shadowing. Currently, we use the median observed value to estimate surface color and brightness. When the PSC-VB displays surfaces, a new set of virtual light sources are applied and the surfaces are shaded appropriately based on the relative directions of light and surface normals. In the future, we will use the full set of sampled values together with surface normals to estimate specularity and bi-directional reflectance properties.

Even for normal anatomical structures there are large individual differences in size and shape. Consequently, if we are to apply a surface texture to different model, we need to determine the point-to-point mapping between the models so we can assign proper texture coordinates. In our current test case we have used a small number of manually positioned landmark points to define an overall smooth warping from the image model to the target volume model.

3. Results and Discussion

The surface model of a humerus recovered from the Wright State QTVR photography has been inserted into the PSC-VB environment for visualization together with the Visible Female data. Figure 6 shows the PSC-VB slice window of a cutting plane through the Visible Female shoulder including the upper part of its humerus. Figure 7 is PSC-VB's context view of the position of the slice with respect to the body surface. In this case the humerus recovered from QTVR source images is superimposed in place of the original Visible Female humerus. This model is intentionally abstract and translucent so users can see how the structures fit together in 3D space.

Figure 8 shows the same humerus model recovered from QTVR surface photography embedded in several surrounding cuts through the Visible Female data. This additional imagery helps the viewer to place the bone model in its proper anatomical context. In this case the bone is in a position that was not directly represented by any of the original QTVR photographs and is shown with its virtual illumination from the upper right rather than the illumination directions that were in the source images. We currently have not included specular reflections, so this bone is simulated as a purely diffuse Lambertian surface. Nevertheless, the result is easily recognizable as bone and does not suffer from the artifacts that occur when sampling voxels from the Visible Human data to build a surface.

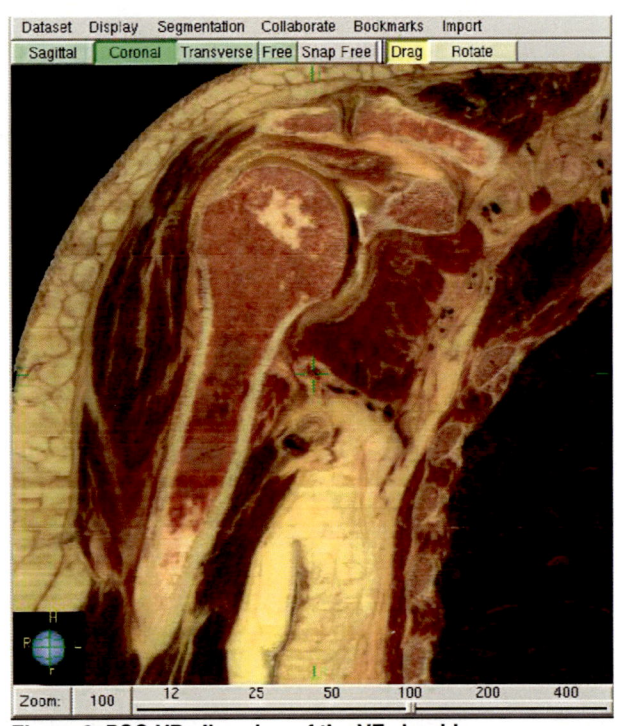

Figure 6. PSC-VB slice view of the VF shoulder

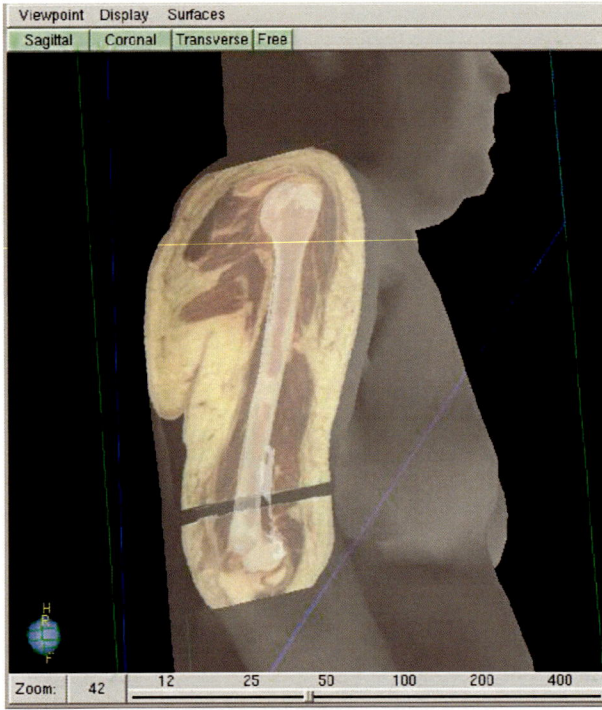

Figure 7. PSC-VB 3D context view

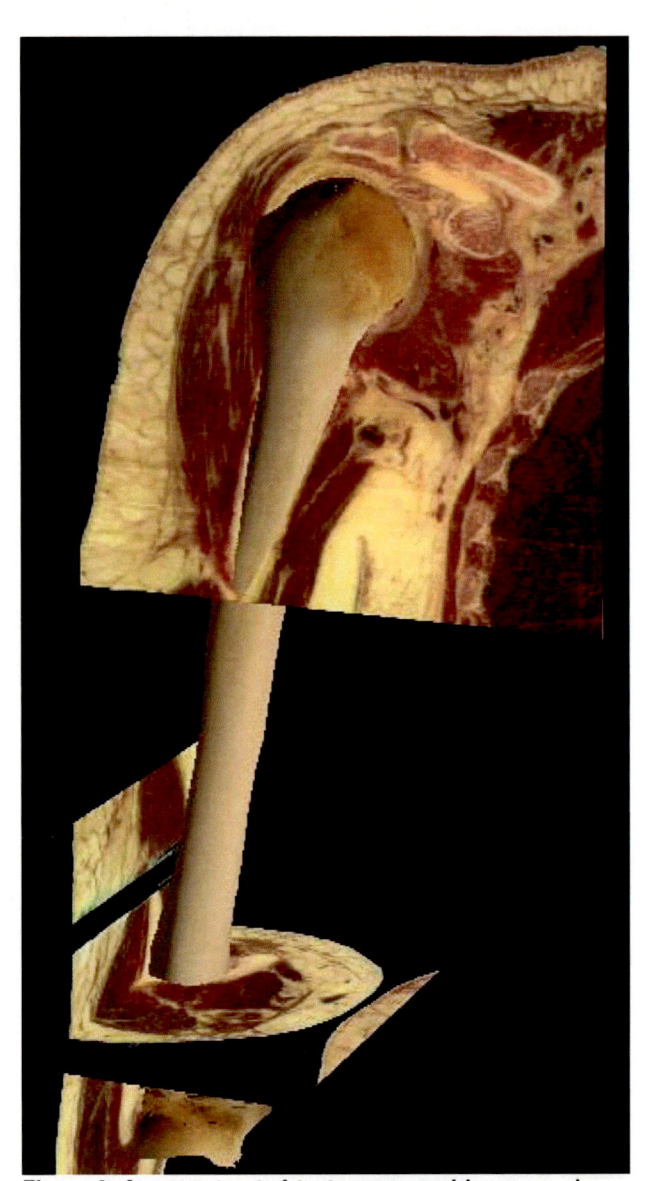

Figure 8. A reconstructed texture mapped humerus shown with a surrounding context of Visible Female slice imagery

Surface models produced by these methods can also be viewed together with new volumetric data sources, such as the Visible Human 2.0 [17], as they become available. Provided that appropriate landmark coordinates are located in these new volumes an existing surface model can be repositioned and warped into alignment with the volume without performing a complete segmentation and model construction from the new volume. Photo-realistic textured models also improve the visual quality of stereoscopic visualization due to the visual details that aid visual stereo fusion.

The availability of low cost high performance graphics hardware that can display 3-dimensional models with texture mapping, illumination shading, and bump mapping in real-time has expanded the range of anatomical representations that can be used for computer assisted instruction. The design approach of PSC-VB combines this graphical capability with computer networking so that students can interactively access large repositories of anatomical data that cannot be easily stored on their own PC. Lesson plans and course materials can be modified without having to distribute CDROM sets to the students. Appropriate visual displays ranging from artistic illustration, to solid or translucent surfaces, voxel surfaces and now photo-realistic textured surfaces can be combined with the display of volumetric data in whatever way best accomplishes the learning goals.

Providing photo-realistic textured surfaces derived from actual structures narrows the cognitive "gap," which reduces the amount of time and effort required for viewers to understand complex anatomical relationships. While computer-generated images may never fully replace the dissection laboratory, the ability to look at realistic images will provide greater insight into bones, organs, and tissues that weave together in an intricate relationship of development, physiology, mechanical movement, and pathology. With the increased cost and decreased availability of donor bodies for dissection, greater emphasis will be placed on alternative forms of teaching (e.g. prosections, plasticized models, digital images).

Requirements for the general public and undergraduate students are different from the requirements for medical students and practicing physicians. The broad anatomical and physiological concepts are what is important for the general public and undergraduate students; thus, the volumetric datasets from the Visible Human Project coupled with highly accurate surfaces from the segmented structures would suffice. The ability to perform virtual dissections would complete the majority of the educational requirements for this group. However, professionals in the medical and biological communities have a greater need to understand differences between many individual bodies.

Extension of this approach to include samples that demonstrate developmental changes, natural variability, or specific pathology states will greatly enhance anatomical education. One can imagine creation of an archive showing a number of natural and compromised tissues, which provides a natural framework for the systematic study of anatomical variation that is not possible using just the two Visible Human specimens. With the availability of a number of examples of a single bone or system (e.g., the hand), one can begin to understand the interdependencies between structure and variability. Potentially the most important part of this study would be the age-related anatomical changes, since donor bodies rarely include age groups ranging from children to middle-aged adults. By creating a database of models that includes all age groups and continuous updates of pathologies, healthcare students and practitioners can be exposed to variations within the populations they will eventually serve. These may differ from the small number they have seen during their studies. Surgical procedures, and developmental and pathological research will be enhanced by the ability to manipulate and hypothesize against an increasing collection of varied anatomy representing the general population.

Methods to accurately represent anatomical structures in their correct positions will be essential as surgical simulation becomes routine. For surgeons, visualizing and understanding spatial relationships is critical. For example, in orthopedic surgery, variability across the width of a humerus must be accurately calculated so that screws used to hold bone plates are of the correct length and placed at the optimal angle. Using virtual simulation with variable models would facilitate the learning, planning, and performing of such surgical procedures [18]. Provided with an appropriate model such as the humerus and its connecting bones, tendons, and ligaments- motion and the effects of structural change due to breaks, displacement, and orthopedic surgery could be viewed and understood. Work being done by Cooper, et. al. [19] on the moving human lumbar spine utilizes 3-dimensional modeling to assess spinal load and motion. In another example, endoscopic surgery has progressed to involve digitization of the pre-, intra-, and postoperative surgery, with the use of 3-dimensional visualizations to plan and practice procedures [20]. Mapping of individual patient structures (created via MRI or CAT scans) to practice models would provide the surgeon or student with information on how the patient variation may affect the procedure, as well as providing research on how procedures performed and how patient outcomes were affected by variability in structure.

The use of digital models to teach basic function and structure, as well as surgical procedures and research use, will expand as telemedicine rises to the forefront of collaborative science and education. This age of information has resulted in tele-education, tele-teaching, tele-training, tele-mentoring, and tele-accreditation across the globe [21]. The need for 3-dimensional models to convey information and provide content in support of medical and biological knowledge domains will demand the techniques to create accurate digital models quickly.

4. Conclusions

We have demonstrated a method for the accurate extraction of shape, color and texture for biological specimens from a systematic series of photographic images. When fused with segmented structures from volumetric datasets, users can see realistic 3D surface models in their proper orientations along with surrounding structures in either mono- or stereo projections and interactively navigate to any vantage point. The use of proper surfaces narrows the viewers' cognitive gap and provides students with accurate tools to supplement dissection. Extensions of this approach will provide a data resource to demonstrate variability in developmental changes, natural variability or specific pathology states.

5. Acknowledgments

The collection of images and development of the QTVR modules (GN, LW) has been supported by an NIH grant (LM06924). The PSC Volume Browser (PSC-VB) was developed (AW, SP, DN, DD) and evaluated in a classroom setting (GD-P, TG) under the auspices of a contract from the NIH (LM03511) to the University of Michigan Visible Human Project led by Dr. Brian Athey. We appreciate the many fruitful discussions and feedback from members of this project; particularly Drs. Fred Bookstein and William Green, whose Edgewarp program provided an initial model for PSC-VB's cutting plane display. Additional enhancements, collaborative features and compression (AW, SP, DN, CZ, ES, DD) to PSC-VB have been made under a second NIH grant (RR06009). We thank Dr. Donald P. Jenkins for his comments and the description of the periosteum and humerus features.

References

[1] Ackerman, M.J., The Visible Human Project. The Journal of Biocommunication, vol. 18, no. 2, pp. 14, 1991.

[2] Spitzer, V.M., Ackerman, M.J., Scherzinger, A.L. and Whitlock, D.G., The visible human male: a technical report. The Journal of the American Medical Information Association, vol. 3(2), pp. 118-30, 1996.

[3] Ackerman M.J. The visible human project: a resource for education. Academic Medicine 74(6):667-670 (1999)

[4] A.W. Wetzel, S.M. Pomerantz, D. Nave, A. Kar, J. Sommerfield, M. Mathis, D.W. Deerfield II, F.L. Bookstein, W.D. Green, A. Ade, B. Athey, "A Networked Environment for Interactively Viewing and Manipulating Visible Human Datasets", Proceedings of the 4th Visible Human Conference, Keystone, Colorado, Oct 17-19, 2002

[5] Bookstein, F., Athey, B.. Wetzel, A.W., and Green, W. Navigating solid medical images by pencils of sectioning planes. In SPIE 45th Annual Meeting, volume 4121, pp 117-121, SPIE 2000

[6] G. Durka-Pelok, S.M. Pomerantz, C. Gadd, T. Weymouth, T. Gest, J. Huang, D. Nave, A.W. Wetzel, S. Lee, B. Athey "Evaluation of a Volume Browser: PSC-VB", Proceedings of the 4th Visible Human Conference, Keystone, Colorado, Oct 17-19, 2002

[7] T. Weymouth, G. Durka-Pelok, T. Gest, J. Huang, S.M. Pomerantz, A.W. Wetzel, C. Burger, B. Athey, "Using a Knowledge Base: The University of Michigan Visible Human Project", Proceedings of the 4th Visible Human Conference, Keystone, Colorado, Oct 17-19, 2002.

[8] http://cpmcnet.columbia.edu/vesalius/

[9] Nieder, G.L., J. Scott, and M.D. Anderson. Using QuickTime VR objects in computer-assisted instruction of gross anatomy: Yorick - The VR Skull. Clinical. Anatomy, 13(4), 287-293 (2000)

[10] Trelease, R.B., G.L. Nieder, J. Dørup, and M.Hansen. Going Virtual with QuickTime VR: New Standardized Tools for Interactive Dynamic Visualization of Anatomical Structures. Anatomical Record - New Anatomist 261:64-77 (2000).

[11] http://www.anatomy.wright.edu/QTVR/index.html

[12] G. Durka-Pelok, T. Gest, G. Nieder, T. Weymouth, Jie Huang, A.W. Wetzel, S.M. Pomerantz, D. Nave, B. Athey, "Creation of an educational visual module: integration of QTVR and the Visible Human Data Set", Proceedings of the 4th Visible Human Conference, Keystone, Colorado, Oct 17-19, 2002.

[13] Nina Amenta, Sunghee Choi and Ravi Kolluri. The power crust. Sixth ACM Symposium on Solid Modeling and Applications 2001, pages 249-260.

[14] http://www.cs.utexas.edu/users/amenta/powercrust/

[15] Heckbert, P. and Garland, M., Optimal Triangulation and Quadric-Based Surface Simplification, Journal of Computational Geometry: Theory and Applications, vol. 14 no. 1-3, pages 49-65, November 1999.

[16] Cooper, R., Cardan, C., and Allen, R. 2001. Computer visualisation of the moving human lumbar spine. Computers in Biology and Medicine 31(6): 451-469

[17] http://splweb.bwh.harvard.edu:8000/pages/ppl/ratiu/vham/

[18] Bernardo, A., Preul, M.C., Zabramski, J.M., and Spetzler, R.F. 2003. A three-dimensional interactive virtual dissection model to simulate transpetrous surgical avenues. Neurosurgery 52(3): 499-504.

[19] Cooper, R., Cardan, C., and Allen, R. 2001. Computer visualization of the moving human lumbar spine. Computers in Biology and Medicine 31(6): 451-469.

[20] Maresceaux, J., Soler, L., Ceulemans, R., Garcia, A., Henri, M., and Dutson, E. 2002. Image merging, virtual reality, robotics and minimally invasive surgery. Their influence on the practice of surgery. CHIRURG 73(5): 422-427.

[21] Malassagne, B., Mutter, D., Leroy, J., Smith, M., Soler, L., and Marescaux, J. 2001.Teleeducation in surgery: European Institute for TeleSurgery experience. World Journal of Surgery 25(11): 1490-1494.

Data Fusion Using Neural Networks

⌘ ⌘ ⌘ ⌘ ⌘ ⌘ ⌘ ⌘

Neural Network Based Skin Color Model for Face Detection

Ming-Jung Seow, Deepthi Valaparla, and Vijayan K. Asari
VLSI Systems Laboratory
Department of Electrical and Computer Engineering
Old Dominion University, Norfolk, VA 23529
Email: {mseow, dvala001, vasari}@odu.edu

Abstract

This paper presents a novel neural network based technique for face detection that eliminates limitations pertaining to the skin color variations among people. We propose to model the skin color in the three dimensional RGB space which is a color cube consisting of all the possible color combinations. Skin samples in images with varying lighting conditions, from the Old Dominion University skin database, are used for obtaining a skin color distribution. The primary color components of each plane of the color cube are fed to a three-layered network, trained using the backpropagation algorithm with the skin samples, to extract the skin regions from the planes and interpolate them so as to provide an optimum decision boundary and hence the positive skin samples for the skin classifier. The use of the color cube eliminates the difficulties of finding the non-skin part of training samples since the interpolated data is consider skin and rest of the color cube is consider non-skin. Subsequent face detection is aided by the color, geometry and motion information analyses of each frame in a video sequence. The performance of the new face detection technique has been tested with real-time data of size 320×240 frames from video sequences captured by a surveillance camera. It is observed that the network can differentiate skin and non-skin effectively while minimizing false detections to a large extent when compared with the existing techniques. In addition, it is seen that the network is capable of performing face detection in complex lighting and background environments.

1. Introduction

Unsupervised surveillance gadgets aided by hi-tech visual information indexing and retrieval systems are proving to be indispensable in the existing terror environment. Real-time applications such as frontal view face detection [1], tracking faces in natural scenes [2] and adult content filters [3] rely heavily on computationally inexpensive and adaptive face localization schemes which work in unconstrained environments. Face localization is the preliminary step towards recognition and identification of human facial characteristics in a visual scene. Contemporary approaches have built skin detectors based on histograms [4], which have the expensive time constraint. Skin color model based on the Gaussian distribution have not been able to deal with the variation of the skin distribution in non-uniform lighting environments [5]. Robust skin segmentation involves the formulation of an efficient mathematical model [6] to represent the skin color distribution. Segmenting skin from real-world images is a difficult task even though human skin is known to possess a unique color range, which is but a fraction of all the possible color combinations. The advantage of using the RGB color space in skin detection methods has been emphasized by Shin et al. [7]. in their comprehensive evaluation of existing color space transformations using four different separability criteria based on the scatter matrix and histogram analysis. Elimination of the illumination content by normalization [8] worsened the discriminating power due to projection of image data into lower dimensional space.

Face detection using statistical models in [9 and 10] have been strongly undermined by their inability to apply higher global constraints on the face template. In addition to that they have not been able to negate the influence of noise or changes in facial expressions on the extracted features. Neural network based face detection [11] tests for the existence of human faces using a retinally connected neural network, which requires scanning of the entire image for faces of different sizes and rotations thereby resulting in loss of valuable computation time. We propose a novel scheme in section 2 to model skin color, by training a three-layered network with skin and non-skin examples, using the back propagation algorithm. The trained network shown in Figure 1 is used to estimate the probable skin regions in a three-dimensional color cube and interpolate to provide a reasonable estimate of

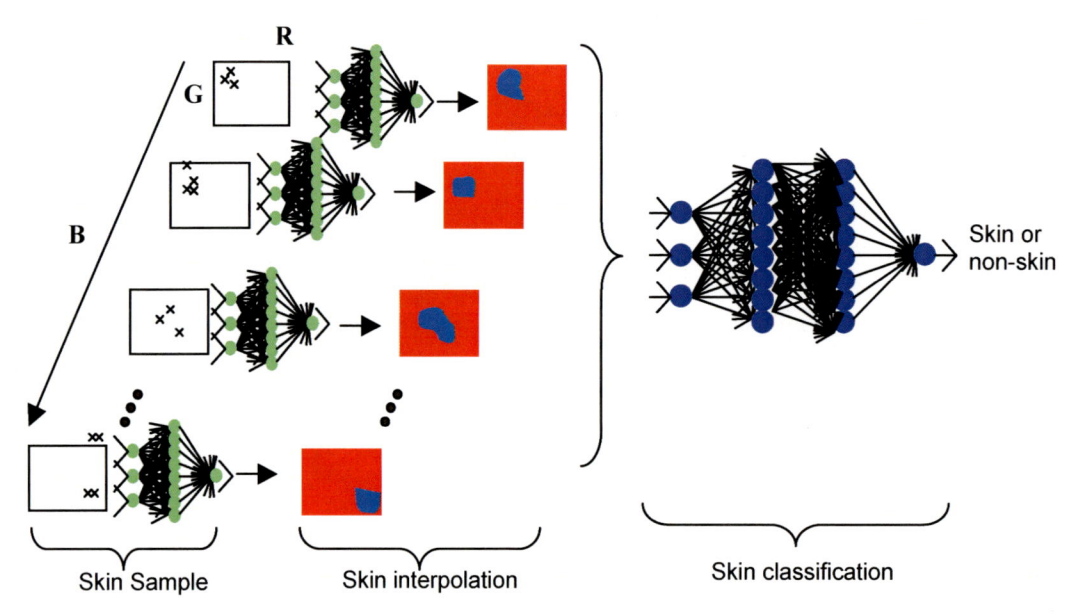

Figure 1. Overview of the algorithm

the skin color distribution. A new technique for face detection has been proposed in section 3 that significantly enhances the computational speed for real-time applications. Section 4 provides a comprehensive look into the simulation and performance analysis of the proposed model. Section 5 concludes with an insight into the issues of human face tracking and improving the proposed model.

2. Modeling skin color in the RGB color space

Training a neural network for the skin color detection is challenging because of the difficulty in characterizing non-skin color. It is easy to get a representative sample of images, which contain skin color, but it is much harder to get a representative sample of those, which do not, since objects can have color similar to the skin color. The training of the skin color model based on neural networks composed of three stages: skin color collection, skin color interpolation, and skin color classification. Figure 1 illustrates the proposed method for training, extraction and classification using the skin color model.

2.1. Skin Database Compilation

Skin colors from various races of the world are collected from the Internet in the form of 10 × 10 pixels per skin sample for each individual from each image. 410 such samples were collected. As a result, there are 41,000 skin pixels having different illuminations in our skin color database used for training the neural network. The skin obtained was used to compute a three-dimensional histogram and assess the extent of skin color in the color cube comprising of all the possible color combinations. Figure 2 shows that the human skin is a fraction of the actual color cube, roughly about 0.25 % of the total colors present.

2.2. Skin color interpolation

Since the skin color samples we have collected do not represent the skin color population, we need to interpolate for the skin color that we don't have using the skin color we have.

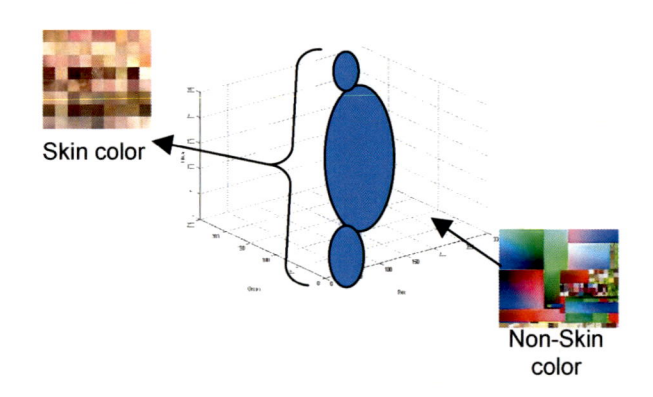

Figure 2: Histogram of the skin region

Multilayer perceptron trained using the back-propagation learning algorithm is used for skin color interpolation. Figure 3 illustrates the back propagation minimize the mean square error between the desired output and the actual output. The back propagation algorithm uses supervised learning where the training of the network is done with known input and output data. Once the network is trained, its weights can be used to compute outputs for new input values. We generated a 256×256×256 color cube to represent all the possible color combinations. Training the network involved learning of skin and non-skin examples. The primary color components of each of the 256 slices of the cube are fed to a three-layered network, trained using the back-propagation algorithm, to extract the skin regions (the crosses/ skin samples in Figure 1) from the slices and interpolate them so as to provide an optimized decision boundary for the skin regions (blue regions in Figure 1).

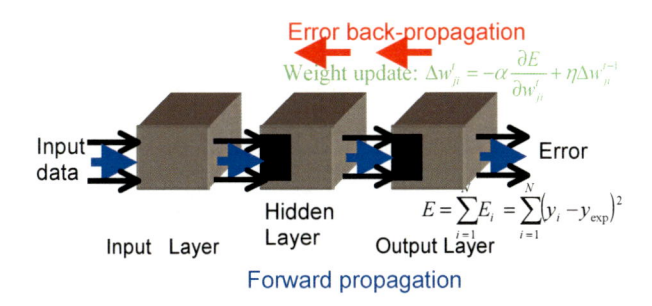

Figure 3: Back propagation algorithm

2.3. Skin color classification

Once the skin is interpolated it is used to train the three layer network for skin color classification. A three layered network is used since it is conceived from the color cube that the probable skin regions can be encapsulated by the complex decision boundaries such as the ones depicted in Figure 4, probably a hexagon.

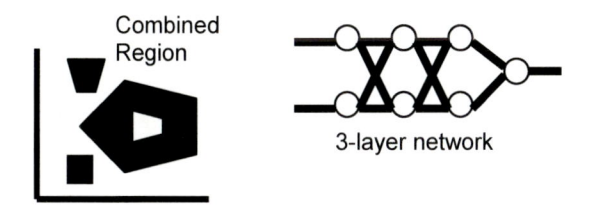

Figure 4: Optimized decision boundary

3. Face Detection

The proposed face detection technique analyzes the skin regions from each skin-segmented frame with a 20×20 mask similar to the one shown in Figure 5. Probable face regions in the images are divided into 9 regions according to the scheme shown in the figure. Nine different back propagation networks are used to decide the proximity of each of the 9 regions to a face region. The votes from each of the back propagation networks are used to decide if the probable face region is a face.

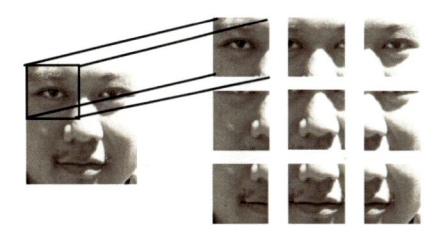

Figure 5. Architecture of the network

Result of the skin segmentation is used by the mask to scan for the face by the scanning process shown in Figure 6. Each of the 9 regions obtained by using the mask on a pixel-by-pixel scan of the image is subjected to a threshold function to decide if it corresponds to a facial feature. The presence of 4 facial features in the regions is needed for it to be detected as a face.

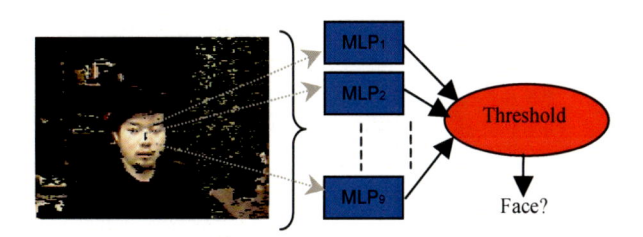

Figure 6. Illustration of the scanning process.

4. Simulation and Results

In addition to the skin samples that were collected during the skin database compilation, about 200 test images of individual persons and 150 images containing group photos were collected. Experiments were conducted in a Windows NT environment using Microsoft Visual C++ on a set of still images and video sequences. The first part of the simulation shows two still images with people of different races. The proposed method extracts skin very well irrespective of color of the skin as is evident from the results in Figures 7 (b) and 7 (d). The system was also used to detect and track human faces in real-time video sequences captured by an off the shelf Logitech camera, as is evident from Figure 8. It was able to detect faces in varying lighting environments too. The proposed face detection routine performed very well when compared to Rowley's method [11]. The reason being that the method does not need to scan the entire image every time. The skin detector reduces the search area considerably, saving a lot of computation time and enhancing the speed of the system.

7(a)

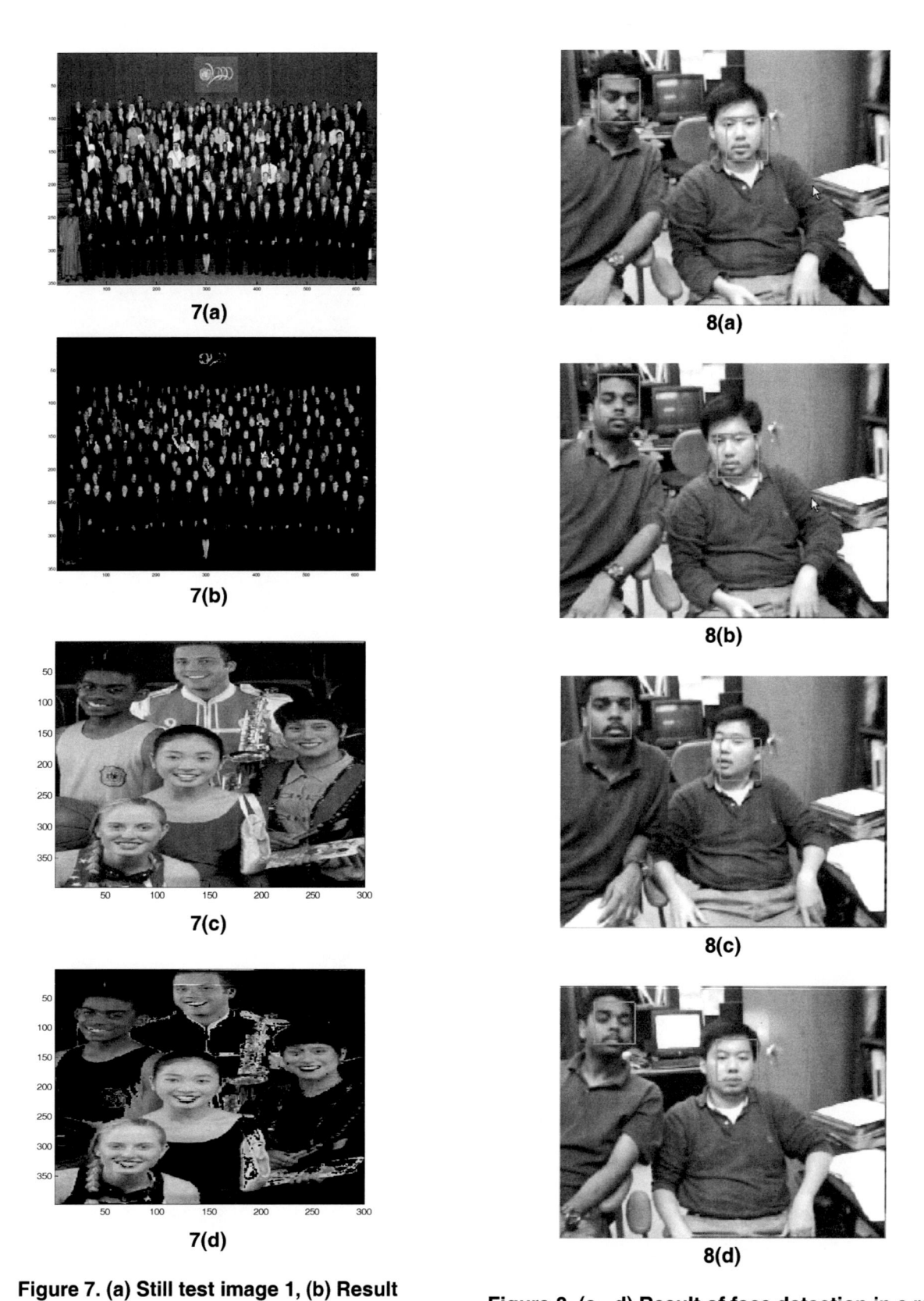

7(b)

7(c)

7(d)

Figure 7. (a) Still test image 1, (b) Result (c) Image 2, (d) Result

8(a)

8(b)

8(c)

8(d)

Figure 8. (a - d) Result of face detection in a real-time video sequence

144

5. Conclusion

A novel neural network based skin color model has been presented in this paper. The method has incorporated the concept of the color cube, back propagation and a novel filter based face detection technique to provide an accurate skin color model. The model has been used to segment still images and track faces in real-time video sequences in non-uniform lighting conditions. The computation time has been reduced considerably when compared to conventional techniques facilitating real-time applications. Further work is in progress to develop a face recognition system to identify and index individuals for surveillance purposes.

6. References

[1]. A. Eleftheriadis and A. Jacquin, "Automatic face location detection and tracking for model-assisted coding of video teleconferencing sequences at low bit-rates," *Signal Processing: Image Communication*, No. 7, 1995, pp. 231-248.

[2]. Y. Raja, S. J. McKenna and S. Gong, "Tracking and segmenting people in varying lighting conditions using color," *Proc. International Conference on Face and Gesture Recognition*, pp. 228-233, 1998.

[3]. M. M. Fleck, D. A. Forsyth and C. Dregler, "Finding naked people," *Proc. European Conference on Computer Vision*, 1996, pp. 593-602.

[4]. R. Kieldsen, J. Kender, "Finding skin color in images," *Proc. International Conference on Automatic Face and Gesture Recognition*, 1996, pp. 312-317.

[5]. S.J McKenna, S. Gong, Y. Raja, Modelling facial colour and identity with Gaussian mixtures, *Pattern Recognition*, vol. 31, no. 12, 1998, pp. 1883–1892.

[6]. J.C. Terrillon, M. David, S. Akamatsu, "Automatic detection of human faces in natural scene images by use of a skin color model and invariant moments," *Proc. International Conference on Automatic Face and Gesture Recognition*, 1998, pp. 112–117.

[7]. M. C. Shin, K. I. Chang, and L. V. Tsap, "Does Colorspace Transformation Make Any Difference on Skin Detection?," *IEEE Workshop on Applications of Computer Vision*, Orlando, FL, Dec 2002.

[8]. J. Yang and A. Waibel, "Tracking human faces in real-time," *Proc. IEEE Workshop on Applications of Computer Vision*, 1996.

[9]. K.C.Yow and R. Cipolla, "Feature-based human face detection," *Image and Vision Computing*, 1997, vol. 15, no. 9, pp. 713–735.

[10]. S. H. Jeng, Y. Y. M. Liao, C. C. Han, M. Y. Chern, Y. T. Liu, "Facial feature detection using geometrical face model: an efficient approach," *Pattern Recognition*, 1998, vol. 31, no. 3, pp. 273–282.

[11]. H. Rowley, S. Baluja, and T. Kanade, "Neural network based face detection," *IEEE Trans. Patt. Recog. Mach. Intell.*, January 1998, vol. 20, no. 1, pp. 23–38.

Real Time Face Detection from Color Video Stream Based on PCA Method

Rajkiran Gottumukkal and Vijayan K. Asari

VLSI Systems Laboratory
Department of Electrical and Computer Engineering
Old Dominion University, Norfolk, VA 23529

Abstract

We present a face detection system capable of detection of faces in real time from a streaming color video. Currently this system is able to detect faces as long as both the eyes are visible in the image plane. Extracting skin color regions from a color image is the first step in this system. Skin color detection is used to segment regions of the image that correspond to face regions based on pixel color. Under normal illumination conditions, skin color takes small regions of the color space. By using this information, we can classify each pixel of the image as skin region or non-skin region. By scanning the skin regions, regions that do not have shape of a face are removed. Principle Component Analysis (PCA) is used to classify if a particular skin region is a face or a non-face. The PCA algorithm is trained for frontal view faces only. The system is tested with images captured by a surveillance camera in real time.

1. Introduction

Automatic detection of the human faces has been an area of active research for the past few years. Although detection of faces does not seem to present any difficulties for most human observers, computerized face detection systems fail to achieve satisfactory performance due to numerous variations in expression, illumination and pose of human faces. A general statement of the problem can be defined as follows: Given a still or video image, detect and localize an unknown number (if any) of faces. The solution to the problem involves segmentation, extraction, and verification of faces and possibly facial features from an uncontrolled background. This task, therefore, still presents a significant challenge and is considered as one of the fundamental problems in computer vision and pattern analysis. In addition to the importance of the face detection from a research point of view, it has a number of commercial and law enforcement applications such as entrance control in buildings, access control for computers in general or for automatic teller machines in particular, day-to-day affairs like withdrawing money from a bank account or dealing with the post office, or in the prominent field of criminal investigation.

There are two main approaches for face detection. The techniques in the first category make explicit use of face knowledge and follow the classical detection methodology in which low level features are derived prior to knowledge-based analysis [1, 2]. The apparent properties of the face such as skin color and face geometry are exploited at different system levels. Typically, in these techniques face detection tasks are accomplished by manipulating distance, angles, and area measurements of the visual features derived from the scene. Since features are the main ingredients, these techniques are termed the feature-based approach. Taking advantage of the current advances in pattern recognition theory, the techniques in the second group address face detection as a general recognition problem. Image-based [3] representations of faces, for example in 2D intensity arrays, are directly classified into a face group using training algorithms without feature derivation and analysis. Unlike the feature-based approach, these relatively new techniques incorporate face knowledge implicitly [2] into the system through mapping and training schemes.

The development of the feature-based approach can be further divided into three areas. Given a typical face detection problem in locating a face in a cluttered scene, low-level analysis first deals with the segmentation of visual features using pixel properties such as gray-scale and color. Because of the low-level nature, features generated from this analysis are ambiguous. In feature analysis, visual features are organized into a more global concept of face and facial features using information of face geometry. Through feature analysis, feature ambiguities are reduced and locations of the face and facial features are determined. The next group involves the use of active shape models. These models ranging from *snakes*, proposed in the late 1980s, to the more recent point distributed models (PDM) have been developed for the purpose of complex and non-rigid feature extraction such as eye pupil and lip tracking.

It has been shown that face detection by explicit modeling of facial features has trouble due to the unpredictability of face appearance and environmental conditions. Although some of the recent feature-based attempts have improved the ability to cope with the unpredictability, most are still limited to head and shoulder and quasi-frontal faces (or are included as one of the techniques in a combined system). There is still a need for techniques that can perform in more hostile scenarios such as detecting multiple faces with clutter-intensive backgrounds. This requirement has inspired a new research area in which face detection is treated as a pattern recognition problem. By formulating the problem as one of learning to recognize a face pattern from examples, the specific application of face knowledge is avoided. This eliminates the potential of modeling error due to incomplete or inaccurate face knowledge. The basic approach in recognizing face patterns is via a training procedure, which classifies examples into face and non-face prototype classes.

In this work we segment skin regions in an image based on the color of the pixels. Under normal illumination conditions, skin color takes small regions of the color space. By using this information, we can classify each pixel of the image as skin region or non-skin region. We then use template-matching scheme to identify faces in the skin regions. The rest of this paper is organized as follows. In Section 2, we describe the skin segmentation procedure. We discuss template matching based on PCA method in Section 3. In Section 4, we present the face detection results obtained. Finally, a conclusion is drawn in section 5.

2. Skin segmentation

It was found that different human skin color gives rise to a tight cluster in color spaces even when faces of difference races are considered [4, 5, 6]. This means color composition of human skin differs little across individuals.

Color segmentation can basically be performed using appropriate skin color thresholds where skin color is modeled through histograms or charts.

Choosing a color space was one of the first issues that had to be dealt with. Previous skin detectors have used a variety of color spaces, for reasons ranging from efficiency to illumination independence. Some color spaces are intuitive, and their components easily relate to the physical world. We experimented with various color spaces and decided to use the $YC'_bC'_r$ color space proposed in [6]. This color space is obtained by nonlinearly transforming the YC_bC_r color space to make the skin region luma-independent. Digital color images are normally represented in the RGB color space. From this color space we transform into the YC_bC_r color space as shown below:

$$Y = 16+(0.2549 \times R)+(0.5059 \times G)+(0.0980 \times B)$$
$$Cb = 128-(0.1451 \times R)-(0.2902 \times G)+(0.4392 \times B) \quad (1)$$
$$Cr = 128+(0.4392 \times R)-(0.3647 \times G)-(0.0706 \times B)$$

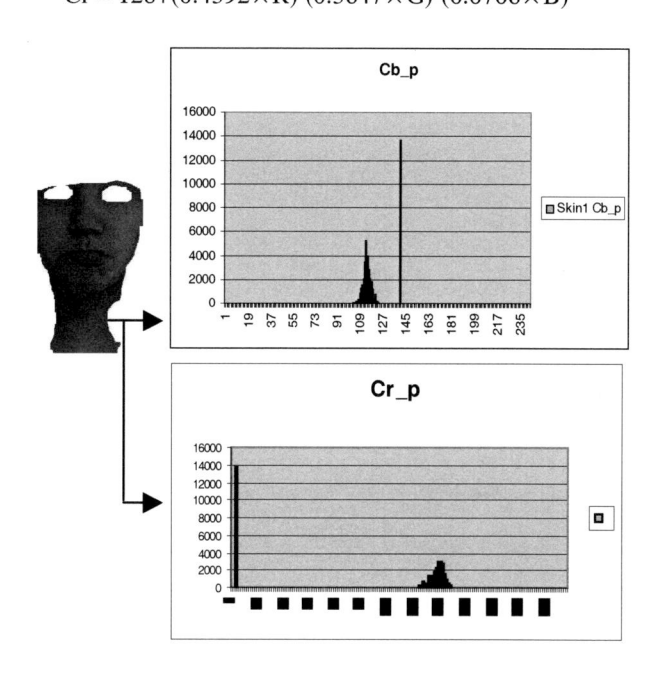

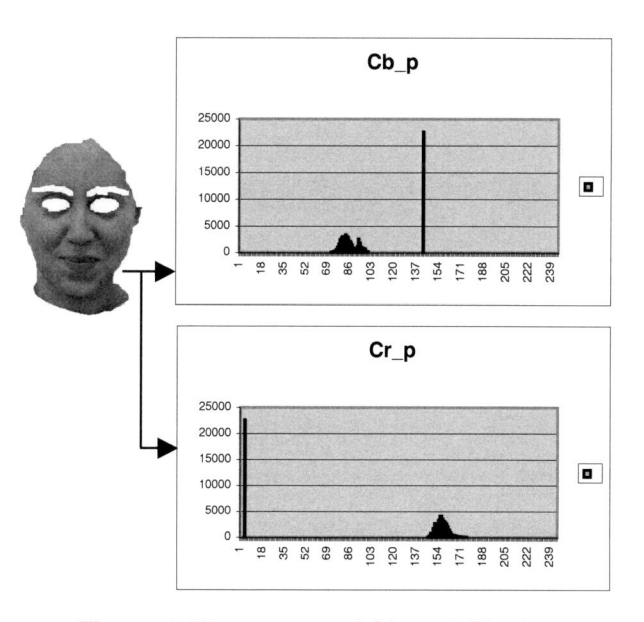

Figure 1. Histograms of C'_b and C'_r of two skin-regions.

By using the above equations we convert each pixel in the image from RGB color space to YC_bC_r color space. In this color space the skin color cluster is more compact. In order to make this color space luma-independent we modify the C_b and C_r components as described in [6]. After obtaining the $YC'_bC'_r$ color space, the histograms of C'_b and C'_r were plotted to determine the skin color threshold. Histograms obtained for a few skin-regions are shown in Figure 1.

The spike observed in the histograms shown in Figure 1 was caused by the white used to mask the non-skin regions hence it may be ignored. Based on the histograms obtained for various skin-regions a threshold for C'_b was set as 71 to 128, and for C'_r it was set between 130 to165. Hence all the regions in an image, which do not fall in this range, are removed. Figure 2 shows the result of skin segmentation, the image on the right is the original image and the image on the left is the skin segmented image.

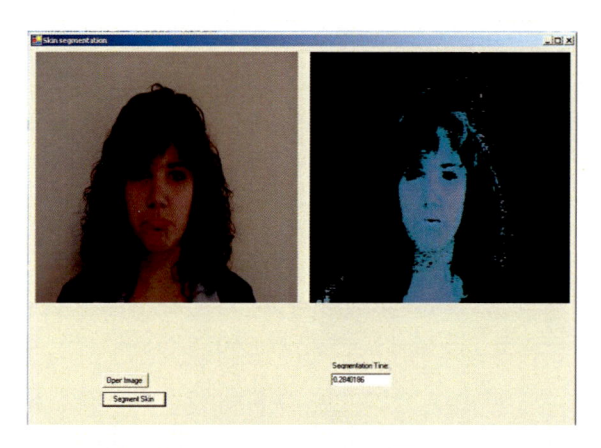

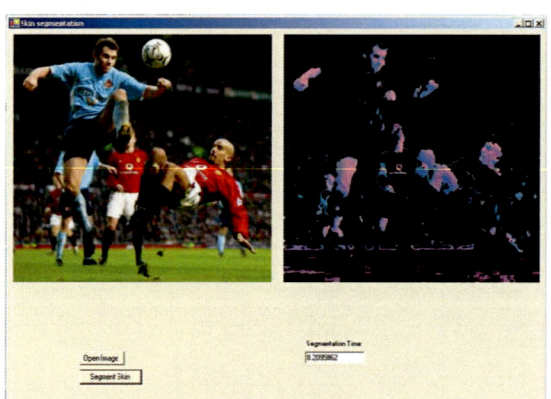

Figure 2. Results of skin segmentation. Images on the left are the original images, and images on the left are the skin segmented images.

After performing skin segmentation the image is further analyzed to eliminate non-face like regions. The skin-segmented image is scanned from left to right and top to bottom. If a row of continuous skin pixels is encountered with the number of skin pixels being greater than or equal to 32, a square region is considered with the row of skin pixels forming the first row of the square region. If the number of skin pixels is greater than twice the number of non-skin pixels in the square region, it is considered for further analysis to determine if it's a face or non-face. This procedure is used to eliminate skin regions, which are too small or whose shape doesn't fit the shape of a face. The screen captures shown in Figure 3 show the intermediate results obtained after performing this procedure. Template matching using PCA is performed on the skin regions which are not eliminated; the next section describes this procedure in detail.

Figure 3. The images on the left are the skin-segmented images, and on the right are obtained after eliminating non-face like skin regions.

3. Template matching based on PCA

The template-matching scheme used is known as principle component analysis (PCA). This technique is based on the Karhunen-Loève transformation and was introduced into face processing by Kirby and Sirovich [7]. Since then it has been used widely in appearance-based applications such as face detection and recognition [8, 9, 10]. We use PCA to further distinguish faces from other non-face objects that have the same skin color. It mainly consists of two parts, training to compute the weight vector, and classification to determine if skin regions are faces or non-faces.

3.1. Training

In this phase we take a set of frontal face images and compute the mean weight vector from them using PCA.

The face images are chosen such that the eyes, nose and mouth are visible but care is taken not to include hair and background. The images used for training were obtained from the AR face database and are shown in Figure 4. The procedure of computing the weight vector from the training images is described below:

Let $I_1, I_2, ..., I_M$ be the set of face images, size of each image being $L \times L$, in the face training set. We histogram equalize all the images and represented them as row vectors of size L^2. Then the average face can be computed as

$$A = \frac{1}{M} \sum_{i=1}^{M} I_i \qquad (2)$$

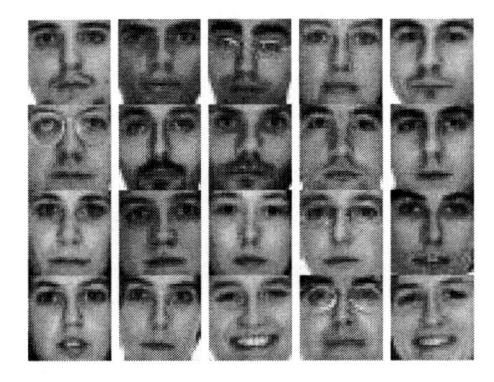

Figure 4. Images used for training.

In our case there are 20 face images in the face training set, each of dimension 32×32. The average face obtained is shown in Figure 5.

Figure 5. Mean face image.

Each face differs from the average face by the vector $Y_i = I_i - A$. The covariance matrix C is constructed from these vectors as

$$C = \frac{1}{M} \sum_{i=1}^{M} Y_i \cdot Y_i^T \qquad (3)$$

where the dimension of C will be $L^2 \times L^2$. The eigenvectors of the covariance matrix are computed and the M' significant eigenvectors are chosen as those with the largest corresponding eigenvalues. The eigenvectors are represented as $E_1, E_2, ..., E_{M'}$, where each eigenvector is a row vector of size L^2. The weight vector for each image in the face database is computed from the eigenvectors as shown below:

$$W_{ir} = E_r^T \cdot (I_i - A) \qquad \forall i, r \qquad (4)$$

where E_r's are the eigenvectors corresponding to the M' largest eigenvalues of C and r varies for 1 to M', M' being 20 in our case and i varies from 1 to M, M being the number of face images in the training set. Then the mean weight vector is computed as shown below:

$$T_r = \frac{1}{\Gamma} \sum_{i=1}^{M} W_{ir} \qquad \forall r \qquad (5)$$

The eigenvectors and the mean weight vector obtained after training are stored and used for classifying a skin region as a face or non-face.

3.2. Classification

In this phase a decision is made if the skin region is a face or non-face. The square regions obtained after eliminating the non-face regions are resized to 32×32 blocks and histogram equalized. The weight vector of these blocks is computed as shown below:

$$Wskin_r = E_r^T \cdot (Itest - A) \qquad \forall r \qquad (6)$$

It is important to note that the eigenvectors E_r and the average image vector A were computed offline in the training phase.

To classify the skin region, the city block distance of the weight vector of the skin region from the mean weight vector is computed as shown below:

$$D = \frac{1}{M'} \sum_{r=1}^{M'} |T_r - Wskin_r| \qquad (7)$$

If the distance is less than or equal to a threshold the skin region is classified as a face. On the other hand if the distance is greater than the threshold the skin region is classified as a non-face. The threshold was determined during the training phase by finding the distances of some know faces and non-faces from the mean weight vector. Observing these distances the threshold is set such that most of the face distances will fall below the threshold and most of the non-face distances will lie above the threshold. A square is drawn on skin regions classified as faces. As can be seen from the Figure 4 in the training phase, only frontal view faces were used for training. Hence classification of faces from non-faces can be performed effectively only on frontal view faces.

4. Face detection system

The system consists of a computer for image processing and one CCD camera mounted on the wall, an overview of the system is shown in Figure 6. The computer captures video streams from the CCD camera. The video cable is used to transfer the frames from the camera to the computer, and the camera can be controlled from the computer through the RS232C cable.

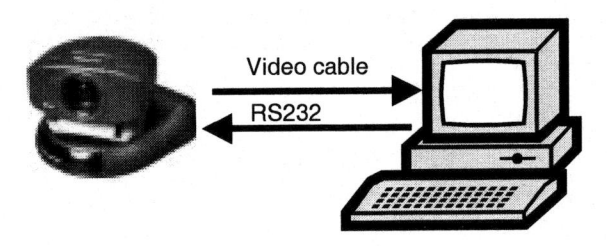

Figure 6. System overview.

The system is capable of detecting faces in approximately 200ms. Since the algorithm looks for faces in skin like regions, the detection time can very depending on the amount of skin like regions in the frame. Figure 7 shows the detected faces in a few frames.

Figure 7. Face detection results in a video stream.

5. Conclusion

Face detection was performed on a video stream from a surveillance camera. The skin regions were segmented from the frame and faces were detected by matching face-like regions with a face template. The face template was obtained by considering faces in frontal view hence the system is effective in detecting faces in frontal view only. We are in the process of extending this method for all views by training the PCA algorithm for other views.

6. References

[1] R. Brunelli and T. Poggio, "Face recognition: Feature versus templates", *IEEE Trans. Pattern Anal. Mach.Intell.* 15, 1993, 1042–1052.

[2] D. Valentin, H. Abdi, A. J. O'Toole, and G. Cottrell, "Connectionist models of face processing: A survey", *Pattern Recog.* 27, 1994, 1209–1230.

[3] M. Hunke and A. Waibel, "Face locating and tracking for human-computer interaction", *28th Asilomar Conference on Signals, Systems and Computers, Monterey, CA, 1994.*

[4] S. McKenna, S. Gong, and J. J. Collins, "Face tracking and pose representation", *British Machine Vision Conference, Edinburgh, Scotland, Sept. 1996.*

[5] J. Yang and A. Waibel, "A real-time face tracker", *IEEE Proc. of the 3rd Workshop on Applications of Computer Vision, Florida, 1996.*

[6] R.-L. Hsu, M. Abdel-Mottaleb, and A. K. Jain, ``Face detection in color images," *IEEE Trans. Pattern Analysis and Machine Intelligence*, vol. 24, no. 5, pp. 696-706, May 2002.

[7] M. Kirby and L. Sirovich, "Application of the Karhunen–Loeve procedure for the characterization of human faces." *IEEE Transactions on Pattern Analysis and Machine Intelligence*, 12 (1), 103–108, 1990.

[8] M. A. Turk and A. P. Pentland. "Face recognition using eigenfaces." In *Proceedings of IEEE Computer Society Conference on Computer Vision and Pattern Recognition*, pages 586–591, Hawaii, June 1991.

[9] B. Moghaddam and A. Pentland. "Probabilistic visual learning for object representation." *IEEE Transactions on Pattern Analysis and Machine Intelligence*, 7:696–710, July 1997.

[10] K.-K. Sung and T. Poggio. "Example-based learning for view-based human face detection." *IEEE Transactions on Pattern Analysis and Machine Intelligence*, 20(1):39–51, 1998.

Associative Memory Based on Ratio Learning For Real Time Skin Color Detection

Ming-Jung Seow and Vijayan K. Asari
VLSI Systems Laboratory
Department of Electrical and Computer Engineering
Old Dominion University, Norfolk, VA 23529
Email: {mseow, vasari}@odu.edu

Abstract

A novel approach for skin color modeling using ratio rule learning algorithm is proposed in this paper. The learning algorithm is applied to a real time skin color detection application. The neural network learn, based on the degree of similarity between the relative magnitudes of the output of each neuron with respect to that of all other neurons. The activation/threshold function of the network is determined by the statistical characteristic of the input patterns. Theoretical analysis has shown that the network is able to learn and recall the trained patterns without much problem. It is shown mathematically that the network system is stable and converges in all circumstances for the trained patterns. The network utilizes the ratio-learning algorithm for modeling the characteristic of skin color in the RGB space as a linear attractor. The skin color will converge to a line of attraction. The new technique is applied to images captured by a surveillance camera and it is observed that the skin color model is capable of processing 420×315 resolution images of 24-bit color at 30 frames per second in a dual Xeon 2.2 GHz CPU workstation running Windows 2000.

1. Introduction

Automatic human face recognition, a technique, which can locate and identify human faces automatically in a video surveillance and authentication system and determine "who is who" from a database are gaining more and more attentions in the area of computer vision and pattern recognition over the last two decades. Although face recognition is a fundamental part in a fully automated facial analysis system, the first important step in recognizing faces in video sequences is to find where they are located in an image frame captured by a surveillance camera. This is called face detection or face tracking in the case of video sequences. Most of the existing face detection methods use gray scale values to detect faces [1-6]. However, it is well known that the majority of images acquired today are colored and the skin color feature should be an important source of information for discriminating faces from the background. Only a few face detection methods use color as a feature [7-9]. In these systems, color is modeled as a Gaussian function in some color space where intensity plays no role and the whole information is provided by hue and saturation. The reason for using such color spaces is that human skin color varies more in intensity than in chromatic feature itself between different ethnic groups [10]. This fact gives rise to a relatively well-clustered cloud of skin samples even for training sets containing people from different races. As a result, there have been several attempts to model the sample distribution with a single Gaussian probability density function. [7-9]

We propose a novel approach for skin color modeling using ratio rule learning algorithm [11] in this paper. The proposed method is a neural network method, which learns, based on the degree of similarity between the relative magnitudes of the output of each neuron with respect to that of all other neurons. The activation/threshold function of the network is determined by the statistical characteristic of the input patterns. Theoretical analysis shows that the network is able to learn and recall the trained patterns. It can be proved mathematically that the network system is stable and converges in all circumstances for the trained patterns. The network utilizes the ratio-learning algorithm for modeling the skin color in the RGB space. The skin color will converge to a line of attraction. Conversely, the non-skin color diverges away from the line attractor. Skin samples collected from various sources are used for training the network. The network generalizes the skin samples and uses its generalization for detecting skin color based on the RGB combination.

2. Ratio rule

Let the relationship of two neurons be described as

$$W_{ij}^s = \frac{b_i^s}{a_j^s} \quad (1)$$

for stimulus-response pair (a_j^s, b_i^s) and the resultant memory W_{ij}^s. The term b_i^s/a_j^s represents the ratio between the state values of two neurons. This ratio finds the degree of similarity between each neuron with other neurons. Therefore, W^s can be written as:

$$W^s = \begin{bmatrix} w_{11}^s & w_{12}^s & \cdots & w_{1N}^s \\ w_{21}^s & w_{22}^s & \cdots & w_{2N}^s \\ \vdots & \vdots & \vdots & \vdots \\ w_{N1}^s & w_{N2}^s & \cdots & w_{NN}^s \end{bmatrix} = \begin{bmatrix} \frac{b_1^s}{a_1^s} & \frac{b_1^s}{a_2^s} & \cdots & \frac{b_1^s}{a_N^s} \\ \frac{b_2^s}{a_1^s} & \frac{b_2^s}{a_2^s} & \cdots & \frac{b_2^s}{a_N^s} \\ \vdots & \vdots & \vdots & \vdots \\ \frac{b_N^s}{a_1^s} & \frac{b_N^s}{a_2^s} & \cdots & \frac{b_N^s}{a_N^s} \end{bmatrix} \quad (2)$$

To combine W^s, which is each pattern to form a memory matrix W; we need to utilize statistical methods. The approach to this problem is to use the training samples to estimate the unknown probabilities and probability density, and then use resulting estimation as if they were the true values. To see how maximum-likelihood method applies to a specific case, we can reasonably assume that the values of b_i^s/a_j^s is drawn for a multivariate normal density with mean μ, although we do not know the exact value of these quantities. This knowledge simplifies the problem for estimating an unknown function as estimating the parameter μ. Let the log-likelihood of a single point b_i^s/a_j^s be

$$\ln\left[P(\frac{b_i^s}{a_j^s}|\mu)\right] = -\frac{1}{2}\ln(2\pi)^d|\Sigma|$$
$$-\frac{1}{2}\left(\frac{b_i^s}{a_j^s} - \mu\right)^t \Sigma^{-1}\left(\frac{b_i^s}{a_j^s} - \mu\right) \quad (3)$$

where Σ is the covariance matrix. We usually find the value of μ that maximized $\ln\left[P(\frac{b_i^s}{a_j^s}|\mu)\right]$ by differentiating it by the component μ and setting the result to zero [12]:

$$\nabla \ln\left[P(\frac{b_i^s}{a_j^s}|\mu)\right] = \Sigma^{-1}\left(\frac{b_i^s}{a_j^s} - \mu\right) \quad (4)$$

The maximum likelihood estimation for μ can be obtained by

$$\sum_{i=1}^{P} \Sigma^{-1}\left(\frac{b_i^s}{a_j^s} - \mu\right) = 0 \quad (5)$$

Multiplying (5) on both left and right side by Σ and rearranging, we obtain the following maximum-likelihood estimation for μ.

$$\mu = \frac{1}{P}\sum_{s=1}^{P}\frac{b_i^s}{a_j^s} \quad (6)$$

Equation (6) shows that the maximum likelihood estimate for the unknown population mean is just the arithmetic average of the training samples. Figure 2 shows the weight graph illustrating the concept of training based on (6). A weight graph is a graphical representation of the relationship between the ith neuron and the jth neuron for P patterns. Utilization of the weight graph may help visualize the behavior of one neuron pair.

Based on the above theory, the memory matrix for the N neuron network can be obtained as:

$$w_{ij} = \frac{1}{P}\sum_{s=1}^{P}\frac{x_i^s}{x_j^s} \quad for \ 1 \leq i,j \leq N \quad (7)$$

where $x_m \in \{1, 256\}$ can be the magnitude of the input at m^{th} neuron. The learning algorithm can be interpreted as the mean ratio between two neurons. The network architecture is a single layer fully connected recurrent neural network. The net output of the network can be computed as (Figure 1)

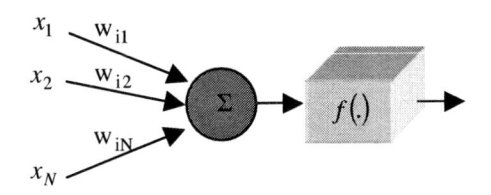

Figure 1. Simplified model of a neuron with threshold function

$$Net_i = \frac{1}{N}\sum_{j=1}^{N}w_{ij}x_j \quad (8)$$

where N is the number of neurons. The Net_i can be thresholded considering the region of distance of the weight components in the weight graph shown in Figure 2.

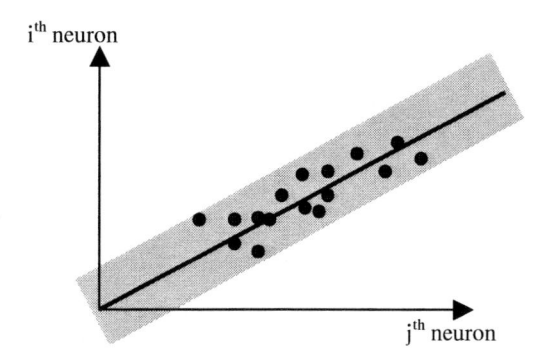

Figure 2. Weight graph describing the relationship of the ith neuron with respect to the jth neuron

That is, w_{ij} gives a linear approximation for all the points x_i^s / x_j^s. In order to preserve each pattern, we need to find the region where the threshold can preserve each pattern. The region in Figure 2 describes such a distance. Mathematical representation of the threshold function can be expressed as

$$o_i^{new} = f(Net_i^{new})$$
$$= \begin{cases} o_i^{old} & \text{if } winL_i \leq Net_i^{new} - o_i^{old} \leq winR_i \\ Net_i^{new} & \text{otherwise} \end{cases} \quad (9)$$

Where $winL_i$ and $winR_i$ is the window function for thresholding. They can be expressed as:

$$winL_i = \alpha \frac{1}{N} \sum_{j=1}^{N} Tl_j \quad (10)$$

$$winR_i = \alpha \frac{1}{N} \sum_{j=1}^{N} Tr_j \quad (11)$$

where α is a constant and $0 < \alpha \leq 1$ and Tl_j and Tr_j can be expressed as:

$$Tl_j = \text{Min}(w_{ij}x_j - x_i) \text{ for } 1 \leq i \leq N \quad (12)$$

$$Tr_j = \text{Max}(w_{ij}x_j - x_i) \text{ for } 1 \leq i \leq N \quad (13)$$

The window width between $winL_i$ and $winR_i$ decides if the o_i^{old} should be updated or not. That is, the $winL_i$ and $winR_i$ calculate the mean of the maximum distance from the approximate functions, which is also the maximum error from the approximate function of the x_i and use it as a function of threshold. Figure 3 shows the activation function for each neuron.

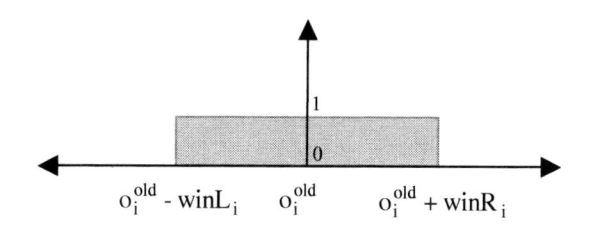

Figure 3. Windows function for activation

3. Associability

The proposed learning algorithm is defined as:

$$W_{ij} = \frac{1}{P} \sum_{s=1}^{P} \frac{x_i^s}{x_j^s}$$

Given $X = \{x^s : s = 1..P\}$, ideally, we would want

$$X^\beta = f(WX^\beta) \quad (14)$$

if X^β is one of the trained patterns. So, let us assume:

$$x_i^\beta = \frac{1}{N} \sum_{j=1}^{N} w_{ij} x_j^\beta$$

$$= \frac{1}{N} \sum_{j=1}^{N} \left(\frac{1}{P} \sum_{s=1}^{P} \frac{x_i^s}{x_j^s} \right) x_j^\beta$$

$$= \frac{1}{N} \frac{1}{P} \sum_{j=1}^{N} \sum_{s=1}^{P} \frac{x_i^s}{x_j^s} x_j^\beta$$

$$= \frac{1}{N} \frac{1}{P} \sum_{j=1}^{N} \left[\sum_{\substack{s=1 \\ s \neq \beta}}^{P} \frac{x_i^s}{x_j^s} x_j^\beta + \frac{x_i^\beta}{x_j^\beta} x_j^\beta \right]$$

$$= \frac{1}{N} \frac{1}{P} \sum_{j=1}^{N} \left[\sum_{\substack{s=1 \\ s \neq \beta}}^{P} \frac{x_i^s}{x_j^s} x_j^\beta + x_i^\beta \right]$$

$$= \frac{1}{N} \frac{1}{P} \sum_{j=1}^{N} \sum_{\substack{s=1 \\ s \neq \beta}}^{P} \frac{x_i^s}{x_j^s} x_j^\beta + \frac{1}{N} \frac{1}{P} \sum_{j=1}^{N} x_i^\beta$$

$$= \frac{1}{N} \frac{1}{P} \sum_{j=1}^{N} \sum_{\substack{s=1 \\ s \neq \beta}}^{P} \frac{x_i^s}{x_j^s} x_j^\beta + \frac{1}{P} x_i^\beta \quad (15)$$

As a result, we could see that when

$$\frac{1}{N}\frac{1}{P}\sum_{j=1}^{N}\sum_{\substack{s=1\\s\neq\beta}}^{P}\frac{x_i^s}{x_j^s}x_j^\beta = \frac{P-1}{P}x_i^\beta \qquad (16)$$

which also implies that if

$$\frac{x_i^s}{x_j^s} = \frac{x_i^\beta}{x_j^\beta} \qquad (17)$$

or sufficiently close as defined in (9), the learning algorithm will be able to correctly recall the stored patterns.

4. Stability

Before simulating and testing the new algorithm, it has to be verified that the new learning rule will be stable over a finite number of iterations. The energy due to a single neuron i is:

$$E_i = \sum_{j=1}^{N} w_{ij} x_j o_i \qquad (18)$$

From (18), we can derive the change in energy due to the update from o_i^{old} to o_i^{new} as:

$$\Delta E_i = -\frac{1}{2}\sum_{j=1}^{N} w_{ij}x_j o_i^{new} - \left(-\frac{1}{2}\sum_{j=1}^{N} w_{ij}x_j o_i^{old}\right) \qquad (19)$$

which can be simplified as

$$\Delta E_i = \left(o_i^{new} - o_i^{old}\right)\left(-\frac{1}{2}\sum_{j=1}^{N} w_{ij}x_j\right) \qquad (20)$$

Now we can consider 3 cases:

(1) If $winL_i \leq Net_i^{new} - o_i^{old} \leq winR_i$, then by (9) and (20), ΔE_i will become 0,

$$\Delta E_i = (0)(-) = 0$$

(2) If $\left(o_i^{new} - o_i^{old}\right) > winR_i$ and according to (9), the change in energy ΔE_i from (20) will be less than 0, and

$$\Delta E_i = (+)(-)(+) = -$$

(3) If $\left(o_i^{new} - o_i^{old}\right) < -winL_i$, and according to (9). the change in energy ΔE_i from (20) will be greater than 0, and

$$\Delta E_i = (-)(-)(+) = +$$

Condition 1 and 2 clearly demonstrate that the network converges for every consecutive iteration. On the other hand, condition 3 states that when a neuron changes its state to a lower magnitude, the energy increases. But in the next iteration, it will have a tendency to go to higher magnitude or stay at the same level to capture its final state if the input pattern is closer to one of the trained patterns. Otherwise, if the input pattern is an untrained pattern, the network goes to an unstable state.

5. Skin color modeling

RGB is a color space originated from cathode-ray tube (or CRT) display applications, when it was convenient to describe color as a combination of three colored rays (red, green and blue). It is one of the most widely used color spaces for processing and storing of digital image data. Color is an important feature on Human Face. Using Skin color as a feature for detecting a face, recognizing a face, and tracking a face have many advantages because processing skin color is much more faster than processing other feature such as eyes, nose, and mouth. Under certain lighting conditions, color is orientation invariant. Figure 4 shows a face image and the skin color occurrences in the RGB space (256×256×256). It can be observed that the skin colors are cluster in the RGB space, that is, it is possible to describe the skin color in a human face mathematically using ratio learning algorithm.

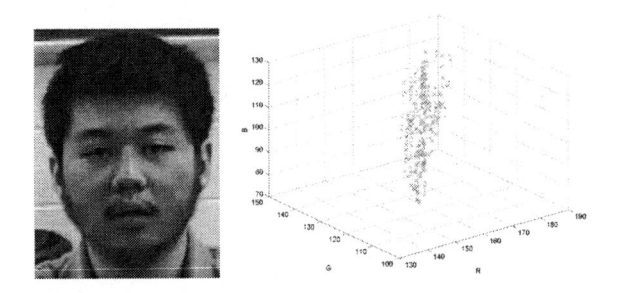

Figure 4. An Example of skin color occurrences in the RGB scatter plot

For skin color modeling, we have used the proposed ratio-learning rule. The training set is consisting of 4,000 skin samples randomly collected from the World Wide Web (WWW). The collected skins include Caucasian, African, Asian, and many other races. The skin pixel distribution obtained is shown in Figure 5(b). The collected skin samples are used for training in the ratio rule learning algorithm using equation (7). Figure 6-8 show the decision surfaces of the ratio rule. It can be seen that the ratio learning algorithm is able to encapsulate the data into skin and non-skin region with only the skin data.

(a) Skin Samples from difference races

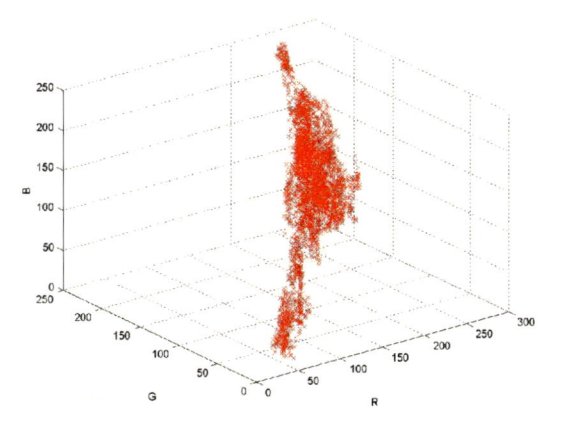

(b) RGB 3-D scatter graph of skin distribution

Figure 5. Skin samples collected from the WWW

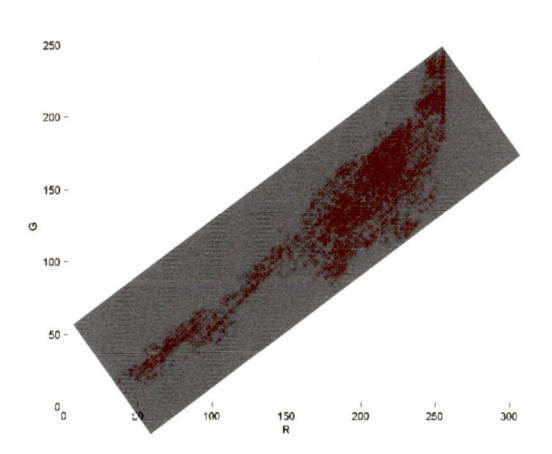

Figure 6. RG 2-D scatter plot for skin segmentation using Ratio Rule

6. Experimental results

We have implemented the skin segmentation application trained using the proposed ratio learning rule. In the first experiment, we have applied the models to a set of 100 images from the Internet, which contain people from white to black skins in different levels of background complexity and luminance variation. Figure 9 shows the example results of the skin color detection. It can be observed that the ratio network can distinguish skin color for Caucasian, African, and Asian people without any problem.

The second experiment tests the speed and performance of the network when it is applied to Sony EVI-D30 surveillance camera at 30 fps for 420 × 315 resolution images of 24-bit color. The network is able to process the frames without any problem. Figure 10 shows the sequence of images from the camera.

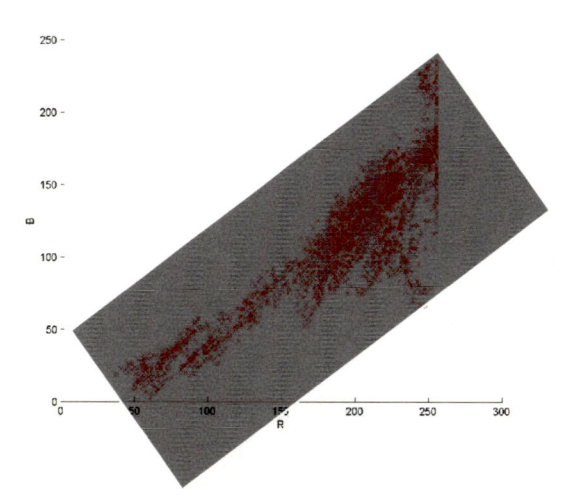

Figure 7. RB 2-D scatter plot for skin segmentation using Ratio Rule

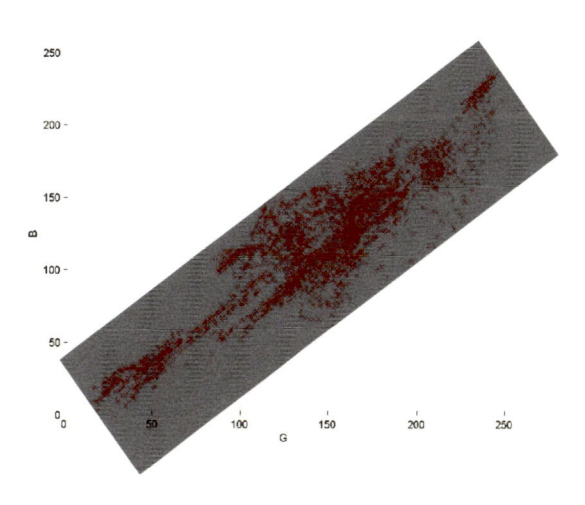

Figure 8. GB 2-D scatter plot for skin segmentation using Ratio Rule

Figure 9. Skin segmentation for still image

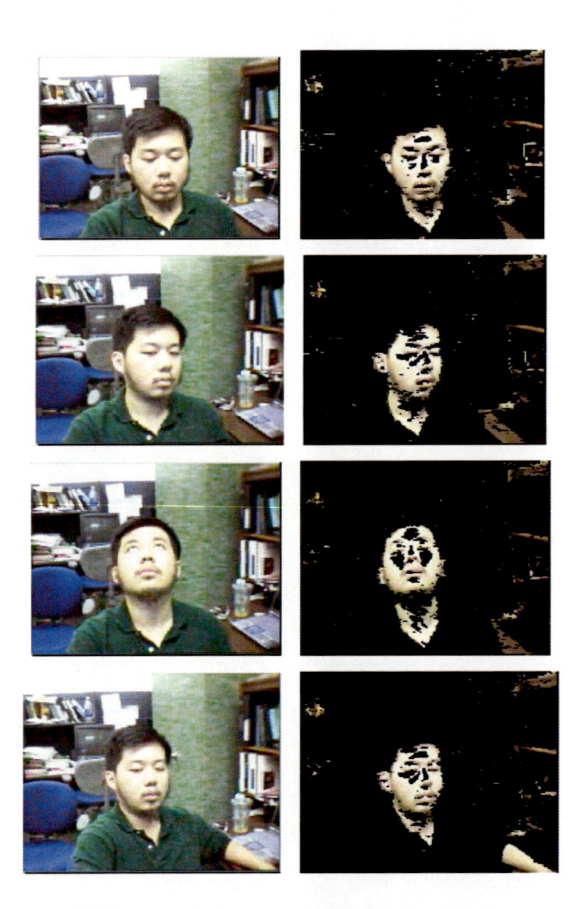

Figure 10. Skin segmentation for video sequences

7. Conclusion

A ratio rule based training algorithm suitable for skin color detection has been presented in this paper. The ratio rule learns by minimizing the maximum distance of the statistical properties of the relative magnitudes of two neurons. The threshold function has been represented by the statistical characteristic of the input patterns. Theoretical analysis and empirical evidence of the neural network with ratio rule have shown that the network is stable and is capable of detecting skin color from Caucasian, African, and Asian people satisfactorily.

8. References

[1] T.K. Leung, M.C. Burl, P. Perona, Finding Faces in cluttered scenes using random labeled graph matching, Proceedings of the 5th. Int. Conf. on Computer Vision, 1995, pp. 637-644.

[2] H. A. Rowley, S. Bluja, T. Kanade, Neural network based face detection, IEEE Trans. on Patt. Anal. Mach. Int. 20 (1) 1998, 23-38.

[3] K.-K. Sung, T. Poggio, Example-based learning for view-based human face detection, IEEE Trans. Patt. Anal. Mach. Int. 20 (1) 1998, 39-51.

[4] K.C. Yow, R. Cipolla, Feature-based human face detection, Image and Vision Computing 15 (1997) 713-735.

[5] K.C. Yow, R. Cippola, A probabilistic framework for perceptual grouping of features for human face detection, Proceedings of the 2nd. Int. Conf. on Automatic Face and Gesture Recognition, Vermont, USA, 1995.

[6] M.C. Burl, T.K. Leung, P. Perona, Face locatization via shape statistics, Procee-dings of the First International Workshop on Face and Gesture Recognition, Zurich, Switzerland, 1995.

[7] J. Cai, A. Goshtasby, Detecting human faces in color images, Image and Vision Computing, 18 (1999) 63-75.

[8] E. Saber, A.M. Tekalp, Frontal-view face detection and facial feature extraction using color, shape and symmetry based cost functions, Pattern Recognition Letters 19 (1998) 669-680.

[9] J-G. Wang, E. Sung, Frontal-view face detection and facial feature extraction using color and morphological operations, Pattern Recognition Letters 20 (1999) 1053-1068.

[10] Y.A. Waibel, A real-time face tracker, Proceedings of WACV'96, Sarasota, USA, 1996.

[11] Ming-Jung Seow and Vijayan K. Asari, Associative Memory using Ratio Rule for Multi-valued Pattern Association, IEEE International Joint Conference on Neural Networks – IJCNN 2003, Portland, Oregon, USA, July 20-24, 2003

[12] R. O. Duda, P. E. Hart, and D. G. Stork. "Pattern classification," John Wiley & Sons, 2nd ed. Edition. 2000.

Performance Evaluation of Color Based Road Detection Using Neural Nets and Support Vector Machines

Patrick Conrad and Mike Foedisch
National Institute of Standards and Technology, Gaithersburg, MD 20899
conrad@cme.nist.gov , fodisch@cme.nist.gov

Abstract

We present a comparison of two methods for color based road segmentation. The first was implemented using a neural network, while the second approach is based on support vector machines. A large number of training images were used with varying road conditions including roads with snow, dirt or gravel surfaces, and asphalt. We experimented with grouping the training images by road condition and generating a separate model for each group. The system would automatically select the appropriate one for each novel image. Those results were compared with creating a single model with all images. In another set of experiments, we added the image coordinates of each point as an additional feature in the models. Finally, we compared the results and the efficiency of neural networks and support vector machines of segmentation with each combination of feature sets and image groups.

1. Introduction

A vehicle autonomously traveling often benefits from driving on roads, as it allows increased safety and speed of travel. Driving on paved roads is a well-studied problem, and several vehicles have driven successfully over long distances. [1] However, driving on unpaved roads, and in adverse weather conditions is not well studied.

On paved roads, a simple lane following algorithm is often sufficient. However, many dirt or gravel roads have no clear markings on the edges of the road. They often blend into the surrounding area, and have greatly varying colors and surface materials. Adverse weather conditions can render models created for clear weather useless, because the colors of the environment change, as in rain or snow.

It has previously been shown [2] that color histograms over small sections of the image provide enough information for classification into road or non-road categories. The previous methods made no allowance for the expected shape of the road, which seemed to generate incorrect road labels for some trees or dark patches far outside the road area. In an attempt to lessen this type of error, we included the image coordinates as part of the feature vectors, and evaluated the changes created by this alteration.

As different road types have dramatically disparate visual structures, we attempted to classify images first by type, as paved, dirt and gravel, or snow. A first stage analysis determined the road type and picked the appropriate second stage classification parameters.

Since the goal is to classify the images, neural networks (NN) and Support Vector Machines (SVM) are possible approaches for implementation. Within each classification method, we tried variations using pixel color and image coordinates as inputs to the classifiers. We also compared the classification with and without a first stage classifier that selected the appropriate second stage parameters.

The data we discuss in this paper was collected from a camera mounted on a modified High Mobility Multipurpose Wheeled Vehicle (HMMWV) as part of the Army's Demo III project [3]. In the following sections we discuss the basic classification methods, the alterations and their effects, and perform an overall evaluation between neural nets and SVMs.

2. Implementation

First, we selected 93 images from several sets of data collected from a camera mounted on a High Mobility Multipurpose Wheeled Vehicle (HMMWV) driving on paved, dirt, and snow-covered roads. In an attempt to test this system to

Figure 1. Sample images from dataset

its fullest, we chose difficult images, with shadows, multi-colored paved surfaces, and poorly-defined borders. Several examples are shown in Figure 1. For each image, independent histograms of the red, green, and blue color channels were generated over 31x31 pixel areas, sampled every 10 pixels, leaving a border to ensure they all lie entirely within the image. The histograms were then normalized. The images were 720x480 pixels, yielding 3105 feature vectors per image. For training purposes, we manually generated labels by selecting a single polygon to define the region that should be labeled as road. In several instances, roads that had vegetation growing in their centers required complex shapes to include only the road surface.

We worked with four groups of images: dirt and gravel, paved, snow, and all images at once. Within each group, we randomly selected ¾ of the images to use for training of the classification methods, and the last ¼ for evaluation.

The neural networks we discuss were trained using the Matlab Neural Network Toolbox [4]. The neural nets had 20 hidden units in one layer, and weights were updated using conjugate-gradient back-propagation, with the "tansig" activation function. With the training portion of each set, we used a cross-validation method to help improve accuracy. We trained four nets, each using a different ¾ of the training set, and estimated the network's accuracy over the remaining ¼. The network with the best accuracy was kept. [2] This net was then applied to the evaluation portion of the data set, and the resulting accuracy is the performance cited in the tables for each network.

The second classification approach made use of Support vector Machines (SVMs). To train the SVMs, we used the SVMlite software [5]. The SVMs were trained using the radial basis function with gamma term 10. The SVM learned using the training portion of each set. The accuracy cited in the tables is over the evaluation portion of the given set.

Table 1. Results of including position data; fraction correct, false positive (FP), and false negative (FN)

	Correct	FP	FN
NN w/o pos	0.781	0.115	0.105
NN w/ pos	0.8729	0.041	0.086
SVM w/o pos	0.836	0.109	0.055
SVM w/ pos	0.894	0.069	0.037

3. Results

Including Image Coordinates When we examined the classification of the first set of data, it appeared that the system was making some very large errors, labeling patches of road in the sky and in dark portions of the background. We decided to include the image coordinates as part of the feature vectors, because we believed it might capture the average road shape in the models. The coordinate used was the upper left corner of the 31x31 pixel sampling block.

In the neural net approach, the image coordinates were tacked onto the front of the feature vector, and the networks were retrained. For Support Vector Machines, simply adding the coordinates to the input vector introduced significant error because the image coordinates were orders of magnitude larger than the normalized histogram values. We decided to divide the image coordinate by the total width or height of the image as appropriate, to bring it down to the same scale as the other data, and added these to the feature vectors. This brought SVM accuracies to a reasonable level. We tried making the same change to the neural networks, but it did not seem to have a positive effect.

As shown in Table 1, including position information results in a significant increase in the classification accuracy. In particular, it helped to lower the percentage of erroneously labeling background features as road. This improvement was evident throughout all of our data. Using position information helped to localize most of the error in regions near the road border, where the error is of less importance. Figure 2 shows this effect in one of the more dramatic examples.

Table 2. Results of one model per road type showing fraction correct

	All	Snow	Dirt	Paved
NN	0.8729	0.9	0.8791	0.917
SVM	0.894	0.9	0.903	0.94

It is important to note that including the image coordinates in this way builds into the system the assumption that the vehicle is on, and looking down, the road it is supposed to identify.

One Model per Road Type We first generated one model for each road type; dirt and gravel, paved, and snow. We found that including the pixel position still increased the accuracy of these data sets, so we continued to use this as part of the feature vector. Table 2 shows that each of the single type models performed equally well or better than the model for all images using the same implementation.

To create a switch to automatically pick the appropriate road type model, we selected three pixels near the bottom of the image that would likely be road (given the assumption that the vehicle is on a road). We created a new image set as the union of the image sets used to train each of the three road type models, and another as the evaluation set for each road type.

To prepare the data for training the switch network, each of those three pixels was given a three bit binary label. Each bit represented one of the three types of road, where a positive bit indicated that pixel was that type of road. One and only one of the bits for each pixel was marked positive. In order to create single output networks, three models were trained, where each one took the data from all three pixels, and their bits representing a single road type. This resulted in three networks, one to report the similarity of a given pixel to each of the three road types.

To classify a novel image, each of the three pixels is passed through each network independently, creating a similarity score to each of the three types. These scores are reduced to a single set of scores for the entire image by averaging the road type scores for each of the three types. The largest of the image scores is determined to be the road type in the novel image, and the single road type model for that type is selected for segmentation.

This switch only chose the correct road type with 82% accuracy over the evaluation set. When used to select the single type model for segmentation of the road over the new validation image set, it created a final road segmentation

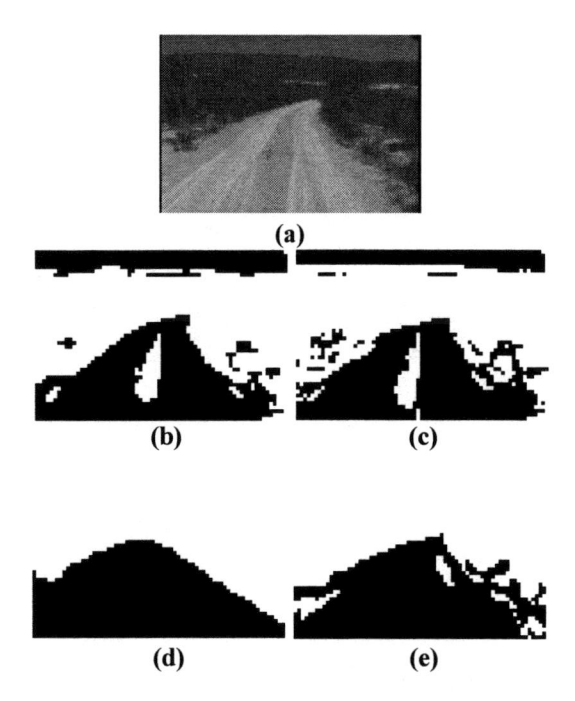

Figure 2. Comparison of the identified road shape with and without coordinates and by classification method; (a) raw image (b) NN without coordinates (c) SVM without coordinates (d) NN with coordinates (e) SVM with coordinates

accuracy of 88%. Unfortunately, this was little better than the single neural network model for all types, and is slightly worse than the SVM version of the model for all types. Had the switch worked perfectly, the road segmentation results would have only improved slightly, to 89%.

We were unable to create a switch using Support Vector Machines that produced results with an accuracy acceptable for further testing.

We believe that the disappointing results of these experiments were caused by our selection of the classes for the road type classification. While the difference used to discriminate them was apparent to the human eye, those sets may not be any more homogenous to the computer than the combination of all the images. This would account for the lack of increase in performance from separating the images by type, and possibly explains why SVMs could not classify them correctly. A better set of classes, possibly automatically generated, would likely improve results.

Comparison of SVM and Neural Networks

Overall, the percentage accuracy difference between SVMs and Neural Networks was not large. The SVM tended to be equal or higher by a few points at most, but this was not its greatest strength. When we examined images labeled by both systems, the SVM often appeared more accurate. It correctly identified more of the road, and marked sections as not road more precisely. More of the error seemed to concentrate near the border of the road, where we preferred it. In particular, the neural networks seemed to fail with two-tracked roads when position data is included, because the position information overrides color information in the area immediately in front of the camera. This effect was shown in the mound shape of (d) in Figure 2, where the shape, though mostly correct, does not include areas outside those that are most commonly road. In (d) of Figure 2, the inclusion of image coordinates is successful, because while the neural net lost some of the road shape near the top, it did correct for some large misclassifications. In (e) the SVM model kept a few errors after coordinates were introduced, but still showed much improvement.

The primary failing of SVMs were their speed. It took several seconds for the SVM to classify an image, while neural nets took less than one second. This makes neural networks a much better option for implementing a real time system, because the accuracy drop is not large for such a speed gain. Additionally, a robust real-time system with a high refresh rate such as we have implemented in the past could most likely tolerate the additional errors.

4. Conclusions

We presented a system for color based road segmentation. This system seemed to perform quite well, generating high accuracies with the inclusion of image coordinates in the feature vector. The individual models and the switch did not provide much improvement, but merits further investigation with autonomously defined classes. Support Vector Machines outperformed neural networks slightly, but the long calculation time weighs heavily against them as a practical method. Experimentation with optimization of the SVM should be tried, to determine if the speed could be increased while continuing to keep a high accuracy. As work continues, we hope to test this method on a very large set of images, to see if these promising results will scale up to a more universal system.

5. Acknowledgments

Thanks to Christopher Rasmussen, who first developed this system, and determined the methods for SVM and neural net generation.

6. References

[1] M. Bertozzi, A. Broggi and A. Fascioli, "Vision-based Intelligent Vehicles: State of the Art and Perspectives," in Robotics and Autonomous Systems 32, 2000.

[2] C. Rasmussen, "Combining Laser Range, Color, and Texture Cues for Autonomous Road Following," in *Proc. IEEE Inter. Conf. on Robotics & Automation, Washington, DC*, 2002.

[3] C. Shoemaker and J. Bornstein, "The Demo III UGV Program: A Testbed for Autonomous Navigation Research," in *Proc IEEE Int. Symp. Intelligent Control*, 1998.

[4] H. Demuth and M. Beale, "Matlab Neural Network Toolbox User's Guide, Version 4.0," The MathWorks Inc., 2000.

[5] Thorsten Joachims, "Learning to Classify Text Using Support Vector Machines." Dissertation, Kluwer, 2002.

Posters

⌘⌘⌘⌘⌘⌘⌘⌘

Defect Detection on Patterned Jacquard Fabric

Henry Y.T. Ngan*, Grantham K.H. Pang*, S.P. Yung[†], Michael K. Ng[†]
*Department of Electrical and Electronic Engineering, [†]Department of Mathematics,
The University of Hong Kong, Pokfulam Road, Hong Kong.
Email:gpang@eee.hku.hk   Phone: 852-2857-8492   Fax: 852-2559-8738

Abstract

The techniques for defect detection on plain (unpatterned) fabrics have been well developed nowadays. This paper is on developing visual inspection methods for defect detection on patterned fabrics. A review on some defect detection methods on patterned fabrics will be given. Then, a new method for patterned fabric inspection called Golden Image Subtraction (GIS) is introduced. GIS is an efficient and fast method, which can segment out the defective regions on patterned fabric effectively. An improved version of the GIS method using wavelet transform is also given. This research result will contribute to the development of an automated fabric inspection machine for the textile industry.

1. Introduction

Defect detection by automated fabric inspection machine nowadays is only for plain and twill fabrics, which are called the 'unpatterned' fabrics. Many methods have been developed for on this kind of fabric. Examples are Gabor filters [1], Fourier Transform [2], Neural Network [3] and Wavelet Transform [4], [5], [6], [7], [8]. The existing automatic fabric detection methods can recognize around 95% of defects on the plain 'unpatterned' fabric. However, there has not been much research on patterned fabric so far. We define the 'patterned' fabric with repetitive patterned units on its design. Under the class of the 'patterned' fabric, there are still many categories among them. Defect detection on the patterned fabric is difficult due to the design of the repetitive pattern on fabric. Fabrics can be classified into two main categories, namely the non-patterned fabric and the patterned fabric. For the non-patterned fabric, the plain and twill fabric are two common examples. The patterned fabric and the non-patterned fabric are distinguished by the appearance of repetitive unit on fabric. For example, there can be a flower or graphic logo on the fabric. Figure 1 illustrates the classification of fabrics. In section 2, a new method for defect detection on patterned fabric is given. An extension of the method using wavelet transform is given in section 3. A summary with conclusions is finally presented in section 4. Lastly, conclusions are presented in section 5.

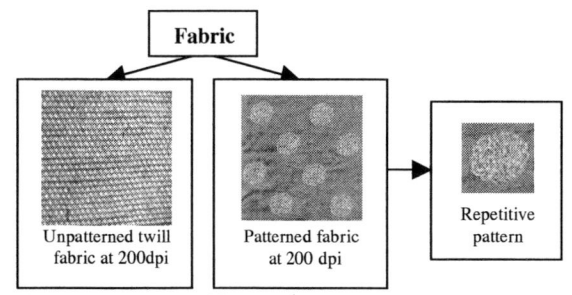

Fig. 1 Classification of fabrics

In this paper, a new defect detection method is developed and applied on one common kind of dot-patterned designed jacquard, which is shown in Figure 2. It has many repetitive units within the acquired image as our classification mentioned above. At this preliminary stage, three reference detective free samples were collected for training the threshold value and then used it to classify whether a testing image contains a defect. Only three reference samples are chosen at the training stage for the threshold value.

Fig 2. Dot-patterned designed jacquard

Fig. 3 Sample of histogram Equalized defective free image

There are three reference images (e.g. see Fig. 3) and eight defective images images with Netting (D1, D2), Broken Yarns (D3, D4, D5), Oil Stains (D6, D7) and Knots (D8). (e.g. see Fig. 7) in the experiments. All images for reference and testing have 256 x 256 pixels with grey level scale and they are all processed with histogram equalization in order to get better contrast.

2. The Golden Image Subtraction (GIS) Method

In this section, the steps of GIS (Fig. 4) are described for defect detection on a type of patterned fabric, which is a dot-patterned designed jacquard. Firstly, histogram equalization will be applied on all scanned images in order to enhance the contrast of the images. Secondly, this section will outline how GIS is applied on testing images. Thirdly, after GIS, a thresholding process will be performed and then there is a discussion on how the thresholding value is obtained from the training samples. Lastly, this section will show how the noise is removed by median filter and Wiener filter.

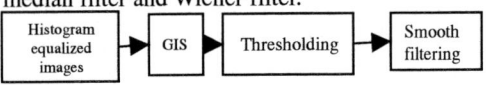

Fig. 4 The stages of the GIS method

Details of Golden Image Subtraction method

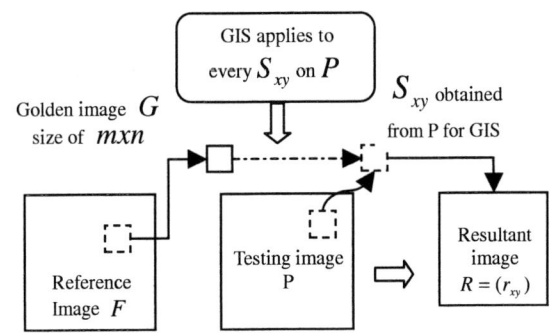

Fig. 5 Idea of the method of Golden Image Subtraction

A reference patterned fabric's image F of size MxN is picked up and then a golden image $G = (g_{ij})$ with size of mxn pixels (larger than one repetitive unit) is obtained from that reference image. Using this golden image, the computer can perform the GIS method on the testing image P. For every subtraction done in the testing image P, it calculates the mean of sum of absolute value of all pixels in every subtracted image which is mxn dimension. So, every mxn size subtracted image

$$S_{xy} = S_{xy}(i,j) = (s_{ij})$$

where $x=1,...M-m+1, y=1,...,N-n+1, i=1,...,m$ and $j=1,...,n$ ($0 < n \leq N, 0 < m \leq M$) will generate a value r_{xy}. (See Fig. 5) We define this value as the Energy of Golden Image Subtraction,

$$R=(r_{xy})=\frac{1}{m \cdot n}\sum_{i=1}^{m}\sum_{j=1}^{n}|s_{ij}-g_{ij}| \quad (1)$$

where $x=1,...M-m+1$ and $y=1,...,N-n+1$

As a consequence, after applying the methods of GIS on the entire testing image, it will return an $(M-m+1)x(N-n+1)$ matrix for the Energy of Golden Image Subtraction, which defined as a resultant image, $R = (r_{xy})$. Then, it will generate a plot of periodic hills and valleys if no defective region is found. Otherwise, there will be a subtle change in the plot if a defective region exists.

Thresholding

For a reference image, periodic hills and valleys will appear on the plot from resultant image R. A thresholded image $D = (d_{ij})$ is defined as

$$d_{ij} = \begin{cases} 1 & if\ r_{ij} > T \\ 0 & if\ r_{ij} \leq T \end{cases}$$

where $i=1,...,M-m+1$ and $j=N-n+1$ where r_{ij} is the energy value of resultant image R and T is the moderate threshold value. This image can be considered as a binary image and give the information on defects. A direct way to get the threshold value is to select the peak value of those hills and assume all hills have same peak in principle. For the defective samples, subtractions on defective area will make a distinguish jump on the plot as above. So, it will outline the defective region if a precise threshold value is known. Therefore, a training stage for obtaining the threshold value is essential. The method to train threshold value is firstly to collect a large amount of reference samples F_k where $k=1,...,w$, i.e. w reference samples. Using the same golden image, we process GIS on every sample. In principle, we should obtain $T_k = \max(r_{xy})$ where $x=1,...,M-m+1$ and $y=1,...,N-n+1$, the maximum value of Energy of GIS of every reference samples for $k=1,...,w$. However, there exists noises in those resultant images R_k, where $k=1,...,w$. Therefore, it needs to be eliminated by truncating some highest portion of peak values for each T_k. For example, the T_k will be 0.95 of original peak value in R_k if there is 5% noise. Afterward, averaging all the peaks $(T_1, T_2,...,T_w)$ will give us the **moderate threshold value T**, where $T = (T_1 + T_2 + ... + T_w)/w$. Using this threshold value, the defective region can be found on a testing image P.

De-noising process / Filtering process

After the threshold value is determined by the training samples, it can be used to threshold the testing images. As mentioned above, there will be some white impulse noises appeared when the testing image is passing a threshold value. So, we need to apply filtering techniques on thresholded image D in order to remove the noise and enhance the picture for defect on D. After trying several types of filters, Median filter [14] is chosen. Median filter is effective in dealing with bipolar and unipolar impulse. With the help of an appropriate filter, the result of thresholded image D would be improved to an appreciated level.

Results and Discussions

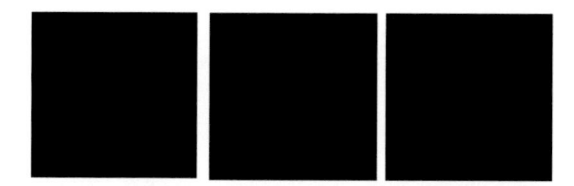

Fig.6 Filtered three reference images with median filter of size [5 5].

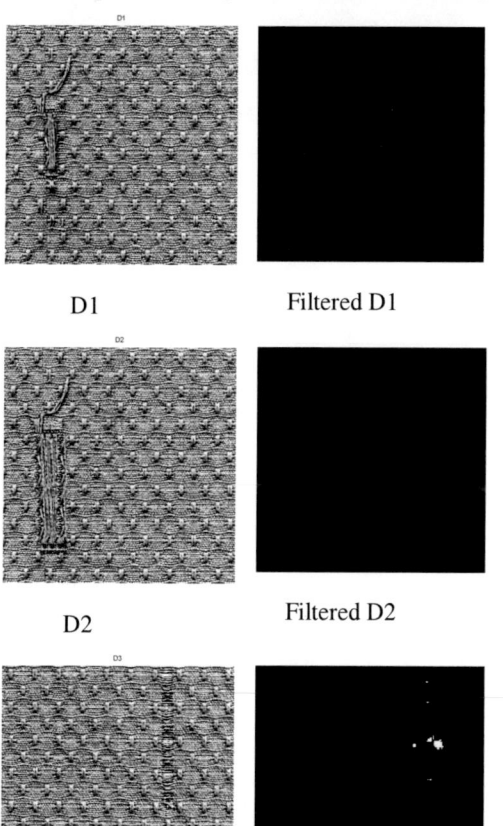

D1 Filtered D1

D2 Filtered D2

D3 Filtered D3

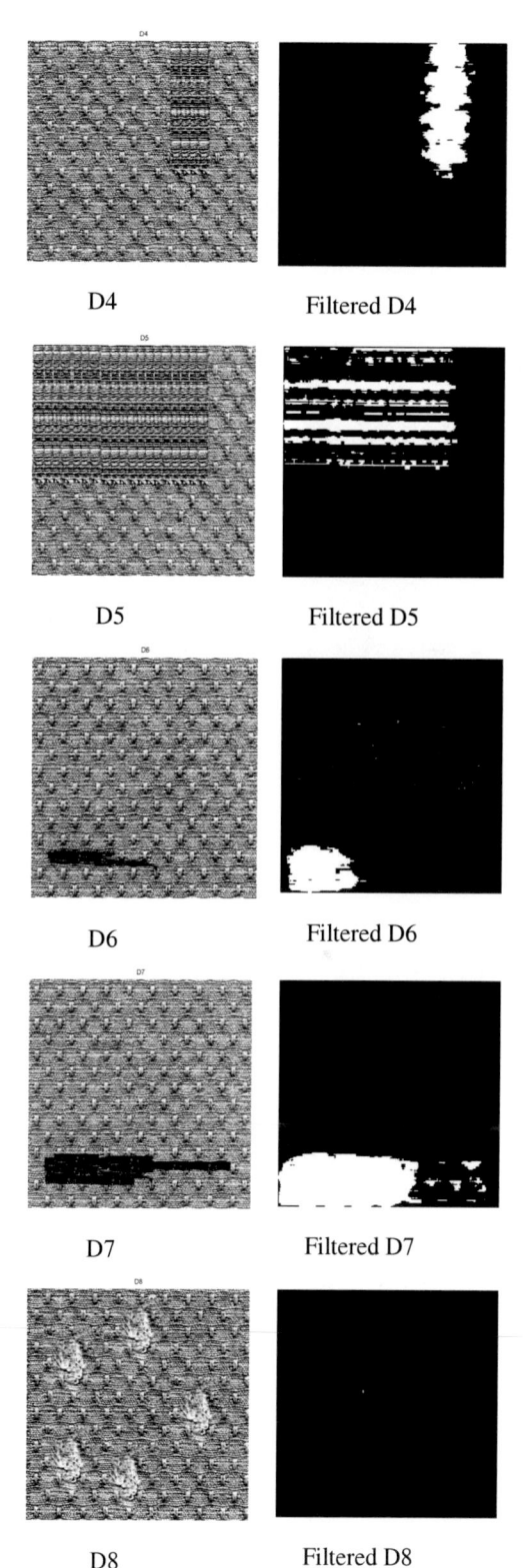

D4 Filtered D4

D5 Filtered D5

D6 Filtered D6

D7 Filtered D7

D8 Filtered D8

Fig. 7 Filtered eight defective images (D1, D2, ..., D8) with median filter of size [5 5].

Using three reference images and eight defective images, the size of the golden image is 47 x 40, approximately equivalent to five repetitive units in the Dot-patterned designed jacquard. Using the method of GIS, it can segment out the defect from the background by a thresholding value. The final results are shown in Fig. 6 for reference images and Fig. 7 for defective images. The results showed the defects with larger areas, e.g., D4 and D5 (broken yarn) and with high contrast compared to the background, e.g. D6 and D7 (oil stain) giving the significant results. The defective regions could be illustrated after thresholding and smoothing filtering. For those defects, e.g., D1, D2, D3 and D8, with small size or with low contrast compared to the background, only GIS is not enough.

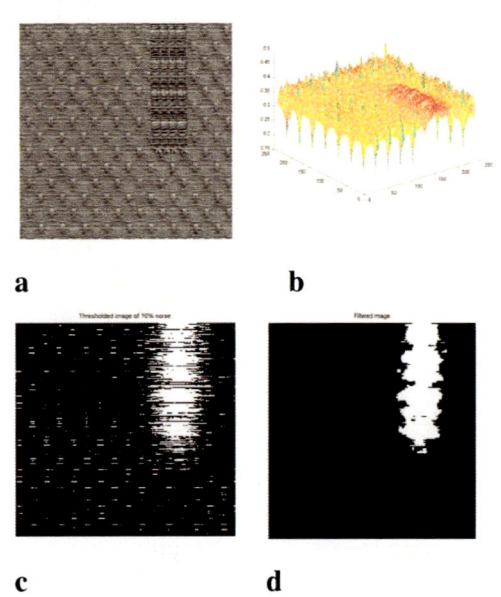

Fig 8 (a) Histogram equalized testing sample with *broken yarn*. (b) Mesh diagram after GIS. (c) Thresholded subtracted image (d)Using median filter of size[5 5] on thresholded image.

For more details, there is one sample from **broken yarn** from the testing images that are commonly found in the process of weaving jacquard. The results of these three samples are illustrated in Figures 8.

Effect due to noise levels in thresholded images

As mentioned above, by assumption, there is a small amount of noise existing in the thresholded image D. So, noise should be eliminated in order to give the best result on detecting for defects. Figure 9 shows that 10% noise level is the most appropriate level for the testing sample, broken yarn. If the noise level was adjusted to be too little, ie.1%, it would not give any result for defect detection.

When the noise level is adjusted to 10%, the output would be the most outstanding among all. However, the noise level could not be assumed too high. Otherwise, the thresholded image would be in white colour since the threshold value might reach the middle level of hills and valleys of resultant image.

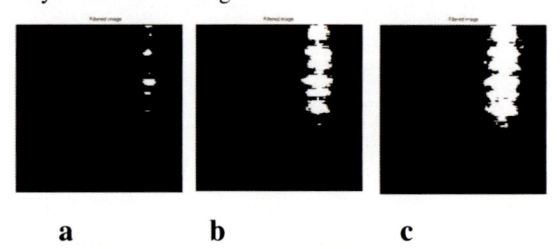

Fig.9 Histogram equalized testing sample with *broken yarn*. (a) 1% noise, (b) 5%noise, (c) 10% noise in thresholded image after using Median filter

Effect due to Size of Golden image

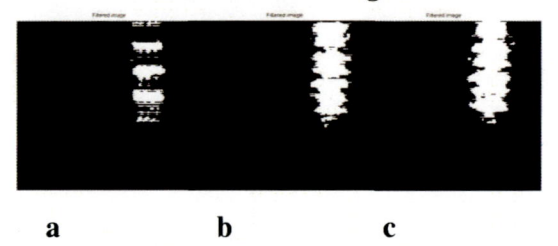

Fig.10 Applying median filter on 10% noise thresholded image of broken yarn of pixel size (a) 25x15, (b) 35x28, (c) 47x40, golden images

Choosing a golden image is a key step for the GIS method. The size of golden image cannot be chosen too small. Without chosen a size bigger than or equal to a repetitive pattern, the detection would not be succeeded. Yet, if any size of golden image bigger than a repetitive pattern is chosen, the result would be similar with those only approximately same size of one repetitive pattern. Size in half(10x9), one(25x15), two(35x28) and five(47x40) repetitive units of golden image are tested and the size in 47x40 shows the best result. The results of choosing different sizes of repetitive unit are shown on Figure 10.

3. Combination of Wavelet Transform (WT) and GIS

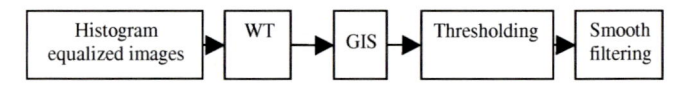

Fig.11 Combination of WT and GIS

From above results, it is shown that noise on the patterned fabrics is a big obstacle for our detection method in section 2. So, in order to tackle this problem, we rearranged our method 1 into a new procedure as shown in Figure 11.

Wavelet transform [5], [9] can be considered as a preprocessing tool as used to remove the noise impulse in scanned images. At this stage, its multiresolution and translation invariant properties are used and applied on the patterned fabric. It is a preprocessing tool is by selecting the first level approximation after the histogram equalized image passing Haar Wavelet Transform. The subimage of level 1 approximation is generated by passing by two low pass filters on the original image so that the noise on that subimage can be removed. Then, applying GIS on this image would enhance the detection result. From Section 2, a good golden image of size 47x40 size for GIS and 10% noise level for thresholding after GIS would generate a good result.

Fig. 12 Filtered three reference images with median filter of size [5 5].

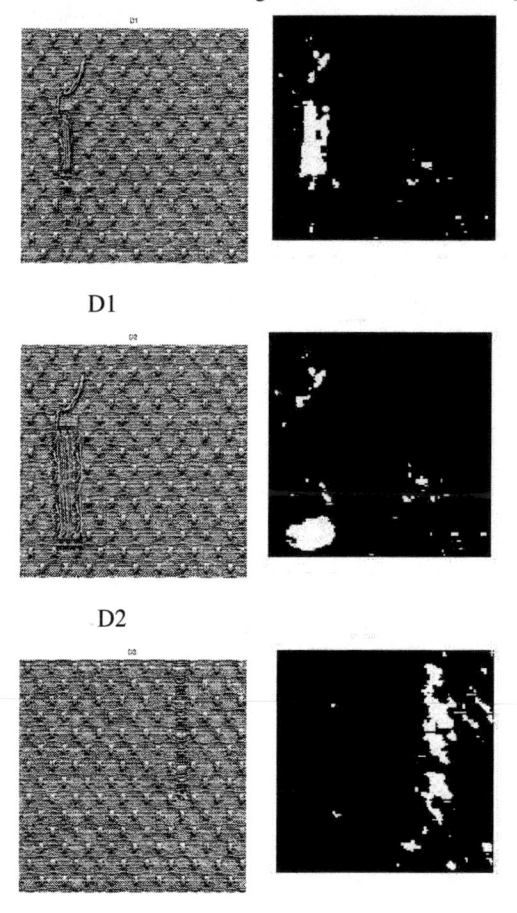

D1

D2

D3

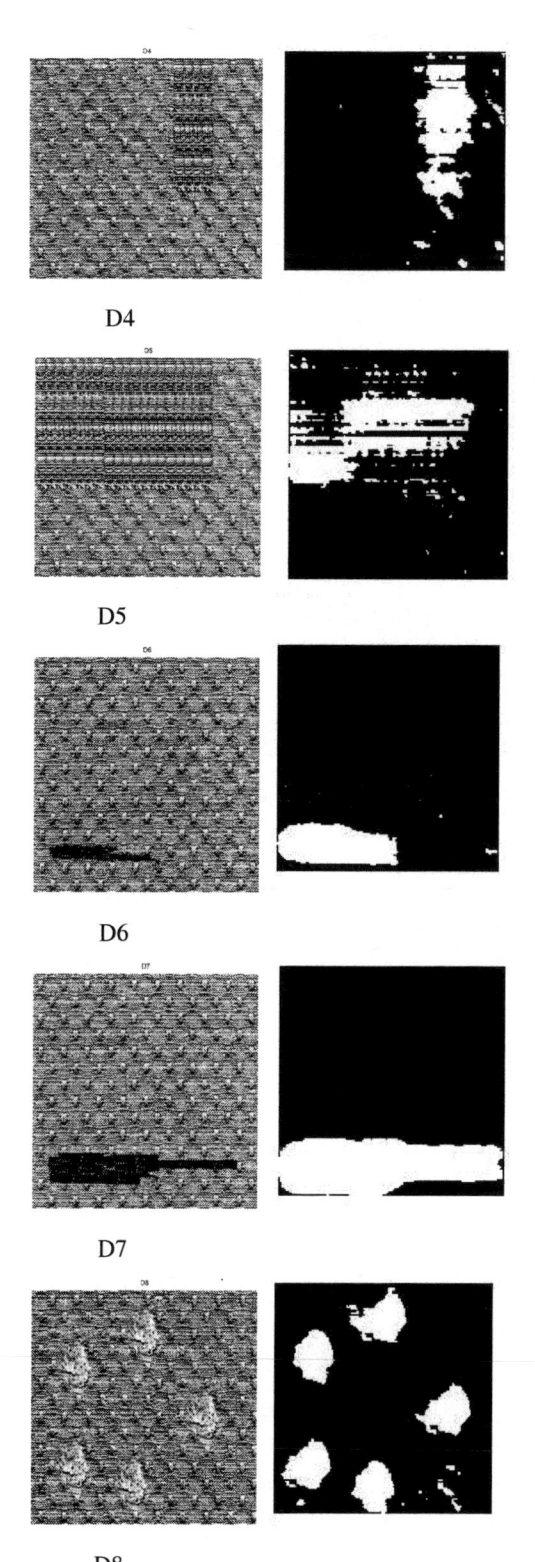

D4

D5

D6

D7

D8

Fig. 13 Filtered eight defective images (D1, D2,...,,D8) with median filter of size [5 5].

The resultant images of smooth filtering are shown in Fig.12 for reference images and Fig. 13 for defective images. It is impressive that eight defective images are detected. We conclude the result because the Haar wavelet's low pass filter can retain useful information after smoothing the original images.

4. Summary

Defect	Method 1 (GIS)	Method 2 (GIS with WT as preprocessing)
1	Not detected	Detected
2	Not detected	Detected
3	Not detected	Detected
4	Detected	Detected
5	Detected	Detected
6	Detected	Detected
7	Detected	Detected
8	Not detected	Detected
Total Number of defects detected	4	8

Fig. 14 Comparison of the detection results from the two methods.

Figure 14 summarized the two methods we investigated above and give us a clear idea that GIS should be combined with other methods in order to generate the best detection result. Method 2 can correctly detect all the defects and give outstanding outline for each defect. Finally, Figure 15 makes an overall conclusion for the two methods.

(Method) Main idea	Noise Level for threshold	Complexity	Comments for defect detection On dot-patterned jacquard
(1) GIS	10%	Low	Not successful
(2) Combination of WT and GIS	10%	Higher, but still low since the algorithm is simple and direct	Successful

Fig.15 Overall conclusion of the two methods addressed in this paper.

5. Conclusions

It can be concluded that the method of GIS is an effective way to detect defects on the periodic patterned fabric. With a moderate threshold value and an appropriate filter, a defect existing on testing sample can be found easily. Also, the size of golden image can be freely chosen by the user. It is useful in some cases if the repetitive unit is too small in some patterned fabric. The method of GIS can show both the shape and location of defect to the user. If we apply some pattern recognition techniques later on, we believe the classification of different defects can be easily achieved. On the other hand, there are some weaknesses for GIS. GIS cannot be applied on the right and bottom borders of the testing image. It is difficult to find a way to extend the border by suitable padding since the pattern of fabric sometimes is too complicated to be duplicated. The subtraction may also be done starting from the last pixel of last row in a backward approach as a second time. However, in a real situation, the borders of fabric are not important for detection so that we can neglect this problem. To conclude, with the outstanding results of method two, the combination of GIS with Wavelet Transform, defect detection on the dot-patterned fabric provides a satisfactory result.

Acknowledgement:
S.P. Yung's Research supported in part by a CRCG Grant 25500/301/01 and Michael K. Ng's Research supported in part by Hong Kong Research Grants Council Grant Nos. HKU 7130/02P and 7046/03P, and HKU CRCG Grant Nos. 10203501, 10203907 and 10204437.

References:

[1] A.Kumar, G.K.H., Pang, "Defect detection in textured materials using Gabor filters", *IEEE Trans. on Industry Applications,* Vol.: 38 Issue: 2, Page(s) 425 -440, Mar-Apr 2002

[2] Chi-ho Chan, G.K.H. Pang, "Fabric Defect Detection by Fourier Analysis," *IEEE Trans. on Industry Applications,* Vol.36, No.5, Sept/Oct, 2000

[3] L.H. Hoffer, F. Francini, B.Tiribilli, and G. Longobardi, "Neural networks for the optical recognition of defects in cloth," *Opt. Eng.*, Vol. 35, pp. 3138-3190, Nov. 1996

[4] G.Lambert, F.Bock, "Wavelet Methods for Texture Defect Detection," Image Processing, 1997. Proceedings, International Conference on, Vol:3, 26-27Page(s): 201-204, Oct 1997.

[5] A. Latif-Amet, A.Ertuzun, A.Ercil, "An efficient method for texture defect detection: sub-band domain co-occurrence matrices," *Image and Vision Computing,* Vol.18, pages 543-553, 1999

[6] Hamed Sari-Sarraf, James S.Goddard, "Vision System for On-Loom Fabric Inspection," *IEEE Trans. on Industry Applications*, Vol. 35, No. 6, Page(s): 1252-1259, Nov/Dec 1999

[7] Xuezhi Yang, G.K.H.Pang, Nelson. Yung, "Fabric Defect Detect Classification Using Wavelet Frames and Minimum Classification Error Training," Industry Applications Conference, 2002, 37th IAS Annual Meeting. Conference Record on the, Vol: 1, Page(s) 290-291, 13-18 Oct, 2002

[8] Xuezhi Yang, G.K.H.Pang, Nelson. Yung, "Fabric Defect Detection Using Adaptive Wavelet," Acoustic, Speech and Signal Processing, Proceedings (ICASSP'01) 2001 IEEE Conference on Vol:6,7-11 May 2001, Page(s)3697-3700, 2001

[9] D.M.Tsai, Bo.Hsiao, "Automated surface inspection using wavelet rescontruction." *Pattern Recognition*, Vol. 34, Page(s)1285-1305, 2001

A Hybrid Approach to Character Segmentation of Gurmukhi Script Characters

Neena Madan Davessar
M.Tech. (Comp. Sc. & Engg.)
Lecturer
Guru Nanak Dev University
Amritsar, India
Email: nmadan70@rediffmail.com

Sunil Madan
M.Tech. (Comp. Sc. & Engg.)
Email: sunilmadan@hotmail.com

Hardeep Singh
M.S. (Comp. Sc. & Engg.)
Reader
Guru Nanak Dev University
Amritsar, India

Abstract

A new approach to segmentation of machine printed Gurmukhi text has been suggested. This approach can easily be extended to other Indian language scripts such as Devnagri and Bangla. Most of the characters in these scripts have horizontal lines at the top called headlines. Besides, there are cases in which the characters are found touching in the scanned image, just below the headline. To resolve these issues, a two-pass mechanism is used. In pass-one it approximates the segmentation point, while in pass-two the cutting point is optimized. This approach has been very successful in segmenting a pair as well as triplets of touching characters.

1. Introduction

Written language recognition is the task of transforming language represented in its spatial form of graphical marks into its symbolic representation. For the past 30 years, there has been a mounting interest among researchers in the problems related to written language recognition. The subject has attracted immense research interest not only because of the challenging nature of the problem, but also because it provides a means for automatic processing of large volumes of data such as postal codes, automatic cheque amount reading in banking environments and for office automation. The basic problem is to assign the digitized character into its symbolic class. In the case of a print image this is referred to as Optical Character Recognition (OCR). In the case of handprint, it is referred to as Intelligent Character Recognition (ICR).

Character segmentation is an operation that seeks to decompose an image of a sequence of characters into sub-images of individual symbols. It has been verified experimentally[1] that it is less erroneous to recognize separated characters than otherwise. Character segmentation is one of the decision processes in a system for optical character recognition. It's decision, that a pattern isolated from the image is that of a character (or some other identifiable unit), can be right or wrong. It is therefore very important to minimize the errors in character segmentation process so as to reduce the error rate of character recognition process, as the success of recognition is based on that of segmentation.

2. Segmentation strategies

According to a survey of vast literature done by Casey *et. al.*[1] and according to Shridhar *et. al.*[2], there are three pure strategies for segmentation, plus numerous hybrid approaches that are weighted combination of these three. The elementary strategies are:
- *The Classical Approach*, in which segmentations are identified based on character-like properties. This process of cutting up the image into meaningful components is called *dissection*.
- *Recognition Based Segmentation,* in which the system searches the image for components that match classes in alphabet.
- *Holistic Methods,* in which the system seeks to recognize words as a whole, thus avoiding the need to segment into characters.

There are many strategies for segmentation, which are combinations of one or more of above three *pure* ones.

We can show these three strategies to occupy orthogonal axes. Hybrid methods can be represented as weighted combinations of these lying at points in the intervening space (Figure. 1).

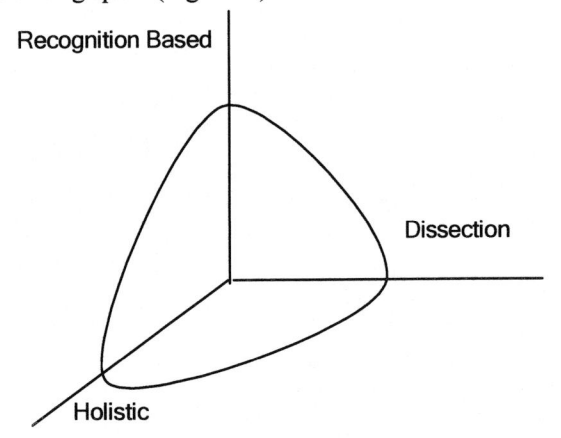

Figure 1: A three dimensional space representing the strategies of segmentation

3. Properties of Gurmukhi script

The Gurmukhi script alphabet consists of 40 consonants and 12 vowels. The writing style is from left to right. The concept of upper/lower case is absent. Most of the characters have a horizontal line at the upper part. Mostly this line called *headline* connects the characters of words. A word in Gurmukhi script can be partitioned into two horizontal zones. The upper zone denotes the region above the headline, while the lower zone represents the area below the headline (Figure 2). The major part of the characters is located in the lower zone.

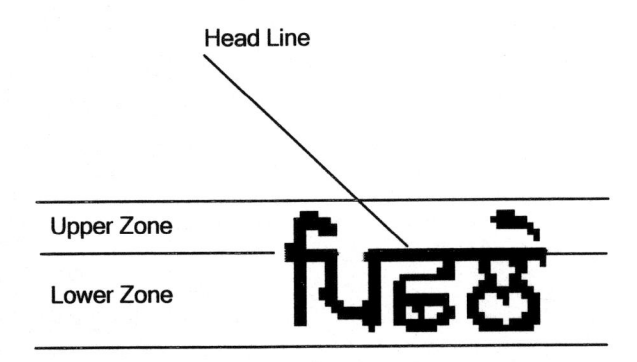

Figure 2: Upper and lower zones of a word in Gurmukhi script

4. Character segmentation for Gurmukhi script

Gurmukhi scripts characteristics like the *headline* make it difficult for segmentation. Some work has already been done on this by Parminder[3]. The technique he used involves separating the words from the text, and then finds the headline. After that it searches for a vertical white space. The point where it finds white space becomes the candidate cutting point.

5. Touching characters problem in Gurmukhi script

In Gurmukhi also, like other scripts, touching characters are a major source of errors for character segmentation. The technique by Parminder[3], does not address this problem.

It has been observed that, mostly, the touching characters of Gurmukhi Script are either of the form of twins (Figure 3), or, triplets (Figure 4). Further there can be a combination of characters having same width or one or more of these characters may have smaller width (Figure 5).

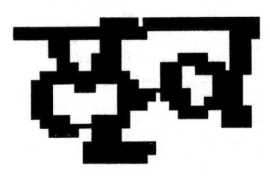

Figure 3: Pair of touching characters of equal width

Figure 4: Triplet of touching characters

Figure 5: Pair of touching characters of unequal width

6. Proposed segmentation technique

6.1 A hybrid approach

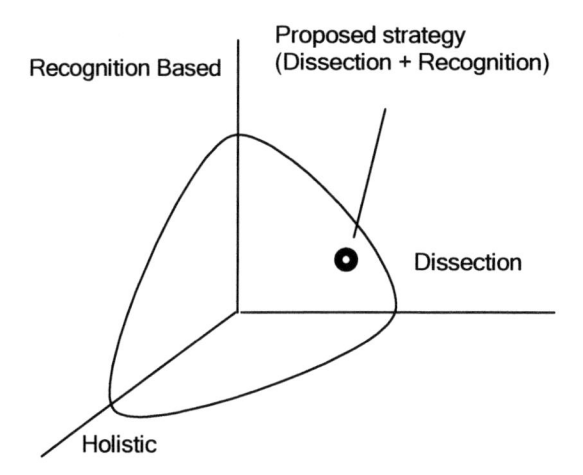

Figure 6: Proposed technique in 3-D segmentation space

Conventional segmentation strategies (discussed in section 2) do not suffice for Gurmukhi script. While the segmentation methodology for Gurmukhi script (Parminder[3]), handles the segmentation of Gurmukhi characters well, but fails to separate touching characters. Proposed technique has been chosen to be the hybrid approach. It combines dissection as well as the recognition-based approaches.

We can show the proposed technique in the 3-D representation of segmentation strategies as on the recognition-dissection plane (Figure 6).

6.2 Dissection (Pass One)

First pass exploits the structural feature of Gurmukhi that all its characters are joined at headline, and there is vertical white space after the baseline. The key issue is to find the baseline. This is found by taking horizontal pixel densities (the line with maximum density would be marked as headline) (Figure 7).

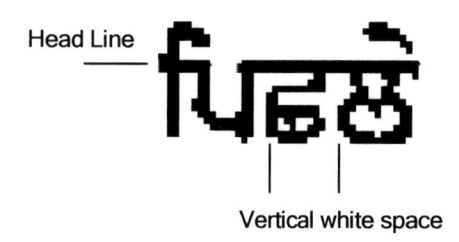

Figure 7: Locating the headline & vertical white space

After locating the headline, vertical white spaces are found and marked. Up to this point, the technique is same as the one used by Parminder[3].

6.3 Handling the touching characters (Pass Two)

The touching characters do not have any in-between vertical white space, after the headline (Figures 3,4 & 5). To separate such characters, aspect ratio of the characters has been used (Aspect ratio is the width of a character divided by its length). The width of characters is known (from pass one), while, the length is also known from the headline calculations. So, aspect ratio for every character is calculated. If it is greater than (the experimentally chosen figure), that means the width is greater than length and hence a candidate touching characters pair. The approximate cut is made in the half of touching character pair. But, actual cut is made after optimizing the cutting point. This is done to cope up with the problem of a touching character pair including one small character (Figure 5) or symbol, and to handle the touching characters' triplet (Figure 4).

Optimal cutting point is found by checking vertical pixel densities after headline in the constant width window around the approximate cut-point. The cut is made at a point having minimum density. The window width is chosen to be of the order of the width of characters. And the window is placed such that half of it is to the left of approximate cutting point, and half to its right. Let us consider the touching character pair of figure 3. The results of two-pass mechanism were found to be as shown in figures 8 & 9.

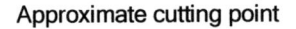

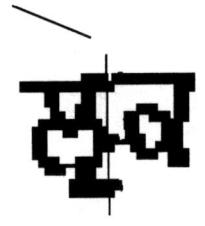

Figure 8: Pass-one - Got approximate cutting point

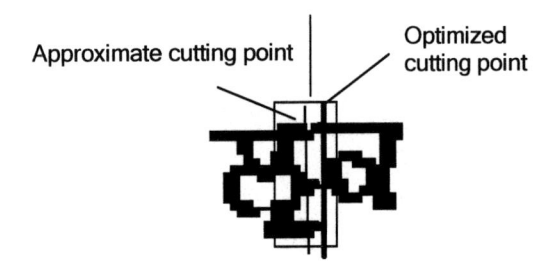

Figure 9: Pass-two - Cutting point optimized

For touching triplets we got approximate cutting point as shown in figure 10.

Figure 10: Pass-one - Got approximate cutting point

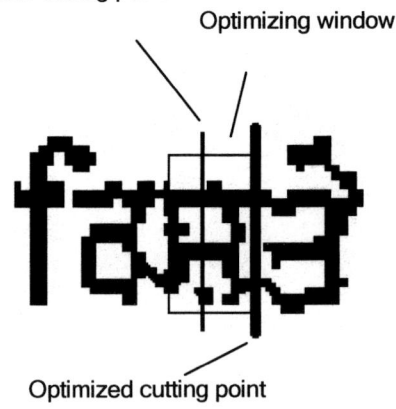

Figure 11: Pass-two - optimized cutting point

After separating the two components obtained in pass-two, both the components are again put for aspect ratio analysis. We found further approximate cutting point in this analysis (Figure 12).

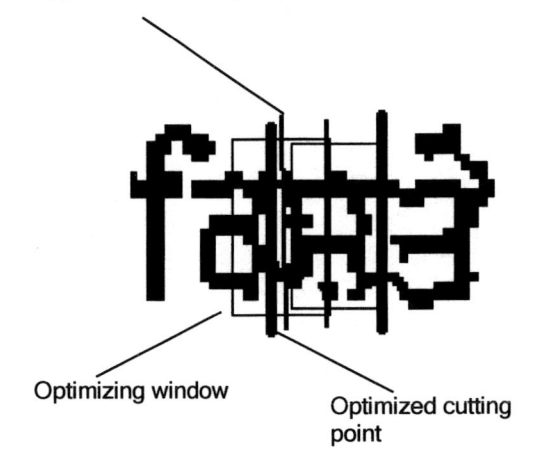

Figure 12: Pass-two - repeated to find another optimized cutting point

This process is repeated until all the segments obtained are through the aspect ratio analysis. In the same way we can separate any number of touching characters using the proposed strategy. The experimental results of the above segmentation strategy, when applied to a printed text sample of Gurmukhi are shown in figure 13 (after pass-one) and figure 14 (after pass-two).

Figure 13: Pass-one

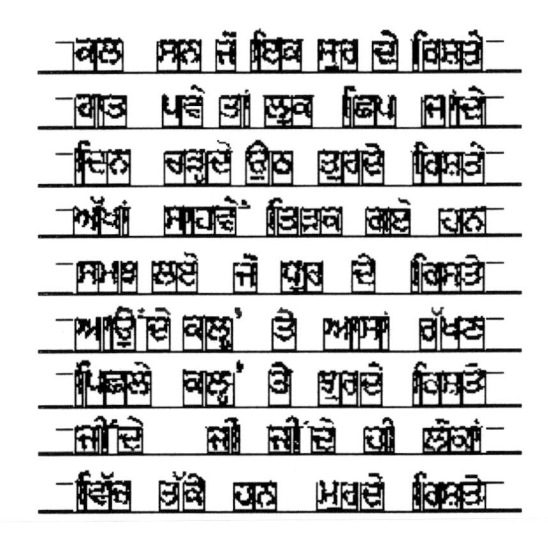

Figure 14: Pass-two

7. References

[1] Casey, R.G. and Lecolinet, E., "A Survey of Methods and Strategies in Character Segmentation", *IEEE Transactions on Pattern Analysis and Machine Intelligence,* 1996, vol.18, no.8, pp.690-706.

[2] Liang, S.; Shridhar, M. and Ahmadi, M., "Segmentation of Touching Characters in Printed Document Recognition", *Pattern Recognition,* 1994, vol.27, no.6, pp.825-840.

[3] Perminder Singh, "A Technique for Preprocessing and Segmentation of Printed Text in Gurmukhi Script", *An M.Tech. thesis submitted to Deptt. of Comp. Sc. & Engg., Punjabi University, Patiala.,* 1997.

[4] Fujisawa, H.; Nakano, Y. and Kurino, K., "Segmentation Methods for Character Recognition: From Segmentation to Document Structure Analysis" *Proceedings of the IEEE,* 1992, vol.80, no.7, pp.1079-1091.

[5] Lu, Y., "Machine Printed Character Segmentation - An Overview", *Pattern Recognition,* 1995, vol.28, no.1, pp.67-80.

[6] Wang, J. and Jean, J., "Segmentation of Merged Characters by Neural Networks and Shortest Path", *Pattern Recognition,* 1994, vol.27, no.5, pp.649-658.

[7] Weissman, H.; Schenkel, M.; Guyon, I.; Nohl, C. and Henderson, D., "Recognition-based Segmentation of On-line Run-on Handprinted Words: Input vs. Output Segmentation", *Pattern Recognition,* 1994, vol.27, no.3, pp.405-420.

[8] Pavlidis, T., "Recognition of Printed Text Under Realistic Conditions", *Pattern Recognition Letters,* 1993, vol.14, no.4, pp.317-326.

[9] Kahan, S.; Pavlidis, T. and Baired, H.S., "On The Recognition of Printed Characters of Any Font and Size", *IEEE Transactions on Pattern Analysis and Machine Intelligence,* 1987, vol.PAMI-9, no.2, pp.274-288.

[10] Seni, G. and Edward, C., "External Word Segmentation of Off-line Handwritten Text Lines", *Pattern Recognition,* 1994, vol.27, no.1, pp.41-52.

[11] Srihari, S.N. and Lam, S.W., "Character Recognition",*http://www.cedar.buffalo.edu/Publications/TechReps/OCR/Ocr.htm,* 1992, pp.1-8.

Modified Luminance Based MSR for Fast and Efficient Image Enhancement

Li Tao and Vijayan Asari
VLSI Systems Laboratory
Department of Electrical and Computer Engineering
Old Dominion University, Norfolk, VA 23529
Email: (ltaox001, vasari)@odu.edu

Abstract

A luminance based multi scale retinex (LB_MSR) algorithm for the enhancement of darker images is proposed in this paper. The new technique consists only the addition of the convolution results of 3 different scales. In this way, the color noise in the shadow/dark areas can be suppressed and the convolutions with different scales can be calculated simultaneously to save CPU time. Color saturation adjustment for producing more natural colors is implemented. Each spectral band can be adjusted based on the enhancement of the intensity of the band and by using a color saturation parameter. The color saturation degree can be automatically adjusted according to different types of images by compensating the original color saturation in each band. Luminance control is applied to prevent the unwanted luminance drop at the uniform luminance areas by automatically detecting the luminance drop and keeping the luminance up to certain level that is evaluated from the original image. Down-sized convolution is used for fast processing and then the result is re-sized back to the original size. Performance of the new enhancement algorithm is tested in various images captured at different lighting conditions. It is observed that the new technique outperforms the conventional MSR technique in terms of the quality of the enhanced images and computational speed.

1. Introduction

Image enhancement is a very important preprocessing stage in many fields, such as Face Detection and Face Recognition. After enhancement, we can get all the details of an image especially under extremely dark background. So far, linear enhancement methods have been utilized, e.g. gain/offset correction method, histogram equalization method. Gain/offset correction is a linear processing, which linearly makes wide dynamic range of the images so as to span the full intensity range of the display medium. However, this processing does not always provide a good visual representation from the original scenes. Histogram equalization is based on transforming the input image to an output image, which contains a uniform distribution of intensity. This method works well when the original images have a unimodal or weak bi-modal histograms, but not so well for the images with strong bi-modal histograms. As for MSR (multi-scale retinex), it works well under most lighting conditions. However, the MSR technique still needs to be improved on the following issues:

- The color restoration output may be unpredictable and unnatural.
- Chromatic noise in dark/shadow areas tends to be enhanced as well.
- Near the border between the bright and dark areas, an artifact of a dark band can be seen on the darker side while a bright band can be seen on the brighter side.
- For images with large bright areas, the features in the small dark regions are usually not enhanced sufficiently.
- The convolution of large images and large scales needs long CPU time.
- Need to set many parameters.
- Lack of edge sharpness.

In order to improve these problems, we propose a Luminance Based MSR (LB_MSR) approach for image enhancement. The processing is simplified by adding the convolution results of luminance and different scale Gaussians instead of multiplying the convolution results of each color value and the different scale Gaussian. Based on this, we propose two speed-up methods, one is to downsize the original image to its half size while convolving it with the largest scale Gaussian. In this way, the scale of Gaussian can also be downsized to its half size. The other speed-up method is to use the arithmetic mean of the image instead of convolving this image with the largest scale Gaussian. In this way, the dynamic range can be mostly compressed. By doing the modified MSR on the luminance of an image instead of doing MSR on each of the 3 bands, the process elapse time is dramatically reduced, which leads to real-time image enhancement.

LB_MSR algorithm has fewer arbitrary parameters that are more flexible, maintains color fidelity, and still preserves the contrast-enhancement benefits of the conventional MSR method. Moreover, by using our new algorithm, SNR of the enhanced result is more than the conventional MSR. Since we add the results of different scale convolution instead of multiplying them, the chance of enhancing the noise of the original image will get reduced. When enhancing that kind of 'whole black background' images, which already have a lot of noise, the enhanced result is clearer. Compared to the conventional MSR, this algorithm is more suitable to 'black objects with bright background' images due to one of our speed-up methods viz. using the arithmetic mean of the image instead of convolving this image with the largest scale Gaussian. In this way, the dynamic range can be mostly compressed without 'edge effect' (shadow around the edge of the bright object in a dark background) generated by convolution. In this method, color restoration is a linear correction, which will achieve relatively more colorful and clearer results, which is more suitable for Face Detection and Recognition.

The paper is organized as follows: In section 2, we describe the outline of our theoretical approach. In section 3, we describe the investigation of the speed-up processing methods. In section 4, we give the experimental results and comparisons with the conventional MSR algorithm. Finally in section 5, we conclude and mention about the ongoing research.

2. Theory of operations

We propose a luminance based MSR method that can improve the performance of the conventional MSR. The details of LB_MSR are the following:

- The luminance of the image is achieved through a standard procedure as in Eq. (1)
- The convolution of the luminance is conducted with one 2-D distribution Gaussian function that is a sum of the two Gaussian functions with two smaller scales.
- The convolution of the luminance with the Gaussian function with the largest scale is calculated. Both the image matrix and the 2-D Gaussian function are downsized in half to accelerate the calculation. After convolution, the result is upsized by 2 to obtain the average luminance with the original pixel number.
- The two convolution results are added together and ready for the luminance enhancement computation.
- The luminance enhancement is implemented by the logarithmic computation described in Eq. (6) followed by a gain/offset operation.
- A comparison between the original luminance and the enhanced luminance is applied to assure that the enhanced luminance has no luminance drop for any pixels, see Eq. (8).
- The image colorization method is a linear process that is described in Eq. (9).
- Finally, color saturation adjustment is used to make the color looks more natural, see Eq. (10).

This algorithm is composed of independent steps of dynamic range compression and color balance. In the former MSR method, we do MSR for each band: R, G and B in order to compress the dynamic range of each band by considering the 24-bit color values as our processing object. Although this processing works well in compressing an image's dynamic range, it needs a lot of computations, which are very expensive. Meanwhile, it compresses the color's dynamic range also, that's why even after using the color restoration method, the processed image is still kind of 'graying out'. Sometimes 'graying out' is not bad especially when the original image is in extremely black background, because the 'graying out' result is more natural, but not suitable for further research on Face Detection and Recognition, which depends to some extent on the color of the skin region. So, in our new algorithm, we apply MSR processing on an appropriately defined luminance of the original color image first as,

$$I(x,y) = R \times \frac{R}{(R+G+B)} + G \times \frac{G}{(R+G+B)} + B \times \frac{B}{(R+G+B)} \quad (1)$$

Having computed the luminance, LB-MSR processing is now applied to it. Before doing that, let's recall the conventional MSR which is by doing the following computations:

$$R_{MSR2}(x,y) = \sum_{i=1}^{3} W_i \{\log I(x,y) - \log[I(x,y) * F_i(x,y)]\} \quad (2)$$

W_i: weight associated with the ith scale (the default number of scales is 3: a small scale to enhance fine details, a large scale to provide color tonality, and a medium scale to provide a bridge)

Empirical values: $W_1 = 0.40$, $W_2 = 0.30$, $W_3 = 0.30$ (if one more scale is added, the weighting factor is changed to

0.25, since there are four scales now and the weights for all four scales are equal.)

Gaussian function: $F(x,y)=K\exp(-(x^2+y^2)/c^2)$

K determined by:

$$\iint K \exp(-(x^2+y^2)/c^2)dxdy = 1$$

C is the Gaussian surround space constant:

$C_1 = 5$, $C_2 = 20$, $C_3 = 240$

In Eq. (2), I represent the luminance of the original image. In this way, we get a luminance version of conventional MSR. Here the luminance is in a space, which is locally approximately linear, and thus the image, which requires little or no change, should look more natural. If $W_i = 0.33$, we can further expand the equation as in Eq. (3):

$$R_{MSR2}(x,y) = \frac{1}{3}(\log\frac{I(x,y)}{I(x,y)*F_1(x,y)} + \log\frac{I(x,y)}{I(x,y)*F_2(x,y)} + \log\frac{I(x,y)}{I(x,y)*F_3(x,y)}) \quad (3)$$

Further, we can get,

$$R_{MSR2}(x,y) = \frac{1}{3}(\log\frac{I(x,y)\cdot I(x,y)\cdot I(x,y)}{(I(x,y)*F_1(x,y))\cdot(I(x,y)*F_2(x,y))\cdot(I(x,y)*F_3(x,y))}) \quad (4)$$

From this equation, we can see the denominator of log function is the product of three convolutions by luminance and three different scale Gaussians. In this way, although we can compress the dynamic range, the noise of the original image is also enhanced because of the multiplication relationship of each of the three convolution results. So we change Eq. (4) to Eq. (5):

$$R_{MSR2}(x,y) = \frac{1}{3}(\log\frac{I(x,y)\cdot I(x,y)\cdot I(x,y)}{(I(x,y)*F_1(x,y))+(I(x,y)*F_2(x,y))+(I(x,y)*F_3(x,y))}) \quad (5)$$

which is equal to::

$$R_{MSR2}(x,y) = \frac{1}{3}(\log\frac{I(x,y)\cdot I(x,y)\cdot I(x,y)}{I(x,y)*(F_1(x,y)+F_2(x,y)+F_3(x,y))}) \quad (6)$$

F_1 represents the Gaussian with scale 5, F_2 represents the Gaussian with scale 20, F_3 represents the Gaussian with scale 240. The size of the scale determines the output of the single scale retinex. Sizes from 1% - 5% of the image size bring out fine details; sizes from 10% - 15% a mixture of details and color, and sizes from 30% - 50% of the image size provide color balance. We can bring out more fine details by adding another small scale (scale size 1% - 5% of image dimensions) to the luminance image or by changing the weight associated with the smallest scale. By using Eq. (6), we can lower the chance of enhancement of the noise in the original image by adding the convolution results. Meanwhile, the process speed can be reduced by only computing one convolution instead of three convolutions.

Next-step is to apply the histogram based gain-offset method to R_{MSR2}. In this way, we map the pixels into the output range, typically [0, 255], recalling that the zero point is already set by the bottom clipping of the intensity. The contrast (gain) and brightness (offset) are experimental values. A high contrast value is equivalent to a brighter, high contrast output; it can provide a sharp image that captures fine details in the original image, but at the cost of more noticeable noise. As for the brightness (offset), increasing its magnitude results in the ability to see deeper into the dark regions but at the cost of loss in sharpness as:

$$R_{MSR\,2'}(x,y) = G \times (R_{MSR\,2}(x,y) + b) \quad (7)$$

gain: $G = 150$ offset: $b = 0.6$

In order to assure that the enhanced luminance have no luminance drop for any pixels, we compare the original luminance and the enhanced luminance, then by applying Eq. (8), we can always get the larger value between $R_{MSR2'}(x,y)$ and $I(x,y)$. That is to say, we always can keep the brightness of the bright region in the image.

$$R_{MSR2''}(x,y) = \left(\frac{|R_{MSR2'}(x,y)-I(x,y)| + R_{MSR2'}(x,y)-I(x,y)}{2}\right) + I(x,y) \quad (8)$$

Thus having determined the desired relative intensity, we set each channel to the same chromaticity as in the input by Eq. (9):

$$R_j(x,y) = \sum_{j=1}^{3} R_{MSR\,2''}(x,y)\frac{I_j(x,y)}{I(x,y)}\cdot \lambda \quad (9)$$

j = 1: Red component, j = 2: Green component,
j = 3: Blue component,
λ: Flexible adaptive constant between 0 and 1.

The processing so far has been designed to maintain color fidelity. We introduced a parameter λ here in order to adjust the saturation of each band, which will be useful for further Face Detection and Recognition research. But this kind of saturation is not enough. In order to let the output looks more natural, we introduce a second step of color saturation. Actually, different images taken from different types of cameras have different color saturation requirements. For example, images taken from a digital camera (Canon Powershot G1) already have relatively good color effect. So after enhancement, we should do some operations to suppress the color saturation in order to let the result looks more close to the natural color, then the output is more suitable for face detection procedure.

The saturation can be adjusted by the following computations:

$$R_a = \frac{R_1(x,y) + R_2(x,y) + R_3(x,y)}{3} \quad (10a)$$

R_a: Average color value of each pixel after enhanced

$$R_j(x,y) = R_j(x,y) + (R_a - R_j(x,y)) * \kappa_j \quad (10b)$$

$R_j(x,y)$: Enhanced value in each band of each pixel, where j = 1: Red band, 2: Green band, 3: Blue band
$\kappa_1 = 0.15$, $\kappa_2 = \kappa_3 = 0.3$

So, if the intensity of each band of a pixel is smaller than the average color value of each pixel, we increase the value of that intensity in that band. If the case is on the contrary, we lower the value of that intensity in that band. In this way, we can flexibly adjust the saturation.

2.1. Speed-up method

The processing of the conventional MSR takes a long time, because of the larger size of the third Gaussian. Convolving that Gaussian with the luminance will cost 70% of the processing time. In our method, computations performed only on luminance space can save time. Furthermore, by downsizing the original image ('Downsize' speed up method) to its half size while convolving with the largest scale Gaussian, we can downsize this scale 240 to its half size 120 too. After convolution, the result is upsized by 2 to obtain the average luminance with the original number of pixels.

Another way to speed-up ('Mean' speed up method) is an approximate method by calculating the arithmetic mean of the luminance of the original image instead of doing the largest scale convolution. As we know, when an image passes through a wide window Gaussian filter, we get most of the low frequency components of the image, which is approximately equal to the arithmetic average value of the image. Hence, Eq. (6) can be simplified as:

$$R_{MSR2}(x,y) = \frac{1}{3}(\log\frac{I(x,y) \cdot I(x,y) \cdot I(x,y)}{I(x,y)*(F_1(x,y)+F_2(x,y))+Mean(x,y)})$$

where $Mean(x,y)$ is the arithmetic average value of the luminance of the original image.

3. Experimental results and discussion

In this section, image enhancement by LB_MSR is compared with that by conventional MSR. Test results have been illustrated in Figures 1 and 2. It can be seen that multi scale retinex (MSR) is a reasonably good method of image enhancement that simultaneously provides dynamic range compression, color consistency and lightness rendition. Its color restoration process may provide good color rendition in images that violate the gray-world assumption. However, it can be observed from the figures that MSR with color restoration does not work well for images with complex lighting environment. It tends to enhance the chromatic noise in shadow/dark areas. It is unable to predict the output of the color restoration process and it may produce unnatural images. Small dark areas with large bright background cannot be enhanced satisfactorily by this procedure. In addition, it needs large computational load for several convolution operations. It can be seen from the figures that the LB_MSR rectifies the issues in the conventional MSR by performing major operations in the luminance space instead of that in the chrominance space.

In Figure 1, the original image has a large and bright background while the object is darker and underexposed because of the limited dynamic range of the camera. The difference between the two results from the two algorithms is significant. First, LB_MSR has a much higher luminance improvement than the conventional MSR. That's why the girl's face gets brighter after enhanced by LB_MSR. We can clearly see her eyes after enhancement, which originally are hidden in the shadow of her hat. Secondly, in the image produced by the conventional MSR, the luminance of the sky (the brightest area) drops after enhancement compared to the original image; but by applying LB_MSR, a luminance control routine has been introduced to prevent the luminance drop at pixels in the brighter region. Finally, as it is mentioned earlier, due to the color-saturation adjustment feature in LB_MSR, it produced more natural colors of the output image as we can see from the girl's face after enhancement. Since luminance enhancement has a lot to do with the largest-scale convolution, it is reasonable to adjust the scale of the Gaussian function for convolution in order to achieve the best luminance enhancement.

In Figure2, the original image was taken at night with most of the areas underexposed. When the two enhanced results are analyzed, it can be seen that the color rendition looks somewhat different in the conventional MSR and LB_MSR techniques. For example, the building in the image produced by the conventional MSR method is much bluer than that in the image processed by LB_MSR method. In reality, the real color of the building is more close to that in the image created by LB_MSR, since the color restoration used with the conventional MSR can often over-enhance the color contrast and color saturation. But on the contrary, LB_MSR comes with a color saturation adjustment routine that makes the color looks more natural and more close to the true color. Another significant difference in those images is in the enhancement of chromatic noises.

Original image 1

Original image 2

LB_MSR

LB_MSR

Conventional MSR

Conventional MSR

Figure 1. LB_MSR and conventional MSR algorithms applied to an image with darker objects in brighter background.

Figure2. LB_MSR and conventional MSR algorithms applied to an image captured at night to illustrate the effectiveness in suppressing enhancement of noise components.

The conventional MSR produces more color noises that are quite well pronounced anywhere in the dark areas, such as the sky above the building, the ground and the tree. The noise reduction in the results produced by LB_MSR is a result of the fact that the sum of the three convolutions, instead of the product of them, is used as the denominator for the logarithmic operation. But in the case of conventional MSR the noise could also be enhanced during the process of multiplication. The third difference between the two results is that in the conventional MSR, due to the largest scale convolution operation, there appears 'edge effect' between the border of the brighter object (building) and the darker background (sky). But in LB_MSR, by using the arithmetic average of the original image instead of passing it through the largest scale Gaussian filter, no 'edge effect' exists.

In general, LB_MSR incorporates more luminance and color saturation control features than the conventional MSR, and all these features help to produce higher quality enhanced images with higher processing speed.

4. Real-time implementation

We implemented LB_MSR algorithm for real time image enhancement. Images used for the experiments were captured by a commercial Digital Video Camcorder - Canon NTSC 2R65 MC. The size of the image is 640×480 pixels and all images have three spectral bands with 8 bits per band. In this real time environment for nonlinear enhancement of the images, processing time is measured by computer simulation in a Pentium4 (2.26GHz) personal computer, with RAM size of 512 Mbytes in Windows-XP platform. LB_MSR algorithm has been implemented by using Visual C. The processing rate under these conditions was 3 frames/sec.

5. Conclusion

A luminance based multi scale retinex algorithm for the enhancement of darker images has been presented. The LB_MSR not only maintains the dynamic range compression benefits of conventional MSR, but is also precise with respect to color and has the ability to adjust the color saturation. This algorithm works effectively in the 'whole black background' image and 'darker objects with brighter background' images. LB_MSR provides better color fidelity, has fewer parameters to specify, less noise enhancement, and provides flexible saturation adjustment. The enhancement can be well performed for the 'dark' objects in 'bright' background, but keep the 'bright' background unaffected. In addition, it is computationally effective since it performs convolutions only on the luminance space, and also due to the 'downsize' and 'mean' speed-up methods.

6. References

1. D.J.Jobson, Z.Rahman and G.A Woodell " A multisacle Retinex for Bridging the Gap Between Color Images and the Human Observation of Scenes," *IEEE Transaction on Image Processing,* vol.6, no.7, pp. 965-977, 1997.

2. D.J.Jobson, Z.Rahman and G.A Woodell "Properties and Performance of a Center/Surround Retinex," *IEEE Transaction on Image Processing,* vol.6, no.3, pp. 451-462, 1997.

3. Kobus Barnard and Brian Funt "Analysis and Improvement of Multi-Scale Retinex" *IS&T/SID Fifth Color Imaging Conference: Color Science, Systems and Applications*, Scottsdale, Arizona, pp. 221-226, 1997.

4. Tatsumi Watanabe, Yasuhiro Kuwahara, Akio Kojima, Toshiharu Kurosawa "Improvement of color quality with modified linear multi-scale retinex" *Proceedings of the 15th SPIE Symposium on Electronic Imaging*, Santa Clara, CA, pp. 59-69, 2003.

5. K.Barnard, G.Finlayson, and B.Funt, "Color constancy for scenes with varying illumination," *Proceedings of the 4th European Conference on Computer Vision,* pp. II: 1-15, 1996.

6. Z.Rahman, D.J.Jobson, and G.A.Woodell, " A Multiscale Retinex for Color Rendition and Dynamic Range Compression," *SPIE International Symposium on Optical Science, Engineering and Instrumentation, Applications of Digital Image Processing XIX*, Proceedings SPIE 2825, Andrew G. Tescher, ed., 1996.

7. D. J. Jobson, Z. Rahman and G. A. Woodell, "Retinex Image Processing: Improved Fidelity To Direct Visual Observation," *Proc. of the IS&T/SID Fourth Color Imaging Conference: Color Science, Systems and Applications,* November, pp.124-126, 1996.

8. E. H. Land, " An Alternative Technique for the Computation for the Designator in the Retinex Theory of Color Vision," *National Academy of Science,* vol.83, pp.3078-3080, 1986.

Fusion for Registration of Medical Images- A Study

Rajiv Kapoor
Punjab Engg College
Chandigarh, India
raj_himani@hotmail.com

Aditya Dutta
NSIT
New Delhi, India
adutta@ice.nsit.ac.in

Deepak Bagai
Punjab Engg. College
Chandigarh
dbagai@yahoo.com

TS Kamal
SLIET
Longowal, Pb, India
tskamal@yahoo.com

Abstract

The paper is a study demonstrating the application of discrete multiwavelets in Medical image registration. The idea is to improve the image content by fusing images like MRI, CT and SPECT images, so as to provide more information to the doctor. The process of fusion is not new but here the results of study have been compared with the results from FCM algorithm used for similar application. Multiwavelets have been used for better clustering, as their decomposition results were better than Daubechies decomposition. A new feature based fusion algorithm has been used. This method shows results better than other methods for image registration when the images have been taken for the same person at a particular angle. The selective fusion not only gives more information but also helps in disease detection.

Keywords: Image Fusion, Wavelet Transforms, Super resolution, Image Clustering.

1. Introduction

With the availability of multisensor images in many fields, fusion has emerged as a new and promising research area. Multisensor image fusion can be performed at three different levels namely pixel level, feature level, and decision level. In this paper, multi sensor image fusion is pixel-level fusion for MRI-SPECT images and Feature level for CT-MRI , where the fusion process generates a single image containing a more accurate description than any individual source image. The simplest image fusion method is to take the average of the two source images pixel by pixel. However when this method is applied, several undesired effects, including reduced feature contrast appear. To solve this problem, sophisticated approaches based on multiscale transforms, such as gradient pyramid, Laplacian pyramid, morphological pyramid, and wavelet transform, have been proposed in the recent years [9]. Multiresolution wavelet transforms can provide good localization in both frequency and space domains. Compared with other multistage transforms, the discrete wavelet transform (DWT) is more compact, and able to provide directional information in the low-low, high-low, low-high, and high-high bands, and contains unique information at different resolutions - Image fusion based on the DWT can provide better performance than fusion based on other multiscale methods listed above. Multiwavelets are an extension from scalar wavelets, and have several advantages over scalar wavelets for image processing [27]-[30] . In this paper, we will demonstrate the application of the discrete multiwavelet transform (DMWT) to multisensor image fusion, and propose a new fusion algorithm based on it. This image fusion method provides an effective way to enable more effective analysis of multisensor data.

2. Literature Survey

Computed Tomography and Magnetic Resonance (MR) reveal the anatomic structure of an organ, while single photon emission computed tomography (SPECT) and positron emission tomography (PET) provide the functional and metabolic information. Thus, in clinical applications those images are frequently fused together to improve the diagnostic accuracy, assess lesion progression, or treatment effectiveness, and aid surgical and/or radio therapeutic planning. Image registration is the most important step of an image fusion task since images may be obtained when the patient is at different geometric relation with the imaging device. Algorithms for retrospective medical image registration have been extensively studied in the past decades. They have recently been reviewed and classified [1]. Earlier work—prior to 1993—has also been reviewed [2], [3]. Fitzpatrick and his colleagues evaluated 13 of those algorithms visually as well as objectively [4]–[6]. The voxel-similarity approaches to image registration have attracted significant attention since these full-volume-based registration algorithms do not rely upon data reduction, require no segmentation, and involve little or no user interactions. More importantly, they can be fully automated and quantitative assessment becomes possible. Reference [1] lists the reported paradigms and [7], [8] compares some of them. Among those different approaches, entropy-based algorithms, the mutual-information approach in particular, are the most prominent [9]–[16]. In this paper, we apply another information-theoretic mea-sure, cross-entropy (CE), also known as relative entropy and Kullback–Leibler distance, to image registration. It is a measure quantifying the difference between two probability density functions (pdfs) of random variables. CE minimization as a principle was formally established by Shore and Johnson [17], [18]. They also studied the properties of CE minimization [19]. This measure has been applied to diverse areas, including spectral analysis [20], image reconstruction [21], biochemistry [22].

3. Discrete Multiwavelet Transform & Image Fusion

Multiwavelets are an extension from wavelets, and several mother wavelet functions are used to expand a function. The GHM multiwavelet has several remarkable properties. Its scaling functions have short support. Both scaling functions are symmetric, and the multiwavelets form a Symmetric/antisymmetric pair. This is not possible for a single orthogonal wavelet. The application of multiwavelets requires that the input signal first be vectorised, namely pre-processing . Here, the pre-processing is based on Strela's algorithms. A pre-processing scheme is described based on the approximation properties of the multiwavelets. This scheme is connected with the GHM multiwavelet. We apply the discrete multiwavelet transform (DMWT) to image, fusion so as to create new fused images that have more information than the source images, and are more suited to the purposes of human visual perception, object detection and target recognition. Because the Source images have been obtained from different sensors they present different resolutions, sizes and spectral characteristics. A prerequisite for successful image fusion is that the source images have to be correctly aligned on a pixel-by-pixel basis. Many methods of multi-sensor image registration have been presented (13-15), and they can be used in multifold sorting of source images. We assume here that the images to be combined are already perfectly registered so that corresponding features coincide. First, multiwavelet processing and decomposition of the each input source image are computed at different levels (or scales). The source image is decomposed into sub bands, which can be treated as sub images: The pixels of the sub images consist of corresponding multiwavelet decomposition coefficients. Except for the low-low sub bands which all have positive transform values, all the other sub bands contain transform values that fluctuate around zero. The low-low sub bands block shows an image's approximate part. The low-high sub bands block, the high-low sub bands block and the high-high sub bands block show detail parts of the image in horizontal, vertical and diagonal directions, respectively. The next step decomposes the 'low-low' sub bands in the next level. With increasing level, the source image can be decomposed into a series of sub images, to construct a pyramid. Second, a pyramid is formed for the composite image by selecting multiwavelet decomposition coefficients from the source image pyramids. Large absolute values of multiwavelet decomposition coefficients correspond to sharper brightness changes and thus to salient features in the image such as edges, lines and regional boundaries. In the proposed image fusion scheme, we present a new feature-based fusion rule to combine source sub images and to form a pyramid for the composite image. In the source images, multiwavelet decomposition pyramid, the low-low sub bands block shows the image's approximate characteristic, so that the cluster formed by the extrema density points using the nearest neighborhood approach is the feature point for fusion. We select coefficients belonging to the feature-cluster-block between two source images', corresponding sub bands to form the coefficient of composite sub bands. The selected cluster-contour coefficients must represent the salient features in the sub bands of the source image. The other in this specific case has done this to avoid overlapping of useful information cluster. Finally, the fused image is constructed by successively performing reconstruction and the post filtering on the combined coefficients. Because multi-wavelets have many advantages, an image decomposed by multiwavelets will show the image's interior information adequately. The fusion rules take into account the various characteristics of the sub image so that the proposed method gives better results.

4. Experimental results

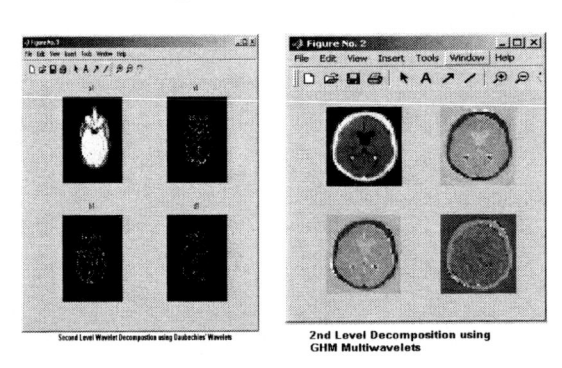

(a) (b)

Figure 1. 2nd Level Decomposition Process Comparison(a)Daubechies(b) GHM Multiwavelets

(2)　　　　　　　　(3)

(4)

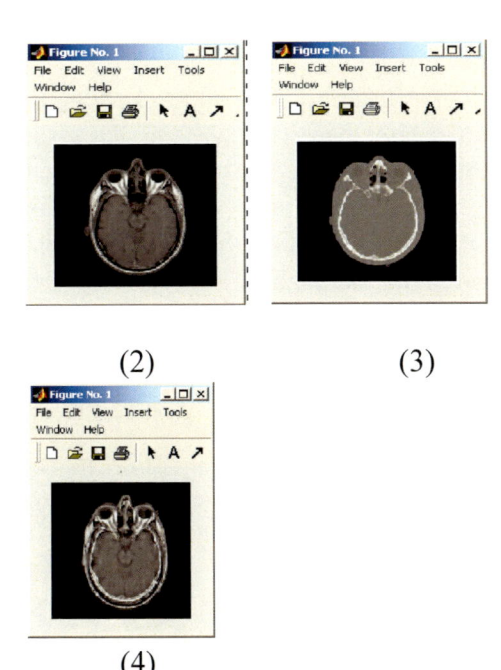

Figure 2. MRI Image Figure 3. CT Image Figure 4. Fused Image

Similar fusion principle was applied to the CT, MRI and the SPECT images to get the best results. Results of these have been shown in figures (1-5).

(a)　　　　　　　　(b)

(c)

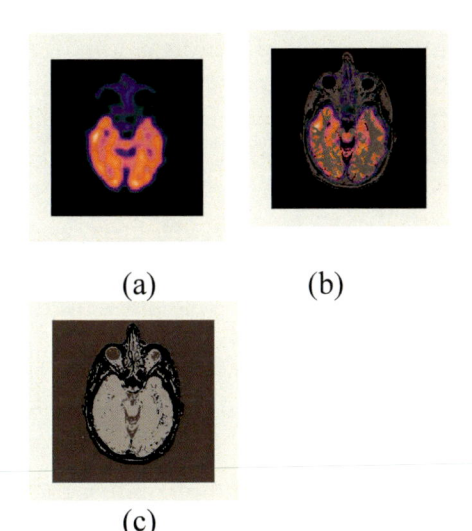

Figure 5 Fusion using FCM (a) SPECT Image (b) Fused Image (c) MRI Image

5.　Conclusions

Multiwavelet offer advantages of combining symmetry, orthogonal, and short support, which cannot be achieved by scalar two-channel wavelet systems at the same time. Fusion method has been proposed for performing the pixel-level fusion of spatially registered images. This fusion method is based on the discrete multiwavelet transform (DMWT). Fusion results obtained through Multiwavelets are easily comparable to the results obtained through FCM Algorithm and are much better in case of DMWT. Two kinds of data have been taken for verification. The first is the MRI, CT and SPECT Images, which have complex structure. These images have been shown so as to highlight the performance of the approach. The DMWT method is not only better than FCM approach but also better than any other Wavelet technique, which has also been demonstrated (comparison with Daubechies wavelet). Later on the method was applied to the Document images and the results are better than earlier approaches. To compare fusion effects, several methods were used to merge images with different resolutions. Based on the experimental results, the conclusion can be drawn that this image fusion algorithm gives more satisfactory results than other methods.

References

[1] J. B. A. Maintz and M. A. Viergever, "A survey of medical image registration," Med. Image Anal., vol. 2, no. 1, pp. 1–36, 1998.

[2] P. A. van den Elsen and M. Λ. Viergever, "Medical image matching—A review with classification," *IEEE Eng. Med. Biol. Mag.*, vol. 12, pp. 26–39, Mar. 1993.

[3] C. R. Maurer and J. M. Fitzpatrick, "A review of medical image registration," in *Interactive Image-guided Neurosurgery*, R. J. Maciunas, Ed. Parkridge, IL: Amer. Assoc. Neurological Surgeons, 1993, pp. 17–44.

[4] J. West, J. M. Fitzpatrick, M. Y. Wang, B. M. Dawant, C. R. Maurer, Jr., R. M. Kessler, R. J. Maciunas, C. Barillot, D. Lemoine, A. Collignon, F. Maes, P. Suetens, D. Vandermeulen, P. A. van den Elsen, S. Napel, T. S. Sumanaweera, B. Harkness, P. F. Hemler, D. L. G. Hill, D. J. Hawkes, C. Studholme, J. B. A. Maintz, M. A. Viergever, G. Malaandain, X. Pennec, M. E. Noz, G. Q. Maguire, Jr., M. Pollack, C. A. Pelizzari, R. A. Robb, D. Hanson, and R. P. Woods, "Comparison and evaluation of retrospective intermodality brain image registration techniques," *J. Comput. Assist. Tomogr.*, vol. 21, pp. 554–566, 1997.

[5] J. M. Fitzpatrick, D. L. G. Hill, Y. Shyr, J. West, C. Studholme, and C. R. Maurer, Jr., "Visual assessment of the accuracy of retrospective registration of MR and CT images of the brain," *IEEE Trans. Med. Imag.*, vol. 17, pp. 571–585, Aug. 1998.

[6] J. West, J. M. Fitzpatrick, M. Y. Wang, B. M. Dawant, C. R. Maurer, Jr., R. M. Kessler, and R. J. Maciunas, "Retrospective intermodality registration techniques for images of the head: Surface-based versus volume-based," *IEEE Trans. Med. Imag.*, vol. 18, pp. 144–150, Feb.1999.

[7] C. Studholme, D. L. G. Hill, and D. J. Hawkes, "Automatic three-dimensional registration of magnetic resonance and positron emission tomography brain images by multiresolution optimization of voxel similarity measures," *Med. Phys.*, vol. 24, no. 1, pp. 25–35, Jan. 1997.

[8] G. P. Penney, J. Weese, J . A. Little, P. Desmedt, D. L. G. Hill, and D. J. Hawkes, "A comparison of similarity measures for use in 2D–3D med-ical image registration," *IEEE Trans. Med. Imag.*, vol. 17, no. 4, pp. 586–595, 1998.

[9] A. Collignon, D. Vandermeulen, P. Suetens, and G. Marchal, "3D multi-modality medical image registration using feature space clustering," in *Computer Vision, Virtual Reality and Robotics in Medicine*, N. Ayache, Ed. Berlin, Germany: Springer-Verlag, 1995, pp. 195–204.

[10] W. M. Wells, III, P. V. Viola, H. Atsumi, S. Nakajima, and R. Kikinis, "Multi-modal volume registration by maximization of mutual information," *Med. Image Anal.*, vol. 1, no. 1, pp. 35–51, 1996.

[11] F. Maes, A. Collignon, D. Vandermeulen, G. Marchal, and P. Suetens, "Multimodality image registration by maximization of mutual information," *IEEE Trans. Med. Imag.*, vol. 16, pp. 187–198, Apr. 1997.

[12] C. R. Meyer, J. L. Boes, B. Kim, P. H. Bland, K. R. Zasadney, P. V. Kison, K. Koral, K. A. Frey, and R. L. Wahl, "Demonstration of accuracy and clinical versatility of mutual information for automatic multimodality image fusion using affine and thin-plate spline warped geometric deformations," *Med. Image Anal.*, vol. 1, no. 3, pp. 195–206, 1996.

[13] B. Kim, J. L. Boes, K. A. Frey, and C. R. Meyer, "Mutual information for automated unwarping of rat brain autoradiographs," *Neuroimage*, vol. 5, pp. 31–40, 1997.

[14] F. Maes, D. Vandermeulen, and P. Suetens, "Comparative evaluation of multiresolution optimization strategies for multimodality image registration by maximization of mutual information," *Med. Image Anal.*, vol.3, no. 4, pp. 373–386, 1999.

[15] C. Studholme, D. L. G. Hill, and D. J. Hawkes, "An overlap invariant entropy measure of 3D medical image

alignment," *Pattern Recogn.*, vol. 32, pp. 71–86, 1999.

[16] N. Ritter, R. Owens, J. Cooper, R. H. Eikelboom, and P. P. van Saarloos, "Registration of stereo and temporal images of the retina," *IEEE Trans. Med. Imag.*, vol. 18, May 1999.

[17] J. E. Shore and R. W. Johnson, "Axiomatic derivation of the principle of maximum entropy and the principle of minimum cross-entropy," *IEEE Trans. Inform. Theory*, vol. IT-26, Jan. 1980.

[18] R. W. Johnson and J. E. Shore, "Comments on and correction to 'Axiomatic derivation of the principle of maximum entropy and the principle of minimum cross-entropy,' *IEEE Trans. Inform. Theory*, vol. IT-29, Nov. 1983.

[19] J. E. Shore and R. W. Johnson, "Properties of cross-entropy minimization," *IEEE Trans. Infor. Theory*, vol. 27, no. 4, July 1981.

[20] J. E. Shore, "Minimum cross-entropy spectral analysis," *IEEE Trans.Acoust., Speech, Signal Processing*, vol. ASSP-29, pp. 230–237, 1981.

[21] T. G. Zhuang, Y. M. Zhu, and X. L. Zhang, "Minimum cross-entropy algorithm (MCEA) for image reconstruction from incomplete projection," *SPIE*, vol. 1606, pp. 697–704, 1991.

[22] E. Yee, "Reconstruction of the antibody-affinity distribution from experimental binding data by a minimum cross-entropy procedure," *J. Theor.Biol.*, vol. 153, no. 2, pp. 205–227, Nov. 1991.

[23] L. C. Alwan, N. Ebrahimi, and E. S. Soofi, "Information theoretic framework for process control," *Eur. J. Operational Res.*, vol. 111, no. 3, pp. 526–542, Dec. 1998.

[24] N. C. Das, S. K. Mazumder, and K. De, "Constrained nonlinear programming:
A minimum cross-entropy algorithm," *Eng. Optimization*, vol. 31, no. 4, pp. 479–487, 1999.

[25] J. Antolin, J. C. Cuchi, and J. C. Angulo, "Minimum cross-entropy estimation of electron pair densities from scattering intensities," *Phys. Lett.* A, vol. 26, pp. 247–252, Sept. 1999.

[26] Yang-Ming Zhu," Volume Image Registration by Cross-Entropy Optimization" IEEE TRANSACTIONS ON MEDICAL IMAGING, VOL. 21, NO. 2, FEBRUARY 2002.

[27] Mallat, S.G, "A theory for Multi-Resolution Signal Decomposition : The wavelet representation", IEEE-TPAMI, 1989,11,(7),pp.674-693.

[28] Daubechies. I, "The wavelet Transform, time , frequency localization and signal analysis", IEEE-Trans. On Information Theory,1990, 36,(9),pp.961-1005.

[29] Tham. J.Y,Shen. L, Lee.S.L and Tan. H.H, "A general approach for analysis and application of discrete Multiwavelet transforms", IEEE-Trans. On Signal Processing,2000,48,(2),pp. 457-464.

[30] Strela V,Hellers.P.N, Strang G, Topiwala P, and Heil C, "The application of Multiwavelet filter bank to image-processing",IEEE-trans. On Image Processing,1999,8(4),pp.548-563.

Visual Learning in Humans and Machines

⌘⌘⌘⌘⌘⌘⌘⌘

Visual Literacy: An Overview

James Aanstoos
Cary Academy
Jim_Aanstoos@caryacademy.org

Abstract

Visual literacy may be defined as the ability to recognize and understand ideas conveyed through visible actions or images, as well as to be able to convey ideas or messages through imagery. Based on the idea that visual images are a language, some authors consider visual literacy to be more of a metaphor, relating imagery interpretation to conventional literacy, than a well-defined and teachable skill. However, the field is credited with the development of educational programs that enhance students' abilities to interpret and create visual messages, as well as improvement of reading and writing skills through the use of visual imagery.

This paper presents a broad overview of the concept of field literacy, focusing on its interdisciplinary nature and varied points of view.

1. Introduction

Since this paper is being presented at a conference focused on the design of systems for understanding imagery using data fusion techniques, it is worth mentioning that the greatest example of a system for performing data fusion based image understanding is the human brain. Indeed, many artificial image analysis systems are based on theories of how the brain perceives and learns from imagery. The higher-level aspects of image interpretation in humans are less well understood, but the importance of cultivating these skills as our society makes ever greater use of visual communication has been recognized and strongly advocated over the last few decades, giving rise to the concept of visual literacy.

The area of study known as visual literacy and the movement that spawned it are very interdisciplinary in nature, encompassing the fields of art, education, psychology, linguistics, computer science, and even philosophy. This broad cross section leads to a fascinating variety of points of view on just what it means to be "visually literate" and whether this ability can or even should be taught and if so how. Contributors to this field seem to be much more in agreement as to the need for visual literacy skills than they are on exactly what these skills comprise and how they are acquired.

2. Defining visual literacy

The simple definition of visual literacy given above is but one of many encountered in the literature, and this so-called "definition problem" is given a considerable amount of attention. This problem no doubt arose in large part to the varied disciplines contributing to this field, and can be an obstacle to effective collaboration within it. Some lament that visual literacy lacks an operational definition, which is an impediment to effective research on the topic. The closest thing to an "official" definition is that due to Fransecky and Debes [1] which has been adopted by the International Visual Literacy Association: "a group of vision competencies a human being can develop by seeing and at the same time having and integrating other sensory experiences. The development of these competencies is fundamental to normal human learning. When developed, they enable a visually literate person to discriminate and interpret the visual actions, objects, and/or symbols, natural or man-made, that are [encountered] in [the] environment. Through the creative use of these competencies, [we are] able to communicate with others. Through the appreciative use of these competencies, [we are] able to comprehend and enjoy the masterworks of visual communications."

More recently Brill, Kim and Branch [2] suggested that the assumptions underlying a concept of visual literacy are that "images communicate meaning, and literacy means being able to read and compose". They conducted a study to solicit a working definition of visual literacy. The consensus of the visual literacy scholarly community resulting from their research defines visual literacy as follows: "A group of acquired

competencies for interpreting and composing visible messages. A visually literate person is able to:
  (a) discriminate, and make sense of visible objects as part of a visual acuity,
  (b) create static and dynamic visible objects effectively in a defined space,
  (c) comprehend and appreciate the visual testaments of others, and
  (d) conjure objects in the mind's eye."

These capabilities tie in well with Randhawa's [3] categorization of three "sub-concepts" of visual literacy which can be used to provide operational constructs: Visual Thinking, Visual Learning, and Visual Communication. These are further characterized by their "directionality" with respect to self and others, as depicted in Figure 1.

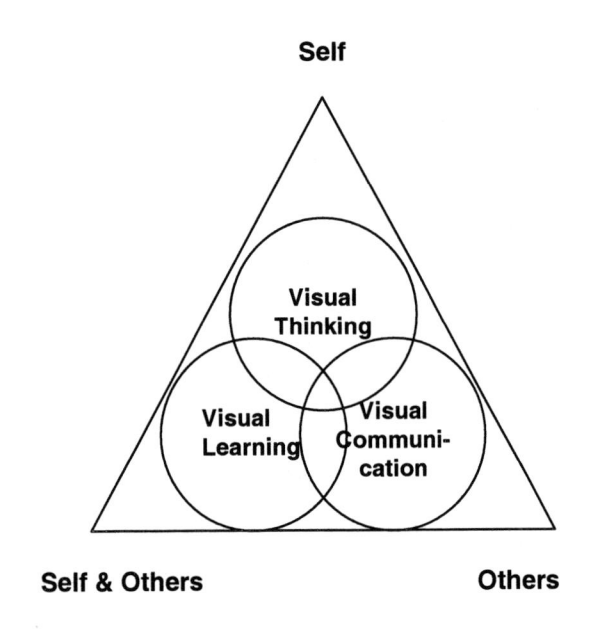

Figure 1. Directionality of VL components.

2.1 Visual Thinking

Visual thinking refers to visualization through images – mental pictures of sensory experiences, perceptions, or conceptions [4]. Arnheim describes visual thinking as the unity of perception and conception which calls for the ability to see visual shapes as images. He further characterizes it as preconscious, metaphorical thought. [5]

Arnheim and others bemoan the fact that our educational system is based so strongly on the study of "words and numbers," while the arts are neglected or relegated to second-class status. He believes that practice in "perception-based reasoning" such as comes from the study of art can improve overall learning.

2.2 Visual Learning

Visual learning, according to Seels [4], refers to the acquisition and construction of knowledge as a result of interaction with visual phenomena. Thus it covers both the creation of visuals to aid in learning as well as the ability to learn from such visuals. Much has been published in this field dealing with the design of instructional visuals, such as the compilation by Fleming and Levie [6].

2.3 Visual Communication

Seels [4], defines visual communication to be "using visual symbols to express ideas and convey meaning." By visual symbols she means "pictorial and graphic symbols" and it is clear that this includes both drawings and photographs, as well as both still pictures and video or animation. It should be quite clear that messages can be communicated by visual works, and the ability to convey and understand such messages is a component of visual literacy.

3. The need for visual literacy

Studies show that the average US elementary school student watches between 5 and 6 hours of TV a day. By the time he graduates from high school, this student has watched some 22,000 hours of television [7]. The motivation for teaching visual literacy skills most frequently cited in the literature is based on the increasing use of imagery and video in our culture. Doomsday predictions worried that TV would replace printed text. A more constructive reaction to the proliferation of TV and images is to ensure that our children learn critical and independent thinking skills applied to interpreting what they see as well as what they read. This is an important part of what it means to be visually literate.

Some authors refer to this particular component of visual literacy as *media literacy*. Sutton distinguishes media literacy from visual literacy, defining the former more broadly to be "the ability to decode, analyze, evaluate and produce communication in a variety of forms." [8]

The awareness of ways in which messages conveyed by pictures can be manipulated enhances one's ability to critically interpret such messages. Even photographs, which in a simplistic sense can be thought of as mere snapshots of reality, can be manipulated to influence the viewer. Such manipulation can be subtle, such as by the choice of viewing angle, lighting conditions, or simply the choice of which moment in time to capture. Or it can be more overt, such as by actually changing the picture after it has been captured.

A famous example of the former type of manipulation is the widely publicized photograph of the April 2000 taking of the Cuban boy Elian Gonzalez from the house in Miami where he had been illegally kept from immigration authorities intent on returning him to his father. The proximity of a heavily armed, combat-dressed, US marshal to the small frightened child discovered hidden in a closet certainly conveyed a range of messages and emotions to the viewer—but is it reality and does it tell the whole story? An article in Slate magazine about the use of images in telling this story contrasted this photo with the one released shortly thereafter of a smiling Elian reunited with his father, criticizing the point of view that these two pictures told the whole story: "Nonsense. Reality is one thing. Pictures are another. To confuse the two, you'd have to be blind." [9]

An infamous example of the more overt manipulation possible in using photographs to convey a message is the TIME magazine cover photo of O.J. Simpson during his murder trial. TIME took the mug shot of Simpson when he was arrested and changed it. They darkened the photo and created a five o'clock shadow and a more sinister look. The National Press Photographers Association wrote of this incident: "They decided Simpson was guilty so they made him look guilty." [10]

4. A failed metaphor?

The term visual literacy is clearly a metaphor, equating the reading and writing skills of conventional or "verbal" literacy with the ability to understand and convey messages through imagery. Cassidy and Knowlton [11] argue that this is a failed metaphor, and point out several problems as they see it with the whole concept.

One major flaw they point out is the lack of a well-defined syntax for pictures as language. VL proponents seem to use terms like syntax and other linguistic concepts rather loosely when applying them to the codification and analysis of messages using imagery.

In the case of verbal literacy, writing is used to encode speech. It is pointed out that this involves taking one type of sensory input (auditory) and encoding it for processing by another sense (vision). There is no such analog for visual literacy, so these authors claim.

Literacy implies learning, say Cassidy and Knowlton, and they claim that the ability to understand images is acquired naturally as a form of "maturation" of the mind rather than it being a learned skill. Verbal literacy, on the other hand, is clearly learned – as evidenced by the fact that all cultures have spoken languages, but not all cultures develop written language. Another piece of evidence they present is the results of studies of humans who were born blind but later in life had their sight restored. In such cases, unless the sight was restored at a very young age, the individuals were never able to process what they saw properly The conclusion drawn from this was that we must be presented with visual stimuli during the maturation process of our visual system in order for it to develop normally, otherwise no amount of teaching can restore the visual perception skills which were missed.

Finally, these authors point to the well known left-brain right-brain duality as evidence of the unsuitability of the visual literacy metaphor. The left brain is known to be responsible for language, logic, symbols, and analytical processing; the right brain for visio-spatial processing, among others. We do not "know how to teach the right brain, or if it 'needs' teaching, or if indeed it is even teachable" say these researchers. [11]

5. Theory of dual coding

Visual Literacy proponents answer brain-duality based criticisms by pointing to Pavio's theory of dual coding, which proposes an explanation for the purpose and use of this structure in the brain. This theory states that the brain involves independent yet interdependent systems so concepts can flow seamlessly between their linguistic labels and their visual representations [12]. This is used to explain why the use of visuals with written text increases comprehension

This theory shows the benefit of improving visual literacy and incorporating more visuals in instruction, but does not address the question of whether the skill can actually be taught. It seems to say however, that even if "the right brain cannot be taught," improvements in the skills attributed to visual literacy are really enhancing right-left brain communication, which would seem to be very beneficial.

Different visually literate individuals may get distinctly different "messages" from looking at the same pictures, based on their stored knowledge about the relevant domain. This is true even of pictures of natural scenes; for example the picture of the Grand

Canyon shown in Figure 2. The typical individual might simply appreciate the beauty of the scene, while someone with specialized geological knowledge might be thinking more along the lines of the labeling in Figure 3 and the "story" it tells. This figure also illustrates the use of the dual-coding principle explicitly in instructional materials, which reinforces the knowledge being conveyed.

Figure 2. Grand Canyon scene.

Figure 3. How a geologist might view it.

6. Art and visual literacy

When the human brain is viewing a scene and creating a representation of it to be stored in memory, it searches for "essentials" or "constancies" of the objects in the scene. These could be characteristics of the objects that do not change with viewing angle or lighting conditions for example. Engineers creating computer vision systems often devise algorithms to extract what are called invariants – which are merely mathematical formalisms of the same concept, being features that are preserved through transformations like rotation for example. Zeki makes the point that just as the brain searches for constancies and essentials, so does art. Supporting this point he quotes French art critic Jacques Rivière (1912): "The true purpose of painting is to represent objects as they really are, that is to say differently from the way we see them... this is why the image it forms does not resemble their appearance" [13]

Different styles or art movements may or may not adhere to this goal, and even when they do they vary greatly in the way they may attempt to achieve it. Viewers of art often attempt to find meaning in a given work, but at least one artist points to the futility of that task with regard to his work, which is decidedly not trying to convey any particular message. René Magritte said: "My painting is visible images which conceal nothing; they evoke mystery and, indeed, when one sees one of my pictures, one asks oneself this simple question 'What does that mean'? It does not mean anything, because mystery means nothing either, it is unknowable." [14]

Many educators argue that an image-rich curriculum can reach more students and teach them more quickly than traditional text-based, verbal instruction and written student reports ever could. They advocate that schools adopt an arts-integrated education system "where teachers are energized and students are empowered across the curriculum." It is claimed that integrating the multi-sensory experiences of art, music, and drama into the curriculum results in better scores on standardized tests of basic skills. [15]

7. Where to get more information

In addition to the references cited in this article, there are some excellent starting points on the Internet for learning more about visual literacy or going into any of its many facets in greater depth. One is the web site of the International Visual Literacy Association:

http://www.ivla.org/

In another, Dr. Mahmood Abdulnabi Al-Mousawi, a professor of mass communication, has collected and posted on his web site an excellent and very thorough visual literacy bibliography entitled "Visual Communication: A Taxonomy and Bibliography". The address of this page currently is:

http://www.al-mousawi.org/bib.html

8. Summary

Among all the writings about visual literacy, and the connections they make with art appreciation, philosophy, left and right brain duality, etc., a message attributed to a young child [15] ties it all together nicely. He may have seen a sunset like that pictured in Figure 4 when he wrote:

Dear God,
I didn't think orange went with purple until I saw the sunset you made on Tuesday. That was cool.
--Eugene

Figure 4. The essence of visual literacy.

10. References

[1] R.B. Fransecky and J.L. Debes, *Visual literacy: A way to learn -- A way to teach*, Association for Educational Communications and Technology, Washington, DC, 1972.

[2] J.M. Brill, D. Kim, and R.M. Branch, "Visual literacy defined: the results of a Delphi study - can IVLA (operationally) define visual literacy?" in Griffen, R.E., V. S. Williams, and J. Lee (Eds.), *Exploring the visual future: art design, science and technology*, Blacksburg, VA: The International Visual Literacy Association, pp. 9-15.

[3] B.S. Randhawa, "Visual trinity: An overview", in B.S. Randhawa and W.E. Coffman (Eds.) *Visual Learning, Thinking, and Communication*, Academic Press, New York, pp. 191-211.

[4] B. Seels, "Visual Literacy: The Definition Problem", in D.M. Moore and F.M. Dwyer (Eds.) *Visual Literacy: A Spectrum of Visual Learning*, Educational Technology Publications, Englewood Cliffs, NJ, 1994, pp 97-112.

[5] Arnheim, R., *Visual Thinking*, Univ. of California Press, Berkeley, CA, 1969.

[6] M. Fleming and W.H. Levie (Eds.), *Instructional message design: Principles from the behavioral and cognitive sciences (2nd ed.)*, Educational Technology Publications, Englewood Cliffs, NJ, 1993.

[7] J.L. Dunn, "Television Watchers", *Instructor*, 103, no.8, April 1994, pp 50-54.

[8] R.E. Sutton, "Information Literacy Meets Media Literacy and Visual Literacy", in R. Braden, J.C. Baca, D. Beauchamp (Eds.), *Art, Science and Visual Literacy*, The International Visual Literacy Association, Inc., Blacksburg, VA 1993.

[9] W. Saletan, "The Elián Pictures", *Slate*, http://slate.msn.com/id/81142/, posted April 24, 2000.

[10] J. Long, "Ethics in the Age of Digital Photography", National Press Photographers Association, September 1999, http://www.nppa.org/services/bizpract/eadp/eadp2.html.

[11] M.F. Cassidy, J.Q. Knowlton, "Visual Literacy: A Failed Metaphor?", Educational Communication and Technology Journal, 31, 1983, pp 67-90.

[12] A. Pavio, "Mental Representations: A dual coding approach", Oxford University Press, New York, 1986.

[13] S. Zeki, Semir, Inner Vision. Oxford University Press, 1999.

[14] The Magritte web site, http://www.magritte.com/, 2003.

[15] Burmark, L., *Visual Literacy: Learn to see, See to Learn*, Association for Supervision and Curriculum Development, Alexandria, Virginia, 2002.

Children's Understanding of Imagery in Picture Books

Lori M. Levin
Kansas State University
llevin@ksu.edu

Abstract

This discussion focuses on beginning readers' perceptions and observations of picture book images they encounter in both school and home literacy environments. The data gathered from the subjects were organized in order to describe how visual literacy develops simultaneously with conventional literacy. Beginning with what research tells us about what strategic readers do in order to comprehend print, the current study seeks to understand if similar competencies are used when beginning readers view or "read" pictures in children's books.

1. Introduction

Researchers have concluded that students can be taught about the existence of reading strategies through informed direct instruction. It has been suggested that a model of comprehension instruction should include explicit description, modeling, collaborative use, guided practice, and independent use of the selected strategy. Other research has developed a comprehensive synopsis of strategic reader research organized around seven comprehension strategies that consistently surface in research about strategic readers. These strategies are described as a comprehension curriculum and form the basis for a model of the process of reading comprehension. So the question this study seeks to answer is how do the reading strategies identified in the comprehension model look when applied to images in picture books?

2. Images in children's literature

An analysis of children's literature, across genres, by readability level suggests that the number of images decreases as readers gain greater competency and skill (see Figure 1). The very first books that children are exposed to are called board books and consist mainly of images with little to no text. Board books have images on every page and can be entirely wordless. The genre called picture books varies in the amount of total text from only one to three words per page to hundreds, yet they all share in common images on every page. Finally, chapter books designed for beginning readers have larger amounts of text and fewer images with not more than 25% of the book's content devoted to images.

Whether these books are read aloud, or read by beginning readers, the images play an important role in the comprehension of the text. For young children, images are the primary medium for conveying the meaning of the text or the story. As children's reading ability increases, the need for images to aid comprehension decreases, and we see a decline in the total amount of images in books.

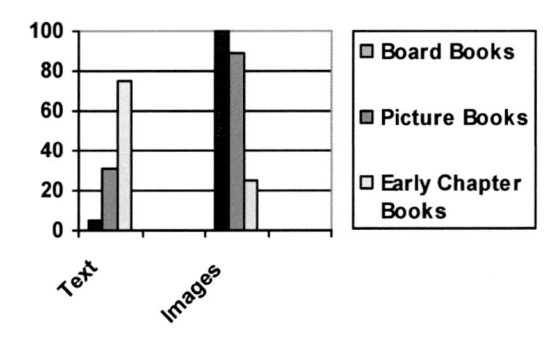

Figure 1. Comparison of percentages of text and images in children's books

3. Strategic readers of printed text

One approach to answering the question of how children comprehend images is to begin with what we know about strategic readers of printed text: They tend to use a set of comprehension strategies [4; 9]. Research has focused on identification and instruction of such strategies because poor readers seem to lack them and to be unaware of when and how to apply the knowledge they do possess. (See Pressley & Afflerbach, [11] and Block & Pressley, [2] for reviews of much of the research on good readers' comprehension.) Paris, Cross, and Lipson [8] concluded that students can be taught about the existence of reading strategies through informed direct instruction. Duke and Pearson [6] suggested that a model of comprehension instruction should include explicit description, modeling, collaborative use, guided practice, and independent use of the selected strategy.

Pearson, Roehler, Dole, and Duffy [11] developed a comprehensive synopsis of strategic reader research organized around seven comprehension strategies that consistently surface in research about strategic readers (Figure 2). These strategies are described as a comprehension curriculum and form the basis for a model of the process of reading comprehension.

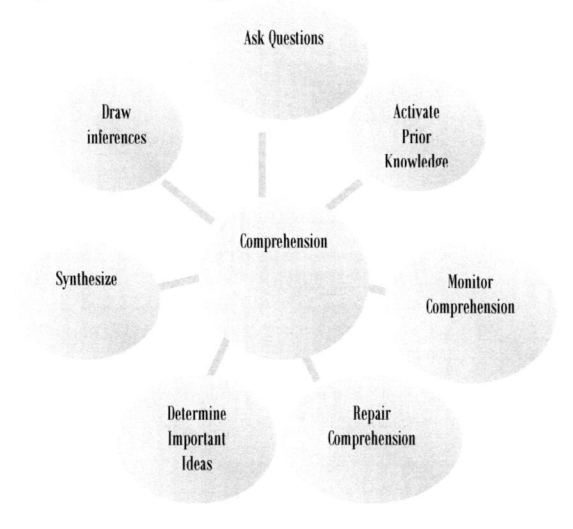

Figure 2. Seven comprehension strategies for reading comprehension

Pearson et al. [11] found these seven components of comprehension to be the factors that distinguish between expert and novice readers—between skilled and less able readers. Recent uses of this model focused on the teaching of strategies in context [5] and teaching them in collections or packages as a way to help students develop better comprehension [6].

3. Connections between literacy and visual learning

Literacy and visual learning converge when students read picture books. The skills required to comprehend text (both narrative and expository text) are used when students read picture books. To be adept at seeking, evaluating, and using information found in books, readers must navigate through text and apply their knowledge of the reading process as they view the pictures. The merging of these skills is seen when the reader uses the images during a reading act to aid their understanding of the printed text. How do the reading strategies identified in the comprehension model [11] look when applied to viewing and understanding images? Beginning readers are reading narrative and expository text in books where ideas are connected by images and graphics. Through observation and interviewing of young readers, it appears that they attempt to apply similar comprehension strategies when viewing images as those used with printed text reading. Figure 2 describes the reading strategies identified in the comprehension model and compares how these strategies are used when viewing images.

Table 1. Comparison of reading strategies

	Text	Image
Repair Comprehension	Reader adjusts reading rate depending on the purpose for reading.	Images help reader to get clues to repair meanings.
Activate Prior Knowledge	Reader recalls experiences and information related to the topic.	Images spark memories or help readers to connect existing ideas to the text.
Ask Questions	Questions give purpose to reading by motivating the reader to continue	Images provide a means to check understanding and make connections through comparison.
Determine Important Ideas	Reader analyzes text to determine which parts are important for developing an understanding of the text.	Images feature important ideas and give the reader a way to confirm predictions.
Draw Inferences	Reader reads between the lines using background knowledge and text to help fill in the gaps.	Images provide inferential clues to supplement the readers understanding of the text.
Monitor Comprehension	Reader recognizes when they are confused or when the text does not make sense.	Images give the reader a checkpoint to see if he is understanding what he reads.
Synthesize	Reader sifts important from unimportant details to determine the kernel of an idea.	Images illustrate important details that may not be described in the text.

4. Strategic Readers of Picture Books

Observations and interviews with beginning readers provide examples of the comprehension strategies these readers apply to the reading of text with images. The students completed a reading task where they were asked to select a book from several choices that interested them. They were then asked to read the book aloud, or if they were unable to read it, with assistance from the interviewer. Finally, the interviewer asked the subjects several questions about the books and the pictures. Through their own words, these readers share how they applied comprehension strategies to books with images.

4.1. Activate prior knowledge

When presented with a book he has never seen before, six-year old Ethan was able to draw upon his prior knowledge from social studies class and other readings he did outside of class. Ethan said, "Well, I know a lot about ancient Egypt already because I want to be an Egyptologist when I grow up. I can tell this book is going to be about mummification and pyramids."

Ethan activates and reactivates his prior knowledge in his attempts to locate the necessary information through out the book. Although he selected a book that was too difficult for his reading level, he negotiated understanding by "reading" the pictures and drawing upon his background knowledge.

Background knowledge is vital to a student's ability to comprehend text or images. Without the activation of background knowledge, children can not comprehend fully enough to create meaning of printed text or images. Consider seven-year old Amy's reaction to a picture (Figure 3) in the book, *Hooray for Diffendoofer Day* [14], by Dr. Seuss: "I have no idea what this picture is about, but it doesn't look very happy", Amy said. Amy could not relate anything familiar from her prior experiences to the image, and thus, had difficulty making any inferences as to the meaning of the picture. The text in the title of the book did little to help her make sense of the image because it too was foreign to her set of background experiences.

Figure 3. Illustration from *Hooray for Diffendoofer Day*

4.2. Monitor comprehension

Amy, a second grader, uses the pictures in *Junie B. Jones* [9] books to check her comprehension and see if what she is reading makes sense. When she sees a word or phrase that might be a clue to the information represented in a picture, she returns to the page with an illustration and reads more carefully, paying closer attention to the details in the picture. Amy said, "I read the story and then I like to look at the picture to see what is happening in the story." Amy moves from page to page to look at small details in the illustrations, always with a focus on monitoring comprehension when reading.

4.3. Repair comprehension

Allison is a slow and careful reader. Her initial reading of a book might be a slow one, with slightly more time spent than she would spend if she were just looking at the pictures. If her reading results in confusion, she reads the entire page more carefully and then returns to reread specific sections that might have the required information. Each time she encounters difficulty, she pauses reading to search the picture for clues to help her repair or revise her understanding. She says, "Sometimes I just like to look at the pictures to get some help with the story."

4.4. Determine important ideas

Ethan uses the images in the book to help him determine the important ideas. In his reading of the book, *Ethan Cleans* [7], a simple text supports his reading attempts, but the pictures guide his reading more than the text. He attends to the pictures on each page in order to find the main idea presented in the text on each page (Figure 4). When asked why he is looking at the pictures and not the words, he says, "The pictures are clues for what the words say. I read the pictures because it reminds me more what's happening."

Figure 4. Illustration from *Ethan Cleans*

4.5. Synthesize

Amy pauses during her reading of an information book about Rocks and Minerals to summarize what she has read about the quartz crystals and put the somewhat difficult language from the book into her own words: "These are very hard rocks that come in many different colors." Amy seems to confirm her own understanding by orally pulling together the ideas from the text she has read and the images she has viewed.

4.6. Draw inferences

Ethan makes an inference when listening to a read aloud of the book, *The Mitten,* by Jan Brett [3]. Brett's books feature foreshadowing that is only apparent in the illustrations. When asked questions about what might happen next, Ethan determines what will be happening: "This is it. This picture is giving me clues so I know what animal will be next. So this is the right place for me to search." Ethan skims the page and quickly draws the conclusion that he needs to move on to another page to draw more inferences.

4.7. Ask questions

Amy questions herself during reading as a way to check her understanding of information about the sinking of the Titanic in a *Magic Tree House* book [13]. She wonders aloud if the information is what she needs to answer her question: "Would Jack and Annie, the main characters, make it off the ship before it sinks? The illustration shows the ship beginning to sink, but I don't see Jack and Annie anywhere." Amy can check her understanding and make connections by questioning what she sees in the pictures and comparing it to what she reads in the text.

5. Connecting Conventional and Visual Literacy

These beginning readers have taken the strategies used for understanding printed text and applied them to the comprehension of visual images. Along with knowing how to read print, they also know how to "read" images through use of their prior knowledge about the topic to enhance their understanding. Beginning readers are learning to read text accompanied by visual images in a format where ideas are connected to visual graphics. It appears that students do apply similar comprehension strategies for "reading" the picture images as those used with print text reading.

By fusing two types of data, text and images, the interplay of both on children's comprehension structures becomes clearer. Young readers are gaining sophistication in their abilities to comprehend, or make sense of, both printed text and images. When the images that accompany the text match exactly the action taking place or the events being described, the understanding is heightened. It appears that the images can give a child a greater understanding of the text because the pictures often have much greater detail represented than is present in the text.

When adults read novels with no pictures, the imagery we see in our minds comes from our ability to activate background knowledge and link existing schemata stored in our memories to draw a mental image. The imagery that takes place in adult literature is literary rather than visual. Young readers have a limited set of background knowledge along with a limited reading ability, and thus must rely on picture images to convey meaning.

6. The importance of background knowledge

The most striking finding from this research is the importance of activating background knowledge in order for comprehension to occur. When Amy read *The Bravest of Us All* [1], a book about a little girl who was afraid of nothing until a tornado bears down on her house, she had a wealth of background knowledge from which to draw. Growing up in Kansas has afforded her multiple opportunities to learn and hear about tornadoes. She has tornado drills in school and has even had to rush to her basement when the town tornado sirens sounded. She was able to comprehend the images in thorough manner due to the rich set of background knowledge she can connect with the text and the images. When viewing the image pictured in Figure 5, she could identify with the children's sense of panic as they raced for the storm cellar.

Figure 5. Illustration from *The Bravest of Us All*

7. Conclusions

Findings suggest that young children use written text to assist their comprehension of images, as well as using the images to help them decode unknown words. Parents and teachers should create opportunities for children to draw upon their background knowledge in order to help them comprehend images and printed text. Images can be used as a means to help children make predictions and ask questions about the text in order to gain deeper understanding beyond what is printed on the page.

Young children need to be made aware that the images in books they read or have read to them have meaning. They also could benefit from direct instruction using the seven reading strategies to gain greater comprehension of images. The implications from this research with beginning readers could also be applied to older, more competent readers. Older students who struggle with literacy could benefit from texts that feature rich illustrations in order to activate their background knowledge. Indeed, comprehension instruction should include explicit description, modeling, collaborative use, guided practice, and independent use of the selected strategy.

Implications for further research could include a quantitative analysis of children's comprehension of images. Children could be asked to a series of higher level comprehension questions in response to viewing images from children's books. The responses could be analyzed to search for patterns in the ways children use the seven comprehension strategies to comprehend images.

Educators can guide students to be successful readers by helping them recognize their experiences with various types of text and applying this knowledge to the viewing of visual images. Literacy and technology are converging in classrooms where teachers provide opportunities for students to gain information from reading on the Internet where visual images abound. Through modeling and instruction, teachers can begin to build the bridge connecting conventional literacy and visual literacy.

8. References

[1] Arnold, M.D., *The Bravest of Us All*, Dial Books for Young readers, New York, 2000.

[2] Block, C.C., M. Pressley, *Comprehension instruction: Research-based best practices.* Guilford, New York, 2001.

[3] Brett, J. *The Mitten: a Ukranian folktale,* Putnam, New York, 1989.

[3] J.A. Dole, G.G. Duffy, L.E. Roehler, P.D. Pearson, "Moving from the old to the new: Research on reading comprehension instruction", *Review of Educational Research,* 1991, pp. 239–264.

[5] S.L. Dowhower, "Supporting a strategic stance in the classroom: A comprehension framework for helping teachers help students to be strategic," *The Reading Teacher, 52,* 1999, pp. 672–683.

[6] N.K. Duke, P.D. Pearson, "Effective practices for developing reading comprehension", In A.E. Farstrup & S.J. Samuels (Eds.), *What research has to say about reading instruction* (3rd ed., pp. 205–242). Newark, DE: International Reading Association, 2002.

[7] Hurwitz, J, B. Floca, *Ethan Cleans*, Candlewick Press, Cambridge, MA, 2003.

[8] S.G. Paris, D.R. Cross, M.Y. Lipson, " Informed strategies for learning: A program to improve children's reading awareness and comprehension", *Journal of Educational Psychology, 76,* 1984, pp. 1239–1252.

[9] Park, B., *Junie B. Jones is a graduation girl*, Random House, New York, 2001.

[10] Pearson, P.D. "Changing the face of reading comprehension instruction", *The Reading Teacher, 38,* 1985, pp. 724–737.

[11] Pearson,P.D., L.R. Roehler, J.A. Dole, G.G. Duffy, "Developing expertise in reading comprehension.", In S.J. Samuels & A.E. Farstrup (Eds.), *What research has to say about reading instruction* (2nd ed., pp. 145–199). Newark, DE: International Reading Association, 1992.

[12] Pressley, M., P. Afflerbach, *Verbal protocols of reading: The nature of constructively responsive reading,* Hillsdale, NJ: Erlbaum, 1995.

[13] Osbourne, M.P., *Tonight on the Titanic*, Random House,NewYork,1999.

[14] Seuss, T.G., *Hooray for Diffendoofer Day*, Knopf, New York,1998.

Spectral Histogram Representations for Visual Modeling

Xiuwen Liu and Qiang Zhang
Department of Computer Science, Florida State University
Tallahassee, FL 32306
{liux,zhang}@cs.fsu.edu

Abstract

We present spectral histogram representations for visual modeling. Based on a generative process, the representation is derived by partitioning the frequency domain into small disjoint regions and assuming independence among the regions. This gives rise to a set of filters and a representation consisting of marginal distributions of those filter responses. A distinct advantage of our representation is that it can be effectively used for different classification and recognition tasks, which is demonstrated by experiments and comparisons in texture classification, face recognition, and appearance-based 3D object recognition. The marked improvement over existing methods justifies our principle that effective a priori knowledge should be derived from physical generative processes.

1. Introduction

With the recent development of sophisticated learning algorithms, it has been realized that the performance of a classification and recognition system critically depends on the underlying representation [3, 2]. Geman and Bienenstock suggested that "the fundamental challenges are about representation rather than learning" [3].

How could we obtain a representation that is effective for classification and recognition applications? Theoretically one could learn a representation from a large amount of data as suggested by recent studies on natural image statistics [10]. In practice, however, one could incorporate *a priori* knowledge to reduce the number of training data needed and also regularize the learning process. Does there exist a principle to derive *a priori* knowledge in general for classification and recognition of images? In this paper, we advocate that *a priori* knowledge should be derived by analyzing the physical generative processes underlying images pioneered by Grenander [4] who proposed *pattern theory*. The most effective *a priori* knowledge should then be derived by integrating out factors that do not matter or are too complicated if made explicit.

Within this paradigm, we derive a representation for classification and recognition of images based on a simple generative process. The obtained representation, however, has demonstrated to be very effective for a variety of classification and recognition problems. While these problems have been studied separately in the literature, they can be unified under this framework.

This paper is organized as follows. Sect. 2 derives our representation based on a generative process. Sect. 3 presents our experimental results on three problems, namely, 3D object recognition, face recognition, and texture classification. Sect. 4 concludes the paper with discussion on a number of issues related to our approach.

2. Spectral Histogram Representations

The starting point of our representation is the following scenario. Suppose that we have a large of number of different objects which may appear on a uniform background according to a Poisson process and the objects are not known explicitly in any other way. We are interested in a translation invariant statistical feature that can be used to characterize the appearance of images. In other words, the derived feature should be able to classify and recognize the large number of objects based on the observed images.

An obvious choice is the histogram of the given image, which is translation invariant. However, for a large number of objects, their histograms can be very close or even identical, making the histogram not sufficient for recognition and classification. If all the pixel values are statistically identical and independent, then the histogram is the only choice. In practice, this assumption of independence is not valid as the pixels belonging to one object are dependent. Another obvious choice is to build a joint probability model of all the pixels. However, the dimension of the joint space is too high computationally.

Here we seek a compromise between the two extreme choices. Instead of assuming that the pixels are independent, we assume that small disjoint regions in the frequency domain are independent. In other words, we partition the frequency domain into small disjoint regions and model each region by its histogram, or marginal distribution.

How shall we partition the frequency domain? One sensible way is to partition it into rings with a small range of radial frequencies, as shown in Fig. 1(a). Another way is to partition it into regions with a small range of radial center frequencies and orientations, as shown in Fig. 1(b). Yet another way is to partition it into regions with a small range of orientation, which is not explored in this paper.

These small regions give rise to ideal band pass filters in the spatial domain with infinite support. To make the corresponding spatial filters local and compact, we use a Gaussian window function to make the filter coefficients go down quickly from the center. It can be shown that each ring in Fig. 1(a) leads to a difference of Gaussian filter, which can be implemented using a Laplacian of Gaussian (LoG) filter.

$$LoG(x,y|T) = (x^2 + y^2 - T^2)e^{-\frac{x^2+y^2}{T^2}}, \quad (1)$$

where $T = \sqrt{2}\sigma$ determines the scale of the filter and σ is the variance of the Gaussian function. These filters are referred to as $LoG(T)$. It also can be shown that each small region in Fig. 1(b) leads to a Gabor filter. The Gabor filters with both sine and cosine components are given by

$$\begin{aligned} Gabor(x,y|T,\theta) = \\ e^{-\frac{1}{2T^2}(4(x\cos\theta+y\sin\theta)^2+(-x\sin\theta+y\cos\theta)^2)} \\ e^{-i\frac{2\pi}{T}(x\cos\theta+y\sin\theta)}, \end{aligned} \quad (2)$$

where T is a scale. The cosine and sine components of these filters are referred to as $Gcos(T,\theta)$ and $Gsin(T,\theta)$ respectively. Fig. 1(b) shows several Gabor filters with different orientation and frequency in the spatial and frequency domain. Gabor filters are sensitive to both orientation and radial center frequency.

While the constructed filters may not be independent, the independence is valid to a certain extent for natural images, as recent numerical studies show that Gabor filters are independent components of natural images [10, 7]. Assuming that their responses are independent, the Kullback-Leibler distance between two joint distributions is the sum of their corresponding marginal distributions as shown, by the following equation, where $p_i(x_1, \cdots, x_n)$ is the joint distribution and $p_i(x_j)$ the jth marginal distribution:

$$\begin{aligned} &KL(p_1(x_1,\cdots,x_n), p_2(x_1,\cdots,x_n)) \\ &= \int_{x_1} \cdots \int_{x_n} p_1(x_1,\cdots,x_n) \log \frac{p_1(x_1,\cdots,x_n)}{p_2(x_1,\cdots,x_n)} dx_1 \cdots dx_n \\ &= \sum_{i=1}^{n} \int_{x_i} p_1(x_i) \log \frac{p_1(x_i)}{p_2(x_i)} dx_i \\ &= \sum_{i=1}^{n} KL(p_1(x_i), p_2(x_i)) \end{aligned} \quad (3)$$

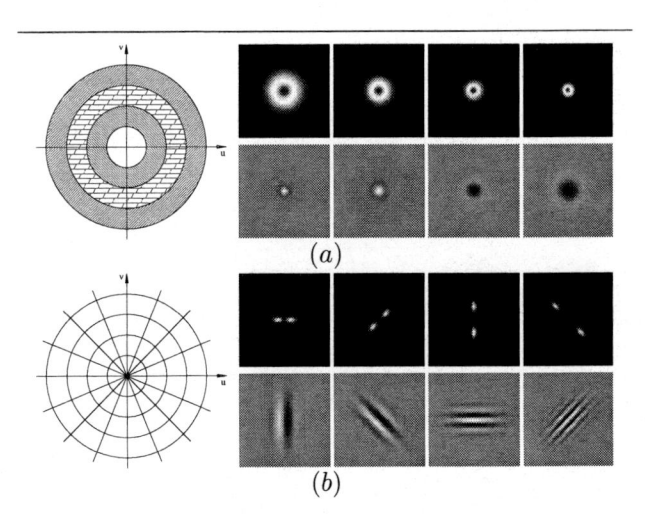

Figure 1. Two ways of partitioning the frequency domain. (a) Ring structures and the corresponding LoG filters in the frequency and spatial domain. (b) Small regions and the corresponding Gabor filters in the frequency and spatial domain.

This gives rise to the following representation. We partition the frequency domain into small regions and derive the corresponding spatial filters. For a given image, we convolve it with every filter and compute the marginal distribution of the resulting filtered image. Then we combine the marginal distributions together. So each image is represented by a vector consisting of all the marginal distributions. We shall call this representation *spectral histogram representation* of the image with the selected filters.

The generative process used here can be seen as a simplified version of the *transported generator* model proposed by Grenander and Srivastava [5]. The derived representation has also been suggested through psychophysical studies on texture modeling [1], and has been used in the texture modeling and synthesis [6, 14].

To demonstrate the effectiveness of the spectral histogram representation for recognition applications, we visualize 500 images (some of which are shown in Fig. 3) in the image space and the spectral histogram representation space. To visualize the images, we apply the principal component analysis technique on the data set in image space and in spectral representation space. Fig. 2 shows the 500 images in image space and in spectral representation space respectively, where only the two most prominent dimensions are shown. This example shows clearly that images from one class cluster together in the spectral histogram space while images from any class do not form clusters in the image space.

The spectral histogram representation is also effective in charactering appearance of objects other than textures. To

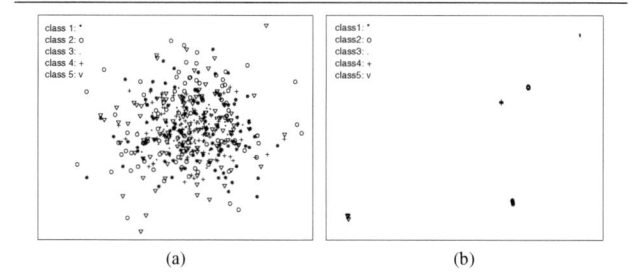

Figure 2. The PCA result of 500 images belonging to 5 classes as shown in Fig. 3 (100 images of each class) in image space (a) and in spectral histogram representation space (b). Note that many points of the same class overlapped in (b).

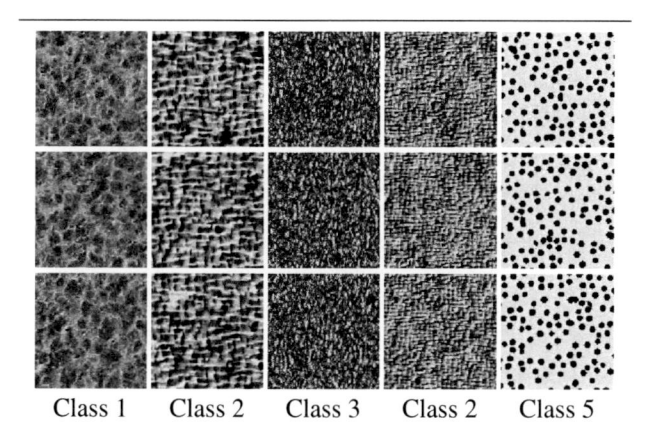

Figure 3. the five classes of images, 3 images are shown for each class.

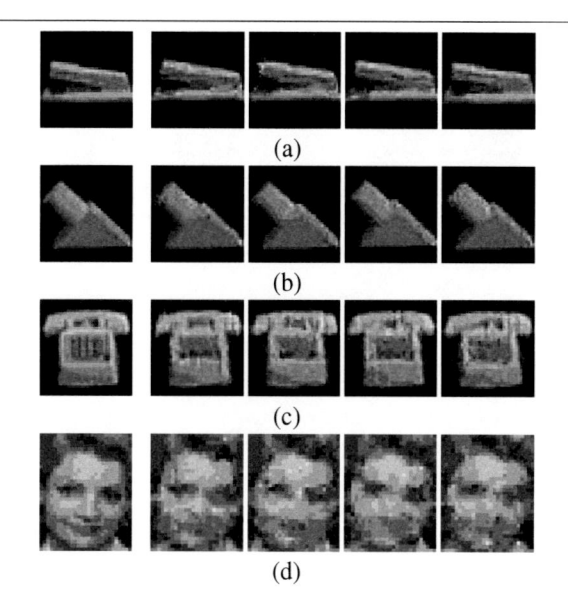

Figure 4. Observed images (left) and four synthesized images. (a) A stapler. (b) A wood object. (c) A telephone. (d) A face.

demonstrate this, we synthesize images by matching the spectral histogram representation of the given image using a Gibbs sampler. Fig. 4 shows the observed image and the corresponding synthesized images. One can see that the synthesized images are perceptually similar to the observed images, demonstrating that spectral histogram representation captures the global topological structures as well as local structures.

3. Experimental Results

In this section, we demonstrate the effectiveness of our proposed method on three different problems. For all the datasets used here, we start with 40 filters including: (i) Laplacian of Gaussian filters at different scales, and (ii) Gabor filters at different scales with multiple orientations at each scale. We exclude the intensity filter, corresponding to the histogram of the input image, to make our representation illumination invariant. While the proposed representation can be used directly to characterize rigid objects, objects are often subject to deformations. Here we adopt the learning from examples methodology and use a standard multiple-layer perceptron to learn a classifier for each image type based on this representation. We also use a filter selection algorithm to choose a subset from the given ones by maximizing the performance.

3.1. 3D Object Recognition

We have applied our method to appearance-based 3D object recognition. For evaluation of our method and comparison with existing methods, we use the Columbia Object Image Library (COIL-100)[1] dataset, which consists of the color images of 100 3-D objects with varying pose, texture, shape and size. For each object there are 72 images taken at different view angles with $5°$ apart. Therefore there are 7,200 color image in the entire dataset. Fig. 5 shows 20 selected objects from the database.

A number of appearance-based schemes have been proposed to recognize 3D objects. Murase and Nayar [9] proposed a parametric method to recognize 3D objects and estimate the pose of the object at the same time. Recently Pontil and Verri [11] applied Support Vector Machines (SVM) to appearance-based object recognition and their method was tested using a subset of the COIL-100 dataset with half for training and the other half for testing. As pointed out by

---

[1] Available at http://www.cs.columbia.edu/CAVE.

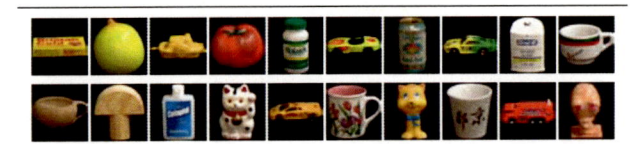

Figure 5. Selected 3-D objects in the COIL database. Each image is a color image of 128×128**.**

	# of training / test views per object		
Methods	36/36	18/54	8/64
Our Method	100.00%	99.50%	96.33%
SNoW[13]	95.81%	92.32%	85.13%
Linear SVM[13]	96.03%	91.30%	84.80%
Nearest Neighbor[13]	98.50%	87.54%	79.52%

Table 1. Recognition results of different methods on the COIL-100 dataset.

Yang et al.[13], this dense sampling of training views made the recognition less challenging. Yang et al. [13] applied Sparse Network of Winnows (SNoW) to recognition of 3D objects and they used the full set of COIL-100 dataset and compared with SVM methods.

As in [13], we vary the number of training views per object to make the 3D recognition more challenging. Given the images in the training set, we apply our filter selection algorithm starting with 40 filters. It is interesting to note the filters selected by our algorithm. It first chose a LoG filter at the largest scale and then chose four Gabor filters at the largest scale with different orientations and then another LoG filter and a Gabor filter at a smaller scale. This seems consistent with our intuition. Those objects do not prefer a particular orientation and the global patterns and shapes are the most effective for recognition as most of the objects contain uniform surfaces, making the local patterns ineffective for discrimination among different objects.

With the chosen filters, a network is trained and the learned network is then used to recognize the testing images at novel views. The unit with the highest output is taken as the result from the system. Table 1 shows our recognition results using different number of training views along with the results reported in [13]. With eight views for training, our system gives a correct recognition rate of 96.3%. If we allow the correct to be within the closest five, the correct recognition rate is 99.0%.

It is interesting to compare our recognition results with other methods in [13]. Our method gives the best result under all the test conditions and improves significantly when fewer training views are used. This improvement is essentially because our representation is more meaningful than pixel- and edge-based representations [13]. This is also consistent with the nearest neighbor result based on pixel-wise distance between two images.

3.2. Face Recognition

In recent years, the problem of face recognition has been studied extensively in the literature. Our method is very different from most of the current methods for face recognition in that it is a general method for image classification and recognition. However, due to the perceptually meaningful representation, our method is also very effective for face recognition as demonstrated using a face recognition dataset.

Here we use the ORL database of faces[2]. The dataset consists of faces of 40 different subjects with 10 images for each subject. The images were taken at different times with different lighting conditions on a dark background. While only limited side movement and tilt were allowed in this dataset, there was no restriction on facial expression. Because there are only 10 faces per subject, we use 5 of them as training and 5 for testing. Because some images are more representative for a subject than others, we randomly choose training faces to avoid the potential bias on the performance. Then we repeat the same procedure many times to have a better evaluation. Table 2 shows the recognition results for 100 trials. Here we report the average performance, the best and worst among the 100 trials. On average we have achieved over 95% correct recognition rate.

Criterion	Average	Best	Worst
Correct to be the first	95.4%	98.5%	90.5%
Correct within the first three	98.9%	100%	96.0%

Table 2. Recognition results on the ORL face dataset.

3.3. Texture Classification

Without any change, we have also applied our method to the problem of texture classification, which has been studied extensively as a separate topic in computer vision. We argue that texture models should be consistent with perceptual models for objects as they need to be addressed within one generic recognition system; we demonstrate here that our method can be applied equally well to the texture classification problem.

---

2 http://www.uk.research.att.com/facedatabase.html

To demonstrate the effectiveness of our approach, we use a dataset consisting of 40 textures[3]. Each texture image is partitioned into non-overlapping patches with size 32×32 and then all the obtained patches are divided into a training set and a test set with no common patch between the two sets. As for 3D object recognition and face recognition, we start with the same 40 filters and apply our filter selection algorithm on the training set. The network trained with the chosen filters is then used to classify the patches in the test set. To avoid a bias due to the choice of the training set, we randomly choose the training set for each texture and run our algorithm many times for a better evaluation. We also change the number of patches in the training set to demonstrate the generalization capability of our representation.

Compared to the filters chosen for COIL-100 and ORL datasets, our algorithm chose filters whose scale is comparable with dominant local texture patterns. Table 3 shows the classification result with 100 trials for each setting. This dataset is very challenging in that some of textures are perceptually similar to other textures in the dataset and some are inhomogeneous with significant variations. With as few as 8 training patches, our method achieves a correct classification rate of 92% on average. With half patches used for training, we achieve an average classification rate over 96%. Table 4 is more convincing, which shows the correct classification rate when the correct is within the closest three. The worst performance is above 97%, demonstrating the good generalization of our system.

Training / test	Average	Best	Worst
8/56	92.07%	94.20%	90.22%
16/48	94.74%	95.83%	93.07%
22/42	95.64%	96.73%	94.35%
32/32	96.36%	97.42%	95.16%

Table 3. Classification results on the 40-texture dataset.

To further demonstrate the effectiveness of our method and compare with existing methods, we apply our method to two datasets that were shown to be very challenging for all the methods included in a recent comprehensive comparative study[12]. Randen and Husoy[12] studied and compared close to 100 different methods for texture classification. For the dataset shown in Fig. 11(h) in [12], Fig. 6(a) shows the correct classification rate of all the methods in [12] with average 52.55% and best 67.70%. Similarly, for the other dataset shown in Fig. 11(i) in [12], the average

Training/test	Average	Best	Worst
8/56	98.70%	99.42%	97.86%
16/48	99.32%	99.69%	98.70%
22/42	99.52%	99.94%	99.11%
32/32	99.62%	99.92%	99.14%

Table 4. Classification results of the correct to be within the closest three on the 40-texture dataset.

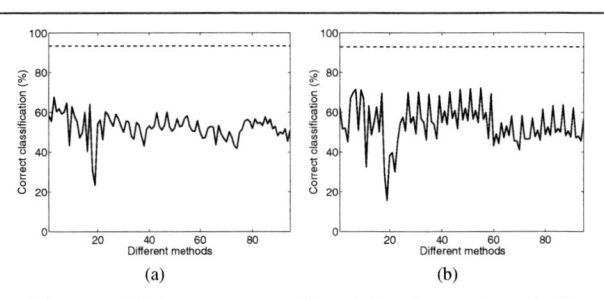

Figure 6. The correct classification rate of all the methods studied in [12] on the texture dataset shown in Fig. 11(h) of [12] (a) and Fig, 11(i) (b). The dashed line shows our result for comparison.

correct classification rate is 54.02% with the best 72.20% as shown in Fig. 6(b). For datasets of 10 textures, a classification error of 33.3% is very significant. For a fair comparison, we apply our method to the same dataset[4]. As in the original experiment setting, we use a training set to train the neural network with filter selection. Then the learned network is applied to a separate test set. Because the texture images are perceptually quite similar, an accurate perceptual texture model is needed in order to classify the textures correctly. In addition, two different sets of textures for training and testing make the classification even more difficult. On the two data sets, our method gives a correct classification of 93.49% and 92.96% respectively as shown in Fig. 6. The significant improvement demonstrates the necessity of a perceptually meaningful model for texture classification such as the one proposed here.

3.4. Mixed Dataset

To further demonstrate the generality of the spectral histogram representation, we have applied our method on a dataset consisting of 40 texture types, 100 3-D object classes, and 40 face classes by combining the datasets to-

---

[3] Available at http://www-dbv.cs.uni-bonn.de/image/texture.tar.gz

[4] Available at http://www.ux.his.no/~tranden

	Training/Test		
	5080 / 5080	2560 / 7600	1300 / 8860
Correct to be the first	99.37%	97.53%	92.87%
Correct within the first three	98.60%	99.34%	99.92%

Table 5. Recognition rate for the combined dataset

gether. Table 5 shows the result, which shows clearly the proposed representation can effectively characterize different kinds of objects for recognition applications.

4. Discussion

In this paper we presented a spectral histogram representation for recognition applications of images derived from a generative process. While our model is simple, it is very effective for different problems that have been primarily studied separately in computer vision. The marked improvement of our method over existing ones justifies our principle that *a priori* knowledge should be derived from physical generative processes. Not only our approach is generic as demonstrated through different datasets of real images, the representation also provides other advantages such as illumination, rotation, and scale invariance by choosing proper filters.

Our representation along with the filter selection algorithm provides a unified framework for appearance-based object recognition and image classification. Within this framework, the difference among general object recognition, face recognition, and texture classification is the choice of most effective filters. While filters with large scales are most effective for face recognition as faces are topographically very similar, filters whose scales are comparable with texture elements are most effective for texture classification. Our filter selection algorithm chooses the most effective set of filters in this regard. This may lead to a system that is effective for different types of images, which is a key requirement for a generic recognition system.

Our representation has been derived and proposed not as an ultimate solution to the classification and recognition problem. Rather, it is proposed as an effective bottom-up feature statistic which can prune irrelevant templates for more accurate top-down matching methods. In this regard, the filter responses can also be used as top-down templates, an example of which was implemented by Lades et al. [8] for object recognition in general and face recognition in particular. This is also consistent with our generative process discussed in Sect. 2. With marginal distributions as bottom-up feature statistics and filter responses as templates, the top-down and bottom-up solutions can be integrated in a coherent framework.

Acknowledgments

The authors would like to thank Prof. Anuj Srivastava for many insightful discussions and suggestions. This research was supported in part by NIMA NMA 201-01-2010, NSF IIS-0307998, and NSF DMS-0345242.

References

[1] J. R. Bergen and E.H. Adelson, "Early vision and texture perception," *Nature*, vol. 333, pp. 363–367, 1988.

[2] C. M. Bishop, *Neural Networks for Pattern Recognition*, Oxford University Press, Oxford, UK, 1995.

[3] S. Geman and E. Bienenstock, "Neural networks and the bias/variance dilemma," *Neural Computation*, vol. 4, pp. 1-58, 1992.

[4] U. Grenander, *General Pattern Theory*, Clarendon Press, Oxford, 1993.

[5] U. Grenander and A. Srivastava, "Probability models for clutter in natural images," *IEEE Transactions on Pattern Analysis and Machine Intelligence*, vol. 23(4), pp. 424-429, 2001.

[6] D. J. Heeger and J. R. Bergen, "Pyramid-based texture analysis/synthesis," in *Proceedings of SIGGRAPHS*, pp. 229–238, 1995.

[7] A. Hyvärinen and E. Oja, "Independent component analysis: Algorithms and applications," *Neural Networks*, vol. 13, pp. 411–430, 2000.

[8] M. Lades, J. C. Vorbruggen, J. Buhmann, J. Lange, C. von de Malsburg, R. P. Wurtz, and W. Konen, "Distortion invariant object recognition in the dynamic link architecture," *IEEE Transactions on Computers*, vol. 42, pp. 300-311, 1993.

[9] S. K. Murase and S. K. Nayar, "Visual learning and recognition of 3-d objects from appearance," *International Journal of Computer Vision*, vol. 14, pp. 5-24, 1995.

[10] B. A. Olshausen and D. J. Field, "Emergence of simple-cell receptive field properties by learning a sparse code for natural images," *Nature*, vol. 381, pp. 607-609, 1996.

[11] M. Pontil and A. Verri, "Support vector machines for 3D object recognition," *IEEE Transactions on Pattern Analysis and Machine Intelligence*, vol. 20(6), pp. 637-646, 1998.

[12] T. Randen and J. H. Husoy, "Filtering for texture classification: A comparative study," *IEEE Transactions on Pattern Recognition and Machine Intelligence*, vol. 21(4), pp. 291–310, 1999.

[13] M. H. Yang, D. Roth, and N. Ahuja, "Learning to recognize 3D objects with SNoW," in *Proceedings of the Sixth European Conference on Computer Vision*, vol. 1, pp. 439-454, 2000.

[14] S. C. Zhu, Y. N. Wu, and D. Mumford, "Minimax entropy principle and its application to texture modeling," *Neural Computation*, vol. 9, pp. 1627–1660, 1997.

A Survey of Recent Developments in Theoretical Neuroscience and Machine Vision

Jeffrey B. Colombe
Dept. of Cognitive Science and Artificial Intelligence
The MITRE Corporation
7515 Colshire Drive, McLean VA 22102
jcolombe@mitre.org

Abstract

Efforts to explain human and animal vision, and to automate visual function in machines, have found it difficult to account for the view-invariant perception of universals such as environmental objects or processes, and the explicit perception of featural parts and wholes in visual scenes. A handful of unsupservised learning methods, many of which relate directly to independent components analysis (ICA), have been used to make predictive perceptual models of the spatial and temporal statistical structure in natural visual scenes, and to develop principled explanations for several important properties of the architecture and dynamics of mammalian visual cortex. Emerging principles include a new understanding of invariances and part-whole compositions in terms of the hierarchical analysis of covariation in feature subspaces, reminiscent of the processing across layers and areas of visual cortex, and the analysis of view manifolds, which relate to the topologically ordered feature maps in cortex.

1. Introduction

Conventional computer-science approaches to automated image analysis have met with little success when compared with even rudimentary visual analysis capabilities of children or animals, and much less when compared with trained image analysts. Past efforts have been based on the *knowledge engineering* approach to software design, in which logical or geometric heuristics based on scientific knowledge of the problem domain (or the intuition of the software engineer) are used to analyze image data. The adaptability and performance of human analysts, however, does not primarily result from their brains being preordained with domain knowledge about the physics and natural history of image generation. Human brains develop expertise primarily as a function of exposure to information from the sensory environment, and from innate rules implemented at the level of neural circuits and synapses for organizing and retaining that information during learning. This paper reviews several key findings from neuroscience about the functional architecture of the visual cortex, and several neuromimetic machine learning approaches to modeling these findings.

1.1. Cognition as probabilistic control

Cognition may be thought of broadly as the sensorimotor signal-processing aspect of survival. A cognitive agent is coupled to its environment in a sensorimotor feedback loop, the function of which is to regulate environmental conditions in ways that favor the survival of the agent's design. As with all control systems, corrective influences are generated in response to deviations of target environmental variables from their desired values. A trivial but familiar example of a feedback control system is a thermostat which, importantly, must sense temperature in order to control it effectively. If an agent were able to directly measure its environment, and the environment were static in its properties, a deterministic optimal control policy could be developed and hard-wired into the agent. However, the environment is constantly changing due to the presence of nonstationarities like evolving species, learning organisms, and advancing technology. In addition, the organism only has access to the proximal sensory stimulus, and cannot directly observe the true degrees of freedom in the environment or their causal constraints on each other. Perceptual processing thus becomes necessary.

Perception is widely regarded as the preprocessing of sensory signals for behavior. Sensory input is transformed into an alternate representation that is more suitable for the regulation of behavior. Preprocessing is needed because behaviorally relevant target variables in the environment are only implicit in sensory signals, but need to be made explicit for efficient behavioral learning. Further, it is generally useful, particularly in organisms that can afford high compute-density nervous systems, to develop a predictive model of causality in the environment for planning and problem-solving. In the absence of a prior innate model, and/or when the environment is nonstationary, target variables of interest in the environment must be estimated from the statistical properties of the sensory data. Thus, I argue that the most generally useful kind of perceptual system, as a first approximation, would apply unsupervised learning to the statistics of natural sensory scenes to model exploitable redundancies in the environment.

1.2. Invariance and sensory semantics

The human brain uses both sensory and linguistic processing to understand and communicate sensory events. One of the grand challenges of artificial intelligence has been to understand how noisy, continuous-valued sensory signals can be effectively mapped into the symbolic representations typical of language. In particular, one might ask how statistical properties of the sensory data may suggest, or warrant, the formation of descriptive classes in language, specifically nouns, modifiers, and verbs, in an unsupervised framework. An active area of research proposes that objects can be identified from the topologically organized manifolds of their views [1-3]. During live viewing, subsequent views of an object are related by their spatiotemporal continuity and their similarity in sensor space (e.g., the Cartesian coordinate space of pixel intensities) from one moment to the next [4-6]. Neural architectures that learn a variety of views, and group those that are spatiotemporally adjacent, can thus potentially identify manifolds corresponding to "natural" object classes, in other words those suggested by the structure of unlabeled sensory data. Such grouping of views provides a basis for learning *nouns*. Figure 1A shows a *viewing sphere*, indicating the set of views obtained by rotating a point of view around a rigid object in three dimensions. The author notes that an object's view manifold may also include degrees of freedom that result from deformation of the object, for example facial expression, and other sources of view variation such as illumination.

Linguistic *modifiers* may be thought of as pose or state variables to describe the configuration of an object, corresponding to the position of the current view within that object's manifold. These attributes may systematically apply to a class of individual object manifolds; for example, a description of the state of horizontal rotation of a head may apply to any number of individuals' heads. In Figure 1B, each row of images corresponds to an object (noun) manifold in which there is an object-identity analogy between images, wheras the columns correspond to a pose variable that has analogous meaning across object identities. Figure 1C shows systematic temporal trajectories through pose space, which provide a basis for learning "natural action" classes and their corresponding *verbs*. In this framework, a parsimonious representation of natural scenes is suggested in which object identity and pose are factorized as relatively independent sources of image variability, and actions are temporal features in the resulting pose spaces. One of the major difficulties of this approach is that views of two different objects may be more similar (closer together in sensory space) than two views of the same object. Thus, simple distances between disjoint views are not sufficient for separating object manifolds from each other.

1.3. Composition hierarchies of parts and wholes

It is important in a wide range of perceptual and behavioral tasks to be able to identify parts and wholes in visual scenes (e.g., both a car and its wheels), and to identify part-to-whole relations, or *compositions*, within the scenes. In addition, it can be easier to learn larger patterns if one is able to have previously learned the parts that compose it, and then recognize the wholes as relatively simple assemblies of familiar parts [8]. The local data compression that results from summarizing covariation among several inputs with a single feature may provide a process compression effect in the use of that signal in downstream processing, by helping to avoid the curse of dimensionality in inferences that span larger numbers of sensory variables. A variety of recognition tasks are thus likely to be greatly simplified if they can be broken up into several hierarchical processing stages, each of which models sensory structure with some degree of inclusiveness over the set of sensory variables. Recognizing objects despite occlusion by the foreground (e.g., a tiger behind tall grass) can be made more tractable if the local features that describe all of the unoccluded parts can be assembled by higher-order pattern detectors that use the outputs of the lower-level components as input, with some tolerance for missing parts or expected deviations from a "best" pattern. An important consideration is that monotonic scalar variables (approximating the rate or phase properties of spiking neurons, for example) have limited representational capacity in a single-layer architecture. Decision manifolds, for example between perceptual classes, may be too complex to be modeled in a single layer of linear or nonlinear monotonic processing. Hierarchical networks make it possible for complex decision manifolds, or partitions, to be built up in several stages using simple transfer functions.

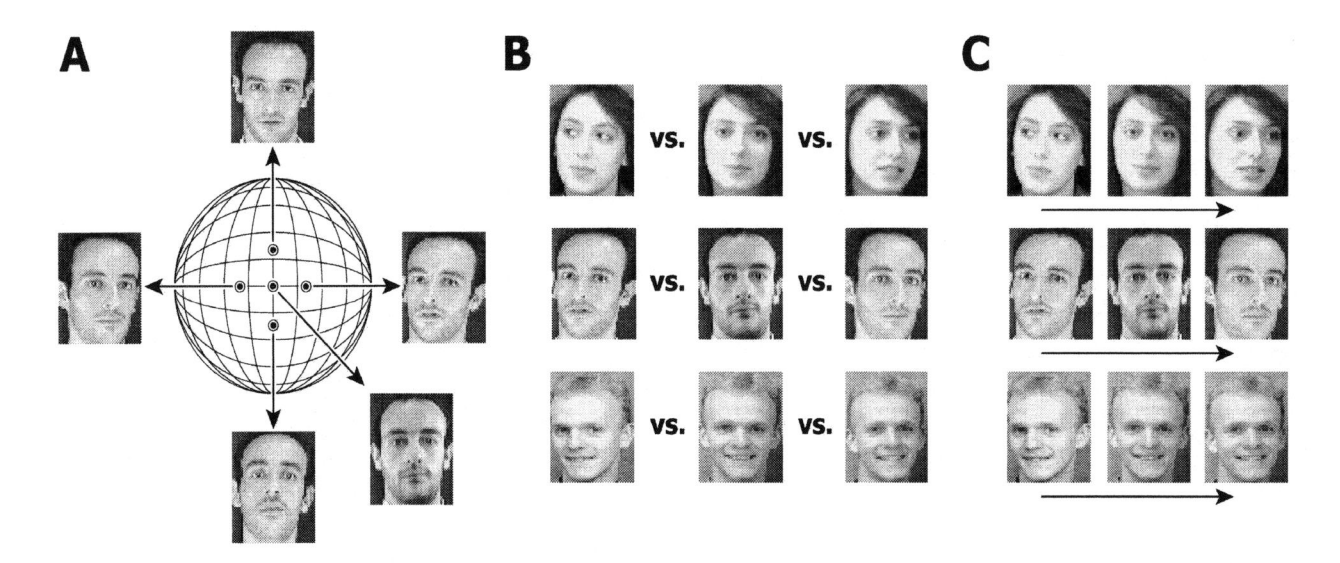

Figure 1. Viewing manifolds and their potential linguistic decompositions. (A) A viewing sphere for a 3D object is a manifold of views around an object in which positionally (in this case, rotationally) adjacent views have similar coordinates in the Cartesian space of input variables (in this case, pixel intensities). (B) Objects versus pose variables. Rows correspond to members of the same object manifold that are analogous across pose variables, and columns correspond to systematic pose variables that are analogous across objects. (C) Analogous trajectories through pose space. (Face images are from the publicly available Database of Faces from AT&T Laboratories Cambridge [7]; http://www.uk.research.att.com/facedatabase.html).

Finding an appropriate transformation from sensory signals to such a representation has proven to be elusive, but there are clues from neurobiology about how the brain executes such a transformation. One of the key issues in studying biological systems is to determine which of their properties are critical for cognition in general, and which properties are merely implementational consequences of the particular hardware medium used by natural systems, or that reflect constraints imposed by the evolutionary sequence from which the design properties were derived. For example, it is clear that the evolution of spiking in neurons was needed to send nondegrading signals over long cellular distances; it is less clear what precise role spikes play in the computation of perceptual and behavioral activity in animals; and it seems implausible in the extreme that spiking *per se* is required for cognition at an algorithmic or functional level of description. Numerical or statistical modeling of neural systems provides an opportunity to clarify which properties are likely to be intrinsic to cognition, and which implementational.

2. Findings from neuroscience

If the brain is not born an expert image analyst, how does it become one? Mammalian nervous systems are capable of learning to extract statistically relevant structure from sensory data in ways that abbreviate and compress the information in sensory data. These learned representations are able to abbreviate structure by making hypothetical models of the causal processes that appear to have generated the data. Such models allow predictive inferences to be made about currently obscured environmental conditions across differences in space or time. This predictive model-building capability of the cerebral cortex appears to operate relatively independently of sensory modality, whether imagery, sound, tactile and postural signals, chemical sensing, etc. [e.g., 9]. Further, the local circuit architecture of the cerebral cortex has important basic similarities over all of the areas of the brain that process different senses [10]. A compelling suggestion from neuroscience research is that a general-purpose representational algorithm is embodied in the cortex (with some built-in areal specializations), and that what is learned from cortical area to cortical area, and from one brain to another, is largely the result of the same basic operator applied to different modalities, and different sets, of sensory data. Using a simple computational principle, if it is an appropriate principle, it should be possible for all of what is learned in an intelligent perceptual system to be generalized from the informational structure, or statistical redundancy, of the sensory data itself.

This shift of focus in perceptual modeling from *a priori* logical and geometric computation, to *a posteriori* statistical analysis of the properties of sensory data, has grown partly out of efforts to model the anatomy and physiology of the brain, and out of efforts to use biologically inspired neural network algorithms to solve engineering problems. The early clues from neuroscience suggested several algorithmic and implementational approaches for neural processing, including massive parallelism using nearly identical and fairly simple processors, distributed representations (also called population codes), analog signal processing, local feature analysis, hierarchical organization with feedback between levels, and statistical learning. In the early 1990s, biologically-inspired neural network methods were explicitly cast in the larger framework of statistical learning theory and conditional probability [11-13]. Around this same time, attention in the neuroscience community began to turn in earnest toward a study of the statistical properties of natural sensory scenes, which necessarily constrain *a posteriori* function [14-18].

In the primate cerebral cortex, there are over 30 identified areas that are sensitive to visual stimuli. After visual signals are processed in the retina, they project through a relay nucleus and into the primary visual cortex (or area V1), then on to a large set of other processing stages. The two major processing streams in primate visual cortex, the dorsal (motion and location) pathway and the ventral (form) pathway, are each composed of a hierarchy of cortical areas, each of which has broader spatial receptive fields than the areas beneath it in the hierarchy [19,20]. The features in higher areas tend to be qualitatively more specific than those below; more invariant to translation, scaling, and other sources of variation; and less frequently observed (e.g., curved contours of a given size and orientation are less frequently seen than the edgelets that make them up, which themselves appear in a variety of other contours). Other sensory modalities have a similar hierarchical organization (e.g., in auditory cortex [21]; and in somatosensory cortex [22]). Object-like representations are built up in these several hierarchical stages in visual cortex, and at each stage there are topologically organized maps of features, where nearby neurons in the two-dimensional sheet of cells in a cortical area show qualitatively and quantitatively similar responses to local image content.

3. Neuromimetic machine learning findings

There are a handful of new machine learning approaches to the above research problems that show promise. Several of these build on or relate to prior work in independent components analysis (ICA), an unsupervised source separation method that learns a single-layer transformation of sensory data whose output signals adapt to become as statistically independent from each other as possible over the set of training data [23-25]. The set of features found using ICA extract important local structure from sensory data. When applied to image data, these learned features are substantially similar to processing in so-called *simple cells* in the primary visual cortex of mammals [26-28]. The simple cell encoding of visual information is the first transformation applied to visual information in the cerebral cortex. It resembles a Gabor wavelet basis, similar to that used in image compression techniques that compactly summarize image structure. When provided with visual input that has stereo information from two retinas and multiple color channels, ICA learns stereo disparity-tuned features [29] and color-opponent features [29,30], as in mammalian simple cells. When provided with moving visual input from natural video sequences, ICA learns space-time receptive field properties typical of simple cells, such as direction-selectivity, velocity tuning, and reversal [31,32].

Higher-level percepts, such as contours, shapes, and objects, are built up by further processing the outputs of simple cells, both within the primary visual cortex and in a hierarchically organized sequence of other cortical areas with similar local circuit architecture throughout [19]. Several new approaches to modeling the relationships between simple cells, and the stages of processing that follow simple cells, has opened the possibility of understanding the nature of high-level vision problems from simple characterizations of low-level visual processing, particularly if mechanisms responsible for low-level perception can be applied in hierarchical architectures across successively more global portions of the sensory field.

3.1. Subspace methods and slow feature learning for local invariance

A collection of related methods, called *subspace-norm* or *adaptive subspace* methods, assign features (*syn.* units, neurons, basis vectors, filters) into groups, or subspaces, prior to learning. The synaptic weights of all features are adapted so that the norm (e.g., the Euclidean length) of the activities within each subspace is as independent as possible from the norms of other subspaces. The importance of the norm is that it allows the subspace features to represent related image structures that vary in some systematic way, like being shifted in space by degrees, while the norm over the group is *invariant* to this shift. When applied to images, such responses are analogous to the transformation performed by *complex cells* in the primary visual cortex of mammals [26,33]. Complex cell responses are the first stage of processing in the cortex that cannot be explained by a linear transformation from pixel intensities on the retina, but which require a nonlinear disjunction over the responses of groups of simple cell-like features. Complex cell modeling is an important frontier in understanding how invariant responses are built up mechanistically in the cerebral cortex. Some versions of subspace methods impose a network topology or *map* on the set of features, forcing the learning of similar features in nearby parts of the map, as also occurs in cortex [34]. Adaptive subspace methods are beginning to show use in automated image description and retrieval [35].

Another approach to modeling local invariances does not impose subspaces on a network *a priori*, but lets them emerge in a principled way. Wherever invariant features are seen in perceptual cortex, invariances tend to appear strongest with respect to those aspects of the stimulus that are most likely to vary, or that have the highest local variance, due to normal movement of the stimulus [e.g., 36,37]. Finding invariances over typical scene motion is analogous to adaptive image stabilization, performed locally, and has been referred to as *slow feature learning* [38,39]. Complex cell responses are built up from simple cell responses under slow feature learning, because subsets of phase-varying simple cells are most likely to lead and follow each others' activities on short timescales. The second layer of complex cells learns to integrate over these phase-varying simple cell subspaces so that the set of complex cell outputs can show persistent, but relatively independent, activities in response to input. The complex cell code developed in this way can be thought of as a representation that predicts from one state of the lower-level representation (simple cells) what the next lower-level state is likely to be, by bridging over a learned subspace of these states. Another method, referred to as *temporal coherence* learning, seeks components that have some temporal correlation with their own activities over relatively short time periods, in response to natural video sequences [40]. Simple cell receptive fields show a kind of temporal invariance because their own activities persist or recur over short timescales, and thus are predictive of their own activities on those timescales. Similar principles have been used to develop invariance to moving edges [4], and to novel views of familiar rotating 3-dimensional objects, using temporal "trace" learning to associate temporally contiguous views [41]. All of these methods exploit the persistence of physical objects, and the temporal contiguity and high likelihood of seeing adjacent views over various timescales, as model-independent clues for the unsupervised discovery of objects in the environment.

3.2. Learning generator functions and space-time receptive fields for invariance

One approach for learning to recognize objects regardless of "nuisance parameters" or sources of image variability, such as translation, dilation, rotation, and variations in the illumination or deformation of objects, is to model these sources of variability explicitly and separate that information from the residual identity of the object. The result is a set of multiple maps, for example a map of object identity and another map of object pose. The total information about the object and the scene is preserved in such a representation, but the statistically separable sources of variability are factored into separate but interacting representations.

The set of visual cortical areas in human and nonhuman primates are divided into processing streams that report different aspects of visual scenes [19]. The ventral stream progressively extracts shape information with a limited degree of invariance to the position, pose, and lighting of the object. The dorsal stream progressively extracts estimates of the position and movement of the visual scene with some invariance to the identity of objects. Rao and Ballard [42,43] modeled a similar factorization of object identity from object transformation using a method that learns canonical images in one pathway, and systematic image transformations in another pathway, as a result of having been trained on a variety of systematically transformed canonical images (see also [44]). The method then seeks to explain novel images as systematically transformed canonical images (but see also [45]). While the method is currently limited in that it has only been demonstrated to perform global affine transformations of images, the idea shows promise in the modeling of locally modulated transformations that may include deformation and articulation. A general approach seeks to find *generator functions* that systematically transform images by a small amount along an invariance path or manifold in the pixel or representation state-space [46]. Specific deviations of novel images from recognizable, previously learned images can be generatively corrected, globally or locally, using a sequence of small linear transformations. In Rao and Ballard [42,43], these transformations were selected by joint gradient descent with the selection of canonical images from a learned set.

In visual cortex, neurons that receive visual inputs with several different degrees of delay from the original stimulus show *space-time receptive fields*, with response properties that represent input structure not only across input variables but over some interval of time [31]. These motion and change-sensitive cells show direction selectivity, velocity tuning, and occasionally simple reversal in polarity of on- and off-sensitive regions. ICA models provided with several sets of serially delayed pixel inputs learn features that model similar temporal structure [32]. Such receptive fields, although local, could be coordinated and used in a generative modeling capacity to enact the transformations that they recognize, providing a new inroad to the learning of perceptual invariances. The generator functions of Rao and Ballard [42,43] are collections of local difference operators, similar in form to spatial receptive fields, that are multiplicatively coordinated in groups by higher-order neurons representing the learned global affine transformations (rotation, translation, dilation). These coordinated groups of local transforming features alter canonical image content additively. If short-term, local image transformations are learned as a set of motion-sensitive feature detectors, these same features could be used in a generative framework to perform a shift operation for transformation invariance.

3.3. Joint statistics of filters and dependent components analysis

The filters learned by independent components analysis do not result in coefficients that are truly independent. There is a body of research focused on fixed banks of feedforward filters that are similar to those learned using ICA, perhaps the most well-known of which is the steerable wavelet pyramid [47]. A wavelet pyramid is a set of derivative filters, sensitive to edges at a variety of positions, orientations, phases and scales, analogous to processing in primary visual cortex. The same set of filters are scanned over an image centered on each pixel in sequence, and the set of spatial frequencies are filtered by scanning the same set of filters over duplicates of the image that have been blurred and subsampled at several different scales. Recent work has shown that the coefficients of these filter banks show characteristic statistical dependencies with each other over sets of natural images [48-50]. Filter outputs (coefficients) that are distant from each other in an image relative to the size of their receptive fields have joint activity histograms that are well-fit by a diamond-shaped Laplacian function. The coefficients of components whose receptive fields have a common center (but, for example, different spatial frequency) have a joint histogram that is well-fit by a radially symmetric Laplacian. Components with some overlap in their receptive fields have a joint histogram that is intermediate between diamond-shaped and circularly symmetric. The circularly symmetric joint isoprobability surface of concentric receptive fields indicates an increased likelihood that both coefficients will have high values, when compared with the diamond-shaped isoprobability surfaces of distant receptive fields.

Importantly, the coefficients contributing to a diamond-shaped Laplacian joint distribution are factorially independent, whereas the coefficients of a circularly-symmetric Laplacian are not independent. It may be expected that overlapping receptive fields that are not orthogonal will show dependency because they are similarly driven by some of the same inputs, as measured by the inner dot-product of their weight vectors. Depending upon their orientations, filters that are several wavelengths away from each other in the image plane also tend to show smaller characteristic dependencies with each other, that correspond to the appearance of extended edges and contours in natural scenes [18,51,52].

A family of models has been developed that use long-range "horizontal" or "lateral" excitatory connections between filters, to allow those filters with high coactivation probability to boost each others' activity in a way that is consistent with the suggestions of human psychophysics [53,54], the correlated anatomy and physiology of primary visual cortex [55,56], for example involving the synchronization of neuronal oscillations [57-59], in order to subserve contour popout and/or contour completion. Such models make use of the deviations from statistical independence between individual filters to perform inferences, whether or not this is explicitly stated as motivation for these models. Under these models, occlusions or breaks along the length of a contour are treated as 'dirty' or uncharacteristic measurements, and corrected using lateral inference between filters. Nonlinear gain control mechanisms that adapt to the conditional dependencies of filter outputs can be used to reduce or eliminate those dependencies [51,60,61]. These models also use recurrent connections between filters that are intended to model horizontal intra-area connections in cortex.

There have been some recent efforts to develop unsupervised learning methods that learn filters whose coefficients show specific types of dependencies with each other. The general problem of dependencies between variables has been addressed in terms of the *co-information lattice*, which describes the information between variables in an arbitrarily structured graphical model [62], although the problem of tractably finding dependency graphs is not addressed. *Tree-dependent* component analysis [63] finds sets of components whose dependencies can be modeled using an analytically tractable tree-structured graphical model. Child components are allowed to be dependent upon their parent components via a bivariate density model, while correlations between adjacent parents and children are minimized. An extension of this method proposes *forest-structured* graphical models in which clusters contain sets of tree-dependent components, while components across clusters seek independence during learning [64]. One concern with conventional graphical models that use density estimation techniques to model conditional distributions is that they appear to depart from the biologically more plausible monotonic, weighted-sum inference mechanisms of neural systems, which although less general an approach are nonetheless more computationally efficient.

3.4. Compositional and hierarchical feature analysis

Compositionality is a relatively undeveloped area of study in neuroscience and machine learning. Early work identified the need for compositional analysis methods and the compositional hierarchy (CH) representation structures that result [65,66], although these have so far largely resulted in methods based on formal grammars or heuristic learning methods applied to symbolic representations of sensory data [67-70]. A desirable property of composition parse hierarchies is that lower-level features should approach independence given the activity of the higher-level features that represent, and thus account for, the lower-level dependencies (Geoffrey Hinton, *personal communication*).

The idea of explicit integrative feature hierarchies appears to have originated with the Panedmonium model [71], in which signal-processing "demons" reported on their input signals in a sequence of layers that ultimately converged on behavioral decisions. This notion was later cast in terms of neural architectures with the Neocognitron, which used a sequence of processing steps to develop translation-invariant visual pattern recognition [72]. One recent example of a composition parse hierarchy used for feature analysis is the multilayer HMAX method for object recognition [73,74]. A hand-wired multilayer architecture used alternating layers of conjunction-finding units ('S' for simple) and MAX-tuned disjunctive units ('C' for complex). The simple units responded to specific patterns in their input and the complex units responded in proportion to the strongest (the MAX) of a set of transformation-related inputs, such as a set of phase-varying edges. Objects were learned only at the highest level of view-tuned units. This algorithm worked well for learning to associate the multiple views of rotated 'paper-clip' objects, which are artificial images generated using 2-dimensional projections of 3-dimensional rigid objects made up of line segments. Another example of a composition parse hierarchy used for adaptive feature analysis used the outputs of a model of simple and complex cells to learn extended contour features [75].

A framework for generative hierarchical factor analysis was outlined by Dayan [76], although because there is no method for adapting the graphical structure of models, this approach depends on a user-specified fixed architecture, and thus does not address the issue of finding optimal representational architectures or graphs. There has been very little progress in the area of finding optimal graphical architectures for hierarchical, factorial analysis in an unsupervised learning framework. Important issues include the tesselation density of features at any level, principled ways in which model neurons might reorganize their connections to establish layers and streams, and the factors upon which objectives for adaptive architectures should be based, including the relevant statistical properties of sensory data and the desired feature extraction and inference functions of the network.

3.5. Manifold modeling

Tenenbaum *et al.* [2] and Roweis and Saul [3] proposed similar methods for embedding high-dimensional manifolds in lower-dimensional subspaces where the true dimensionality of the degrees of freedom in sensory data can be explicitly parameterized and visualized. Both methods are based on local neighborhood relationships between observed sensory data points. Interestingly, interpolations within these embedded manifolds all generate plausible sensory images if the density of observed points is high enough. Positions within the manifolds thus appear to describe the viewing state of an object, and trajectories within the manifolds appear to correspond to typical object actions. These approaches offer promise for adjacency mapping of noun classes, the parameterization of position within noun manifolds for learning modifier classes, and the mapping of trajectories for the learning of verb classes.

4. Summary

Independent components analysis, and more recently, dependent components analysis approaches to modeling the structure of the sensory environment are being extended in hierarchies, and in parallel processing streams, to handle the invariances and compositionality properties of natural object classes. Manifold embedding methods and the modeling of spatiotemporal transition features show promise for identifying manifolds corresponding to natural object classes, natural attribute classes, and natural action classes for mapping sensory data into linguistic representations.

5. Acknowledgements

This review was supported by NIMA. The opinions expressed here are those of the author, and are not endorsed by NIMA or the United States Government.

6. References

[1] Lee DD and Seung HS (2000) Cognition. The manifold ways of perception. *Science* 290:2268-2269.
[2] Tenenbaum JB, de Silva V and Langford JC. (2000) A global geometric framework for nonlinear dimensionality reduction. *Science* 290:2319-2323.
[3] Roweis ST and Saul LK (2000) Nonlinear dimensionality reduction by locally linear embedding. *Science* 290:2323-2326.
[4] Földiák P (1991) Learning invariance from transformation sequences. *Neural Computation* 3:194-200.
[5] Rhodes P (1992) The long open time of the NMDA channel facilitates the self-organization of invariant object responses in cortex. *Society for Neuroscience Abstracts* 18:740.
[6] Bartlett MS and Sejnowski TJ (1996) Unsupervised learning of invariant representations of faces through temporal

association. In: *Computational Neuroscience: International Review of Neurobiology Suppl. 1.* J.M. Bower, ed. Academic Press, San Diego, CA, pp317-322.

[7] Samaria F and Harter A (1994) Parameterization of a stochastic model for human face identification. *Proceedings of 2nd IEEE Workshop on Applications of Computer Vision*, Sarasota FL, December 1994.

[8] Biederman I (1987) Recognition-by-components: A theory of human image understanding. *Psychological Review* 94:115-147.

[9] Sur M, Garraghty PE and Roe AW (1988) Experimentally induced visual projections into auditory thalamus and cortex. *Science* 242:1437-1441.

[10] Rockel AJ, Hiorns RW and Powell TPS (1980) The basic uniformity in structure of the neocortex. *Brain* 103:221-244.

[11] White H (1989) Learning in artificial neural networks: A statistical perspective. *Neural Computation* 1:425-464.

[12] Geman S, Bienenstock E and Doursat R (1992) Neural networks and the bias/variance dilemma. *Neural Computation* 4:1-58.

[13] MacKay D (1992) A practical bayesian framework for backprop networks. *Neural Computation* 4:448-472.

[14] Atick JJ (1992) Could information-theory provide an ecological theory of sensory processing? *Network: Computation in Neural Systems* 3:213-251.

[15] Field DJ (1987) Relations between the statistics of natural images and the response properties of cortical cells. *Journal of the Optical Society of America A* 4:2379-2394.

[16] Field DJ (1994) What is the goal of sensory coding? *Neural Computation* 6:559-601.

[17] Ruderman DL and Bialek W (1994) Statistics of natural images: Scaling in the woods. Physical Review Letters 73:814-817.

[18] Coppola DM, Purves HR, McCoy AN and Purves D (1998) The distribution of oriented contours in the real world. *Proceedings of the National Academy of Sciences USA* 95:4002-4006.

[19] Felleman DJ and Van Essen DC (1991) Distributed hierarchical processing in the primate cerebral cortex. *Cerebral Cortex* 1:1-47.

[20] Wiskott L (2003) How does our visual system achieve shift and size invariance? In *Problems in Systems Neuroscience*, van Hemmen JL and Sejnowski TJ, eds., Oxford University Press (to appear).

[21] Read HL, Winer JA and Schreiner CE (2002) Functional architecture of the auditory cortex. *Current Opinion in Neurobiology* 12:433-440.

[22] Toda T and Taoka M (2002) Hierarchical somesthetic processing of tongue inputs in the postcentral somatosensory cortex of conscious macaque monkeys. *Experimental Brain Research* 147:243-251.

[23] Jutten C and Herault J (1991). Blind separation of sources, part I: An adaptive algorithm based on neuromimetic architecture. *Signal Processing* 24:1-10.

[24] Comon P (1994) Independent component analysis, a new concept? *Signal Processing* 36:287-314.

[25] Bell AJ and Sejnowski TJ (1995) An information-maximization approach to blind separation and blind deconvolution. *Neural Computation* 7:1129-1159.

[26] Hubel D and Wiesel T (1962) Receptive fields, binocular interaction and functional architecture in the cat's visual cortex. *Journal of Physiology* 160:106-154.

[27] Olshausen BA and Field DJ (1996). Emergence of simple-cell receptive field properties by learning a sparse code for natural images. *Nature* 381:607-609.

[28] Bell AJ and Sejnowski TJ (1997) The 'independent components' of natural scenes are edge filters. *Vision Research* 37:3327-3338.

[29] Hoyer PO and Hyvärinen A (2000) Independent component analysis applied to feature extraction from colour and stereo images. *Network* 11:191-210.

[30] Lee T-W, Wachtler T and Sejnowski TJ (2002) Color opponency is an efficient representation of spectral properties in natural scenes. *Vision Research* 42:2095-2103.

[31] DeAngelis GC, Ohzawa I and Freeman RD (1995) Receptive-field dynamics in the central visual pathways. *Trends in Neurosciences* 18:451-458.

[32] van Hateren JH and Ruderman DL (1998) Independent component analysis of natural image sequences yields spatio-temporal filters similar to simple cells in primary visual cortex. *Proceedings of the Royal Society of London B Biological Sciences* 265:2315-20.

[33] Hyvärinen A and Hoyer P (2000) Emergence of phase- and shift-invariant features by decomposition of natural images into independent feature subspaces. *Neural Computation* 12:1705-1720.

[34] Kohonen T, Kaski S and Lappalainen H (1997) Self-organized formation of various invariant-feature filters in the adaptive-subspace SOM. *Neural Computation* 9:1321-1344.

[35] de Ridder D, Lemmers O, Duin RPW and Kittler J (2000) The adaptive subspace map for image description and image database retrieval. In *Proc. S+SSPR 2000*, 94-103, Berlin, IAPR, Springer-Verlag.

[36] Pasupathy A and Connor CE (2001) Shape representation in area V4: Position-specific tuning for boundary conformation. *Journal of Neurophysiology* 86:2505-2519.

[37] Tanaka K (2003) Columns for complex visual object features in the inferotemporal cortex: Clsutering of cells with similar but slightly different stimulus selectivities. *Cerebral Cortex* 13:90-99.

[38] Wiskott L and Sejnowski TJ (2002) Slow feature analysis: Unsupervised learning of invariances. *Neural Computation* 14:715-770.

[39] Einhäuser W, Kayser C, König P and Körding KP (2002) Learning the invariance properties of complex cells from natural stimuli. *European Journal of Neuroscience* 15:475-86.

[40] Hurri J and Hyvärinen A (2003) Simple-cell-like receptive fields maximize temporal coherence in natural video. *Neural Computation* 15:663-691.

[41] Stringer SM and Rolls ET (2002) Invariant object recognition in the visual system with novel views of 3D objects. *Neural Computation* 14:2585-2596.

[42] Rao RPN and Ballard DH (1996) A class of stochastic models for invariant recognition, motion, and stereo. *Technical Report 96.1, National Resource Laboratory for the Study of Brain and Behavior*, University of Rochester, June 1996.

[43] Rao RPN and Ballard DH (1998) Development of localized oriented receptive fields by learning a translation-invariant code for natural images. *Network: Computation in Neural Systems* 9:219-234.

[44] Perrett D and Oram M (1993) Neurophysiology of shape processing. *Image & Vision Computing* 11, 317–333.

[45] Olshausen BA, Anderson CH, and Van Essen DC (1995) A multiscale dynamic routing circuit for forming size- and position-invariant object representations. *Journal of Computational Neuroscience* 2:45-62.

[46] Jebara T (2003) Convex invariance learning. *Artificial Intelligence and Statistics, AISTAT 2003 (submitted)*.

[47] Adelson EH, Simoncelli E and Hingorani R (1987) Orthogonal pyramid transforms for image coding. *Proceedings of the SPIE: Visual Communications and Image Processing II*, Cambridge, MA, 845:50-58.

[48] Simoncelli E (1999) Modeling the joint statistics of images in the wavelet domain. *Proceedings of the SPIE 44th Annual Meeting, vol 3813, Denver, Colorado, July 1999*.

[49] Parra LC, Spence C and Sajda P (2000) Higher-order statistical properties arising from the non-stationarity of natural signals. *Advances in Neural Information Processing Systems* 12:786-792.

[50] Wainwright MJ and Simoncelli EP (2000) Scale mixtures of Gaussians and the statistics of natural images. *Advances in Neural Information Processing Systems 12. Solla SA, Leen TK and Muller K-R, eds. MIT Press, Cambridge, MA, May 2000*.

[51] Dimitrov A and Cowan J (1998) Spatial decorrelation in orientation-selective cortical cells. *Neural Computation* 10:1779–1795.

[52] Geisler WS, Perry JS, Super BJ and Gallogly DP (2001) Edge co-occurrence in natural images predicts contour grouping performance. *Vision Research* 41:711-724.

[53] Field DJ, Hayes A and Hess RF (1993) Contour integration by the human visual system: Evidence for a local 'association field'. *Vision Research* 33:173-193.

[54] Kovacs I and Julesz B (1993) A closed curve is much more than an incomplete one: Effect of closure in figure-ground segmentation. *Proceedings of the National Academy of Sciences* 90:7495-7497.

[55] Bosking WH, Zhang Y, Shofield B and Fitzpatrick D (1997) Orientation selectivity and the arrangement of horizontal connections in tree shrew striate cortex. *Journal of Neuroscience* 17:2112-2127.

[56] Walker GA, Ohzawa I and Freeman RD (1999) Asymmetric suppression outside the classical receptive field of the visual cortex. *Journal of Neuroscience* 19:10536-10553.

[57] Singer W and Gray CM (1995) Visual Feature Integration and the Temporal Correlation Hypothesis. *Annual Review of Neuroscience*, 18:555-586.

[58] Wang D and Terman D (1997) Image segmentation based on oscillatory correlation. *Neural Computation* 9:805-836.

[59] Yen S-C and Finkel LH (1998) Extraction of perceptually salient contours by striate cortical networks. *Vision Research* 38:719-741.

[60] Schwartz O and Simoncelli EP (2001) Natural signal statistics and sensory gain control. *Nature Neuroscience* 4:819-25.

[61] Shriki O, Sompolinsky H and Lee DD (2001) An information maximization approach to overcomplete and recurrent representations. *Advances in Neural Information Processing Systems* 13:612:618.

[62] Bell AJ (2003) The co-information lattice. *4th International Symposium on Independent Component Analysis and Blind Signal Separation (ICA2003)*, April 2003, Nara, Japan.

[63] Bach FR and Jordan MI (2002) Tree-dependent Component Analysis. *Uncertainty in Artificial Intelligence Conference Proceedings, Edmonton, Canada, August 2002*.

[64] Bach FR and Jordan MI (2003) Beyond independent components: trees and clusters. *Journal of Machine Learning Research (in press)*.

[65] Utans J (1993) Learning in compositional hierarchies: Inducing the structure of objects from data. In: *Advances in Neural Information Processing Systems* 6:285-292. Cambridge, MA: MIT Press.

[66] Bienenstock E and Geman S (1995) Compositionality in neural systems. In: *The Handbook of Brain Theory and Neural Networks*, Arbib M, Ed., Bradford Books/MIT Press, 223-226.

[67] Bienenstock E, Geman S and Potter D (1997) Compositionality, MDL priors, and object recognition. In: *Advances in Neural Information Processing Systems 9*, Mozer MC, Jordan MI, and Petsche T, Eds., MIT Press, 838-844.

[68] Potter DF (1999) *Compositional Pattern Recognition*. Ph.D. thesis, Division of Applied Mathematics, Brown University.

[69] Pfleger K (2000) Learning predictive compositional hierarchies. *Technical Report, KSL-01-09, Computer Science Department, Stanford University*.

[70] Pfleger K (2002) On-line learning of predictive compositional hierarchies. *Ph.D. dissertation, Computer Science Department, Stanford University, Stanford CA*.

[71] Selfridge OG (1959) Pandemonium: A paradigm for learning. In: *Proceedings of the Symposium on Mechanisation of Thought Processes*, Blake DV and Uttley AM, Eds., pp511-529, London: H M Stationary Office.

[72] Fukushima K (1980) Neocognitron: A self-organizing neural network model for a mechanism of pattern recognition unaffected by shift in position. *Biological Cybernetics* 36:193-202.

[73] Riesenhuber M and Poggio T (1999) Hierarchical models of object recognition in cortex. *Nature Neuroscience* 2:1019-1025.

[74] Knoblich U, Riesenhuber M, Freedman DJ, Miller, EK and Poggio T (2002) Visual categorization: How the monkey brain does it. In: *Biologically Motivated Computer Vision*, Lee SW, Buelthoff HH, and Poggio T, Eds. Second IEEE International Workshop, BMCV 2002, Tuebingen, Germany, December 2002.

[75] Hoyer PO and Hyvärinen A (2002) A multi-layer sparse coding network learns contour coding from natural images. *Vision Research* 42:1593-605.

[76] Dayan P (1997) Recognition in hierarchical models. In: *Foundations of Computational Mathematics*. Cucker F and Shub M, Eds., Berlin, Germany: Springer.

Homeland Security

⌘ ⌘ ⌘ ⌘ ⌘ ⌘ ⌘ ⌘

Perspectives on the Fusion of Image and Non-image Data

David L. Hall
School of Information Sciences and Technology
The Pennsylvania State University
dhall@ist.psu.edu

Abstract

Increasingly, multi-sensor systems are being developed to collect, process, and disseminate image and non-image data. Applications include homeland security, monitoring of facilities, and military situation assessment. Fusion of image and non-image data has traditionally been performed with extensive human-in-the-loop involvement. Typically the image data are used as the "fundamental" data source with non-image data simply overlaid on the image data, or conversely the non-image data are treated as fundamental, and the image data are used to confirm the identity of observed entities. This paper discusses the problem of multi-sensor fusion and argues that new techniques are emerging that will allow fusion of image and non-image data at multiple levels of inference from the "raw" data level, to the feature level, decision-level, and knowledge level.

1. Introduction

Numerous multi-sensor systems have been developed to collect, process, and disseminate image and non-image data ([1], [2], [3] and [4]). For applications such as homeland security, monitoring of facilities, and military situation assessment, new mobile platforms are being developed and deployed for monitoring and surveillance. These include mobile robots, unmanned aircraft, and ground-based sensors [5]. Modern sensor suites may include image sensors (e.g., visual and infrared image collection), non-image sensors (collection of radio frequency signals from emitters, acoustic emissions, etc.), and the ability to include reports from human observers (e.g., textual messages that provide interpretation information). Wideband communication links increasingly enable the dissemination of large amounts of image and non-image data across a distributed sensing/processing system.

The goal of multi-sensor fusion is to achieve inferences about the observed environment or situation that cannot be achieved by a single sensor or source of information. Conceptually, information about the observed situation (viz., the specific domain of interest for the application at hand) are combined to achieve high-level inferences. This is illustrated in Figure 1. Data from sensors or sources are transformed from raw data (e.g., signals, images, and vectors) to intermediate products such as state vectors (target tracks), declarations of target/entity identity, and an understanding of the relationships among these entities and the environment to achieve a sense of the situation or threat. As illustrated in figure 1, multiple techniques may be used to achieve these high level inferences.

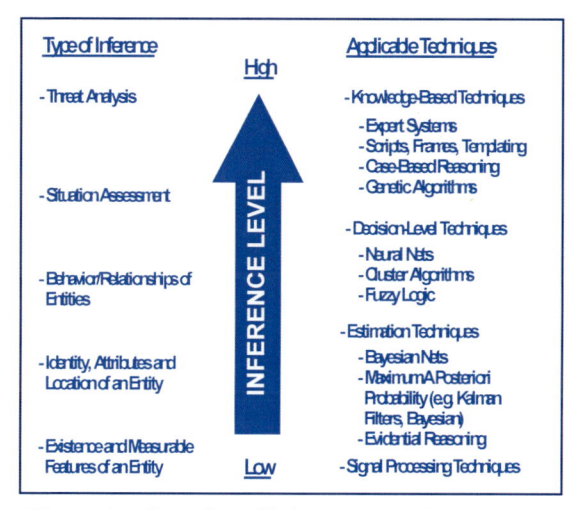

Figure 1: Hierarchy of inference techniques [1]

If multiple sensors or sources are used in the inference process, in principle, they could be fused at one of three levels in the hierarchy; (1) data level fusion, (2) feature-level fusion; or (3) state-vector or decision-level fusion. Data level fusion involves fusion of raw data; for example, the combination of multiple images into one fused image, from which inferences are made. Techniques for data level fusion include model-based methods, statistical estimation methods, and techniques such as least-squares methods. In feature-level fusion, each data source is pre-processed to extract representative features. For example, signal data may be processed to obtain information about an emitter's direction and emission characteristics, while image data may be processed to obtain information about the size and shape of an observed object (which contains or hosts the emitter). Feature level fusion combines the feature data (e.g., concatenates multiple feature vectors from different sources into a larger feature vector) and processes the combined feature vector using pattern recognition techniques such as cluster algorithms or neural networks. Finally, decision level fusion involves pre-processing each source of data to obtain an estimate of an entities position, velocity, attributes, and identity (viz., a vector that describes the target's state). Given these state vectors from different sources, the information is fused at the state vector or decision level using methods such as statistical estimation, Bayesian inference or Dempster-Shafer's method. Subsequently, automated reasoning techniques may be employed to interpret the meaning of these entities and their inter-relationships.

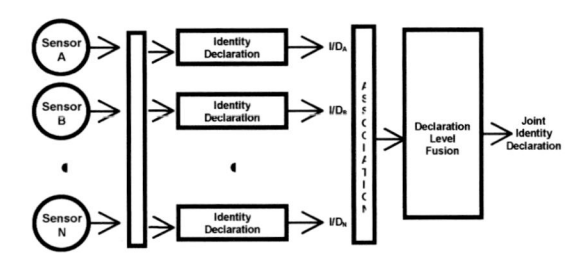

Figure 2: Example of decision-level fusion [1]

An example of decision-level fusion is provided in Figure 2. A general discussion of the tradeoffs of these different architectures is provided in [6].

2. Challenges in Fusing Image and Non-Image Data

Traditionally, automated fusion of image and non-image data has been performed at the feature-level or state-vector level. Alternatively the data fusion was performed manually by a human-in-the-loop. In this approach, the image data are used as the "fundamental" data source with non-image data simply overlaid on the image data, or conversely the non-image data are treated as fundamental, and the image data are used to confirm the identification of observed entities.

Why is it difficult to fuse image and non-image data? Why can't image and non-image data be fused the same way as commensurate sensors (commensurate sensors are those sensors that observe the same physical phenomena)? There are several basic reasons for this. First, physical models are not generally available to allow the accurate prediction of multi-spectral phenomena. For example, in observing an object such as a aircraft, models are generally not available to simultaneously predict radar cross section (as a function of aspect angle), visible spectral characteristics, infra-red spectra, and phenomena associated with the emitters associated with the aircraft. It is difficult for a single model (or even suite of models) to predict all of the observable phenomena associated with an entity (and observed by multiple, non-commensurate sensors). Hence, data level fusion using statistical estimation techniques such as Kalman filters cannot be used for heterogeneous multi-sensor tracking and identity estimation at the "raw" data level.

Second, fusion of "raw" data across heterogeneous sensors requires very accurate cross-sensor association and correlation. This is a challenging problem [7] that requires precise sensor co-registration and accurate models of platform and sensor pointing, environmental effects on signal propagation, and an unambiguous link between observational data and targets/entities of interest. Association and correlation at the state vector or decision-level is much easier than at the "raw" data level.

Finally, the fusion of image and non-image data is challenging because the problem of object recognition is hermeneutical. That is, if we know the context in which an image is observed (viz., we have a description of the environment, situation, context, and circumstances) of an image, it becomes easier to interpret the content of the image (i.e., to identify possible targets or entities). Conversely, if we know the targets or entities contained within an image, then it is easier to interpret the context of the image data.

If fusion could be performed at multiple levels in the inference hierarchy (illustrated in Figure 1), then non-image data would assist in the interpretation and extraction of information from image data. By the same token, if image data were available to provide contextual information for non-image data, then the processing of the single-source non-image data would be more effective. Hence, improvements could be achieved for both image-processing, and processing of non-image data if they could be fused at multiple levels of the inference hierarchy. Ideally, one would like to emulate the ability of humans to interpret visual scenes using their "naïve" visual physics [8] and to engage contextual reasoning at the semantic level [9].

3. Enabling Technologies to Improve the Fusion Image and Non-image data

Three developments are emerging that appear to provide the potential for improved multi-level fusion of image and non-image data. These include, (1) new methods for automatically interpreting image data and associating descriptive semantic labels, (2) improvements in physics-based modeling, and (3) new hybrid reasoning models. These are summarized below.

Semantic labeling of images – The ability to automatically transform image data to semantic concepts is becoming available using techniques developed by Wang ([10]). Wang has developed an approach to label images using a gestalt-type approach and associative pattern matching. The approach represents images using features based on hierarchical wavelet transforms. The features are extracted from an entire image, rather than on a segmented subset of the image or an extracted object. The features are mapped to general semantic terms to describe or characterize the content of the image. The concept is illustrated in Figure 3.

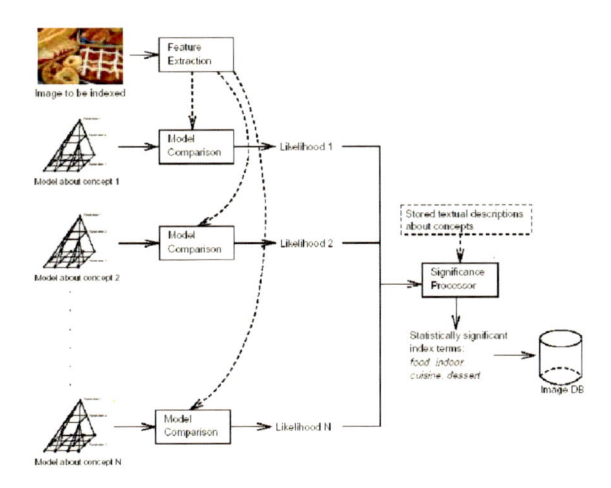

Figure 3: Semantic labeling of image data [10]

In his SIMPlicity tool kit, Wang demonstrated the ability to train a classifier to link several semantic concepts (from a list of about 600 semantic terms) to 500,000 images selected from the web. Wang uses a neural network approach to link semantic terms to extracted features. After training the classifier (using about 40 images per semantic concept), the user can use terms such as "European", "sports", "people", "clothing" and other general terms to search for images in a large set of images. Conversely, the user can supply an image and use the classifier to automatically annotate the image with descriptive terms.

The use of such a capability enables images to be processed at a higher level of semantic interpretation than basic segmentation and object recognition. Given the image data and associated semantic labels, automated reasoning may be applied to perform fusion at the knowledge level (even above the decision level). Moreover, automated labeling of images provides content information to guide algorithms for improved image processing and object recognition within the image [11]

Improved physics based models – New developments in computing power enable the development of increasingly sophisticated physical models to predict observational data that crosses multiple sensor types. The defense technology area plan related to sensors and electronics cites the evolution of increasingly sophisticated physics-based models for sensors and signal propagation. Moreover, new smart sensors are beginning to incorporate built-in models to improve the sensor performance and reporting of the sensor data.

Emergence of hybrid models – Finally, new hybrid reasoning methods are being developed that incorporate both explicit information (e.g., information available via physical models or representation of human expert knowledge) and implicit knowledge obtained using computer learning algorithms to process exemplar data. Hall and Garga [12] developed such techniques for understanding heterogeneous sensor information observing a complex mechanical situation. The hybrid reasoning approach is shown conceptually in figure 4.

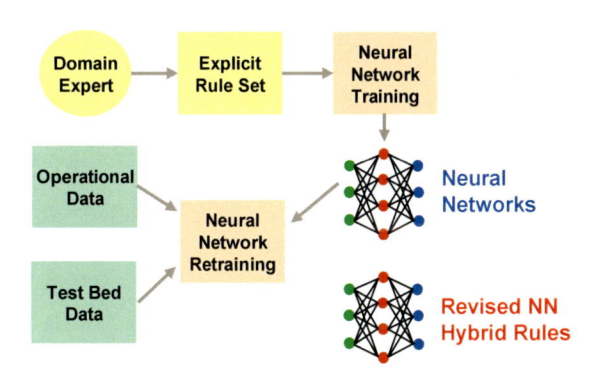

Figure 4: Example of hybrid reasoning [12]

In the hybrid reasoning method, information from physical models or expert knowledge encoded via rules are learned by a neural network. This provides a "background education" for the automated reasoning system. Subsequently, the neural net is provided with examples of real data (e.g., from specific targets or situations) and trained to evolve to incorporate not only knowledge from the basic education as well as lessons from real observations.

The result is a robust automated reasoning system that combines the benefits of expert knowledge, physical models, and examples of real data.

4. Summary

Emerging techniques in hybrid reasoning, semantic labeling of images and improved physical models provide the opportunity for new methods of fusing image and non-image data. In particular,

- Transformation of image data to semantic labels allows image data to be fused with non-image data at the semantic (or knowledge level) – beyond the state-vector level.
- Transformation of image data to semantic labels provides context-based information to improve processing of image data.
- Improved physical models provide the opportunity for data level fusion of heterogeneous sensor data.
- Hybrid reasoning models provide a method to incorporate semantic level information, as well as data or feature level information.

The result of these emerging techniques is a broader perspective on how to develop fusion architectures for combining image and non-image data. Techniques analogous to those used for interacting multiple model (IMM) estimation filters [13] might be used to allow fusion of image and non-image data at multiple inference levels with subsequent comparison and fusion of the results provided by the different models.

5. References

1. Hall, D., *Mathematical Techniques in Multisensor Data Fusion*. 1992, Norwood, MA: Artech House, Inc.
2. Hall, D. and J. Llinas, eds. *Handbook of Multisensor Data Fusion*. 2001, CRC Press: New York.
3. Nichols, M., *A survey of multisensor data fusion systems*, in *Handbook of Multisensor Data Fusion*, D. Hall and J. Llinas, Editors. 2001, CRC Press: Boca Raton, FL.
4. Hall, D., R.J. Linn, and J. Llinas. *Survey of data fusion systems*. in *SPIE Conference on Data Structure and Target Classification*. 1991. Orlando, FL: SPIE.
5. Swanson, D.C. and D. Hall. *Real-time data fusion processing of internetted acoustic sensors for tactical applications*. in *1994 IEEE International Conference on Multisensor Fusion and Integration for Intelligence Systems*. 1994. Las Vegas.
6. Bowman, C. and A. Steinberg, *A systems engineering approach for implementing data fusion systems*, in *Handbook of Multisensor Data Fusion*, D. Hall and J. Llinas, Editors. 2001, CRC Press: New York.
7. Llinas, J.e.a., *Engineering guidelines for data correlation algorithm characterization*. 1996, State University of New York at Buffalo: Buffalo, NY.
8. Pinker, S., *How the Mind Works*. 1997, London: Penguin Books.
9. Pinker, S., *The Language Instinct: How the Mind Creates Language*. 2000: Harper Perennial.
10. Wang, J.Z., J. Li, and G. Wiederhold, *SIMPLicity: Semantics-sensitive Integrated Matching for Picture Libraries*. IEEE Transactions on PAMI, 2000. **23**: p. 1-21.
11. Frank, R., *Understanding Smart Sensors*. 1995, Norwood, MA: Artech House, Inc.
12. Hall, D. and A. Garga. *Hybrid reasoning techniques for automated fault classification*. in *Society for Machinery Failure Prevention, 51st Meeting*. 1997.
13. Semerdjiev, E., et al., *Interacting multiple model algorithm for maneouvering ship tracking based on new ship models*. Information and Security, 1999. **2**.

Quick Response Airborne Deployment of Viper Muzzle Flash Detection and Location System During DC Sniper Attacks

M. Pauli[**], M. C. Ertem[*], E. Heidhausen[*],
[**]Naval Research Laboratory, [*]University Research Foundation MADL
pauli@ninja.nrl.navy.mil, madl@ertem.com, cheeks@urf.com

Abstract

The VIPER infrared muzzle flash detection system was deployed from a helicopter and an airship in response to the Washington, DC area sniper attacks in October 2002. The system consisted of a midwave IR camera, which was used to detect muzzle flash and cue a visible light camera on a gimbal to the detected event. The helicopter installation was done to prove that a manned airborne installation of the VIPER detection system would work. Within 36 hours of the request to deploy the system, it had been modified, approved by the FAA inspector and flown. Testing at the Ft. Meade rifle range showed that in the helicopter installation the system worked at least as well as the ground based system. Because of the limited endurance that a helicopter allows, the system was then installed aboard a Navy leased airship. It was flown at Elizabeth City, NC and was tested against live fire.

In response to the Washington, DC sniper shootings, the OSD had tasked a parallel effort to deploy a 20" WesCam gyro stabilized gimbal on the same airship. Software was developed in the field to interface the WesCam gimbal to the VIPER system so that it could automatically slew over to a detection event. The airship installation also added GPS based moving map display capability. That was completed within four days of the first request to deploy. The next four days were spent coordinating a concept of operations for working with law enforcement agencies and getting flight clearances to bring the airship into the DC-Richmond corridor. After the sniper suspects were caught, the airship was taken to Patuxent River Naval Air Station and the muzzle flash detection system was tested there against live rifle fire.

These were the first flights of the airborne VIPER payload. It has since been flown numerous times on helicopters and tested against various guns, mortars, and artillery. The Naval Research Laboratory has demonstrated multiple payloads, each of which flew in manned helicopters and all controlled from a single ground station.

1. Introduction

The VIPER infrared muzzle flash detection system [1][2] uses a midwave infrared camera to detect and locate the discharge of firearms. Work on this system has been carried out by the Naval Research Laboratory and the Maryland Advanced Development Laboratory of University Research Foundation [3]. The system has been in continuous development since 1995, and has gone through many configuration changes. This paper describes the configuration as used during the October 2002 period.

1.1. Sensor and Optics

Several midwave IR camera / lens configurations have been used as the sensor for the VIPER system. The configuration used in the events described here consisted of an InSb midwave camera with an anamorphic lens that resulted in an approximately 140 x 20 degree field of view. The camera has a 14 bit digital output that gives it a high dynamic range that allows operation at a fixed gain. This makes it easier to operate the system in a 'NUC and forget' mode, where once a non-uniformity correction (NUC) has been done on the focal plane array / lens configuration, the system can be used with no further sensor adjustment. Earlier configurations of the system had used cameras with analog video output which required continuous control of pedestal and gain settings to keep the scene levels within the small dynamic range of the sensor. The wide field of view anamorphic lens results in a large difference in optical gain between the lens axis and pixels around the edges of the image. The system nonuniformity correction is important. This is especially true for a camera that is installed on a moving platform, since any spatial nonuniformity will appear as a temporal signal when the camera moves. For a stationary camera the quality of the NUC is of much less concern.

1.2. Detection Algorithms

The detection system in VIPER consists of spectral, temporal, spatial and morphological filters to discriminate IR flashes due to gunfire from background noise and clutter. Spectral filtering increases the signal to background ratio in the video collected from the IR camera. Temporal filtering is done by a matched FIR filter that has taps optimized for detecting the signature of a typical muzzle flash. The spatial filters include a low pass adaptive background estimator that tracks the localized signal energy at each pixel to account for dynamic activity in the scene, and a high pass filter that is used to discriminate small flashes. (At the ranges of interest and with the fields of view used, the muzzle flash signal typically has a spatial extent of at most a few pixels.) These filters are followed by morphological filters. The first one of these is a selectable global background filter. When this filter is on, it implements an IIR low pass threshold adjustment based on the entire scene. It acts to raise the detection threshold if there is excessive signal energy at the output of the preceding detection stages. Hard upper and lower bounds are used to limit how much the threshold can change. The global background filter was developed to reduce false alarms in cases where the camera makes sudden or high rate turns, or when there is activity in the near field. This filter is usually turned off. Another morphological filter detects and rejects tracks. This is normally on, and is used to reject false alarms due to far field objects transitioning the scene at high speed. The system can be set to display those events rejected by the track filter. These "false" events are from activity in the scene that although is not due to muzzle flash, is still of interest to the operator.

The detection algorithms were implemented on a computer equipped with a commercial image processor card. The temporal and spatial filters were run on the image processing card, while the morphological filters were executed using the host processor. The image processor card also had the camera interface on board.

The entire suite of detection algorithms ran at a rate of 120 frames per second. With the fixed number of taps in the temporal filter, this allows the system to declare detection in less than 100 milliseconds of the gun flash. (This means that a detection occurs before a supersonic bullet has traveled 50 meters from the weapon.)

1.3. Response to Detections

The system declares a detection in several ways. An operator alarm consisting of an audible 'ding' sound is initiated. It has been observed that if the shooter is at a range of more than about 300 meters from the system, the audio alarm gives enough warning for a trained user to duck before the round arrives. (The system does not require that the shot be fired in its direction. It works at all aspect angles, as long as there is a line of sight to the muzzle flash.) The typical sequence of events is 'ding, bang, boom' with a supersonic round.

The x,y pixel coordinates of the alarm, and the calculated azimuth and elevation angles in camera coordinates are displayed in numeric form and graphically.

The system is attached to a gimbal with a visible light video camera installed. When a detection occurs, this camera can be set to automatically slew to and zoom in on the bearing of the target. The operator then sees where the declared target is, and the video is recorded for intelligence or judicial use later.

2. The BOUNCE Project

The original VIPER system was developed for ground use with a stationary camera. A follow on project called Battlespace Ordnance Understanding - Net Centric Environment (BOUNCE) was under way in 2002. The goal of BOUNCE was to extend the VIPER technology to detect and locate ordnance from a low flying unmanned air vehicle (UAV). The reasoning was that a low cost low flying UAV would be able to fly under the clouds to detect and locate targets such as mortars, artillery, and even rifles and get this information to the warfighter in real time.

A data collection and feasibility analysis was done in 1998 by flying an early version of VIPER aboard an experimental NRL UAV [4]. The recorded data was post processed and it was shown that reliable detection of gunfire could be performed in an airborne system. An airborne system was also seen as a logical next step in the development of motion control algorithms for muzzle flash detection. The fact that for a camera installed on an aircraft all objects in the scene are in the far field means that image motion is constrained to translation and rotations. Even for the very wide field of view anamorphic lenses used, it would be easier to determine the optical flow vectors as the aircraft moved. In a ground system, on the other hand, since there are so many object in the foreground, it is a much more complex task to estimate camera motion, and to predict the next image given a sequence of images. BOUNCE would be a good intermediate project to work on developing motion algorithms.

The BOUNCE project also involved algorithms for geolocating a target once it was detected. This is done by using an inertial measurement unit (IMU) on board the UAV, and tracking the attitude and position of the aircraft. Upon detection a simple geometric transformation would draw a bearing line from the UAV position to target. BOUNCE had a gimbal on the aircraft with a laser rangefinder. Geolocation is done in several ways. One uses a digital terrain map to calculate where the detection bearing line intersects the surface of the earth. This is immediate, but is potentially the least accurate method, depending on the grazing angle and accuracy of the terrain data available. The second method uses the laser rangefinder to geolocate the target. The third method is to get multiple lines of bearing to the target. The second and third methods are more accurate, but require the operator to visually identify and track the target using gimbal video. (All three methods have since been implemented and tested [5].)

3. Washington, DC Sniper Emergency

In October 2002, the area around Washington DC was affected by a series of sniper shootings. The immediate reaction to this was to evaluate how this technology and assets at hand could be used to aid in the investigation.

Just finished was implementing algorithms for detection, for a moving airborne camera, for slewing a gimbal to detection, and for calibrating this camera and gimbal coordination. There was one system for software development and a single available camera with a wide field of view lens. The system had been in a vehicle but had not yet started any airborne tests. The UAVs that BOUNCE would use had not yet been flown or certified. It seemed that the only option would be to deploy from the ground. Considering the area under potential threat (roughly a triangle between Frederick, MD, Baltimore, and Richmond) it was realized that chances of being at the same neighborhood and within line of sight of the sniper at the time of a shot was infinitesimally small.

On the afternoon of Wednesday October 16, 2002 an investigation was initiated to determine if a quick response deployment from an aircraft was possible. A trip was made to Tipton airfield, at Ft. Meade, MD to determine if the system could be installed on a JetRanger helicopter. It was required to fly both the system and the operator, as data links for ground operation in BOUNCE had not yet been implemented. That night and Thursday were spent on building the mechanical interface, resolving the power supply issue, and working to get emergency FAA certification. On the morning of Friday, October 18, 2002 the system was ready to operate. The IR camera and a visible light camcorder were mounted to look out the left side of the helicopter with the left door removed. The operator squeezed in to the right of the rack of equipment. [Fig 1]

The helicopter had FAA clearance to operate over the Fort Meade rifle range, which is immediately adjacent to Tipton airfield. Detection tests were carried out at the rifle range against .223 caliber sniper rifles [Fig 2]. The helicopter orbited the shooter at altitudes of up to 1000 feet and detections were obtained. It was noticed that above approximately 100' altitude the false alarm rate was acceptably low at several per hour. Below this altitude objects on the ground blowing about because of rotor downwash caused false alarms. However any operational aircraft would have to fly at a minimum of 1000' altitude due to FAA restrictions and reliable detections from that altitude were demonstrated on this flight.

That same afternoon the system was taken to Elizabeth City, NC to deploy on a US Navy leased airship. On the morning of Saturday October 19, 2003 the system was installed on the Airship 600 [Fig 3]. Since there was much better space, power, and weight capabilities on the airship, it was possible to install the visible camera verification gimbal as well. The system was installed to look out the left side of the airship [Fig 4].

In addition to the system, a WesCam stabilized gimbal was installed by another contractor in response to the OSD request for quick response to the sniper emergency. That gimbal had much better optics than the Viper's and it was stabilized. An operator normally manually controlled it, but in discussion with the WesCam engineers it was discovered that their gimbal would take positioning commands over a standard RS-232 port. Modifications were made to the software to issue WesCam gimbal commands so that in addition to the Viper gimbal, it was possible to auto slew the WesCam gimbal to the detection bearing. [Fig 5]

It was realized that no concept of operations had ever been developed for an airship outfitted with a sniper detector. In parallel with writing code to drive the WesCam gimbal, there was writing of a CONOPS that dealt with contingencies such as how to communicate detection, procedures for geolocation and even scenarios such as what to do if the airship was fired on.

On Sunday October 20, 2003 was performed the first detection test from the airship while tethered. This was also done to calibrate the visible light gimbals to IR camera coordinates. The system worked as expected and with satisfactory detection and false alarm rates.

On Monday, October 21, 2003 the code to interface to the WesCam gimbal was finished. Also added was a separate processor and GPS receiver to run a moving map display to assist in geolocating any detections [Fig 6]. The geolocation capability in BOUNCE had not been coded yet.

At this point, the system was fully operational, five days after the initial request. Coordination was done for a full up flight test with the Elizabeth City Coast Guard Station at the Pasquotank Sheriff's Department shooting range. The system was flight tested and demonstrated detection and location of rifle fire from operational altitudes.

It proved to be more challenging to coordinate the operation of the airship in the threat region, especially since it meant flying inside the Washington, DC Temporary Flight Restriction Area. Tuesday October 22, 2003 was spent working on procedures and clearances. Clearance was obtained to depart Elizabeth City, NC for Manassas, VA. That night sniper suspects were caught, before the airship was deployed.

The airship was subsequently flown to Patuxent River NAS and another test flight was conducted. The experience obtained during this week in October 2002 allowed transition to airborne testing of the BOUNCE system. [5]

4. References

[1] Caulfield, J.T.; Gower, P.W.; Moroz, S.A., Burchick, D.A., Ertem, M. C., Pierson, R.B.; " *Performance of the Vectored Infrared Personnel Engagement and Return Fire (VIPER) IRFPA Muzzle Flash Detection System*", IRIS 1996

[2] Gower P.W., Moroz S. A., Burchick D.A., Ertem M. C., Pierson R.B. " *The Vectored Infrared Personnel Engagement and Returnfire (VIPER) System and Its Counter Sniper Application* ", IRIS Passive Sensors 1997

[3] US Patent # 6,496,593 - Optical Muzzzle Blast Detection and Counterfire Targeting System and Method

[4] S. A. Moroz, R.B. Pierson, M. C. Ertem, D. A. Burchick, Sr., T. Ippolito, *"Airborne Deployment of and Recent Improvements to the Viper Counter Sniper System",* IRIS Passive Sensors Symposium, March 1999

[5] M Pauli, S Moroz, C. Ertem, E. Heidhausen, D. Burchick *"Infrared Detection and Geolocation of Gunfire and Ordnance Events from Ground and Air Platforms"* , National Military Sensing Symposia, October 2003

Figure 1 - First flight. Processor is strapped down in yellow rack, IR and visible cameras are on stand, and batteries are on floor under plywood frame.

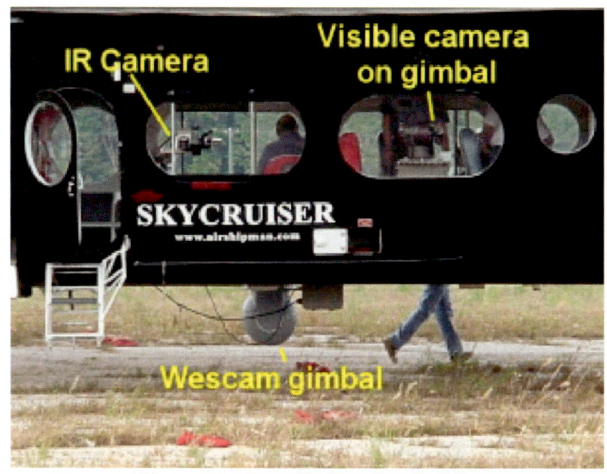

Figure 4 - Installation in airship.

Figure 2 - Fort Meade rifle range from helicopter at 1000' with video captured at time of detections.

Figure 5 - IR detection suite on left, consisting of visible camera on gimbal, operator station, detection camera. WesCam operator station on right.

Figure 3 - Airship 600 at Weeksville, NC

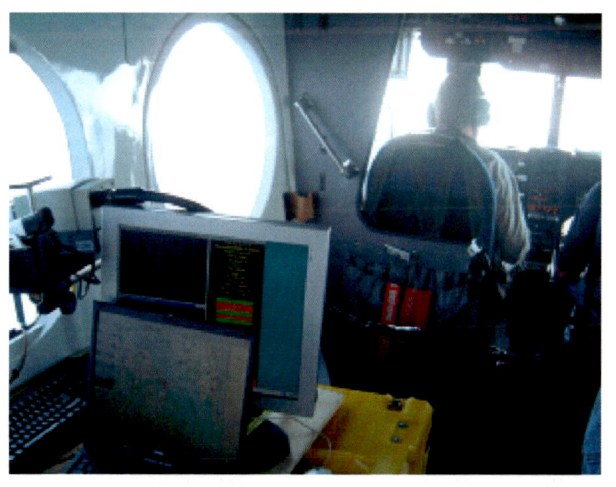

Figure 6 - Test flight with IR detection suite, moving map geolocation on laptop.

Fusing Face and ECG for Personal Identification

Steven A. Israel[1], W. Todd Scruggs[1], William J. Worek[1], John M. Irvine[2]
[1] SAIC, 4001 Fairfax Drive, Suite 450, Arlington, Virginia 22203
[2] SAIC, 20 Burlington Mall Road, Suite 130, Burlington, Massachusetts 01803
steven.a.israel@saic.com

Abstract

Single modality biometric identification systems exhibit performance that may not be adequate for many security applications. Face and fingerprint modalities dominate the biometric verification / identification field. However, both face and fingerprint can be compromised using counterfeit credentials. Previous research has demonstrated the use of the electrocardiogram (ECG) as a novel biometric. This paper explores the fusion of a traditional face recognition technique with ECG. System performance with multimodality fusion can be superior to reliance on a single biometric, but performance depends heavily on the fusion technique. In addition, a fusion-based system is more difficult to defeat, since an imposter must provide counterfeit credentials for both face and cardiovascular function.

1. Introduction

Biometric techniques offer the possibility of improving security in a number of settings including facilities access, computer system access, law enforcement, and homeland defense. Traditional biometric methods, such as fingerprint and face recognition, have been employed with varying degrees of success for these applications. A major weakness of relying on a single biometric modality is that relatively simple methods exist for spoofing or defeating many biometric systems. The fusion of two or more biometric techniques offers the prospect of improving system performance, while also being more difficult to defeat.

This paper explores the fusion of traditional face recognition techniques with a novel biometric based on the subject's electrocardiogram (ECG). Because acquisition of the ECG information requires contact sensing, this technique is best suited to verification and identification tasks for cooperative subjects. In principle, ECG and face should be independent sources of information about the subject. Consequently, fusion of the two data sources should outperform either source alone.

The remainder of the paper is structured in the following manner. Section 2 discusses the processing of the raw ECG data to generate attributes. Section 3 highlights face recognition technologies and those functions performed for this experiment for attribute creation. Section 4 describes the role of fusion and fusion methodologies. Section 5 provides the experimental set-up and results, which is followed by a discussion of the experiment in Section 6.

2. ECG

The electrocardiogram signal measures the change in electrical potential over time. The trace of each heartbeat consists of three complexes: P, R, and T. These complexes are defined by the fiducial that is the peak of each complex. The labels in Figure 1 document the commonly used medical science ECG fiducials. Additional fiducials used by this team are noted with apostrophe (α').

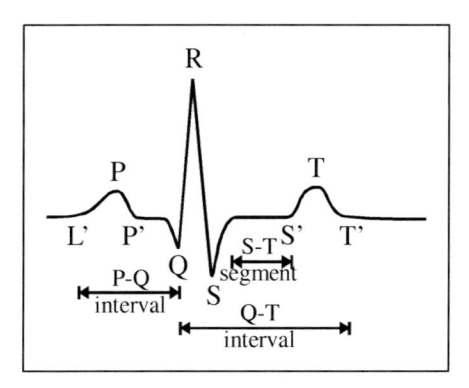

Figure 1. Ideal ECG Signal: Fiducial points and medically significant segments of a heartbeat.

The ECG is measured with respect to an arbitrary baseline. Its magnitude varies with the electrode placement relative to the heart. The ECG trace contains a wealth of information. However, only in the last 20 years have researchers been able to apply digital analysis to the data [1]. The most common digital application is heart rate variability (HRV) [2]. Researchers have applied numerical methods to more complex diagnostic interpretation tasks such as mother – fetal signal demixing [3], identifying atrial and ventricular fibrillation [4, 5], myocardial infarction [6] and recently to identify individuals [7-9].

2.1. Data Collection

The data were collected using commercial hardware at SAIC's laboratory. The data for each subject were collected at 256 Hz and quantized to 7 bits. The data rate was sufficient to resolve the ECG fiducials. The population consisted of thirty-five men and women between the ages of 18 and 44. Several of the subjects were measured across multiple sessions; however, only single session information was used here. The experimentation consisted of two 2-minute tasks. The tasks were the subject's baseline and an arithmetic stressor. For the stressor, subjects were asked to continually subtract seven from an initial large number.

2.2. Data Processing

A two-minute sequence of heartbeats was used to determine the subject's average waveform. Bandpass filtering eliminated nearly all the electrical, A-to-D, and thermal noise. Individual heartbeats were extracted and aligned by the peak of their R waves. The waterfall diagram (Figure 2) is offset to the start of the heartbeat, the firing of the sino-atrial node (the heart's primary pacemaker), which is the L' position (Figure 1).

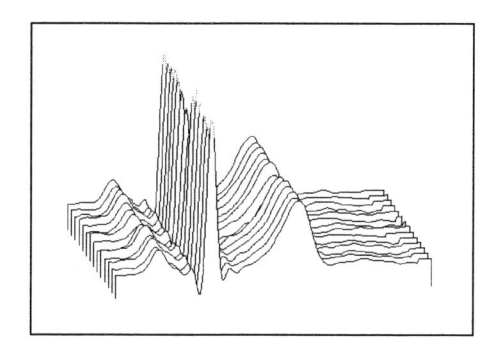

Figure 2. ECG Waterfall Diagram

The relative distances between the peak and trough of the three component complexes to the peak of the R wave and the distance among the complexes were extracted. A total of 15 time intervals were extracted from each heartbeat and normalized by the L'T' distance (Figure 1). The normalized attributes are the inputs to the identification system. Since the expression of the ECG changes with sensor placement, electrode contact quality, and muscle contractions, magnitude attributes were not exploited. After heartbeat alignment, involuntary muscle flexion noise and low signal-to-noise ratio were observed in several individuals. To satisfy the operational requirement for speed, fusion was performed using information from between 1 and 5 heartbeats. The start of the heartbeat block was selected at random.

3. Face

For cooperative individuals, face recognition supports both verification and identification. The application of face recognition to general security and surveillance missions is far more challenging, due to variations in subject pose and lighting conditions. Often, verification is performed in a controlled environment, while identification tasks are not [10].

Researchers have performed experiments for both human cognition [11] and computer processing of face [12]. For computer processing, the face must be detected from its background [13], normalized into a common structure for the verification or identification algorithm [14], features extracted [15], and finally algorithms applied to the data [16, 17]. This study collected facial imagery from cooperative subjects under controlled conditions.

3.1. Data Collection

The data input for the facial recognition algorithm consisted of two frontal images for each of the subjects taken prior to and immediately after the collection of the ECG data. Facial expression was unregulated. The images were collected indoors using uncontrolled diffuse overhead lighting.

Figure 3. Raw input image

The images were collected using a commercially available digital camera. Raw images were 1168×1760×3 pixels and jpeg compressed with minimum loss (Figure 3). The images were acquired so that there were 200-250 pixels between the subject's pupils. The orientation of the subject's head ranged between $\pm 10°$ azimuth and $\pm 5°$ in elevation with respect to the viewing axis.

3.2. Data Transformation via Principal Components Analysis

A number of feature extraction and recognition algorithms have been applied to facial imagery [17-19]. For this project, the data were transformed using the principal components analysis (PCA) [20]. From the eigenvectors, the attributes were compared using the Euclidian distance.

PCA (also known in the literature as eigenfaces) is a statistical method that reduces the dimensionality of an input dataset while retaining the majority of the variance in the dataset. In fact, PCA is optimal in that it uses the projection directions that maximize the variance of the *training* input set. Specifically, given a set of *n* centered (zero mean, unit variance) images $\bar{x}_k$ the covariance matrix

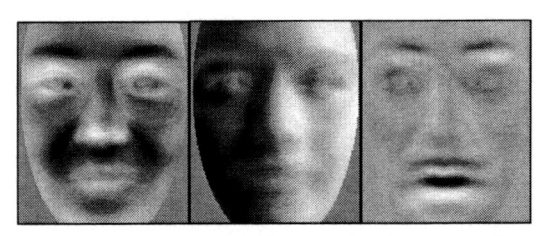

Figure 4. Eigenfaces 1st, 8th, and 15th

$$\Omega = \frac{1}{m}\sum_{i=1}^{n}\bar{x}_i\bar{x}_i^T, \quad (1)$$

is constructed. The projection directions that maximize the variance are the eigenvalues of the covariance matrix that correspond to the largest eigenvalues (i.e. solutions, v, of the eigenvalue problem $\Omega\lambda = \lambda v$ for eigenvalues $\lambda > 0$) (Figure 4). This calculation of the optimal projection directions is the training process for eigenface methods.

Next, a new centered face image, $\bar{w}$, is transformed into eigenspace using the eigenvectors, which represent a set of orthogonal vectors, via the simple operation

$$\hat{w}_i = v_i^T \cdot \bar{w}, \quad i = 1,\ldots,m. \quad (2)$$

Here, the attribute vector $\hat{w}$ is the projected face image and $m<n$ is the number of nonzero eigenvalues. In this experiment, 15 eigenvalues were retained.

This experiment used the two frontal images of each subject. Borrowing terminology from Phillips *et al.* [21], the initial image of each subject were the *probe* set, P, and the post-ECG image of subjects were the *gallery* set, G. The PCA algorithm was trained using a third set of 500 images for the FERET database[1]. First, each FERET image was normalized using standard image processing techniques to try to minimize variations due to illumination, facial pose, resolution (i.e. pixels on face), facial position, etc.

The raw color images were reduced to 256 graylevels. The face was centered in the image and the images were scaled to a standard number of pixels between the eyes. Finally, the background was masked and the spatial information was rectified to 130 x 150 pixels.

These normalized images were then used to train the PCA algorithm using the process described previously. Next, each probe and gallery image was normalized, centered, and projected into eigenspace using Equation 2.

[1] http://www.itl.nist.gov/iad/humanid/feret/feret_master.html

Finally, a similarity matrix, S, was constructed whose elements s_{ij} represent the similarity between the *i*th probe image, p_i, and the *j*th gallery image g_j. Specifically, we used the Euclidean norm

$$s_{ij} = \|p_i - g_j\|_2. \quad (3)$$

The performance of the algorithm was quantified by analyzing the similarity matrix. Specifically, we report the *Rank 1* percentage (i.e. the percentage of times that the diagonal element s_{ii} of S was the smallest value in its row). Here, we labeled images so that p_i and g_i both correspond to the *i*th subject.

4. Fusion

Fusing disparate information sources into a common recognition system has a number of advantages. Fused systems, in principle, perform better than single streams systems [22]. Multichannel or multimodality systems can be more capable handling exceptions and may be tuned to operate in an "either/or" capacity to increase its usability. The disadvantages to multisensor systems are the increased cost, computational load, and sensing requirements.

There are three basic techniques for fusing data: combining attributes, merging decisions, and voting (Figure 5). Combining attributes is a straightforward fusion technique. A single identification algorithm is generated using feature vectors containing all of the attributes [23]. In other words, the two feature vectors are concatenated to form a new features vector, which is fed to the classifier. Combining attribute techniques assume that the identification algorithms can handle a relatively larger number of inputs, possible differences in the input format; i.e, real, nominal, ordinal, etc., and the inputs are registered and synchronized.

Decision fusion occurs when a set of classifiers generates a score from each sensor's attributes. The outputs from the individual classifiers are amalgamated using various weighting parameters based upon their belonging or membership to each output [24]. Decision fusion is ideal for cases when sensor data are of different types or formats and in cases when interaction across modalities are not expected.

Voting fusion is a simplification of decision fusion. With voting each classifier makes a decision, i.e., votes on the assignment for each input record generating a rank. Final assignment for each record is based the majority of output decisions [25]. Voting fusion is simpler than decision fusion since the outputs of the individual classifiers do not require any interclassifier calibration. However, secondary selection rules are necessary when classifiers' votes are split.

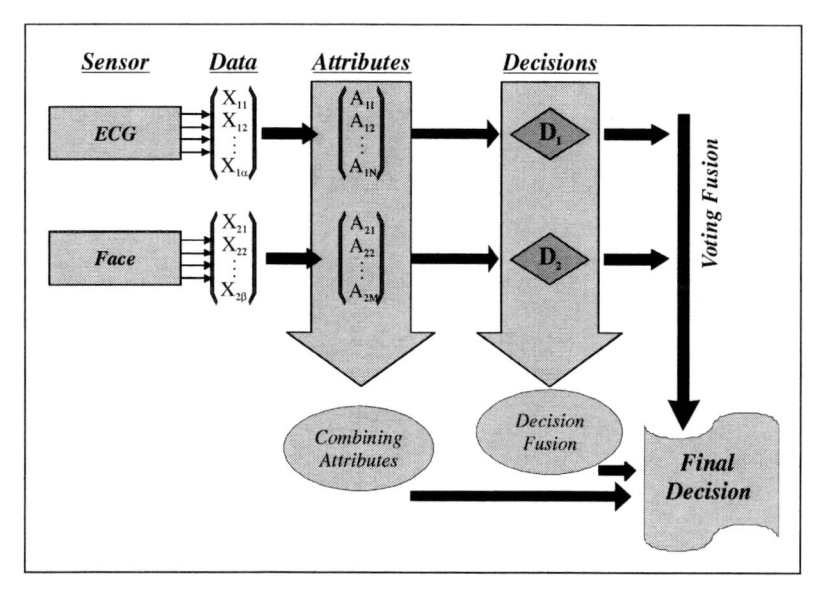

Figure 5. Fusion Types

5. Experimentation

This section describes the experimental procedures and the results. All experiments were performed with the identification paradigm, one-to-many comparisons. The population was 35 individuals. The data consisted of 15 ECG attributes and 15 eigenface attributes. To remove non-fusion influences from the experimentation, the attributes were scaled between [0, 1], the Euclidian distance was used to identify individual in all experiments, and no attribute selection/downsampling was performed. After the data registration, no additional data processing was performed. Confidence intervals are determined using the binomial distribution. Performance is based upon Rank 1 output values.

5.1 Baseline Classifiers

As ECG has not been applied to an operational system, the first question to answer was: "How many heartbeats are required?" We conjecture that an individual's tolerance is 5 seconds for data collection, less is better. The attributes were extracted from the heartbeats individually and averaged. The results show a trend of increasing performance with increasing the number of heartbeats, where no significant difference exists between four and five heartbeats at 54 and 55±11% correctly classified individuals (Figure 6). In previous experiment, a linear discriminant function showed the same trend of heartbeat and performance with four and five heartbeats having 80 and 81±9%, while a large number of heartbeats improved to 89±7% with the dataset.

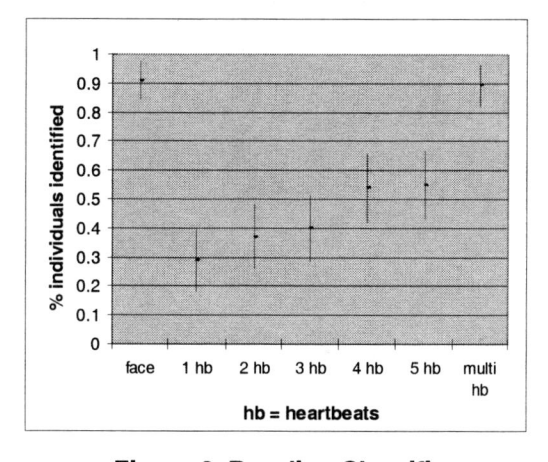

Figure 6. Baseline Classifiers

The face data performed significantly better than the 5 heartbeat ECG data at 91±7%. The remaining experiments are compared to the 5 heartbeat and face performance. The multi-hb experiment on Figure 6 is the result of identifying subjects by applying linear discriminant analysis to approximately 40 heartbeats per subject.

5.2 Combining Attributes

For combining attribute fusion, the entire vector of 30 (15 face and 15 ECG) attributes was used as inputs to the Euclidian distance metric. No additional weighting was performed. The combined attribute identified 99±2% of the subjects (Figure 7). This precision is significant compared to the face at the 0.1 level.

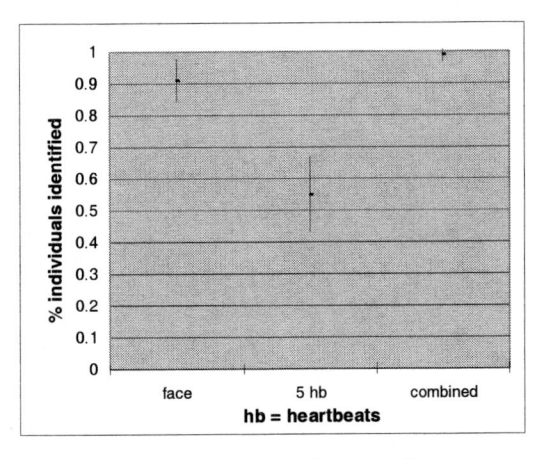

Figure 7. Combining Attributes

5.3 Decision Fusion

With decision fusion, the output Euclidian distances are combined rather than the input attributes used in combining attribute fusion. The output distances were combined using two techniques: multiplying and adding the corresponding values. The results for both multiplication and addition decision fusion were identical at 94±6% and not significantly better than using face alone (Figure 8).

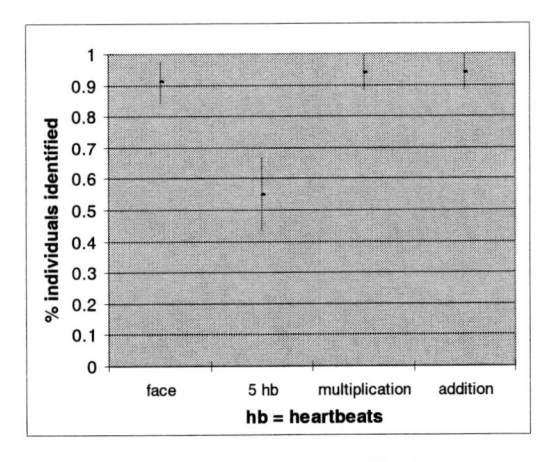

Figure 8. Decision Fusion

5.4 Voting Fusion

For Euclidian distance, all of the subject data are compared to all of the other subject data and the ranks are combined based on the minimum rank among all subjects. With two voting modalities, face and ECG, a likely occurrence is that the vote splits. For split votes, a secondary rule is required, which was to average according to rank. The averaged rank was computed using unweighted and weighted combinations of the baseline experiments. The weightings were based upon the performance of the baseline experiment. In both cases, voting fusion was significantly worse than face recognition alone (Figure 9) at 60 and 66±11% for unweighted and weighted respectively.

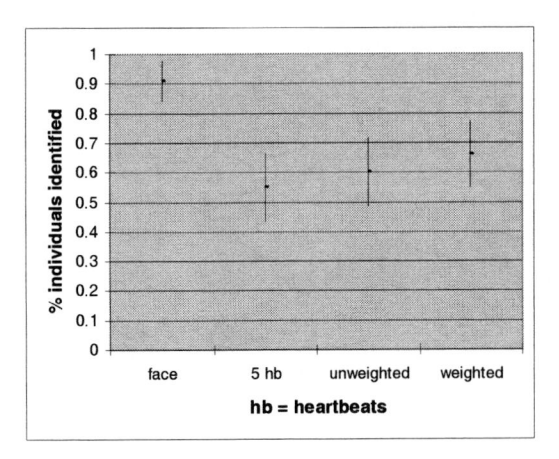

Figure 9. Voting Fusion

6 Discussion

This paper presents the initial efforts to fuse face recognition with a novel biometric based on the ECG. The face recognition procedure employed a standard PCA approach documented in the literature. The ECG analysis employed Euclidian distance to facilitate merging with the face recognition procedure. This approach exhibits substantially lower performance for ECG than other classifiers (see [7]). The result is not surprising since the ECG feature space, subjects are often not linearly separable and more sophisticated classifiers are appropriate.

The fusion analysis demonstrates two important pitfalls of fusion-based methods. First, re-casting ECG processing into a framework suitable for fusion with face sacrifices performance of the single modality. More importantly, the benefits of fusions depend heavily on the fusion method. Only attribute level fusion shows an improvement relative to face recognition alone. Voting fusion shows a substantial loss in performance compare to face alone. The implications are clear: Fusion is not a panacea for poor single-modality performance. Realizing the benefits of fusion depends critically on the approach and implementation.

7. References

[1] D. P. Golden Jr, R. A. Wolthuis, and G. W. Hoffler, "A Spectral Analysis of the Normal Resting Electrocardiogram," *IEEE Transactions on Biomedical Engineering*, vol. BME 20, pp. 366-373, 1973.

[2] M. Malik, "Heart Rate Variability: Standards of Measurement, Physiological Interpretation, and Clinical Use," *Circulation*, vol. 93, pp. 1043-1065, 1996.

[3] L. De Lathauwer, B. De Moor, and J. Vandewalle, "Fetal Electrocardiogram Extraction by Blind Source Subspace Separation," *IEEE Transactions on Biomedical Engineering*, vol. 47, pp. 567-572, 2000.

[4] E. Tatara and A. Cinar, "Interpreting ECG Data by Integrating Statistical and Artificial Intelligence Tools," *IEEE Engineering in Medicine and Biology*, vol. January/February, pp. 36-41, 2002.

[5] J. Carlson, R. Johansson, and B. Olsson, "Classification of Electrocardiographic P-Wave Morphology," *IEEE Transactions on Biomedical Engineering*, vol. 48, pp. 410-405, 2001.

[6] M. Ohlsson, H. Holst, and L. Edenbrandt, "Acute Myocardial Infarction: Analysis of the ECG Using Artificial Neural Networks," presented at Artificial Neural Networks in Medicine and Biology (ANNIMAB-1), Goteborg, Sweden, 2000.

[7] J. M. Irvine, S. A. Israel, M. D. Wiederhold, and B. K. Wiederhold, "A New Biometric: Human Identification from Circulatory Function," presented at Joint Statistical Meetings of the American Statistical Association, San Francisco, 2003.

[8] L. Biel, O. Pettersson, L. Philipson, and P. Wide, "ECG Analysis: A New Approach in Human Identification," *IEEE Transactions on Instrumentation and Measurement*, vol. 50, pp. 808-812, 2001.

[9] J. M. Irvine, B. K. Wiederhold, L. W. Gavshon, S. A. Israel, S. B. McGehee, R. Meyer, and M. D. Wiederhold, "Heart Rate Variability: A New Biometric For Human Identification," presented at International Conference on Artificial Intelligence (IC-AI'2001), Las Vegas, Nevada, 2001.

[10] A. Jain, R. Bolle, and S. Pankanti, "BIOMETRICS Personal Identification in Networked Society." Norwell, Massachusetts: Kluwer Academic Publishers, 1999, pp. 411 pages.

[11] P. Ekman, "Facial Expressions of Emotion: An Old Controversy and New Findings," *Philosophical Transactions of the Royal Society of London B*, vol. 335, pp. 63-69, 1992.

[12] R. W. Frischholz and U. Dieckmann, "BioID: A Multimodal Biometric Identification System," *IEEE Computers Magazine*, vol. February, pp. 64-68, 2000.

[13] O. Ayinde and Y. H. Yang, "Region-Based Face Detection," *Pattern Recognition*, vol. 35, pp. 2095-2107, 2002.

[14] B. Takacs and H. Wechsler, "A Dynamic and Multiresolution Model of Visual Attention and Its Application to Facial Landmark Detection," *Computer Vision and Image Understanding*, vol. 70, pp. 63-73, 1998.

[15] K. M. Lam and H. Yan, "Locating and Extracting the Eye in Human Face Images," *Pattern Recognition*, vol. 29, pp. 771-779, 1996.

[16] K. K. Sung and T. Poggio, "Example-Based Learning for View-Based Human Face Detection," *IEEE Transactions on Pattern Analysis and Machine Intelligence*, vol. 20, pp. 39-51, 1998.

[17] D. Q. Dai and P. C. Yeuen, "Regularized Discriminant Analysis and its Application to Face Recognition," *Pattern Recognition*, vol. 36, pp. 845-847, 2003.

[18] P. Flocchini, F. Gardin, G. Mauri, M. P. Pensini, and P. Stofella, "Combining Image Processing Operators and Neural Networks in a Face Recognition System," *International Journal of Pattern Recognition and Artificial Intelligence*, vol. 6, pp. 447-467, 1992.

[19] P. J. Phillips, "Matching Pursuit Filters Applied to Face Identification," *IEEE Transactions on Image Processing*, vol. 7, pp. 1150-1164, 1998.

[20] M. Turk and A. Pentland, "Eigenfaces for Recognition," *Journal of Cognitive Neuroscience*, vol. 3, pp. 71-86, 1991.

[21] P. J. Phillips, H. Moon, P. J. Rauss, and S. Rizvi, "The FERET Evaluation Methodology for Face Recognition Algorithms," *IEEE Transactions on Pattern Analysis and Machine Intelligence*, vol. 22, 2000.

[22] D. L. Hall, *Mathematical Techniques in Multi-sensor Data Fusion*. Norwood, MA: Artech House, Inc., 1992.

[23] L. I. Kuncheva, "Switching Between Selection and Fusion in Combining Classifiers: An Experiment," *IEEE Transactions on Systems, Man, and Cybernetics - Part B: Cybernetics*, vol. 32, pp. 146-156, 2002.

[24] P. C. Smits, "Multiple Classifier Systems for Supervised Remote Sensing Image Classification Based on Dynamic Classifier Selection," *IEEE Transactions on Geoscience and Remote Sensing*, vol. 40, pp. 801-813, 2002.

[25] J. Kittler and F. M. Alkoot, "Sum Versus Vote Fusion in Multiple Classifier Systems," *IEEE Transactions on Pattern Analysis and Machine Intelligence*, vol. 25, pp. 110-115, 2003.

Image Formation Through Walls Using a Distributed Radar Sensor Array

Allan R. Hunt

AKELA, Inc., 5276 Hollister Avenue, Suite 263, Santa Barbara, CA 93111
ahunt@akelainc.com

ABSTRACT

Through the wall surveillance is a difficult but important problem for both law enforcement and military personnel. Getting information on both the internal features of a structure and the location of people inside improves the operational effectiveness in search and rescue, hostage, and barricade situations. However, the electromagnetic properties of walls constrain the choices available as sensor candidates.

We have demonstrated that a high range resolution radar operating between 450 MHz and 2 GHz can be used with a fixed linear array of antennas to produce images and detect motion through both interior and exterior walls. While the experimental results are good, it has been shown that the linear array causes signal processing artifacts that appear as ghosts in the resultant images. By moving toward a sensor concept where the antennas in the array are randomly spaced, the effect of ghost images can be reduced and operational and performance benefits gained.

1. Introduction

There are many situations in both peace keeping and law enforcement operations where there is a need to not only determine if there is someone inside a building structure but also to know where they are. These situations arise during searches for suspects, hostage and barricade incidents, and tactical surveillance. While in many cases the objective is to make contact with a suspect to defuse a potentially violent situation, not all suspects are cooperative.

This often leads to the necessity of entering a building in order to take a suspect into custody. Unfortunately, most operations conclude with a physical search with personnel under a great deal of stress and subject to a high possibility of physical harm. Military operations in urban terrain face this same set of issues, but greatly magnified by the scope of operations and the presence of unarmed, noncombatant, civilians. Taking away the ability of suspects to hide, and providing command elements with better information, changes the operational tactics used, reducing the risk and increasing the probability that an operation will successfully conclude without casualties.

The technology available to military and law enforcement personnel to assist them in securing a building is rapidly changing. A new generation of techniques is being developed that will enhance the capability to look into buildings at standoff distances and build a picture of the tactical situation. Among those is AKELA's high range resolution radar and scanned antenna array technique.

2. Technical issues

Sensors that are designed to create images of the interior of an object most often use tomographic image reconstruction. While the type of energy used to probe the object varies, the basic method of reconstructing an image of the inside of the object consists of collecting data over a range of orientations and using backward propagation algorithms to remove ambiguities in the location of objects that scatter the probing radiation. In this way, a picture of the inside of the object showing the relative location of scattering objects is formed.

In order to create an image of the interior of an object, the illuminating radiation must be able to pass through the object with little attenuation. For through the wall surveillance systems the material properties of the wall determine the degree to which a system will be successful. The major considerations are the absorption and refraction losses for the penetrating radiation.

Data taken by Frazier[1] show that most building materials are relatively transparent from 250 MHz to 3 GHz. Figure 1 is based on Frazier's data and shows the approximate one way transmission loss through specific building materials as a function of frequency. As can be seen in the graph, because the attenuation through concrete increases monotonically, a system that uses frequencies below 2 GHz has the best chance of seeing through walls. Above 3 GHz, the attenuation in all the materials begins to increase rapidly. This makes higher frequency imaging methods unsuitable for through the wall surveillance.

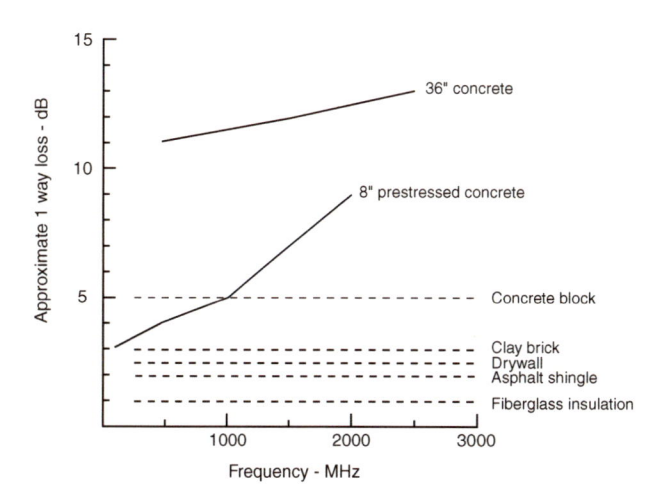

Figure 1. Attenuation of common building materials[1].

The frequency band of interest for through the wall surveillance is very wide in comparison to that required for traditional radar systems, spanning a decade in frequency. Even ultra wide band radars used by the U.S. military for foliage penetration span less than two octaves[2]. Either frequency or time domain techniques can be used to generate this wide band of frequencies.

To achieve two dimensional image reconstruction requires being able to resolve scattering objects in both the range and cross range directions. The methods used vary, depending on the method of illumination and the nature of the radiation. For a stepped frequency waveform, range resolution is determined by the bandwidth of the waveform and follows the relation $\Delta R = c/2n\Delta f$, where c is the speed of light, n the number of frequency steps in the waveform, and Δf is the frequency step size. As with pulsed radar waveforms, there is range ambiguity associated with a stepped frequency waveform. The unambiguous range limit $R_u = c/2\Delta f$.

Resolution in the cross range direction can only be achieved by varying the illumination over the field of view of the sensor system. At low frequencies, directional antennas become too large to be practical. The common practice in this case is to move the radar taking data at various intervals, and then to synthesize an antenna aperture to obtain crossrange resolution.

For most through the wall surveillance situations, while this type of operation is possible, it is operationally less desirable, since there is not always easy access for a vehicle mounted system. In addition, detecting individuals moving inside a building from a moving platform, as well as doing image reconstruction, makes the processing effort more difficult and increases the cost of the system.

Rather than move the radar, it is possible to keep the radar at a single location and synthesize an aperture from an array of antennas arranged as a phased array with a single receiver, or as a synthetic array with multiple receivers. Figure 2 shows a comparison of the antenna patterns of a single antenna, a four element phased array, and the same four element array scanned from end to end as a synthetic array. The array is made up of antennas with patterns that are the same as that of the single antenna. The decrease in beamwidth achieved with the array techniques is noticeable, and it improves the ability of the system to resolve scatterers in the cross range direction.

While range resolution is constant, cross range resolution degrades with distance. This is because the width of the antenna beam naturally diverges with distance. Cross range resolution is a function of the wavelength at the lowest operating frequency of the radar, the length of the physical antenna aperture, and the distance to the target being imaged. Figure 3 shows a set of charts that illustrate the system dependence of cross range resolution. The cross range resolution shown in the figure is a measure of how close two targets can be to one another and still be resolved as two targets by the radar.

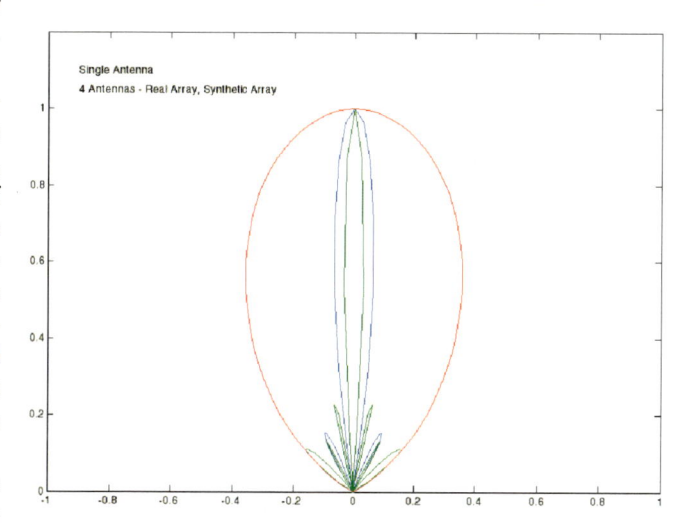

Figure 2. Scanning a multiple element array improves cross range resolution.

3. Experimental hardware and results

AKELA has demonstrated imaging and motion detection through walls using a stepped frequency radar and a linear antenna array. This demonstration was done with the support of the National Institute of Justice and the Air Force Research Laboratory under contract F30602-00-C-0205 using the imaging radar shown in Figure 4. The antenna array is 2.2 m wide when fully extended and collapses

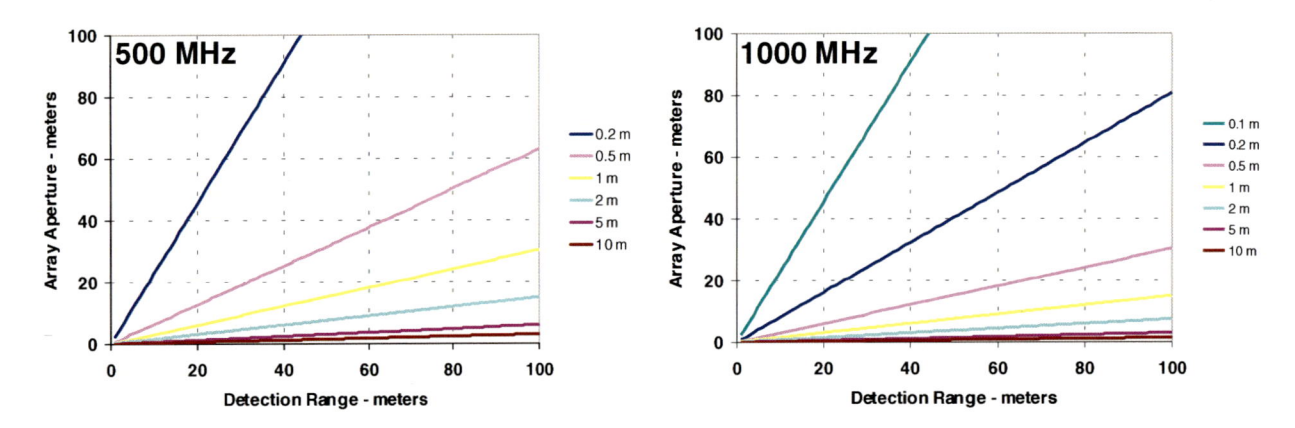

Figure 3. Cross range resolution depends on system operating parameters.

to a size approximately 16" wide, 25" long, and 14" tall. The radar weighs less than 20 pounds, has a power output of 50 mW, and operates on battery power for up to 8 hours. The radar design is CW, bistatic, and stepped frequency operating over the range of 450 MHz to 2 GHz.

The operating range was selected on the basis of both technical and operational considerations. Low frequency cutoff was determined primarily by the size of the antenna needed to radiate efficiently at that frequency. High frequency cutoff was determined primarily by the availability of modestly priced electronic components.

Data is collected by scanning the elements of the array one antenna pair at a time. One antenna is used for transmitting while the other receives. With 4 antennas we get 12 independent combinations. Image reconstruction is accomplished by the Fourier transform method. Taking the Fou-

Figure 4. Experimental through the wall imaging radar system.

rier transform of the stepped frequency data for an individual transmit/receive antenna pair creates a range profile for all of the scatterers in the antenna field of view. The bistatic range to each pixel in the image map is used to index into the range profile to find the value of the in phase and quadrature components of the scattered field from that range. For a different antenna pair, the bistatic range to the same pixel will be different. The values from all of the antenna pairs from the scanned array are summed for each pixel in the image map. Where there are objects in the image that result in scattering, the individual observations from the antennas will be in phase and sum to a large value. Where there are no objects, the individual observations will be out of phase and tend to sum toward zero. The magnitude of the summation depends on the radar cross section of the scattering object and the distance from the antenna array. Figure 5 shows a schematic view of the reconstruction of a single point in the image map for a 4 element array with the same dimensions as the experimental radar.

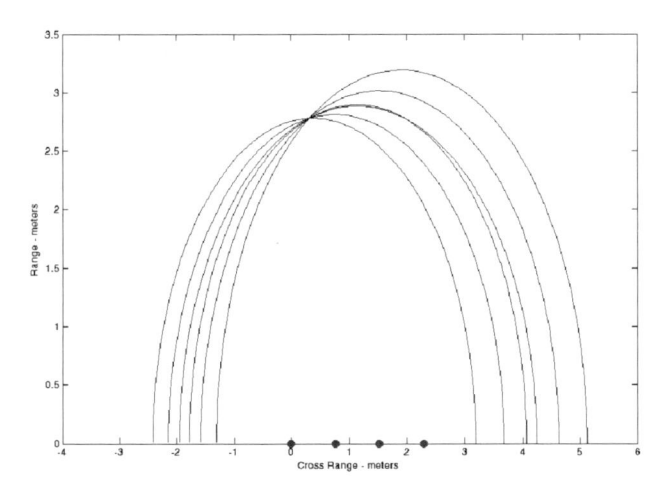

Figure 5. Reconstruction of a point in the image map.

This radar was used to explore the technical and operational issues associated with through-the-wall sensor systems by performing imaging and motion detection experiments under a variety of conditions. Figure 6 shows an example image from the experimental testing. In the image shown, a set of three 2.4 m x 2.4 m (8 ft x 8 ft) stud walls covered with drywall were placed in an open ended room configuration 5 m in front of the imaging radar. Resolution of the image is good enough to see the individual studs in the closest walls. Other tests, including those on a double wide trailer being used as an administrative area and a conference room with 12" thick walls of poured, steel reinforced concrete, also showed good results.

4. Limitations

This testing showed some of the limitations associated with our technique. The most notable issue from an imaging point of view is the presence of ghost images. This is related to the use of a linear array with a fixed distance between antennas. Figure 7 shows this limitation. The image to the left in the figure is of one of the stud walls just described. The wall is parallel to the boresite of the imaging radar array and lined up approximately with the left edge of the array. Each of the studs is clearly evident in the image.

However, note that there are also three other similar patterns in the image. We first believed that these patterns were caused by grating lobe effects that are well known for systems that use arrays of antennas and narrower bands of frequencies. A simulation of the image reconstruction technique was performed and showed that the ghosts are associated only with the geometry of the linear array and the spacing of the studs in the wall. The results of this simulation are shown to right in the figure. There are ghost intersections in the same locations as those that show up in the experimental data and there are no frequency dependent effects.

One method of reducing the effect of ghosts is to use additional processing within individual images. A median filter can be used to apply a weighting function that varies inversely as the standard deviation of the individual antenna observations at pixels associated with potential targets. Observations for direct path scatterers tend to have very small standard deviations while those for ghosts have a much wider variation. The median filter is not a linear algorithm and is relatively complicated to implement for complex value images.

An easier method is to use a random spacing for the array of antennas. The image reconstruction algorithms do not require an even spacing. Figure 8 shows an image reconstruction simulation that was performed to demonstrate the effect of random spacing within an array. The top left image in the figure shows the regularly spaced array of Figure 7. The remainder of the images show different random locations of the four element array and the resulting reconstructions. While the three random array patterns show good results, it is important to note that not all random patterns produce good results.

The best solution would be to allow the antennas to move periodically thus providing varying views of the image space and a variable aperture that will also improve cross range resolution. In this type of scheme it is necessary to be able to determine the positions of the individual antennas in order for the image reconstruction to be successful. In a bistatic system, the direct path signal between the transmitter and receiver is the strongest and can be used to determine the distance between antennas.

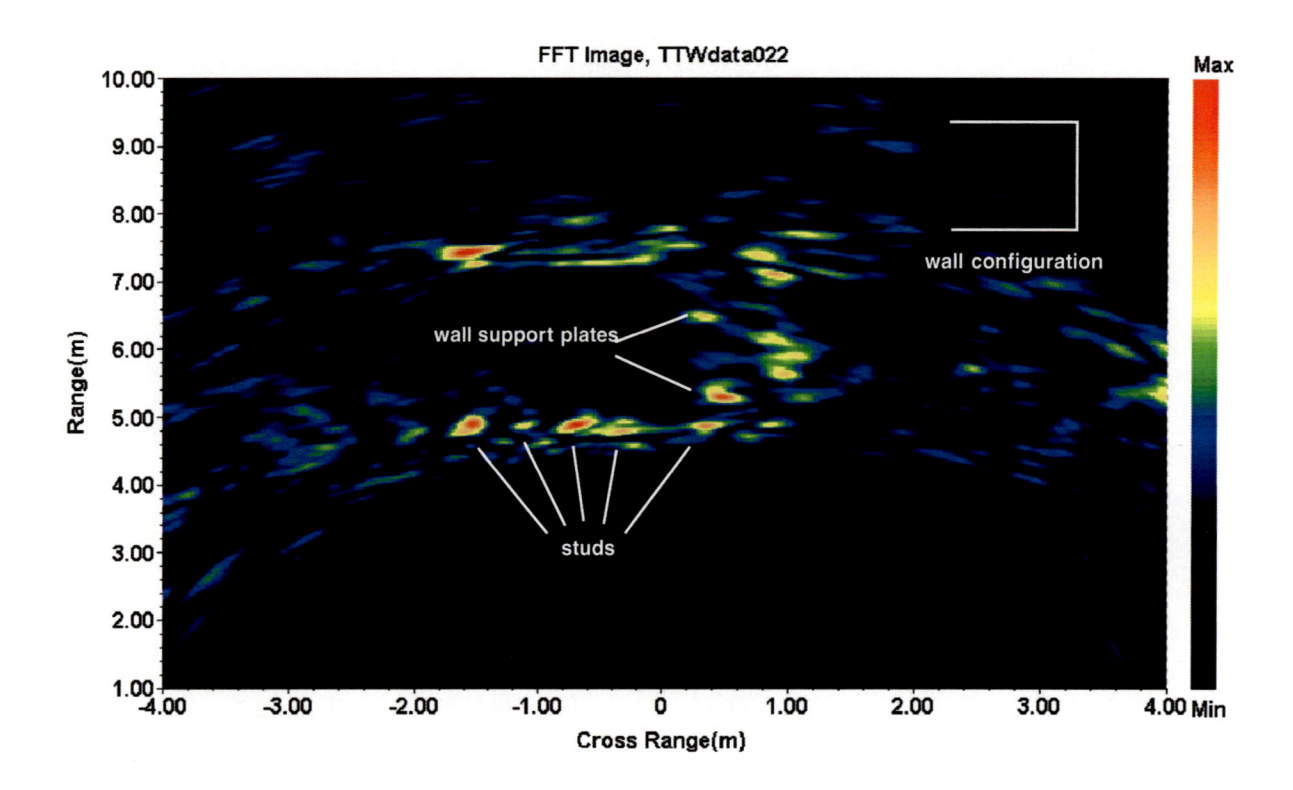

Figure 6. Experimental data.

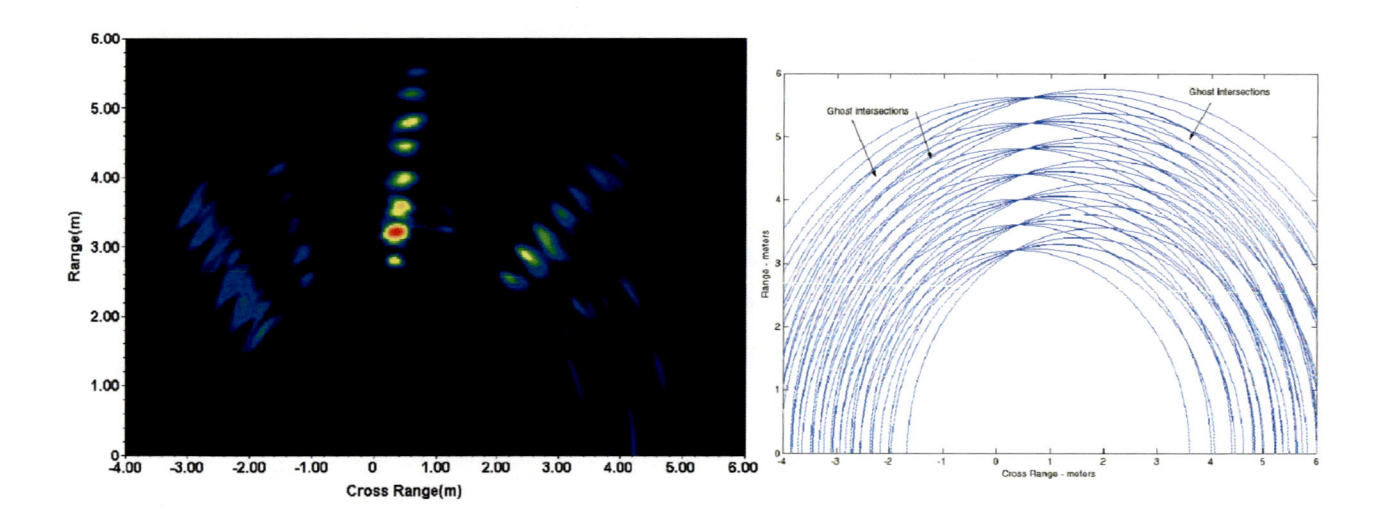

Figure 7. Image ghosts are due to regular spacing of antennas and wall studs.

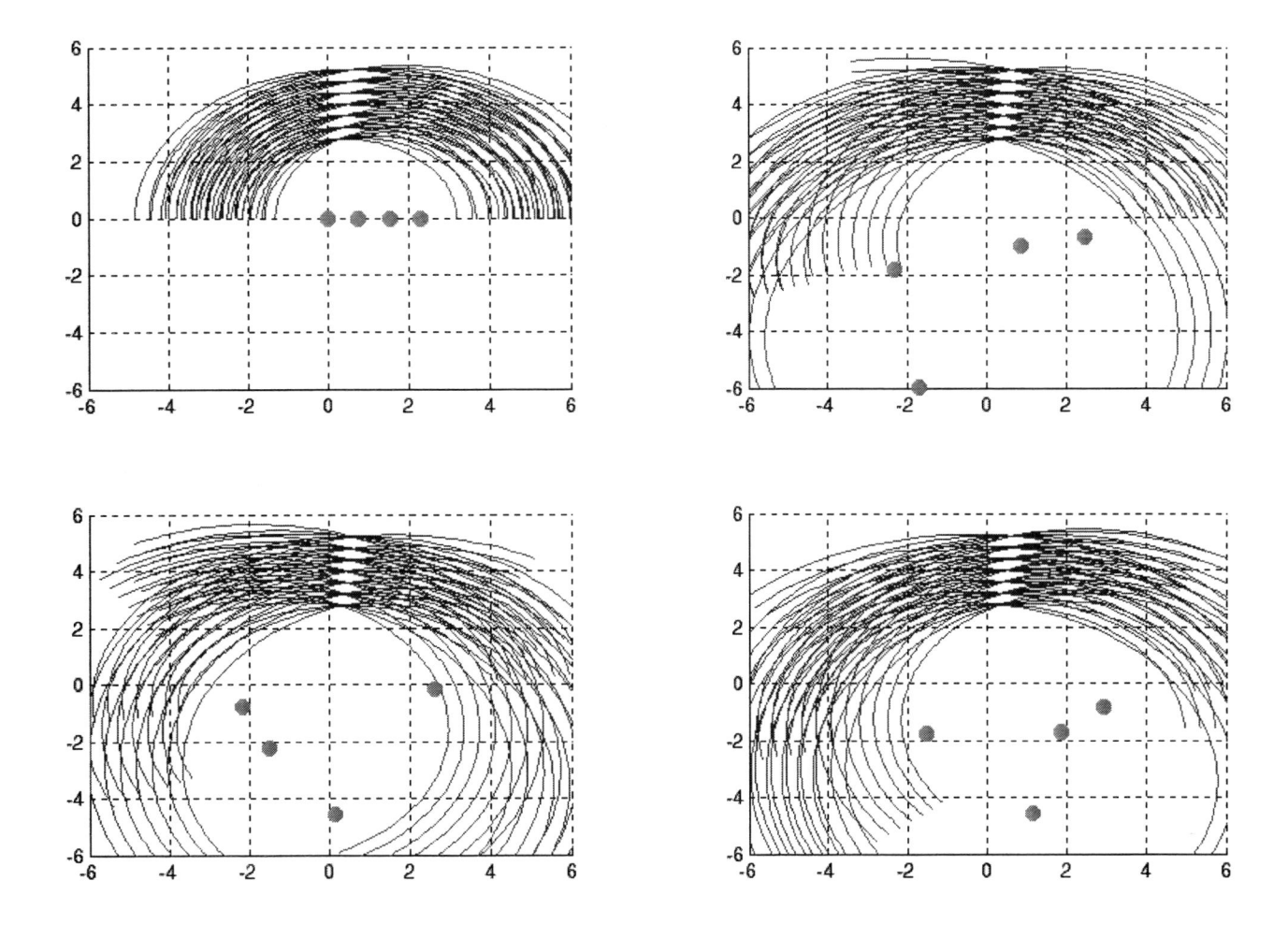

Figure 8. Random placement of antennas reduces the effect of ghost images.

5.0 Conclusion

The physics and technology associated with through the wall imaging are well understood. Our experimental imaging system has demonstrated with real data that there are no fundamental principles that limit success. Commercial technology exists to implement a robust system. While we have demonstrated good results with a system using a fixed linear antenna array, it is clear that performance can be improved by using an array with randomly spaced antennas.

Implementing a system with randomly spaced antennas imposes an additional processing burden associated with using sensor data to perform geolocation. Allowing sensor movement requires additional attention to timing and control. However, the operational flexibility gained to place antennas wherever desired, the improvement in cross range resolution from a variable aperture, and the increased failure tolerance of such a system are attractive benefits.

This type of system would allow military, peacekeeping, and law enforcement personnel to gain a situational awareness advantage by denying the adversary the use of cover.

References

[1] L. Frazier, "MDR for Law Enforcement", IEEE Potentials, Vol. 16, No. 5, pp. 23 - 26, 1998.

[2] M. Soumekh, D. A. Nobles, M. C. Wicks, and G. J. Genello, "Signal Processing of Wide Bandwidth and Wide Beamwidth P-3 SAR Data, IEEE Trans. on Aerospace and Electronics Systems, Vol. 37, No. 4, pp. 1122 - 1140, 2001.

Access Control System with High Level Security Using Fingerprints

Younhee Gil, Dosung Ahn, Sungbum Pan, Yongwha Chung[1]
Information Security Research Division
Electronics and Telecommunications Research Institute
{yhgil, dosung, sbpan}@etri.re.kr
[1] *Dept. of Computer and Information Science*
Korea University
ychungy@korea.ac.kr

Abstract

Biometric based applications guarantee for resolving numerous security hazards. As a method of preserving of privacy and the security of sensitive information, biometrics has been studied and used for the past few decades. Fingerprint is one of the most widely used biometrics. A number of fingerprint verification approaches have been proposed until now. However, fingerprint images acquired using current fingerprint input devices that have small field of view are from just very limited areas of whole fingertips. Therefore, essential information required to distinguish fingerprints could be missed, or extracted falsely. The limited and somewhat distorted information are detected from them, which might reduce the accuracy of fingerprint verification systems. In the systems that verify the identity of two fingerprints using fingerprint features, it is critical to extract the correct feature information. In order to deal with these problems, compensation of imperfect information can be performed using multiple impressions of enrollee's fingerprints.

In this paper, additional three fingerprint images are used in enrollment phase of fingerprint verification system. Our experiments using FVC 2002 databases show that the enrollment using multiple impressions improves the performance of the whole fingerprint verification system.

1. Introduction

Traditionally, verified users have gained access to their property or service via dozens of PIN/password, smart cards and so on. However, these knowledge based, token based security methods have crucial weakness that can be lost, stolen, or forgotten. In recent years, there is an increasing trend of using biometrics. X9.84 [1] standard defines terminology of biometrics as 'A measurable biological or behavioral characteristic, which reliably distinguishes one person from another, used to recognize the identity, or verify the claimed identity, of an enrollee'. The fingerprint is one of widely used biometrics satisfying uniqueness and permanency [2]. Thus a number of fingerprint verification approaches have been proposed until now. Jain et al. [3] presented a minutiae-based verification, which aligns minutiae using Hough transform and performs minutiae matching by bounding box. Ross et al. [5] proposed hybrid matching method of local-based matching and global-based matching to enhance the performance. Pan et al. proposed an alignment algorithm using limited processing power and memory space to be executed in a smart card, and showed the possibility of match-on-card [4]. In the match-on-card system, as entire verification operation is executed on the smart card, the system doesn't have to maintain central database and the biometric template is prevented from being streamed out of the smart card. Therefore, it can prevent biometric templates from being misused by the fraud.

Although it is true that technical improvement has been achieved, there still exist challenging problems relating to the quality of fingerprint images and reliability of extracted minutiae. Most of input devices get fingerprint images having fingerprints being pressed on it not rolled, as a result, the area of fingerprint images can not help being very limited. Fingerprint mosaicking [6] uses multiple fingerprint images to generate template, augmenting minutiae sets from plural fingerprint images on enrollment stage. But, it does not check the reliability of each fingerprint images.

We proposed enrollment using multiple fingerprint images to extend enrolled fingerprint image and also guarantee the reliability of each fingerprint image. And we have tested our algorithm on the first FVC 2002 database [7,8].

This paper is organized as follows. Section 2 describes fingerprint verification system and the enrollment using plural fingerprints briefly. Section 3 explains proposed methods. The experimental results are shown in Section 4. Finally, Section 5 contains conclusion.

2. User Verification Using Fingerprint

It is widely known that the fingerprint is unique, and invariant with aging, which implies that user authentication can be relied on the comparing two fingerprints [2]. In general, a professional fingerprint examiner relies on details of ridge structures of the fingerprint in order to make fingerprint identifications. And the structural features are composed of the points where ridges end or bifurcate, that are called minutiae. Figure 1 shows small part of an enlarged fingerprint image and two types of minutiae pointed by square marker and circle marker. The minutia marked by square is bifurcation, and that by circle is ending point, and the branch from minutia represents the direction of the minutiae. Usually, each minutia is described by the position in the coordinate, the direction it flows and the type, whether it is ridge ending or bifurcation.

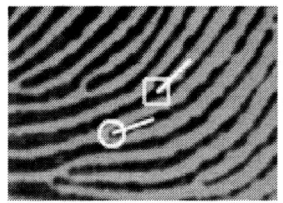

Figure 1: Fingerprint minutiae

Figure 2 presents a fingerprint verification system, which consists of two phases: enrollment and verification. In the off-line enrollment phase, at first, the fingerprint image of an enrollee is acquired and preprocessed. Then, the minutiae are extracted from the raw image and stored as enrolled template. And in the on-line verification phase, it reads the fingerprint from a claimer, and detects the minutiae information through the same procedure as in the enrollment phase. Then, it estimates the similarity between the enrolled minutiae and the input minutiae.

Image preprocessing refers to the refinement of the fingerprint image against the image distortion occurred during the image acquisition and transmission. Minutiae extraction refers to the detection of features in the fingerprint image and finding out of their information, i.e., position, direction and type

Based on the minutiae, the claimed fingerprint is compared with the enrolled fingerprint. Generic minutiae matching is composed of alignment stage and matching stage. In order to match two fingerprints captured with unknown direction and position, the differences of direction and position between two fingerprints should be evaluated, and alignment between them needs to be preceded. In the alignment stage, transformations such as translation and rotation between two fingerprints are estimated, and two minutiae sets are aligned according to the estimated alignment parameters. If the alignment procedure is performed accurately, the remaining matching stage is referred to point matching simply. In matching stage, two minutiae are compared based on their position, direction, and type. Then, a matching score is computed.

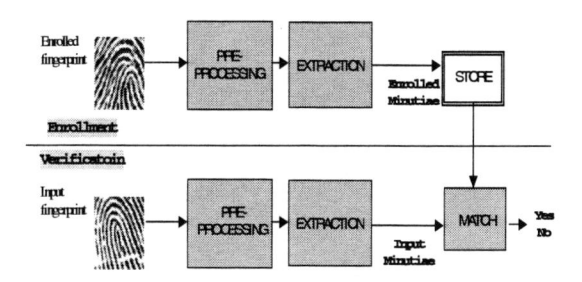

Figure 2: User authentication system using fingerprint

2.1. Minutiae Extraction

Our minutiae extraction algorithm mainly consists of four components: generation of direction map, binarization of fingerprint image, detection of minutiae, and removal of false minutiae.

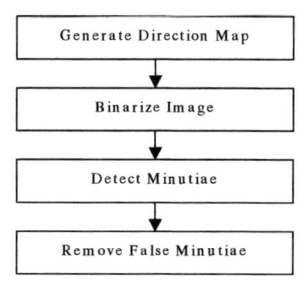

Figure 3: Minutiae Extraction

Besides these steps, it is critical to analyze the image and determine the areas that are degraded and likely to cause problem because the image quality of a fingerprint may vary. Several characteristics can be measured that convey information regarding the quality of localized regions in the image. These include detecting regions of low contrast and determining directional flow of ridges. Using this information, the unstable areas in the image where minutiae detection is unreliable can be distinguished.

Generation of Direction Map. One of the fundamental steps in minutiae extraction is deriving a directional ridge flow map. The purpose of this map is to represent areas of the image with sufficient ridge structure. Well-formed and clearly visible ridges are essential to reliably detecting minutiae. In addition, the direction map records the general direction of the ridges as they flow across the image. The directional information are estimated based on the 8 8 pixel sized windows and their range is 0~15. And background that has no variation of intensity is set as -1. This information can be used to segment images.

Binarization of Image. As our minutiae detection algorithm is working on bi-level image, every pixel in the grayscale input image must be binarized. A pixel is assigned as a binary value based on the ridge flow direction associated with the block the pixel is within. In order to determine whether current pixel should be set to black or white, the pixel intensities of 7 9 pixel grid rotated according to the orientation of it, which surround the current pixel, are analyzed. Grayscale pixel intensities are accumulated along each rotated row in the grid, forming a vector of row sums. The binary value to be assigned to the center pixel is determined by multiplying the center row sum by the number of rows in the grid and comparing this value to the accumulated grayscale intensities within the entire grid. If the multiplied center row sum is lower than the total intensity of the grid, the center pixel is set to black. Otherwise, it is set to white.

Detection of Minutiae and Removal of False Minutiae. Before minutiae are detected, the binarized image should be thinned, and the detection step scans the thinned image with some kernels that can detect minutiae. After detection of minutiae, candidate minutiae points are detected. Usually, many false minutiae are included in the candidate list, therefore, removal of them are necessary to increase the performance of the fingerprint verification system. The step includes removing islands, lakes, holes, minutiae in regions of poor image quality, hooks, overlaps, minutiae that are too wide, and minutiae that are too narrow. The more details about minutiae extraction can be found in [2].

2.2. Enrollment with Plural Fingerprint Images

As automatic fingerprint identification and authentication systems rely on representing the two most prominent minutiae, i.e., bifurcation and ridge ending, a reliable minutiae extraction algorithm is critical to the performance of the system. However, although minutiae are detected through not only extraction process but also false minutiae removal process, it is still possible to detect false minutiae and miss true ones. These faults can cause matching failure. In particular, if they occur during enrollment phase and are stored as enrolled template, it will be serious problem, because they will affect the matching phase continuously. In the other word, if the system ensures there are neither false minutiae nor missed minutiae, its reliability will be increased.

We suggested using plural fingerprint images on the enrollment phase to discard the false minutiae and compensate the missed minutiae. The system that adopts the enrollment using multiple fingerprint images is shown in figure 4. As this figure presents, enrolled minutiae are generated from several genuine fingerprint images.

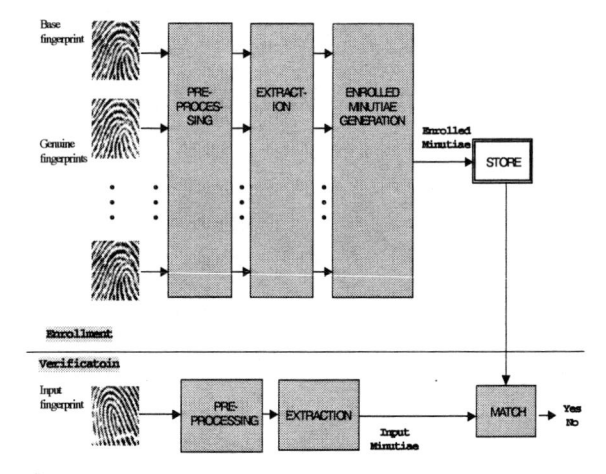

Figure 4: User Authentication system that adopts the enrollment using plural fingerprint images

2.3. Minutiae Matching Algorithm

As mentioned before, minutiae matching is composed of alignment stage and matching stage. In order to make the explanation easier, we define the notation of two minutiae sets extracted from enrolled and claimed fingerprint images two minutiae sets as P and Q respectively.

$$\begin{aligned} P &= \{(p_x^1, p_y^1, \alpha^1), \ldots, (p_x^P, p_y^P, \alpha^P)\} \\ Q &= \{(q_x^1, q_y^1, \beta^1), \ldots, (q_x^Q, q_y^Q, \beta^Q)\} \end{aligned} \quad (1)$$

where (p_x^i, p_y^i, α^i) and (q_x^j, q_y^j, β^j) are the three features (spatial position and direction) associated with the *i*th and *j*th minutia in the set P and Q respectively, and *P* and *Q* are the number of elements in the P and Q set.

The alignment stage gets two minutiae sets, P and Q, as input and estimates how their differences of position and orientation were when the two fingerprints were captured. And then, transforms minutiae set Q for the claimed fingerprint to have same locality as the enrolled fingerprint according to the estimated difference. We denote aligned minutiae set Q as Q^a. For the purpose of proper alignment, the estimation of the rotation and translation parameters must precede. In order to estimate transformation parameters, we find out $(\Delta x, \Delta y)$ and $\Delta \theta$ satisfying formula (2) according to the formula (3).

$$F_{\theta, \Delta x, \Delta y}((q_x, q_y, \beta)^T) = (p_x, p_y, \alpha)^T \quad (2)$$

$$F_{\theta, \Delta x, \Delta y}\begin{pmatrix} x \\ y \\ \theta \end{pmatrix} = \begin{pmatrix} \cos\Delta\theta & \sin\Delta\theta & 0 \\ -\sin\Delta\theta & \cos\Delta\theta & 0 \\ 0 & 0 & 1 \end{pmatrix}\begin{pmatrix} x \\ y \\ \theta \end{pmatrix} + \begin{pmatrix} \Delta x \\ \Delta y \\ \Delta \theta \end{pmatrix} \quad (3)$$

where ($\Delta x, \Delta y$) and $\Delta \theta$ are the translation and rotation parameters; $(p_x, p_y, \alpha)^T$ represents the enrolled minutiae and $(q_x, q_y, \beta)^T$ represents the claimed minutiae.

The evaluated transformation parameters $(\Delta x, \Delta y, \Delta \theta)^T$ are used to align claimed minutiae by

$$\begin{pmatrix} q_x^a \\ q_y^a \\ \beta^a \end{pmatrix} = \begin{pmatrix} \cos\Delta\theta & \sin\Delta\theta & 0 \\ -\sin\Delta\theta & \cos\Delta\theta & 0 \\ 0 & 0 & 1 \end{pmatrix}\begin{pmatrix} q_x \\ q_y \\ \beta \end{pmatrix} + \begin{pmatrix} \Delta x \\ \Delta y \\ \Delta \theta \end{pmatrix} \quad (4)$$

where $(q_x^a, q_y^a, \beta^a)^T$ is the aligned of the claimed minutiae.

After alignment step, the comparison of the information of two minutiae sets, P and Q^a, is accomplished by point pattern matching in the polar coordinate system with respect to the center of foreground. Such a point matching can be accomplished by placing bounding box [3] around enrolled minutiae. When an aligned minutia is placed within the bounding box, the minutia is considered as a candidate of the mated one with the enrolled minutiae. And two additional conditions will be checked: whether the difference between their directions is below predetermined tolerance, and whether their types are the same. Their results affect the matching score. It depends on the size of bound box that how many candidates match. The smaller the size is, the stricter matching stage gets and it can be happened that the rate of falsely non matching is increased, and the opposite case is the same way likewise. It is possible that there is more than one candidate for one enrolled minutia. In this case, the candidate with the largest score is selected as mated minutiae. Figure 5 shows an example of mating of two minutiae. Assume that m_1, m_2 are enrolled minutiae and n_1, n_2 are input minutiae to be mated and the kinds of four minutiae are same. The direction of each minutia is marked as branch from minutia, and they are assumed to be similar enough so that their difference is within the tolerance. Then, consider the mating result. In this case, it is reasonable that n_1 is mated with m_1 and n_2 with m_2. Although both n_1 and n_2 are candidates of the mated minutiae with m_2, n_2 must be regarded as mated minutia with m_2 because n_2 is nearer to m_2 than n_1. Also, correlation of n_1 with m_1 should be considered. Even if n_1 is a mated candidate of not only m_1 but also m_2 and it is nearer to m_2 than m_1, it should be mated with m_2, as m_2 has been mated with n_1 already.

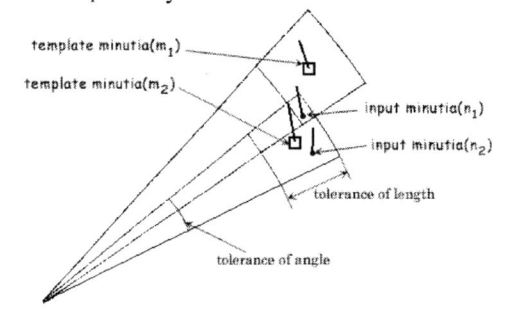

Figure 5: Mating of minutiae

3. Multiple Fingerprint Images and Enhanced Matching Method

Usually, even superior extraction process including removal of false minutiae have some false minutiae remained still. And it can miss the true ones. The performance of fingerprint verification is influenced by both of them. Figure 6 is enlarged part of fingerprint images and shows some extracted minutiae. In Figure 6 (a), examples of false minutiae are presented being pointed out with black arrows. They are neither the bifurcation nor the ending of ridges, are just points on the middle of ridges. They should not have been detected. These are caused by couple of reasons such as failure in extraction stage or noise of fingerprint image itself. However, these can be eliminated based on the fact that they are temporal and no false minutia on the same position in one image as another fingerprint image may merely be detected. Therefore, plural fingerprint images are used on the enrollment phase in order to discard the false minutiae.

(a) (b)

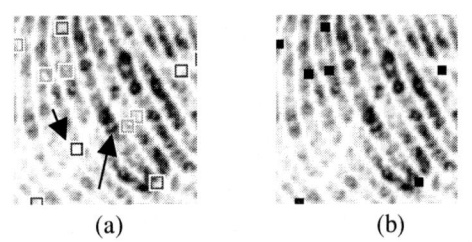

Figure 6: Extracted minutiae including false minutiae superimposed on the enlarged fingerprint image and discarded result of false minutiae

In the enrollment phase using multiple impressions, at first, one fingerprint image is acquired and set as base image, and minutiae from it are extracted. Then after segmentation of image, find out the center of foreground, which will be the reference point of polar coordinate system. And then, minutiae set from base fingerprint image are transformed into polar coordinate system. Once finishing above processes to the base image, a few genuine fingerprint impressions are acquired. And minutiae from each fingerprint image are extracted, and each minutiae set is aligned with base fingerprint image. Then, they are converted into polar coordinate system with respect to the center of base image. Now, each minutia from one fingerprint image is examined if it can be mated with the minutia from the other fingerprint image. To do this, it is required to compute similarity between two minutiae. The minutia is regarded as false minutia if it has been mated with no minutia during whole examinations, and discarded. Figure 6 (b) shows the false minutiae have been discarded through our false minutiae discard step. The simple flowchart of false minutiae discard algorithm is shown in Figure 7.

Another factor reducing the accuracy of the verification is limited contact area of fingerprint scanner. As input device is getting smaller, the size of window acquiring image has been shrunk. And owing to the tiny window, the verification system use only partial regions of fingerprint images. Therefore, two identical fingerprint images can be misjudged they are from different fingerprints if two images are scanned from the opposite parts of the fingertip. Besides the extreme case like this, when the overlapped area of two images is small, it causes low matching score.

In order to compensate one minutiae set from the identical fingerprint images that have little common area, padding method of minutiae in non-overlapped area is used. This method first measures the overlapped area of two fingerprint images, and then finds out minutiae pairs in the area. To estimate the intersected area, segmentation of two images should precede. Next, it estimates the ratio of minutiae pairs to total enrolled minutiae. It regards two fingerprint images as ones from the same finger when the ratio is over the predetermined threshold. And in the case when two minutiae sets are determined to be identical, it appends the enrolled minutiae in the non-overlapped area to the claimed minutiae set. Then more mated pairs can be found and it will improve matching performance.

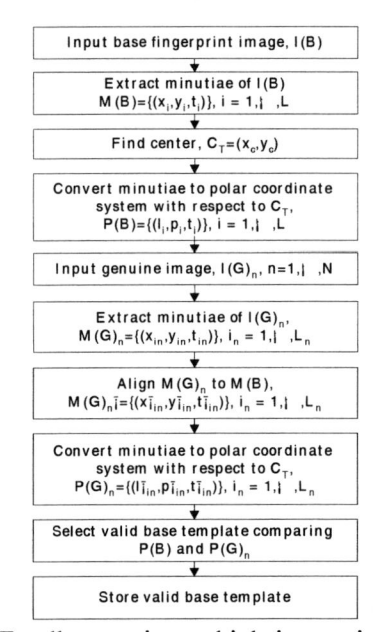

```
Input base fingerprint image, I(B)
        ↓
Extract minutiae of I(B)
M(B)={(x_i,y_i,t_i)}, i = 1,…,L
        ↓
Find center, C_T=(x_c,y_c)
        ↓
Convert minutiae to polar coordinate
system with respect to C_T,
P(B)={(l_i,p_i,t_i)}, i = 1,…,L
        ↓
Input genuine image, I(G)_n, n=1,…,N
        ↓
Extract minutiae of I(G)_n,
M(G)_n={(x_in,y_in,t_in)}, i_n = 1,…,L_n
        ↓
Align M(G)_n to M(B),
M(G)_n'={(x'_in,y'_in,t'_in)}, i_n = 1,…,L_n
        ↓
Convert minutiae to polar coordinate
system with respect to C_T,
P(G)_n={(l'_in,p'_in,t'_in)}, i_n = 1,…,L_n
        ↓
Select valid base template comparing
P(B) and P(G)_n
        ↓
Store valid base template
```

Figure 7: Enrollment using multiple impressions

4. Experimental Results

We have tested our fingerprint verification algorithm using one of the FVC 2002 databases [7,8]. There are four different databases in the FVC 2002 databases, each of which were collected by different scanners or generated by using SFinGE software. Hence, they have different image size and resolution. Every database consists of two classes, set A for evaluation and set B for training. Set A is composed of eight fingerprint images per one finger from 100 individuals for a total of 800 fingerprint images and set B from 10 individuals for a total of 80 images. The details about FVC 2002 databases are in [8]. Among them, A set of DB1 was used in our experiment. The size of fingerprint images of DB1 was 388 374 at 500dpi.

For the enrollment, the first four fingerprint images among eight were used, and the remaining four were used for verification. Therefore, when a matching was labeled GENUINE if the matching was performed between fingerprint images from same finger, and IMPOSTER otherwise, 400 GENUINEs were able to be performed. And 9900 IMPOSTERs were performed, i.e., 99 IMPOETERs have been tested for one fingerprint using the other 99 fingerprints.

We performed two matching tests in order to show the effect of the adoption of enrollment using multiple impressions, matching after enrollment using single impression and matching after enrollment using multiple impressions. Figure 8 presents the distribution of false match rate and false non-match rate. Vertical axis represents the normalized distribution of matching scores, and horizontal axis represents the score ranging from 0 to 100. As shown in the curve of Figure 8 (b), it is observed that equal error rate is lower by 1.38% when using multiple impressions on enrollment than when using single impression.

When false non-match rate is set 1%, false matches happen at the rate of about 40% in the former. In the other hand, the false match rate of the latter is 6.15%.

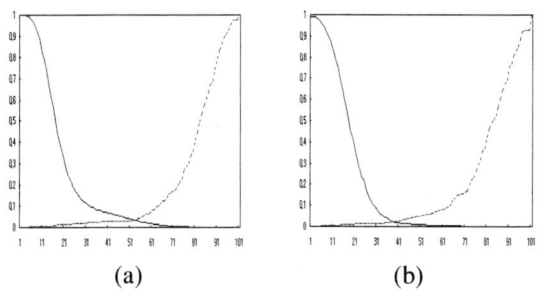

Figure 8: FMR/FNMR curve, (a) case when using one fingerprint image on the enrollment, (b) case when using four fingerprint images on the enrollment

5. Conclusion and Future Work

This article shows the comparison between matching performances when using single fingerprint image on enrollment phase and when using multiple fingerprint images. If plural fingerprint images are used during enrollment, extracted and stored minutiae can be quaranteed becuase false minutiae are discarded and missed ones are added in the final minutiae set. And we confirmed this by experiments. On using multiple impressions on enrollment, equal error rate decreased by 1.38% as compared with the case when using single impression, and its FMR 100[7] is 6.15%.

The enrollment phase using multiple impressions can be part of match-on-cord [4] system. The match-on-card system is shown in Figure 9. In the match-on-card system, the whole matching step should be executed in the smart card and the processing power of smart card is very limited [4]. Therefore, it is essential to extract reliable minutiae in order to make matching more accurate even though matching step uses only simple information of minutiae such as the position, direction and type.

Although the performance of matching adopting the proposed enrollment was improved considerably, the result is not satisfied yet. Thus, it is required to enhance the algorithm and study new method.

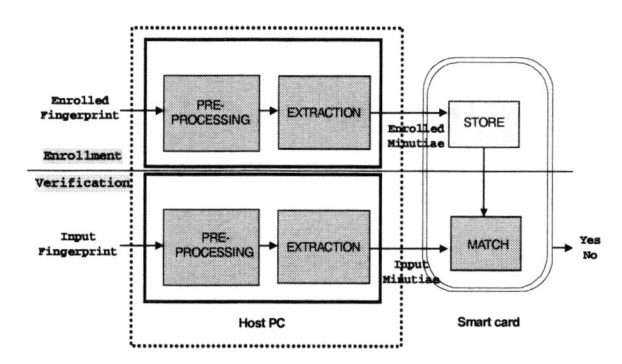

Figure 9: Fingerprint based Match-on-Token

References

[1] ANSI web site, http://www.ansi.org/
[2] Jain, L.C., Halici, U., Hayashi, I., Lee, S.B., Tsutsui, S.: Intelligent Biometric Techniques in Fingerprint and Face Recognition, CRC Press LLC, (1999)
[3] Jain, A., Hong, L., Bolle, R.: On-line Fingerprint Verification. IEEE Trans. on Pattern Analysis and Machine Intelligence, Vol.19, No.4 (1997) 302–313
[4] Pan, S.B., Gil, Y.H., Moon, D., Chung, Y., Park, C.H.: A Memory-Efficient Fingerprint Verification Algorithm using A Multi-Resolution Accumulator Array, ETRI Journal, Vol. 25, No. 3, (2003) 179–186
[5] Ross, A., Jain, A. K., Reisman, J.: A Hybrid Fingerprint Matcher, Pattern Recognition, Vol. 36, No. 7, (2003) 1661-1673
[6] Jain, A. K., Ross, A.: Fingerprint Mosaicking, Proc. ICASSP, (2002)
[7] FVC 2002 web site, http://bias.csr.unibo.it/fvc2002
[8] Maio, D., Maltoni, D., Cappelli, R., Wayman, J.L., Jain, A.K.: FVC2002:Second finger-print verification competition, Proc. ICPR, (2002)

Geo-spatial Active Visual Surveillance on Wireless Networks

Terrance E. Boult
Univ. of Colorado at Colorado Springs and Guardian Solutions, Inc

Keywords: Detection, Tracking, video surveillance, video motion detection Geo-spatial, rules, ESRI, security, wireless video

Abstract

This paper reviews some of the history of automated visual surveillance, from the second and third generation VMD days of the early 1990s, to the current state of the art. It discusses the inherent limitations that resulted in an nearly negligible "increase" in performance throughout the 1990s and still exist in commercially available systems. Then we review an approach that overcomes these limitations – active visual surveillance with geo-spatial rules.

Active visual surveillance uses data from computer controlled Pan/Tilt/Zoom (PTZ) units combined with state of the art video detection and tracking to, in a cost effective manner, provide active assessment of potential targets. This active assessment allows an increase in the number of pixels on target and provides a secondary viewpoint for data fusion, while still allowing coverage of a very large surveillance area. This active approach and multi-sensor fusion, not a new concept, was developed as part of the DARPA Video Surveillance and Monitoring (VSAM) program in the late 90's. While we have continued to expand upon it since that time, there has been no commercial video surveillance, before Guardian Solutions, that provided these important abilities.

The core ideas in this paper address limitations of the original VSAM designs, briefly introducing our enhancements including geo-spatial rules for wide area multi-sensor fusion, and key design issues to allow us to support wireless networks.

1. Background & Previous Research

Visual Surveillance is a broad area and no amount of review in this paper will cover it adequately. In addition to the papers cited herein, a good review of many state-of-the-art visual surveillance systems can be found in a special issue of the *Proceeding of the IEEE* (Oct. 2001) as well as recent IEEE Workshops on Visual Surveillance and Workshops on Performance Evaluation of Tracking Systems.

In [1], Ringer and Hoover of Sandia National Lab present a detailed evaluation of the (then) commercially available exterior digital Video Motion Detectors (VMDs). These systems used specialized hardware, some were boards in a PC, other were standalone units, to allow real-time processing. This study was extremely well done, analyzing 13 different commercial systems in a controlled outdoor study (on a clean dirt background within a double fenced area). The stated detection criterion of the evaluation was 90% probability of detection (pd) at 95% confidence. Another requirement was an average of 10 or fewer false/nuisance alarms in 24 hours on a day with few clouds, bright sunny and calm weather. Only 6 of the 13 systems achieved the stated goals. In more challenging lighting conditions (still on dirt background), they developed 24 hours of "test tape" to test systems. (This set of tapes is still available and a good place to start for static VMD type system evaluation.) On the test tapes, the 6 systems that "passed" the clear-day tests averaged over 50 nuisance alarms. Even with the testing on simple dirt backgrounds, their final conclusions were that "VMDs in general, when used in an outdoor environment, are susceptible to nuisance alarms from environmental effects ... all had some problems rejecting nuisance alarms". Applying them in even more complex environments, such as grass, water, woods, where the backgrounds are themselves moving, would have been even more problematic.

As the Sandia study was ongoing, DARPA as developing its plans for the Video Surveillance and Monitoring (VSAM) program. That program, which funded research in video surveillance in the late 90's, sought to move beyond single camera VMD, to networks of video sensors, [2]. Most of the research was focused at higher level analysis like classifying activities as uncommon[3], seeking particular patterns of (indoor) activity[4] and reasoning about human movements [5, 6, 7, 8]. Unfortunately, most of the work in VSAM did not stress the detection capabilities – it was done in good lighting with color cameras and moderate size targets (approximately .1% to 1% of the image (between 300 and 3000 pixels on target), with those doing human modeling often having the target represent 10% of the image. Furthermore, most of the groups exploited color (which cannot be used at night or in thermal video) to simplify detection and tracking.

The main efforts with a significant focus on low-level detection were the work of Sarnoff [9], which addressed detection/tracking from a moving plane and [10] which addressed lighting independent background subtraction (though it was not tested on complex outdoor scenes). The VSAM work at Maryland [11, 12] included non-parametric models for background subtraction and low-level people tracking, but all the examples were color imagery with simple lighting and large targets. Finally, our work, [13], addressed detection/tracking in omni-directional video and included analysis in very challenging situations including snipers.

There have been a few projects which have explicitly addressed lighting, which is a major issue outdoors, with a few important projects in Europe. Again there is too much to site in a workshop paper, but a few important works include PASSWORDS project, [15] uses an illumination change compensation algorithm to allow it to work in outdoor settings, and Riddler, et.al., [16], which uses Kalman filtering for adaptive background estimation which takes into account changing illumination so as not to mistake lighting as objects of interest. A similar approach is used in [17]. In [18], an approach was explored that used local order statistics to detect significant lighting changes. While each of these approaches was moderately effective for dramatic changes, none of them work well for a fast moving localized cloud shadow, and none of them discussed use at night, were moving "lights", illuminating static scene elements, are the often the only visible sign of an intruder.

To be viable systems, however, automated video surveillance needs to be able to work at night (maybe its most critical time), with small and non-distinctive targets that are as far away as possible. (Distance translates to response time – the goal is not just to record events but to respond to them while they are happening). None of the aforementioned systems discudded on nocturnal video, [17] and our own work has seriously addressed gray-scale data, the only type available at night (low-light or thermal).

For many current US government projects, the requested goal is to produce less than 3 false alarms (FA) per day. For these military applications, undetected targets could be, literally, deadly, so the miss detection (MD) rates also need to be low, with stated goals ¡ 5distant targets (1-2km). With each NTSC video containing 10^{20} potential target regions per camera per day achieving these performance goals place very strong demands on the low-level processing of the system. In [19, 20, 21], we investigated FA and MD rates for this type of problem. These papers analyzed the grouping algorithm that has allowed us to address the "signal-level" FA and impacts of random noise. However, they did not address nuisance alarm (NA) rates, where lighting, water, grass or trees produce real changes that are not "significant" motion.

How then does one reduce the impact of FA and NA? One approach, which we are pursuing, is active surveillance with geo-spatial models. This approach combines sensor-fusion with active sensor control and calibration information to allow the system to use multiple sensors to analyze an event. Thus providing added information that can significantly reduce the FA and NA rates.

2. Active Geo-spatial surveillance

One of the issues addressed in the VSAM project was the importance of situational awareness and the role of geo-spatial information in providing that awareness for a large facility.

We content that, while geo-spatial information has much more to offer than just "situational awareness", we consider it the key to scalability and robustness of a video surveillance system, see 1. How to calibrate cameras and do ray intersection is well known for regular cameras, and for omni-directional cameras we discussed the geometric calibration and back-projection in [22].

For scalability we need to provide coverage with fewer cameras. One aspect of this is to detect targets at greater ranges, but then the targets will be too small in the image for assessment. By using the geo-spatial information, the camera that detected the target can "handoff" to another sensor with greater optical magnification for assessment. For high-end cameras, e.g. a thermal camera with 300mm lens which might cost $250,000, making efficient use of that camera for assessment is important to scalability. A similar issue arises with having fixed cameras watching choke points – using active PTZ control, it can then "hand-off" a target to a PTZ when that target begins leaving the choke region. With active tracking, the PTZ can then follow the target through a large open area. The geo-spatial sensor-to-sensor hand-off was demonstrated as part of the VSAM project, with hand-offs from the Lehigh OmniCamera to the CMU PTZ systems and multiple CMU fixed to PTZ hand-offs.

For robustness, 3D provides significant advantages that were not exploited in the VSAM project. In addition to the back-projected position, the calibrated cameras and geo-spatial information allows computation of the targets approximate size, speed and heading in meaningful world coordinates. In most perspective images for surveillance, the variations in "image" size of targets makes it difficult to define a "pixel" size that is meaningful. E.g. the feet of the subject behind the truck (¡ 1sq.ft of target) in the foreground of figure 3, take up almost as much area as the backhoe out-

Figure 1. 3d is the key to scalability and robustness. From a single calibrated camera, one can intersect rays with a digital terrain model. The simplest model, a local plane, is sufficient for many settings. Back-project of the ray from the camera to the ground plane produces target location. It also produces a distance which can be used to scale the pixels on the target to approximate size in square feet (or meters). Using true 3D positions it also allows computing speed in mph and heading (degrees from north).

Figure 2. An example of a situational awareness display with an 8 camera system showing a fixed to PTZ hand-off. Without the map, it is difficult to understand that the two images with targets (boxed regions upper left and lower right) are showing the same thing. On the map are shown the FOVs of the different cameras and the recent locations of the target (shown as question marks, ????, since it did not know the type.). This this knowledge it is clear there are two cameras with overlapping FOVs that are looking at the same target. In this case the fixed camera was loosing the target and "handed off" to the PTZ to continue following it.

lined in black in the far part of the scene (¿ 50sq.ft of target). A small motion of the brush in the front of the scene would generate a motion target much larger than the backhoe. But by using 3D information, one can filter the detect objects in a more meaningful size. Our approach, implemented in GuardianWatch, is to use an image-map such as figure 4, where each region has associated XML rules describing the targets of interest (i.e. what sets of an alarm rather than just what moves).

Guardian represents its rules in two different forms. The first is as ESRI shape files (ESRI is a trademark of ESRI incorporated, www.esri.com). The ESRI shape file format allows sharing geo-spatial information (we can back-project the coordinates of the regions) in a form that quickly is becoming the de-facto standard for government GIS. (Internally it is really just a DB3 database with special column attributes). For simpler interfaces with other tools, we also use an XML format with an associated image.

A partial XML rule-set might look like:

```
<rule_set>
 <sensor_ruleset id="0x01 0x01">
  <image> manatee-alarm-0.ppm </image>
  <rule name="Parking exit ">
   <alarm_id> 230-230 </alarm_id>
   <threatcon> 0-5 </threatcon>
   <days_of_week> sun-fri </days_of_week>
   <start_time> 0:00 </start_time>
   <duration> 24:00 </duration>
   <size> 5-25 sqft </size>
   <speed> .1-5 mph </speed>
   <angle> 240-270 degrees </angle>
   <gps_poly> .. (saveing space) </gps_poly>
  </rule>
  <!-- ship boarding sat 10am-4pm,
       handle it separately, rules not shown -->
  <!-- We ignore people on saturdays..
       too busy with passengers, crew -->
  <rule name="People in parking area ">
   <alarm_id> 230-230 </alarm_id>
   <threatcon> 0-5 </threatcon>
   <days_of_week> sun-fri </days_of_week>
   <start_time> 0:00 </start_time>
   <duration> 10:00 </duration>
   <size> 2-5 sqft </size>
   <speed> 0-5 mph </speed>
   <angle> 0-360 degrees </angle>
   <!-- handoff syntax is
       camid dlat dlon dalt zoom_fov_degrees -->
   <handoff> 0x8 0 0 0 5 </handoff>
   <gps_poly> .. (saveing space) </gps_poly>
  </rule>
  <!-- ... rest rules -->
<rule_set>
```

The move to geo-spatial representations allows us to not only have rules for targets based on their position in the image, but our patent-pending approach allows us to define

Figure 3. As is well known, distant targets appear smaller than near-by targets. The feet of the person behind the truck have more pixels than the backhoe in the distance. The perspective effect makes image-based rules difficult to apply in filtering nuisance alarms.

Figure 4. An alarm map associates rules with pixels in the image. The red (small vertically striped region on left) has rules that activated only for cars leaving (not entering) off-hours. The yellow (lighter region in parking lot) has rules that alarm for people-sized targets anytime. The yellow region hands-off to a PTZ so a guard can assess what the human is doing. The blue regions (sky and lower corners) are ignored. The remaining regions will detect/track targets but do not set off alarms.

rules in a map-based geo-spatial nature and then use it to filter targets for any cameras that are looking at the area. This allows rules to apply to PTZ cameras as well as fixed cameras. As the PTZ follows a target it will have better estimates of size and speed and can have more certainty about it.

While the VSAM project investigated some uses of geo-spatial information for situational awareness and camera coordination, the biggest advantage of 3D, filtering nuisance went unstudied. Using geo-spatial information allows the video surveillance system to ignore a wide range of "nuisance" alarms (e.g. most lighting, many birds, blowing trash), that would otherwise render the systems unusable. While some of these can be ignored using 2D information, the 3D information makes it far simpler for the end user to understand. Combining 3D analysis with the sophisticated detection/tracking from [20] has allowed us to detect and track small targets on very complex moving backgrounds, such as a zodiac on water in figure 6, with 30 pixels on target. Zodiac was 700ft away in 2ft waves using a 320x240 thermal sensor with 50mm lens. Guardian Solutions commercialized this technology and now has multiple commercial clients who are using automated video surveillance on a 24/7/365 basis.

3. Wireless video surveillance

Our approach to video surveillance has been, from the beginning, intended for distributed processing. With the data demands of real-time video processing, it simply makes sense to push the processing as close to the camera as possible. The VSAM project also embarrassed the "networked" approach. The original VSAM communication protocol, [23], provided rudimentary means for communication of the necessary data, but it was not particularly efficient. Once the video surveillance system has the ability to decide salient motion and use rules to decide what is important, it has the inherent ability to filter not just "alarms", but also the vast streams of video data it has analyzed.

With moderate analysis as that described above and a significantly extended network protocol, we can support video surveillance on lower-bandwidth networks. The GuardianWatch software has implemented a basic adaptive bandwidth control with priority filtering. Using the "significance" of the motion along with the alarm rules, the system can decide the priority of each video item.

To support efficient adaptive bandwidth management, the system uses a sprite-based representation.

The system represents each moving target separately (as a jpeg chip) on a reference background (a full size jpeg). The detection system then queues up the video chips, their geo-spatial position, shape descriptions etc, and the system can decide what it can afford to send. The "video" encoding is, in spirit, similar to sprites in Mpeg4 (which almost no one supports), but we drop all the inter-frame motion coding both to make it easy to dynamically drop data, and so writing display code is easier. (The approach/protocol supports differential motion coding but we have not found it

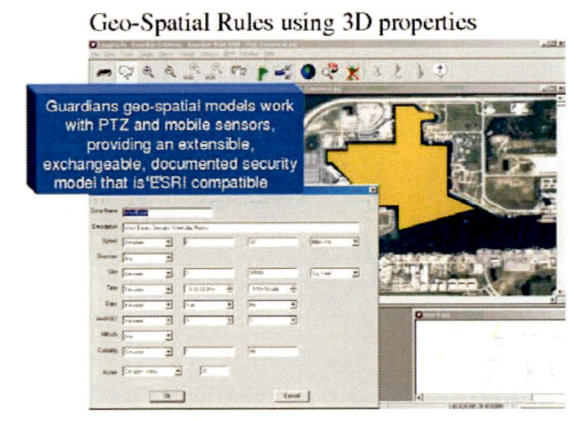

Figure 5. An example showing a geo-spatial alarm zone and the GUI interface for defining the alarm rule associated with that polygon. The geo-spatial rules can apply to any camera watching the area, including PTZs that follow the target into the area.

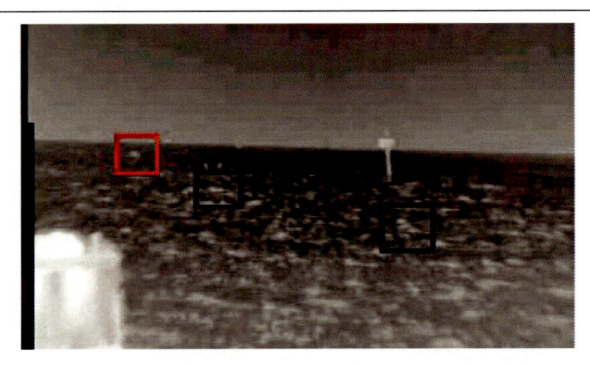

Figure 6. Zodiac tracking example from thermal video. Zodiac is detected as a confident target (red/light gray box). Two other boxes (black) show hypothesis of potential targets. Using 3D information, the waves never become confident.

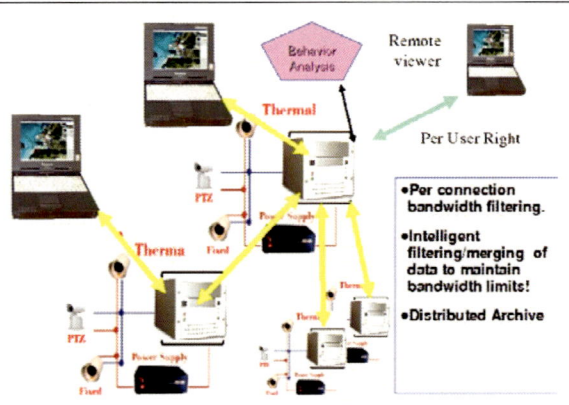

Figure 7. The communication architecture for GuardianWatch. Each computer processes video, stores video and geo-spatial data, and then filters data based on both a priority allocated bandwidth and the currently available bandwidth. The geo-spatial data is analyzed by the Behavioral Analysis node which implements the overall geo-spatial rule engine. The system supports encryption and per user/node access rights.

necessary). If there is minimal bandwidth (e.g the 8 camera hand-off example above was monitored over a 33Kbps dialup link), then the reference background images are sent very infrequently (often ¡ 1 per min) and significant chips are sent more frequently. In the zodiac example, more and more of the hypothesis chips would be pruned as the bandwidth was reduced. At the same time, the target position and other (very small) descriptors are passed around so we can maintain situational awareness.

The system's processors/communication nodes forms a "tree", see figure 7, with communication filtering as data moves up the tree. If the user is mobile and near one of the clusters of cameras, e.g. the guard truck pulls up near a terminal in the port, they have more available bandwidth and get more of the video chips and faster reference frames. If the local first responders (e.g. police) are examining an alarm via their Internet connection, the data might be bouncing off a commercial "Internet" satellite with much lower bandwidth. The first responders will still get a good situational awareness but it will be far from "full motion video". However rather than degrading all the data uniformly, the "chips" of potential targets will have much higher quality than the less significant data. If the communication links between the processors are wireless, as they are at many of Guardian Solutions commercial and military clients, then the "storage" of archival video also needs to be distributed. The extended VSAM protocol supports the necessary "DVR" features as well. In August of 2003, an 88 camera installation of Guardian Solutions automated video surveillance system went "online" at Port Canaveral, the largest Cruise ship port in the country. The system communicates the processed results from these cameras back to the central monitoring and the mobile monitoring stations using COTS 802.11 technology. Two guards can manage this large set of cameras because they are not watching them unless something significant is happening.

4. Conclusion & Future work

Studies the early 90's pointed to the problem of nuisance alarms, yet little of the research since that time has really focused on addressing this issue. While many researchers have been trying to "recognize" complex human activities, the ability to ignore simple nuisances such as birds, lighting and trash, have been largely ignored. This paper discussed how to use geo-spatial rules and filtering using 3D propertie to reduce or reject the nuisance alarms. It also briefly discussed how advanced "filtering" can produce data that supports more efficient situational awareness of video-based systems on wireless networks.

Even with 3D filtering, there are many situations where nuisances still arise. More advanced algorithms that fuse the data from multiple complimentary sensors can reduce these even farther. Already our system can use its "confidence" to filter its alarms, so a fixed sensor could detect a target, but uncertain about its properties, it can hand-off to another sensor to automatically assess the target. But adding multiple sensors could reduce the nuisance alarm rate even farther, e.g. with good lighting a thermal and visible sensor would see a human target with similar size, but would see "trash" very differently. The issue of nuisance from large animals (deer) is more problematic (especially in woods where target shape cannot be used because of the frequency of occlusion). But sensitive acoustic/seismic sensors that could monitor the "footsteps" might be able to distinguish them. Our future work includes multiple issues in multi-sensor integration and cueing.

References

[1] C. Ringler and C. Hoover, "Evaluation of commercially available exterior digital vmds," tech. rep., SANDIA, Sept. 1998. SAND94-2875 UC-706. (Printed June 1995).

[2] T. Kanade, R. Collins, A. Lipton, P. Burt, and L. Wixson, "Advances in cooperative multi-sensor video surveillance," in *Proc. of the DARPA IUW*, pp. 3–24, 1998.

[3] W. Grimson, C. Stauffer, R. Romano, and L. Lee, "Using adaptive tracking to classify and monitor activities in a site," in *Proceedings of IEEE Conference on Computer Vision and Pattern Recognition*, pp. 22–29, 1998.

[4] B. Flinchbaugh and T. Olson, "Autonomous video surveillance," in *25th AIPR Workshop: Emerging Applications of Computer Vision*, May 1996. See also DARPA IUW May 1997.

[5] J. Davis and A. Bobick, "The representation and recognition of human movements using temporal templates.," in *Proceedings of IEEE Conference on Computer Vision and Pattern Recognition*, pp. 928–934, 1997.

[6] C. Wren, A. Azarbayejani, T. Darrell, and A. Pentland, "Pfinder: Real-time tracking of the human body," *IEEE Tran. on Pattern Analysis and Machine Intelligence*, vol. 19, no. 7, pp. 780–785, 1997.

[7] A. Lipton, H. Fuijiyoshi, and R. Patil, "Moving target detection and classification from real-time video," in *Proc. of the IEEE Workshop on Applications of Computer Vision*, 1998.

[8] I. Haritaoglu, D. Harwood, and L. Davis, "W^4: Real-time surveillance of people and their activities," *IEEE Tran. on Pattern Analysis and Machine Intelligence*, pp. 809–830, August 2000.

[9] L. Wixson, "Detecting salient motion by accumulating directionally-consistent flow," *IEEE Tran. on Pattern Analysis and Machine Intelligence*, pp. 774–781, August 2000.

[10] Y. Ivanov and A. Bobick, "Fast lighting independent background subtraction," *International Journal of Computer Vision*, vol. 37, no. 2, pp. 199–207, 1998.

[11] I. Haritaoglu, D. Harwood, and L. Davis, "W^4s: A real-time system for detecting and tracking people in 2.5D," in *Computer Vision—ECCV*, 1998.

[12] A. Elgammal, D. Harwood, and L. Davis, "Non-parametric model for background subtraction," in *FRAME-RATE Workshop*, IEEE, 1999. Eletronic (only) proceedings at www.eecs.lehigh.edu/FRAME.

[13] T. Boult, C. Qian, W. Yin, A. Erkin, P. Lewis, C. Power, and R. Micheals, "Applications of omnidirectional imaging: Multi-body tracking and remote reality," in *Proc. of the IEEE Workshop on Computer Vision Applications*, Oct. 1998.

[14] T.E.Boult, R.Micheals, X.Gao, P.Lewis, C.Power, W.Yin, and A.Erkan, "Frame-rate omnidirectional surveillance and tracking of camouflaged and occluded targets," in *Second IEEE International Workshop on Visual Surveillance*, pp. 48–55, IEEE, 1999.

[15] M. Bogaert, N. Chleq, P. Cornez, C. Regazzoni, A. Teschioni, and M. Thonnat, "The passwords project," in *ICIP*, pp. 1112–1115, IEEE, 1996.

[16] C. Riddler, O. Munkelt, and H. Kirchner, "Adaptive background estimation and foreground detection using kalman filtering," in *ICRAM*, pp. 193–199, 1995.

[17] G. Foresti, "Object detection and tracking in time-varying and badly illuminated outdoor environments," *SPIE Journal of Optical Engineering*, vol. 37, no. 9, pp. 2550–2564, 1998.

[18] B. Xie, V.Ramesh, and T. Boult, "Sudden illumination change detection using order consistency," in *Workshop on Statistical Methods in Video Processing (in conjunction with ECCV2002)*, 2002.

[19] X. Gao, T. Boult, F. Coetzee, and V. Ramesh, "Error analysis of background adaption," in *Proceedings of IEEE Conference on Computer Vision and Pattern Recognition*, June 2000.

[20] T.E.Boult, R.Micheals, X.Gao, and M. Eckmann, "Into the woods: Visual surveillance of noncooperative and camouflaged targes in complex outdoor settings," *Proceeding of the IEEE*, vol. 89, pp. 1382–1402, October 2001.

[21] X. Gao, V. Ramesh, and T. Boult, "Statistical characterization of morphological operator sequences," in *Computer Vision—ECCV*, May 2002.

[22] T.E.Boult, X.Gao, , R.Micheals, and M.Eckmann, "Omnidirectional visual surveillance," *Image and Vision Computing*, 2004. to appear.

[23] A. Lipton, T. Boult, and Y. Lee, "Video surveillance and monitoring communication specification document 98-2.2," tech. rep., CMU, Sept. 1998. http://www.cs.cmu.edu/~vsam/Documents as vsam_protocol_98_22.ps.gz.

A Real-time Wide field of View Passive Millimeter-wave Imaging Camera

Stuart Clark, Chris Martin,
Vladimir Kolinko, John Lovberg
Trex Enterprises, Inc
sclark@trexenterprises.com

Peter J. Costianes
*Air Force Research Laboratory,
Information Directorate*
costianesp@rl.af.mil

Abstract

With the current upsurge in domestic terrorism, suicide bombings and the like, there is an increased interest in high technology sensors that can provide true stand-off detection of concealed articles such as guns and, in particular, explosives in both controlled and uncontrolled areas.

The camera discussed in this paper is based upon passive millimeter-wave imaging (75.5-93.5 GhZ) and is intrinsically safe as it uses only the natural thermal (blackbody) emissions from living beings and inanimate objects to form images with. The camera consists of four subsystems which are interfaced to complete the final camera. The subsystems are Trex's patented flat panel frequency scanned phased array antenna, a front end receiver, and phase and frequency processors to convert the antenna output (in phase and frequency space) into image space and in doing so form a readily recognizable image. The phase and frequency processors are based upon variants of a Rotman lens.

1. Introduction.

The proposed MMW imager known as the PMC-2 is a follow on to two previous grants funded by the National Institute of Justice (NIJ). This second generation imager uses the Trex Enterprises patented flat panel antenna and millimeter-wave signal processors to enable a 30 by 20 degree instantaneous field of view true real time (30 Hz) sensor with a 2 Kelvin instantaneous thermal sensitivity, to be built in a 2 foot square by 10 inch deep package. The frequency scanned phased array flat panel antenna is coupled to MMW low noise amplifiers (LNA's), to produce enough signal to allow a two-dimensional MMW Rotman lens (comprised of one phase processor lens and 192 frequency processor lenses), to perform the Fourier transform that is needed to go from the antenna (pupil plane) to the image plane. Custom detector diodes and A/D chips are then used to detect and digitize the image plane MMW signal. The digitized signal is then fed to a high performance PC for processing and display.

2. Overall system operation

The overall system block diagram is shown in Figure 1. The MMW radiation enters the system through an antenna (Figure 2) which is composed of a single sheet of 30-mil-thick polyethylene dielectric, with copper cladding on both sides and a sequence of small slots photolithographically etched on one side. The antenna can be thought of as a parallel plate dielectric filled waveguide, with the top and bottom cladding acting as a big flat waveguide and the polyethylene acting as a dielectric filler material. The slotted square antenna essentially samples the incident wavefront and sets up a field within the parallel plates. This field is channeled into the processing elements of the system amplified by the LNA's and Fourier transformed by the two Rotman lenses. The Fourier transformed aperture function (i.e. the image) is then detected by the MMW diodes. The resulting electrical signal is digitized and processed into a video image of up to 30 frames/sec displayed on the host PC.

3. Detailed system operation

3.1 Receiving Antenna

The incident MMW radiation is coupled into the antenna by an array of rectangular slots. These slots are

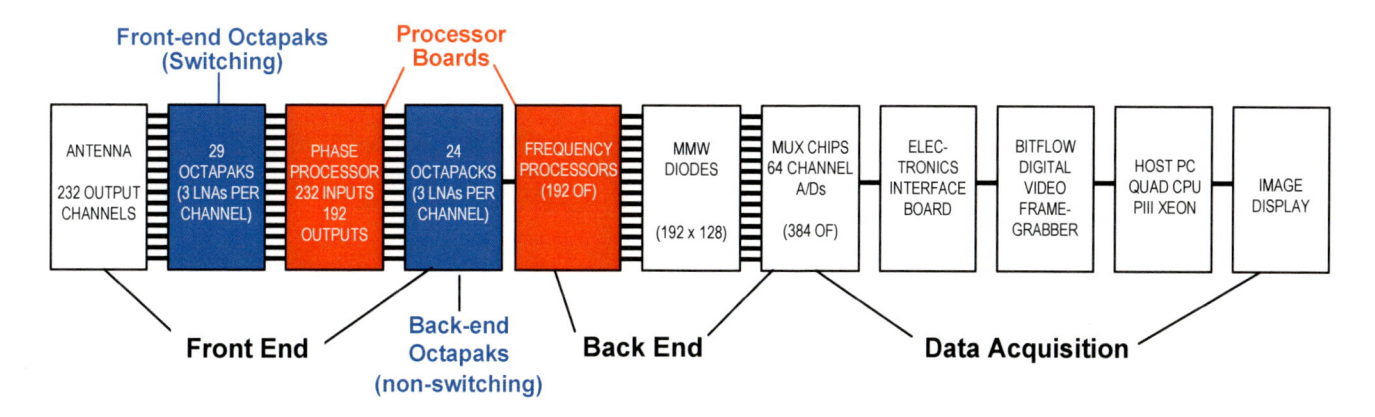

Figure 1. PMC-2 System Flowchart showing the various sections of the imager from front to back and can be broken down into three main sections (front end, back end and data acquisition) together with various sub-sections.

large enough to allow sufficient energy to couple into the antenna but small enough to permit sufficient broadband response. Incident radiation is sampled by this array of slots and each slot may be considered as an individual radiation source within the antenna. The field within this large square waveguide is then determined by how each source (slot) constructively or destructively interferes with each other source. The radiation reaching the feeds at the bottom of the antenna may be simply characterized both in phase and frequency.

The phase is determined by the angle of incidence of the radiation in a horizontal direction. Radiation incident normal to the antenna will produce a phase at the feeds which is constant across the input. As the horizontal angle of incidence is moved beyond the normal, the phase changes linearly with increasing slope. There are 232 feeds from the antenna into the first stage of amplifiers. The particular phase of the radiation into the 232 feeds translates into a horizontal position of the object/image. This will be seen more clearly when we look at the operation of Phase processor (Rotman lens).

The frequency is determined by the angle of incidence of the radiation in a vertical direction. In this case, the frequency of the radiation coupled into the antenna is governed by the following expression

$$n\,d + d \sin \theta = k\lambda$$

where n = index of refraction of the dielectric
   d = the slot spacing
   θ = angle of incidence
   k = integer
   λ = wavelength

The slot spacing is selected so that only the k=1 mode can exist. For example, a slot spacing of d=78 mils, n=1.55, and a λ = 139 mils (85 GHz) will form a beam at θ = 13.43 degrees. For the 75 GHz to 95 GHz range this will give a field of view (or beam scan) from 28 to 2.56 degrees and falls within the design goals of the PMC-2 imager.

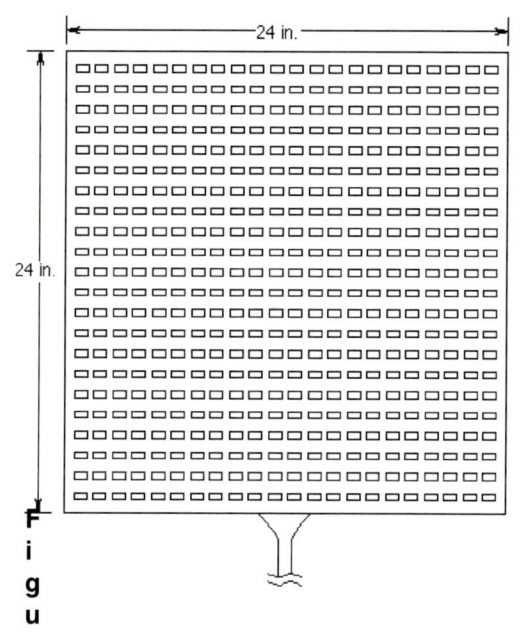

Figure 2. WR-10 Waveguide to W-band receiver. Parallel plate waveguide with 30 mil polyethylene dielectric sandwiched between two copper sheets. edge of the antenna, for imaging or radar applications.

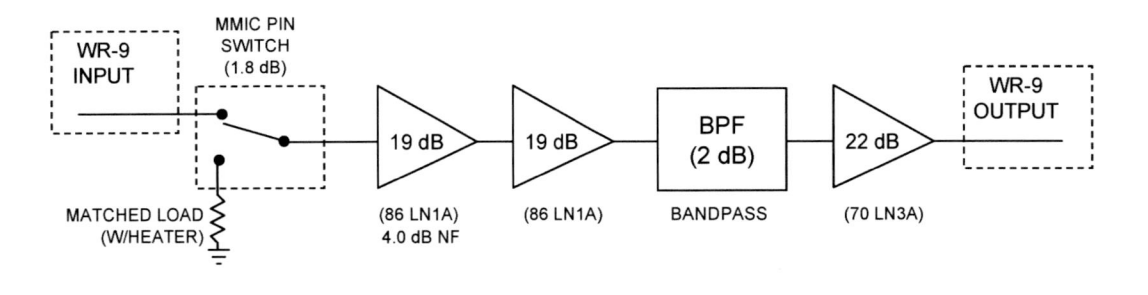

Goals:

- \> 53 dB small-signal gain
- 86 GHz center frequency
- 18 GHz bandwidth
- < 6 dB noise figure
- ± 3 dB gain flatness
- Output power (P_{1dB}) > 0 dBm

Results Summary (to date):

55.0 dB

84.5 GHz

18 GHz

6.8 dB

± 4 dB max

0 dBm

Figure 3. Schematic and performance of a receiver channel.

3.2 Amplification Stages.

Before entering the Phase processor the 232 feeds from the antenna are amplified using Hughes Research Labs (HRL) Low Noise Amplifiers (LNA's). The LNA's are fabricated and packaged in sets of eight channels per package (Octapaks). Each channel is made up of 3 individual LNA chips that each have a gain of about 20 db giving a total gain of around 55 db (after accounting for losses). The performance goals and actual performance results are given in Figure 3. Much effort was expended to eliminate cross-talk and ringing between these high gain amplifiers due to their close proximity in the Octapaks. The Octapak gain and noise figure data is given in Figure 4.

3.3 Phase Processor

The phase processor is a Rotman lens which is used to perform the phase based transform that is needed in the horizontal direction to remove the position to phase mapping that the antenna applies to the incident MMW signal. The lens consists of a convex surface on the input side and a concave surface on the output side (Figure 5). In order to maintain the same phase distribution at the input to the Rotman lens as there is at the ouptut of the phase processor, there is a bootlace section that feeds the convex surface. The bootlace ensures that the distance from each input feed line from the antenna to each point on the convex surface is such that the phase distribution from the antenna is unaltered on the convex surface.

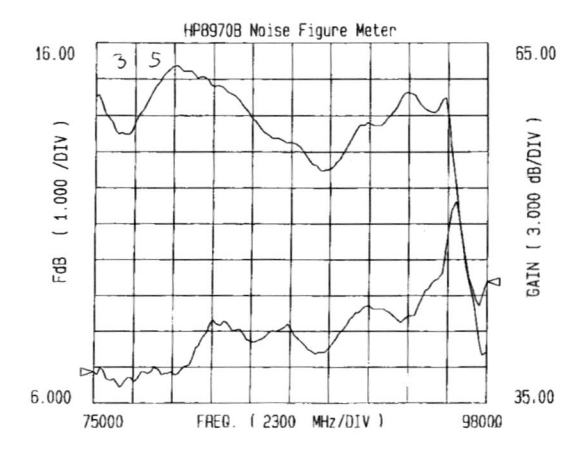

Figure 4. Octapak gain and noise figure data while running at typical drain bias.

Each of these 232 sources propagate to the concave surface forming an interference pattern. For example, if the original incident wave is normal to the antenna, then this constant phase distribution across the convex surface constructively interferes at the center of the concave output surface. For all radiation that is incident within the rest of the field of view in the horizontal direction, constructive interference will occur depending on the slope of the linear phase distribution resulting from the off-axis incidence at the antenna. These 192 output lines are then amplified again and sent to the frequency processor.

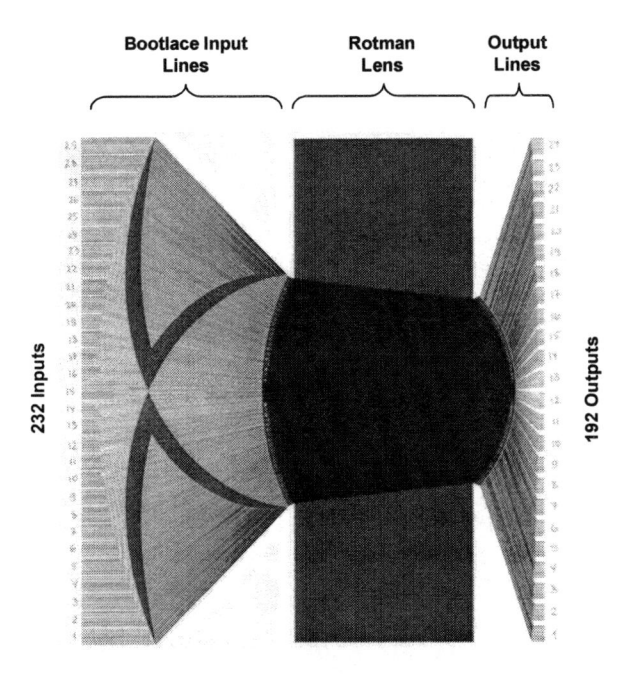

Figure 5. PMC-2 phase processor design.

3.4 Frequency Processor

For a Rotman lens to be a frequency processor it must be able to remove the position to frequency mapping that the antenna applies in the vertical direction to the incident MMW signal. Since a Rotman lens works on phase alone, a way must be found to convert a frequency based mapping back to a phase based mapping. This is accomplished by using a tapped delay line section added to the input side of the lens.

3.5 Frequency Processor Board components

On the output side of the frequency processor board, MMW detector diodes are required to convert the MMW signal (90+ GHz) into a near-dc-voltage that can be measured and digitized. The diodes (Figure 6) are highly custom parts made by HRL and based on vertical AlSb heterostructures. The near dc signal produced by the detector diodes is digitized, using custom 64-channel 7-bit (instantaneous) ultra low noise MUX chip built for Trex by Indigo Systems of Santa Barbara, CA.

To improve performance and substantially reduce cost, the chip was designed with a 7-bit digitizer and a sampling time of 1/64th of a standard 33 ms frame, i.e., approximately 0.5 ms per sampling interval. By using 63

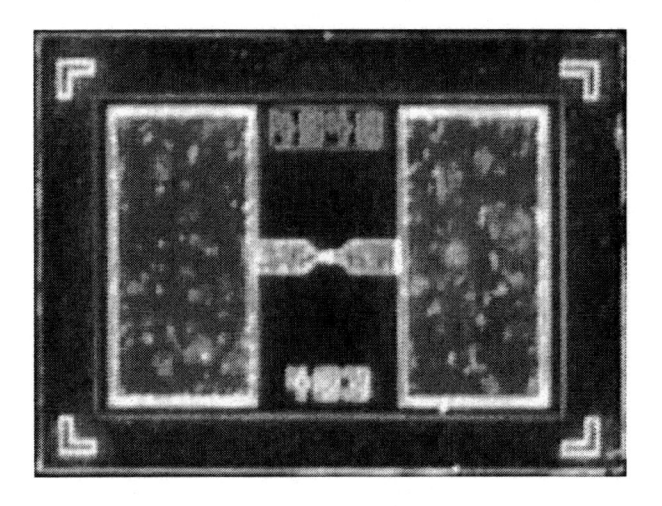

Figure 6. High magnification picture of W-band detector diode from HRL.

of the possible 64 sampling intervals that are present in a standard 33 ms (30 Hz) frame, the output signal resolution is effectively increased to 10 bits. Data is transferred from buffers on the chip to a readout board during the remaining sampling interval. A custom readout board that takes the parallel outputs from the 384 MUX chips that are present in a PMC-2 imager and converts it to a single serial output in RS-422 digital video format was designed and built by Indigo Systems. This readout board makes extensive use of FPGA chips to buffer and then re-format the parallel signals into a single serial signal.

3.6 Data Acquisition System

To Allow for a degree of sensor fusion and for comparison purposes, the ability to simultaneously capture MMW, visible and IR image of the same scene taken at the same time is built into PMC-2 by using RS-422 compatible digital visible and IR cameras. Digital framegrabber boards from Bitflow Corp of Boston, MA coupled with appropriate software from Bitflow and Microsoft is then used to run a custom C based program developed by Trex to control all aspects of the imager.

The imager code which runs to tens of thousands of lines of code, runs under Windows NT. Due to the loading that the three data streams place on the PCI bus that is currently standard on PC's, the PC that controls the PMC has two independent PCI buses and four processors. The code, which is multi-threaded, allows for each sensor's date to be acquired and processed on its own processor, with one processor left to actually display the data vial calls to the appropriate windows API functions. Standard and custom real-time algorithms for various calibration and image processing functions have been developed and implemented as part of the code.

4. Processor Performance

4.1 Phase Processor

Initial measurements showed that, when left uncorrected, the errors in path length are about a $1/6^{th}$ of a wave which is not small enough to give good near diffraction limited imagery. Correction is achieved by use of high dielectric constant material that is inserted into the waveguide cavity of the transition that is used to couple the output of the antenna (after amplification by the front end Octapaks) to the input of the phase processor. With this and other techniques it has been possible to bring performance up to expected levels and produce near diffraction limited performance.

4.2 Frequency Processor

The performance of the frequency processor board involved inserting a source signal of known amplitude and frequency into the board and measuring the output response of the board at each of the 128 channels. In theory a perfect (diffraction limited) board would produce the classic "sinc squared" output in response to a single frequency input that is within its pass band of 75 to 93 GHz. Results for two separate frequencies showed the following results at the measured peak powers: Design freq = 81.96 GHz with a measured freq = 81.18 GHz; Design freq = 83.9 GHz with a measured freq = 83.77 GHz. This shows a relatively good agreement with design (i.e. theoretical) performance.

5. Future Plans

The final PMC-2 system is scheduled for delivery in January 2004. Testing will be conducted by the Air Force Research Laboratory, Information Directorate at the Rome Research Site.

6. Acknowledgements

This effort was funded by the National Institute of Justice (NIJ) Concealed Weapons Detection Program (CWDP). The work was performed by Trex Enterprises Corporation, San Diego, CA, under Contract Number F30602-01-C-0154 with the Air Force Research Laboratory (AFRL), Information Directorate (IF). The AFRL/IF, Intelligence and Information Exploitation Division provided the technical monitoring for this effort.

Figure 7. PMC-1 Image taken outside. The subject is wearing a shirt over a concealed pistol.

Sensor and Classifier Fusion for Outdoor Obstacle Detection: an Application of Data Fusion To Autonomous Off-Road Navigation

Cristian S. Dima, Nicolas Vandapel and Martial Hebert
Carnegie Mellon University
The Robotics Institute
Pittsburgh, PA 15217, USA
cdima,vandapel,hebert@ri.cmu.edu

Abstract

This paper describes an approach for using several levels of data fusion in the domain of autonomous off-road navigation. We are focusing on outdoor obstacle detection, and we present techniques that leverage on data fusion and machine learning for increasing the reliability of obstacle detection systems.

We are combining color and IR imagery with range information from a laser range finder. We show that in addition to fusing data at the pixel level, performing high level classifier fusion is beneficial in our domain. Our general approach is to use machine learning techniques for automatically deriving effective models of the classes of interest (obstacle and non-obstacle for example). We train classifiers on different subsets of the features we extract from our sensor suite and show how different classifier fusion schemes can be applied for obtaining a multiple classifier system that is more robust than any of the classifiers presented as input.

We present experimental results we obtained on data collected with both the Experimental Unmanned Vehicle (XUV) and a CMU developed robotic vehicle.

1. Introduction

Numerous military and civilian applications call for dependable autonomous vehicles that can navigate off-road. Robotic vehicles can help remove people from dangerous missions, can reduce costs and the time required for deployment. One of the more challenging aspects of autonomous navigation is perception in unstructured or weakly structured outdoor environments such as forests, small dirt roads and terrain covered by tall vegetation. We focus on obstacle detection, where we consider an obstacle to be any region that a vehicle should not attempt to traverse (e.g. humans, trees, big rocks, large holes, large amounts of water). Unfortunately, the difficulty of the problem is such that even human performance in this domain is not perfect.

We believe that in order to achieve acceptable levels of autonomy, vehicles operating in off-road conditions will need to rely on redundancies both at the sensor level and in the decision-making process. Essentially, obstacle detection can be seen as an inference problem: there exists no sensor that will directly indicate if a region in space is an obstacle or not. As a result, we will need to use the available information about such a region to *infer* if it is safe to traverse it or not. Intuitively, having more information should lead to better inferences, which translate in turn to higher degrees of reliability of the obstacle detection system.

Another reason for which outdoor navigation should benefit from having several sensing modalities is that their failure modes are often different. Even if a good quality color image can generally provide a lot of information, limitations in the dynamic range of existing cameras make it hard to extract information from images which contain shadows and bright spots, or from images taken at dusk or dawn. A laser range finder is not sensitive to such issues. Similarly, there are times of the day when an infrared camera - which can normally provide great information for detecting humans, water and vegetation - does not produce very useful information. A more diverse set of sensing modalities would increase the chances that at least some of the sensors can produce useful information allowing the autonomous vehicle to pursue its mission.

In addition to data fusion, our approach relies quite heavily on machine learning. Detecting obstacles in environments that are as complex as the ones we are considering requires complex decision schemes which involve large numbers of parameters. Deriving such schemes manually can be an extremely tedious process. We believe that manually optimizing the performance of a system with many parameters is not a satisfactory solution. We would like our robots to be easily adaptable to new environments and operating conditions, and for this purpose we will use automated methods for tuning our systems.

Using several sensing modalities or machine learning are certainly not new ideas in the mobile robotics field. A quick look at the previous work shows that sensor fusion has been a constant presence in this area from the earliest mobile robots to the plaforms that define the current state of the art. Begining with the indoor HILARE robot in 1979 [7], Moravec's Stanford Cart and CMU Rover ([14], 1983) and continuing with the outdoors Ground Surveillance Robot [10, 9], the Autonomous Land Vehicle [5], the NAVLAB series of autonomous vehicles [22, 8] and the Demo I-II-III project [23], numerous groups have used sonars, TV cameras, IR sensors, contact switches and laser range finders in order to tackle the obstacle detection problem.

In 1992, Pomerleau [17] demonstrated the first successful application of machine learning methods to the problem of mobile robot navigation. Soon after Davis and Stentz [6] proposed the MAMMOTH system which employed a neural network to learn how to combine steering angles produced by other neural networks using image and laser data.

It is interesting to contrast the machine learning techniques used in early robotic systems such as NAVLAB to more recent approaches such as the Demo III project [1]. While the early systems tried to achieve autonomy by solving one monolithic learning problem (training a neural network to map from grey level images to steering angles in the case of Pomerleau's ALVINN [17]), more recently the trend has been to make intensive use of human domain knowledge and only use learning for those aspects of the problem that are hard to pre-program. For example, in [1] the authors describe a system which uses manually derived rules to identify geometric obstacles, and then filters the results through a color-based classifier that tries to identify the false geometric obstacles caused by vegetation. This latter classifier is trained by fitting a mixture of Gaussians to humanly labeled data.

The approach we propose is located somewhere between the two extremes we just described. We believe that in certain cases it is a good idea to try to go directly from low-level data to an obstacle/non-obstacle decision but we would also like to be able to improve our results by using classifiers produced by human experts. Essentially, we would like to build a "black-box" in which we can feed our data and some other classifiers (trained or pre-programmed, that solve the entire obstacle detection problem or just part of it). The black-box should combine its inputs in such a way that the obstacle/non-obstacle decisions it produces as an output are more likely to be correct than those of any other classifier provided as an input. In this paper we will present results based on several classifier combination techniques and show that such a black-box can be built in practice.

In the following sections we will describe in more detail our problem setup (section 2) and the fusion techniques we have experimented with (section 3). In section 4 we present our experimental results and we draw conclusions and discuss future research directions in section 5.

2. Problem Setup

Considering the large variety of sensing equipment used in outdoor mobile robotics, we will attempt to describe the main assumptions we make about the robotic platform.

Two elements are important for our approach: we assume that the robot is equipped with some form of 3D range sensing (such as a laser range finder or a stereo vision setup), and that it has relatively good pose estimation. The pose estimation requirement can be relaxed, since it is only required for accumulating sensor data over time as the robot moves. In the worst case in which no pose estimation is available, we could still attempt to navigate using a "blindfolded robot" approach: we can ignore all history and make all decisions based on current data.

In addition to range sensing it is frequently the case that robots are equipped with some cameras (e.g. color, black and white, infrared). Our goal will be to combine the range and camera data in order to perform reliable outdoor obstacle detection.

2.1. Data Association

Fusing multisensor data at low-level requires solving the data association problem, which consists of establishing correspondences between the measurements returned by the different sensors. In our case we will need to find such correspondences between our laser data and the images from the color and IR cameras.

The initial step of our calibration procedure consists in determining the intrinsic paramters of our color and IR cameras, for which we use the Matlab Camera Calibration Toolbox ([3]). A relatively simple laser-camera calibration process – consisting of extracting the corners of a checkerboard calibration target in both the laser data and our images – allows us to recover the 3D transformation between the reference frame attached to the laser range finder and the frame of each camera. Using this transformation we can transform all the range measurements from the laser to the camera frames and then use the intrinsic parameters of our cameras in order to find the pixel coordinates where each 3D measurement should project. Thus, for all the laser points that happen to be in the field of view of our cameras we can obtain color and IR information.

Note that if we assume that the position of our robot in a fixed world frame is known we can accumulate laser points expressed in this frame. When a new set of images is captured we can transform these points to the current frame of the cameras and obtain image information for all the accumulated points that are visible.

2.2. Obstacle Detection as a Classification Problem

Assuming that the data association step is completed, there is a choice regarding the space in which we will perform obstacle detection: we can use the 3D space or the image space.

Using a 3D voxel representation for our analysis requires a mapping of the features extracted from images to 3D locations in the world. Using the 3D coordinates of the laser points that project close to a certain location in the image we can map the image properties extracted from that small area to a specific voxel in the 3D representation. The 3D voxels can then be classified as obstacle/non-obstacle voxels using their laser and image-based features.

Performing the analysis in the image space requires the opposite process: one of the images selected as reference is divided into a grid of rectangular patches and all the available 3D measurements are projected into it. Each image patch will contain zero or more laser points, which we can use to extract "laser features" such as range statistics or height in the vehicle frame. The laser features together with the image features (such as texture and color statistics) are the inputs to a classifier which will decide if the image patches as corresponding to an obstacle in the scene or not. The 3D points that project into each patch can be used to estimate the locations of the patches classified as obstacles, a step necessary for obstacle avoidance.

While the two representation models are essentially equivalent, we have chosen to use the image space classification which is more convenient for both labeling data and visualization of the classification results. This is not a limiting factor for the obstacle detection algorithms that we can use in our classifier fusion approach: any labeling of 3D voxels can be converted to a labeling of image patches and vice-versa.

The setup we have presented reduces the problem of obstacle detection to the one of binary classification of image patches in the obstacle/non-obstacle classes. For each image patch we extract color, texture, IR and various laser statistics features which can be used as inputs to our classification methods.

The learning methods used for the experiments presented in this paper are all supervised algorithms. We produce manually labeled data by selecting area of interest in images and classifying them as obstacles or non-obstacles.

3. Classifier Fusion

3.1. Motivation

We have described a method for extracting information (or "features") from several different sensors and using them as inputs to classification algorithms. If we reduced ourselves to simply concatenating all the feature vectors we would essentially perform a simple form of data fusion at the pixel (or more precisely image patch) level. In many mobile robotics applications it is beneficial to be able to also include already existing classifiers that might incorporate significant amounts of domain knowledge. As we have stated in the introduction, we would like to have the capability to automatically learn when to use certain classifiers and how to combine them with and based on the available input data.

The reasons for which classifier combination might be desirable in robotics applications include:

- Several research groups might work on obstacle detection algorithms, making possibly different assumptions about the scene and about the sensors. It is likely that the failure modes of their algorithms will be slightly different, which leads to the question whether by aggregating the decisions of all the classifiers in the pool we could do better on average than any individual algorithm.

- Certain types of obstacles can be particularly difficult to detect: thin wires and negative obstacles (such as holes and trenches) are good examples. While in such cases it might hard to implement a general obstacle detection algorithm that "learns" how to detect them, human understanding of the constraints specific to the obstacle to be detected can lead to much more effective *specialized* detectors. Learning classifier fusion automatically would enable us to determine the weights and rules that should be used with such specialized classifiers without manually tuning parameters based on their false alarms and detection rates.

3.2. Algorithms

In this paper we will discuss three algorithms for classifier combination: committees of experts ([15, 2]), stacked generalization ([27]) and a slight variation of the AdaBoost algorithm ([20]). While our classifier fusion experiments are not limited to these specific algorithms, we consider them to be different enough from each other to be representative for the results one could expect from applying classifier fusion in our domain.

1. **Commitees of Experts**

   Initially described as a method for improving regression estimates in [16, 15], a committee of experts can be used for both regression and classification. The idea behind the algorithm is simple: if we have a pool of L experts that estimate a target function $f(x)$, we can linearly combine their outputs as $f_{COE}(x) = \sum_{i=1}^{L} \alpha_i f_i(x)$, where $f_i(x)$ is the estimate produced by the ith expert. Under this model it can easily be shown [16, 15, 2] that the optimal (in the mean squared error sense) α_i's are given by

   $$\alpha_i = \frac{\sum_{j=1}^{L}(\mathbf{C}^{-1})_{ij}}{\sum_{k=1}^{L}\sum_{j=i}^{L}(\mathbf{C}^{-1})_{kj}}$$

   where $\mathbf{C}$ is the error correlation matrix. It can be shown that the mean squared error of the committee is always smaller than or equal to the average mean squared error over the classifier pool. In fact, if we assume that the experts make uncorrelated zero mean errors the error decreases by at least a factor of L. Obviously, this is overly optimistic: in reality the errors of the classifiers are going to be correlated so the reduction in error will be much smaller. However, given the simplicity of the method it is very attractive to use it. The assumption that needs to be made for the COE fusion approach is that the classifiers in the pool are trying to solve the same problem. As a result, this technique has the limitation of not being able to support specialized classifiers.

2. **Stacked Generalization**

   Introduced by Wolpert in 1990 [27], stacked generalization (or "stacking") was initially presented as a method for combining multiple models learned for classification. Since then, stacking has also been used for regression [4] and even unsupervised learning [24].

   Despite being an extremely simple algorithm, stacked generalization is quite difficult to describe. To make the task easier, we describe what stacked generalization (SG) would be equivalent to if we are willing to assume that a very large amount of training data is available, and then explain the actual algorithm.

   In the form described by Wolpert in [27], stacked generalization is a two stage classifier. Just like in the case of committees of experts we will assume that we have a pool of L trainable experts that estimate a target function $f(x)$. These classifiers are what Wolpert calls the "level-0 generalizers", and are trained in the first stage of SG. The second stage consists of training a classifier that takes as inputs the outputs of the level-0 generalizers and tries to produce the correct label as an output.

   This classifier is called the "level-1 generalizer", and its purpose is to learn the biases of the level-0 generalizers.

   The crucial element of stacked generalization is that the level-1 generalizer should be trained using data that is "new" to the level-0 generalizers, since we are interested in learning about their generalization properties and not their ability to overfit. In the ideal case where very large amounts of training data were available, this could simply be achieved by splitting the training data and reserving half of it (for example) for training the second stage classifier. The only difference about the stacked generalization algorithm and the method we just described is that in the real algorithm a cross-validation scheme is used so that all the data is used for training both stages of the classifier.

   Stacked generalization works surprisingly well in practice, and it has been applied successfully in other domains such as ATR ([26]).

3. **AdaBoost with Classifier Selection**

   AdaBoost is an algorithm that has been shown to be somewhat similar to the popular support vector machines, in that it tries to maximize the separation margin. Shapire and Freund [20] proposed a clever iterative algorithm that solves the margin maximization problem with the only requirement that a so-called "weak classifier" –a learning algorithm that can perform better than a random one– is available.

   The intuitive idea behind AdaBoost is to train a series of classifiers and to iteratively focus on the hard training examples. The algorithm relies on continuously changing the weights of its training examples so that those that are frequently misclassified get higher and higher weights: this way, new classifiers that are added to the ensemble are more likely to classify those hard examples correctly. Aside from this intuition, AdaBoost's training scheme corresponds to performing gradient descent on an error function that exponentially penalizes small classification margins [13, 21].

   Our small variation to the regular form of Adaboost consists in allowing the algorithm to choose at each iteration which *type* of weak classifier to train. Assuming that we have a pool of classifiers and that some of them can be trained, we allow the algorithm to examine all the classifiers in our pool –training the ones that are trainable– and select the one that can best classify the training examples given their current weight distribution. Thus, AdaBoost will select one of the classifiers available at each iteration.

   Note that while this is not the regular procedure for training AdaBoost, we are not modifying any of the assumptions that the algorithm is based on. A similar application of AdaBoost was successfully demonstrated by Tieu and Viola [25] in the context of automated image retrieval.

4. Experimental Results

4.1. Features

In order to validate the techniques described so far we have performed experiments with both the XUV and another CMU robotic platform. While the two vehicles are equipped with different sensors and have different geometries, we have used the same approach (described in section 2) to extract information about the scenes. For each patch in our image grids we have computed the following features:

- **Color.** The images are converted to the LUV color space; we extract the mean and standard deviation of the pixels in a patch for each channel, obtaining 6 color features.

- **Texture.** The FFT representation of each patch is computed, and it is then divided into 6 bins for frequency and 6 for the orientation. The means and standard deviation of the energy in each bin are computed, resulting in a total of 24 texture features.

- **Infrared.** The mean and standard deviation of the IR pixel values for each patch are computed, resulting in 2 IR features. The correspondence between the color patches (used as reference) and IR patches is established using the 3D information provided by the laser points that project in the color patch.

- **Laser (simple statistics).** Using the laser points that project into each image patch we estimate the average height expressed in the vehicle frame, and the standard deviations in the XYZ directions relative to the vehicle frame. This results in 4 simple laser features.

- **Laser (Vandapel-Hebert features and classification [11]).** As a good example of a specialized classifier we might want to incorporate into our system, we have used an implementation of the technique described in [11] for terrain classification. The method looks at the local point distribution in space and uses a Bayes classifier to produce the probability of belonging to 3 classes - vegetation, solid surface and linear structure. The method takes as input a sparse set of 3-D points. At each point the scatter matrix is computed using a predefined support region. The decomposition in principal components of this matrix leads to the definition of three saliency features characterizing the 3-D points spatial distribution as "random", "linear" and "surface". We use both these saliencies and the probabilities of belonging to each class, which results in a number of 6 features. We will refer to these features as "Laser VH".

4.2. Experiment 1

The first experiment we will present is based on data collected with the XUV robotic platform. The vehicle is equipped with a laser range finder unit, two 640x480 Sony color cameras and an infrared camera with the same resolution. The laser unit and the cameras are mounted inside a pan-tilt platform.

We have evaluated the performance of the various feature sets and the benefit of the different fusion strategies by attempting to solve a problem that is very important for outdoor mobile robotics: detecting dirt roads. While the road detection is not an instance of an obstacle detection problem, notice that our setup is essentially solving binary classification problems and as such can also be used for terrain classification.

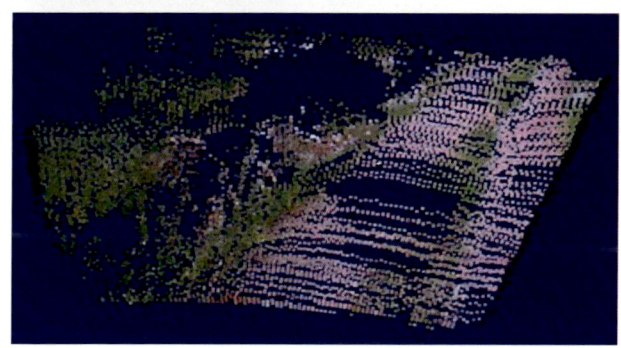

Figure 1. A typical scene from the road detection dataset: the color image (top-left), the IR image (top-right), the 3D point cloud in which points are colorized based on the color image (bottom).

The data logs used for this experiment were collected at the ARL Fort Indiantown Gap robotics facility. Each data log contained color and infrared images, together with vehicle position and range data from the vehicle. We have used 3 independent datasets (2 merged into the training set,

1 used as a test set). The corresponding images were manually labeled in the two classes of interest. We have only used image patches that contained laser points, which resulted in 18963/8582 patches in the train/test datasets. The percentage of road patches was 0.62/0.63.

After labeling the data and extracting the features we have trained several classifiers on this problem. More specifically, we compared the performance of neural networks trained on subsets of our full feature vector (such as color, texture, IR, laser simple and laser VH) with the performance of a neural network that has access to the full vector. We also compared their performance to two of our classifier fusion algorithms, stacked generalization and committees of experts. The numerical results are presented in Figure 2, while Figure 3 presents a graphical representation of the average error rates.

Name	Mean	Std Dev
SG	2.89	0.44
CoE	3.77	0.54
Color	9.45	2.79
Texture	28.73	2.02
IR	12.33	5.22
Laser Simple	17.33	5.29
Laser VH	11.72	3.13
All Features	3.19	0.61

Figure 2. Error rates for the road detection experiments. From the first row down we have stacked generalization, committees of experts, and color, texture, infrared, laser simple, laser VH, and all feature based neural networks.

In order to estimate the error rates and standard deviations we performed 10 fold cross-validation without prior randomization of the patches. We chose not to use randomization in order to avoid getting overly optimistic results: since there is high degree of correlation between neighboring image patches, splitting them randomly would lead to unrealistic similarities between the training and testing datasets. We have also performed experiments with completely separate training and test datasets (i.e. without cross-validation) and the error rates we obtained were similar to the ones produced by cross-validation.

Overall our results are encouraging: they confirm that performing both low-level data fusion and classifier fusion can significantly improve classification performance. The fact that committees of experts and stacked generalization performed as well as a neural network that has access to the full feature vector is very positive. While in this case we had full access to all the features (including the ones pro-

Road Detection

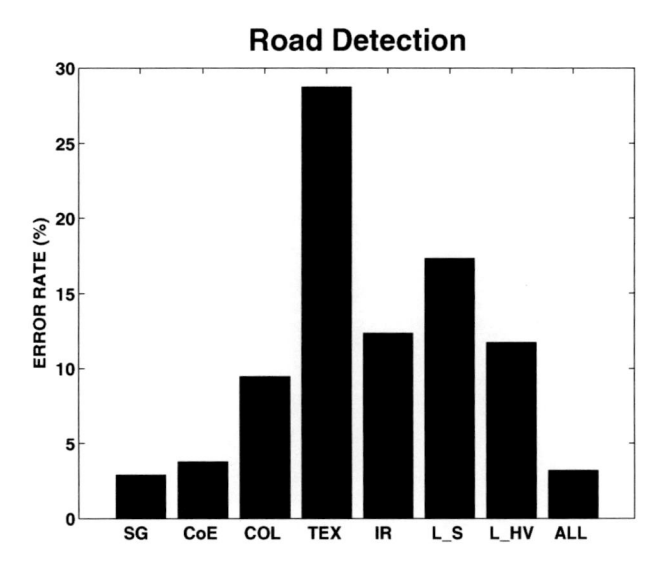

Figure 3. Error rates on the road detection problem. The bars represent in order: (SG) Stacked Generalization, (CoE) committees of experts, (COL) Color, (TEX) Texture, (IR) Infrared, (L_S) Laser simple, (L_VH) Laser VH and (ALL) all features based neural networks.

duced by the VH classifier) which reduces the importance of classifier fusion, it is important to confirm that algorithms like COE and SG can learn to combine input classifiers very effectively.

It is interesting to notice that the VH features (which effectively represent a form of specialized classifier) perform significantly better than the simple laser statistics, despite the fact that exactly the same laser points are used as inputs in both cases. This is a perfect example of why one would like to be able to fuse several classifiers.

4.3. Experiment 2

The second experiment we present uses data collected with a CMU developed robotic platform (a large tractor). The vehicle is equipped with two Sony DFW-SX900 high-resolution color digital cameras producing 1280x960 images and two laser range finder units which are based on mechanically scanned SICK LMS units. At the time the data logs were recorded the vehicle did not have an IR camera.

The experiment we performed on CMU data used the same types of features as the ones based on XUV data, except for the laser VH and the IR features which were not available. The cameras and the laser units have performance characteristics that are quite different from those of the XUV sensors. This makes the experiment even more interesting: we are claiming that using automated learning makes our fusion techniques applicable to many different vehicles and sensor configurations. This is an example of such an application of the same techniques fusion techniques on significantly different vehicles.

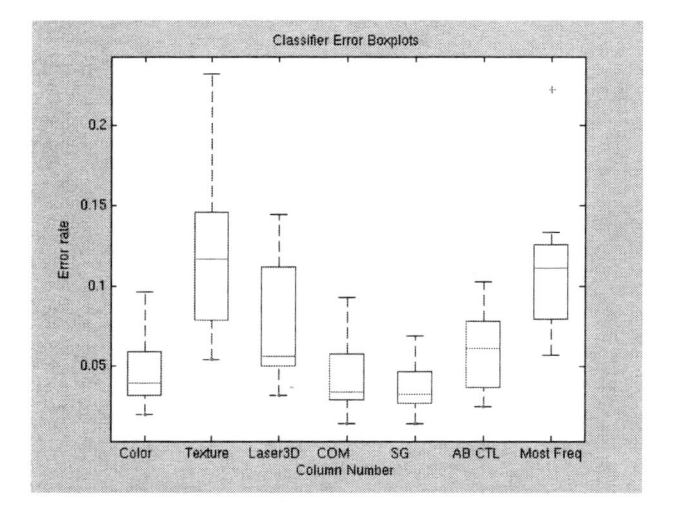

Figure 4. Box plots representing the classification performance on the obstacle detection problem. The rectangle for each classifier represents the interquartile range and the horizontal line is the median. From left to right we have the color, texture and laser based classifiers, the committee of experts (COM), stacked generalization (SG), AdaBoost (AB CTL) and Most Frequent, a classifier that always predicts the most frequent class without using any features.

The problem we attempted to solve in this case was obstacle detection, using a dataset in which the obstacle was a human walking in front of the moving vehicle in an area with tall vegetation. To make the problem non-trivial the human was wearing a camouflage jacket. The raw classifiers were neural networks, this time using color, texture and simple laser features. The classifier fusion strategies we compared were stacked generalization, a committee of experts and the version of AdaBoost we described. The dataset we used contained 22989 non-obstacle and 2893 obstacle image patches (we used 20x20 patches).

The results presented in Figure 4 were obtained performing 10 fold cross-validation on our dataset. Since the two classes (obstacle/non-obstacle) were so unbalanced, we presented the error rate of a "constant" classifier that always predicts the most frequent class. Since only 12 percent of our data represents the obstacle class the reader should be aware that an error rate of 10 percent does not necessarily represent good performance.

In this experiment the color classifier performed extremely well, followed by the laser features and the texture which was mostly irrelevant. The explanation is that the vegetation was slightly dry, which made the color of the camouflaged jacket different from the background. Stacked generalization and the committee of experts were able to learn to focus on the color-based predictions and to use the laser information to slightly improve upon the color performance. A t-test based on our cross-validation data showed this slight improvement to be statistically significant.

The boosting algorithm performed slightly worse than the best input classifier. Our analysis indicated that the problem lies in the exponential penalty that AdaBoost "charges" for small classification margins. The algorithm focuses on increasing the margin on a small number of very difficult training examples while actually reducing the margin of the others; as a result, its generalization performance is reduced. A solution to this problem would be to use "soft-margin" AdaBoost variations such as the one described in [18].

5. Conclusions

We have presented a system that uses multisensor data fusion at both the pixel level and the classifier level in order to improve obstacle detection performance for outdoor mobile robots. Our experiments –on different platforms, sensors and feature configurations– confirm the intuition that combining data from multiple sensing modalities can dramatically improve classification performance. Furthermore, we have shown that automatically combining different classifiers in order to leverage on their particular strengths and provide performance that is better than that of any classifier in the pool is possible. We anticipate that this type of approach will have important applications in mobile robotics. We will continue our experiments in order to analyze the performance of our system on different classification problems and with more complex classifier combination schemes such as hierarchical mixtures of experts [12].

The weakest link of our current setup is the fact that we rely on supervised learning. Labeling data for large scale problems is tedious and expensive, and we are currently developing active learning solutions for alleviating the data labeling requirements. The main direction of our effort is to adapt anomaly detection techniques from the data mining field to our domain, but we are also experimenting with methods such as the one described in [19] to iteratively select the next "most informative" data to label. Since in most robotics applications it is usually inexpensive to collect very large amounts of unlabeled data, we believe that active learning has the potential to open numerous new possibilities for the successful application of machine learning in robotics.

6. Acknowledgements

We would like to acknowledge the valuable support of Carl Wellington in developing some of the infrastructure used for these experiments.

This paper was prepared through collaborative participation in the Robotics Consortium sponsored by the U. S. Army Research Laboratory under the Collaborative Technology Alliance Program, Cooperative Agreement DAAD19-01-2-0012. The U. S. Government is authorized to reproduce and distribute reprints for Government purposes notwithstanding any copyright notation thereon.

References

[1] P. Belluta, R. Manduchi, L. Matthies, K. Owens, and A. Rankin. Terrain perception for DEMO III. In *Proceedings of the IEEE Intelligent Vehicles Symposium*, pages 326–331, October 2000.

[2] C. M. Bishop. *Neural Networks for Pattern Recognition*. Oxford University Press, 1997.

[3] J.-Y. Bouguet. Camera calibration toolbox for matlab. http://www.vision.caltech.edu/bouguetj/calib_doc/.

[4] L. Breiman. Stacked regressions. *Machine Learning*, 24(1):49–64, July 1996.

[5] M. Daily, J. Harris, D. Keirsey, K. Olin, D. Payton, K. Reiser, J. Rosenblatt, D. Tseng, and V. Wong. Autonomous cross-country navigation with the ALV. In *Proceedings of the International Conference on Robotics and Automation*, pages 718–726, 1988.

[6] I. Davis and A. Stentz. Sensor fusion for autonomous outdoor navigation using neural networks. In *Proceedings of the IEEE International Conference On Intelligent Robotic Systems*, volume 3, pages 338–343, August 1995.

[7] A. de Saint Vincent. A 3-D perception system for the mobile robot HILAIRE. In *Proc. IEEE Int. Conf. Robotics and Automat.*, pages 1105–1111, San Francisco, 1986.

[8] Y. Goto and A. Stentz. The CMU system for mobile robot navigation. In *Proc. IEEE Int. Conf. Robotics and Automat.*, pages 99–105, Raleigh, North Carolina, 1987.

[9] S. Harmon, G. Bianchini, and B. Pinz. Sensor data fusion through a distributed blackboard. In *Proc. IEEE Int. Conf. Robotics and Automat.*, pages 1449–1454, San Francisco, 1986.

[10] S. Y. Harmon. The ground surveillance robot (GSR): An autonomous vehicle designed to transit unknown terrain. *IEEE Journal of Robotics and Automation*, RA-3(3):266–279, June 1987.

[11] M. Hebert and N. Vandapel. Terrain classification techniques from ladar data for autonomous navigation. In *Collaborative Technology Alliance Workshop*, 2003.

[12] M. I. Jordan and R. A. Jacobs. Hierarchical mixtures of experts and the em algorithm. *Neural Computation*, (6):181–214, 1994.

[13] L. Mason, J. Baxter, P. Bartlett, and M. Frean. Boosting algorithms as gradient descent. In S. Solla, T. Leen, and K.-R. Muller, editors, *Advances in Neural Information Processing Systems*, volume 12, pages 512–518. MIT Press, 2000.

[14] H. P. Moravec. The Stanford Cart and the CMU Rover. In *Proceedings of the IEEE*, volume 71, pages 872–884, 1983.

[15] M. P. Perrone. *Improving Regression Estimation: Averaging Methods for Variance Reduction with Extensions to General Convex Measure Optimization*. PhD thesis, Brown University, May 1993.

[16] M. P. Perrone and L. N. Cooper. When networks disagree: Ensemble methods for hybrid neural networks. In R. J. Mammone, editor, *Neural Networks for Speech and Image Processing*, pages 126–142. Chapman-Hall, 1993.

[17] D. Pomerleau. Progress in neural network-based vision for autonoumous robot driving. In *Proc. of the Intelligent Vehicles '92 Symposium*, pages 391–396, 1992.

[18] G. Rätsch, T. Onoda, and K.-R. Müller. Soft margins for AdaBoost. *Machine Learning*, 42(3):287–320, Mar. 2001.

[19] N. Roy and A. McCallum. Toward optimal active learning through monte carlo estimation of error reduction. In *Proceedings of the International Conference on Machine Learning*, June 2001.

[20] R. E. Schapire. A brief introduction to boosting. In *Proceedings of the Sixteenth International Joint Conference on Artificial Intelligence 1999*, 1999. read.

[21] R. E. Schapire. The boosting approach to machine learning. MSRI Workshop on Nonlinear Estimation and Classification, 2002.

[22] S. Shafer, A. Stentz, and C. Thorpe. An architecture for sensory fusion in a mobile robot. In *Proc. IEEE Int. Conf. Robotics and Automat.*, pages 2002–2011, San Francisco, 1986.

[23] C. M. Shoemaker and J. A. Bornstein. The Demo III UGV program: A testbed for autonomous navigation research. In *Proceedings of the 1998 IEEE ISIC/CIRA/ISAS Joint Conference*, pages 644–651, Gaithersburg, MD, 1998.

[24] P. Smyth and D. Wolpert. An evaluation of linerly combining density estimators via stacking. Technical Report 98-25, Information and Computer Science Department, University of California, Irvine, July 1998.

[25] K. Tieu and P. Viola. Boosting image retrieval. In *Proceedings of the IEEE Conference on Computer Vision and Pattern Recognition*, 2000.

[26] L.-C. Wang, L. Chan, N. M. Nasrabadi, and S. Der. Combination of two learning algorithms for automatic target recognition. In *Proceedings of the International Conference on Image Processing*, volume 1, pages 881–884, October 1997.

[27] D. H. Wolpert. Stacked generalization. Technical Report LA-UR-90-3460, Los Alamos, NM, 1990.

Stereo Mosaics with Slanting Parallel Projections from Many Cameras or a Moving Camera

Zhigang Zhu

Department of Computer Science, The City College of New York, New York, NY 10031
zhu@cs.ccny.cuny.edu

Abstract

This paper presents an approach of fusing images from many video cameras or a moving video camera with external orientation data (e.g. GPS and INS data) into a few mosaiced images that preserve 3D information. In both cases, a virtual 2D array of cameras with FOV overlaps is formed to generate the whole coverage of a scene (or an object). We propose a representation that can re-organize the original perspective images into a set of parallel projections with different slanting viewing angles. In addition to providing a wide field of view, there are two more benefits of such a representation. First, mosaics with different slanting views represent occlusions encountered in a usual nadir view. Second, stereo pair can be formed from a pair of slanting parallel mosaics thus image-based 3D viewing can be achieved. This representation can be used as both an advanced video interface for surveillance or a pre-processing for 3D reconstruction.

1. Introduction

It is a commonplace to generate a 2D panoramic mosaic of the 3D scene from a moving camera, with a single multiple-viewpoint viewing direction [1,2], but 3D information and/or surface information from other viewing directions is lost in such a representation. A digital elevation map (DEM) generated from aerial photometry consists of a sampled array of elevations (depths) for a number of ground positions at regularly spaced intervals [3]. It usually only has a nadir viewing direction, hence the surfaces from other viewing directions cannot be represented. However, in some applications such as surveillance and security inspection, a scene or an object (e.g. a vehicle) needs to be observed from many viewing directions to reveal the abnormal areas hidden in unusual views. Stereo panoramas [4,5] have been presented to obtain the best 3D information from an off-center rotating camera. In the case of a translating camera, various layered representations [6-8] have been proposed to represent both 3D information and occlusions, but such representations need 3D reconstructions.

This paper presents an approach of fusing images from many spatially distributed video cameras or a moving video camera with external orientation data (e.g. GPS and INS data) into a few mosaiced images that preserve 3D information. In both cases, a virtual 2D array of cameras with FOV overlaps is formed to generate the whole coverage of a scene (or an object). As a matter of fact, many viewing directions are included in the original camera views. X-slit mosaics with non-parallel rays [9] have been proposed using this property to generate mosaics for image-based rendering. In this paper we propose a representation that can re-organize the original perspective images into a set of parallel projections with different slanting viewing angles (in both the x and the y directions of the 2D images). Such representations provide a wide field of view, 3D information for stereo viewing and reconstruction, and the capability to represent occlusions. This representation can be used as both an advanced video interface for surveillance or a pre-processing for 3D reconstruction and scene representation.

As the organization of this paper, we first present the stereo mosaicing representations with a set of slanting parallel projections in both directions. Second we show how to construct a 2D (virtual) camera array in three different cases. Third we present the Parallel Ray Interpolation for Stereo Mosaicing (PRISM) approach for generate mosaics under real camera setups and for arbitrary 3D scenes. Then we analyze the advantages of such representations in stereo viewing and 3D reconstruction. Finally experimental results are given for two important applications – aerial video surveillance and under vehicle inspection. In the aerial video case, a moving camera is accompanied by GPS and INS measurements to provide orientation data. In the under vehicle inspection system, a pre-calibrated 1D array of cameras are used to scan the bottom of a vehicle when the vehicle is driven over the camera array. Finally a brief summary is given.

2. 2D Slanting Parallel Projection

A normal perspective camera has a single viewpoint, which means all the rays pass through a common nodal point. On the other hand, an orthogonal image with parallel projections in both the *x* and *y* directions has all the rays parallel to each other. Imagining that we have a sensor with parallel projections, we could rotate the sensor to capture images with different *slanting* angles (including nadir and oblique angles) in both directions so that we can create many pair of parallel stereo images with two different slanting angles, and observe surfaces that could be occluded in a nadir view.

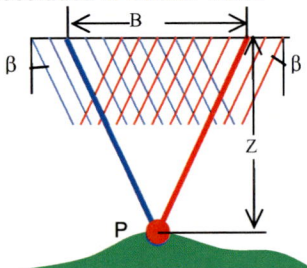

Fig. 1. Depth from parallel stereo with multiple viewpoints: 1D case.

Fig. 1 shows the parallel stereo in a 1D case, where two slanting (oblique) angles are chosen to construct stereo geometry. The depth of a point can be calculated as (Fig. 1)

$$Z = \frac{B}{2tg\beta} \quad (1)$$

where 2β is the angle between the two viewing directions, and B is the adaptive baseline between the two viewpoints that construct the triangulation relation. It has been shown by others [10] and by us [11, 12] that parallel stereo is superior to both conventional perspective stereo and to the recently developed multi-perspective stereo with concentric mosaics for 3D reconstruction (e.g., in [5]), in that the adaptive baseline inherent in the parallel-perspective geometry permits depth accuracy independent of absolute depth in theory [10,11] and as a linear function of depth in stereo mosaics from perspective image sequences [12].

We can make two extensions to this parallel stereo. First, we can select various slanting angles for constructing multiple parallel projections. By doing so we can observe various degrees of occlusions and can construct stereo pairs with different depth resolution via the changes of baselines. Second, we can extend this 1D parallel projection to 2D (Fig. 2): we can obtain a mosaiced image that has a nadir view (Fig. 2a), slanting angle(s) only in one direction (Fig. 2b and c) or in both the *x* and the *y* directions (Fig. 2d).

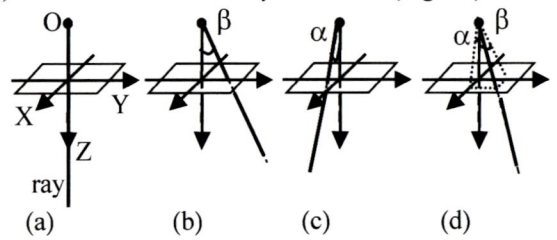

Fig. 2. Parallel projections with two slanting angles α and β (in the *x* and *y* directions). (a) Nadir view (α=β=0); (b) y-slanting view (α=0, β≠0); (c) x-slanting view (α≠0, β=0) and (d) dual-slanting view (α≠0, β≠0). Parallel mosaics can be formed by populating the single selected ray in each case in both the *x* and *y* directions.

3. 2D (Virtual) Array of Cameras

It is impractical to use a single sensor to capture orthogonal images with full parallel projections in both *x* and *y* dimensions for a large scene, and with various oblique directions. However we could have at least three practical approaches in generate images with slanting parallel projections with existing sensors: a 2D sensor array of many spatially distributed cameras, a "scanner" with a 1D array of cameras, and a single perspective camera that moves (Fig. 3).

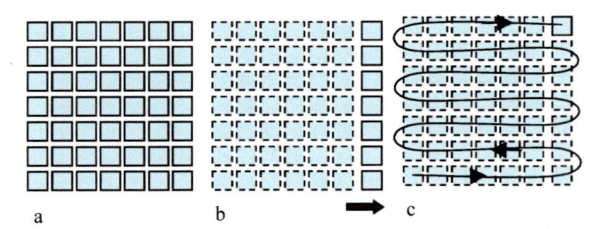

Fig. 3. Parallel mosaics from 2D bed of cameras. (a) 2D array; (b) 1D scanning array and (c) a single scanning camera.

With a 2D array of many perspective cameras (Fig. 3a), we first assume that the optical axes of all the cameras point to the same directions (inside the paper in Fig 3a), and the viewpoints of all cameras are on a plane perpendicular to their optical axes. Then we can reorganize the perspective images into mosaiced images with any slanting viewing angles by extract rays from the original perspective images with the same viewing directions, one ray from each image. If the camera array is dense enough, then we can generate densely mosaiced images.

If we only have a 1D linear array of perspective cameras (Fig. 3b), we can translate the camera to scan over the scene to synthesize a virtual 2D bed of camera array. Then we can still generate stereo mosaic pairs with slanting parallel projections, given that we can accurately control the translation of the camera array. We have actually used this approach in an Under Vehicle Inspection System (UVIS) [13, 14, 18].

Even if we just use a single camera, we can still generate a 2D virtual bed of cameras by moving the cameras in two dimensions, along a 2D scanning path shown in Fig. 3c. This is the case for aerial video mosaics [11, 12, 15, 17].

4. PRISM: Video Mosaicing Algorithm

In real applications, there are two challenging issues. First, it is difficult to have all cameras point to the same directions, with their viewpoints in a plane. Second, it is impractical to have such a dense camera array (or such a dense scan) to generate dense parallel mosaics. However, we can still generate dense parallel mosaics after we solve the following two main problems.

The first problem is camera orientation estimation (calibration). It is well known that camera calibration is a hard problem, especially for a moving camera. In our previous study of aerial video application, we used external orientation instruments, i.e., GPS, INS and laser profiler to ease the problem of camera orientation estimation [11, 12]. In this paper, we assume that the extrinsic and intrinsic camera parameters are known at each camera location.

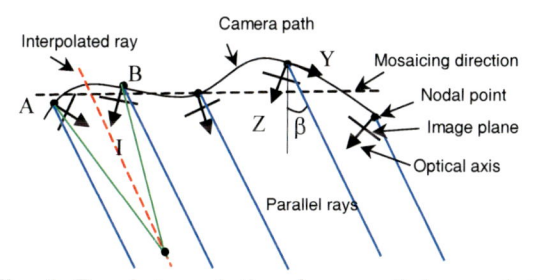

Fig. 4. Ray interpolation for parallel mosaicing from an arbitrary camera array.

The second problem is to generate dense parallel mosaics with a sparse, uneven, camera array, and for a complicated 3D scene. To solve this problem, a Parallel Ray Interpolation for Stereo Mosaics (PRISM) approach has been proposed [11]. While the PRISM algorithm was originally designed to generate parallel-perspective stereo mosaics (parallel projection in one direction and perspective projection in the other), the core idea of *ray interpolation* could be used for generating mosaics with full parallel projection of any slanting angles.

Fig. 4 shows how the PRISM works for 1D images. The 1D camera has two axes – the optical axis (Z) and the Y-axis. Given the known camera orientation at each camera location, one ray with a given slanting angle β can be chosen from the image at each camera location to contribute to the parallel mosaic with the same slanting angle β. The slanting angle is defined against the direction perpendicular to the *mosaicing direction*, which is the mean direction of the camera path (Fig. 4). But the problem is that the "mosaiced" image with only those existing rays will be sparse and uneven since the camera array cannot be regular and very dense. Therefore interpolated parallel rays between a pair of parallel rays from two successive images should be generated by performing local matching between these two images, or other additional images. The assumption is that we can found at least two images to generate the parallel ray. Such an interpolated ray is shown in Fig 4, where Ray I is interpolated from Image A and Image B.

One interesting property of the parallel mosaics is that all the (virtual) viewpoints are in infinite. Therefore, even if the original camera path has large deviation in the direction perpendicular to the mosaicing direction, we can still generate full parallel mosaics. However, we should note that in practice, too large deviation in the perpendicular direction will result in a captured image sequence with rather different image resolutions, hence the resulted mosaics will have an uneven spatial resolution.

The extension to 2D images (particular to the X direction of the cameras) of the above approach is straightforward, and a similar region triangulation strategy as in [11] can be applied here to deal with 2D images. However, one practical issue here is the selection of neighborhood images of each image for ray interpolation. For example, with a 1D scan sequence of a single camera, it is hard to generate full parallel projection in the X direction perpendicular to the motion of the camera, since the interpolated parallel rays far off the center of the images in the x direction have to use rays with rather different oblique angles in the original perspective images.

5. Stereo Viewing and 3D Reconstruction

Parallel mosaics with various slanting angles represent scenes from the corresponding viewing angles with parallel rays, with virtually endless fields of view. There are two obvious applications of such representation. First, a human can perceive the 3D scene with a pair of mosaics with different slanting angles (e.g. using polarized glasses) without any 3D recovery. If we have mosaics with various slanting angles in both the x and the y direction, we can generate a virtual fly/walk-through – the translation in the *xy* plane can be simulated by shifting the current displayed mosaic pair, the rotations around the X and the Y axes can be simulated by selecting different pairs of mosaics, and the rotation around the optical axis only needs to rotate the pair of mosaics in their image planes.

Second, for 3D recovery, matches are only performed on a pair of mosaics, not on individual video frames. Stereo mosaic methods also solve the baseline versus field-of-view (FOV) dilemma efficiently by extending the FOV in the directions of mosaicing – in both the *x* and *y* directions. More important, the parallel stereo mosaics have fixed "disparities" and optimal/adaptive baselines for all the points, which leads to uniform depth resolution in theory and linear depth resolution in practice. For 3D reconstruction, epipolar geometry is rather simple due to the full parallel projections in the mosaic pair.

6. Experimental Examples

We present results of stereo mosaics for two applications: airborne videography for aerial surveillance, and 1D video array for under-vehicle inspection.

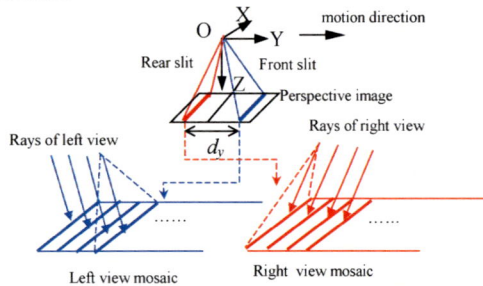

Fig. 5. Parallel-perspective stereo mosaics with a 1D scan path of camera motion.

6.1. Video mosaics from aerial video

First we assume the motion of a camera is an ideal 1D translation, the optical axis is perpendicular to the motion, and the frames are dense enough. Then, we can generate two spatio-temporal images by extracting two columns of pixels (perpendicular to the motion) at the front and rear edges of each frame in motion (Fig. 5). The mosaic images thus generated are *parallel-perspective*, which have perspective projection in the direction perpendicular to the motion and parallel projection in the motion direction. In addition, these mosaics are obtained from two different oblique viewing angles of a single camera's field of view, so that a stereo pair of left and right mosaics captures the inherent 3D information. Note that we do not generate parallel projection in the *x* direction for this 1D scan case due to the difficulty mentioned in Section 4.

In the aerial video application, a single camera is mounted in a small aircraft undergoing 6 DOF motion, together with a GPS, INS and laser profiler to measure the moving camera locations and the distances of the terrain [11, 12]. So we can generate seamless stereo parallel-perspective video mosaic strips from image sequences with a 1D scan path, but with a rather general motion model, using the proposed parallel ray interpolation for stereo mosaicing (PRISM) approach [11]. In the PRISM approach for large-scale 3D scene modeling, the computation is efficiently distributed in three steps: camera pose estimation via the external measurement units, image mosaicing via ray interpolation, and 3D reconstruction from a pair of stereo mosaics.

In principle, we need to match all the points between the two overlapping slices of the successive frames to generate a complete parallel-perspective mosaic. In an effort to reduce the computational complexity, we have designed a fast PRISM algorithm [11] based on the proposed PRISM method. It only requires matches between a set of point pairs in two successive images, and the rest of the points are generated by warping a set of triangulated regions defined by the control points in each of the two images. The proposed fast PRISM algorithm can be easily extended to use more feature points (thus smaller triangles) in the overlapping slices so that each triangle really covers a planar patch or a patch that is visually indistinguishable from a planar patch, or to perform pixel-wise dense matches to achieve true parallel-perspective geometry.

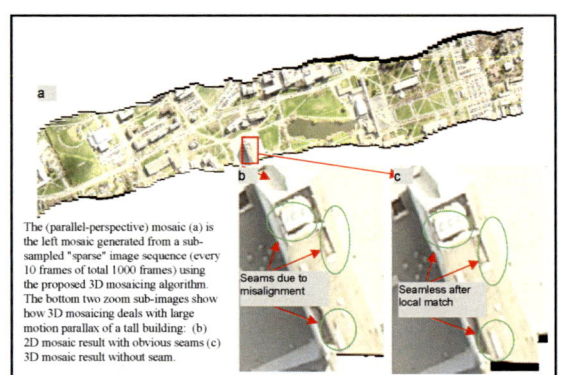

Fig. 6. Parallel-perspective mosaics of a campus scene from an airborne camera.

Fig. 6 shows mosaic results from an aerial video sequence of a cultural scene. Please compare the results of parallel-perspective mosaicing via the

PRISM approach [11] vs. 2D mosaicing via similar approach as the manifold mosaicing [2], by looking along many building boundaries associating with depth changes in the entire 4160x1536 mosaics at our web site [15]. Since it is hard to see subtle errors in the 2D mosaics of the size of Fig. 6a, Fig. 6b and Fig. 6c show close-up windows of the 2D and 3D mosaics for the same portion of the scene with the tall Campus Center building. In Fig. 6b the multi-perspective mosaic via 2D mosaicing has obvious seams along the stitching boundaries between two frames. It can be observed by looking at the region indicated by circles where some fine structures (parts of a white blob and two rectangles) are missing due to misalignments. As expected, the parallel-perspective mosaic via 3D mosaicing (Fig. 6c) does not exhibit these problems.

Fig. 7. Stereo mosaics and 3D reconstruction of a 166-frame telephoto video sequence. (a) Left mosaics (b) right mosaics (c) depth map and (d) stereoscopic viewing using left-blue/right-red glasses.

As another example, Fig. 7 shows a real example of stereo mosaics (with two y-slanting angles) generated from a telephoto camera and 3D recovery for a forest scene in Amazon rain forest. The average height of the airplane is $H = 385$ m, and the distance between the two slit windows is selected as 160 pixels (in the y direction) with images of 720 (x) *480 (y) pixels. The image resolution is about 7.65 pixels/meter. The depth map of stereo mosaics in Fig. 7c was obtained by using a hierarchical sub-pixel dense correlation method [16], where the range of depth variations of the forest scene (from a stereo fixation plane) is from -24.0 m (tree canopy) to 24.0 m (the ground). Even before any 3D recovery, a human observer can perceive the 3D structure of the scene with a stereo pair (Fig. 7d).

We have used the same instrumentation package (GPS/INS/Video camera) to generate multiple slanting parallel-perspective mosaics, each of them has parallel projection (with a slanting angle) in the direction of the camera path and perspective projection perpendicular to that direction. Multiple slanting parallel-perspective mosaics can be used for image-based rendering as discussed in Section 5. A mosaic-based fly-through demo may be found at [17], which uses 9 slanting mosaics generated from real video sequence of the UMass campus. This demo shows *parallax, occlusion and moving objects* in multiple parallel-perspective mosaics. We note that the rendering shows parallel-perspective rather than true perspective perception. However, a true perspective fly-through will be enabled by 3D reconstruction from the multiple mosaics.

6.2. Video mosaics for under-vehicle inspection

The slanting parallel projection has been also applied to a 2D (virtual) camera array where viewpoints of the original images are distributed in a 2D array, which will further extend the FOV in two spatial directions, with parallel projections in both the x and y directions.

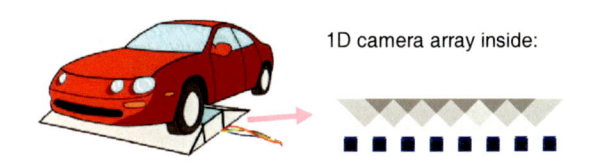

Figure 8. 1D camera array for under-vehicle inspection [13, 14]

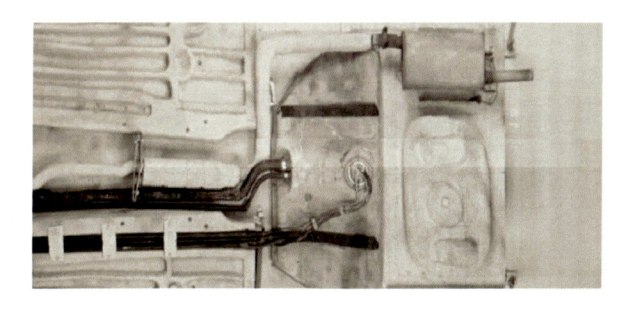

Figure 9. Full parallel projection mosaics with a bed of 2D array of cameras

As one of the real applications of full parallel stereo mosaics, we have generated an approximate version of mosaics with full parallel projection from a virtual bed of 2D camera arrays by driving a car over a 1D array of cameras in an under-vehicle inspection system

(UVIS) [13, 14, 18]. The Under Vehicle Inspection System (UVIS) is a system designed for checkpoints such as those at borders, embassy's, large sporting events, etc. It is an example of generating mosaics in very short-range video so a 2D array of camera is necessary for full coverage of the objects (under-vehicles). Fig. 8 illustrates the system setup where a array of cameras is housed in a platform. When a car drives over the platform, several mosaics with different slanting angles of the underside of a car are created. The mosaics can then be viewed by an inspector to thoroughly examine the underside of the vehicle from different angles. Figure 6 shows such a mosaic generated from four overlapping image sequences taken by four moving cameras side by side – which simulates the motion of the vehicle. A PPT demo of five oblique parallel views of the mosaics can be found at [18] where different "occluded" regions under a pipe can be observed by changing to different mosaics.

In the case of 1D camera array, we can pre-calibrated the fixed cameras, and correct the geometric and photometric distortions of those wide FOV cameras. However challenges remain since (1) the distance between cameras are large compared to the very short viewing distances to the bottom of the car; and (2) without the assistance of GPS/INS for pose estimation, we need to determine the car's motion by other means, e.g. tracking line features on the car. The proposed ray interpolation approach needs to take these two factors into consideration.

7. Conclusions

This paper presents an approach of fusing images from many video cameras or a moving video camera with external orientation data into a few mosaiced images with slanting parallel projections. In both cases, a virtual 2D array of cameras with FOV overlaps is formed to generate the whole coverage of a scene (or an object). The proposed representation provides wide FOV, preserves 3D information, and represents occlusions. This representation can be used as both an advanced video interface for surveillance or a pre-processing for 3D reconstruction. We have shown real examples of stereo mosaics for two important applications - aerial video surveillance and under-vehicle inspection.

8. Acknowledgements

This work is partially supported by AFRL through a grant on multimedia display in surveillance (Award No. F33615-03-1-63-83). The experimental examples are mainly based on some previous work in the Computer Vision Lab at the University of Massachusetts Amherst, under a NSF environmental monitoring using aerial videography (Grant Number EIA- 9726401), and an industrial sub-contract Under Vehicle Inspection System (UVIS). The supports and collaborations of Prof. Edward Riseman and Prof. Allen Hanson and their UMass research team are greatly appreciated. The author also thanks Prof. George Wolberg and Prof. Izidor Gertner at the City College of New York for their discussions with applications in multiple ONR research projects for image registration, target detection and human-computer interaction.

9. References

[1] J. Y. Zheng and S. Tsuji, Panoramic representation for route recognition by a mobile robot, IJCV, 9(1), 1992: 55-76

[2] S. Peleg, B. Rousso, A. Rav-Akha and A. Zomet, Mosaicing on adaptive manifolds, *PAMI*, 22(10), October 2000: 1144-1154.

[3] USGS Digital elevation Models (DEM), http://data.geocomm.com/dem/

[4] S. Peleg, M. Ben-Ezra and Y. Pritch, OmniStereo: panoramic stereo imaging, *PAMI*, March 2001:279-290.

[5] H.-Y. Shum and R. Szeliski, Stereo reconstruction from multiperspective panoramas, *ICCV'99*: 14-21.

[6] S. Baker, R. Szeliski and P. Anandan, A layered approach to stereo reconstruction. *CVPR'98:* 434-441

[7] J. Shade, S. Gortler, L. He. and R. Szeliski, Layered depth image. *SIGGRAPH'98:* 231-242

[8] Z. Zhu and A. R. Hanson, 3D LAMP: a New Layered Panoramic Representation, *ICCV'01:* II 723-730.

[9] A. Zomet, D. Feldman, S. Peleg and D. Weinshall, Mosaicing new views: the crossed-slits projection, *PAMI* 25(6), June 2003.

[10] J. Chai and H. -Y. Shum, Parallel projections for stereo reconstruction, CVPR'00: II 493-500.

[11]. Z. Zhu, E. Riseman, A. Hanson, Parallel-perspective stereo mosaics, *ICCV'01*, vol I: 345-352.

[12] Z. Zhu, A. Hanson, H. Schultz and E. M. Riseman, Generation and error characteristics of parallel-perspective stereo mosaics from real video. In *Video Registration*, M. Shah and R. Kumar (Eds.), Kluwer, 2003: 72-105.

[13]. P. Dickson, J. Li, Z. Zhu, A. Hanson, E. Riseman, H. Sabrin, H. Schultz and G. Whitten, Mosaic generation for under-vehicle inspection. *WACV'02*:251-256

[14] http://vis-www.cs.umass.edu/projects/uvis/index.html

[15] http://www-cs.engr.ccny.cuny.edu/~zhu/StereoMosaic.html

[16] H. Schultz, Terrain reconstruction from widely separated images, SPIE 2486, April 1995: 113-123.

[17] http://www-cs.engr.ccny.cuny.edu/~zhu/CampusVirtualFly.avi

[18] http://www-cs.engr.ccny.cuny.edu/~zhu/mosaic4uvis.html

License Plate Surveillance System Using Weighted Template Matching

Mi-Ae Ko, Young-Mo Kim
Electrical Engineering and Computer Science
KyungPook National University, Daegu, 702701, KOREA
koma@palgong.knu.ac.kr, ymkim@ee.knu.ac.kr

Abstract

This paper presents a simple and robust algorithm for vehicle's license plate recognition system. Based on template matching, this algorithm can be applied for real time recognition of license plates for vehicle surveillance system. The working principle is weight feature based hierarchical template evaluation. The performance of the proposed system has been evaluated on images acquired in real traffic conditions.

1. Introduction

The current paper proposes a hierarchical matching method for the license plate character recognition of the real time image surveillance system. There are a number of techniques used so far for recognition of license plates such as neural network [1][2][3], template matching [4][5][6][7] etc. Template matching methods are widely used for recognizing vehicle characters, for example, [1][4] using a feature vector with a gray input image, [5] applying template matching to a region of characters in binary mode identified using geometrical location characteristics, and [6] using pattern matching with a cross-correlation operator. In these cases, the performance of character recognition system is based significantly on using the recognition feature. For speeding up template matching, the existing methods have been investigated using several approaches such as two-dimensional generalization [8], covariance matrix of a feature point [9], sum of absolute value of differences measure [10], and condensation template tree [11] etc. Though these previous study's good point, we have need to get more simple and more fast algorithms by utilizing license plate specific characteristics. Therefore, the proposed license plate character recognition is used by the method of simple and smart real time template matching based on feature weight. The proposed template matching method only uses parts of the relative template data according to the weight of an image as features, thereby minimizing the data handling and promoting fast and efficient processing under various illumination, exposure conditions and real time conditions.

As such, the correlation of the template data among different characters is used to define the similarity and dissimilarity between candidate characters, minimizes the influence of external noise, and increases the recognition accuracy. In addition, by stages, as opposed to sequential, proposed template matching enables the target recognition object to be traced quickly and efficiently.

We designed the license plate surveillance system considering with some importance target principles. First, to relieve traffic congestion, we have to get the recognition result in real time. Second, the recognition rate could be maintained in spite of a part of the license character area is cropped, hidden or damaged license plates by accessory etc. Third, when we take a side view of the vehicle, the vehicle character should be recognized with good result. We can find and define the feature from license character's distribution and its characteristics befitting for the license plate surveillance system. For the first principle, we propose the hierarchical feature template matching. For the second principle, feature template should have the relative weight. For the third principle, we collect raw images within the limits of the possible camera angle view. It's used to construct basis template data. We have considered the camera's installation position in a license plate surveillance system from a front view to a side view.

The rest of the paper is organized as follows: section 2 discusses about the proposed vehicle surveillance system architecture and considerations inherent in license plate recognition, section 3 explains the proposed algorithm for real time recognition of number plates, section 4 presents some experimental results and finally section 5 concludes the paper with references.

2. License Plate Surveillance System

The main object of the proposed system is to recognize the vehicle number from real time images. Figure 1 shows the main flow of the license plate surveillance system. It consists of two main processes: The feature construction and the recognition processes. The feature construction process consists, mainly of the development of feature map of weighted character coordinates and the construction of a relative weight feature between character candidates used for confidence and verification. The recognition process, on the other hand, consists of the vehicle plate character localization inside in the real time vehicle image, vehicle plate character segmentation, noise filtering and brightness adjustment to improve the recognition rate, character normalization and character recognition using the hierarchical feature-based weighted template matching, which parameters were determined during the feature construction process. Then, through the result estimation and verification process, we can get the final recognition result of license plate number.

The weighted template data is based on statistical feature points for both the character area and the background area of a particular character previously sampled with the high probability from real vehicle images. The matching probability was compared with the first step template matching results. However, since the first candidates can still include some noise excluded from the basis data, if the value of the matching probability is greater than a threshold value set in advance, the relevant characters are judged to be the first step candidates.

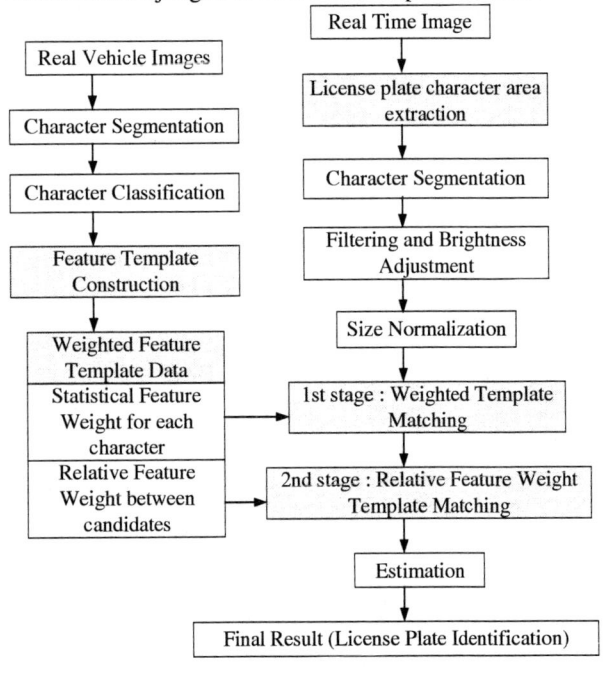

Figure 1. Propose license plate surveillance system

In the second stage template matching, each possible combination of candidates is processed with using the relative template weight. In this step, the template is composed of a weight value for each coordinate based on the difference characteristics between each candidate. The feature points between candidates do not overlap.

As a result of dispersing the data distribution, recognition is effective even though the image may be partially damages by sunlight, noise etc., plus the rate of recognition is increased through hierarchical matching.

3. Weighted Template Matching

Weighted template matching is a pattern classification method that detects particular features in a character image using operators called templates and weights. A template is devised, for example, via a training set collected from real vehicle images, while a weight is an operator based on a specific distance or similarity between characters. Weighted-template matching uses the raw data as a feature coordinate concentration.

Despite the good enhancement of normalized character images, many sources of potential noise and distortion could be existed. And it's impossible to make exact matching to a prototype and to process direct template matching. Therefore, a weight operator is used to determine the relative importance of each potential template location. As such, the similarity and distance are measured using a template, the correlation weight, and the raw image. The point of maximal similarity and maximal distance between characters is selected as the feature location and used as the coordinates and concentrated distribution for the weighted template matching. Plus, to standardize and simplify the feature vector of the gray level input raw data, a reduced gray level image is included. Then, to detect the existence of a specific object within an examined image, a template weight operator is applied between a sub-area of the normalized image and each prototype. In order to feed the feature construction functionality, real vehicle images are at first collected from various surroundings, and each character coordinate templates are constructed from segmented character maps. Finally, the statistical distribution weight maps of the feature coordinate are extracted.

3.1. Construct Basis Feature Template

To construct features map and to weight features down with distinctive characteristics, the feature template array for each pixel of a character created by exploring original images of license plates in an acquired training set. In this process, it makes a template map from the probability of the statistical features for the inter-coordinate points. Figure 2 shows each character's statistical template maps. These are used for basis template data. And figure 3 shows the layered weight maps for numeric characters.

In the case of the numeric character category, each template matrix is made up of the weight maps extracted from the similarity and dissimilarity between one character and all the other characters. In other words, the coordinates with black in Figure 2 has the high probability. These result calculated with efficient coordinates for a specific characters as shown in the figure 3. It was defined as layered gray level weight. If the depth of gray is darker, the feature coordinates has lower weight and high similarity.

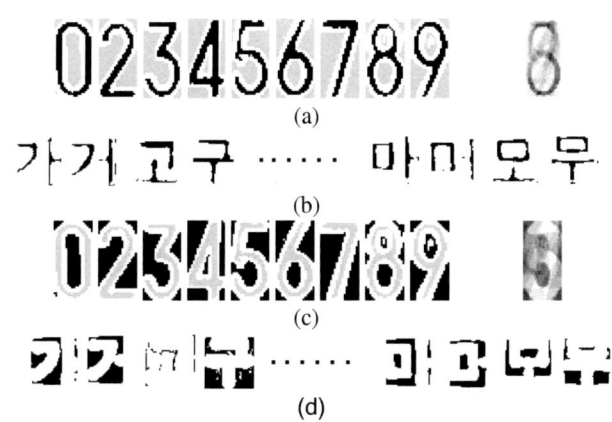

Figure 2. Basis template data (a) character areas with high probability in every numeric character(black) and its total concentration (b) character area in every Korean 'HANGUL' letter(black) (c) background areas with high probability in every numeric character(black) and its total concentration (d) background area in every Korean 'HANGUL' letter(black)

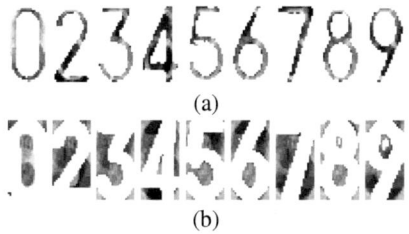

Figure 3. Layered weight basis template map for numeric characters (a) character area basis feature map (b) background area basis feature map

As such, the similarity template consists of some coordinates that always overlap between characters and other coordinates that always overlap with the background, whereas the dissimilarity template consists of some coordinates which do not overlap between similar candidates. Therefore, the next step is to construct key template map based on relative feature weight. And it is used to separate the final candidate from similar candidates.

3.2. Construction of the weight template

With character recognition by pattern matching, building the proper template is very important. This template data is prepared and applied to the second template matching. The relative feature map is $_{10}C_n$ and 'n' is the resulting number of candidates. If there are two candidates, the compared data set is $_{10}C_2 = 45$ for the numeric characters from 0 to 9. Let a template in the first step as the reference character r can be denoted by Tr. The relative template TB as the reference character $r1, r2$ be denoted by $TB_{r1,r2}$ which means the coordinates for classifying $r1$ and $r2$ accurately and this process is created from all combinations of 45, as given in the following Eq.(1).

$$TB_{r1,r1} = \{(m,n) \cdots | T_{r1} \cap (T_{r1} \cap T_{r2})^C \} \quad (1)$$

Figure 4. Relative feature map with weight for numeric characters 3 and 5 (a) feature weight maps of '5' and '3' respectively (b) unprocessed relative feature weighted map for foreground and background between '3' and '5' (c) processed relative feature weighted map for '3' and '5'.

Figure 4 shows an example of the relative feature coordinate matching matrix and its weight after applying the relative feature combinations.

The point of maximal match has the weight of the local maxima for similarity and the local minima for dissimilarity. That is, the distance measure for the same template is an exact match. From the relative feature map, we can figure out the condensation distribution between each character, which utilizes that feature coordinates appear in specific positions, respectively, represent a possible match. The resulting coordinate data set is the weight template data. At this point, when many similar template features exist, a coordinate will have a different relative importance among characters, called a feature weight.

3.3. Hierarchical Template Matching

The first step in template matching consists of calculating the probability of a pixel in a character. As shown in Figure 5, an object image that has been sampled on a real-time basis by a video camera and the template image of a number and character set are prepared. The weighted feature point information is based on the statistical relative distribution of these template image data, which is the point information that differentiates one character from another. This result is the first step candidates related to the template data. We can extract the concentrated common feature's matching map from the first candidates. The coordinates of this result is no more used as the feature because of its overlapping.

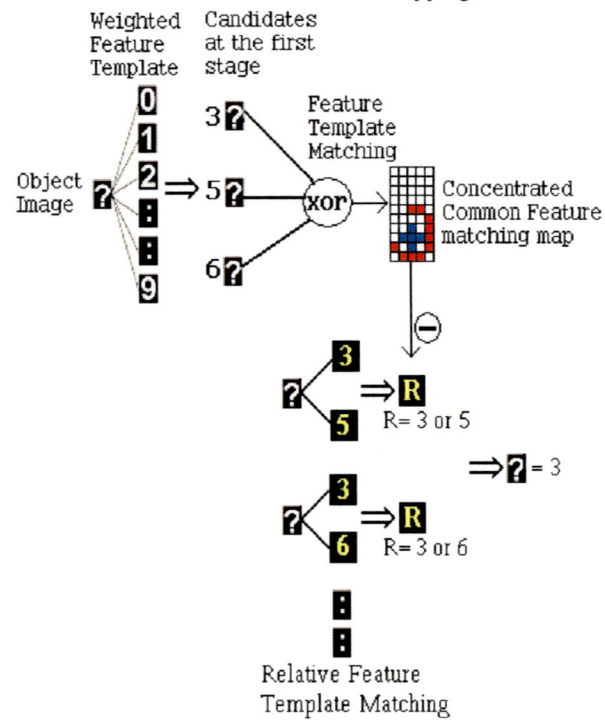

Figure 5. Hierarchical Template Matching

Next, the number of data sets that advance to the second stage template matching is the number of combinations of the candidates from the first stage. In the second stage template matching, the candidate with the high probability is selected after template matching with the normalized input object image. Even though a candidate may have had the second or the third highest probability in the first template matching, it can be reordered to the first candidate position through the second stage template matching.

In the case of character recognition to 'HANGUL', the Korean language, the first step of feature point extraction from a 'HANGUL' character is based on template data of a character with the same vowel. Next, feature points are sampled that differentiate the consonant from the recognized vowel. Therefore, proposed template matching can produce 'HANGUL' character recognition with a little effort. The structure of the 'HANGUL' is composed of the combination of consonant letter and vowel letter as shown in Figure 6.

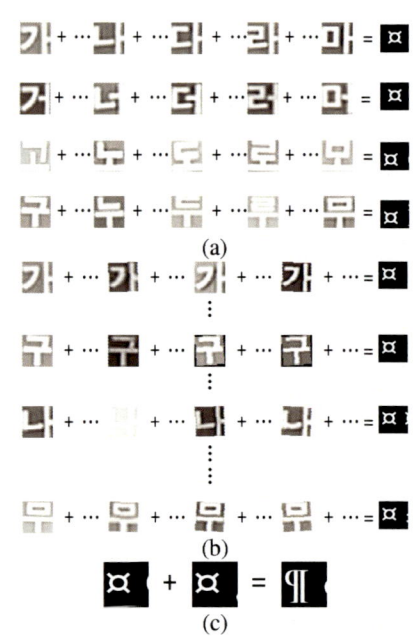

Figure 6. Recognition process of 'HANGUL' characters (a) vowel feature recognition (b) consonant recognition (c) a character recognition

4. Experimental Results

The proposed system has been tested using collections of vehicles at a gateway of a parking lot with various camera angle views. Figure 7 shows the process of identifying the number plate character's location by taking edge variation characteristics in the image. Horizontal lines within the range of vehicle motion are traced at regular intervals as shown in the Figure 7.

(a)

(b)

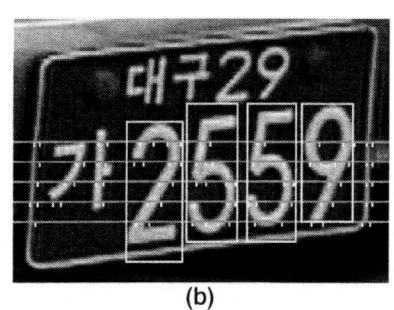

Figure 7. Capture image from real time environment (a) horizontal line scanning across the captured image (b) Character segmentation before fitting (optimized image cropping)

The variation of embossing of characters was used to find character feature point under horizontal tracing. The brilliant points are the extraction result of character area candidates.

In the character segmentation process, the method by using histogram such as [12] is so weak for tilted license plate. As shown in the Figure 7(b), each character is segmented by utilizing embossing repetitions of a specific character. Going through the process of segment fitting, the segmentation area was cut square to fit character just right.

When we try template matching to recognize segmented characters inside a plate, difficulties can be caused by inclination, distortion, and reflection. Moreover, the internal parts of characters in a plate can have different sizes, different positions, and different compositions.

To solve this, multistage preprocessing using conventional techniques is performed as follows: brightness histogram filtering and stretching, segment fitting, and size normalization of each segmented character. There is no necessary to process the adjustment of inclined license plate because feature template was trained including inclined license plates from the angle of –3 to 3. Since the pattern of character observed on a license image depends on the relative placement between the camera and the vehicle, the allowable inclination was limited for the template training set.

The normalized characters are then used as the input data for the template matching. And 25 test patterns were used for 'HANGUL'character usage and 10 test patterns are used for the numeric classification of registration numbers. Experiments were proceeded for day and night at a gateway of parking lot. The experimental images were collected under various conditions, with a permitted inclination limit angle of –5 to 5 and angle view was approximately 0 to 30 degrees. As the main focus of the current paper is character recognition, the described cognitive power was separated from the rate of license plate extraction.

A weighted template set is constructed with 30 images to each character, and the following test phase was performed on about 400 vehicle images. The obtained results were satisfactory enough for real time efficiency, and the accuracy rate of recognition was obtained close to 98% for these images.

From these experiments, even though the brightness of the license plate was very low and if it was uniformly distributed, the license plate was successfully recognized. Even if a part of character image was cropped or partially noised in dust, if there were remaining feature points of the character, it will be still correctly recognized because the template feature information was impartially distributed. For example, Figure 8 (a) shows the good identification result to mashed characters.

(a)

(b)

(c)

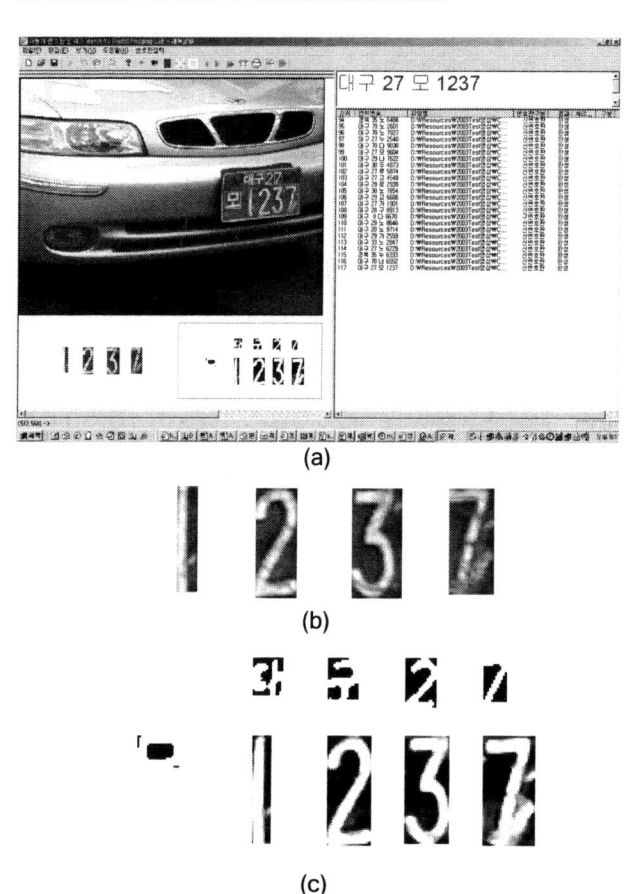

Figure 8. License plate surveillance system application software (a) main program (b)successfully segmented characters (c)converted from 256 level to 8 level gray scale for faster data processing

Conversely, if the feature points were severely damaged or irregular reflection exhibited or an accessory included with the segmented character, recognitions were failed. After the first step template matching, the incorrectly recognized images were characters with a similar template. In the case of 3 and 7 as shown in the Figure 8, if the bottom region of 7 was cropped by illegal segmentation, the remaining template characteristics appeared to be those of 3 or 2 or 7. If a part of the upper half region of 7 was cropped, the remaining template characteristics appeared to be those of 7 or 9. However, after the second template matching, the recognition rate increased because of a discriminative weight.

To verify the recognition precision of the recognition algorithm proposed in the current paper, a verification procedure is also included. The results prove that the function used to estimate and verify license numbers is very helpful in increasing the recognition rates. After the second template matching of the examined characters, the character image with the highest value of probability is referenced as a previous result.

5. Conclusion

In this paper a real time vehicle's license plate recognition system is presented. The originality of this work lies in the extraction of specific character features of vehicle license plate to obtain real time recognition. This proposed system applicable to a real time license plate surveillance system. The simple weight feature refinement and matching deliver precise results at a very low price in terms of computational power and time.

The proposed hierarchical template matching system is real-time, robust, and simple. The license plate surveillance system has been discussed with identifying the steps involved in recognition process. Initially, the character locations of vehicles license plate are detected looking for specific patterns and characteristics. Since this first step could be affected by the presence of illumination or diffused reflection or weather condition or angle view, the second phase based on a simplified feature template matching algorithm is performed to validate results and to accurately recognize vehicle character.

The experiment that has been carried out, clarified the proposed system as a simple and smart algorithm for real time recognition. The prototyped system will be integrated to the license plate surveillance system for some application specific purposes such as vehicle access control to restricted places, parking billing, stolen vehicle detection etc. It is also possible to adapt the basic algorithm to recognizing foreign license plates by correcting the composition of the feature information.

6. References

[1] N.Vazquez, M.Nakano and H.Perez-Meana, "Automatic System for Localization and Recognition of Vehicle Plate Numbers", *Journal of Applied Research and Technology*, Vol.1 No.1 April 2003, pp. 63-77

[2] Wu Wei, Yuzhi Li, Mingjun Wang, "Research on number-plate recognition based on neural networks", *Neural Networks for Signal Processing XI,2001. Procs.of the 2001 IEEE Signal Processing Society Workshp*, 10-12 Sept.2001, pp.529-538

[3] S.Draghici, "A Neural Network based Artificial Vision System for License Plate Recognition", *Int.J.Neural Syst.*, Vol.8 No.1 Feb.1997, pp.113-126

[4] P.Comelli, P.Ferragina,M.N.Granieri, and F.Stabile,, "Optical recognition of motor vehicle license plates", *IEEE Trans. Veh. Technol.*, Vol.44, No.4 1995, pp.790-799

[5] Christoph Busch, Ralf Doner, Christian Freytag and Heike Ziegler, "Feature based Recognition of Traffic Video Streams for online Route Tracing", *VTC'98. IEEE International Symposium on*, 1998, pp.: 1790 –1794

[6] Takashi Naito, Toshihiko Tsukada, Keiichi Yamada, Kazuhiro Kozuka and Shin Yamamoto,"Robust License-Plate Recognition Method for Passing Vehicles Under Ouside Environment", *IEEE Trans. Veh. Technol.*, Vol.49,No.6,2000, pp.: 2309 –2319

[7] Yamaguchi K., Nagaya Y., Ueda K.,Nemoto H., Nakagawa M., " A method for identifying specific vehicles using template matching", *Intelligent Transportation Systems,1999*, Proceedings.1999 IEEE/IEEJ/JSAI International Conference on,1999,pp. 8 –13

[8] Mendonca,A.P., da Silva,E.A.B., "Two-dimensional discriminative filters for image template detection", *Image Processing,2001.Proceedings.2001 International Conference on.* ,Vol.3, 7-10 Oct.2001,pp.680-683

[9] Kanazawa.Y., Kanatani.K., "Do we really have to consider covariance matrices for image features?", *Computer Vision,2001. ICCV2001.Proceesings.Eighth IEEE International Conference on.*,Vol.2, 7-14 July.2001,pp.301-306

[10] Mikhail J.Atallah, "Faster Image Template Matching in the Sum of the Absolute Value of Differences Measure", *IEEE Transactions on Image Processing*, Vol.10, No.4, April 2001,pp.659-663

[11] Brown R.L., "Accelerated template matching using template trees grown by condensation", *Systems, Man and Cybernetics,IEEE Transactions on*, Vol.25, Issue.3, March 1995, pp.523-528

[12] Choudhury A.Rahman, Wael Badawy and Ahmad Radmanesh, " A Real Time Vehicle's License Plate Recognition System", *Proceedings of the IEEE Conference on Advanced Video and Signal Based Surveillance,AVSS03*,2003

Tracking and Handoff Between Multiple Perspective Camera Views[1,2]

Sadiye Guler, *Member, IEEE*, John M. Griffith and Ian A. Pushee
Northrop Grumman Information Technology / TASC
55 Walkers Brook Road
Reading, Massachusetts 01867
{ sguler, jmgriffith, iapushee}@tasc.com

Abstract—We present a system for tracking objects between multiple uncalibrated widely varying perspective view cameras. The spatial relationships between multiple perspective views are established using a simple setup by using tracks of objects moving in and out of individual camera views. A parameterized Edge of Field of View (EoFOV) map augmented with internal overlap region boundaries is generated based on the detected object trajectories in each view. This EoFOV map is then used to associate multiple objects entering and leaving a particular camera's FOV into and out of another camera view providing uninterrupted object tracking between multiple cameras. The main focus of the paper is robust tracking and handoff of objects between omni-directional and regular narrow FOV surveillance video cameras without the need for formal camera calibration. The system tracks objects in both omni-directional and narrow field camera views employing adaptive background subtraction followed by foreground object segmentation using gradient and region correspondence.

Index Terms—Multiple camera tracking, camera handoff Omni-directional video tracking, video surveillance.

I. INTRODUCTION

ROBUST tracking of moving objects in a multiple camera environment has become a requirement for advanced video surveillance systems. In a typical video surveillance system multiple cameras cover the surveyed site as conventional cameras have very limited FOV, and events of interest may take place over multiple camera FOV's. In this regard, omni-directional viewing cameras [1, 2 and references therein] have attracted a great deal of attention recently. Omni-directional viewing cameras can provide an (almost) uninterrupted coverage for a wide area, and are being used in surveillance and autonomous navigation applications. Even with omni-directional viewing more than one camera view is necessary to cover the blind spot that falls right under the sensor (Figure 1) or to provide more detailed surveillance for some specific areas within the omni view. Hence, an intelligent surveillance system must track objects and perform accurate object handoff between different camera views to be able to analyze video events over multiple streams. Tracking and handoff of objects over multiple views has been researched over the last decade and approaches ranging from reconstructing 3D scene models of the environment using multiple calibrated camera views [3] to ones that do not require any camera calibration but discover spatial relationships between cameras from the video streams [4] have been developed. In between the more formal approach of [3] and highly practical approach of [4] other methods have also been proposed and used such as in [5], the problem of automatic external relative calibration of multiple cameras is tackled without explicit calibration requirements for each camera. The object trajectories are used to obtain an "extended scene" to track moving objects over multiple scenes. In [6] camera calibration for each view is estimated without any camera parameter requirements using the coordinates of image and ground point pairs. Then the absolute positions of objects are used to guide the handoff between views, even if there is no overlap between the two views.

Camera calibration is in general an expensive process and in real life surveillance applications measurements of camera parameters are not readily available. Edge of Field of View (EoFOV) concept introduced in [7] and extended in [4] is a practical alternative to inconvenient camera calibration. EoFOV is simply described as finding and marking the limits of FOV of a camera as visible in other cameras. Edges of FOV lines are fitted thru observations that are collected either using a simple setup with an object moving in and out of overlapping camera views [7] or without a setup using a statistical approach based on examining all candidate object correspondences in multiple overlapping views [4]. Here we adopt and generalize the EoFOV concept to the camera handoff problem between sensors that may have significantly different viewing angles and noticeably different frame rates. To handle object correspondence between camera views with

---

[1] This work was partially supported by the Advanced Research and Development Activity (ARDA). Any opinions, findings and conclusions or recommendations expressed in this material are those of the authors and do not necessarily reflect the views of the U.S. Government.

[2] This work was partially supported by Northrop Grumman Information Technology Internal Research and Development Program Advanced Digital Video Project.

different frame rates we propose to use the edges of the overlap region between different views. To facilitate camera views that have significantly different viewing angles, we generalize the EoFOV lines to be represented by curves instead of straight lines and allow all four sides of a camera view to be embedded in another camera view. To accomplish these we developed an approach to parameterize EoFOV lines.

The rest of this paper is organized as follows: In the next section our object tracking algorithm and tracking in the omni-directional camera view are briefly described, the handoff problem between multiple perspective cameras is introduced. In section 3, proposed extensions to EoFOV concept are described and formalized. Some experimental results are presented in section 5 and finally conclusions are drawn in section 6.

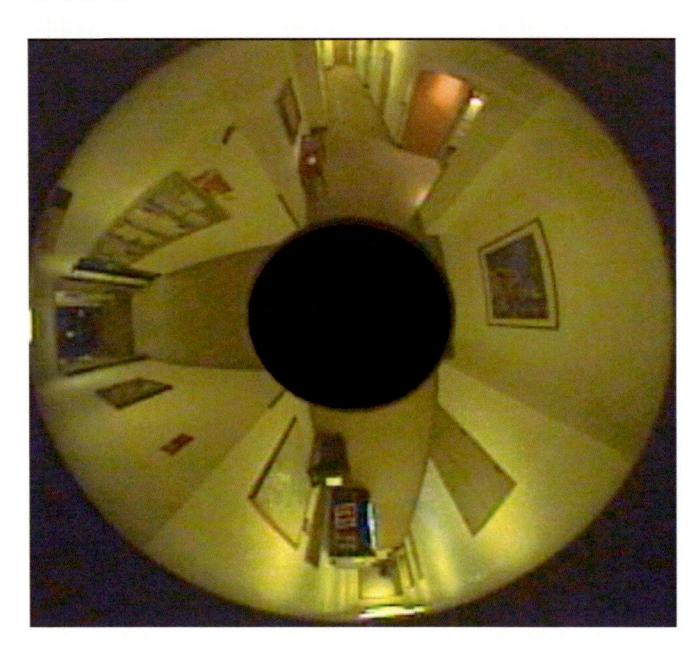

Figure 1: Omni-directional camera view

II. OBJECT DETECTION AND TRACKING

A. General Description

To track objects between multiple camera views the tracking in each view has to be performed first. We developed a robust object detection and tracking algorithm [8] that uses adaptive background subtraction similar to that of [9] followed by foreground object segmentation using edge and region based correspondence. Our background model constitutes mixture of Gaussians for R, G and B channels. After background subtraction candidate foreground object pixels are grouped by using connected components and object regions are reinforced by edges. Observed object velocities, color make-up and a few geometric features are used to track objects in consecutive frames. Each detected object is assigned a unique ID number and the ID number is preserved as long as an object is tracked in a view.

B. Object Tracking in Omni View and Re-association through the Blind Spot

Object detection and tracking in the omni-directional camera is similar to the general algorithm described above except for a few differences. One such difference is in the use of geometrical features for tracking because of the geometric distortion in the omni view. However the most important difference is the need for object re-association through the "blind spot". Most omni-directional cameras have a blind spot beneath the camera, causing the loss of tracking information for the objects moving through. Much like with a known occlusion in the scene, to preserve the tracking information, we use objects' physical and motion characteristics to re-associate them as they travel through the blind spot. Using appearance models for re-association is viable for this case because the re-association is being preformed within a single camera. Within the omni camera, we keep track of an object's average scaled size, color makeup, and average velocity vector. The velocity vector information of an object entering the blind spot is used to determine the most probable direction vector for that object as the it travels thorough the blind spot. Objects leaving the blind spot are then compared with the occluded object's features as well as their proximity to the occluded object's probable direction vector. When a match is found, the object exiting the blind spot is re-associated with the corresponding object ID, and tracking continues unhindered.

C. Object Tracking and Handoff Between Multiple Views

Use of appearance models to associate objects across multiple camera views or for the camera handoff problem is not plausible as different camera characteristics and perspectives would affect the objects' appearances. In this case, one can only rely on object's position correspondence between multiple views. To obtain accurate position correspondence tracking all four edges of a camera FOV may be necessary for sensors with significantly different perspectives. One such sensor combination is an omni-directional and a narrow FOV regular surveillance camera and the two basic viewing configurations that are of special interest are:

1) Blind Spot Coverage: In this configuration the goal would be to provide uninterrupted tracking of objects throughout the omni view camera by covering the blind spot with a narrow FOV camera as shown in Figure 2.

2) Detailed Surveillance Area Enclosed in an Omni View: In this camera arrangement, the goal would be to have detailed surveillance of an area of high interest (outside the blind spot) while tracking the history of objects into and out of that area as depicted in Figure 7. Extending this scenario, one could easily have several areas of interest within the omni view that can be covered by using several narrow FOV cameras.

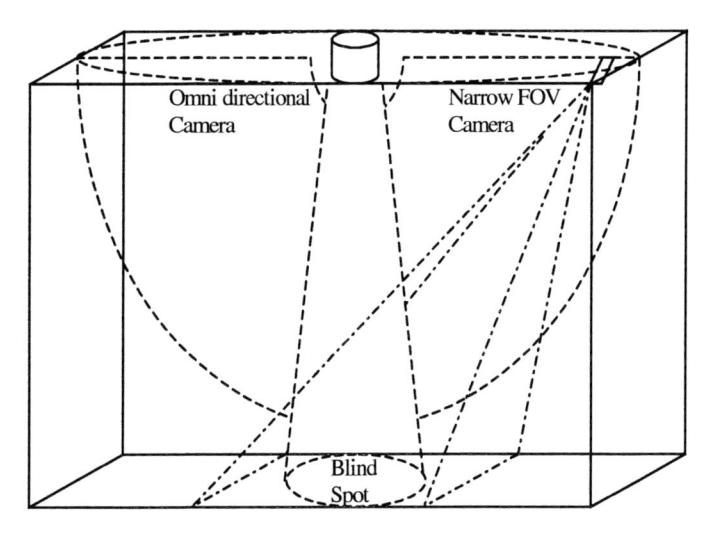

Figure 2: Diagram of Blind Spot Coverage

associated edge of the camera view respectively. In Figure 4, the FOV line (circle) shown delimits the edge of the omni-directional camera's blind spot.

2) Overlap Lines: Using only the EoFOV lines is not sufficient for accurate handoff between two cameras that have noticeably different frame rates. For example, consider the case where an object is crossing an EoFOV line, moving out of a camera view into another camera view with a significantly lower frame rate. By the time this object is detected in the slower view it may have already left the first view, creating ambiguity in the object correspondence. The *overlap lines* can be obtained in a camera view by using the edges of the overlapping region that does not correspond to EoFOV lines. Hence, for each EoFOV line a view creates in another view, an overlap line is created in the first view, represented as $O^{i,S}$ as shown in Figures 3 and 4. In $O^{i,S}$ the first and second superscripts indicate the corresponding camera view and the associated edge of the camera view respectively. Using overlap lines together with the EoFOV lines the ambiguity described above can be resolved.

III. EXTENSION OF EoFOV MAPPING TO MULTIPLE PERSPECTIVE VIEWS

In the multi camera configurations described above, the EoFOV lines are best represented by curves due to the imaging geometry. The processing frame rates may be noticeably different for regular and omni view cameras, causing delays in detection of objects as they move in and out of a view in related views. These delays may create ambiguities in object handoff as by the time an object detected in the view with the slower frame rate, the corresponding object may not be visible in the first view or another object may be in close proximity causing a wrong association for handoff. In the following we extend the EoFOV concept to address these requirements. Although, we use the omni and regular view cameras for the descriptions the concepts are applicable to other camera combinations with widely varying perspectives.

A. Edge of Field of View and Overlap Lines

To accomplish accurate object handoff between cameras with different frame rates, we use of *overlap lines* defined below to mark the exit-entry of FOV of a camera internally, in addition to EoFOV lines that mark the limits of other camera views. EoFOV and *overlap lines* and their estimation are described next.

1) EoFOV Lines: EoFOV lines are the limits of a camera's field of view as seen in another camera's view. In Figures 3 and 4, we present the corresponding views seen by the omni-directional and narrow FOV cameras depicted in Figure 2. In Figure 3, the EoFOV lines, labeled with EoFOV, are the edges of the field of view (L:Left, R:Right, T:Top and B:Bottom) of the narrow FOV (camera 2) as seen in the omni-directional view (camera 1). In $EoFOV^{i,S}$, the first and second superscripts indicate the corresponding camera view and the

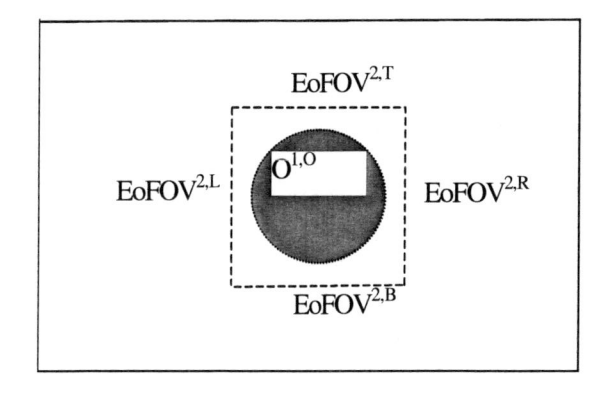

Figure 3: Camera 1 (Omni-directional) View, EoFOV and Overlap(O) Lines.

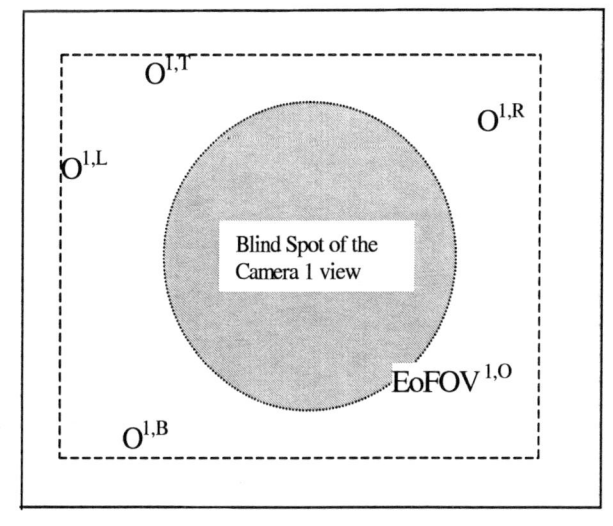

Figure 4: Camera 2 (Narrow FOV) View, EoFOV and Overlap (O) Lines.

277

By marking the *overlap lines i.e.,* edge of a camera's field of view within that camera itself, the objects can be tagged as they enter or leave the field of view across that edge. When an object is in contact with an overlap line of camera 2, camera 1 is notified that the object is in the process of crossing into or out of the narrow FOV camera's view. This allows compensating for the delays in detecting the same object in views with different frame rates.

3) *Estimation of EoFOV and Overlap Lines:* The EoFOV and Overlap Lines are estimated by using the same method described in [7]. As a single object is allowed to move across the edges of the FOV's of different cameras (into or out of a camera's field of view), the (x, y) coordinates of the midpoint of the object bounding box at the point it disappears or appears in the current view and the coordinates at the time of disappearance along its trajectory in the other view are recorded. The edge that the entity crossed while disappearing is determined by finding the intersection of the velocity vector and the frame edges of the current view. Then the point in the current view is added to the intersecting edge's associated overlap line and the point in the associated view is added to the EoFOV line for the current camera and edge crossed.

In order to maintain EoFOV and overlap lines for all four edges, it becomes necessary to determine through which edge an object entered or exited the particular view. Using a common tracking point such as the center of the bottom of the object's bounding box, along with the proximity of the object and its direction near the edge, which edge the object has crossed when entering or leaving the camera FOV can be accurately determined.

B. Parameterization of FOV and Overlap Lines:

While mapping camera views with very different perspectives onto one another straight lines will not well represent the actual EoFOV and overlap lines. We generalize the EoFOV lines to be cubic segments and parameterize the data points before fitting the EoFOV lines. As the parameter we use the x or y coordinates of the point of intersection between object's velocity vector (projected from the center bottom of the object's bounding box) and the edge over which the object is crossing. For example, if the object is determined to be crossing the top or bottom edge of the field of view, the x coordinate would be used as the parameter value for the point, and if the object is determined to be crossing the left or right edge of the view, the y coordinate would be used as the parameter for the data point.

In Figure 5, the calculation of the parameter value is illustrated graphically. An entity crosses out of the narrow FOV camera view on the right hand edge between time t=2 and t=3. We record the (x, y) coordinates of the last location of the center of the bottom of the bounding box for the entity in this view. Since the entity crossed out of the view on the right edge, we use the varying coordinate of that edge, y, as the value for the parameter, p, for that point. In the omni view, the

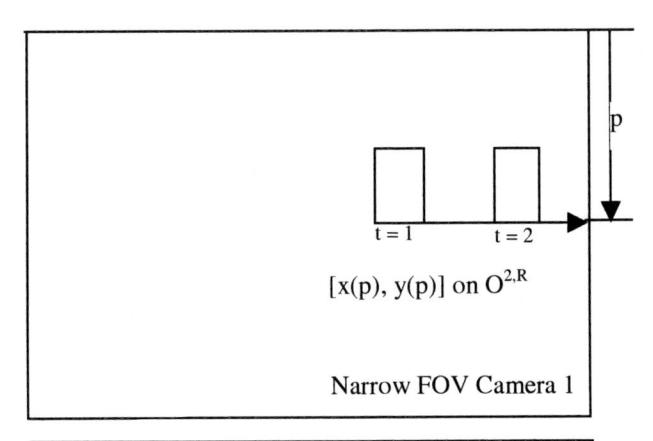

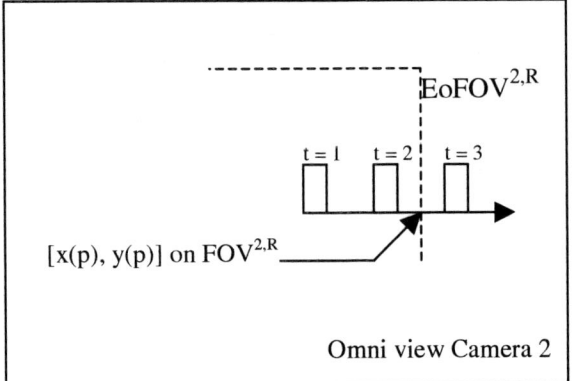

Figure 5: Parameter Calculation for an Exiting Object

(x, y) coordinate at time t=2.5 is calculated and the parameter value p from the camera 1 view is associated with the y coordinate of the intersection point.

Once at least four points have been recorded and calculated for both an EoFOV line and the associated overlap line, a least squares fit can be performed to calculate the coefficients of the cubic segment that is used to describe the lines. The parameterized cubic equations used to describe the overlap and EoFOV lines for each edge are as follows:

$$x(p) = A_x \cdot p^3 + B_x \cdot p^2 + C_x \cdot p + D_x$$
$$y(p) = A_y \cdot p^3 + B_y \cdot p^2 + C_y \cdot p + D_y$$

where A_x, B_x, C_x, D_x, A_y, B_y, C_y, and D_y are the sought coefficients. Once the points and their parameters are collected and calculated, the least squares method can be used to fit a parametric curve to the data for each of the edges in both camera views. Using the above equations for describing the lines, the set of simultaneous equations to be solved in order to obtain the least squares fit of the data for the x coordinate is given below. The coordinates of the collected data points (the corresponding coordinates of the midpoint of the object bounding box) is used to calculate the summations on the RHS's, then the coefficients A_x, B_x, C_x, D_x, A_y, B_y, C_y, and D_y

are solved for.

$$A_x \sum_n p^6 + B_x \sum_n p^5 + C_x \sum_n p^4 + D_x \sum_n p^3 = \sum_n xp^3$$

$$A_x \sum_n p^5 + B_x \sum_n p^4 + C_x \sum_n p^3 + D_x \sum_n p^2 = \sum_n xp^2$$

$$A_x \sum_n p^4 + B_x \sum_n p^3 + C_x \sum_n p^2 + D_x \sum_n p^1 = \sum_n xp^1$$

$$A_x \sum_n p^3 + B_x \sum_n p^2 + C_x \sum_n p^1 + D_x \sum_n p^0 = \sum_n xp^0$$

C) Multiple Objects Crossing Between Views:

Once the parameterized curves representing the EoFOV and Overlap lines have been obtained, they can be used to distinguish between objects crossing between views at the same time. When two distinct objects cross into a view simultaneously, each will have a distinct parameter value from their contact points with the EoFOV curve in the associated view. In the entered view, the two new objects will also have parameter values from the associated overlap curve. Since the parameter values of the EoFOV and overlap curves correspond with one another, the parameter values associated with the objects can be used to create object correspondence between the views to achieve accurate handoff.

D) In-View Occlusion

In real world, the camera FOVs do not necessarily end neatly at the edge of a camera's field of vision due to in scene occlusions. Consider for example the scenario presented in Figure 6, the occlusion in camera 1 view alters the perceived EoFOV line for camera 1 in camera 2 view, hence changing the overlap region for two cameras. To prevent ambiguities in object tracking and handoff across two cameras, we also mark and label the occlusion edges and use them in the EoFOV mapping. Even though they do not correspond to any of the four edges of the picture, by recording this *occlusion edges* in both views, it is possible to create object correspondences between the views at all times. The occlusion edges are estimated much like the EoFOV lines during the setup time when a single object moving through the view disappears form the original camera (while remaining in the overlapping view) near the occlusion, that point is added to the *occlusion edge* data in both views.

IV. EXPERIMENTAL WORK

The extensions to EoFOV described in section 3 are implemented as part of a multi camera tracking system [8]. We present some preliminary experimental results for the *detailed*

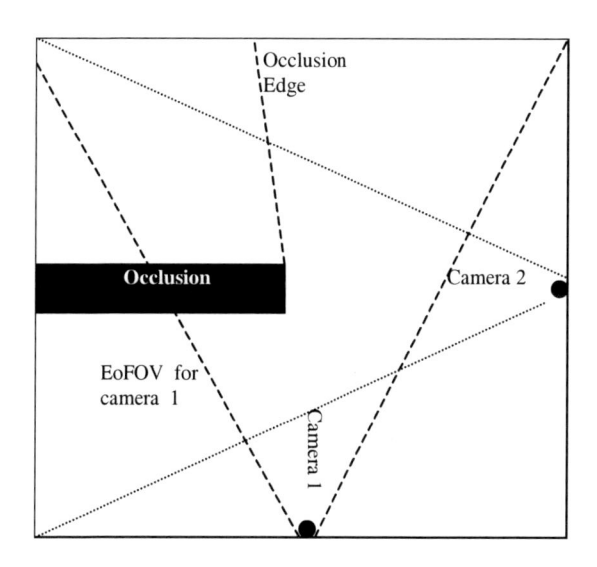

Figure 6: In-View Occlusion Edge

surveillance camera enclosed in an omni view case as shown in Figure 7 and explained in section 3. The omni-directional camera used in our experiments is provided by RemoteReality[3]. It is a catadioptric system that uses both mirrors and lenses [2]. A simple overview of the imaging geometry is given in the Appendix. Detection and tracking in each individual view is very accurate in both narrow FOV (camera 2) and omni view (camera 1) as this is a controlled indoor setting. All the objects that are in any of the scenes are detected and correctly tracked in each individual view. The experiment presented here focuses on object handoffs between the views. In this scenario, the omni-directional camera is viewing the entire laboratory, with the narrow FOV camera viewing the door to the equipment room to identify the people and the equipment going in and out of the room. All four sides of the narrow FOV camera view is in the omni-directional camera view, however we only need to track and handoff objects through the Left, Right and the Bottom edges of the narrow FOV.

In this configuration the omni-directional camera outputs video at a much lower frame rate than the narrow FOV camera. Hence, it is possible that a person could cross into or out of the camera 2 view before they are seen and detected at the EoFOV line in the omni-directional view. By the time a person is near the EoFOV line in the omni-directional view, they could have already crossed well into the camera 2 view. Trying to associate that person to someone near the edge of camera 2 will no longer result a valid correspondence. Since we have the overlap line marked in the camera 2 view, we can

---

[3] RemoteReality builds of advanced omni-directional video surveillance products for security, anti-terrorism and force protection. www.remotereality.com

add the parameter *p* (described in section 4.B) to the features of the object. This parameter is stored until the omni-directional (camera 1) view updates and has an opportunity to process what has happened. The same process works in reverse (for a slower standard and faster omni-directional camera), only with the omni-directional camera saving the edge crossing information for the 2nd camera's retrieval and use. In Figure 7 the EoFOV lines for the narrow FOV camera as they are estimated in the omni view, and the corresponding overlap lines (drawn in the same color) in the narrow FOV camera are shown. The image shows object 27 in camera 2 view crossing over the blue overlap line, a few frames later, in Figure 8 the same object becomes visible in camera 1 view and is correctly associated with its occurrence in camera 2, hence takes the same ID number (27) in this view as well. Due to the differences in frame rates, by the time this object is detected in omni view, it is already in the middle the narrow view. Without the use of parameterized overlap and EoFOV lines and using the parameter as an added object feature, this association could not have been accomplished if especially there was another object in camera 2 view near the bottom left corner of the scene. Figure 9 shows the object 27 close to the overlap line in camera 2 view as it is leaving the narrow FOV, and in Figure 10, when the object is detected as crossing the EoFOV line for camera 2 in omni view, at this instant the object is no longer visible in camera 2. We repeated this experiment with different objects and with multiple objects in the scenes with consistent results.

As seen from the figures, even though the omni view provides an uninterrupted coverage to track objects around a

Figure 7: Object in narrow FOV camera.

Figure 9: Tracking associated object in omni view and narrow FOV cameras.

Figure 8: Handoff between an omni view and a narrow FOV cameras.

Figure 10: Handoff between an omni view and a narrow FOV cameras.

large area the due to the resolution and the look angle distortions the objects are not easily identifiable. If the tracking and handoff between the views is handled correctly, placing a narrow FOV camera to an area of high interest provides the necessary detail, while the objects are tracked around a large area.

V. CONCLUSIONS

We presented a system for tracking objects between multiple uncalibrated widely varying perspective view cameras. In particular we focused on robust tracking and handoff of objects between omni-directional and regular surveillance video cameras without the need for formal camera calibration. However the concepts developed are applicable to other camera combinations with widely varying perspectives such as near top down view and side view camera combinations. We generalized the EoFOV concept to the camera handoff problem between sensors that may have significantly different viewing angles and noticeably different frame rates and developed an approach to parameterize EoFOV lines. To handle object correspondence between camera views with different frame rates we use the edges of the overlap region between different views, i.e., the overlap lines. To facilitate camera views that have significantly different viewing angles, we generalized the EoFOV lines to be represented by cubic segments and allow all four sides of a camera view to be embedded in another camera view. The spatial relationships between multiple perspective views are established using a simple setup by using tracks of objects moving in and out of individual camera views. A parameterized Edge of Field of View map augmented with overlap lines is generated based on the detected object trajectories in each view. This EoFOV map is then used to associate multiple objects entering and leaving a particular camera's FOV into and out of another camera view providing uninterrupted object tracking between multiple cameras. Our system can robustly track objects in both omni-directional and narrow field camera views employing adaptive background subtraction followed by foreground object segmentation using gradient and region correspondence. Multiple objects can be accurately handed off and tracked through multiple perspective and varying frame rate cameras without the knowledge of the scene geometry.

APPENDIX

A simplified geometry of the omni-directional imaging system is depicted in Figure A-1. A paraboloidal mirror M collects the light rays directed towards the focus of parabola. The rays are then reflected parallel to the optical axis and collected by a telecentric imaging system, producing a point projection.

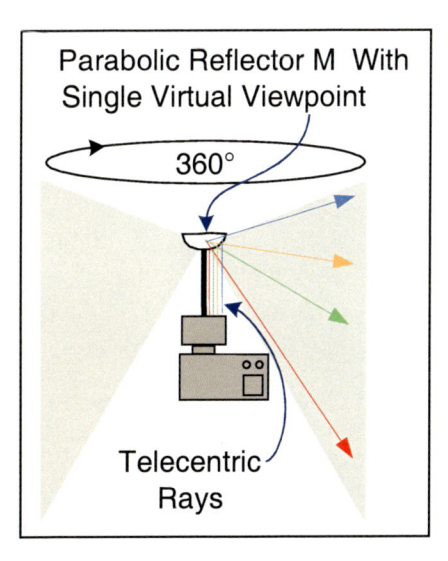

Figure A-1: Imaging geometry of the double reflector omni-directional camera (courtesy Remote Reality Inc.).

ACKNOWLEDGMENTS

Authors would like to thank RemoteReality for providing the Omni-directional viewing sensor, to Mr. J. A. Silverstein for his work on Northrop Grumman IT Internal Research and Development Program Advanced Digital Video Project on object detection and tracking and, to Mr. Randy Paul for electing research in this area under the ARDA/VACE program extension.

REFERENCES

[1] S. K. Nayar. "Catadioptric Omnidirectional Camera", In International Conference on Computer Vision and Pattern Recognition 1997, Puerto Rico USA, IEEE Computer Society Press, June 1997, pp. 482-488.

[2] S. Nayar and V. Peri. "Folded Catadioptric Cameras", In Conference on Computer Vision and Pattern Recognition, Fort Collins, Colorado, volume II, Los Alamitos, CA, USA, June 1999. IEEE Computer Society Press, pp. 217-223.

[3] P.H. Kelly, A. Katkere, D.Y. Kuramura, S. Moezzi, S. Chatterjee and R. Jain, " An Architecture for Multiple Perspective Interactive Video," Proc. ACM Conference on Multimedia, 1995, pp.201-212.

[4] S. Khan, O. Javed, M. Shah, "Tracking in Uncalibrated Cameras with Overlapping Field of View", *Performance Evaluation of Tracking and Surveillance PETS 2001*, (with CVPR 2001), Kauai, Hawaii, Dec 9th, 2001

[5] L. Lee, R. Romano, and G. Stein, "Monitoring Activities from Multiple Video Streams: Establishing a Common Coordinate Frame," *IEEE Trans. Pattern Analysis Machine Intelligence*, vol. 22, no. 8, Aug. 2000, pp. 758-767.

[6] S. Guler, "Scene and Content Analysis From Multiple Video Streams", in *Proc. 30th AIPR*, Washington D.C., Oct 1-12, 2001.

[7] S. Khan, O. Javed, Z. Rasheed, M. Shah, "Human Tracking in Multiple Cameras," *The Eighth IEEE International Conference on Computer Vision*, Vancouver, Canada. July 9-12, 2001

[8] S. Guler and J.A. Silverstein, "Advanced Digital Video Solutions", Northrop Grumman IT, Internal Research and Development Program Report, Dec, 2001.

[9] C. Stauffer and W.E.L. Grimson, "Learning Patterns of Activity Using Real-time tracking', *IEEE Trans. Pattern. Anal. Mach. Intell.* vol. 22, no. 8, Aug. 2000, pp. 831-843.

Personal Authentication Using Feature Points on Finger and Palmar Creases

Junta Doi and Masaaki Yamanaka
Chiba Institute of Technology, Department of Computer Science
2-17-1 Tsudanuma, Narashino, 275-8588 Japan
doi@cs.it-chiba.ac.jp and jnd@bb.exite.co.jp

Abstract

A new and practical method of reliable and real-time authentication is proposed. Finger geometry and feature extraction of the palmar flexion creases are integrated in a few numbers of discrete points for faster and robust processing. A video image of either palm, palm placed freely facing toward a near infrared video camera in front of a low-reflective board, is acquired. Fingers are brought together without any constraints. Discrete feature point involves intersection points of the three digital (finger) flexion creases on the four finger skeletal lines and intersection points of the major palmar flexion creases on the extended finger skeletal lines, and orientations of the creases at the points. These metrics define the feature vectors for matching. Matching results are perfect for 50 subjects so far. This point wise processing, extracting enough feature from non contacting video image, requiring no time-consumptive palm print image analysis, and requiring less than one second processing time, will contribute to a real-time and reliable authentication.

1. Introduction

Biometrics is defined as measurable physiological and/or behavioral characteristics to verify the identity of an individual. It is the technology using image processing and pattern recognition in the security field. Recently biometric technologies are rapidly evolving and becoming security options to verify the true identity of an individual in the wide areas of businesses and organizations.

Biometric authentication requires comparing an enrolled biometric sample against a newly acquired biometric sample. The biometric system authenticates a person's claimed identity from their previously enrolled pattern. It involves confirming or denying a person's identity. An identity is claimed by inputting PIN or presentation of a token and then presenting a live sample for comparison, resulting in a match or no match according to predefined parameters. This is called "one-to-one" matching. In the identification, biometric system identifies a person from the entire enrolled population by searching a database for a match based solely on the biometrics. This is called "one-to-many" matching.

Among the physical features measured are face, fingerprints, palm prints, hand or palmar geometry, retina and iris, and vein. Behavioral features are signature or handwriting, keystroke patterns, gait motion, gesture and voice in behavioral aspect [1-8].

Hand or palmar geometry involves measuring and analyzing the shape of the hand or palm. These include geometric parameters of length, width, thickness, surface area and so on. The biometric system offers a good balance of performance characteristics and is relatively easy to use in various applications.

Accuracy can be very high if desired and flexible performance tuning and configuration can accommodate a wide range of applications. Ease of integrating into other systems makes this geometry an obvious first step for many biometric projects. The personal authentication, using the hand geometry based on the back and side images of hand, has long history. Besides general personal authentication it is frequently used in physical access control application, in time and attendance recording [9-12].

The palm prints are thought to be personal similar to fingerprints. Heredity may influence the path followed by major flexion creases and minor finger flexion creases through genetic programming of the volar pads. The palm creases are persistent and variable enough to individualize.

There are a variety of researches on palm print verification. Some of them try to emulate the traditional police method of matching minutiae. Others are straight pattern matching approaches. Image acquisition and feature extraction of palm prints are complicated and difficult comparing to those of fingerprints.

1.1. Previous work

A number of literatures on the palm print analysis are reported so far [13-18]. Most of them deal with the pattern analysis similar to the fingerprint analysis and are rather

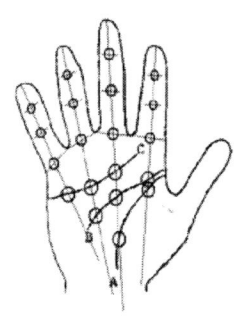

Fig. 1. Intersection points with circles. A; Thenar crease, B; Proximal transverse crease, C; Distal transverse crease.

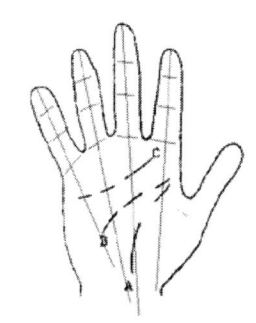

Fig. 2. Illustration of the tangents at the intersecttion points. Creases may be reconstructed by tracing these tangential vectors sequentially.

time consumptive, not suitable to the authentication that requires faster response of, for instance, one second or so. No palm print analyses seem to be reported so far for use of the real-time authentication. As for the fingerprint feature extraction widely used for the authentication, a limited area, for instance the forefinger tip area is processed locally. As the hand geometry is not unique and distinctive, a multimodal biometric system, which combines other traits of face and fingerprint, is reported so far [19].

1.2. Proposed feature extraction

We have proposed an authentication method, an image- and video-based dual biometric processing, which integrates the palmar geometry with the palm print feature extraction [20]. Image acquisition of a palm gives both data for the palm geometry and the palm print for feature extraction simultaneously. In the method feature of the palm prints are extracted at the discrete points determined in relation to the finger geometry, not by using pattern processing of the palm print. This makes the palm print feature extraction simple and reliable, and accelerates to get a real-time result for authentication within one second or so. Concept of the feature points in our processing are illustrated in Figures 1 and 2. They are discussed later in section III. Kumar et. al [21] proposed similar multimodal method but palm print pattern is processed in a limited area. More detailed reviews on the previous palm print analysis are included in the article.

This paper proposes a dual biometric system, but not using the straight pattern matching of the palm print itself, and here an easy to practice procedure of the personal authentication system, requiring a short processing time, is reported based on our previous work.

2. Palmar image acquisition

A video image of either palm is acquired. Images are taken by using a mono-chrome and/or color video camera. Higher resolution is not necessary for the faster response and for the major crease detection. Detailed finger and palm patterns are not necessary or rather harmful. They are rather too sensitive to noises and/or daily variations. The palm placed freely toward the video camera in front of a low-reflective plate.

In the image acquisition, non-touching image input is made except that the back of the hand slightly touches some small knobs on the plate. The knobs are attached with magnet to indicate the desired hand position. They do not need to be touched, but only indicates the desired hand position.

Such dedicated devices as pegs, usually used popular hand scanners, to control the finger alignment for an appropriate placement of the hand, are not required by instead using an image of a finger-closed-together palm [20]. Heavily ringed hand is unable to be authenticated. Variously ringed finger is difficult to be processed. In this paper rings are slipped off and the extent of ring wear is a future problem.

2.1. CCD camera with a polarizing filter

Besides the normal use of usually used CCD cameras, video cameras or digital cameras, a polarizing filter is tested and observed better result to enhance the images of finger and palmar creases that run perpendicular to the finger axis. Also lighting with a tungsten lamp from a direction of 45 degrees wrist side is observed effective to enhance them. A focused lighting, with or without the polarizing filter contributes a little to the enhancement.

2.2. Near infrared CCD camera

A near infrared CCD camera (Hamamatsu C3077-78), having spectral sensitivity between 800 nm and 1100 nm, is found more effective than the above filtered CCD camera to detect the finger and palmar creases. Some of

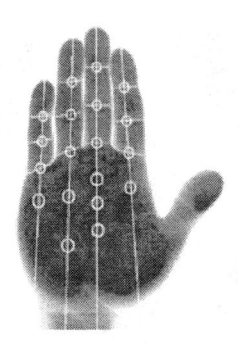

Figure. 3. Feature extraction at the intersection points on skeletal lines. Fingers brought together.

the common CCD cameras have usually infrared limiting filter in front of the sensor array for preventing thermal damages. Removal of the filter of this type will be similarly effective. In this near infrared acquisition no specific light source is observed conspicuously effective for the enhancement.

An example of our video image of the finger-closed-together palm is in Figure 3 with the marked extracted feature points. Orientations at the points are illustrated in Figure 4.

The image processed area is a VGA of 640 x 480 pixels with eight-bit gray levels. Noise reduction is made using a binary noise removal algorithm with repetitive morphological operations of erosions and dilations. Some hand made routines for thinning, 2D masking and template matching filters are used. A directional enhancing filter for the crease detection is applied, but the enhancement at the image acquisition stage is most effective. No such image processing devices as DSP (Digital Signal Processor) for acceleration are used.

3. Palmar feature point definition

According to the previous examination we concluded that the feature extraction points on the palm is to be decided in relation to the finger geometry and that they should be effective enough to authenticate, but small enough in number to shorten the overall processing time, and to achieve a real-time operation within one second or so [20].

Our feature extraction is at the intersection points of each finger (digital) skeletal line and finger creases. And also the intersection points of the extended finger skeletal line and the major palmar creases are the feature points concerning each of the four fingers. Schematic illustration is shown in Figure 1, where the intersection points are marked with circles. Positions of the intersection point define a feature vector for matching.

In the figure, typical three major palmar flexion creases, those are prominent and usually classified into the

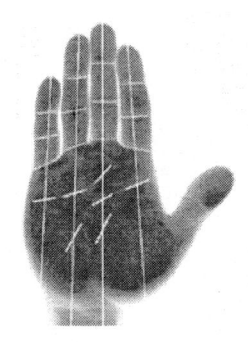

Figure. 4. Orientations at the intersection points. The same as Figure 3.

thenar crease (A), the proximal transverse crease (B) and the distal transverse crease (C), are shown. Some minor or secondary flexion creases or patterns are occasionally detected. In our authentication the creases are not limited to these three and more or less creases are detected and processed.

Tangential angles between the creases and the extended skeletal lines are other feature parameters. They are shown with short line segments in Figure 2. If a crease line and a skeletal line intersect nearly parallel, the position of the intersection is not reliable. So in the case, we judge the tangent is significant rather than the position. And the positional data are treated as they have some ranges.

The finger skeletal line should be extracted from the finger image using the skeletonization or thinning algorithm. But we approximated it by simply connecting the distal digital crease center and the proximal digital crease (palmo-phalangeal creases) center for faster processing. The palmar crease image is thinned until a line segment or curve segment of one pixel width. Then the intersection point is searched using a two-dimensional matrix operator. This matrix also gives an approximate intersection angle.

4. Palmar feature extraction

Feature points on the palm when the fingers are closed together are shown in Figure 3 as an example. The tangents at the intersection points are shown in Figure 4. Fingertip points are not always significant because they are affected by nail images. Intersection points of the palmar creases deviate due to the finger spreading. Orientations accordingly deviate.

It is found that if the fingers are brought together, intersection points on the palm print are stable. And the middle finger skeleton remains unchanged in the same line even if the fingers are spread apart and accordingly the position of the intersection points on the middle finger axis little affected. When the fingers are brought together,

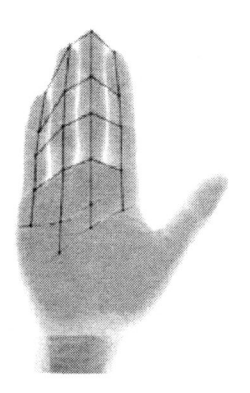

Figure 5. Mesh generated for the enrolled palm A, overlaid with the palm image.

loosely or tightly, the skeletal lines little deviate and accordingly the palmar intersection points can be reliably detected as feature points.

Following the segments, some major palmar creases are traced and reproduced, suggesting that the palmar crease feature is well sampled and detected by the orientation segments, though points are limited in number.

In Figure 1 or in Figure 3, each position of the intersection point on the palmar creases is measured from the point (origin) that is the intersection point of the proximal digital crease and each finger skeletal line or the center of the digital crease. Successive point-to-point distance is not used here, because lack of points or additional points on the extended skeletal line in the palm region may occur in the new entry.

From these examinations it is concluded that the matching is best performed for the palm with the four fingers brought together, requiring no constraints such as the pegs to align the fingers. The middle finger matching is found to be most reliable among the four.

5. Feature matching on skeletal line

The first feature vector consists of each center point of the three finger (digital) creases of the middle finger, and the intersection points of the major palmar flexion creases or prominent creases on the extended skeletal line of the finger (origin), and orientations at the intersection points. The second, third and fourth feature vectors includes similar parameters concerning the fore-finger, the ring finger and the little finger, respectively. Total feature points are from 20 to 30 for a single palm depending on each person. These points are small in number and small enough to shorten the processing time but adequate enough to reliably authenticate.

6. Feature matching on skeletal mesh

For further matching, a mesh is proposed and constructed by connecting laterally the adjacent corresponding intersection points on the skeletal lines, as shown in Figure 5 for subject A. In the figure the mesh is overlaid with the palm binary image. Lateral line to line distance depends on the thickness of each finger. Over all lateral line distances depend on the palm width. Mutual distances between the three consecutive finger creases are the finger segment lengths. They depend on the finger length. All of these are personal and are combined with the oriented palmar intersection points. Small in number but enough features are represented in the mesh.

Figure 6 is a mesh, proposed for feature extraction, for the subject B. A mesh of the palm B is compared with the enrolled A in Figure 7 as an example. The middle finger skeleton is selected to align the meshes for the two. Differences are clearly observed. In general, the positional deviation between the two is evaluated by calculating the root mean square deviation (rmsd). The parameter rmsd is given as follows,

$$\text{rmsd} = (\Sigma \delta_i^2 / N)^{1/2}$$

where, δ_i is positional difference at each mesh point and N is the total number of the mesh point to be compared. Magnitude of the difference is calculated in pixels and thereafter normalized by the finger length parameter and palm width parameter. Alignment for the comparison is made on the middle finger skeletal line based on our previous observation.

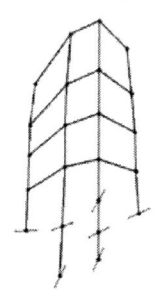

Figure 6. Mesh generated for the palm B.

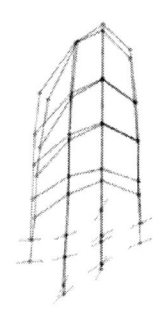

Figure 7. Comparison of meshes A and B

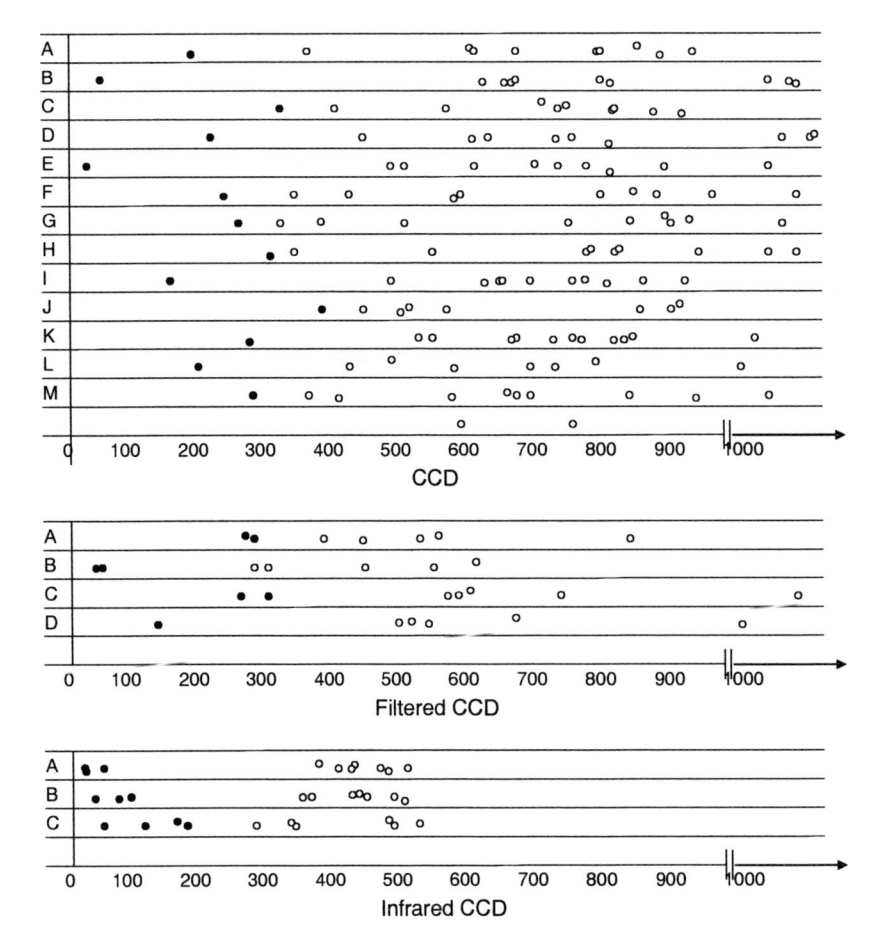

Figure 8. Rsmd values for CCDs. Solid circles are the new of the same enrolled palm. Circles are other palms. The filtered CCD and the infrared CCD camera bring about large threshold margins for discrimination. The infrared CCD gives the best performance among the three.

7. Results and discussion

In our method palmar feature sampling points are determined with respect to the finger geometry, not solely depending on the palm print pattern itself. If the fingers are brought together, how tightly they are brought together is not so sensitive. The method is that, as defined by the first feature vector concerning the middle finger and by the four finger mesh, the discrete point matching is reliable.

The palmar features are expressed in terms of the discrete points on the extended finger skeletal lines from the finger characteristic points, the proximal digital crease centers (origins), and also of the angular displacements at the corresponding points of intersection. The overall time, from image acquisition to the matched result output for each subject is about 0.9 seconds using a 2.0 GHz Pentium 4 processor.

Figure 8 shows distributions of the rmsds for the common CCD, the polarizing filter attached CCD and the infrared CCD cameras. Solid circles are for the same palm with the enrolled. The new images of the enrolled palm vary a little time to time, but deviation represented by the rmsd is small. From the point of views of the margin of the rmsd values from those of other palm images, and also of the palm image quality, it is concluded that the filtered CCD image is better and the infrared is the best.

Results are perfect so far, though the number of subjects is limited to 50 at present in a laboratory environment and though rings are slipped off. Furthermore, even the single usage of positions and orientations of the palmar feature points on the middle finger skeleton has brought about a faster, simpler, and still reliable authentication. For the palm where the margin is small, additional matching parameters, such as more detailed geometric parameters, are applicable to ensure the desirable performance. Paired comparison between the both hands skeletal line points result in a more reliable authentication.

8. Concluding remarks

We have proposed a practical personal authentication method that integrates geometric characteristics of the digitals or fingers and the palm print, at a few sampling points, for instance 20 to 30, for real-time processing, but enough feature extraction for reliable authentication.

In the palmar image acquisition no finger constraint is required. Fingers are just brought together and palmar is facing toward a video camera without any constraints such pegs, usually used for the positional alignment in many hand geometry devices. Fingers brought together are found to be able to replace the constraints for alignment.

Feature points to be extracted are determined with respect to the finger geometry, independent of the palm print pattern itself. In this method, intersection points of the palmar flexion creases and the extended skeletal line of the fingers are defined as the palmar feature points, where the angles of intersection are also defined as the significant feature parameters. This point wise feature extraction enables the sophisticated, time consumptive and not robust analysis of the palm print pattern omissible and the robust real-time matching achievable.

The discrete mesh points having the oriented points of intersection on the four finger skeletal lines, not using other finger and palmar parameters, have brought about reliable results, perfect for 50 subjects at present. Even the single matching of the middle finger parameters has resulted in a satisfactory authentication. Our results are encouraging though subjects are limited in a laboratory environment and rings are slipped off.

The integration of the finger geometry with the discrete intersection method is easy to practice because the finger geometry and the palmar image analysis are of the image- and video-based and the image acquisition is made simultaneously.

Further examinations for more subjects, for ringed fingers and for a simple authentication device construction are required. We expect this proposal will have some considerable utility in practical usage.

9. References

[1] K. L. Kroeker, "Graphics and security: Exploring Visual Biometrics", *IEEE Computer Graphics and Applications*, pp. 16-21, July/August, 2002.

[2] S. Pankanti, R. M. Bolle, and A. K. Jain, "Biometrics-The Future of Identification", *IEEE Computer*, vol 33, pp. 46-49, 2000.

[3] S. Liu and M. Silverman, "A practical guide to biometric security technology", *IT Professional*, 2001, URL: http://www.computer.org/itpro/homepage/jan_feb01/ security3_printer.htm.

[4] S. Nanavati, M. Thieme, and R. Nanavati, *Biometrics*, Identity Verification in a Networked World, Wiley, 2002.

[5] Biometric Consortium, An introduction to biometrics, URL: http://www.biometrics.org/html/introduction.html.

[6] F. L. Podio, Biometrics-Technologies for highly secure personal authentication,
URL: http://www.itl.nist.gov/lab/ bulletns/ bltnmy01. htm.

[7] A. Ross and A. K. Jain, Biometrics Research,
URL: http:// biometrics. se.msu.edu/index.html.

[8] A. K. Jain, R. Bolle and S. Pankanti, *Biometrics; Personal Identification in Network Society*, Kluwer Academic Publishers, 1999

[9] A. K. Jain, A. Ross and A Prototype Hand Geometry- based Verification System", in *Proc. 2nd Int'l Conference on Audio- and Video-based Biometric Personal Authentication (AVBPA)*, pp. 166-171, March, 1999.

[10] A. K. Jain and N. Duta, "Deformable matching of hand shapes for verification", in *Proc. IEEE Int'l Conference on Image Processing*, October, 1999.

[11] Biometric Systems Laboratory-Cesena, Hand Geometry, URL:http://bias.csr.unibo.it/research/biolab/bio_ tree.html.

[12] N. Duta, A. K. Jain, and K. Mardia, "Matching of Palmprint", *Pattern Recognition Letters*, vol. 23, pp. 477-485, 2002.

[13] A. K. Jain and A. Ross, "Learning User-specific Parameters in a Multibiometric System", in *Proc. Inter-national Conference on Image Processing (ICIP)*, Rochester, New York, September, 2002.

[14] L. C. Jain, U. Halici, I. Hayashi, S. B. Lee and S. Tsutsui, Eds, *Intelligent Biometric Techniques in Fingerprint and Face Recognition*, CRC Press, 1999.

[15] G. W. Jones, *Introduction to Fingerprint Comparison*, Staggs Publishing, 2000.

[16] D. R. Ashbaugh, *Quantitative-Qualitative Friction Ridge Analysis, An Introduction to basic and advanced ridgeology*, CRC press, 1999.

[17] N. Duta, A. K. Jain, and K. Mardia, "Matching of Palmprint", *Pattern Recognition Letters*, vol. 23, pp. 477-485, 2002.

[18] W. Li, D. Zhang, and Z. Xu, "Palmprint Identification by Fourier Transform", *International Journal of Pattern Recognition and Artificial Intelligence*, vol. 16, no. 4, pp. 417-432, 2002.

[19] A. Ross, A. K. Jain, and J. Z. Qian, "Information Fusion in Biometrics", in *Proc. 3rd International Conference on Audio- and Video-Based Person Authentication (AVBPA)*, pp. 354-359, June, 2001.

[20] M. Yamanaka and J. Doi, "Personal Authentication by Integrating Palmar Geometry and Flexion Crease Analysis", in *Proc. SPIE' 8th Annual International Symposium on Nondestructive Detection Evaluation for Health Monitoring and Diagnostics, Vol. 5048*, pp. 83-90, San Diego, USA, March, 2003.

[21] A. Kumar, D. C. M. Wong, H. C. Shen and A. K. Jain, "Personal Verification Using Palmprint and Hand Geometry Biometric", in *Proc. of 4th Int'l Conf. on Audio- and Video-Based Biometric Person Authentication (AVBPA)*, pp. 668-678, Guildford, UK, June, 2003.

Author Index

32nd Applied Imagery Pattern Recognition Workshop — AIPR 2003

Aanstoos, J. 189	Downs, A. 45
Ahn, D. 238	Du, H. 93
Asari, V. 141, 146, 151, 174	Durka-Pelok, G. 131
Bagai, D. 180	Dutta, A. 180
Beach, G. 39, 51	Easton, R. 111
Blake, P. 99	Ertem, M. 221
Bomberger, N. 11	Evans, J. 3
Bonneau, R. 62, 66	Fay, D. 11
Bose, N. 81	Foedisch, M. 157
Boult, T. 244	Gest, T. 131
Brown, T. 99	Gil, Y. 238
Butman, J. 119	Goldberg, A. 73
Caulfield, J. 7	Gottumukkal, R. 146
Christens-Barry, W. 111	Griffith, J. 275
Chung, Y. 238	Guler, S. 275
Clark, S. 250	Gupta, N. 21, 73
Cohen, C. 39, 51	Hall, D. 217
Colombe, J. 205	Hebert, M. 255
Conrad, P. 157	Heidhausen, E. 221
Costianes, P. 250	Henry, M. 51
Czanner, S. 131	Hilger, J. 56
Davessar, N. 169	Hinnrichs, M. 73
Deerfield, D. 131	Hong, T. 45
Dima, C. 255	Hunt, A. 232
Doi, J. 282	Irvine, J. 226

Israel, S.	226	Poland, A.	3
Ivey, R.	11	Pomerantz, S.	131
Kamal, T.	180	Pushee, I.	275
Kapoor, R.	180	Qi, H.	33, 93
Kim, Y.	269	Ramanath, R.	33, 93
Knox, K.	111	Rebmann, A.	119
Ko, M.	269	Rizvi, S.	27
Kolinko, V.	250	Schaum, A.	87
Levin, L.	194	Scruggs, W.	226
Liu, X.	199	Seow, M.	141, 151
Loew, M.	56	Shirey, E.	131
Lomont, C.	39	Singh, H.	169
Lovberg, J.	250	Snyder, W.	33, 93
Madan, S.	169	Tao, L.	174
Madhavan, R.	45	Valaparla, D.	141
Martin, C.	250	Vandapel, N.	255
Miao, Y.	125, 125	Wagner, L.	131
Moody, G.	51	Walli, K.	103
Nasrabadi, N.	27	Wang, X.	93
Nave, D.	131	Waxman, A.	11
Ng, M.	163	Wetzel, A.	131
Ngan, H.	163	Withbroe, G.	3
Nieder, G.	131	Worek, W.	226
Pan, S.	238	Yamanaka, M.	282
Pang, G.	163	Yung, S.	163
Pauli, M.	221	Zhang, Q.	199
Perconti, P.	56	Zhu, Z.	263

Notes

IEEE Computer Society

IEEE

Press Operating Committee

Chair
Mark J. Christensen
Independent Consultant

Editor-in-Chief
Michael R. Williams
Department of Computer Science
University of Calgary

Board Members

Roger U. Fujii, *Vice President, Logicon Technology Solutions*
Richard Thayer, *Professor Emeritus, California State University, Sacramento*
Linda Shafer, *UT Software Quality Institute*
John Horch, *Independent Consultant*
James M. Conrad, *Associate Professor, University of North Carolina at Charlotte*
Deborah Plummer, *Book Series Manager, IEEE Computer Society Press*
Thomas Baldwin, *Proceedings Manager, IEEE Computer Society Press*

IEEE Computer Society Executive Staff

David Hennage, *Executive Director*
Angela Burgess, *Publisher*

IEEE Computer Society Publications

The world-renowned IEEE Computer Society publishes, promotes, and distributes a wide variety of authoritative computer science and engineering texts. These books are available from most retail outlets. Visit the CS Store at *http://computer.org* for a list of products.

IEEE Computer Society Proceedings

The IEEE Computer Society also produces and actively promotes the proceedings of more than 160 acclaimed international conferences each year in multimedia formats that include hard and soft-cover books, CD-ROMs, videos, and on-line publications.

For information on the IEEE Computer Society proceedings, please e-mail to csbooks@computer.org or write to Proceedings, IEEE Computer Society, P.O. Box 3014, 10662 Los Vaqueros Circle, Los Alamitos, CA 90720-1314. Telephone +1-714-821-8380. Fax +1-714-761-1784.

Additional information regarding the Computer Society, conferences and proceedings, CD-ROMs, videos, and books can also be accessed from our web site at *http://computer.org/cspress*

Revised: 4 December 2003